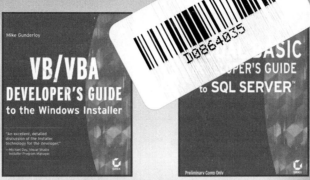

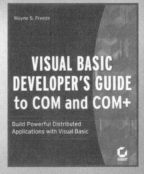
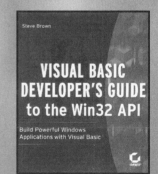

Oracle® and Visual Basic® Developer's Handbook™

Jim Fedynich
Jenny Besaw
Mark Tomlinson

SYBEX®

San Francisco • Paris • Düsseldorf • Soest • London

Associate Publisher: Richard Mills
Contracts and Licensing Manager: Kristine O'Callaghan
Acquisitions & Developmental Editor: Melanie Spiller
Editor: Raquel Baker
Production Editor: Shannon Murphy
Technical Editor: Amy Sticksel
Book Designer: Kris Warrenburg
Graphic Illustrator: Tony Jonick
Electronic Publishing Specialist: Nila Nichols
Proofreaders: Laurie O'Connell, Nancy Riddiough, Laura Schattschneider, Suzanne Stein
Indexer: Matthew Spence
CD Coordinator: Kara Schwartz
CD Technician: Keith McNeil
Cover Designer: Design Site
Cover Illustrator: Jack D. Meyers
SYBEX and the SYBEX logo are trademarks of SYBEX Inc. in the USA and other countries.

Developer's Handbook is a trademark of SYBEX Inc.

Screen reproductions produced with Collage Complete.
Collage Complete is a trademark of Inner Media Inc.

The CD interface was created using Macromedia Director, COPYRIGHT 1994, 1997–1999 Macromedia Inc. For more information on Macromedia and Macromedia Director, visit http://www.macromedia.com.

TRADEMARKS: SYBEX has attempted throughout this book to distinguish proprietary trademarks from descriptive terms by following the capitalization style used by the manufacturer.

The author and publisher have made their best efforts to prepare this book, and the content is based upon final release software whenever possible. Portions of the manuscript may be based upon pre-release versions supplied by the software manufacturer(s). The author and the publisher make no representation or warranties of any kind with regard to the completeness or accuracy of the contents herein and accept no liability of any kind including but not limited to performance, merchantability, fitness for any particular purpose, or any losses or damages of any kind caused or alleged to be caused directly or indirectly from this book.

Library of Congress Card Number: 00-102847

ISBN: 0-7821-2476-3

Manufactured in the United States of America

10 9 8 7 6 5 4 3 2 1

My contributions to this book are dedicated to the memory of Bradford T. Partain, January 25, 1981–June 23, 1998.

-J.B

To Al Stevens, Charles Petzold, Dale Rogerson, Jeff Richter, and all the many other great programmer/writers without whom I would have found life much harder. I hope this helps someone else in return.

-M.T.

ACKNOWLEDGMENTS

As with any book, this one wouldn't have been possible without the contributions of many people behind the scenes. First of all, we'd like to thank our developmental editor Melanie Spiller for laying a solid foundation for the project. In addition, we'd like to thank our editor Raquel Baker for all of her hard work, patience, and enthusiasm for the project. There are many others at Sybex we'd like to thank, as well, including all the folks in publishing, production, and administration. But, we must mention a few names: thanks to Electronic Publishing Specialist Nila Nichols for the speediest and most elegant layout in town, to Production Editor Shannon Murphy for managing everything with amazing clarity and grace, and to the proofreaders who worked hard to make sure it all made sense after we read it too many times to know the difference.

CONTENTS AT A GLANCE

CONTENTS

INTRODUCTION

Welcome to *Oracle and Visual Basic Developer's Handbook*. This is one of the first books that illustrates how to work with Oracle8i's new features using Visual Basic.

Oracle Objects for OLE (OO4O) is a middleware product developed by Oracle as a way for third-party applications to interface with an Oracle database. Unlike other middleware products, such as ADO or ODBC, this product allows you to leverage the full functionality of the Oracle8i RDBMS and its new features. This book illustrates using OO4O in Microsoft's Visual Basic IDE.

The topics covered in the chapters range from basic setup information to some of the more advanced features, including the new features of Oracle8i and OO4O. We begin by walking you through the installation of an Oracle client and creating an initial OO4O connection to an Oracle8i database in Visual Basic. We go on to discuss working with the Oracle Data Control, handling errors, and using multi-user concurrency and transactional control. As you progress through the chapters, you will become more exposed to OO4O's new features, as well as to some of the advanced features. Some of the advanced topics include working with LOBs, collection types, and Advanced Queuing. Many of these features were previously unavailable to the VB programmer.

About the Book

Visual Basic provides a powerful front-end for multi-platform solutions, but many programmers may not be aware of all of the middleware products that can provide programming help. In this book, you'll learn to use OO4O as a tool to connect Visual Basic to an Oracle database. The topics covered include

- Installing and configuring an Oracle client (Chapter 1)
- Connecting to an Oracle database (Chapter 3)
- Viewing and manipulating data (Chapter 4)
- Using the Oracle Data Control (Chapter 5)

- Trapping and handling application errors (Chapter 6)

- Creating solutions in a multi-user environment (Chapter 7)

- Working with Oracle8i collection types (Chapter 8)

- Working with LOBs (Chapter 10)

- Using Connection Pooling and Multiplexing (Chapter 11)

- Deploying your application (Chapter 13)

- Working with Oracle's OLE Provider (Chapter 14)

This book is *not* product specific. That is, whether you're using Microsoft Office 2000 or any other product that hosts VB 6 or later, you'll be able to take advantage of the code in this book.

In addition to introducing you to a powerful new tool with new functionality, we also hope to provide you with useful code that you can modify and extend it to come up with the perfect functionality for your specific needs. We hope that the code and information in this books gets you started in working with programmatic interfaces.

Who Is This Book For?

This book is for the Visual Basic programmer or application developer who is

- Looking for a middleware product that interfaces with an Oracle8i database

- New to Oracle8i or OO4O

- An experienced Oracle programmer who is interested in Oracle8i or OO4O's new and advanced functionality

If you are looking for a middleware product to integrate with Visual Basic that allows you to interface with an Oracle8i database, this book will cover the different aspects of OO4O, including the basic setup, general features, as well as the new features. If you compare OO4O with other middleware products, you will find that not all middleware products on the market are capable of interfacing with as many Oracle8i database features as OO4O. This ability makes OO4O a very powerful tool.

If you have not used OO4O before, this book walks you through a client installation such that when the installation is complete, you will not only have an Oracle client installed but will also have an understanding of what makes up an Oracle client.

If you are an experienced OO4O programmer, there is still a wealth of information to learn. The first chapter will get you acquainted with the new version of the Oracle Installer, called the Universal Installer. The chapters on advanced features and new features will allow you to make changes to your code to take full advantage of Oracle8i's features.

What You Need to Know

Because we wanted to get to the powerful functionality of using OO4O with an Oracle client, we had to dispense with introductory material. If you're not sure where to put the code in this book, how to create a module, or even what the different variable types are in VB and Oracle, please refer to the reference materials that come with Oracle and the VB host that you're working with. Make sure you have a good grasp of the following topics before jumping into this book:

- Creating modules
- Creating procedures
- Variables and their data types
- VB syntax (including If…Then, For…Next, and other control structures)
- SQL statements

We assume that you have a solid understanding of these concepts. Where appropriate, we have pointed you to additional reference materials so that you can get the most out of the information presented in this book.

Required Products

In order to follow along with the code examples in the book, you will need the following:

- Windows NT, 95, or 98
- Microsoft Visual Basic Version 6

- Oracle Objects for OLE (OO4O)

- Oracle's OLE Provider (for final chapter)

- An Oracle client CD-ROM (for the installation chapter)

- An Oracle8i database

This book presumes that you are working on a machine that already has Visual Basic and the appropriate operating system installed. It also assumes that you have access to an Oracle8i database.

If you have these materials but aren't sure of the installation procedure, don't worry, Chapter 1 takes you step by step through installing the Oracle client and OO4O.

Chapter Descriptions

This book discusses both concepts and specific functionality. Where applicable, the Visual Basic projects, code listings, and applications from the chapters are also available on the CD-ROM that accompanies this book.

Setup and General Introduction

Chapter 1 uses the Oracle8i 8.1.5 Enterprise Edition CD-ROM and walks you through a Custom installation of the client components. After the installation, you will have established a native database connection without using VB or OO4O.

Chapter 2 provides an overview of some different middleware components, including

- ODBC (Open Database Connectivity)

- Data Access objects

- Remote Data objects

- OLE DB and Microsoft ActiveX Data objects

Chapter 2 also provides examples of interfacing with each.

The Initial Connection and Simple Data Manipulation

In Chapters 3 through 5, you start working with VB and OO4O. Chapter 3 discusses OO4O's two connection objects: the OraSession and OraServer objects. Chapter 3 provides an introduction to the OraServer object. This object is covered more thoroughly in the Multiplexing chapter. The focus of Chapter 3 is on the more commonly used OraSession object and its methods and properties.

Chapter 4 dissects the OraDynaset object, providing ways to navigate and manipulate it. Chapter 4 also provides two detailed examples. One illustrates navigating through an OraDynaset, and the other illustrates a typical master-detail relationship.

Chapter 5 covers the properties, methods, and events for the Oracle Data Control. This chapter also provides two in-depth examples that illustrate working with the data control.

Application Concepts

With all the different products available that allow for so-called rapid design or development of applications, it appears that more and more developers focus less and less on the actual design of an application and jump right into creating code without first analyzing the entire environment. Chapters 6 and 7 cover two topics that many developers overlook. Chapter 6 focuses on error handling. If you take two identical applications and modify one to provide user-friendly and useful error checking and error handling and give the other application poor error-handling methods, you will find that the way errors are handled is often the key to a superior application. Chapter 6 also includes a number of common errors that users may run into, as well as solutions.

Chapter 7 covers the other topic that many developers overlook, which is how an application actually functions in a multi-user environment. How many times have you seen an application that functions flawlessly during development, but once it is released to the user community, problems are encountered? Chapter 7 discusses how Oracle and OO4O function in a multi-user environment and how to control transactions.

Advanced Use and New Features

Chapters 8 through 12 contain a wealth of information on the advanced features of OO4O and on how OO4O interfaces with Oracle8i's new data types and features. Although other chapters mention new features, these chapters each concentrate on a new topic or feature. Chapter 8 introduces objects types and collection types in the Oracle8i database. It also covers OO4O's new types, which interface with Oracle8i types. If you have worked with Oracle8i object and collection types in other applications, you know how complex it can be and will appreciate how intuitive OO4O makes working with these types.

Chapter 9 covers advanced OO4O functionality and also includes a couple of traditional topics that tend to cause confusion.

Chapter 10 provides an introduction to the LOB data types in the Oracle8i database and goes in depth into the new OO4O data types that interface with database LOBs.

Chapter 11 covers Connection Pooling and Multiplexing and includes two examples on how to implement each method of handling database connections.

Chapter 12 covers another new feature called Advanced Queuing.

Deploying Your Application

Chapter 13 walks you through using the Package and Deployment Wizard to deploy your application.

A Few Final Topics

As this book was nearing completion, Oracle 8.1.6 was nearing the end of its beta cycle. It was too late to include any of the new 8.1.6 features for OO4O because, at the time of this writing, it was still undetermined which, if any, new features would be included when the beta went to production.

One new product that we are certain will be released with 8.1.6 is Oracle's first version of its OLE DB Provider. Chapter 14 gives you a good overview of the Oracle OLE DB Provider and its use in the Visual Basic 6 IDE. The topics covered range from getting connected to using the Provider's advanced functionality, such as reading and writing LOB data. This chapter provides you with the means to start writing ADO/OLE DB applications that access an Oracle database. Basically,

Chapter 14 follows the same path as the other chapters that discuss OO4O: It discusses all the areas related to writing client-server database applications.

The Default Schema and Demo Data

On a standard installation of an Oracle database, a number of accounts and schemas are automatically created. Not only are the Sys and System accounts created for you, but also a user named Scott. The Scott account has a number of tables already created and populated with data. We will be using one or two of these default tables in this book.

Of course, you will need a password to connect as user Scott. Don't worry: The database takes care of this, as well. The password for the user Scott is Tiger. In fact, it's quite common to refer to the Scott account as Scott/Tiger. So, whenever you hear someone ask you to connect to your Scott/Tiger account, you will know what they are talking about.

If your database was installed with a Custom option, the Scott account is not created. But don't feel left out, you can ask your database administrator to create a Scott account for you. As far as creating the tables and data, an installation of OO4O provides a `Demobld7.sql` file. This file is an SQL script and can be executed from SQL*Plus to create the necessary tables and data. Keep in mind that you don't have to create a user Scott and that the `Demobld7.sql` file can be executed in any user's account. Chapter 2 discusses running the required SQL scripts in more detail.

Conventions Used in This Book

This book uses various conventions to present the information in as readable a form as possible. Tips, Notes, and Warnings, shown here, appear throughout the book to call your attention to special highlights.

TIP   This is a tip. Tips contain specific techniques on using the features presented in the text.

| **NOTE** | This is a note. Notes contain important background information or provide references to additional material on the topic. |

| **WARNING** | This is a warning. Warnings call attention to bugs, design problems, or other trouble spots. |

This book also uses several font styles. **Bold font** in text indicates something that the user types. A monospaced font is used for program code, URLs, SQL statements, filenames, and directory paths.

Using the Chapter Examples

Each chapter that has example applications has a folder included on the CD-ROM that accompanies this book. In each folder, you'll find all the example files used in the chapter. Use the code to work through the exercises in the book. To use the code, simply click the Code.exe, and the code will be unzipped to the desired subdirectory. For more information, please refer to the Readme.txt file included on the CD-ROM. A few examples require detailed setup. These instructions are described in the Readme.txt file in that chapter's folder. Be sure to refer to these files to set up each project successfully.

About the CD-ROM

The CD-ROM includes the following useful demos and tools:

Assistant Series   FinSys has created a useful software suite to assist end users and developers in finding source database columns, automatically joining tables, and building queries. The Assistant Series software suite includes Research Assistant, Join Assistant, Query Assistant, SQL Assistant, and AOL Assistant modules. You can also transfer and copy information between Oracle instances.

EZSQL   EZSQL is a powerful, easy-to-use Oracle database development and administration tool. With it, you can create and alter database objects, reorganize table data, monitor database performance, export data to text files, extract DDL statements, and much more.

Oracle 8 SQL Help   Is a very useful online compilation of SQL syntax. It provides a convenient cheat sheet for SQL syntax without having to search through heavy manuals.

SQL Designer 1.4   SQL Designer is a simple program for executing, testing, and debugging SQL and PL/SQL statements with Oracle RDBMS. You must have Oracle 8 or 8i to run this program.

Time to Win   The MCR Co. supplies a number of utilities aimed at Access developers. We've included some of these on this CD-ROM, and you'll find others on their Web site at http://www.trigeminal.com.

WinSQL   From Summit Data Group, this is a shareware evaluation version of the WinSQL product, which offers many exciting features, such as data export, catalog printing, parameterized queries, and extended command-line options.

Look for the Readme.txt file in the CD-ROM's root directory for installation instructions for each of these products.

Why This Book Is Useful

We hope you now have a clear idea of what this book covers. Simply stated: the ease of creating applications with Visual Basic combined with a middleware capable of implementing Oracle8i functionality makes for a very robust development environment.

This book is a valuable resource for all developers wishing to get the most out of their Oracle and Visual Basic development tools. We hope that we have succeeded in creating a valuable reference that enhances your knowledge of use OO4O with Visual Basic.

Our sincerest thanks go to you for choosing this book. We hope it serves you well. We welcome comments, criticisms, and suggestions. Please see the next section for details on how to contact us.

Sybex Technical Support

If you have questions or comments about this book (or other Sybex books), please contact Sybex.

For the Fastest Reply

E-mail us or visit the Sybex Web site! You can contact Sybex through the Web by visiting http://www.sybex.com and clicking Support. You may find the answer you're looking for on this site in the FAQ (Frequently Asked Questions) file.

When you reach the support page, click support@sybex.com to send Sybex an e-mail. You can also e-mail Sybex directly at support@sybex.com.

Make sure you include the following information in your e-mail:

Name   The complete title of the book in question. For this book, it is *Oracle and Visual Basic Developer's Handbook.*

ISBN number   The ISBN that appears on the bottom-right corner of the back cover of the book. This number looks like this:

0-7821-2476-3

Printing   The printing of the book. You can find this near the front of the book at the bottom of the copyright page. You should see a line of numbers as in the following:

10 9 8 7 6 5 4 3 2 1

Tell us what the lowest number is in the line of numbers. This is the printing number of the book. The example here indicates that the book is the first printing.

> **NOTE**   The ISBN number and printing are very important for Technical Support because they indicate the edition and reprint that you have in your hands. Changes may occur between printings. Don't forget to include this information.

Page number   Include the page number where you have a problem.

For a Fast Reply

Call Sybex Technical Support and leave a message. Sybex guarantees that they will call you back within 24 hours, excluding weekends and holidays.

Technical Support can be reached at (510) 523-8233, ext. 563.

After you dial the extension, press 1 to leave a message. Sybex will call you back within 24 hours. Please leave a phone number where you can be reached.

Other Ways to Reach Sybex

You may also reach Sybex through the mail at the following address:

SYBEX Inc.

Attention: Technical Support

1151 Marina Village Parkway

Alameda, CA 94501

Again, it's important that you include all of the following information to expedite a reply:

Name   The complete title of the book in question.

ISBN number   The ISBN that appears on the bottom-right corner of the back cover of the book and looks like this:

0-7821-2476-3

Printing   The printing of the book. You can find this near the front of the book at the bottom of the copyright page. You should see a line of numbers as in the following:

10 9 8 7 6 5 4 3 2 1

Tell us what the lowest number is in the line of numbers. This is the printing number of the book. The example here indicates that the book is the first printing.

NOTE   The ISBN number and printing are very important for Technical Support because they indicate the edition and reprint that you have in your hands. Changes may occur between printings. Don't forget to include this information.

Page number   Include the page number where you have a problem.

No matter how you contact Sybex, Technical Support will try to answer your question quickly and accurately.

chapter 1

Installing and Configuring an Oracle Client

- Understanding the Oracle installer

- Configuring an Oracle client

- Creating a connect string

- Installing the Oracle client

Before actually asking you to perform the installation, this chapter discusses some of the basic changes to the installer, as well as what components can be found on any machine that has Oracle installed. It then discusses the information required to create a connect string. After the installation directions are complete, the chapter continues with a simple overview of changes to the machine. The chapter closes with a quick glance of the products installed, along with a discussion of the Oracle Objects for OLE (OO4O) documents.

Overall, you need three things before doing the tasks outlined in this chapter. The first is an Oracle 8i database to connect to, the second is administrator privileges, and the third is the information to create a connect string.

Keep in mind that there are different types of Oracle8i installation CD-ROMs. One is the Enterprise Edition, which contains the components for both a client and a server installation. Another is the Personal Oracle8i CD-ROM, which contains the Personal Oracle database plus client installation, and another type is the Oracle8i Client CD-ROM, which contains the components required for a client installation. This chapter was written using the Oracle8i Enterprise Edition CD-ROM. Regardless of which CD-ROM you use, not only will the general installation and initial dialog boxes be the same, but the concepts discussed in the beginning of this chapter will also apply generically. So don't think that you must have the Enterprise Edition CD-ROM to follow along with this chapter.

NOTE   This chapter was completed using the Oracle8i Enterprise Edition CD-ROM. No matter which CD-ROM you use for your installation, not only will the general installation and initial dialog boxes be the same, but the concepts discussed in the beginning of this chapter will also apply generically to all the different CD-ROMs.

General Installer Information

With this new version of Oracle comes a new version of the Universal Installer. The new installer is written in Java. For this reason, you will notice that a number of Java components, including a version of the Java Runtime Environment (JRE), get installed automatically by the installer.

In addition to the Oracle Home directory you designate, the installer will create the following three directories under its own Oracle directory:

- JRE
- BIN
- Inventory

The Oracle directory created by the installer is under the Program Files directory on the default system drive (usually drive C). If the Program Files directory does not already exist, the installer will create that directory along with the others.

The JRE directory contains the JRE required to run the installer. The JRE directory is the only directory out of the three in which the installer will allow the installation location to be modified. This prompt will be visible only on the initial installation of Oracle on a given machine.

The BIN and Inventory directories hold not only other installer components but also contain information about the products that are currently installed on the machine.

Generic Client Configuration

There are two Oracle components that need to be installed for any client machine to connect to an Oracle database:

- Net8 (or SQL*Net for version 7.*x*)
- An application

The first component is the *Net8 layer,* which is a layer of adapters that allow Oracle to talk on the network layer that is already installed on the machine.

The second component is basically any application that attempts to connect to an Oracle database. An excellent example would be SQL*Plus. SQL*Plus is an Oracle-specific application tool that allows a user to connect to an Oracle database and execute different SQL and PL/SQL commands. SQL*Plus is used throughout the book to generate tables, stored procedures, and stored functions, as well as other database objects. SQL*Plus will be the Oracle application used to test and validate your connection later in the chapter.

Net8 and SQL*Plus are basic Oracle components and are available on just about every Oracle CD-ROM. Certainly, any CD-ROM that contains OO4O will contain these components.

Users who have worked with earlier versions of Oracle may be wondering why the Required Supported Files (RSFs) were not mentioned as one of the required components. This is because with Oracle8i, the RSFs have been bundled with the Net8 component. This is a very important item to note because OO4O is linked very closely with particular versions of the RSFs. In fact, many problems that arise when executing an OO4O application that is distributed from a development machine to production machines are due in large part to incorrect versions of the RSFs being installed. A simple check of the RSFs' version numbers can save many hours of troubleshooting. If you ever need to obtain the version of the RSFs installed on a given machine, simply check the version of the Net8 component, as they are one and the same.

TIP   OO4O is linked very closely with particular versions of the RSFs. Many problems with executing an OO4O application are caused by having the wrong version of the RFS installed. To check the version of the RSF that is installed on your machine, check the version of theNet8 component—they'll be the same.

Creating a Connect String

Discussing how to create a connect string may seem a bit premature at this time, especially since there are no Oracle products installed. But an overview is vital because creating a database alias is actually part of the installation process.

The documentation on Oracle versions 7.*x* and 8.0.*x* refers to connect strings as either a database alias or simply an alias. Oracle8i not only uses the old term *alias* for its database connect string, but it also includes a new term, *service name*. Both the alias and service name can be created using the Oracle tools that get installed with the Net8 component. You can create an alias to connect to both Oracle8i and earlier versions of Oracle, but a service name is capable of connecting only to an Oracle8i database. During the installation process, this book will step through configuring a service name. For further information between the two connect strings (alias and service name), you can review the Net8 Administrator's Guide.

Items Required to Create an Alias

Creating a service name is not difficult at all. It is something that is usually configured on a fresh installation and is very seldom modified in a production environment. The installation of the Net8 component includes a couple of tools to maintain the service name by either modifying existing names or by creating new ones.

Before creating a service name, you need to know three things:

- The server name
- The Oracle instance (SID) or global database name
- The port

The first item is easy. It's simply the server name. Think of it as the name of the machine where the database is located. Actually, either the server name or the IP address for the machine can be used.

The second item can be one of two things depending on whether a database alias or a service name is being created. If an alias is being created, the Oracle Instance (SID), which is the name of the database, is required. If a service name is being created, the global database name is required. For the installation in this chapter, the global database name is required.

Figuring out the SID or global database name is not as obvious as finding the server name and may require a phone call or an e-mail to your DBA. The database name is prefixed with INIT and has an ORA extension, such as INIT<SID>.ORA. For example, if I search my machine for INIT*.ORA, I would see INITV8I.ORA, and I would know that my database is named V8I. Keep in mind that I am the only one who works on my machine, so I know what is installed. However, if you search for INIT*.ORA on most servers, more than one file will be returned because there will be more than one database, or there may be multiple database versions. Therefore, to avoid confusion, it's best to ask the DBA for this information.

The third item is less obvious than the first two. This is the port number and usually defaults to 1521. Normally, the default value for the port is valid and once set, it usually will not require changing. The port number is the last bit of information you will have to acquire from your database administrator (DBA).

Once you have these three items, you are ready to start the initial installation.

Installing the Oracle Client

As this is the initial installation, the installer will actually execute in two parts. The first part installs the selected products. Once the products are successfully installed, the installer will continue to the second part of the installation. During the second part of the installation, the installer steps through the configuration of a service name. Since only the initial installation is done in two steps, any subsequent installations by the installer will end when the new component is installed and will not prompt you to configure a service name. Any additions or modification to service names should be done through the Net8 Assistant tool. Once again, after the first installation, you will not be prompted to configure additional service names. With that said, let's begin the installation.

WARNING	You must have administrator privileges to complete the installation.

If you have not already done so, place the Oracle8i CD-ROM in the CD-ROM drive. Before installing any products, you need to go to the Welcome dialog box. This can be done in three ways. First, if the CD-ROM auto starts, you will see the image in Figure 1.1. From there, click the Install/Deinstall Products button. The next screen will be the Welcome dialog box.

FIGURE 1.1
The Initial screen

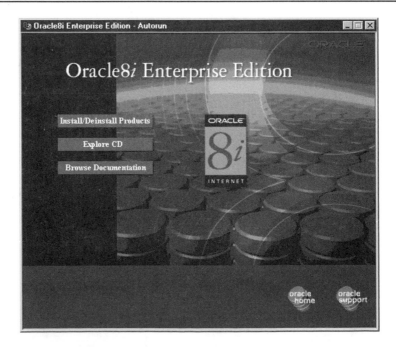

If the CD-ROM happens to be already inserted into the CD-ROM drive, or if the drive did not auto start, you can use Windows Explorer to navigate to the CD-ROM drive and click the drive letter to refresh the screen with the directories and files from the CD-ROM. Figure 1.2 illustrates how the directory structure for this second method of getting to the Welcome dialog box should look.

FIGURE 1.2

The Explorer screen

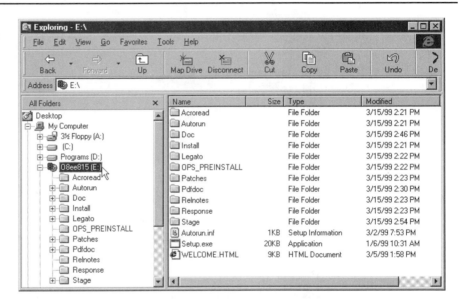

Once the screen has refreshed, you will find a `Setup.exe` file. Figure 1.3 has the `Setup.exe` file highlighted. Execute this file, and the Welcome screen will be the first screen to appear.

FIGURE 1.3
Selecting the Setup.exe file

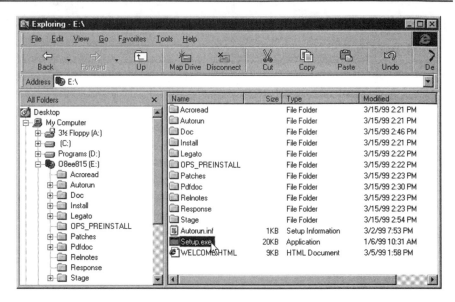

The third method that you can use to initiate the installer is to type **Setup.exe**, preceded by the drive letter, in the Run dialog box. Figure 1.4 illustrates how this would look if the CD-ROM is located on the E drive. When finished, click the OK button, and the installer will display the Welcome screen.

FIGURE 1.4
The Run dialog box

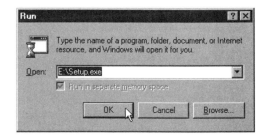

Any of the three methods work. Figure 1.5 illustrates the Welcome screen.

FIGURE 1.5

The Welcome screen

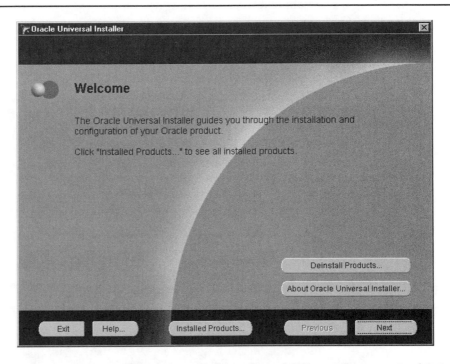

The Welcome screen provides you with a number of different buttons. As this is the first installation, the Deinstall Products and Installed Products buttons will not be very useful. We are looking for the screen to install the client products. To get to this screen, click the Next button.

Figure 1.6 displays the next screen for the installation. The File Locations screen is where you actually provide input. The Source field is the path to the file that lists the available products to install. The Destination field is the section that we are interested in: It includes the pieces required to define the Oracle Home. Here, you must decide on a name for your Oracle Home. This can be just about any name. Feel free to accept the default.

NOTE   If installing on a machine with an existing version of Oracle (version 8.0.x or earlier), make sure you install this version in a separate home.

The Path text box shows the physical path where the products are installed. Once again, you can either create one of your own or accept the default path provided by the installer. Once completed, click the Next button to continue to the next screen.

FIGURE 1.6
The File Locations screen

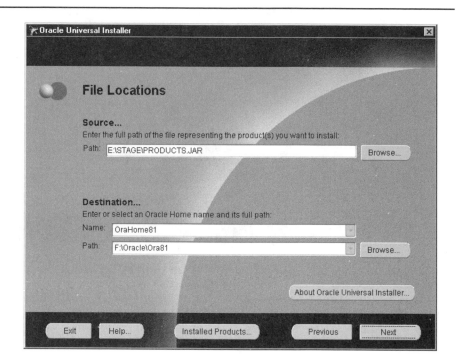

Once the Next button is clicked, you'll see the screen in Figure 1.7 for a brief moment while the installer prepares for the installation.

FIGURE 1.7
The Loading Product Information progress bar

Once the installer is ready, you'll see the screen displayed in Figure 1.8, which provides you with three different installation options and a brief explanation of each. You'll see the following:

- Oracle8i Enterprise Edition 8.1.5.0.0

- Oracle8i Client 8.1.5.0.0

- Oracle Programmer 8.1.5.0.0

NOTE   At the time of this writing, only the Oracle8i Enterprise Edition CD-ROM was available. In the future, there may be an Oracle 8i Client CD-ROM or Programmer CD-ROM. In any case, the previously mentioned options may differ.

To get a list of the components required to connect to the database and install OO4O, select either the Oracle8i Client or the Oracle Programmer. Although either the client or programmer version will install the OO4O product, to follow along with this book, select the Oracle Programmer option and click the Next button.

FIGURE 1.8
The Available Products
screen

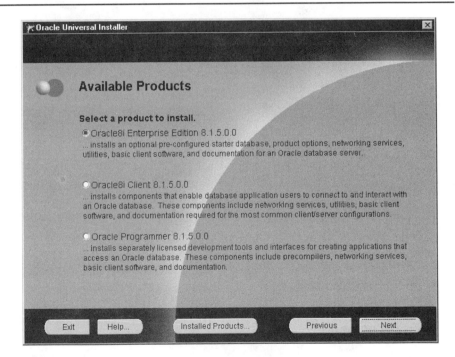

Figure 1.9 displays the next screen, which prompts you for the installation type. The first option is a pre-determined installation, and the second is a custom installation. For our purposes, we'll select a custom installation so that you can see how

the installer operates and what products you need to select to make Oracle work. Select Custom and click the Next button.

FIGURE 1.9
The Installation Types
screen

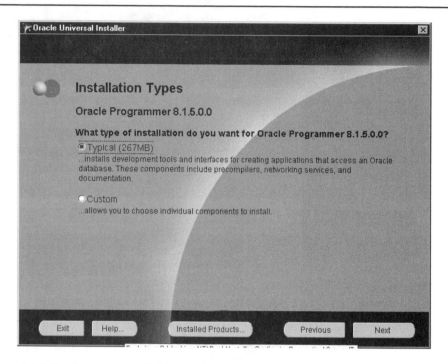

Figure 1.10 displays the available products. These are not all the available products on the CD-ROM, but rather all the available products for an Oracle Programmer installation. Selecting either Oracle8i Enterprise Edition 8.1.5.0.0 or an Oracle8i Client 8.1.5.0.0 displays an even broader list of products. To find out all the products contained within the CD-ROM, you can look at the small booklet located on the inside cover of the CD-ROM case. This little booklet contains a brief overview of the installation types, system requirements, and the supported platforms, as well as a complete list of all the products.

Although the installer provides suggested products that are already checked, you will be selecting only the ones needed to follow along in the book and deselecting any that are not required.

FIGURE 1.10
The Available Product Components screen—Section 1

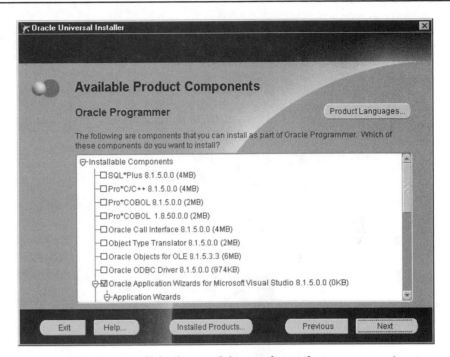

Near the top of the list, you'll find two of the products that you are going to need. The first is SQL*Plus, and the second is Oracle Objects for OLE. Place a check mark in both of these check boxes. The Oracle Application Wizards for Microsoft Visual Studio can be deselected. Figure 1.11 illustrates what this screen should look like with the proper products selected to match the examples in this book. Click the scrollbar to scroll down a page for the continued list of products.

NOTE   You can refer to Figure 1.11 to see how we've configured our installation. Your choices may differ.

FIGURE 1.11

The Available Product Components screen—Section 1 with the selected products

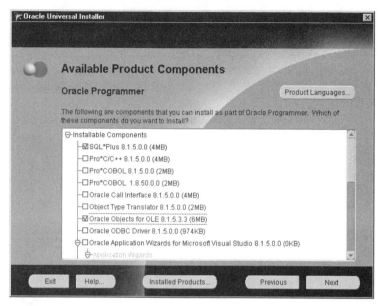

FIGURE 1.11

The Available Product Components screen—Section 1 with the selected products

Scroll down the list to see all of the products. Figure 1.12 displays the next set of products that you'll see as you scroll down. These products are primarily Java related and, as this book is not covering any Java topics, these products can be deselected.

FIGURE 1.12

The Available Product Components screen—Section 2

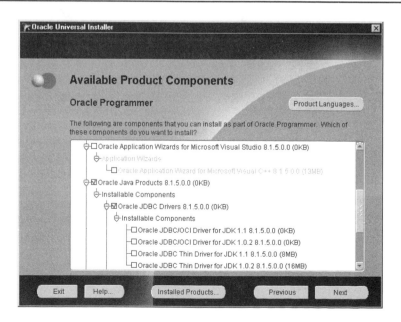

Figure 1.13 illustrates what this screen should look like when you deselect the Java components. Once again, click the scrollbar to scroll down a page for the remaining list of products. Although you may still see check marks in some components' check boxes, as long as the component is grayed out, it will not be installed.

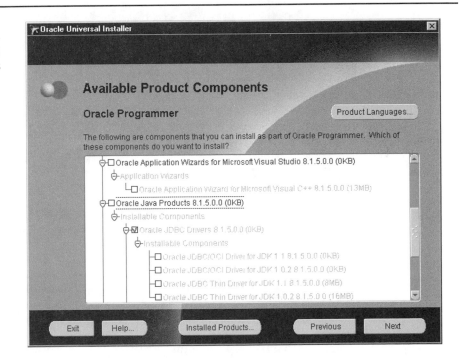

Figure 1.14 displays the last set of products. These are primarily miscellaneous products and can be deselected. As with Figure 1.13, you may still see check marks in some components' check boxes, but as long as the component is grayed out, it will not be installed.

FIGURE 1.14

The Available Product Components screen—Section 3

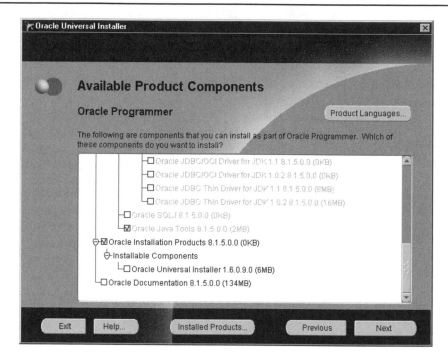

Figure 1.15 illustrates what this screen should look like when you deselect the remaining products. When finished, click the Next button.

FIGURE 1.15
The Available Product Components screen—Section 3 with the selected products

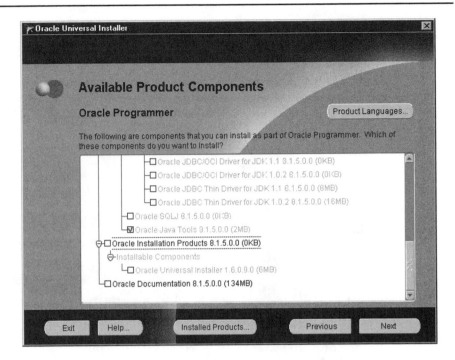

The next screen in the installation process is for component locations. As you can see in Figure 1.16, the only component listed is the Java Runtime Environment. Although we deselected the Java-related products for our installation, the Java Runtime Environment is required for running the Universal Installer. (As mentioned previously, the Universal Installer provided by Oracle is actually written in Java.) Just think of the Java components that you deselected as part of the client installation that is designed for the development of client-side applications and for the current Java Runtime Environment, which is specifically for the Universal Installer. If you click this item, a field appears that allows you to change the directory in which the JRE is installed. Not only that, but if you click the "Show all components to be installed" check box, a list of products and their installation directories are displayed. Keep in mind that the only directory you have control over is the directory in which the JRE will be installed. In fact, you'll only see this screen during the initial installation. The screen in Figure 1.16 will not appear in subsequent installations. For now, accept the defaults and click the Next button.

FIGURE 1.16
The Component Locations
screen

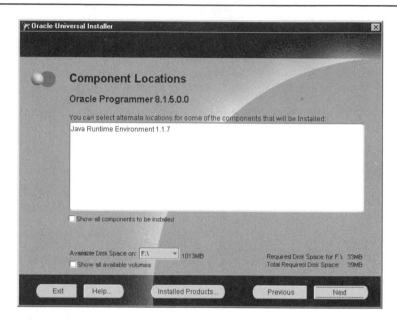

Figure 1.17 displays the Oracle Protocol Support screen. The installer highlights the protocols that are detected on your machine. This is a required protocol, as Oracle must install its own protocol adapters, which enable Oracle to interface with the other existing protocols. The number of protocols displayed on this screen will be determined by the number of protocols detected on the machine.

FIGURE 1.17
The Oracle Protocol Sup-
port screen

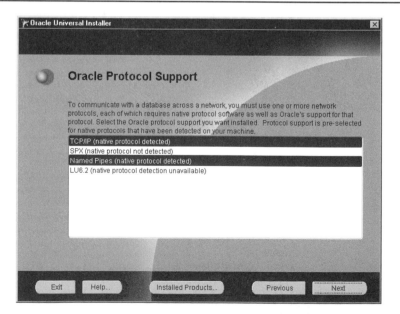

Although you are able to select one or more protocols, Figure 1.18 illustrates the selection of the TCP/IP support. The system searches for known existing protocols and highlights them. Notice whether the system has already selected the correct options for your installation. If TCP/IP is not one of the highlighted protocols on your system, as it is on ours for this book, keep in mind that some of the later dialog boxes may differ. Also, if no protocols are highlighted, you may need someone from your Networking department to install a protocol for you. Once you've got all this checked out, click the Next button.

FIGURE 1.18

The selected protocol

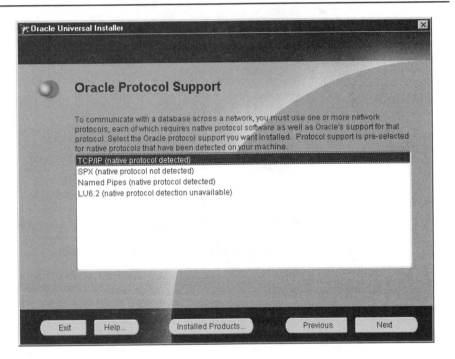

Once the protocols are selected, the installer provides an overview of the components that are going to be installed. Figure 1.19 illustrates the Summary screen with some of these components showing. The Summary screen provides an overview of the products to be installed, along with other information. For example, the Global Settings section provides the locations where the products are installed from and displays the Source location. The Destination is the physical location defined as the Oracle Home. The installer also shows that you opted to do a custom installation, and it displays this information for the Installation Type setting. The installer provides other miscellaneous settings, such as Product Languages and Space Requirements.

More importantly, take a look at what is listed under the New Installations section—there are 14 products in our configuration. Figure 1.19 displays some of the 14 products. Scroll down to see the rest.

FIGURE 1.19
The Summary screen—
Section 1

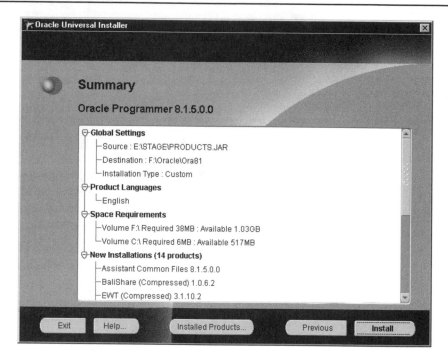

Figure 1.20 displays the remainder of the 14 products. How can selecting only 2 products (SQL*Plus and OO4O) grow to having 14 products in the display? There are actually two reasons. First, remember from the beginning of the chapter that one of the required components for connecting to a database was the Net8 layer? Well, although Net8 was not explicitly selected, the installer knows that it's a required product and automatically makes it a part of the installation. In fact, if you were to go back and look at the figures of available products displayed (Figures 1.10 through 1.15), you would notice that Net8 is not listed as an available option. But this doesn't mean that you must install Net8 through another component. Remember, the type of installation selected was the Oracle Programmer. If the Oracle8i Client was selected, you would have seen Net8 listed as an available product. Don't forget that even though we opted not to install any Java-related products, the Universal Installer will still install the Java components it needs to function.

Once you have gotten a chance to review this screen, click the Install button to start the actual installation.

FIGURE 1.20
The Summary screen—
Section 2

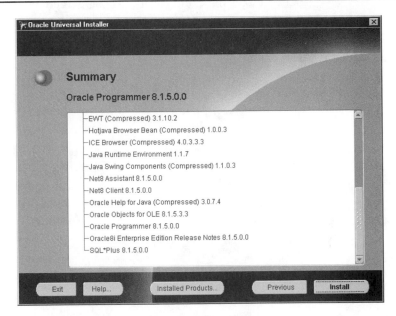

Once the installation is underway, the installer displays the next Install screen. This screen provides a progress bar to monitor the status of the installation. Figure 1.21 shows the screen when the product installation is complete. When finished, the installation process will display the Configuration Tools screen.

FIGURE 1.21
Install screen

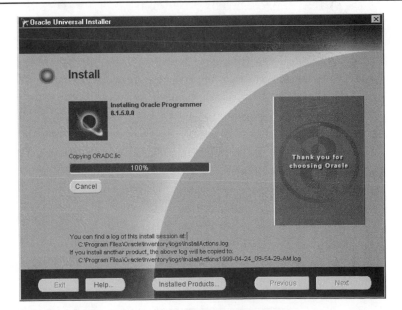

Figure 1.22 is the Configuration Tools screen, which appears when the product installation is complete.

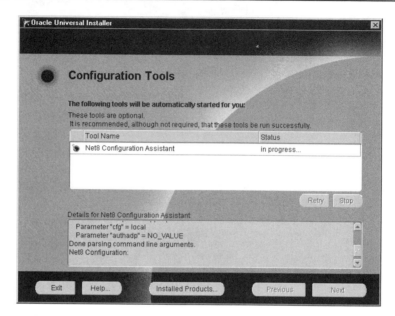

This screen does not yet imply that the installation is complete. Actually, only the first part of the installation is complete. The second part is about to begin. This part of the installation configures Net8 components and creates the connection string.

The Configuration Tools screen displays any additional applications required in configuring the client. In this case, the Net8 Configuration Assistant is invoked when the status is in progress. Keep an eye on the Details For Net8 Configuration Assistant field. Once the configuration is complete, the Details field will display the message "Done parsing command line arguments. Net8 Configuration," and the Welcome screen for the Net8 Configuration Assistant will appear. Figure 1.23 illustrates what the Net8 Configuration Assistant Welcome screen looks like.

NOTE   If the Details section displays "Done parsing command line arguments. Net8 Configuration," and the status is still in progress, and you have not seen the Welcome screen appear after a few moments, you may want to minimize any open windows and move the Configuration Tools screen out of the way. Sometimes the Welcome screen appears behind the Configuration Tools screen. Since the Welcome screen is smaller than the Tools screen, it may appear that the installer is still working when it's waiting for your input.

FIGURE 1.23
The Net8 Configuration
Assistant: Welcome screen

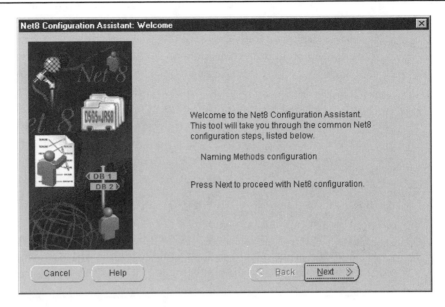

After reading the welcome message, click the Next button. The next screen in the configuration process is the Naming Methods Configuration screen. Figure 1.24 displays what this screen looks like.

FIGURE 1.24
The Net8 Configuration
Assistant: Naming Methods Configuration, Select
Naming Methods screen

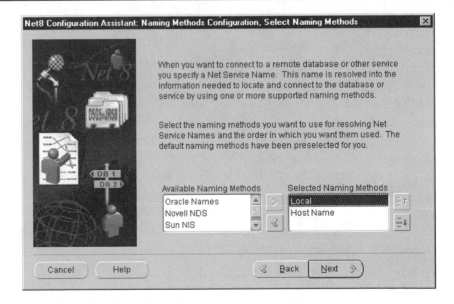

Usually, the selected naming methods that appear are Local and Host Name. The biggest difference between a Local and a Host Name naming method is that one references the TNSNAMES.ORA file, and the other uses DNS. The Local naming method is the most common, and it's the one that uses the local TNSNAMES.ORA file to resolve the name of your connect string. The *connect string* is used in a given application to determine the Oracle database to connect to. The Host Name naming method is similar to the Local naming method, but it does not use the TNSNAMES.ORA file to resolve a connect string. Instead, connect strings are resolved using DNS or by using a similar naming service with HOSTS files. For more information on the different naming methods, review the Net8 Administrator's Guide. To follow along with this book, in the pick list, select the Local naming method. Your screen should look similar to Figure 1.24. Click the Next button to move to the next screen.

Because Local was selected, the installer continues to prompt for more information in order to configure the connect string. Figure 1.25 displays the next screen, which wants to know the version of the database you plan on connecting to.

FIGURE 1.25
The Net8 Configuration Assistant: Net Service Name Configuration, Database Version screen

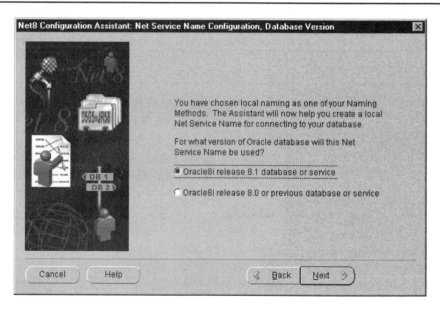

The Net8 Service Name Configuration, Database Version screen provides two options:

- Oracle8i release 8.1 database or service

- Oracle8i release 8.0 or previous database or service

The first option for Oracle8i release 8.1 creates a connect string that is based upon a service name. The second option, for Oracle8i release 8.0 or previous release, creates a connect string that is based upon an alias name. The main difference between the two is that the service name is generic enough to connect to any database on a given machine, and the alias name is based upon a specific database on a specific machine.

In either case, if not already known, the information will have to be acquired from either your network administrator or your database administrator.

For the purpose of this book, select the "Oracle8i release 8.1 database or service" option. Click the Next button to continue to the next screen, which is the Net Service Name Configuration, Service Name screen (see Figure 1.26).

FIGURE 1.26

The Net8 Configuration Assistant: Net Service Name Configuration, Service Name screen

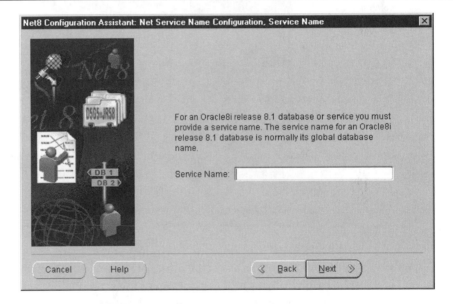

The Net Service Name Configuration screen prompts you for the service name. If you are unsure or do not know which service name to use, you must get this information from your database administrator. As with figuring out the SID, you could look in the Init<SID>.ORA file, but since most people have more than one database or database version installed, it is best to get the information from the DBA. Once a valid service name is entered, click the Next button to continue with the Net8 configuration.

Figure 1.27 shows the next screen, which lists the available protocols to use with the service name that was entered in the previous screen (Figure 1.26). You'll remember from earlier in the installation process that TCP/IP was the protocol adapter selected to install. There is no validation at this point. So, if you select an invalid protocol, you won't find out until you attempt to connect, and an error is returned. If applicable, ensure that only TCP/IP is selected and then click the Next button. This will take you to the next Net Service Name Configuration screen, where you'll configure the TCP/IP protocol (see Figure 1.28).

FIGURE 1.27
The Net8 Configuration
Assistant: Net Service
Name Configuration, Select
Protocols screen

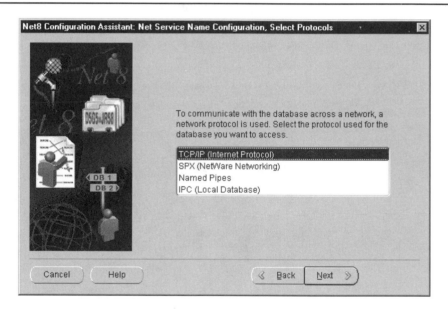

The TCP/IP Protocol screen requires you to enter a host name in the Host Name text box. The *host name* is the name of the server where the database is installed. The radio buttons near the bottom of the screen allow you to change the port number. The port number is determined by the client. Most people use the default port, which is 1521. Although most people accept the 1521 default, if there is more than one database on a given machine, only one database can use 1521, and the other databases will have another port number. Therefore, if you don't already know this information, it should be obtained from the database administrator.

FIGURE 1.28

The Net8 Configuration
Assistant: Net Service
Name Configuration, TCP/
IP Protocol screen

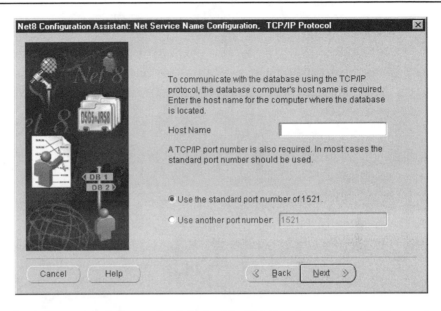

FIGURE 1.28

The Net8 Configuration
Assistant: Net Service
Name Configuration, TCP/
IP Protocol screen

Once the information is entered, click the Next button to continue to the next
Net Service Name Configuration screen, which is displayed in Figure 1.29.

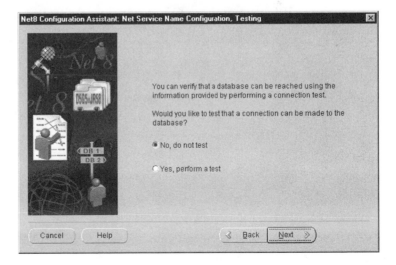

FIGURE 1.29

The Net8 Configuration
Assistant: Net Service
Name Configuration,
Testing screen

The Testing screen provides you with the option of testing the connect string that was just created. It's usually a good idea to do so, so that you can correct an invalid connect string. You need to be able to make a connection to the database to continue following along with this book. To test the connect string, click the "Yes, perform a test" radio button and click the Next button (see Figure 1.30).

FIGURE 1.30

Testing the connect string

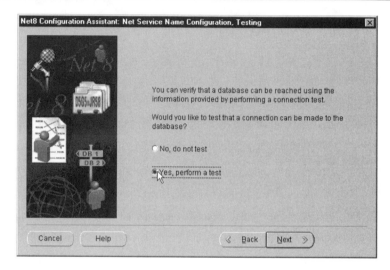

Figure 1.31 shows the next Net Service Name Configuration screen in the configuration sequence. The Testing screen contains a multiline text box and tells you whether or not the test successfully connected to the database. If the test was successful, you can move on. If you get an error saying that you've got an invalid username or password, this is OK, too, because a connection still has to be established to validate the username and password. You may have noticed that the test was executed without prompting you for the username and password. That's because, by default, the username SCOTT and the password TIGER are used. SCOTT is a user created whenever the default settings are used while installing the database. A custom build of an Oracle database does not create this user for you. If this user does not exist or if you wish to test the connection with a different user, you can click the Change Login button to display the Change Login dialog box, shown in Figure 1.32.

FIGURE 1.31
The Net8 Configuration
Assistant: Net Service
Name Configuration,
Testing screen

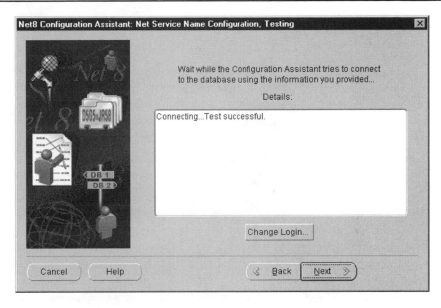

If you want to change the username, click the Change Login button. In the
Change Login dialog box, place the desired name in the Username field, enter the
password in the Password field, and click the Yes button (see Figure 1.32) to continue. Once the Yes button is clicked, a new attempt to connect will automatically
be initiated, and the results will once again be displayed in the multiline Details
text box field, as you saw in Figure 1.31.

FIGURE 1.32
The Change Login
dialog box

Once a successful connection is established, click the Next button to go to the
next Net Service Name Configuration screen, which is the Net Service Name
screen (see in Figure 1.33).

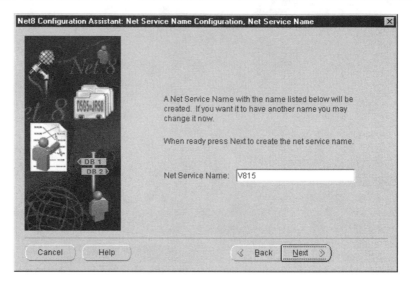

The Net Service Name screen prompts you for the service name you want to create. By default, the installation uses a sub-string of the Global Database name, but this selection can be changed. The name entered here will be the connect string used when connecting to the database either through SQL*Plus or through your OO4O samples. Most of the examples in the book use the service name V8I, so it may be a good idea to use the same name. When finished, click the Next button, which will take you to the Another Net Service Name? screen (see Figure 1.34).

FIGURE 1.34

The Net8 Configuration
Assistant: Net Service
Name Configuration,
Another Net Service Name?
screen

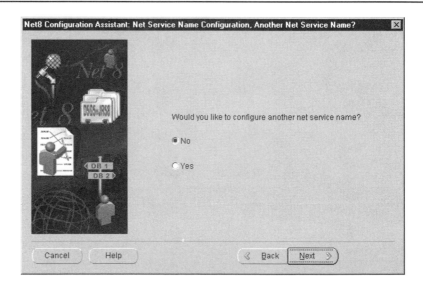

The Another Net Service Name? screen asks if you would like to configure another net service name. Clicking Yes takes you back through the process of configuring a service name. Don't think that this is your one and only chance to do so. Once the installation and configuration in this chapter is complete, you'll be told what product to run in order to configure additional service names. For the time being, accept No and click the Next button, which takes you to the next screen. This screen signifies the completion of the service name configuration. Figure 1.35 shows what the screen looks like.

FIGURE 1.35

The Net8 Configuration Assistant: Net Service Name Configuration Done screen

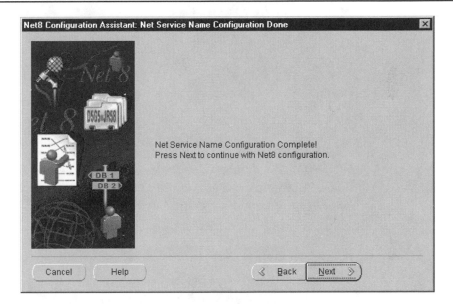

The Net Service Name Configuration Done screen displays a message informing you that the net service name configuration is complete. Just click the Next button to continue. The next screen informs you that the naming method configuration is complete. Figure 1.36 shows what that screen looks like.

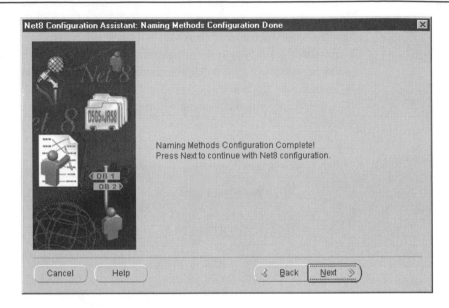

The Naming Methods Configuration Done screen is another information screen, which shows that you've completed an action. After clicking the Next button, another information-only screen appears, as shown in Figure 1.37.

FIGURE 1.37

The Net8 Configuration
Assistant: Done screen

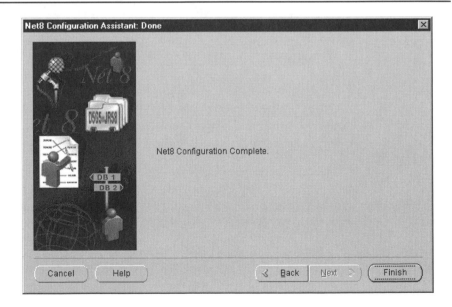

This Net8 Configuration Done screen informs you that the Net8 configuration is complete. Notice that there is now a Finish button at the bottom of this screen, instead of a Next button. When ready, click the Finish button to move to the final screen, as shown in Figure 1.38.

FIGURE 1.38
The End of Installation screen

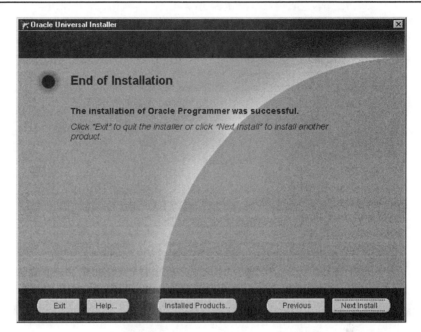

This final screen is the conclusion of the installation of the required components and configuration of the service name. From this screen, you can elect to view the installed products, install additional products, or click the Exit button to exit the installer. Of course, clicking the Exit button will not simply exit the installer. Instead, the installer prompts you, giving you one last chance to change your mind. Figure 1.39 shows what the prompt looks like.

FIGURE 1.39
The Exit dialog box

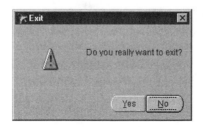

Click the Yes button on the Exit dialog box to exit the installer.

If you installed on Windows NT, you have nothing else to do. If you installed on Windows 95, you must reboot the machine. The reboot needs to be done only after the initial installation. This resets your path to include the `<Oracle Home>\Bin` directory. Subsequent installations will not require a reboot.

NOTE	After the initial installation on Windows 95, the machine must be rebooted.

The Products Installed

Once the installation from the previous section is complete, take a moment to view the changes the installer made to the machine. The first change is the addition of an Oracle directory, as well as subdirectories created beneath the Program Files directory on the C drive, as discussed in the "General Installer Information" section earlier in the chapter.

The second change is the new menu items added to the System menu. These changes can be viewed by clicking the Start button on the desktop and navigating to the Programs menu. From the Programs menu, you can see Oracle—OraHome81 if you accepted the default value. If not, you can still see Oracle, but it will be followed by the name you provided during the initial installation (refer to Figure 1.6). Under this menu, there are two more menu items (Application Development and Network Administrator), which represent the products selected during the installation.

The Application Development menu houses SQL*Plus and OO4O products. Figure 1.40 shows how a menu layout may look. Of course, depending on the products you installed, your menu layout may differ.

FIGURE 1.40

The Application Development menu

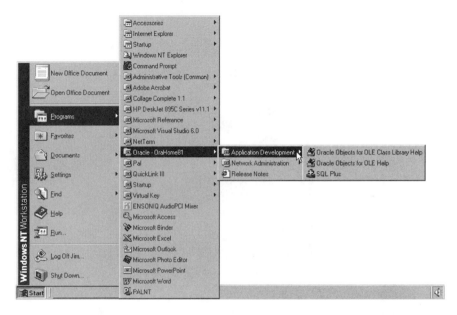

The Network Administrator menu houses the following three applications (see Figure 1.41).

- Net8 Assistant

- Net8 Configuration Assistant

- Net8 Easy Config

Remember that additional connect strings (alias or service names) can be configured any time after the installation? Configuring a new connect string can be done with any of the three applications in the Network Administration menu. Why have three, you ask? Well, although each application can be used for managing connect strings, each exists for different reasons.

The Net8 Assistant is primarily an administrator's tool and is used not only to configure a connect string but also for other client configurations, like the local profile and listeners.

FIGURE 1.41

The Network Administrator menu

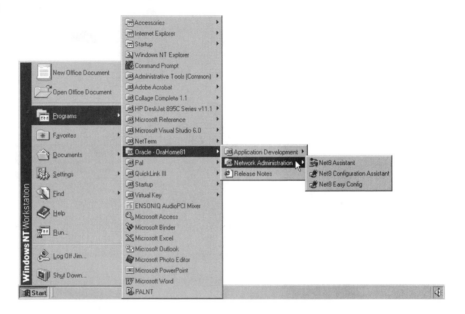

The Net8 Configuration Assistant is very similar to the configuration application embedded in the installer. So, many of the screens that you see in this application will match the screens that you have already seen during the installation process. This application is what Oracle is urging the users on the client side to use when configuring a connect string.

The Net8 Easy Config is a simple tool for configuring connect strings. This application has existed for some time and is included because many people are familiar with it from earlier versions of SQL*Net. Don't get too used to this application because it will not be included in future releases.

Note that the fact that the Bequeath Adapter is no longer supported. So, when using any of the tools discussed here to create your database alias, don't be unduly dismayed that the Bequeath Adapter is not provided as an option.

For further assistance on using any of these applications, review the *Net8 Administrator Handbook*.

Keep in mind that the menu items visible are directly related to the items selected during the installation. The menu items shown in the figures will be visible if you followed the installation procedure from the previous section. If additional products were installed, you will see additional menu items.

Connecting with SQL*Plus

By this time, you should have a service name defined. If you did not test your connection during the installation, now is a good time to test it. If you cannot connect using SQL*Plus, your OO4O application will also fail and you will have to take the time to configure a valid service name because a connection to a database is required if you ever want to retrieve data.

Figure 1.40 shows where SQL*Plus is on the System menu. Locate the SQL*Plus icon and click it to start the application. Once the application starts, you will be prompted with a Log On dialog box, as shown in Figure 1.42.

FIGURE 1.42
The Log On dialog box

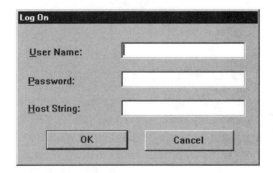

The User Name field is the name of a user in the database. The Password field is the password for the user in the first field. The Host String field is for the connect string, which can be either the alias name or the service name. Once the fields are entered, click the OK button. If the connect was successful, you should see something similar to Figure 1.43.

FIGURE 1.43

The Oracle SQL*Plus screen

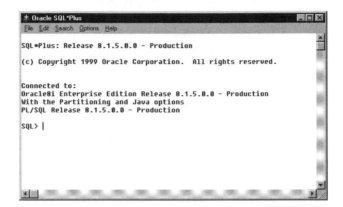

SQL*Plus has many useful purposes beyond being a tool for testing connections. It provides a simple way to test SQL used in your application, and, more importantly, it provides a simple way to create database object, such as tables, arrays, and stored procedures. SQL*Plus is used quite extensively in some of the later chapters of this book. For more information on the capabilities and commands for SQL*Plus, please review the SQL*Plus manual.

Installed OO4O Documents

Before working with OO4O, you should take a moment to become familiar with the available online documentation. The OO4O directory is located in a subdirectory beneath your Oracle Home. Besides other subdirectories, this directory contains a number of files that may be of interest to you. Figure 1.44 illustrates what the listing of directories and files may look like.

FIGURE 1.44
The OO4O directory

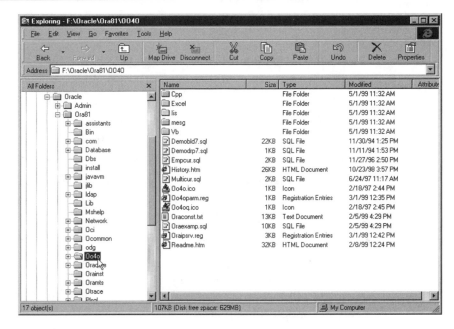

The directories listed are primarily samples, with the exception of the Mesg directory. The following directories contain a number of examples:

Cpp   Contains Visual C/C++ projects that use the OO4O C++ Class Libraries. These samples are not related to the content contained in this book.

Excel   Contains Excel workbooks that retrieve data from Oracle and place the data in a spreadsheet.

Iis   Contains samples using Microsoft's Internet Information Server.

Vb   Contains a number of Visual Basic projects that illustrate various concepts in OO4O.

There are a number of files of interest in the OO4O directory. For example, the files with the SQL extension (for example, `demobl7.sql`) contain SQL commands that you can use to build tables, data, stored procedures, and functions used by the samples.

The `Oraconst.txt` file is OO4O's global constant file and is required when referencing any OO4O predefined variables.

One of the first documents you should review is the Release Notes, which can be found in the Readme.htm file. The Release Notes provide a wealth of information. Here are just some of the topics you will find:

System requirements   Some of the requirements listed pertain to minimum processor speed, minimum memory, and supported databases, along with other information.

New features   A number of new features will be discussed in the book, so it's handy to get a look at what these features are for. For example, one of the many new features listed is the new interface to LOBs and other objects.

Known issues   This is an excellent source for discovering known issues that may be causing problems for you. For example, a very common error, "Error with Visual Basic 6—Runtime Error 5: Invalid Procedure Call or Argument," is new to Visual Basic version 6 and is caused by underlying changes made to the Visual Basic product.

We don't expect anyone to memorize or study the Release Notes, but simply to become familiar with what it contains so that you know the kinds of questions it can answer.

Finally, we come to the online help. If you look back to Figure 1.40, you will see the menu item Oracle Objects for OLE Help. Click this menu item to open the online help. Between the information contained in this book and the online help, you should be able to quickly implement a large portion of OO4O's functionality in a short time.

Summary

This chapter walked you through a simple client installation with the new installer, discussed the information required to create a service name for connecting to an Oracle database, and pointed out where to find some of the required OO4O online documentation. Once you successfully complete the tasks in this chapter, your client machine is ready for its first OO4O application.

chapter 2

An Overview of Data Access Methods from Visual Basic

- Understanding Data Access objects

- Understanding Remote Data objects

- Understanding ActiveX Data objects

- Programming with Oracle Objects for OLE

- Mapping Oracle data types to Visual Basic

- Returning Oracle internal data types

Microsoft offers a variety of data access methods for accessing data from Visual Basic applications. These include the following:

- ODBC (Open Database Connectivity)
- Data Access objects
- Remote Data objects
- OLE DB and Microsoft ActiveX Data objects

Oracle offers a similar data access interface, known as *Oracle Objects for OLE* (OO4O). OO4O is a data access model that provides a specific API to write applications that access data in an Oracle server. OO4O is based on Microsoft's COM Automation and ActiveX technology. COM, or Common Object Model, is a software design methodology for creating components that provide services to clients or applications. The underlying technologies include ActiveX, OLE, and COM Automation. The heart of OO4O consists of an in-process COM server that services requests from your application. Oracle Objects for OLE is compatible with any COM Automation scripting language, such as Visual Basic and VBA-licensed applications like Access and Excel.

Getting Started

In this chapter, you will briefly examine the various interfaces available by writing simple applications that demonstrate the use of each interface, as well as their differences. The example applications introduced will use the sample database schema Scott, which is provided by Oracle after installing the client products. If you have not run the scripts to build the Scott schema, follow these steps:

1. Start SQL*PLUS version 8.1.

2. Log into the database using a system account such as System/Manager.

3. At the SQL prompt, type the following statement to create the Scott user account and to grant Scott appropriate privileges.

```
create user SCOTT identified by TIGER;
grant CONNECT to SCOTT;
grant RESOURCE to SCOTT;
grant DBA to SCOTT;
connect scott/tiger
```

4. At the SQL prompt, type the following to run the script to create the Scott user account and its associated objects. Change the drive letter to the appropriate one for your client installation.

```
@c:\%oracle_home%\0040\demobld7.sql
```

NOTE   The name of the directory where the Oracle client is installed is %Oracle_Home%. By default, the home name is oracle\ora81.

The script will create the Scott schema objects, such as the Emp and Dept tables. You may want to issue a few Select statements, such as those that follow, to test the connection and to ensure that the appropriate objects are created.

```
select * from emp;
select * from dept;
```

In order to build the examples presented in this chapter, you need to install the Oracle ODBC driver and configure a Data Source Name (DSN). Refer to Chapter 1 for details on installing Oracle client components. The ODBC driver component is listed in Figure 1.10. Once you have installed the Oracle ODBC driver, you can configure the DSN that will be used later in this chapter. The tool used to create and manage Data Source Names is the Microsoft ODBC 32-bit Administrator. The following steps will help you configure the DSN for the example applications:

1. Start the ODBC Administrator from either the Control Panel or the shortcut provided in the Oracle – Ora81 folder on the Programs menu.

2. Click the System DSN tab to give it the focus, as seen in Figure 2.1.

FIGURE 2.1
The list of data sources

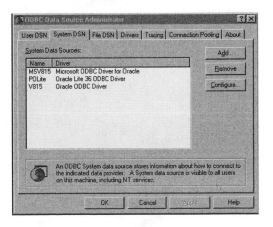

3. Click the Add button to create a new DSN. A list of installed drivers will appear, as shown in Figure 2.2.

FIGURE 2.2
The list of installed ODBC drivers

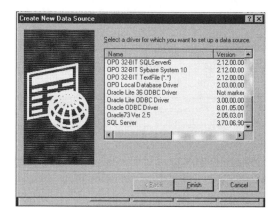

4. Choose the Oracle ODBC driver Version 8.01.05.00 and click OK. The setup routines for the driver will appear, as seen in Figure 2.3.

FIGURE 2.3
The Oracle ODBC driver setup routines

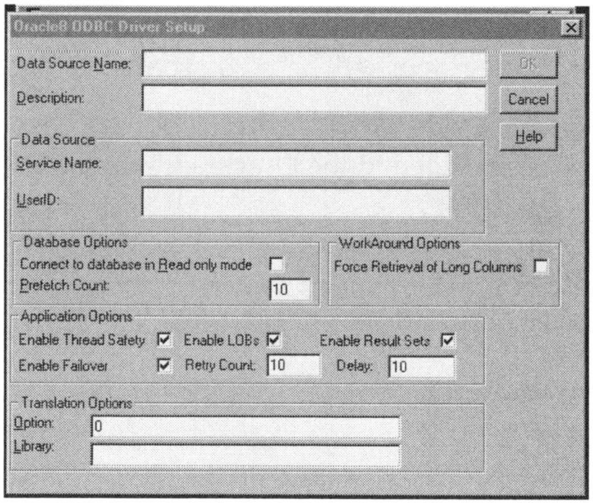

5. Place the text cursor in the Data Source Name field to give it the current focus. Type **v8i**.

6. Place the text cursor in the Server Name field to give it the current focus. Type in the Net8 service name that you configured in Chapter 1.

7. Place the text cursor in the UserID field to give it the current focus. Type **scott**. See Figure 2.4 for how this should look.

FIGURE 2.4
The setup routine with the parameter values

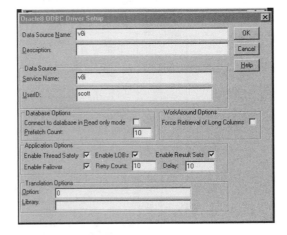

8. Click the OK button to save the newly created DSN.

9. Click the OK button to close the ODBC Administrator.

With the ODBC driver installed, the ODBC DSN configured, and the starter database and Scott schema in place, you are now ready to move forward and take a closer look at the various programmatic interfaces available through Microsoft Visual Basic.

Data Access Objects

Data Access Objects (DAO) provide data access to native Microsoft Jet engine databases and any ODBC data source. The DAO object model is structured after a relational database system. With DAO methods and properties, you can create databases, define tables, define columns, and query and navigate data. The Microsoft Jet database engine translates methods called on DAO objects into database operations and handles all the details of interfacing with the supported databases, including ODBC data sources. Figure 2.5 shows the various components of the DAO model and their hierarchical relationship to each other.

FIGURE 2.5
The Data Access Objects
model

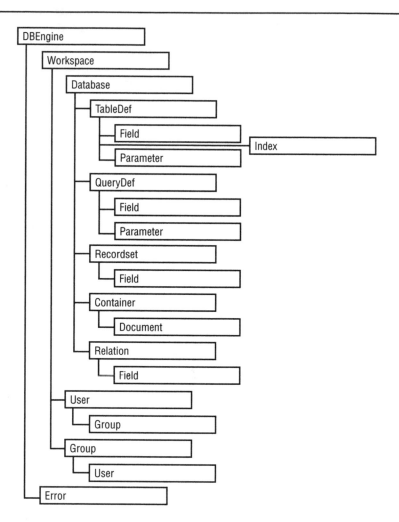

The following list defines the objects in the Data Access Objects model as defined by Microsoft Corporation. They are listed according to their place in the hierarchical model pictured in Figure 2.5. For additional information on each of these objects, please refer to the Visual Basic online documentation.

DBEngine object   The DBEngine object is the base object in the DAO model. All DAO objects are derived from the DBEngine object. This object is automatically created for you by the Visual Basic Runtime.

Workspace object   The workspace object represents a user session. It contains information on connections to open databases.

Database object   The database object represents a database with an open connection.

TableDef object   The table definition object represents a table in the database. It contains field and index objects that are used to describe a database table.

Index object   The index object represents an index on a table in the database.

QueryDef object   The query definition object represents an SQL statement.

Parameter object   The parameter object represents a bind variable that is used with a QueryDef or TableDef object. There are three different types of parameters: input, output, or both.

Recordset object   The recordset object represents the results returned by executing an SQL statement. There are five types of recordsets: table, dynaset, snapshot, forward only, and dynamic.

Container object   A container object represents a set of objects in a database for which you can assign permissions.

Document object   The document object represents information about individual objects in the database, such as tables and queries.

Relation object   The relation object represents relationships between fields in tables and queries. You can use this object to enforce referential integrity, as well as set behaviors such as cascading updates and deletes.

Field object   The field object represents a column or field in a database table. A Field object holds data, and you can use it to read data from or write the column values in a recordset object.

User object   The user object represents a user account. You can use this object to set access permissions.

Group object   The group object represents user accounts that have similar permissions in a workspace. This is very similar to roles in Oracle.

Error object   The error object contains information about an error that occurred during a DAO method call or operation. When a method or operation does not complete successfully, an error is generated and returned as an individual error object.

Workspace objects can contain one or many database objects. The database object represents a connection that has been created against a data source. Of all the DAO objects, applications use the Recordset object the most. Recordsets provide applications with the means to execute SQL statements and to manage and manipulate data. As you can see, the DAO model is very cumbersome and quite complex in that it provides 15 objects used by the Microsoft Jet to manage data from many different data sources.

Using Microsoft Jet isn't always the best appraoch, but the flexibility of its 15 object types can provide you with many different alternatives and options when writing your application. Table 2.1 lists some of the pros and cons of using DAO with a Microsoft Jet workspace.

TABLE 2.1:   The Pros and Cons of Using DAO

Pros	Cons
Flexibility	Difficulty in coding
Support for cursors	Average performance
Support for many different data sources	Tied to Microsoft Jet

Choosing Microsoft Jet or ODBC Direct

DAO can be used either with Microsoft Jet or with ODBC Direct. The Jet Database access engine processes queries, as well as routes them to remote data sources. By using the Microsoft Data Control and data aware controls, such as the DBGRID control, you can create code that is database independent because Jet performs all the translations necessary to access remote data. With DAO, you can write an application that accesses different types of data sources without being tied to specific databases. These data sources could be Open Database Connectivity (ODBC) databases, such as Oracle and SQL Server; or Index Sequential Access Method (ISAM) databases, such as Access, FoxPro, Paradox, or dBase; or other Jet databases.

NOTE   DAO is the only data access method that supports 16-bit operations.

ODBC Direct is another option available when using DAO. ODBC Direct allows you to choose the database source and leaves Jet out of the picture. When you use this type of workspace, DAO uses the RDO (Remote Data Objects) libraries. ODBC Direct maps each DAO object to an RDO object that has similar functionality.

A Simple Demonstration of Using DAO

Let's write a simple DAO application following the steps here. This example uses a Microsoft Jet workspace not ODBC Direct. The steps will guide you through building a simple Visual Basic application that demonstrates how to connect and execute a simple SQL statement using the DAO libraries and the Oracle ODBC driver.

In this example, the DAO object library will be used to bring data to text field controls on Form1. The following steps describe how to create a small DAO application that uses an ODBC data source to establish a connection to an Oracle database. You'll create command buttons to enable the user to move through the recordset easily.

1. Start Microsoft Visual Basic 6.

2. Choose File ➢ New Project.

3. From the Project window, choose Standard EXE for the target type. Click the OK button.

NOTE Make sure the Project Explorer and toolbox are present. If necessary, use the View menu to make them visible.

Now that you have set up a project with a default form, as seen in Figure 2.6, the next step is to draw the user interface for the default form.

FIGURE 2.6

The Visual Basic Designer

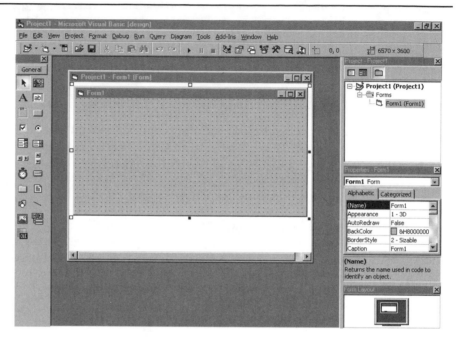

The user interface consists of a form with three text boxes and two command buttons. Command buttons and text boxes are referred to as *controls*, or visual widgets that are bundled with VB. The controls provide functionality for building a user interface. The text boxes are used to present the three pieces of information contained in your recordset to the end user. The command buttons are used to tell the application to move through the recordset and display each new row of information. To build the user interface, follow these steps:

1. Click the command button located on the toolbox, to give this control the current focus.

TIP

You can use the Tool Tips feature to locate the correct control. Position your mouse over a control for a moment or two, and the name of the control will appear.

2. Use your mouse pointer to draw a button on the form by holding down the left mouse button and drawing a rectangle.

3. Repeat the process in step 2 so that you have two command buttons on the form.

4. Click each command button, dragging and positioning each on the bottom center of the form. Refer to Figure 2.7 to check your work.

FIGURE 2.7
The Default form with two command buttons

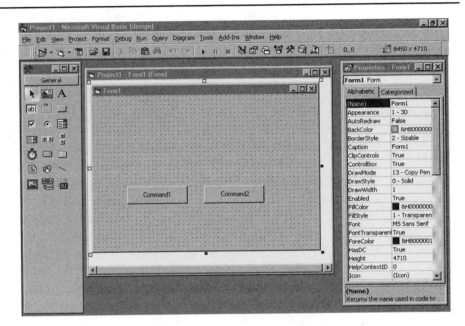

5. Click the first command button to give it the current focus. The default name for the button is Command1. Locate the Properties dialog box on the right-hand side of the Visual Basic Designer.

6. Locate the (Name) property and change the button's name to **MoveForward**. Change the value by positioning the text cursor in the text edit area on the right-hand side of the property name. Use the mouse pointer to highlight the old value. Overwrite the default value by typing the new one.

7. Locate the Caption property and change the button's caption to **MoveNext**.

8. Click the second command button, Command2, giving it the current focus.

9. Locate the (Name) property and change the button's name to **MoveBackward**.

10. Locate the Caption property and change the button's caption to **MoveBack**.

FIGURE 2.8
The user interface with
MoveNext and MoveBack
buttons

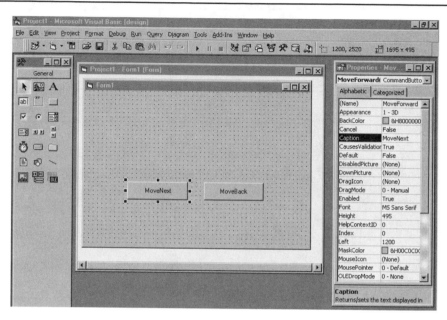

Now that the buttons are drawn and labeled, as seen in Figure 2.8, you are ready to draw the three text boxes. These controls will be used to present data to your end user.

1. Choose the text box located on the toolbox to give this control the current focus.

2. Use your mouse pointer to draw a text box on the form by holding down the left mouse button and drawing the button by pulling a rectangle out of the dotted lines.

3. Repeat the process in step 2 twice more until you have three text boxes on the form.

4. Click each text box in turn, dragging the controls to the center of the form and positioning them in a horizontal row.

5. Click Text1, giving it the current focus.

6. In the Properties dialog box of the Visual Basic Designer, locate the (Name) property and change the text box name to **empno_fld**.

7. Click Text2 to give this object the current focus.

8. Locate the (Name) property and change the text box name to **ename_fld**.

9. Click Text3 to give this object the current focus.

10. Locate the (Name) property and change the text box name to **hiredate_fld**.

The completed design for the user interface is shown in Figure 2.9. The application will provide context-sensitive help and a good error handler to ensure that the user makes the connection successfully. The next step is to add the program code to make the connection to the database. You'll do that in the next section.

FIGURE 2.9
The completed user interface

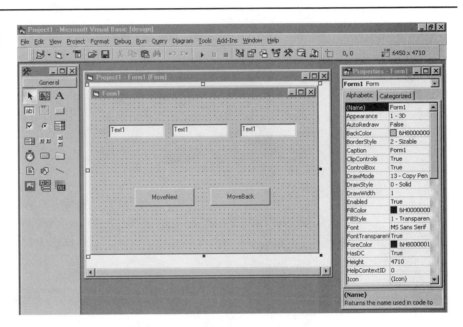

Now that the design of the interface is ready, you can start adding custom code into the event handlers for the controls so that something will actually happen when the user interacts with the text boxes and buttons.

You need to include the reference to the DAO Type Library so that the data types declared in your program are resolved at compile time.

1. Choose Project ➢ References in the Visual Basic Designer.

2. Locate the Microsoft DAO 2.5/3.51 Compatibility Library in the Available References dialog box. Enable the type library by checking the box on the left, as shown in Figure 2.10. Click the OK button.

FIGURE 2.10
Enabling the DAO library in
the Available References
dialog box

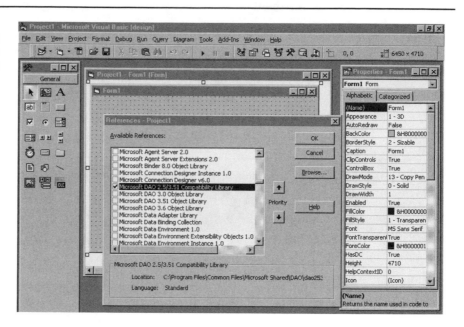

3. Click the form object to give it the current focus.

4. Click the right mouse button to display the pop-up menu for the form.

5. Choose View Code. The Project Code window appears, as seen in Figure 2.11.

FIGURE 2.11
The Project Code window

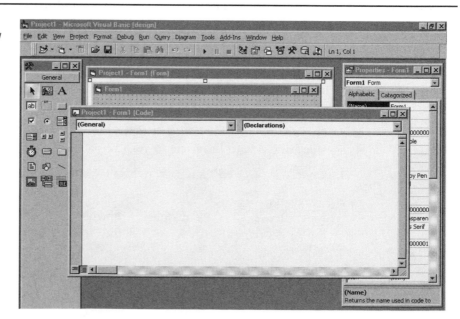

6. In the Project Code window, pull down the Objects pick list and select General.

7. In the Project Code window, pull down the Procedures pick list and select (Declarations).

8. Position your text cursor in the Project Code window and type the following:

```
Dim DAODatabase As Database
Dim DAORecordset As Recordset
```

9. In the Project Code window, pull down the Objects pick list and select Form.

10. In the Project Code window, pull down the Procedures pick list and select Load.

11. Position the text cursor in the Form_Load procedure and type the following lines of code. Figure 2.12 gives you a look at the Project Code window with the code typed in the Form_Load procedure.

```
Set DAODatabase = OpenDatabase _
("",dbDriverNoPrompt,False,"ODBC;DSN=v8i;UID=scott; _
PWD=tiger")
Set DAORecordset = DAODatabase.OpenRecordset ("scott.emp", _
dbOpenDynaset)
DAORecordset.MoveFirst
empno_fld = DAORecordset.Fields("empno").value
ename_fld = DAORecordset.Fields("ename").value
hiredate_fld = DAORecordset.Fields("hiredate").value
```

FIGURE 2.12
The Project Code window with the DAO calls in the Form_Load procedure

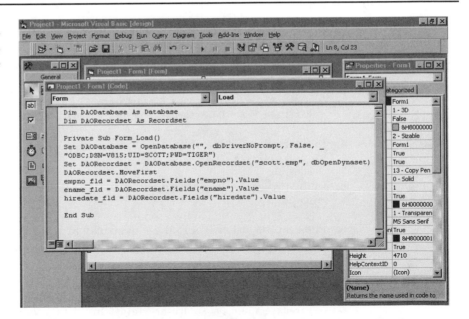

When you run the application at this stage, two things will happen. First, the DBEngine, DAODatabase, and DAORecordset objects will be created. Second, the text boxes will contain the first row of data. Figure 2.13 gives you a look at the results when the application is run in the Visual Basic Designer.

Next, you need to provide the program code for the MoveNext and MoveBack buttons.

FIGURE 2.13
The DAO application displaying the first row of data to the user

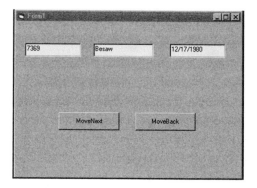

1. In the Project Code window, pull down the Objects pick list and choose MoveForward.

2. In the Project Code window, pull down the Procedures pick list and choose Click.

3. Position the text cursor in the MoveForward_click procedure and type the following lines of code:

```
DAORecordset.MoveNext
empno_fld = DAORecordset.Fields("empno").value
ename_fld = DAORecordset.Fields("ename").value
hiredate_fld = DAORecordset.Fields("hiredate").value
```

4. In the Project Code window, pull down the Objects pick list and choose MoveBackward.

5. In the Project Code window, pull down the Procedures pick list and choose Click.

6. Position the text cursor in the MoveBackward_click procedure and type the following lines of code:

```
DAORecordset.MovePrevious
empno_fld = DAORecordset.Fields("empno").value
ename_fld = DAORecordset.Fields("ename").value
hiredate_fld = DAORecordset.Fields("hiredate").value
```

At this stage, all text boxes and buttons have been coded, and the application is ready to be run. Test the Forward and Backward buttons by scrolling through the first couple of records. Take a look at Figure 2.14 for an example of what the application displays to your end user. You may want to save your work to refer back to at a later time. To save your project, follow these steps:

1. Choose File ➤ Save Project.

2. You will be prompted for a name for both the project and form files. Type **DAOSample** for both the project and form filename.

FIGURE 2.14
The DAO application with the first row of data displayed

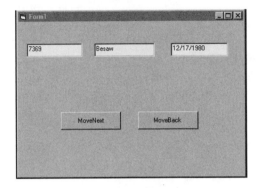

Next, let's examine the RDO model and see how it differs from the DAO model and why you may want to choose this approach when accessing databases through an ODBC data source.

Remote Data Objects

The *Remote Data Objects* (RDO) *model* provides access methods for ODBC data. It was introduced and available for the first time with Visual Basic 5. RDO is similar to DAO but was created specifically for access to SQL databases rather than ISAM files. RDO is a thin layer or wrapper that sits on top of the ODBC API and makes it much easier for developers to write ODBC applications to access relational data. RDO provides the application developer a simpler alternative to writing their applications to the native ODBC API, which requires technical expertise and knowledge of the ODBC specification. RDO is designed to take advantage of SQL database servers that use complex query engines, such as Oracle and SQL Server.

The RDO model includes a number of objects, properties, and methods that allow you to execute SQL statements, call stored procedures, and use bind variables in parameterized queries. Figure 2.15 shows the various components of the model and their relational hierarchy in the model.

FIGURE 2.15

The Remote Data Object model

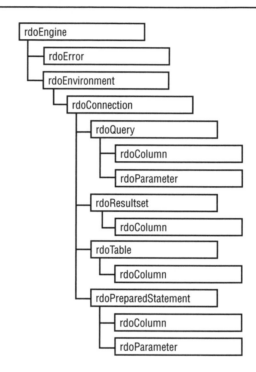

The following list describes the types of objects available in the RDO model as defined by Microsoft Corporation. For additional information on each of these objects that is not presented in this chapter, please refer to the Visual Basic online documentation.

rdoEngine   The rdoEngine object is the base RDO object. All RDO objects are derived from the rdoEngine object.

rdoError   The rdoError object represents an error that has occurred during an RDO operation or method call. You can use this object to trap ODBC errors that may occur.

rdoEnvironment   The rdoEnvironment object represents a set of connections for a specific user. This object also contains information about transaction scopes.

rdoConnection   The rdoConnection object represents a connection a database. This connection may be allocated but not yet open.

rdoQuery   The rdoQuery object represents an SQL statement. This query may or may not have parameters.

rdoColumn   The rdoColumn object represents a column of data in a database table. It holds metadata about the column, such as the data type and size.

rdoParameter   The rdoParameter object represents a bind variable that is associated with an rdoQuery object. You can use three parameters: input, output, or both.

rdoResultset   An rdoResultset object represents the query results returned from an SQL statement.

rdoTable   An rdoTable object represents a database table or view.

rdoPreparedStatement   The rdoPreparedStatement object represents a prepared SQL statement. The rdoPreparedStatement object is obsolete. You should use the rdoQuery object in place of the rdoPreparedStatement object to obtain the same functionality in your RDO applications.

NOTE   RDO's version 1 rdoPreparedStatement and rdoPreparedStatements collection objects are supported by version 2 but only for backward compatibility. You should use the rdoQuery object and rdoQueries collection to provide the same functionality in your RDO applications.

NOTE   RDO is a 32-bit interface only and is designed to work on Windows NT 4 and Windows 98/95.

Table 2.2 lists the pros and cons of choosing RDO over other interfaces, such as Data Access Objects (DAO).

In order to see the differences between RDO and DAO, let's write a simple RDO application. These steps will guide you through building a Visual Basic application that demonstrates how to connect and execute a simple SQL statement using

TABLE 2.2: Pros and Cons of Using RDO

Pros	Cons
Great performance.	No support for ISAM
Aimed at SQL databases, such as Oracle.	No support for Oracle 8/8i features
You can create simple, cursorless result sets.	
You can execute stored procedures that return result sets.	
You can execute action queries that perform data manipulation or data definition operations.	

the RDO libraries and the Oracle ODBC driver. You should use the work completed in the previous section that you saved as DAOSample.

1. Start Microsoft Visual Basic 6.

2. Choose File ➤ Open Project.

3. Select the saved project file, DAOSample, by highlighting the filename.

4. Choose Open.

The user interface consists of a form with three text boxes and two command buttons. The text boxes are used to present the three pieces of information contained in the recordset to the end user. The command buttons are used to tell the application to move through the recordset and display each new row of information. To save this project under a new name so that we can modify its contents to use the RDO libraries, follow these steps:

1. Choose File ➤ Save Project As.

2. You will be asked to enter a new name for the project. Type **RDOSample** for the project filename and click Save.

3. To save the form under the new name, highlight the form object and choose File ➤ Save DAOSample As.

4. You will be asked to enter a new name for the form. Type **RDOSample** for the form filename.

You need to include the reference to the RDO Type Library so that the data types declared in your program will be resolved at compile time.

1. Choose Project ➢ References in the Visual Basic Designer.

2. In the Available References dialog box, locate the Microsoft Remote Data Object 2.0 RDO Type Library. Enable the type library by checking the box on the left, as seen in Figure 2.16. Click the OK button.

FIGURE 2.16
Enabling the RDO Type Library in the Available References dialog box

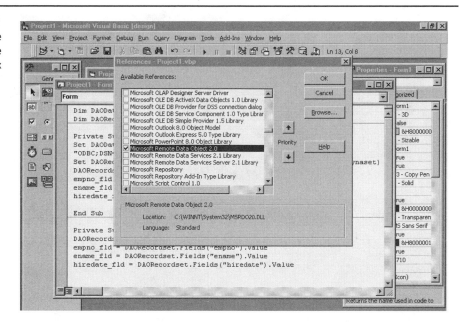

3. Click the form object to give it the current focus.

4. Click the right mouse button to display the pop-up menu for the form.

5. Choose View Code. The Project Code window appears, as seen in Figure 2.17.

6. In the Project Code window, pull down the Objects pick list and select (General).

7. In the Project Code window, pull down the Procedures pick list and select (Declarations).

FIGURE 2.17
The Project Code window

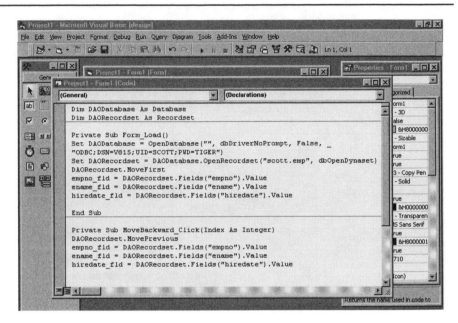

8. Replace the DAO statements with the following RDO statements.

```
Dim OraRdoEnvironment as RdoEnvironment
Dim OraRdoDatabase as rdoConnection
Dim OraRdoRecordset as rdoResultset
```

9. In the Project Code window, pull down the Objects pick list and select Form.

10. In the Project Code window, pull down the Procedures pick list and select Load.

11. Position the text cursor in the Form_Load procedure and replace the DAO statements with the following RDO statements:

```
Set OraRdoEnvironment = rdoEnvironments(0)
OraRdoEnvironment.CursorDriver = rdUseOdbc
Set OraRdoDatabase = OraRdoEnvironment.OpenConnection _
("", rdDriverNoPrompt, False, "DSN=V8i;UID=SCOTT;PWD=TIGER")
Set OraRdoRecordset = OraRdoDatabase.OpenResultset( _
"select * from emp")
OraRdoRecordset.MoveFirst
empno_fld = OraRdoRecordset ("empno").value
ename_fld = OraRdoRecordset ("ename").value
hiredate_fld = OraRdoRecordset ("hiredate").value
```

Figure 2.18 gives you a look at the code that you typed in the Form_Load procedure in the Project Code window.

FIGURE 2.18
The Project Code window with the RDO calls in the Form_Load procedure

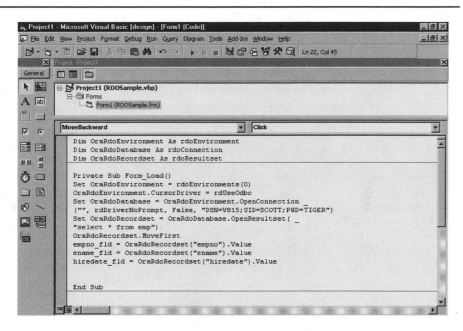

Now, you need to modify the program code for the MoveNext and MoveBack buttons.

1. In the Project Code window, pull down the Objects pick list and choose MoveForward.

2. In the Project Code window, pull down the Procedures pick list and choose Click.

3. Replace the DAO statements with the following RDO statements.

```
OraRdoRecordset.MoveNext
empno_fld = OraRdoRecordset ("empno").value
ename_fld = OraRdoRecordset ("ename").value
hiredate_fld = OraRdoRecordset ("hiredate").value
```

4. In the Project Code window, pull down the Objects pick list and choose MoveBackward.

5. In the Project Code window, pull down the Procedures pick list and choose Click.

6. Replace the DAO statements with the following RDO statements:

```
OraRdoRecordset.MovePrevious
empno_fld = OraRdoRecordset ("empno").value
ename_fld = OraRdoRecordset ("ename").value
hiredate_fld = OraRdoRecordset ("hiredate").value
```

At this stage, all text boxes and buttons have been modified to use the RDO libraries, and the application is ready to run. Take a look at Figure 2.19 for an example of what the application displays to your end user. You may want to save your work to refer back to at a later time. To save your project, perform the following step:

1. Choose File ➤ Save Project.

FIGURE 2.19
The RDO application with the first row of data displayed

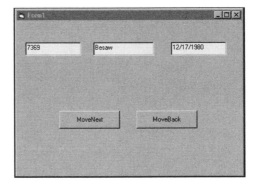

Next, let's examine the ActiveX Data Object (ADO) model and see how it differs from the Data Access Objects (DAO) and Remote Data Objects (RDO) models.

ActiveX Data Objects (ADO)

The *ActiveX Data Objects model* is a high-level interface that sits on top of *Object Linking and Embedding for Databases* (OLE DB). OLE DB is a new database access API specification written by Microsoft. It is the next generation of Open Database Connectivity (ODBC). OLE DB is a complete and separate API from ODBC and is intended for use by applications to retrieve and manipulate data from any persistent store. OLE DB is referred to as a universal strategy for data access. ADO, a COM library, allows you to write an application to access and manage data in a database through an OLE DB or ODBC Provider. Microsoft provides an OLE DB/ODBC bridge, which translates OLE/DB calls from your ADO application to the equivalent ODBC calls. This allows applications written using the ADO interface to access data from a database in which the vendor has not provided a native OLE/DB driver but does provide an ODBC driver. Currently, Microsoft bundles an OLE DB Provider for Oracle databases with Visual Basic 6. Oracle also bundles an OLE DB Provider with the Oracle 8.1.6 client. For additional information on using the Oracle OLE DB Provider, refer to Chapter 14.

The ADO data model is implemented using a COM Automation library. Any language that supports COM and Automation can use ADO. ADO was designed to take the place of DAO and RDO and provide one interface that can be used to access all types of data regardless of where it resides. Universal access is the goal, and ADO is the Microsoft answer. Figure 2.20 shows the various components of the ADO model.

FIGURE 2.20
The ActiveX Data Objects model

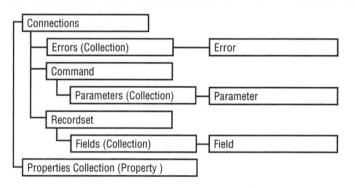

The ADO model contains the following seven objects. The list describes each object as defined by Microsoft Corporation. For additional information on each of these objects that is not presented in this chapter, please refer to the Visual Basic online documentation.

Connection   A connection object represents a connection to a database. It is used to execute queries and manage transactions.

Error   An error object represents an error that has occurred when an ADO operation or method has not completed successfully.

Command   A command object is used to create and execute parameterized queries.

Parameter   A parameter object represents a bind variable in an SQL statement. You can use three types of parameters: input, output, or both.

Recordset   A recordset object represents the query results returned from an SQL statement.

Field   A field object represents a column or field in a database table. A field object holds data, and you can use it to read data from or write the column values in a recordset object.

Property   A property object retrieves information about the characteristics of the connection, command, recordset, and field objects. These are provider-specific properties.

Table 2.3 lists the pros and cons of using ADO as compared to RDO and DAO.

TABLE 2.3:   Pros and Cons of Using ADO

Pros	Cons
Great performance.	The underlying OLEDB provider may not support all features.
Independently created objects are available.	Currently no support for Oracle 8i objects, ADT(s), and LOB data types.
Supports various types of cursors.	
Can execute stored procedures that return multiple result sets.	
Can execute action queries that perform data support for limits on the number of rows returned for tuning purposes.	
Microsoft has created a simpler object model to write applications with. The ADO model is a simple programming model that consists of 7 objects as compared to DAO, which is cumbersome and consists of 14 objects that your application creates and manages.	

To demonstrate the simplicity and power of the ADO model, we will build an ADO application. The following steps show how to establish a connection to an Oracle Database using the ODBC provider and how to open a result set on the Emp table.

1. Start Microsoft Visual Basic 6.

2. Choose File ➢ Open.

3. Select the saved project file, RDOSample, by highlighting the filename.

4. Choose Open.

The user interface will consist of a form with three text boxes and two command buttons. The text boxes will present three pieces of information contained in your recordset to the end user. The command buttons will allow the application to move through the recordset and display a new row of information. Save this project under a new name so that we can modify its contents to use the ADO as we did previously with the RDO example.

1. Choose File ➢ Save Project As.

2. You will be asked to enter a new name for the project. Type **ADOSample** for the project filename and click the Save button.

3. To save the form under the new name, highlight the form object and choose File ➢ Save RDOSample As.

4. You will be asked to enter a new name for the form. Type **ADOSample** for the form filename and click the Save button.

To include the reference to the ADO type library so that the data types declared in your program are resolved at compile time, follow these steps:

1. Choose Project ➢ References in the Visual Basic Designer.

2. Locate the Microsoft ActiveX Data Objects 2.1 Library in the Available References dialog box. Enable the type library by checking the box on the left, as seen in Figure 2.21. Click the OK button.

3. Click the form object to give it the current focus.

4. Click the right mouse button to display the pop-up menu for the form.

5. Choose View Code. The Project Code window appears, as seen in Figure 2.22.

6. In the Project Code window, pull down the Objects pick list and select (General).

7. In the Project Code window, pull down the Procedures pick list and select (Declarations).

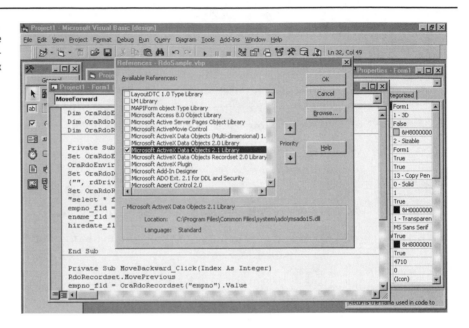

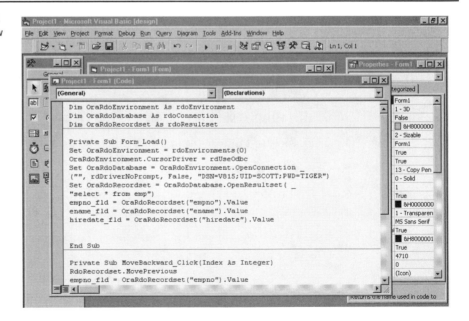

8. Replace the RDO statements with the following ADO statements.

```
Dim adoConnection As ADODB.Connection
Dim adoRecordset As ADODB.Recordset
Dim adoConnectString As String
```

9. In the Project Code window, pull down the Objects pick list and select Form.

10. In the Project Code window, pull down the Procedures pick list and select Load.

11. Position the text cursor in the Form_Load procedure and replace the RDO statements with the following ADO statements:

```
Set adoConnection = New ADODB.Connection
Set adoRecordset = New ADODB.Recordset
adoConnectString = "Data Source = v8i; User id = _
scott;password=tiger"
adoConnection.Open adoConnectString
adoRecordset.CursorType = adUseClient
adoRecordset.Open "EMP", adoConnection, , , adCmdTable
empno_fld = adoRecordset.Fields("empno").value
ename_fld = adoRecordset.Fields("ename").value
hireadte_fld = adoRecordset.Fields("hiredate").value
```

Figure 2.23 gives you a look at the code typed in the Form_Load procedure.

FIGURE 2.23
The Project Code window with the ADO calls in the Form_load procedure

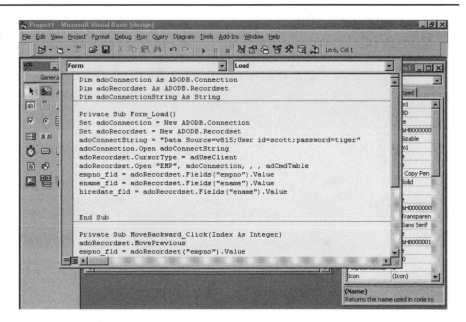

To modify the program code for the MoveNext and MoveBack buttons, follow these steps:

1. In the Project Code window, pull down the Objects pick list and choose MoveForward.

2. In the Project Code window, pull down the Procedures pick list and choose Click.

3. Replace the RDO statements with the following ADO statements.

   ```
   adoRecordset.MoveNext
   empno_fld = adoRecordset.Fields("empno").value
   ename_fld = adoRecordset.Fields("ename").value
   hiredate_fld = adoRecordset.Fields("hiredate").value
   ```

4. In the Project Code window, pull down the Objects pick list and choose MoveBackward.

5. In the Project Code window, pull down the Procedures pick list and choose Click.

6. Replace the RDO statements with the following ADO statements.

   ```
   adoRecordset.MovePrevious
   empno_fld = adoRecordset.Fields("empno").value
   ename_fld = adoRecordset.Fields("ename").value
   hiredate_fld = adoRecordset.Fields("hiredate").value
   ```

At this stage, all text boxes and buttons have been modified to use the ADO libraries, and the application is ready to run. Take a look at Figure 2.24 for an example of what the application displays to your end user. You may want to save your work to refer back to at a later time. To save your project, choose File ➢ Save Project.

FIGURE 2.24
The ADO application with the first row of data displayed

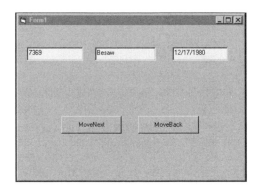

Using the ADO Data Control

Next, you will create a simple application using the ADO Data Control. This demonstrates creating a ready-to-go application in a few easy steps.

The ADO Data Control can be used to bring back data to bound controls with little or no code. The ADO Data Control is very simple to use and performs a lot of the work for your application. The following steps describe how to create a small ADO application that takes advantage of the ADO Data Control.

1. Start Microsoft Visual Basic 6.

2. Choose File ➢ New Project.

3. In the Project window, choose Standard EXE for the target type and click the OK button.

> **NOTE**　　Make sure that the Project Explorer and toolbox are present when you are opening a new project in VB. If necessary, use the View menu to make them visible.

Now that you have set up a project with a default form, as seen in Figure 2.25, the next step is to place the bound control and ADO Data Control on the form.

FIGURE 2.25
The default project with a main form

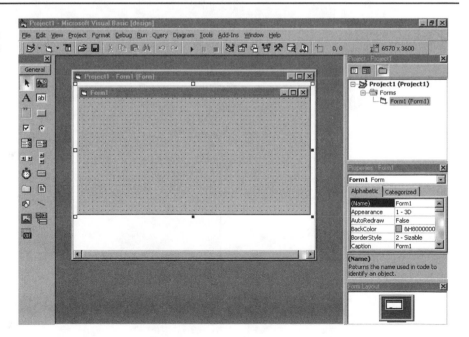

1. Choose Project ≻ Components. Click the Controls tab.

2. In the Components dialog box, choose the ADO Data Control and the ADO DataGrid component by toggling the check box next to each item. Refer to Figure 2.26 to check your work so far.

FIGURE 2.26

A component list with the ADO Data Control and the ADO DataGrid Control selected

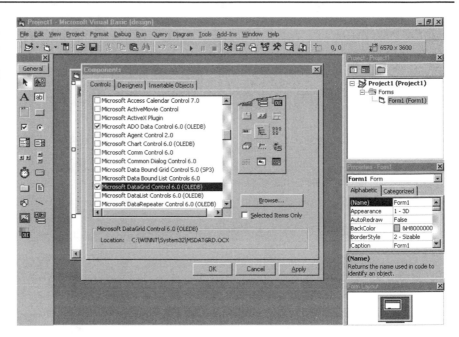

3. Choose the ADO Data Control icon from the toolbox and drag it onto the form (see Figure 2.27).

4. Choose the ADO DataGrid component from the toolbox and drag it onto the form (see Figure 2.27).

5. Choose the DataGrid1 object on the form. Locate the Data Source property and set it to the name of the ADO control on the form. In this case, set it to Adodc1.

FIGURE 2.27
The new toolbox with ADO
Data Control and DataGrid
icons

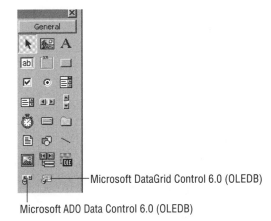

Microsoft DataGrid Control 6.0 (OLEDB)

Microsoft ADO Data Control 6.0 (OLEDB)

TIP   You can use Help to locate a component on the toolbox. Move your cursor over a
component, and the name of it will be displayed.

6. Choose the ADO Data Control object, right-click the button, and choose
ADODC Properties. The Property Pages dialog box will appear, as shown in
Figure 2.28.

FIGURE 2.28
The ADO Data Control
Property Pages dialog box

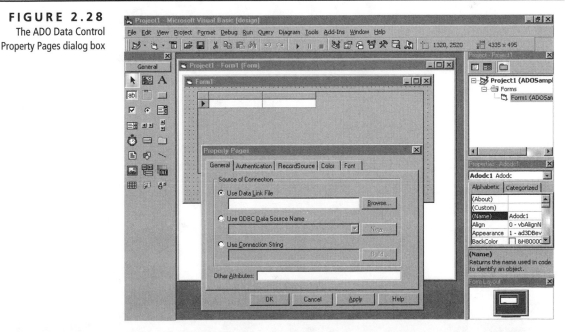

7. Choose the Use ODBC Data Source Name radio button as the source of connection. Pull down the pick list and choose the DSN you created with the Oracle ODBC driver at the beginning of this chapter.

8. In the Property Pages dialog box, choose the Authentication tab. Enter the account information for the database connection in the Authentication Information area. Type **scott** in the User Name text box and type **tiger** in the Password text box. Figure 2.29 demonstrates how this should look.

FIGURE 2.29
The ADO Data Control
Property Pages Authentication tab

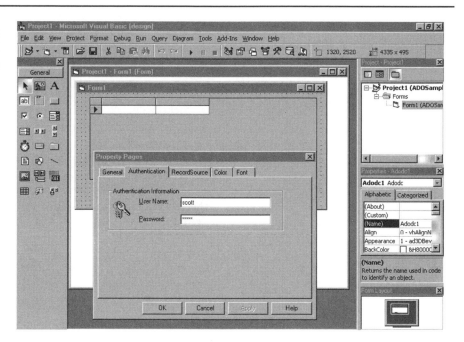

9. Choose the RecordSource tab and enter the SQL statement `Select From Emp` in the Command Text (SQL) text box. Figure 2.30 demonstrates how this should look. In the Command Type pick list, the Command Object Property command type will default to asCmdUnknown, which is acceptable for this type of application. The Table or Stored Procedure Name pick list is not enabled because it is not relevant for the default command type.

FIGURE 2.30
The ADO Data Control
Property Pages Record-
Source tab

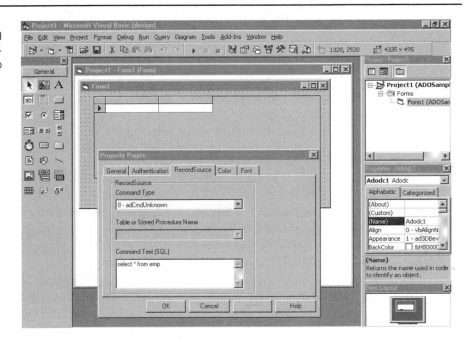

10. Choose Run ➤ Start to launch the form and see the list of employee names displayed in the data grid component. Figure 2.31 shows the correct output.

FIGURE 2.31
The ADO Data Control
application results

Oracle Objects for OLE

Oracle Objects for OLE (OO4O) is a product designed and developed by Oracle Corporation. OO4O allows data access from any language that is OLE enabled and, thus, supports Microsoft ActiveX technology and COM Automation. Some of the OLE-enabled languages include Visual Basic, Visual C++, and IIS Active Server Pages.

The key component of the OO4O programming model is the *Oracle In Process Automation Server* (InProc Server). The InProc Server is actually a set of COM objects used for establishing connections to databases, executing SQL, and calling stored procedures in the database. OO4O is an Oracle solution and cannot be used to access other databases. The OO4O interface provides an API that is tuned for accessing an Oracle database. It also provides a simple way of accessing complex object types and object-oriented database designs. Figure 2.32 shows the various components of the OO4O model.

FIGURE 2.32
The Oracle Objects for OLE model

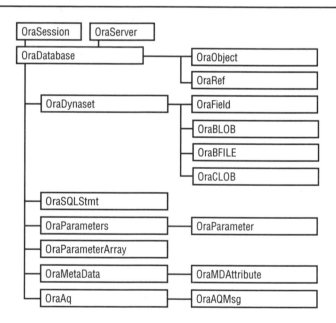

The OO4O model contains the objects in the following list. The list describes each object as defined by Oracle Corporation. For additional information on each of these objects that is not presented in this chapter, please refer to the Oracle Objects for OLE online documentation.

OraSession The OraSession object represents the base object. This object is created when an application starts and creates an instance of the InProc Server. It contains methods for establishing connections to an Oracle database and transaction control of SQL statements.

OraServer   The OraServer object represents a physical connection to an Oracle database. It contains methods for establishing a user session on the server connection it represents.

OraDatabase   The OraDatabase object represents a connection to an Oracle database. This object provides methods for executing SQL statements. It is created by a call to the OpenDatabase method of the OraSession or OraServer objects.

OraSQLStmt   The OraSQLStmt object is used for executing DDL statements, such as `create table`.

OraDynaset   The OraDynaset object represents the results returned from an SQL statement. It is a client-side cursor that can be navigated and manipulated. It is created by a call to the CreateDynaset or the CreateCustomDynaset method of the OraDatabase object.

OraField   The OraField object represents a column in an OraDynaset object. It contains metadata about the column, as well as the value of the column. It can represent any data type supported by the Oracle database, including all primitives and new Oracle 8i types.

OraParameter   The OraParameter object represents a bind variable in an SQL statement. It provides methods for creating and manipulating parameter values.

OraObject   The OraObject object represents an instance of an Oracle object type stored in a column of a table.

OraRef   The OraRef object represents an Oracle reference. It is used as an identifier of an object.

OraBLOB   The OraBLOB object represents a BLOB (Binary Large Object) that is stored in a table of the database. It provides methods and properties to manage BLOBs.

OraCLOB   The OraCLOB object represents a CLOB (Character Large Object) that is stored in a table of the database. It provides methods and properties to manage CLOBs.

OraBFILE   The OraBFILE object represents a BFILE (BLOB file) that is stored in a table of the database. It provides methods and properties to manage BLOBs that are stored as operating system files.

OraParameterArray   The OraParameterArray object represents an array type bind variable in an SQL statement. It provides methods for creating and manipulating parameter values.

OraMetaData   The OraMetaData object is created when the described method of the OraDatabase object is called. It provides the means to get metadata information about a specific schema object, such as the Emp table.

OraMDAttrbute   The OraMDAttrbute object represents an attribute of a value or ref instance of an OraObject or an OraRef.

OraAq   The OraAq object represents a message queue in the database.

OraAQMsg   The OraAQMsg object encapsulates the message to be enqueued or dequeued.

Another key component bundled with OO4O is the *Oracle Data Control*. The Oracle Data Control is an ActiveX Control that will simplify the process of data access in your application. Data can be exchanged between the Oracle database and other data aware controls, such as text, list, or combo boxes and dbgrid controls. These controls are visual and provide a way for the user to interact with the data. The communication between the Oracle Data Control and data aware controls adheres to the protocol specified by Microsoft. The Oracle Data Control will allow you to perform most data-access functions, such as Insert, Delete, and Update operations, without writing a single line of code.

NOTE   The Oracle Data Control is compatible with the Microsoft Data Control bundled with Visual Basic.

Table 2.4 lists the pros and cons of using OO4O.

T A B L E   2 . 4 :   Pros and Cons of Using OO4O

Pros	Cons
Great performance.	Specific to Oracle servers
Oracle Data Control simplifies data access.	No 16-bit support after version 2.1
Optimized API for access to Oracle servers.	

TABLE 2.4: Pros and Cons of Using OO4O *(continued)*

Pros	Cons
Thread safe objects. For additional information on thread safety, please refer to the OO4O online documentation.	
Return of multiple PL/SQL cursors.	
Support for ADT(s). For additional information on ADTs, please refer to the *Oracle 8i Concepts Guide*.	
Support for LOBs.	
Support for Microsoft Transaction Server (MTS) and Internet Information Server (IIS).	
Support for Advanced Queuing. For additional information, refer to Chapter 12.	
Support for Connection Multiplexing and Connection Pooling. For additional information, refer to Chapter 11.	

Listing 2.1 shows how to establish a connection to an Oracle database and return a result set using OO4O. The code in Listing 2.1 is provided to introduce you to OO4O objects. You will use this interface throughout the book, learning simple as well as advanced techniques for accessing data in an Oracle database.

Listing 2.1

```
1  Dim OraSession as Object
2  Dim OraDatabase as Object
3  Dim OraDynaset as Object
4  set OraSession = _
CreateObject("OracleInProcServer.XOraSession")
5  set OraDatabase = OraSession.OpenDatabase( _
       "v8i", "scott/tiger", 0)
6  set OraDynaset = OraDatabase.CreateDynaset( _
       "select * from emp", 0&)
7  msgbox OraDynaset.Fields("ename").Value
```

⊃ **Analysis**

- Line 1 declares the OraSession object.
- Line 2 declares the OraDatabase object.
- Line 3 declares the OraDynaset object.
- Line 4 creates an instance of the InProc Server.
- Line 5 calls the OpenDatabase method to establish a connection to the database.
- Line 6 calls the CreateDynaset method to return a result set.
- Line 7 displays the employee's name.

NOTE The code in Listing 2.1 uses late binding. For additional information on binding OO4O objects, refer to Chapter 3.

New Features of Oracle Objects for OLE

In OO4O version 8i, it is possible for your applications to take advantage of features such as the following:

- Connection Multiplexing (Chapter 11)
- Advanced Queuing (Chapter 12)
- Support for advanced data types (Chapter 8)
- Support for Microsoft Transaction Server (Chapter 7)
- Easy access and manipulation of new data types (LOBs) (Chapter 10)

Each of these features will be discussed in detail in their respective chapters. The next sections provide you with information that you will find valuable as you start writing applications with Oracle Objects for OLE and the Visual Basic scripting language.

Mapping Oracle Data Types to Visual Basic

Mapping Oracle data types to Visual Basic primitive data types is accomplished by using the Type property of an object. The Type property returns a variant type that is associated with the return value of the object. A variant type is a special data type that represents many different types of data. Visual Basic automatically performs the conversions from variant type to the appropriate Visual Basic data type.

Table 2.5 describes the Oracle data type mappings to Visual Basic types that you can expect.

TABLE 2.5:   Oracle Data Type Mapping to Visual Basic Types

Oracle Data Type	Constant	Value	VB Data Type
Char	ORADB_TEXT	10	String
Date	ORADB_DATE	8	Variant
Long	ORADB_MEMO	12	String
Long Raw	ORADB_LONGBINARY	11	String
Number (1–4,0)	ORADB_INTEGER	3	Integer
Number (5–9,0)	ORADB_LONG	4	Long integer
Number (10–15,0)	ORADB_DOUBLE	7	Double
Number (16–38,0)	ORADB_TEXT	10	String
Number (1–15,n)	ORADB_DOUBLE	7	Double
Number (16–38,n)	ORADB_TEXT	10	String
Raw	ORADB_LONGBINARY	11	String
Varchar2	ORADB_TEXT	10	String

Listing 2.2 shows how to return the Visual Basic data type of the object.

Listing 2.2

```
1  Dim OraSession as OraSession
2  Dim OraDatabase as OraDatabase
3  Dim OraDynaset as OraDyanset
4  Dim Data_type as integer
5  Dim sql_stmt as String
6  sql_stmt =  "Select * from emp"
7  Set OraSession = CreateObject( _
   "OracleInProcServer.XOraSession")
8  Set OraDynaset = OraSession.OpenDatabase( _
     "v8i","scott/tiger",0&)
9  Set OraDynaset = OraDatabase.CreateDynaset( _
     sql_stmt,0&)
10 Data_type = OraDynaset.Fields("ename").Type
11 MsgBox Data_type
```

Analysis

- Line 1–3 are Dim statements for the objects being used to connect to the database and create the dynaset.

- Line 4 is the Dim statement for the integer variable that will hold the data type.

- Line 5 is the Dim statement for the string variable that will hold the SQL statement.

- Line 6 assigns the SQL statement `Select From Emp` to the sql_stmt string variable.

- Line 7 creates the OraSession object.

- Line 8 creates an OraDatabase object that establishes the connection to the database.

- Line 9 creates the OraDynaset object from the `Select From Emp` SQL statement.

- Line 10 gets the data type of the Ename column.

- Line 11 displays the data type for the Ename column.

NOTE   Fields of type Date are returned in the default Visual Basic format as specified in the Control Panel, even though the default Oracle date format is *DD-MMM-YY*.

NOTE   Oracle columns defined as Number, instead of being restricted to a specific precision and scale, will be floating point numbers with a precision of 38. The Type property will return a type of ORADB_TEXT for these columns.

Returning the Oracle Internal Data Type

In addition to returning the Visual Basic data type, you can also use the OraI-DataType property to return the Oracle internal data type of an object. Table 2.6 shows the return integer value that is mapped to each of the Oracle internal types. Since Oracle data types do not map directly to Visual Basic types, there are times when you will want to get this type of metadata on a field object in a dynaset. For example, very large numbers will be converted to a string type in your Visual Basic application when the actual type is numeric in the database. This type of information can be retrieved by accessing the OraIDataType property of the OraField object.

TABLE 2.6:   The Return Integer Values Mapped to Oracle Internal Types

Constant	Value	Internal Data Type
ORATYPE_VARCHAR2	1	Varchar2
ORATYPE_NUMBER	2	Number
ORATYPE_LONG	8	Long
ORATYPE_DATE	12	Date
ORATYPE_RAW	23	Raw
ORATYPE_LONGRAW	24	Long Raw
ORATYPE_CHAR	96	Char
ORATYPE_MLSLABEL	106	Mlslabel
ORATYPE_OBJECT	108	Object

T A B L E 2 . 6 : The Return Integer Values Mapped to Oracle Internal Types *(continued)*

Constant	Value	Internal Data Type
ORATYPE_REF	110	Ref
ORATYPE_CLOB	112	CLOB
ORATYPE_BLOB	113	BLOB
ORATYPE_BFILE	114	BFILE
ORATYPE_VARRAY	247	VArray
ORATYPE_TABLE	248	Nested Table

The OraIDataType property only applies to OraField objects. Listing 2.3 demonstrates returning the Oracle internal data type.

Listing 2.2

```
1  Dim OraSession as OraSession
2  Dim OraDatabase as OraDatabase
3  Dim OraDynaset as OraDyanset
4  Dim Data_type as integer
5  Dim sql_stmt as String
6  sql_stmt =  "Select * from emp"
7  Set OraSession = CreateObject( _
   "OracleInProcServer.XOraSession")
8  Set OraDatabase = OraSession.OpenDatabase( _
   "v8i","scott/tiger",0&)
9  Set OraDynaset = OraDatabase.CreateDynaset( _
    sql_stmt,0&)
10 Data_type = OraDynaset.Fields("ename").OraIDataType
11 MsgBox Data_type
```

Analysis

- Line 1–3 are Dim statements for the objects being used to connect to the database and create the dynaset.

- Line 4 is the Dim statement for the integer variable that will hold the data type.

- Line 5 is the Dim statement for the string variable that will hold the SQL statement.

- Line 6 assigns the SQL statement `Select From Emp` to the sql_stmt string variable.

- Line 7 creates the OraSession object.

- Line 8 creates an OraDatabase object that establishes the connection to the database.

- Line 9 creates the OraDynaset object from the `Select From Emp` SQL statement.

- Line 10 gets the internal data type of the Ename column.

- Line 11 displays the data type for the Ename column.

Summary

The 8i features introduced in Oracle Objects for OLE give you the opportunity to work with complex objects and data types, such as BLOBs, CLOBs, and BFILEs. Data Access interfaces (such as DAO, RDO, and ADO) introduced in this chapter each have advantages, but OO4O provides a simple-to-use interface for complex database design and data types that the others are currently lacking. In later chapters, you will see the benefits of OO4O and how easy it is to accomplish tasks such as manipulating BLOB data or using Connection Multiplexing in your Web applications. OO4O for 8i gives you speed, stability, and quick and easy access to objects and complex data types. Table 2.7 summarizes the benefits and features of the four interfaces discussed in this chapter.

NOTE   The ADO interface supports 8.1 features, such as complex data types, only if the vendor of the OLE DB Provider has implemented this functionality. The features listed as supported are based on the Oracle OLE DB Provider version 8.1.6.

TABLE 2.7: Data Access Objects Compared

Benefits	DAO/Jet Direct	RDO	ADO	OO4O
Great performance	No	Yes	Yes	Yes
Specific to Oracle servers	No	No	No	Yes
Support for multiple cursor return	No	No	No	Yes
Optimized for Oracle servers	No	No	No	Yes
Support for complex data types, such as BLOBs, CLOBs, and BFILEs	No	No	Yes	Yes
Support for an object-oriented database design	No	No	No	Yes
Simplifies data access	No	No	Yes	Yes

chapter 3

Getting Connected

- Building OO4O objects

- Establishing a connection in an application

- Using Connection Pooling

- Maintaining database security

Before any SQL or Oracle Objects for OLE (OO4O) commands can be executed, your application must have a connection to an Oracle database. Executing SQL commands at an SQL*PLUS prompt without being connected to the database is not very useful; in fact, SQL*PLUS returns the message "Not Connected" if you try. Since all OO4O commands stem from the OraSession object in one way or another, it makes sense that a session object would have to be established in order to execute any type of SQL. OO4O provides two different objects for establishing a connection:

- OraServer

- OraSession

The *OraServer object* is new to Oracle8i and exposes the Connection Multiplexing features, which are very useful when developing applications for an *n*-tiered distributed environment (where *n* equals a variable number of tiers). *Multiplexing* allows your application to share a single connection object among multiple users. For additional details on Connection Multiplexing, see Chapter 11. In previous releases, a similar concept was known as *Connection Pooling*. Connection Pooling allows a pool of connections to be shared by many clients. These connections are given to an application for use and are returned to the pool when they are no longer needed. Additional information on how and why you would want to use Connection Pooling is given later in this chapter in the section called "A Look Back at Connection Pooling." The OpenDatabase method of the OraSession object is called to establish a connection with the database in Oracle Objects for OLE version 8i. The OraServer object is created implicitly when you call the OraSession.OpenDatabase method.

OraServer and OraSession objects have many properties and methods, some of which are important when establishing connections to the database. Table 3.1 summarizes the OraSession properties and methods that are discussed throughout this chapter. Connection Pooling will be discussed briefly here. The OraServer object, Connection Multiplexing, and Connection Pooling will be discussed in Chapter 11.

TABLE 3.1:   OraSession Properties and Methods

Name	Type	Definition
Connections	Property	Returns the OraConnections collection of the specified session.
DbPoolCurrentSize	Property	Contains the number of currently active database objects in the pool.
DbPoolInitSize	Property	Contains the initial size of the pool.
DbPoolMaxSize	Property	Contains the maximum pool size.
ConnectSession	Method	Returns the OraSession object that is associated with the session's OraClient object.
CreateDatabasePool	Method	Creates a pool of OraDatabase objects.
CreateNamedSession	Method	Creates and returns a newly named OraSession Object.
DestroyDatabasePool	Method	Destroys the database pool.
GetDatabaseFromPool	Method	Returns the next available OraDatabase object from the pool.
OpenDatabase	Method	Establishes a connection to the database.

Binding OO4O Objects

In order to use OO4O objects, there must be a way to declare or bind these types of objects in Visual Basic. This declaration is called *binding*. There are two ways to bind OO4O objects: *early* and *late binding*. Early binding typecasts OO4O objects to their native object types, such as OraSession, rather than to the generic object type provided by Visual Basic. These objects are declared directly as OO4O objects, rather than as generic objects that are later resolved as OO4O objects. Early binding uses the type library information provided at design time to do *parameter checking*. Parameter checking improves performance by reducing frequent access to the OO4O Type Library. An example of early binding looks like the following:

```
Dim OraSession as OraSession
Dim OraDatabase as OraDatabase
Dim OraDynaset as OraDynaset
```

In order to use early binding of OO4O objects, the Oracle InProc Server Type Library must be referenced in your Visual Basic project. The following steps show how to include this in your Visual basic project.

1. Start Microsoft Visual Basic 6.

2. Choose File ➤ New Project

3. In the Project window, choose Standard EXE for the target type and click the OK button.

NOTE Make sure the Project Explorer and toolbar are present. If necessary, use the View menu to make them visible.

Now that you have set up a project with a default form, as seen in Figure 3.1, the next step is to include the reference to the OO4O Type Library so that the data types declared in your program are resolved at compile time.

FIGURE 3.1
The Visual Basic Designer

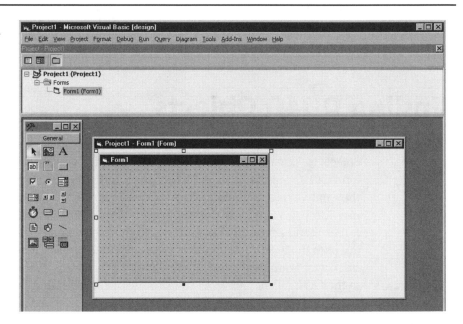

1. Choose Project ➤ References in the Visual Basic Designer.

2. Locate the Oracle InProc Server 3.0 Type Library check box in the Available References dialog box. Enable the type library by checking the box on the left, as seen in Figure 3.2. Click the OK button.

FIGURE 3.2

The Available References dialog box with the Oracle InProc Server 3.0 Type Library enabled

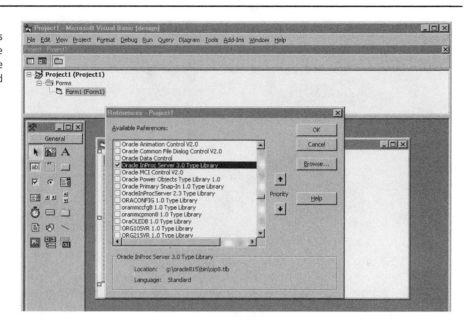

3. Choose File ➢ Save Project.

4. Type **OO4Oproj** for the form filename, as seen in Figure 3.3. Click Save to save the file.

FIGURE 3.3

The Save File As dialog box

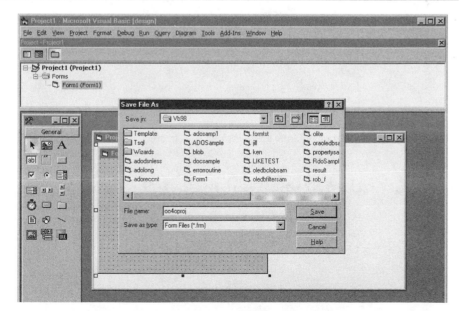

5. Type **OO4Oproj** for the project filename, as seen in Figure 3.4. Click the Save button.

FIGURE 3.4
The Save Project As
dialog box

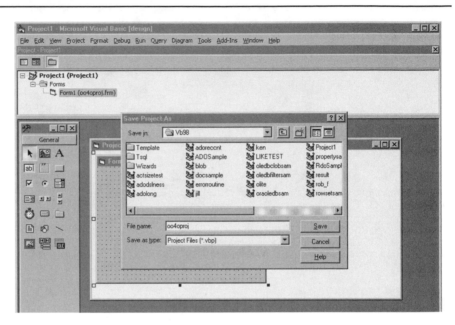

All references to OO4O types are accomplished by including the InProc Server library reference within your Visual Basic Project, as demonstrated in the previous numbered list. Late or generic binding causes the objects to be resolved at application runtime. Late binding uses no parameter checking at design/compilation time. With the late binding approach, the OO4O Type Library is used during the runtime of your application each time an OO4O object is created. This can lead to poor performance. An example of late, or generic, binding looks like the following:

```
Dim OraSession as Object
Dim OraDatabase as Object
Dim OraDynaset as Object
```

Creating the Session Object

The *OraSession object* is the top-level object for an application and is responsible for managing collections of other objects, such as OraDatabase and OraDynaset. OraDatabase and OraDynaset are discussed in greater detail in Chapter 4.

Usually, one OraSession object is created for an application, but you may also want to create named sessions to be shared. The OraSession object is created with the CreateObject Visual Basic API (Application Programming Interface) call that is not an Oracle Objects for OLE (Object Linking and Embedding) method call.

When creating the OraSession object, the argument you supply to the Create-Object() function must always be OracleInProcServer.XOraSession. The left-hand side defines the application name as registered in the system. In this case, it is OracleInProcServer. Listing 3.1 is an example of how the OraSession object is created programmatically.

Listing 3.1

```
1  Dim OraSession as OraSession
2  Set OraSession = _
   CreateObject("OracleInProcServer.XOraSession")
```

Analysis

- Line 1 declares the OraSession object using early binding.

- Line 2 calls the Visual Basic CreateObject method. The CreateObject method returns a reference to the InProc Server, which is stored in the OraSession variable.

Once you have successfully created the OraSession object, the next step is to create the OraDatabase object by calling the OpenDatabase method and passing the following arguments:

Database name	The Oracle SQL*Net database alias or the Net8 service name
User account	The username and password for a valid account
Options	A bit flag used to set different optional modes of the OraDatabase object

Calling the OpenDatabase Method

Calling the OpenDatabase method establishes a direct connection to the database and creates the OraDatabase object for the specified arguments. The *OraDatabase object* is a user connection/session to the database. OraDatabase contains methods for executing SQL statements and creating dynasets, which will be discussed in Chapter 4. Table 3.2 lists the properties of the OraDatabase object.

TABLE 3.2: Properties of the OraDatabase Object

Name	Description
AutoCommit	This property returns or sets AutoCommit behavior. The value can be True or False.
Connect	This property returns the username associated with the OraDatabase object.
Connection	This property returns a pointer to the OraConnection object.
DatabaseName	This property returns the database name or Net8 service name associated with the OraDatabase object.
LastServerErr	This property returns the last Oracle server error that occurred.
LastServerErrPos	This property returns the position of the error in the SQL statement of the OraDatabase object.
LastServerErrText	This property returns the text description of the last server error that occurred.
Options	This property returns the Options flag used to create the OraDatabase object. See Table 4.1 for valid options.
Server	This property returns a pointer to the OraServer object.
Parameters	This property returns a pointer to the Parameters collection object.
RDMSVersion	This property returns the Oracle database version for the OraDatabase object.

Table 3.3 lists the methods of the OraDatabase object. These properties and methods are discussed throughout the book.

The database name is the SQL*Net database alias, sometimes referred to as the SQL*Net connect string. For information on creating a valid alias, please refer to the *Oracle Networking Administration Guide*, which is bundled with the Oracle documentation set, which is located on your Oracle client CD-ROM. The user account you choose is a valid database username and password. Valid examples include entries like Scott/Tiger and System/Manager. The account Scott/Tiger is the schema that gets created when you choose to install the starter database from the

TABLE 3.3: Methods of the OraDatabase Object

Name	Description
BeginTrans	This method starts a new transaction state. This sets the AutoCommit property to False.
Close	This method does not close the OraDynaset object and is provided for compatability purposes. To force the OraDatabase object out of scope, you must it to Nothing.
CommitTrans	This method commits all the transactions to the database.
CreateAQ	This method allows you to create an instance of an OraAQ object.
CreateCustomDynaset	This method allows you to create a custom OraDynaset object with specific Cache and Fetch parameters.
CreateDynaset	This method allows you to create an OraDynaset object. This OraDynaset object will take on the default Cache and Fetch parameters.
CreateOraObject	This method allows you to create an instance of an OraObject object.
CreateSQL	This method allows you to create an instance of an OraSQLStmt object.
Describe	This method allows you to describe a schema or database object. It returns an OraMetaData object.
ExecuteSQL	This method allows you to execute a non-Select SQL statement, such as Insert or Update, or a call to a stored procedure.
LastServerErrReset	This method sets the LastServerErr property to zero.
Open	This method makes a connection to the Oracle server.
RemoveFromPool	This method removes an OraDatabase object form the connection pool.
Rollback	This method causes a rollback to be issued on all the changes in the current transaction.

Oracle product CD-ROM. The Options bit flag is used to set the optional modes of the database. Table 3.4 lists and describes the different modes available and the bit flag values for each one.

NOTE   The examples in this chapter use the Scott schema, which is owned by Oracle Corporation and is bundled with the Oracle8i client software and the OO4O product.

TABLE 3.4: OraDatabase Mode Options and Their Corresponding Values

Mode	Value
Visual Basic Mode (default)	&H0&
Oracle Mode	&H1&
Lock No-Wait Mode	&H2&
Oracle Mode (No Refetch)	&H4&
Non-Blocking Mode	&H8&

The OraDatabase object will exhibit the following predictable behavior when the Options flag is set:

- Visual Basic Mode (default) (&H0&)

    - Column values not explicitly set are null when using the AddNew or Edit methods of the OraDatabase object. The Null values will take precedence over any server column defaults.

    - When using Edit, the OraDatabase object will wait on row locks.

    - Non-blocking functionality is disabled.

- Oracle Mode (&H1&)

    - The database server sets the default column values when using the AddNew method.

    - The default values are retrieved immediately following the AddNew call.

- Lock No-Wait mode (&H2&)

    - The OraDatabase object will not wait on row locks.

    - When you use Edit to update a row that is locked by another user, an error code is returned immediately.

NOTE Lock No-Wait mode affects the way SQL (Sequential Query Language) statements are processed when calling the ExecuteSQL method. For additional information on the ExecuteSQL method, refer to Chapter 4.

- Oracle Mode with No Re-Fetch (&H4&)
  - Like Oracle Mode, but data is not refetched to the local cache, thus improving performance.

WARNING If you edit or change the values of the newly inserted rows, using the No Re-Fetch mode can cause the data to become inconsistent. If you attempt to edit new rows after setting this mode, you will receive error OIP-4119.

- Non-Blocking Mode (&H8&)
  - Non-blocking is enabled.
  - All SQL statements executed with ExecuteSQL, CreateDynaset, and CreateSQL methods are affected.

NOTE The Non-Blocking mode only applies to Windows 3.1. It does not apply to Windows NT, 95, or 98, and therefore it does not apply to Oracle8i. Non-Blocking Mode is included only for backward compatibility.

Listing 3.2 demonstrates how to create the session object and call the OpenDatabase method.

Listing 3.2

```
1  Dim OraSession as OraSession
2  Dim OraDatabase as OraDatabase
3  Set OraSession = CreateObject _
   ("OracleInProcServer.XOraSession")
4  Set OraDatabase = _
   OraSession.OpenDatabase _
   ("v8i","scott/tiger",&H0&)
```

Analysis

- Line 1 declares the OraSession object using early binding.

- Line 2 declares the OraDatabase object using early binding.

- Line 3 calls the Visual Basic CreateObject method. This method returns a reference to the InProc Server, which is stored in the OraSession variable.

- Line 4 calls the OpenDatabase method to establish the connection.

NOTE   When the OpenDatabase method is called, an OraConnection object is implicitly created and appears in the OraConnections collection of the OraSession object.

Building a Custom Logon Application

Now that you have seen the OraSession object and the OpenDatabase method call, let's build a custom logon screen to really get the feel for establishing a connection in the application. You will use Visual Basic 6. Start by building the GUI (Graphical User Interface) form for user interaction.

Designing and Building the GUI Interface for the Logon Application

Follow these steps to create the graphical user interface for the logon application:

1. Start Microsoft Visual Basic 6.

2. Choose File ➢ New Project.

3. In the Project window, choose Standard EXE for the target type. Click the OK button.

NOTE   Make sure the Project Explorer and toolbar are present. If necessary, use the View menu to make them visible.

Now that you have set up a project with a default form, as seen in Figure 3.5, the next step is to draw the user interface for the logon screen.

FIGURE 3.5
The Visual Basic Designer
default Project form

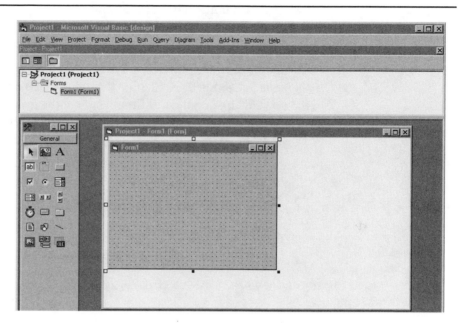

The user interface consists of a form with three text boxes and two command buttons. The text boxes are used to prompt the user for a username, password, and connect string. The command buttons are used to tell the application to either connect to the database or to cancel the request. To draw the user interface for the logon screen, follow these steps:

1. Click the command button located in the toolbox to give this control the current focus.

TIP   You can use the Tool Tips feature to locate the correct control. Position your mouse over a control for a moment or two, and the name of the control will appear.

---

2. Use your mouse pointer to draw a button on the form. To draw the button, hold down the left mouse button and pull the dotted lines into a rectangle.

3. Repeat the process in step 2 so that you have two command buttons on the form.

4. Click each command button, dragging and positioning each button on the bottom center of the form.

5. Click the first command button, Command1, to give it the current focus. Locate the Properties dialog box on the right-hand side of the Visual Basic Designer.

6. In the Properties dialog box, locate the (Name) property and change the button's name to **ConnectBtn**. Change the value by positioning the text cursor in the text edit area on the right-hand side of the property name. Use the mouse pointer to highlight the old value. Overwrite the default value by typing the new name.

7. In the Properties dialog box, locate the Caption property and change the button's caption to **Connect**.

8. Click the second command button, Command2, to give it the current focus.

9. Locate the (Name) property and change the button's name to **CancelBtn**.

10. Locate the Caption property and change the button's caption to **Cancel**.

Figure 3.6 shows the User Interface form with the Connect and Cancel buttons.

FIGURE 3.6
The User Interface form with the Connect and Cancel buttons

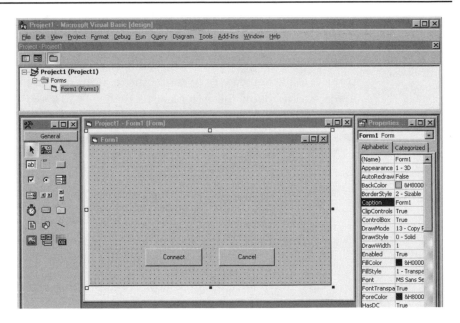

Now that you have the buttons drawn and labeled, you are ready to draw the three text boxes. These controls will capture the user input necessary for the application to make a database connection.

1. Choose the text box located on the toolbox to give this control the current focus.

2. Use your mouse pointer to draw a text box on the form by holding down the left mouse button and pulling a rectangle out of the dotted lines.

3. Repeat the process in step 2 twice more until you have three text boxes on the form.

4. Click each text box in turn, dragging and positioning the controls into a vertical row on the form's right side.

5. Click the TextBox1 object to give it the current focus.

6. In the Properties dialog box, locate the (Name) property and change the text box name to **UserName_fld**.

7. In the Properties dialog box, locate the Text property and change the default text to **scott**.

8. Click TextBox2 to give this object the current focus.

9. Locate the (Name) property and change the text box name to **Password_fld**.

10. Locate the Text property and change the default text to an empty string.

11. Click TextBox3 to give this object the current focus.

12. Locate the (Name) property and change the text box name to **Database_fld**.

13. Locate the Text property and change the default text to **MyDatabase**.

See Figure 3.7 to check your work so far.

FIGURE 3.7

The user interface with text boxes

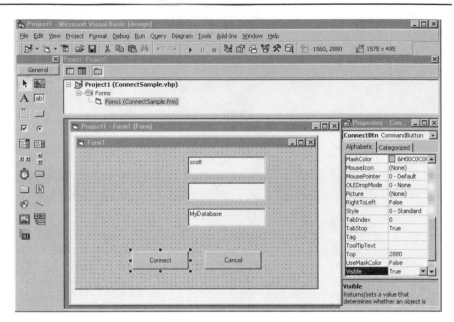

In order to give the user a description of what to type into the text boxes, you can label each one appropriately. To do so, follow these steps:

1. On the toolbox, click Label to give this control the current focus.

2. Use your mouse pointer to draw a label on the form by holding down the left mouse button and pulling a rectangle out of the dotted lines. Position the label to the left of the first text box.

3. Repeat the process in step 2 until there are three labels on the form.

4. Click the Label1 object to give it the current focus.

5. In the Properties dialog box, locate the (Name) property and change the label's name to **UserName_lab**.

6. In the Properties dialog box, locate the Caption property and change the label's caption to **User Name**.

7. Click Label2 to give it the current focus.

8. Locate the (Name) property and change the label's name to **Password_lab**.

9. Locate the Caption property and change the label's caption to **Password**.

10. Click Label3 to give it the current focus.

11. Locate the (Name) property and change the label's name to **Database_lab**.

12. Locate the Caption property and change the label's caption to **Database**.

The completed design for the user interface is shown in Figure 3.8. The next step is to add the program code to make the connection to the database. We'll do that in the next section. The application will provide context-sensitive help and a good error handler to ensure that the user makes the connection successfully.

FIGURE 3.8
The completed User Interface form

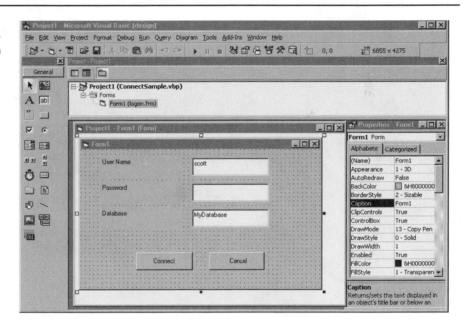

Adding the Program Code

Now that the design of the interface is ready, you can start adding custom code into event handlers for the controls so that something will actually happen when the user interacts with the text boxes and buttons.

In this application, you are going to use early binding. You need to include the reference to the OO4O Type Library so that the types are resolved at compile time (early binding) rather than at runtime (late binding). Early binding will improve performance in the application. To include the reference to the OO4O Type Library, follow these steps:

1. In the Visual Basic Designer, choose Project ➢ References.

2. Locate the Oracle InProc Server 3.0 Type Library in the Available References dialog box. Enable the type library by checking the box on the left. Click the OK button.

3. Click the Form object to give it the current focus.

4. Click the right mouse button to display the pop-up menu for the form.

5. From the pop-up menu, choose View Code. The Project Code window appears, as seen in Figure 3.9.

6. Pull down the Objects pick list and select (General).

7. Pull down the Procedures pick list and select (Declarations).

FIGURE 3.9
The Project Code window

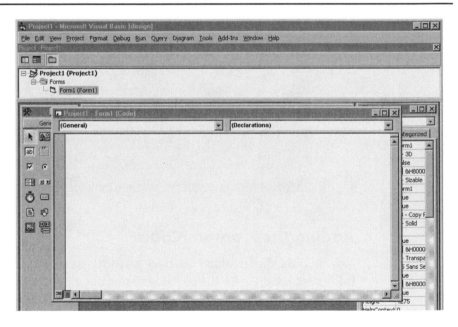

8. Position your text cursor in the Project Code window and type the following code:

```
Dim OraSession as OraSession
Dim OraDatabase as OraDatabase
Dim Connect as String
Dim Database as String
```

9. Pull down the Objects pick list and select Form.

10. Pull down the Procedures pick list and select Load.

11. Position the text cursor in the Form_Load procedure and type the following lines of code:

```
Set OraSession = _
  CreateObject("OracleInProcServer.XOraSession")
'Disable the connect button until all required
'information is entered by the user
ConnectBtn.enabled = FALSE
```

When you run the application at this stage, two things will happen. First, the InProc Server will be created, and second, the Connect button will be disabled. As the user interacts with the text boxes and enters data in the required fields, we want the connect button to be enabled, allowing the user to connect. First, you will add some code to ensure that the user has entered all the fields necessary to make a successful connection to the database. When all the fields have a value, the Connect button will be enabled. The Click event for the Connect button will be coded and an error handler will be provided to trap any errors that may arise from an unsuccessful connection attempt. Finally, the Click event for the Cancel button will need some code to take the appropriate action if the user decides to abort the connection attempt.

1. In the Program Code window, pull down the Objects pick list and choose UserName_fld.

2. Pull down the Procedures pick list and choose Validate.

3. Position the text cursor in the UserName_fld_validate procedure and type the following lines of code:

```
If (UserName_fld <> "") AND _
  (Password_fld <> "") AND _
  (Database_fld <> "") then
    ConnectBtn.enabled = TRUE
End if
```

4. Repeat step 3 for the Password_fld and Database_fld text boxes.

5. Pull down the Objects pick list and choose ConnectBtn.

6. Pull down the Procedures pick list and choose Click.

7. Position the text cursor in the ConnectBtn_click procedure and type the following lines of code:

```
Connect = UserName_fld + "/" + Password_fld
Database = Database_fld
On Error GoTo HandletheError

 Set OraDatabase = OraSession.OpenDatabase( _
    Database,Connect,&H0&)

HandletheError:
If OraSession.LastServerErr = 0 Then
    If Err = 0 Then
     MsgBox("Connected as " & Connect)
    Else
     MsgBox("VB-" & Err & " " & Error)
    End If
Else
    MsgBox(OraSession.LastServerErrText)
End if
```

8. Pull down the Objects pick list and choose CancelBtn.

9. Pull down the Procedures pick list and choose Click.

10. Position the text cursor in the CancelBtn_click procedure and type the following lines of code:

```
'This calls the exit routine for the form
Unload Form1
End
```

At this stage, all text boxes and buttons have been coded and are ready for the user to interaction with. The error handler you provided will display meaningful information to help the user troubleshoot connection problems. Take a look at Figure 3.10 for an example of what the application displays when a user enters an invalid database alias.

FIGURE 3.10
The Logon application with an error message

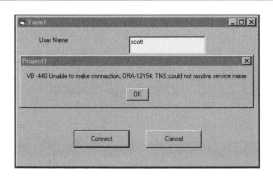

The final step will be to mask the Password field so that other characters are displayed on the screen when the user types the password information. This is done as an extra measure of security to protect the user's account information.

1. In the View Code window, pull down the Objects pick list and select Form.

2. Pull down the Procedures pick list and select Load.

3. In the Form_Load procedure, position the text cursor after the last line of code you already entered and type the following lines of code:

```
'This will mask the characters
'entered by the user and
'replace each one with an asterisk
Password_fld.PassWordChar = "*"
```

4. Run the application and make a successful connection to the database.

5. Enter invalid account information and see how the error handler displays meaningful error messages.

In the next section, you will take a look at Connection Pooling, which is a connection facility manager that was introduced in a previous version of OO4O. Save your project for future reference by following these steps:

1. Choose File ➢ Save Project.

2. You will be prompted for a name for both the project and form files.

3. Type **ConnectSample** for both the project and form filename.

A Look Back at Connection Pooling

OO4O 2.3 introduced a new interface for pooling database connections. This interface is referred to as the Connection Pooling Management Facility. The pool can be created with zero or more OraDatabase objects and can grow to a maximum size. Connections in the pool are automatically closed if they are idle for a specified amount of time. Parameters, such as Maximum Size and Timeout, are set when the pool is first created.

Connection Pooling is a resource manager for OraDatabase objects that contain database connections. The resource manager maintains the Open state on frequently used objects and eliminates the need to create and destroy connections each time a user runs the application. Connection Pooling is very useful in heavily used mid-tier application server components, such as ASP scripts in IIS, that connect to Oracle databases to execute queries every time the page is accessed by a user. These components execute many queries many times, which can certainly take a toll on the performance of the application. With Connection Pooling, new OraDatabase objects are created only if they are needed, saving valuable system resources. This significantly improves performance and provides for scalability.

Calling the CreateDatabasePool method of the OraSession object creates the pool, as shown in Listing 3.3.

Listing 3.3

```
1  Dim InitSize as Integer
2  Dim MaxSize as Integer
3  Dim TimeOutinSecs as Integer
4  DatabaseName as String
5  ConnectInfo as String
6  InitSize = 1
7  MaxSize = 10
8  TimeOutinSecs = 120
9  DatabaseName = "v8i"
10 ConnectInfo = "scott/tiger"
11 OptionsFlag = 0
12 Dim OraSession as OraSession
13 Set OraSession = CreateObject("OracleInProcServer.XOraSession")
14 OraSession.CreateDatabasePool(InitSize,MaxSize, _
   TimeOutinSecs,DatabaseName,ConnectInfo,OptionsFlag)
```

Analysis

- Line 1 declares the integer variable for the Initial Size parameter passed when creating the Database Pool object.

- Line 2 declares the integer variable for the Maximum Size parameter passed when creating the Database Pool object.

- Line 3 declares an integer variable for the Timeout parameter passed when creating the Database Pool object.

- Line 4 declares a string variable for the DatabaseName parameter passed when creating the Database Pool object.

- Line 5 declares a string variable for the Connection parameter passed when creating the Database Pool object.

- Line 6 sets the initial size of the database pool to 1.

- Line 7 sets the maximum size of the database pool to 10.

- Line 8 sets the Timeout parameter of the database pool to 120 seconds.

- Line 9 sets the DatabaseName parameter to our Net8 service name of v8i.

- Line 10 sets the Connection parameter to our sample schema, Scott/Tiger.

- Line 11 sets the Options Flag parameter to zero.

- Line 12 declares the OraSession object using early binding.

- Line 13 calls the Visual Basic method CreateObject.

- CreateObject returns a reference to the InProc Server that is stored in the OraSession variable.

- Line 14 calls the CreateDatabasePool method to create a pool of OraDatabase objects.

    - `InitSize` represents the initial size of the pool.

    - `MaxSize` represents the maximum number of Oradatabase objects in the pool.

    - `TimeOutinSecs` represents the maximum idle time to pass before an OraDatabase object is disconnected.

    - `DatabaseName` is the SQL*Net connect string.

    - `ConnectInfo` is a valid user account, such as Scott/Tiger.

    - `OptionsFlag` is the same as is used in the Open method call (refer to Table 3.4).

NOTE   Only one pool can be created per OraSession object.

To obtain an OraDatabase object from the pool, you must call the GetDatabase-FromPool method. The function in Listing 3.4 returns a reference to an OraDatabase object.

Listing 3.4

```
1 Dim OraDatabase as OraDatabase
2 Dim WaitTime as long
3 WaitTime = 10000
4 Set OraDatabase = _
  OraSession.GetDatabaseFromPool(WaitTime)
```

Analysis

- Line 1 declares the OraDatabase object using early binding.

- Line 2 declares the WaitTime argument as a Long Integer data type.

- Line 3 initializes WaitTime.

- Line 4 calls the GetDatabaseFromPool method to return a reference of an available OraDatabase object.

Wait Time is the number of miliseconds the call should wait for an OraDatabase object if the pool has reached the maximum size and there are no idle OraDatabase objects. The database pool is implicitly destroyed if the Parent Session object that it belongs to is destroyed, or it can be destroyed at any time by invoking the DestroyDatabasePool method, shown here.

```
OraSession.DestroyDatabasePool()
```

The examples shown so far were written using Visual Basic. Next, we will look at Connection Pooling using ASP and IIS. To use OO4O version 8i with OLE Automation and IIS, you need to install IIS 4 or later, including all ASP extensions. An Oracle database must be up and running on the machine on which IIS is running.

The first step is to create the Global.asa code to create the session object and database pool, as illustrated in Listing 3.5 . The database pool will start at a size of 1 and grow to a maximum size of 50 OraDatabase objects. On each call to GetDatabaseFromPool, the application will wait 10 milliseconds for an idle object. The user account and database information is based on the sample schema Scott. The database pool is created when the Global.asa file is executed.

In Listing 3.5, the line numbers are omitted because we are working with VB script and HTML. Each line is explained in the "Analysis" section. Please refer to any HTML or ASP reference book for an explanation of HTML and Visual Basic script.

Listing 3.5

```
<OBJECT RUNAT=Server SCOPE=Application ID=OraSession
PROGID="OracleInProcServer.XOraSession"></OBJECT>
<SCRIPT LANGUAGE=VBScript RUNAT=Server>
Sub Application_OnStart
OraSession.CreateDatabasePool 1,50,100," ", "scott/tiger", 0
End Sub
</SCRIPT>
```

Analysis

- Line 1 declares the Object tag for the InProc Server. This is like calling the CreateObject method in a Visual Basic application and getting a reference to an instance of the InProc Server.

- Line 2 is the scripting language tag.

- Line 3 is the Application_OnStart subroutine, which is called when the Poolsamp.asp file runs.

- Line 4 calls the CreateDatabasePool method of the OraSession object. This creates a database pool with the following parameters:

    - InitSize = 1

    - MaxSize = 50

    - TimeOutinSecs = 100

    - DatabaseName = v8i

    - ConnectInfo = Scott/Tiger

    - OptionsFlag = 0

- Line 5 is the End Sub statement for the Application_OnStart subroutine.

The second step will be to create the ASP file (Poolsamp.asp) that contains the HTML and Visual Basic script to get a connection and execute an SQL statement that returns results back to the Web browser, as shown in Listing 3.6. The line numbers are also omitted, but each line is explained in the "Analysis" section.

Listing 3.6

```
<%@ LANGUAGE = VBScript %>
<HTML>
<BODY BGCOLOR="#FFFFFF"><FONT FACE="ARIAL,HELVETICA">
<HEAD><TITLE>Emp Table</TITLE></HEAD>
<CENTER><H2>Connection Pool Example</H2>
<BR>
<CENTER><H2>Executes Select * from Emp</H2>
<BR>
<%
  Dim OraDatabase
  Dim OraFields
  Dim columnCount
  Dim recCount
  Set OraDatabase = OraSession.GetDatabaseFromPool(10)
  Set OraDynaset = OraDatabase.CreateDynaset( _
  "SELECT * FROM EMP", 0)
  Set OraFields = OraDynaset.Fields
  columnCount = OraFields.count
  recCount = OraDynaset.RecordCount
  Response.Write( _
  "<TABLE BORDER=1><TR bgcolor=""cyan"" align=""center"">")
  For i = 0 To columnCount - 1
    Response.Write("<TD align=center>")
    Response.Write(OraFields(i).Name)
    Response.Write("</TD>")
  Next
  Response.Write("</TR>")
  For j = 0 to recCount - 1
    Response.Write("<TR>")
    For i = 0 to columnCount - 1
      Response.Write("<TD>")
      Response.Write(OraFields(i).Value)
      Response.Write("</TD>")
    Next
    OraDynaset.MoveNext
    Response.Write("</TR>")
  Next
  Response.Write("</TABLE>")
%>
</FONT>
</BODY>
</HTML>
```

Analysis

- Line 1 is the Language tag.

- Line 2 is the HTML tag.

- Line 3 is the Body tag, which sets the background color and font information.

- Line 4 sets up the header to display "Emp Table."

- Line 5 sets the title of the page to display "Connection Pool Example."

- Line 6 is a line break.

- Line 7 sets the title of the page to display "Select * From Emp."

- Line 8 is a line break

- Line 9 starts the Visual Basic script code.

- Line 10 declares the OraDatabase object for the connection.

- Line 11 declares the OraFields collection object.

- Line 12 declares a variable to hold the number of fields in the Fields collection.

- Line 13 declares a variable to hold the record count

- Line 14 calls the GetOraDatabaseFromPool method to get a new OraDatabase object from the connection pool.

- Line 15 calls the CreateOraDynaset method to create a new dynaset object. The call will execute the Select From Emp query.

- Line 16 Creates the Fields collection object.

- Line 17 gets the column count from the OraFields collection object.

- Line 18 gets the total record count from the OraDynaset object.

- Line 19 starts the Table tag for column headers and sets the background color and alignment.

- Line 20 starts a For loop to display the column headers for each field in the OraFields collection.

- Line 21 starts the Table tag and sets the alignment of the column names.

- Line 22 writes the actual column name to the page.

- Line 23 ends the Table tag.

- Line 24 is the Next statement for the outer For loop.

- Line 25 ends the Table tag for the column headers.

- Line 26 starts a for loop to through the number of rows returned by the query select * from emp.

- Line 27 starts the table tag for each column in the emp table.

- Line 28 starts a For loop through each column in the Fields collection.

- Line 29 starts the Table tag to write the individual field value for each column.

- Line 30 writes out the value of the field.

- Line 31 ends the Table tag for each individual field value

- Line 32 is the Next statement for the inner For loop.

- Line 33 calls the MoveNext method of the OraDynaset object to move the row pointer to the next row.

- Line 34 ends the Table tag for each column in the Emp table.

- Line 35 is the Next statement for the outer For loop.

- Line 36 ends the Table tag in line 19.

- Line 37 ends the Visual Basic script code.

- Line 38 ends the Font tag.

- Line 39 ends the Body tag.

- Line 40 ends the HTML tag.

After you create the ASP script, you must create the virtual directory using the Microsoft IIS Console Manager and place all script files in the virtual directory. If you are using the default Web site, I recommend that you place these in the inet-pub/wwwroot default virtual directory of IIS. The next step is to create the HTML file to launch the application by adding a link that looks like the following:

```
<a href="/<the_path>/POOLSAMP.ASP">Run Connection Pool Example</a>
```

If you are running this example from the default virtual directory, the link will look like the follwing:

```
<a href="poolsamp.asp">Run Connection Pool Example</a>
```

You can use the editor of your choice to create this file. Place the `Poolsamp.html` file in the `inetpub/wwwroot` directory along with the `Global.asa` and `Poolsamp.asp` files. Load the HTML file using your Web browser. This can be done by either specifying the complete URL in the address line of your browser or by using Windows Explorer. To use the Explorer, browse to the `inetpub/wwwroot` directory and double-click the `Poolsamp.html` file to see how it works. The application will present the contents of the Emp table to the user by executing the `Select * From Emp` query. The application will present an HTML table of the query results, as seen in Figure 3.11.

FIGURE 3.11
The HTML table of the Emp table query results

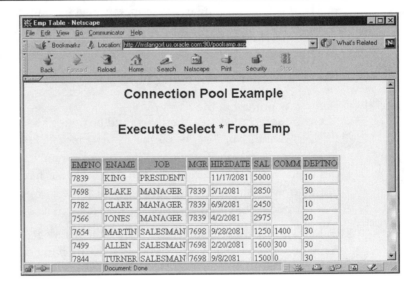

Database Security Issues

Once a user establishes a connection to a database, can the user simply execute any type of DDL (data definition language) or DML (data manipulation language)? No, this would violate the Oracle security model.

Establishing and maintaining database security is very important. Users cannot be permitted to access and change any data they wish. Privileges and roles are the mechanisms used to grant users the permission to see and change data in the database. A *privilege* is the permission to execute a particular type of SQL statement or to access another user's object. A *role* simplifies privilege management by dealing with privileges in bulk.

A few examples of privileges include the permission to

- Connect (create a session)

- Create a table

- Create a view

- Select data from another user's table

The database administrator grants privileges to users so that they can complete specific tasks or jobs. A user can receive a privilege in two ways:

- The administrator grants the privilege explicitly.

- The administrator grants privileges to a role; then the role is granted to one or more users.

Granting privileges explicitly should be done cautiously because certain types of applications can complicate the security model. For example, ODBC applications, specifically the Oracle ODBC drivers, do not use a Product User Profile. A user who has been given explicit privileges could have access to the data outside the normal business applications for which the accounts were created. These business applications could include business logic that could be bypassed by this user.

Roles allow the administrator to manage privileges efficiently by granting a type of permission to a type of user. Roles are named groups of related privileges that the administrator grants to users. It is also used to grant roles to other roles. Roles exhibit the following advantages for the administrator:

- Reduced privilege administration is achieved by applying those privileges to groups of users.

- Application awareness is achieved by querying the data dictionary and enabling and disabling roles when a user executes a database application with a particular username.

- Application-specific security is achieved when applications are created to enable and disable roles when supplied with a correct password.

Roles are created to serve one of two purposes: to manage the privileges for a database application or to manage the privileges for a user group. You grant an application role all the necessary privileges to run a specific database application. Then you grant the application role to specific users. An application can have many roles with each role enabled or disabled, allowing for more or less data access, as shown in Figure 3.12.

FIGURE 3.12
Layers of an
application role

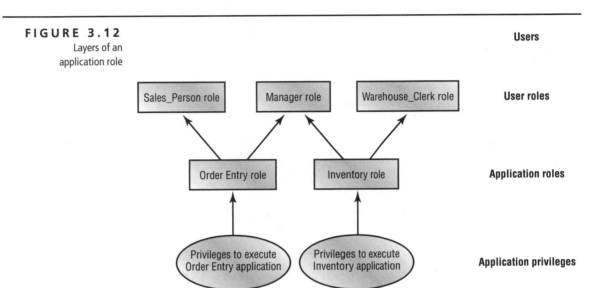

Users

User roles

Application roles

Application privileges

A New Security Feature: Changing the User's Password

Oracle Objects for OLE 8i introduces a new feature that allows you to change the user password when the user's account information has expired or allows the user to change their password periodically for security purposes. Before Oracle 8i, no such feature existed, and this task had to be done by the database administrator. The new method is called ChangePassword and accepts four parameters: database name, username, old password, and new password. Listing 3.7 shows you how to trap the password expiration warning and call the new method ChangePassword, which offers users a simple method to change their passwords.

Listing 3.7

```
1    Dim OraSession As OraSession
2    Dim OraDatabase As OraDatabase
3    Dim username as String
4    Dim password as String
5    Dim newpassword as String
6    Set OraSession = CreateObject _
     ("OracleInProcServer.XOraSession")
7    newpassword = "welcome"
8    username = "scott"
9    password = "tiger"
10   On Error GoTo HandletheError:
11     Set OraDatabase = OraSession.OpenDatabase _
     ("v8i",username & " /" & password, 0&)
12   End
13     HandletheError:
14   If OraSession.LastServerErr = 28001 Then
15       OraSession.ChangePassword _
         "v8i", username,password,newpassword
16     Resume
17     End If
```

Analysis

- Line 1 declares the OraSession object using early binding.

- Line 2 declares the OraDatabase object using early binding.

- Line 3 declares the Username variable as a string.

- Line 4 declares the Password variable as a string.

- Line 5 declares the Newpassword variable as a string.

- Line 6 calls the Visual Basic method CreateObject. This method returns a reference to the InProc Server, which is stored in the OraSession variable.

- Line 7 sets the Newpassword variable to the value of "welcome".

- Line 8 sets the Username variable to the value of "scott".

- Line 9 sets the Password variable to the value of "tiger".

- Line 10 sets up the event to go to the HandletheError block whenever an error occurs.

- Line 11 calls the OpenDatabase method to establish the connection.

- Line 12 closes the If statement block.

- Line 13 begins the code block for the HandletheError block.

- Line 14 starts an If statement, which checks the value of the LastServerErr property and compares it to see if the error is due to the password expiring.

- Line 15 calls the ChangePassword method to change the user's password.

- Line 16 calls Resume, which passes control to the statement after the one that caused the error.

- Line 17 closes the If statement block.

The following steps will guide you in creating a Visual Basic application that allows the user to change their password on demand. This small example can be incorporated into other projects as an added security feature. To create the graphical user interface for the Change Password application, follow these steps:

1. Start Microsoft Visual Basic 6.

2. Choose File ➢ New Project.

3. In the Project window, choose Standard EXE for the target type. Click the OK button.

NOTE   Make sure the Project Explorer and toolbar are present. If necessary, use the View menu to make them visible.

Now that you have set up a project with a default form, as seen in Figure 3.13, the next step is to draw the user interface for the Change Password screen.

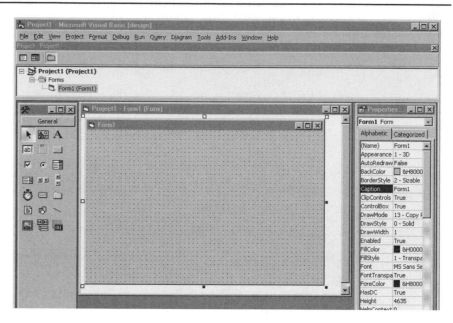

The user interface consists of a form with five text boxes and two command buttons. The first four text boxes are used to prompt the user for a username, password, connect string, and the new password. The fifth text box enables the user to confirm the new password. The two command buttons are Change Password and Cancel Request. The Change Password button tells the application to connect to the database and change the password. The Cancel Request button allows the user to cancel the request if necessary. To continue creating the user interface, follow these steps:

1. Click the command button located in the toolbox to give this control the current focus.

TIP   You can use the Tool Tips feature to locate the correct control. Position your mouse over a control for a moment or two, and the name of the control will appear.

2. Use your mouse pointer to draw a button on the form by holding down the left mouse button and pulling the dotted lines into a rectangle.

3. Use your mouse pointer to draw a second button on the form by holding down the left mouse button and pulling the dotted lines into a rectangle.

4. Click the Command1 command button. Drag it onto the bottom center of the form.

5. Click the Command2 command button. Drag it onto the bottom center of the form, as seen in Figure 3.14.

FIGURE 3.14
The default form with two command buttons

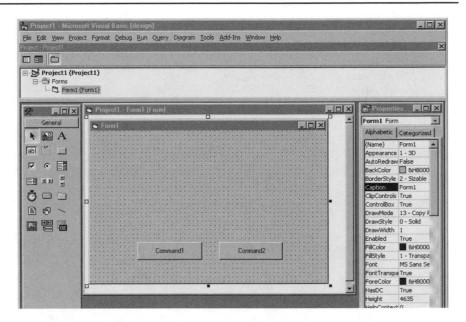

6. Click the Command1 command button to give it the current focus.

7. Locate the Properties dialog box on the right-hand side of the Visual Basic Designer. In the Properties dialog box, locate the (Name) property and change the Command1 button's name to **ChangePassBtn**. Change the value by positioning the text cursor in the text edit area on the right-hand side of the property name. Use the mouse pointer to highlight the old value. Overwrite the default value by typing the new value.

8. Locate the Caption property and change the button's caption to **Change Password**.

9. Click the Command2 command button to give it the current focus.

10. Locate the Properties dialog box on the right-hand side of the Visual Basic Designer. In the Properties dialog box, locate the (Name) property and change the Command2 button's name to **CancelPassBtn**. Change the value by positioning the text cursor in the text edit area on the right-hand side of the property name. Use the mouse pointer to highlight the old value. Overwrite the default value by typing the new value.

11. Locate the Caption property and change the button's caption to **Cancel Request**.

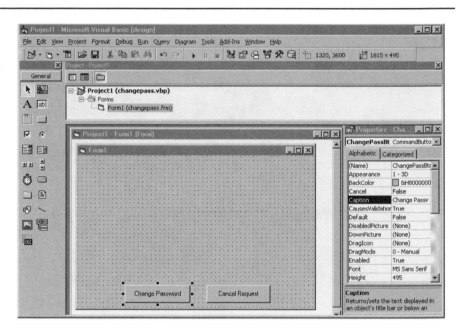

FIGURE 3.15
The User Interface form with the Change Password and Cancel Request buttons

Now that you have the buttons drawn and labeled, as seen in Figure 3.15, you are ready to draw the five text boxes. These controls will be used to capture user input for the application to use when making a call to the ChangePassword method to change the user's password on demand.

1. Choose the text box located on the toolbox to give this control the current focus.

2. Use your mouse pointer to draw a text box on the form by holding down the left mouse button and pulling a rectangle out of the dotted lines.

3. Repeat the process in step 2 four more times until you have five text boxes on the form.

4. Click each text box in turn, dragging and positioning the controls in a vertical row on the form's right side.

5. Click TextBox1 to give it the current focus.

6. In the Properties dialog box, locate the (Name) property and change the text box name to **UserName_fld**.

7. Locate the Text property and change the default text to **scott**.

8. Click TextBox2 to give this object the current focus.

9. Locate the (Name) property and change the text box name to **Password_fld**.

10. Locate the Text property and change the default text to an empty string.

11. Click TextBox3 to give this object the current focus.

12. Locate the (Name) property and change the text box name to **Database_fld**.

13. Locate the Text property and change the default text to **v8i**.

14. Click TextBox4 to give this object the current focus.

15. Locate the (Name) property and change the text box name to **Newpassword_fld**.

16. Locate the Text property and change the default text to **welcome**.

17. Click TextBox5 to give this object the current focus.

18. Locate the (Name) property and change the text box name to **Passwordconfirm_fld**.

19. Locate the Text property and change the default text to **welcome**.

See Figure 3.16 to check your work so far.

FIGURE 3.16
The user interface with its
text boxes

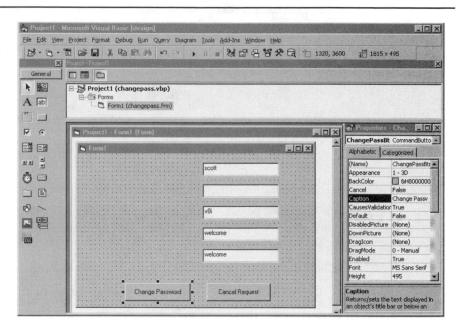

To give the user a description of what should be typed into the text boxes, you can label each one appropriately.

1. On the toolbox, click Text Label to give this control the current focus.

2. Use your mouse pointer to draw a label on the form by holding down the left mouse button and pulling the dotted lines into a rectangle. Position the label to cover the first text box.

3. Repeat the process in step 2 until there is one label over each of the five text boxes on the form.

4. Click the Label1 object to give it the current focus.

5. In the Properties dialog box, locate the (Name) property and change the label's name to **UserName_lab**.

6. In the Properties dialog box, locate the Caption property and change the label's caption to **User name**.

7. Click Label2 to give it the current focus.

8. Locate the (Name) property and change the label's name to **Password_lab**.

9. Locate the Caption property and change the label's caption to **Password**.

10. Click Label3 to give it the current focus.

11. Locate the (Name) property and change the label's name to **Database_lab**.

12. Locate the Caption property and change the label's caption to **Database**.

13. Click Label4 to give it the current focus.

14. Locate the (Name) property and change the label's name to **Newpassword_lab**.

15. Locate the Caption property and change the label's caption to **New Password**.

16. Click Label5 to give it the current focus.

17. Locate the (Name) property and change the label's name to **passwordconfirm_lab**.

18. Locate the Caption property and change the label's caption to **Confirm Password**.

The completed design for the user interface is captured in Figure 3.17. The next step is to add the program code to make the connection to the database and to change the password. The application will provide context-sensitive help and a good error handler to ensure that the user makes the connection successfully and that the password is changed to the new one, as confirmed by the user.

FIGURE 3.17
The completed User Interface form

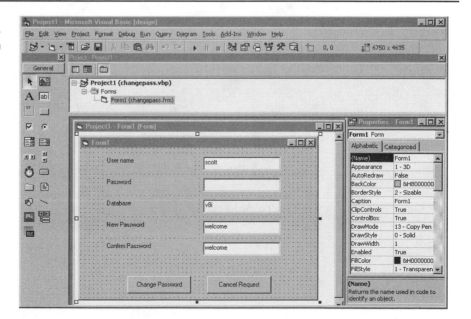

Adding the Program Code

Now that the design of the interface is ready, you can start adding custom code into the event handlers for the controls so that something will actually happen when the user interacts with the text boxes and buttons.

In this application, you are going to use early binding. To do so, you need to include the reference to the OO4O Type Library so that the types are resolved at compile time (early binding) rather than at runtime (late binding). Early binding will improve performance within the application.

1. Choose Project ➢ References in the Visual Basic Designer.

2. Locate the Oracle InProc Server 3.0 Type Library in the Available References dialog box. Enable the type library by checking the box on the left, as seen in Figure 3.18. Click the OK button.

FIGURE 3.18
The Available References dialog box with the OO4O Type Library enabled

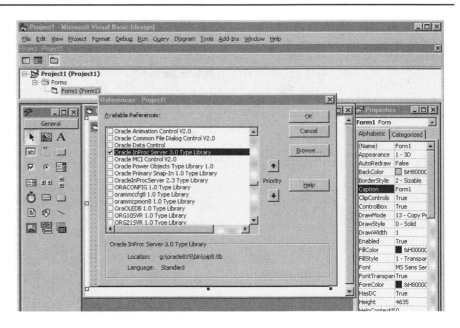

3. Click the Form object to give it the current focus.

4. Click the right mouse button to display the pop-up menu for the form.

5. From the pop-up menu, choose View Code. The Project Code window appears, as seen in Figure 3.19.

6. Pull down the Objects pick list and select (General).

7. Pull down the Procedures pick list and select (Declarations).

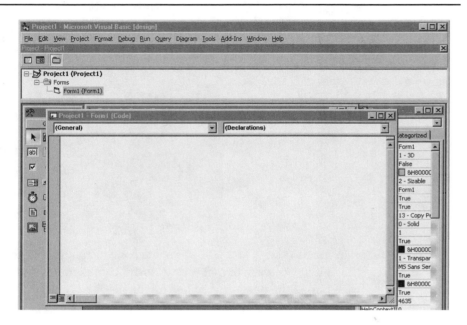

FIGURE 3.19
The Project Code window

8. Position your text cursor in the Project Code window and type the following code:

```
Dim OraSession as OraSession
Dim OraDatabase as OraDatabase
Dim Connect as String
Dim Database as String
Dim NewPassword as String
Dim PasswordConfirm as String
```

9. Pull down the Objects pick list and select Form.

10. Pull down the Procedures pick list and select Load.

11. Position the text cursor in the Form_Load procedure and type the following lines of code:

```
Set OraSession = _
   CreateObject("OracleInProcServer.XOraSession")
'Disable the changepasswprd button until all required
'information is entered by the user
ChangePassBtn.enabled = FALSE
```

When you run the application at this stage, two things will happen. First, the InProc Server will be created, and second, the Change Password button will be disabled, as seen in Figure 3.20. When the user interacts with the text boxes and enters data in the required fields, the button becomes enabled, allowing the user to connect.

FIGURE 3.20

The Change Password form with the Change Password button disabled

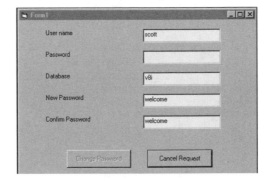

In the next step, you will add some code to ensure that the user has entered all the fields necessary to make a successful connection to the database so that they can change the password. When all the fields have a value, the Change Password button will be enabled. The Click event for the Change Password button will be coded and an error handler will be provided to trap for any errors that may arise from an unsuccessful connection attempt. Lastly, the Click event for the Cancel Request button will need some code to take the appropriate action if the user decides to abort the attempt.

1. In the Project Code window, pull down the Objects pick list and choose UserName_fld.

2. Pull down the Procedures pick list and choose Validate.

3. Position the text cursor in the UserName_fld_validate procedure and type the following lines of code:

```
If (UserName_fld <> "") AND _
   (Password_fld <> "") AND _
   (Database_fld <> "") AND _
   (Newpassword_fld <> "") AND _
   (PasswordConfirm_fld <> "") then
    ChangePassBtn.enabled = TRUE
End if
```

4. Repeat steps 1, 2, and 3 for the Password_fld, Database_fld, Newpassword_fld, and PasswordConfirm_fld objects.

5. Pull down the Objects pick list and choose ChangePassBtn.

6. Pull down the Procedures pick list and choose Click.

7. Position the text cursor in the ChangePassBtn_click procedure and type the following lines of code:

```
On Error GoTo HandletheError
if (NewPassword_fld = PasswordConfirm_fld) then
  Connect = UserName_fld + "/" + Password_fld
  Database = Database_fld
  Newpassword = Newpassword_fld
Else
  Msgbox ("Password Confirmation Failed")
  Exit sub
End if

Set OraDatabase = OraSession.OpenDatabase( _
   Database,Connect,&H0&)
OraSession.ChangePassword _
   "v8i", username_fld,password_fld,newpassword_fld

HandletheError:
If OraSession.LastServerErr = 0 Then
   If Err = 0 Then
    MsgBox("Password successfully changed")
   Else
    MsgBox("VB-" & Err & " " & Error)
   End If
Else
   MsgBox(OraSession.LastServerErrText)
End if
```

8. Pull down the Objects pick list and choose CancelPassBtn.

9. Pull down the Procedures pick list and choose Click.

10. Position the text cursor in the CancelPassBtn_click procedure and type the following lines of code:

```
'This calls the exit routine for the form
Unload Form1
End
```

At this stage, all text boxes and buttons have been coded and are ready for the user's interaction. The error handler thatyou provided will display meaningful information to help the user troubleshoot connection problems. Take a look at Figure 3.21 for an example of what the application displays when a user runs the form.

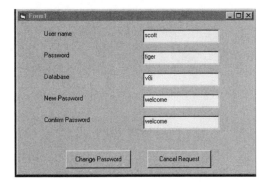

The final step is to mask the Password field so that other characters actually appears on the screen as the user provides the required password information. This is done as an extra security measure to protect the user's account information.

1. In the View Code window, pull down the Objects pick list and select Form.

2. Pull down the Procedures pick list and select Load.

3. Position the text cursor in the Form_Load procedure after the last line of code you already entered and type the following lines of code:

```
'This will mask the characters
'entered by the user and
'replace each one with an asterisk
NewPassword_fld.PassWordChar = "*"
PasswordConfirm_fld.PassWordChar="*"
```

Run the application and change your password to "welcome" on demand, using the sample Scott schema and sample database. Verify that the password has changed by logging into the database with the new password through an application such as SQL*PLUS. You may also want to enter invalid account information to see how the error handler displays meaningful error messages.

Summary

So far, you have seen how to create an instance of the InProc Server and how to establish a connection to the database. In Chapter 4, OraDatabase and OraDynaset objects will be discussed. This chapter will examine in detail the execution of SQL statements that return results to the application. A closer look at dynaset operations will be presented. In Chapter 5, the Oracle Data Control will be examined to see how to exchange data between Oracle databases and Visual Basic controls, such as combo boxes and text boxes. The Oracle Data Control allows you to perform most data access operations without having to write code.

chapter 4

Viewing and Manipulating Data

- Creating dynasets

- Inserting, updating, and deleting data in dynasets

- Navigating dynasets

- Using the ExecuteSQL method

- Creating a OraSQLStmt object

- Building an application with dynaset operations

- Creating a master-detail relationship between two dynasets

The *OraDynaset object* is one of the interfaces used to retrieve data from the database so that it can be browsed and manipulated. The data returned is based on the actual SQL statement used when creating this object. In some ways, the OraDynaset object is like a cursor; it is a pointer to a set of data returned by executing SQL in the database. The methods and properties provided with this object allow you to emulate database operations, such as inserting, updating, and deleting rows. In the following sections, you will learn how to create an object, as well as how to use properties and methods to present and change the data as desired.

The Properties and Methods of the OraDynaset Object

Let's begin with a description of the properties (see Table 4.1) and methods (see Table 4.2) of the OraDynaset object. Then, we'll create dynaset objects.

TABLE 4.1: Properties of the OraDynaset Object

Name	Description
BOF	Determines if the row pointer is positioned before the first row. Can be either True or False.
Bookmark	Sets a bookmark at the current row in the OraDynaset object.
Bookmarkable	Determines if the OraDynaset object supports bookmarks.
Cacheblocks	Can be used to set or get the number of cache blocks of the OraDynaset object.
CacheChanged	Determines if the Cache and Fetch properties have changed. Can be either True or False.
CacheSliceSize	Can be used to set or get the cache slice size of the OraDynaset object.
CacheSlicesPerBlock	Can be used to set or get the cache slices per block of the OraDynaset object.
Connection	Returns a pointer to the OraConnection object.
Database	Returns a pointer to the OraDatabase object.
EOF	Determines if the row pointer is poisitioned after the last row. It can either be True or False.
FetchLimit	Can be used to set or get the fetch array size.
FetchSize	Can be used to set or get the fetch array buffer size.

TABLE 4.1: Properties of the OraDynaset Object *(continued)*

Name	Description
Fields	Returns a pointer to the Fields collection for the current row.
LastModified	Returns a pointer to the row that was last modified in the OraDynaset object.
NoMatch	Determines if a match was found when calling a Find method. It can be either True or False.
Options	Returns the Options flag associated with the OraDynaset object. These options are listed in Table 4.3.
RecordCount	Returns the record count for the OraDynaset object.
RowPosition	Returns the current row number for the position of the row pointer in the OraDynaset object.
Session	Returns a pointer to the OraSession object.
Snapshot	Returns the snapshot identifier for the OraDynaset object.
SQL	Can be used to set or get the SQL statement used to create the OraDynaset object.
Transaction	Determines if the OraDynsaset object will support transactions. It returns either a True or False value.
Updateable	Determines if the OraDynaset object can be updated. It returns either a True or False value.

Table 4.2 describes the methods of the OraDynaset object.

TABLE 4.2: Methods of the OraDynaset Object

Name	Description
AddNew	Adds a new row to the OraDynaset object.
Clone	Makes a read-only copy of an OraDynaset object.
Close	Does not close the OraDynaset object and is provided for compatability purposes. To force the OraDynaset object out of scope, you must set it to "Nothing".
Delete	Allows you to remove rows from the OraDynaset object.
Edit	Allows you to edit fields in the OraDynaset object. This is the same as issuing a `Select For Update` statement.

TABLE 4.2: Methods of the OraDynaset Object *(continued)*

Name	Description
FindFirst	Moves the row pointer to the first row in the dynaset that matches the Find clause.
FindLast	Moves the row pointer to the last row in the dynaset that matches the Find clause.
FindNext	Moves the row pointer to the next row in the dynaset that matches the Find clause.
FindPrevious	Moves the row pointer to the previous row in the dynaset that matches the Find clause.
MoveNextn	Moves the row pointer to the next row offset by *n* in the OraDynaset object.
MovePreviousn	Moves the row pointer to the previous row offset by *n* in the OraDynaset object.
MoveRel	Moves the row pointer to the relative position specified in the OraDynaset object.
MoveTo	Moves the row pointer to the rows in the OraDynaset object that are specified in the call.
MoveFirst	Moves the row pointer to the first row in the OraDynaset object.
MoveLast	Moves the row pointer to the last row in the OraDynaset object.
MovePrevious	Moves the row pointer to the previous row in the OraDynaset object.
MoveNext	Moves the row pointer to the next row in the OraDynaset object.
Refresh	Executes the SQL statement and synchronizes the data in the database with the data in the client cache.
Update	Is used to write the changes in the OraDynaset object to the database.

Creating Dynasets

OO4O provides specific methods for creating dynasets. They are methods of the OraDatabase object. The OraDatabase object was introduced in the previous chapter and defined as a user session to the database. The OraDatabase object methods *CreateDynaset* and *CreateCustomDynaset* allow you to return a set of data based on passing an SQL statement to the Oracle server.

The CreateDynaset Method

The following is an example of the syntax used to call CreateDynaset:

```
Set OraDynaset = _
OraDatabase.CreateDynaset( _
"select empno, ename from emp", 0&)
```

CreateDynaset takes two parameters: an SQL statement and an Options flag. The SQL statement can be any valid Select statement. If the SQL statement that is passed is not a Select statement, an error is returned. The following piece of code would cause an error:

```
Set OraDynaset = _
OraDatabase.CreateDynaset( _
"insert into emp (empno) values (9999)", 0&)
```

The CreateDynaset method expects to receive a pointer to the data. In the case of an Insert statement, no data is returned. In this case, consider using the ExecuteSQL or SQLStmt methods of the OraDatabase object.

The Options flag can contain any of the options listed in Table 4.3.

NOTE   The options listed in Table 4.3 are documented in the OO4O online help and are owned by Oracle Corporation.

TABLE 4.3: Options Flags Available in OraDynaset Objects

Constant	Value	Description
ORADYN_DEFAULT	&H0&	Accept the default behavior.
ORADYN_NO_AUTOBIND	&H1&	Do not perform automatic binding of database parameters.
ORADYN_NO_BLANKSTRIP	&H2&	Do not strip trailing blanks from the character string data retrieved from the database.
ORADYN_READONLY	&H4&	Force the dynaset to be read only.
ORADYN_NOCACHE	&H8&	Do not create a local dynaset data cache. Without the local cache, previous rows in a dynaset are unavailable; however, increased performance results during retrieval of data from the database (Move operations) and from the rows (Field operations). Use this option in applications that make single passes through the rows of a dynaset for increased performance and decreased resource usage.

TABLE 4.3:   Options Flags Available in OraDynaset Objects *(continued)*

Constant	Value	Description
ORADYN_ORAMODE	&H10&	Behaves the same as Oracle mode for a database, except it affects only the dynaset being created. If the database was created in Oracle mode, the dynaset inherits the property from the database for compatibility.
ORADYN_NO_REFETCH	&H20&	Behaves the same as ORADB_NO_REFETCH mode for a database except this mode affects only the dynaset being created. If the database was created in ORADB_NO_REFETCH mode, the dynaset inherits the property for compatibility.
ORADYN_NO_MOVEFIRST	&H40&	Does not force a MoveFirst on dynaset creation. BOF and EOF are both True.
ORADYN_DIRTY_WRITE	&H80&	Update and Delete operations will not check for read consistency.

NOTE   The examples in this chapter set the Options flag by using the integer value. Be sure to include the `oraconst.txt` file in your project when referring to these options as constants to avoid receiving an error. The `oraconst.txt` file is located in the `%Oracle_Home\OO40` directory.

In Table 4.3, the Description column describes the type of behavior you will get when the Option flag is set to that particular constant or value. These options affect dynaset behavior.

The CreateDynaset method also accepts a third parameter that is optional: SnapShotID. When you pass in the SnapShotID parameter, it causes a snapshot descriptor to be created that can be used later to create other dynasets. These snapshots provide the capability for multiple OraDatabase objects to operate simultaneously and create dynasets on the same data. A *snapshot* is a set of data created at a certain point in time, like a timestamp. The life of the snapshot is based on certain configuration parameters in the Oracle database, and they will become invalid at some point. When a snapshot becomes invalid, the following Oracle error is returned to your application: "SnapShot too old." Please refer to the *Oracle8i Concepts* manual for additional details on creating snapshots in the database and on the "SnapShot too old error" message. Listing 4.1 demonstrates the use of the SnapShotID parameter.

NOTE   The examples in this chapter use the Scott schema, which is owned by Oracle and is bundled with the Oracle 8i client and the OO40 product.

Listing 4.1

```
1  Dim OraSession As OraSession
2  Dim OraDatabase As OraDatabase
3  Dim OraDynaset1 As OraDynaset
4  Dim OraDynaset2 As OraDynaset
5  Dim SnapshotID as SnapshotID

6  Set OraSession = _
   CreateObject("OracleInProcServer.XOraSession")
7  Set OraDatabase = _
   OraSession.OpenDatabase( _
   "v815", "scott/tiger",0&)
8  OraDatabase.ExecuteSql( _
   "Update EMP set SAL = 1000 " & _
   where ENAME = 'SMITH'")
9  Set OraDynaset1 = OraDatabase.CreateDynaset( _
   "select SAL from EMP where ENAME = 'SMITH'", 0&)
10  MsgBox "Smith's Salary is" & _
   OraDynaset1.Fields("SAL").Value
11 OraDatabase.ExecuteSql( _
   "Update EMP set SAL = 2000" & _
   "where ENAME = 'SMITH'")
12 Set SnapshotID = OraDynaset1.Snapshot
13 Set OraDynaset2 = _
   OraDatabase.CreateDynaset( _
   "select SAL from EMP where ENAME = 'SMITH'", _
   0&,SnapshotID)
14 MsgBox "Smith's Salary from" & _
   "point of time of OraDynaset1 is" & _
   OraDynaset2.Fields("SAL").Value
15 OraDynaset2.Snapshot = Null
16 OraDynaset2.Refresh
17 MsgBox "Smith's Salary from" & _
   "current point of time is " & _
   OraDynaset2.Fields("SAL").Value
```

```
18 OraDynaset2.Snapshot = SnapshotID
19 OraDynaset2.Refresh
20 MsgBox "Smith's Salary from" &_
     "point of time of OraDynaset1 is " & _
   OraDynaset2.Fields("SAL").Value
```

Analysis

- Lines 1–4 are Dim statements for the objects used to connect to the Oracle8 database and to create the dynaset.

- Line 5 is a Dim statement for the Snapshot object.

- Line 6 creates the OraSession object.

- Line 7 creates an OraDatabase object and establishes the connection to the database.

- Line 8 calls the Execute method for an SQL statement that updates Smith's salary to 1000.

- Line 9 creates the OraDynaset1 object based on the results returned by the SQL statement Select Sal From Emp Where Ename = 'SMITH'.

- Line 10 displays the contents of the Sal field.

- Line 11 calls the Execute method for an SQL statement that updates Smith's salary to 2000.

- Line 12 creates a snapshot of the contents of the first dynaset where Smith's salary is 1000.

- Line 13 creates the OraDynaset2 object based on the results returned by the SQL statement Select Sal From Emp Where Ename = 'SMITH'.

- Line 14 displays the contents of the Sal field from the point in time of OraDynaset1.

- Line 15 sets the Snapshot property for OraDynaset2 to "Null".

- Line 16 calls the Refresh method on OraDynaset2. This executes the SQL Select statement Sal From Emp Where Ename = 'Smith'.

- Line 17 displays the contents of the Sal field from the current point in time.

- Line 18 sets the Snapshot property for OraDynaset2 to the value of SnapshotID.

- Line 19 calls the Refresh method on OraDynaset2, which executes the SQL statement for the snapshot's point of time.

- Line 20 displays the contents of the Sal field from the point of time when OraDynaset1 was created.

Caching the Data on the Client Side

Oracle Objects for OLE uses a caching technique to fetch and store data returned from query results on the client machine where an OO4O application is running. By default, this technique is used unless you create the OraDynaset object with the ORADYN_NOCACHE option to force the data to be returned at the time the OraDynaset object is created. This can have an effect on performance and will result in the OraDynaset being forward scrolling only. When an OraDynaset object is created with the ORADYN_NOCACHE option, previous rows of the OraDynaset object are not available. You may want to consider using this option to turn off caching if your application does not require a bidirectional cursor.

The next section discusses specific parameters that can be changed and tweaked to promote optimal performance when creating OraDynaset objects.

The CreateCustomDynaset Method

The *CreateCustomDynaset method* provides a way to create a dynaset with properties that are specific to that dynaset. These properties are custom cache and fetch settings used for tuning and optimizing the process of retrieving the data for your dynaset.

The following cache settings can be passed when creating a custom dynaset:

Slicesize This entry determines the minimum number of bytes used to store a piece of data in the cache, such as a Field value for a dynaset. Items smaller than this are allocated the same number of bytes as SliceSize.

Perblock This entry specifies the number of slices that are stored in a single block. A single block can be thought of as a unit of memory or the disk allocation used for the cache. Blocks are read and written to the disk cache temporary file as one unit. Assume you have a SliceSize of 256 bytes and a PerBlock of 16, the entire block size is 4096 bytes.

CacheBlocks   This entry specifies the maximum number of blocks held in memory at a given time. When the maximum number of cache blocks is reached, blocks are swapped from memory to the cache temporary file. The blocks that are used the least are swapped out first. The calculation for the total amount of memory used is SliceSize × PerBlock × CacheBlocks.

The following fetch settings can be passed when creating a custom dynaset:

FetchLimit   This entry specifies the number of elements in the array for which data is fetched from Oracle. Be careful to create cache parameters that allow all the data in the fetch arrays to fit into cache memory.

FetchSize   This entry specifies the size, in bytes, of the buffer used to retrieve the data.

You can create a custom dynaset that takes on specific values for the previously mentioned cache and fetch parameters. This allows you to tune and optimize network traffic for a specific query. A dynaset created with the CreateDynaset method takes on the default values for these parameters. You may have to experiment to find optimal settings for the cache parameters in your application and machine environment. Here are some things to think about when setting these parameters:

- As you increase the FetchLimit and FetchSize parameters, you decrease the number of network roundtrips needed to bring in the data that can improve performance. The disadvantage to setting this parameter to a very high value is that it also increases memory requirements on the client side. This can result in additional overhead and can adversely affect application performance. This parameter should be set with the client-side configuration in mind.

- A large SliceSize increases DISK I/O.

- A small SliceSize increases swapping.

- A large CacheBlock increases memory requirements but decreases swapping.

When you create dynasets by calling the CreateDynaset method, the dynaset object takes on global defaults for these parameters. They are located in the Windows Registry at the location HKEY_LOCAL_MACHINE\Software\Oracle\OO40. As an alternative to the Windows Registry, you can create initialization files to specify these customization and tuning settings. The OO4O InProc Server will check both the Oracle.ini and Oraole.ini files.

The default values are as follows:

- SliceSize = 256 bytes

- PerBlock = 16 slices

- Blocks = 20 blocks

- FetchLimit = 100 elements

- FetchSize = 4096 bytes

The order of precedence for determining where the parameter values will be read is as follows:

1. The Windows Registry

2. The Oracle.ini file

3. The Oraole.ini file

NOTE   If you want to experiment with the different cache and fetch settings, I recommend using the CreateCustomDynaset method.

You may want to experiment with these settings in your environment to see how you may be able to improve performance. Certainly tables with small amounts of data will be fine using the defaults. The benefit is seen when large amounts of data are fetched in respect to the number of network roundtrips needed.

NOTE   The FetchLimit does not limit the dynaset to a specific number of rows fetched. These parameters are boundary limits for customizing network traffic. The Fetch limit affects the amount of data contained in a network packet not the number of rows returned by the query.

Along with cache and fetch settings, there are also two additional settings that can be changed in the initialization files or in the Windows Registry. The additional settings are

TempFileDirectory   TThis entry provides a way to specify the disk drive and directory location for the temporary cache files. The files are created in the location determined by the following order of precedence:

1. The TMP Environment variable

2. The TempFileDirectory Environment variable

3. The TEMP Environment variable

4. The current working directory

HelpFile   This entry specifies the location of the Oracle Objects for OLE help.

Inserting, Updating, and Deleting Data

The OraDynaset object provides specific methods for manipulating and changing the data returned to your application, including:

- AddNew
- Edit
- Delete
- Refresh
- Update

Let's look at these methods and see what they do and how they work.

Inserting Records into Your Dynaset

The *AddNew method* allows your application to add new rows to a Dynaset object. After calling the AddNew method, the copy buffer is initialized and an Insert operation is started. The values for the newly inserted row are manipulated through the OraField object. Once the values of the fields are set, the data must be committed by calling the Update method. Examine Listing 4.2 to get a feel for how to insert a new row into a dynaset object.

⟩ Listing 4.2

```
 1  Dim OraSession as OraSession
 2  Dim OraDatabase as OraDatabase
 3  Dim OraDynaset as OraDynaset
 4  Dim sql_stmt as String
 5  sql_stmt = "Select * from emp"
 6  Set OraSesson.CreateObject( _
    "OracleInProcServer.XOrasession" )
 7  Set OraDatabase = OraSession.OpenDatabase( _
    "v8i" ,"scott/tiger" , 0&)
 8  Set OraDynaset = OraDatabase.CreateDynaset( _
    sql_stmt, 0&)
 9   OraDynaset.AddNew
10  OraDynaset.Fields("empno" ).Value = 1000
11  OraDynaset.Fields("ename" ).Value = "ROGERS"
12  OraDynaset.Fields("job" ).Value = "CLERK"
13  OraDynaset.Fields("mgr" ).Value = 7844
14  OraDynaset.Fields("hiredate" ).Value = "19-Sep-98"
15  OraDynaset.Fields("sal" ).Value = 2000
16  OraDynaset.Fields("comm" ).Value = 50
17  OraDynaset.Fields("deptno" ).Value = 10
18  OraDynaset.Update
```

⟩ Analysis

- Lines 1–3 are Dim statements for the objects being used to connect to the database and to create the dynaset.

- Line 4 is a Dim statement for the string variable that holds the SQL statement.

- Line 5 assigns the SQL statement Select From Emp to the sql_stmt string variable.

- Line 6 creates the OraSession object.

- Line 7 creates an OraDatabase object and establishes the connection to the database.

- Line 8 creates the OraDynaset from the SQL statement Select From Emp.

- Line 9 calls the AddNew method of the OraDynaset object.

- Line 10 assigns a value of 1000 to the Empno field.

- Line 11 assigns a value of "ROGERS" to the Ename field.

- Line 12 assigns a value of "CLERK" to the Job field.

- Line 13 assigns a value of 7844 to the Mgr field.

- Line 14 assigns a value of 19-Sep-98 to the Hiredate field.

- Line 15 assigns a value of 2000 to the Sal field.

- Line 16 assigns a value of 50 to the Comm field.

- Line 17 assigns a value of 10 to the Deptno field.

- Line 18 calls the Update method for the OraDynaset method. This commits the data to the database.

NOTE   A call to the Edit, AddNew, or Delete methods will cancel any preceeding Edit or AddNew calls. When you call a new Edit, AddNew, or Delete method, you will lose any changes that were not saved from the call to the preceeding Update method.

Removing Records from Your Dynaset

The *Delete method* enables your application to delete rows from the dynaset object. A call to the Delete method deletes the current row from the dynaset. If the row pointer is not positioned on a valid row, an error will occur. Listing 4.3 demonstrates how to remove rows from the Dynaset object.

Listing 4.3

```
1  Dim OraSession as OraSession
2  Dim OraDatabase as OraDatabase
3  Dim OraDynaset as OraDynaset
4  Dim sql_stmt as String
5  Dim sql_condition as String
6  sql_stmt = "Select * from emp"
```

```
 7  Set OraSession = _
    CreateObject("OracleInProcServer.XOrasession" )
 8  Set OraDatabase = OraSession.OpenDatabase( _
    "v8i" ,"scott/tiger" ,0&)
 9  Set OraDynaset = OraDatabase.CreateDynaset( _
    sql_stmt,0&)
10  OraDynaset.MoveFirst
11  sql_condition = "empno = 1000"
12  If OraDynaset.BOF = FALSE and _
       OraDynaset.EOF = FALSE then
13    OraDynaset.FindFirst sql_condition
14    If OraDynaset.NoMatch Then
15        MsgBox "Couldn't find rows"
16    else
17        OraDynaset.Delete
18      End if
19  End if
```

Analysis

- Lines 1–3 are Dim statements for the objects being used to connect to the database and create the dynaset.

- Line 4 is a Dim statement for the string variable that holds the SQL statement.

- Line 5 is a Dim statement for the string variable that holds the SQL statement Where condition.

- Line 6 assigns the SQL statement Select From Emp to the sql_stmt string variable.

- Line 7 creates the OraSession object.

- Line 8 creates an OraDatabase object and establishes the connection to the database.

- Line 9 creates the OraDynaset object from the SQL statement Select From Emp.

- Line 10 calls the MoveFirst method of the OraDynaset object that moves the row pointer to the first row in the dynaset.

- Line 11 assigns the SQL statement Where clause Empno=1000 to the sql_condition string variable.

- Line 12 checks the EOF and BOF properties of the OraDynaset to make sure that the dynaset is not empty.

- Line 13 calls the FindFirst method of the OraDynaset object.

- Line 14 is an If statement that checks the NoMatch property of the Ora-Dynaset object to see whether any rows were found that match the find criteria.

- Line 15 displays a message if no matching rows were found.

- Line 16 is the Else clause for the inner If statement.

- Line 17 calls the Delete method of the OraDynaset object if a match was found.

- Line 18 is the End If clause for the inner If statement.

- Line 19 is the End If clause for the outer If statement.

NOTE   You cannot restore deleted rows unless you are using transactions. If you wish to roll back changes after calling the Delete method, use BeginTrans and Start a transaction state. For additional information on using transactions, please refer to Chapter 7.

Updating Records in Your Dynaset

The OO4O methods used for updating the data contained in your dynaset are the Edit and Update methods. The *Edit method* is called to make changes to the record-set contents in the local client cache. The *Update method* is called to transfer or write those changes to the database. Listing 4.4 demonstrates how to change the contents of a dynaset and then write those changes from the client-side cache to the database server.

Listing 4.4

```
1  Dim OraSession as OraSession
2  Dim OraDatabase as OraDatabase
3  Dim OraDynaset as OraDynaset
4  Dim sql_stmt as String
```

```
5  Dim sql_condition as String
6  sql_stmt = "select * from emp"
7  Set OraSession = _
   CreateObject("OracleInProcServer.XOrasession" )
8  Set OraDatabase = OraSession.OpenDatabase( _
   "v8i" ,"scott/tiger" ,0&)
9  Set OraDynaset = OraDatabase.CreateDynaset( _
   Sql_stmt,0&)
10  OraDynaset.MoveFirst
11 sql_condition = "empno = 7876"
12 If OraDynaset.BOF = FALSE and _
       OraDynaset.EOF = FALSE then
13   OraDynaset.FindFirst sql_condition
14   If OraDynaset.NoMatch Then
15       MsgBox "Couldn't find rows"
16   else
17       OraDynaset.Edit
18       OraDynaset.Fields("sal" ).value = 500
19       OraDynaset.Update
20   End if
21 End if
```

Analysis

- Lines 1–3 are Dim statements for the objects being used to connect to the database and create the dynaset.

- Line 4 is a Dim statement for the string variable that holds the SQL statement.

- Line 5 is a Dim statement for the string variable that holds the SQL statement Where condition.

- Line 6 assigns the SQL statement `Select From Emp` to the sql_stmt string variable.

- Line 7 creates the OraSession object.

- Line 8 creates an OraDatabase object and establishes the connection to the database.

- Line 9 creates the OraDynaset object from the SQL statement `Select From Emp`.

- Line 10 calls the MoveFirst method of the OraDynaset object that moves the row pointer to the first row in the dynaset.

- Line 11 assigns the SQL statement Where clause Empno = 7876 to the sql_condition string variable.

- Line 12 checks EOF and BOF properties of the OraDynaset to make sure the dynaset is not empty.

- Line 13 calls the FindFirst method of the OraDynaset object.

- Line 14 is the If statement that checks the NoMatch property of the OraDynaset object to see whether any rows were found that match the find criteria.

- Line 15 displays a message if no matching rows were found.

- Line 16 is the Else clause for the inner If statement.

- Line 17 calls the Edit method of the OraDynaset object if a match was found.

- Line 18 sets the Sal field for the current row in the dynaset to 500.

- Line 19 calls the Update method to commit the changes to the database.

- Line 20 is the End If clause for the inner If statement.

- Line 21 is the End If clause for the outer If statement.

When your application calls the Edit method, the contents of the cache buffer (data) are compared to the data on the server. If the data is not the same, an error is raised. The error raised is OIP-4119, which states that the data you are trying to modify has changed on the server side. This error is very common in a client-server environment where many users are running the same application and have access to the same data. Your application must trap this error and refresh the cache if necessary.

The *Refresh method* of the OraDynaset object forces a network roundtrip to the database to synchronize the server data with the client cache. Examine Listing 4.5 to get a feel for how this is done.

Listing 4.5

```
1  Dim OraSession as OraSession
2  Dim OraDatabase as OraDatabase
3  Dim OraDynaset as OraDynaset
4  Dim sql_stmt as String
5  Dim sql_condition as String
6  sql_stmt = "select * from emp"
```

```
7  on error goto HandletheError:
8  Set OraSession = _
   CreateObject("OracleInProcServer.XOrasession" )
9  Set OraDatabase = OraSession.OpenDatabase( _
   "v8i" ,"scott/tiger" ,0&)
10  Set OraDynaset = OraDatabase.CreateDynaset( _
   Sql_stmt,0&)
11 OraDynaset.MoveFirst
12 sql_condition = "empno = 7876"
13 If OraDynaset.BOF = FALSE and _
      OraDynaset.EOF = FALSE then
14   OraDynaset.FindFirst sql_condition
15   If OraDynaset.NoMatch Then
16       MsgBox "Couldn't find rows"
17    else
18       OraDynaset.Edit
19       OraDynaset.Fields("sal" ).value = 500
20       OraDynaset.Update
21    End if
22 End if
23 HandletheError:
24 If Err = 440 Then
25  If strcomp(ERROR$,4119) then
26    MsgBox("The Data has Changed," & _
       "Refreshing the Data Set" )
27    OraDynaset.Refresh
28  else
29    MsgBox ("OLE Automation Error" & ERROR$)
30    End if
31 Else
32    MsgBox (OraDynaset.LastServerErrText)
33 End If
```

⟩ **Analysis**

- Lines 1–3 are Dim statements for the objects being used to connect to the database and to create the dynaset.

- Line 4 is a Dim statement for the string variable that holds the SQL statement.

- Line 5 is a Dim statement for the string variable that holds the SQL statement Where condition.

- Line 6 assigns the SQL statement `Select From Emp` to the sql_stmt string variable.

- Line 7 is the On Error statement that causes execution to branch to the specified line label whenever an error is raised.

- Line 8 creates the OraSession object.

- Line 9 creates an OraDatabase object and establishes the connection to the database.

- Line 10 creates the OraDynaset from the SQL statement `Select From Emp`.

- Line 11 calls the MoveFirst method of the OraDynaset object that moves the row pointer to the first row in the dynaset.

- Line 12 assigns the SQL statement Where clause `Empno=7876` to the sql_condition string variable.

- Line 13 checks the EOF and BOF properties of the OraDynaset to make sure that the dynaset is not empty.

- Line 14 calls the FindFirst method of the OraDynaset object.

- Line 15 is the If statement that checks the NoMatch property of the Ora-Dynaset object to see whether any rows that were found match the find criteria.

- Line 16 displays a message if no matching rows were found.

- Line 17 is the Else clause for the inner If statement.

- Line 18 calls the Edit method of the OraDynaset object if a match was found.

- Line 19 sets the Sal field for the current row in the dynaset to 500.

- Line 20 calls the Update method to commit the changes to the database.

- Line 21 is the End If clause for the inner If statement.

- Line 22 is the End If clause for the outer If statement.

- Line 23 is the Line label for the error handler.

- Line 24 is the If statement that checks to see if an OLE Automation error has occurred.

- Line 25 is the If statement that parses the ERROR$ variable to check the specific OIP number.

- Line 26 displays a message that the client cache is stale and the dynaset needs to be refreshed.

- Line 27 calls the Refresh method of the OraDynaset object.

- Line 28 is the Else clause for the inner If statement.

- Line 29 displays the OLE Automation error if the specified error is not OIP-4119.

- Line 30 is the End If clause for the inner If statement.

- Line 31 is the Else clause for the outer If statement.

- Line 32 displays the LastServerErrText property of the OraDynaset object.

- Line 33 is the End If clause for the outer If statement.

Depending on the SQL statement passed to the Oracle database, you may receive a read-only OraDynaset object. Use the Updateable property of the OraDynaset object to determine if the SQL statement satisfies all the rules that allow it to be updated. Generally, the OraDynaset object will be read only if any of the following are true:

- The SQL statement contains a join and not a simple Select list.

- The OraDynaset object was created with the read-only Options flag.

- The SQL does not conform to the SQL rules for updates of tables and views, so a row ID cannot be determined.

For additional information on the SQL rules for updating tables and views, refer to the *Oracle SQL Reference Manual*.

Listing 4.6 illustrates a violation and returns a read-only OraDynaset object.

Listing 4.6

```
1  Dim OraSession as OraSession
2  Dim OraDatabase as OraDatabase
3  Dim OraDynaset as OraDynaset
4  Set OraSession = CreateObject("OracleInProcServer.XOraSession")
5  Set OraDatabase = _
      OraSession.OpenDatabase("v8i","scott/tiger",0&)
6  Set OraDynaset = OraDatabase.CreateDynaset( _
      "select e.empno,e.ename,d.deptno,d.loc FROM EMP E," & _
      "DEPT D where E.deptno = D.deptno",0&)
7  MsgBox OraDynaset.Updateable
```

⊃ **Analysis**

- Lines 1–3 are Dim statements for the objects being used to connect to the database and to create the dynaset.

- Line 4 creates the OraSession object.

- Line 5 creates an OraDatabase object and establishes the connection to the database.

- Line 6 creates an OraDynaset object from the SQL statement `Select E. empno, E.ename, D.deptno, D.loc From Emp E Dept D Where E.deptno = D.deptno`.

- Line 7 displays the Updateable property of the OraDynaset object.

Navigating Dynasets

There are several methods provided for navigating dynasets. The following navigational methods will be discussed in detail in the next sections.

- Find methods
    - FindFirst
    - FindLast
    - FindNext
    - FindPrevious
- Move methods
    - MovePreviousn
    - MoveNextn
    - MoveRel
    - MoveTo
    - MoveFirst
    - MoveLast
    - MovePrevious
    - MoveNext

Find Methods

The *Find methods* allow you to search a dynaset object and move to the row that matches the criteria specified in the Find clause. You can use the following types of expressions in a Find clause:

- Simple queries, such as `Ename = 'SMITH'`

- Queries involving complex expressions, such as `Sal + Comm > 500`

- SQL function calls, such as `Upper(Ename) = 'SMITH'`

- Sub-queries or nested queries, such as `Deptno = Select Deptno From Dept Where Loc = 'DALLAS'`

FindFirst

The *FindFirst method* finds the first occurrence of a row that matches the Find clause. The Find clause is a string that contains any valid SQL Where condition without the Where keyword. For example, Listing 4.7 will search for the first occurrence of an employee located in Department 10. This expression is considered a simple query.

Listing 4.7

```
1   Dim OraSession as OraSession
2   Dim OraDatabase as OraDatabase
3   Dim OraDynaset as OraDynaset
4   Dim sql_condition as String
5   Set OraSession = _
    CreateObject("OracleInProcServer.XOrasession" )
6   Set OraDatabase = OraSession.OpenDatabase( _
    "v8i" ,"scott/tiger" ,0&)
7   Set OraDynaset = OraDatabase.CreateDynaset( _
    "Select * from emp" ,0&)
8   sql_condition = "deptno = 10"
9   If OraDynaset.BOF = FALSE and _
       OraDynaset.EOF = FALSE then
10    OraDynaset.FindFirst sql_condition
11    If OraDynaset.NoMatch Then
12      MsgBox "Couldn't find rows"
13    else
```

```
14      MsgBox OraDynaset.Fields("ename").Value
15    End if
16 End if
```

Analysis

- Lines 1–3 are Dim statements for the objects being used to connect to the database and to create the dynaset.

- Line 4 is a Dim statement for the string variable that holds the SQL statement Where condition.

- Line 5 creates the OraSession object.

- Line 6 creates an OraDatabase object and establishes the connection to the database.

- Line 7 creates the OraDynaset from the SQL statement Select From Emp.

- Line 8 assigns the SQL statement Where clause Deptno = 10 to the sql_condition string variable.

- Line 9 checks EOF and BOF properties of the OraDynaset to make sure the dynaset is not empty.

- Line 10 calls the FindFirst method of the OraDynaset object.

- Line 11 is the If statement that checks the NoMatch property of the Ora-Dynaset object to see whether any rows found match the find criteria.

- Line 12 displays a message if no matching rows were found.

- Line 13 is the Else clause for the inner If statement.

- Line 14 displays the employee name for the matching row.

- Line 15 is the End If clause for the inner If statement.

- Line 16 is the End If clause for the outer If statement.

For each Find method, the NoMatch property is set to True when the Find clause does not return a match and the row pointer is left unchanged. You can check this property to find out whether a match was found. When the NoMatch property's value is False, a row was successfully found, and the row pointer is moved to the matching row in the dynaset.

To avoid an error, check the BOF (beginning-of-file) and EOF (end-of-file) properties before calling the Find methods. This is demonstrated in Listing 4.7. The BOF and EOF properties are defined in Table 4.1 "Properties of the OraDynaset object."

FindLast

The *FindLast method* finds the last occurrence of a row that matches the Find clause. For example, Listing 4.8 searches for the last occurrence of an employee whose salary plus commission is greater than $1,000. This expression is considered a complex query.

Listing 4.8

```
1  Dim OraSession as OraSession
2  Dim OraDatabase as OraDatabase
3  Dim OraDynaset as OraDynaset
4  Dim sql_condition as String
5  Set OraSession = _
   CreateObject("OracleInProcServer.XOrasession" )
6  Set OraDatabase = OraSession.OpenDatabase( _
   "v8i" ,"scott/tiger" ,0&)
7  Set OraDynaset = OraDatabase.CreateDynaset( _
   "Select * from emp" ,0&)
8  sql_condition = "sal + comm > 1000"
9  If OraDynaset.BOF = FALSE and _
      OraDynaset.EOF = FALSE then
10   OraDynaset.FindLast sql_condition
11   If OraDynaset.NoMatch Then
12     MsgBox "Couldn't find rows"
13   else
14     MsgBox OraDynaset.Fields("ename" ).Value
15   End if
16 End if
```

◯ **Analysis**

- Lines 1–3 are Dim statements for the objects being used to connect to the database and to create the dynaset.

- Line 4 is a Dim statement for the string variable that holds the SQL statement Where condition.

- Line 5 creates the OraSession object.

- Line 6 creates an OraDatabase object and establishes the connection to the database.

- Line 7 creates the OraDynaset from the SQL statement `Select From Emp`.

- Line 8 assigns the SQL statement Where clause `Sal + Comm > 1000` to the sql_condition string variable.

- Line 9 checks the EOF and BOF properties of the OraDynaset to make sure that the dynaset is not empty.

- Line 10 calls the FindFirst method of the OraDynaset object.

- Line 11 is the If statement that checks the NoMatch property of the Ora-Dynaset object to see whether any rows were found that match the find criteria.

- Line 12 displays a message if no matching rows were found.

- Line 13 is the Else clause for the inner If statement.

- Line 14 displays the employee name for the matching row.

- Line 15 is the End If clause for the inner If statement.

- Line 16 is the End If clause for the outer If statement.

FindNext

The *FindNext method* finds the next row in the dynaset that matches the Find clause. Listing 4.9 searches for the next employee located in Department 10.

◯ **Listing 4.9**

```
1  Dim OraSession as OraSession
2  Dim OraDatabase as OraDatabase
```

```
3  Dim OraDynaset as OraDynaset
4  Dim sql_condition as String
5  Set OraSession = _
   CreateObject("OracleInProcServer.XOrasession" )
6  Set OraDatabase = OraSession.OpenDatabase( _
   "v8i" ,"scott/tiger" ,0&)
7  Set OraDynaset = OraDatabase.CreateDynaset( _
   "Select * from emp" ,0&)
8  sql_condition = "deptno = 10"
9  If OraDynaset.BOF = FALSE and _
      OraDynaset.EOF = FALSE then
10     OraDynaset.FindFirst sql_condition
11     OraDynaset.FindNext sql_condition
12   If OraDynaset.NoMatch Then
13     MsgBox "Couldn't find rows"
14   else
15     MsgBox OraDynaset.Fields("ename" ).Value
16   End if
17 End if
```

Analysis

- Lines 1–3 are Dim statements for the objects being used to connect to the database and to create the dynaset.

- Line 4 is a Dim statement for the string variable that holds the SQL statement Where condition.

- Line 5 creates the OraSession object.

- Line 6 creates an OraDatabase object and establishes the connection to the database.

- Line 7 creates the OraDynaset from the SQL statement Select From Emp.

- Line 8 assigns the SQL statement Where clause Deptno = 10 to the sql_condition string variable.

- Line 9 checks the EOF and BOF properties of the OraDynaset to make sure that the dynaset is not empty.

- Line 10 calls the FindFirst method of the OraDynaset object.

- Line 11 calls the FindNext method of the OraDynaset object.

- Line 12 is the If statement that checks the NoMatch property of the Ora-Dynaset object to see whether any rows were found that match the find criteria.

- Line 13 displays a message if no matching rows were found.

- Line 14 is the Else clause for the inner If statement.

- Line 15 displays the employee name for the matching row.

- Line 16 is the End If clause for the inner If statement.

- Line 17 is the End If clause for the outer If statement.

FindPrevious

The *FindPrevious method* finds the previous row in the dynaset starting from the current row that matches the Find clause. For example, the code in Listing 4.10 will search for the previous employee located in Department 10 starting from the last row in the dynaset.

Listing 4.10

```
1  Dim OraSession as OraSession
2  Dim OraDatabase as OraDatabase
3  Dim OraDynaset as OraDynaset
4  Dim sql_condition as String
5  Set OraSession = _
   CreateObject("OracleInProcServer.XOrasession" )
6  Set OraDatabase = OraSession.OpenDatabase( _
   "v8i" ,"scott/tiger" ,0&)
7  Set OraDynaset = OraDatabase.CreateDynaset( _
   "Select * from emp" ,0&)
8  sql_condition = "deptno = 10"
9  OraDynaset.MoveLast
10  If OraDynaset.BOF = FALSE and _
      OraDynaset.EOF = FALSE then
11    OraDynaset.FindPrevious sql_condition
12    If OraDynaset.NoMatch Then
13      MsgBox "Couldn't find rows"
14    else
```

```
15      MsgBox OraDynaset.Fields("ename" ).Value
16   End if
17 End if
```

Analysis

- Lines 1–3 are Dim statements for the objects being used to connect to the database and to create the dynaset.

- Line 4 is a Dim statement for the string variable that holds the SQL statement Where condition.

- Line 5 creates the OraSession object.

- Line 6 creates an OraDatabase object and establishes the connection to the database.

- Line 7 creates the OraDynaset from the SQL statement `Select From Emp`.

- Line 8 assigns the SQL statement Where clause `Deptno=10` to the sql_condition string variable.

- Line 9 calls the MoveLast method of the OraDynaset object.

- Line 10 checks the EOF and BOF properties of the OraDynaset to make sure that the dynaset is not empty.

- Line 11 calls the FindPrevious method of the OraDynaset object.

- Line 12 is the If statement that checks the NoMatch property of the OraDynaset object to see whether any rows were found that match the find criteria.

- Line 13 displays a message if no matching rows are found.

- Line 14 is the Else statement for the inner If statement.

- Line 15 displays the employee name for the matching row.

- Line 16 is the End If clause for the inner If statement.

- Line 17 is the End If clause for the outer If statement.

NOTE   If the value of the Find clause is the same as the previous one, the current Find clause is not reparsed.

Move Methods

The *Move methods* allow you to move the current row pointer in the dynaset. The destination is specified by your application when calling these types of methods.

MovePreviousn

The *MovePreviousn method* moves the row pointer from its current position to the row in the *n*th position prior to the current row in the dynaset. The MovePreviousn method moves the row pointer backward in the dynaset. For example, the code in Listing 4.11 will position the row pointer two rows prior to the current position in the dynaset.

Listing 4.11

```
1  Dim OraSession as OraSession
2  Dim OraDatabase as OraDatabase
3  Dim OraDynaset as OraDynaset
4  Set OraSession = _
   CreateObject("OracleInProcServer.XOrasession" )
5  Set OraDatabase = OraSession.OpenDatabase( _
   "v8i" ,"scott/tiger" ,0&)
6  Set OraDynaset = OraDatabase.CreateDynaset( _
   "Select * from emp" ,0&)
7  OraDynaset.MoveLast
8  OraDynaset.MovePreviousn(2)
9  MsgBox " Row = " & OraDynaset.RowPosition
```

Analysis

- Lines 1–3 are Dim statements for the objects being used to connect to the database and create the dynaset.

- Line 4 creates the OraSession object.

- Line 5 creates an OraDatabase object and establishes the connection to the database.

- Line 6 creates the OraDynaset from the SQL statement Select From Emp.

- Line 7 calls the MoveLast method of the OraDynaset object.

- Line 8 calls the MovePreviousn method of the OraDynaset object.

- Line 9 displays the new row position.

MoveNextn

The *MoveNextn method* moves the row pointer from its current position to the row in the *n*th position after the current row in the dynaset. The MoveNextn method moves the row pointer forward in the dynaset. For example, the code in Listing 4.12 will position the row pointer two rows after the first position in the dynaset.

Listing 4.12

```
1  Dim OraSession as OraSession
2  Dim OraDatabase as OraDatabase
3  Dim OraDynaset as OraDynaset
4  Set OraSession = _
   CreateObject("OracleInProcServer.XOrasession" )
5  Set OraDatabase = OraSession.OpenDatabase( _
   "v8i" ,"scott/tiger" ,0&)
6  Set OraDynaset = OraDatabase.CreateDynaset( _
   "Select * from emp" ,0&)
7  OraDynaset.MoveFirst
8  OraDynaset.MoveNextn(2)
9  MsgBox " Row = " & OraDynaset.RowPosition
```

Analysis

- Lines 1–3 are Dim statements for the objects being used to connect to the database and to create the dynaset.

- Line 4 creates the OraSession object.

- Line 5 creates an OraDatabase object and establishes the connection to the database.

- Line 6 creates the OraDynaset from the SQL statement `Select From Emp`.

- Line 7 calls the MoveFirst method of the OraDynaset object.

- Line 8 calls the MoveNextn method of the OraDynaset object.

- Line 9 displays the new row position.

MoveRel

The *MoveRel method* moves the row pointer from its current position to the row in the *n*th position relative to the current row in the dynaset. The MoveRel method accepts both positive and negative offsets. If the offset is positive, the row pointer is moved forward. The pointer moves backward if the offset is negative. For example, the code in Listing 4.13 will position the row pointer two rows after the first position in the dynaset and then move back to the first position by specifying a negative offset of 2 (rows).

Listing 4.13

```
1  Dim OraSession as OraSession
2  Dim OraDatabase as OraDatabase
3  Dim OraDynaset as OraDynaset
4  Set OraSession = _
   CreateObject(" OracleInProcServer.XOrasession" )
5  Set OraDatabase = OraSession.OpenDatabase( _
   "v8i" ,"scott/tiger" ,0&)
6  Set OraDynaset = OraDatabase.CreateDynaset( _
   "Select * from emp" ,0&)
7  OraDynaset.MoveFirst
8  OraDynaset.MoveRel(2)
9  MsgBox " Row = " & OraDynaset.RowPosition
10  OraDynaset.MoveRel(-2)
11  MsgBox " Row = " & OraDynaset.RowPosition
```

⟳ Analysis

- Lines 1–3 are Dim statements for the objects being used to connect to the database and to create the dynaset.

- Line 4 creates the OraSession object.

- Line 5 creates an OraDatabase object and establishes the connection to the database.

- Line 6 creates the OraDynaset from the SQL statement `Select From Emp`.

- Line 7 calls the MoveFirst method of the OraDynaset object.

- Line 8 calls the MoveRel method of the OraDynaset object with a parameter of 2.

- Line 9 displays the new row position.

- Line 10 calls the MoveRel method of the OraDynaset object with a parameter of –2.

- Line 11 displays the new row position.

MoveTo

The *MoveTo method* moves the row pointer from its current position to the row specified in the offset. For example, the code in Listing 4.14 will position the row pointer to row 6. The MoveTo method always moves the pointer to the exact row specified by the offset unless that row has been deleted. If the specified row is marked as deleted, the row pointer is positioned to the next valid row in the dynaset.

⟳ Listing 4.14

```
1  Dim OraSession as OraSession
2  Dim OraDatabase as OraDatabase
3  Dim OraDynaset as OraDynaset
4  Set OraSession = _
   CreateObject("OracleInProcServer.XOrasession" )
5  Set OraDatabase = OraSession.OpenDatabase( _
   "v8i" ,"scott/tiger" ,0&)
```

```
6  Set OraDynaset = OraDatabase.CreateDynaset( _
   "Select * from emp" ,0&)
7  OraDynaset.MoveFirst
8  OraDynaset.MoveTo(6)
9  MsgBox " Row = " & OraDynaset.RowPosition
```

Analysis

- Lines 1–3 are Dim statements for the objects being used to connect to the database and to create the dynaset.

- Line 4 creates the OraSession object.

- Line 5 creates an OraDatabase object and establishes the connection to the database.

- Line 6 creates the OraDynaset from the SQL statement `Select From Emp`.

- Line 7 calls the MoveFirst method of the OraDynaset object.

- Line 8 calls the MoveTo method of the OraDynaset object with a parameter of 6.

- Line 9 displays the new row position.

MoveFirst

The MoveFirst method moves the row pointer from its current position to the beginning of the dynaset. For example, Listing 4.15 positions the row pointer to the first row in the dynaset.

Listing 4.15

```
1  Dim OraSession as OraSession
2  Dim OraDatabase as OraDatabase
3  Dim OraDynaset as OraDynaset
4  Dim sql_condition as String
5  Set OraSession = _
   CreateObject("OracleInProcServer.XOrasession" )
6  Set OraDatabase = OraSession.OpenDatabase( _
   "v8i" ,"scott/tiger" ,0&)
```

```
7  Set OraDynaset = OraDatabase.CreateDynaset( _
   "Select * from emp" ,0&)
8  OraDynaset.MoveFirst
9  MsgBox " Row = " & OraDynaset.RowPosition
```

Analysis

- Lines 1–3 are Dim statements for the objects being used to connect to the database and to create the dynaset.

- Line 4 is a Dim statement for the string variable that holds the SQL statement Where condition.

- Line 5 creates the OraSession object.

- Line 6 creates an OraDatabase object and establishes the connection to the database.

- Line 7 creates the OraDynaset from the SQL statement Select From Emp.

- Line 8 calls the MoveFirst method of the OraDynaset object.

- Line 9 displays the new row position.

MoveLast

The *MoveLast method* moves the row pointer from its current position to the end of the dynaset. A call to MoveLast will complete the query execution and force all rows to be fetched from the database. Listing 4.16 positions the row pointer at the last row in the dynaset.

Listing 4.16

```
1  Dim OraSession as OraSession
2  Dim OraDatabase as OraDatabase
3  Dim OraDynaset as OraDynaset
4  Set OraSession = _
   CreateObject(" OracleInProcServer.XOrasession" )
5  Set OraDatabase = OraSession.OpenDatabase( _
   "v8i" ,"scott/tiger" ,0&)
```

```
6  Set OraDynaset = OraDatabase.CreateDynaset( _
   "Select * from emp" ,0&)
7  OraDynaset.MoveLast
8  MsgBox " Row = " & OraDynaset.RowPosition
```

⟳ Analysis

- Lines 1–3 are Dim statements for the objects being used to connect to the database and to create the dynaset.

- Line 4 creates the OraSession object.

- Line 5 creates an OraDatabase object and establishes the connection to the database.

- Line 6 creates the OraDynaset from the SQL statement `Select From Emp`.

- Line 7 calls the MoveLast method of the OraDynaset object.

- Line 8 displays the new row position.

MoveNext

The *MoveNext method* moves the row pointer from its current position to the next valid row of the dynaset. Listing 4.17 positions the row pointer at the next row in the dynaset.

⟳ Listing 4.17

```
1  Dim OraSession as OraSession
2  Dim OraDatabase as OraDatabase
3  Dim OraDynaset as OraDynaset
4  Set OraSession = _
   CreateObject("OracleInProcServer.XOrasession" )
5  Set OraDatabase = OraSession.OpenDatabase( _
   "v8i" ,"scott/tiger" ,0&)
6  Set OraDynaset = OraDatabase.CreateDynaset( _
   "Select * from emp" ,0&)
7  OraDynaset.MoveFirst
8  OraDynaset.MoveNext
9  MsgBox " Row = " & OraDynaset.RowPosition
```

Analysis

- Lines 1–3 are Dim statements for the objects being used to connect to the database and to create the dynaset.

- Line 4 creates the OraSession object.

- Line 5 creates an OraDatabase object and establishes the connection to the database.

- Line 6 creates the OraDynaset from the SQL statement Select From Emp.

- Line 7 calls the MoveFirst method of the OraDynaset object.

- Line 8 calls the MoveNext method of the OraDynaset object.

- Line 9 displays the new row position.

MovePrevious

The *MovePrevious method* moves the row pointer from its current position to the previous row of the dynaset. Listing 4.18 positions the row pointer from its current position to the previous row in the dynaset.

Listing 4.18

```
1  Dim OraSession as OraSession
2  Dim OraDatabase as OraDatabase
3  Dim OraDynaset as OraDynaset
4  Set OraSession = _
   CreateObject("OracleInProcServer.XOrasession" )
5  Set OraDatabase = OraSession.OpenDatabase( _
   "v8i" ,"scott/tiger" ,0&)
6  Set OraDynaset = OraDatabase.CreateDynaset( _
   "Select * from emp" ,0&)
7  OraDynaset.MoveLast
8  OraDynaset.MovePrevious
9  MsgBox " Row = " & OraDynaset.RowPosition
```

⟩ **Analysis**

- Lines 1–3 are Dim statements for the objects being used to connect to the database and to create the dynaset.

- Line 4 creates the OraSession object.

- Line 5 creates an OraDatabase object and establishes the connection to the database.

- Line 6 creates the OraDynaset from the SQL statement `Select From Emp`.

- Line 7 calls the MoveLast method of the OraDynaset object.

- Line 8 calls the MovePrevious method of the OraDynaset object.

- Line 9 displays the new row position.

Creating a Dynaset from a Stored Procedure

Oracle Objects for OLE provides a special method for calling a stored procedure that returns a recordset. The method name is CreatePLSQLDynaset. When the CreatePLSQLDynaset method is called, a cursor is returned from a stored procedure, and the resulting dynaset is read only. This method takes three parameters:

- SQL statement
- Cursor name
- Options (bit flag)

The SQL statement is any valid PL/SQL procedure or anonymous block. The cursor is the actual cursor name created in the procedure or anonymous block. The Options flag is the same as described in the previous sections for the Create-Dynaset method. Refer to Table 4.1 for details on what options can be set. The SQL statement must be a procedure name or package.procedure name with the Oracle native Begin...End syntax wrapped around the call. The cursor name must exactly match the cursor created in the procedure.

NOTE You do not bind the cursor name using the OraParameters.Add method. When calling the CreatePLSQLDynaset method, the InProc Server will implicitly bind the cursor parameter for you.

The following code demonstrates how to call the CreatePLSQLDynaset Method. First, you will need to create the stored procedure in SQL*PLUS. Listing 4.19 contains the package specification and body. This PL/SQL package contains the GetEmpData procedure. The GetEmpData procedure accepts a department number as input and will return the data from the Emp table for all employees who are assigned to that particular department. The data is returned as a PLSQL Ref cursor. Once compiled and stored in the database as a program unit, this package will be called from the Visual Basic code in Listing 4.20. For additional information on the CreatePLSQLDynaset method, refer to Chapter 9.

Listing 4.19

```
create or replace package EmployeeData as
cursor e1 is select *  from emp;
type empCur is ref cursor return e1%rowtype;
procedure GetEmpData(indeptno IN NUMBER,
EmpCursor in out empCur );
end EmployeeData;
/
create or replace package body EmployeeData as
procedure GetEmpData(indeptno IN NUMBER,
EmpCursor in out empCur) is
begin
open EmpCursor for select * from emp where deptno = indeptno;
end GetEmpData
end EmployeeData;
/
```

Listing 4.20 is the Visual Basic code that calls the CreatePLSQLDynaset method of the OraDatabase object. This code makes a call to the EmployeeData.GetEmpData procedure you created in Listing 4.19.

Listing 4.20

```
1  Dim OraSession As OraSession
2  Dim OraDatabase As OraDatabase
3  Dim OraDynaset As OraDynaset
4  Set OraSession = _
   CreateObject("OracleInProcServer.XOraSession" )
5  Set OraDatabase = OraSession.OpenDatabase( _
   "v8i" , "scott/tiger" , 0&)
6  OraDatabase.Parameters.Add " DEPTNO" , 10, ORAPARM_INPUT
7  OraDatabase.Parameters( _
   "DEPTNO" ).ServerType = ORATYPE_NUMBER
8  Set OraDynaset = OraDatabase.CreatePLSQLDynaset( _
   "Begin EmployeeData.GetEmpData ( " & _
   ":DEPTNO,:EmpCursor); end;" , "EmpCursor" , 0&)
9  MsgBox OraDynaset.Fields("ENAME" ).Value
10 MsgBox OraDynaset.Fields("EMPNO" ).Value
11 OraDatabase.Parameters("DEPTNO" ).Value = 20
12 OraDynaset.Refresh
13 MsgBox OraDynaset.Fields("ENAME" ).Value
14 MsgBox OraDynaset.Fields("EMPNO" ).Value
15 OraDatabase.Parameters.Remove ("DEPTNO" )
```

Analysis

- Lines 1–3 are Dim statements for the objects being used to connect to the database and to create the dynaset.

- Line 4 creates the OraSession object.

- Line 5 creates an OraDatabase object and establishes the connection to the database.

- Line 6 calls the Add method for the OraParameter collection, which adds a bind parameter for the Deptno column. This line is needed for each bind parameter in the SQL statement except the Ref cursor.

- Line 7 sets the data type of the Deptno bind parameter to Number.

- Line 8 calls the CreatePLSQLDynaset method of the OraDatabase object.

- Line 9 displays the employee name for the first row in the dynaset.

- Line 10 displays the employee number for the first row in the dynaset.

- Line 11 sets the value of the bind parameter to "Deptno = 20".

- Line 12 calls the Refresh method of the OraDynaset object to requery the data for Department 20.

- Line 13 displays the employee name for the first row in the dynaset.

- Line 14 displays the employee number for the first row in the dynaset.

- Line 15 calls the Remove method to delete the Deptno field from the Parameters collection.

NOTE   The OraDynaset created in the example of Listing 4.20 is read only. You cannot insert, update, or delete any data using this process.

Returning Multiple Cursors from a Stored Procedure

Another feature available is the ability to return multiple cursors with a single network roundtrip. The CreatePLSQLDynaset method can return only one cursor. You can use the OraSQLStmt Object when you want to return more than one cursor. When the user wants to view or examine data from two separate queries at the same time, this approach can be useful. The OraParameter object uses a server data type of ORATYPE_CURSOR as an output variable and returns a read-only dynaset.

NOTE   PL/SQL procedures containing cursors as PL/SQL tables are not supported. Your cursor must be of type Ref Cursor. For additional information on Ref cursors, please refer to the *Oracle PL/SQL Programmer's Guide*.

Listing 4.22 returns two different cursors for the Employee and Department tables. One query returns the employee details, such as the employee number and the employee name. The other table returns information on the departments that the employees work in. First, create the PLSQL package specification and body in Listing 4.21.

Listing 4.21

```
create or replace package GetMultiCursors
as
cursor dept1 is select * from dept;
type deptCur is ref cursor return dept%rowtype;
cursor emp1 is select * from emp;
type empCur is ref cursor return emp%rowtype;
procedure GetDeptEmpCur(deptCursor in out deptCur , empCursor in out
empCur);
end GetMultiCursors;
/
show errors
create or replace package body GetMultiCursors as
procedure GetDeptEmpCur(deptCursor in out deptCur , empCursor in out
empCur) is
begin
open deptCursor for select * from dept;
open empCursor for select * from emp;
end GetDeptEmpCur;
end GetMultiCursors;
/
show errors
```

Listing 4.22 is the Visual Basic code that demonstrates how to use the OraSQL-Stmt object and createSQL method of the OraDatabase object to return multiple cursors (queries) from the package created in Listing 4.21.

Listing 4.22

```
1  Dim OraSession As OraSession
2  Dim OraDatabase As OraDatabase
3  Dim DeptDynaset As OraDynaset
4  Dim EmpDynaset As OraDynaset
5  Set OraSession = CreateObject("OracleInProcServer.XOraSession")
6  Set OraDatabase = OraSession.OpenDatabase( _
   "v8i" , "scott/tiger" , 0&)
```

```
7  OraDatabase.Parameters.Add _
   "DEPTCURSOR" , 0, ORAPARM_OUTPUT
8  OraDatabase.Parameters( _
   "DEPTCURSOR").ServerType = ORATYPE_CURSOR
9  OraDatabase.Parameters.Add _
   "EMPCURSOR" , 0, ORAPARM_OUTPUT
10  OraDatabase.Parameters( _
     "EMPCURSOR" ).ServerType = ORATYPE_CURSOR
11 Set OraSQLStmt = OraDatabase.CreateSql( _
   "Begin GetMultiCursors.GetDeptEmpCur( _
   ":DeptCursor,:EmpCursor;end;", ORASQL_FAILEXEC
12 Set DeptDynaset = OraDatabase.Parameters( _
   "DEPTCURSOR" ).Value
13 SetEmpDynaset = OraDatabase.Parameters( _
   "EMPCURSOR"). Value
14 MsgBox "Total number of rows returned _
   from the Dept table = " & DeptDynaset.RecordCount
15 MsgBox "Total number of rows returned _
   from the Emp table = " & EmpDynaset.RecordCount
16 Msg "Department Details are " & _
   DeptDynaset.fields("deptno").Value
17 MsgBox " Employee Details are " & _
   EmpDynaset.fields("empno" ).Value
18 OraDatabase.Parameters.Remove ("DEPTCURSOR")
19 OraDatabase.Parameters.Remove("EMPCURSOR" )
```

⟳ Analysis

- Lines 1–4 are Dim statements for the objects being used to connect to the database and to create the dynaset.

- Line 5 is the Dim statement for the OraSession object.

- Line 6 creates the OraSession object and establishes the connection to the database.

- Line 7 calls the Add method for the OraParameter collection, which adds a bind parameter for the Ref cursor deptCursor. This line is needed for each bind parameter in the SQL statement.

- Line 8 sets the data type of the bind parameter deptCursor to Cursor.

- Line 9 calls the Add method for the OraParameter collection, which adds a bind parameter for the Ref cursor empCursor. This line is needed for each bind parameter in the SQL statement.

- Line 10 sets the data type of the bind parameter empCursor to Cursor.

- Line 11 calls the CreateSQL method of the OraDatabase object that executes the call to the stored procedure.

- Line 12 creates the deptDynaset object for the deptCursor cursor.

- Line 13 creates the empDynaset object for the empCursor cursor.

- Line 14 displays the total number of rows in the deptCursor cursor.

- Line 15 displays the total number of rows in the empCursor cursor.

- Line 16 displays the deptCursor details.

- Line 17 displays the empCursor details.

- Line 18 removes the deptCursor parameter from the OraParameters collection.

- Line 19 removes the empCursor parameter from the OraParameters collection.

NOTE   The OraDynaset created in the Listing 4.22 is read only. You cannot insert, update, or delete any data.

The ExecuteSQL Method

In addition to the CreateDynaset, CreateCustomDynaset, and CreateSQL methods, there is an additional method of the OraDatabase object that enables you to submit SQL to the database. This method is ExecuteSQL. The SQL statement used with this call must be a non-Select statement. If you try to execute a Select statement that returns data, an error will be raised in the application.

NOTE   The ExecuteSQL method should be called when you want to execute SQL statements that do not return any data, such as Insert, Update, or Delete operations, or a call to a PL/SQL stored procedure. If you want to issue a query that selects data, you will need to use the CreateDynaset, CreateCustomDynaset, or CreateSQL methods.

The ExecuteSQL method executes a single non-Select statement or PL/SQL block. This method will automatically issue a commit to the database, so make sure to start a transaction with BeginTrans if you do not want the Auto-Commit behavior to take place. (For additional information on transactions, please refer to Chapter 7.) You can use bind variables in your SQL statements and PL/SQL blocks by declaring them with the OraParameter object Add method. Using bind variables can improve performance because once the statement is parsed on the server, it does not occur again when the same statement is executed with different values. If the SQL statement goes over as a string literal, the statement is parsed each time.

NOTE   Calling the ExecuteSQL method to execute SQL will affect any open dynasets. It is best to use a separate OraDatabase object to ensure that the dynasets that are currently opened will not experience any adverse effects.

Listing 4.23 calls the ExecuteSQL method to update a row in the Emp table.

Listing 4.23

```
1  Dim OraSession As OraSession
2  Dim OraDatabase As OraDatabase
3  Dim OraDynaset As OraDynaset
4  Set OraSession = _
   CreateObject("OracleInProcServer.XOraSession" )
5  Set OraDatabase = OraSession.OpenDatabase( _
   "v8i" , "scott/tiger" , 0&)
6  OraDatabase.Parameters.Add "EMPNO" , 7369, ORAPARM_INPUT
7  OraDatabase.Parameters("EMPNO" ).ServerType _
   = ORATYPE_NUMBER
8  OraDatabase.ExecuteSQL( _
   "update emp set job = 'CLERK' where empno = :empno" )
9 OraDatabase.Parameters.Remove "EMPNO"
```

Analysis

- Lines 1–3 are Dim statements for the objects being used to connect to the database and create the dynaset.
- Line 4 creates the OraSession object.

- Line 5 creates an OraDatabase object and establishes the connection to the database.

- Line 6 creates an OraParameter object for the Empno column with a default value of 7369.

- Line 7 sets the Empno parameter data type to Number.

- Line 8 calls the ExecuteSQL method, which executes the SQL statement `Update Emp Set Job = 'CLERK', Where Empno = :Empno.`

- Line 9 removes the Empno parameter from the OraParameters collection.

When executing PL/SQL blocks or calling stored procedures, you must wrap the call in the Oracle native BEGIN...END syntax as if you were executing an anonymous PL/SQL block.

Listing 4.25 calls the ExecuteSQL method and executes a PL/SQL stored procedure. Listing 4.24 contains the package specification and body. This PLSQL package contains the procedure GetEmpName. The GetEmpName procedure accepts an employee number as input and will return the name of the employee. The data Varchar2 type. Once compiled and stored in the database as a program unit, this package will be called from the Visual Basic code in Listing 4.25.

Listing 4.24

```
create or replace package EmployeeName as
PROCEDURE GetEmpName (inEmpno IN NUMBER, outEmpName OUT
VARCHAR2);
end EmployeeName;
/

create or replace package body EmployeeName as
PROCEDURE GetEmpName (inEmpno IN NUMBER, outEmpName OUT
VARCHAR2) is
BEGIN
SELECT ENAME into outEmpName from EMP WHERE EMPNO =
inEmpNo;
END;
end EmployeeName;
/
```

Listing 4.25 is the Visual Basic code that calls the ExecuteSQL method of the OraDatabase object. The code makes a call to the EmployeeName.GetEmpName procedure you created in Listing 4.24.

Listing 4.25

```
1  Dim OraSession As OraSession
2  Dim OraDatabase As OraDatabase
3  Dim OraDynaset As OraDynaset
4  Set OraSession = _
   CreateObject("OracleInProcServer.XOraSession")
5  Set OraDatabase = OraSession.OpenDatabase( _
   "v8i", "scott/tiger", 0&)
6  OraDatabase.Parameters.Add "EMPNO", 7369, ORAPARM_INPUT
7  OraDatabase.Parameters("EMPNO").ServerType = _
   ORATYPE_NUMBER
8  OraDatabase.Parameters.Add "ENAME", 0, ORAPARM_OUTPUT
9  OraDatabase.Parameters("ENAME").ServerType = _
   ORATYPE_VARCHAR2
10 OraDatabase.ExecuteSQL( _
   "Begin EmployeeName.GetEmpName (:EMPNO, :ENAME); end;")
11 MsgBox "Employee " & _
   OraDatabase.Parameters("ENAME").value
12 OraDatabase.Parameters.Remove "EMPNO"
13 OraDatabase.Parameters.Remove "ENAME"
```

Analysis

- Lines 1–3 are Dim statements for the objects being used to connect to the database and to create the dynaset.

- Line 4 creates the OraSession object.

- Line 5 creates an OraDatabase object and establishes the connection to the database.

- Line 6 creates an OraParameter object with a default value of 7369 for the Empno column.

- Line 7 sets the Empno parameter data type to Number.

- Line 8 creates an OraParameter object with a default value of 0 (zero) for the Ename column.

- Line 9 sets the Ename parameter data type to Varchar2.

- Line 10 calls the executeSQL method, which executes the PL/SQL statement `Begin EmployeeName.GetEmpName (:Empno, :Ename); End`.

- Line 11 displays the employee name that is returned.

- Line 12 removes the Empno parameter from the OraParameters collection.

- Line 13 removes the Ename parameter from the OraParameters collection.

OraSQLStmt Object

The OraSQLStmt object represents a single SQL statement. It can be a Select query, as well as a non-Select statement. Use the OraDatabase CreateSQL method to create an OraSQLStmt object. The CreateSQL method takes two parameters: SQL statement and Options. The SQL statement is a string containing a valid SQL statement. The Options parameter is a bit flag, which can be set to the values shown in Table 4.4.

NOTE   The options listed in Table 4.4 are documented in the OO4O online help, which is owned by the Oracle Corporation.

T A B L E   4 . 4 :   Values for the Option Parameter

Constant	Value	Description
ORASQL_NO_AUTOBIND	&H1&	Do not perform automatic binding of database parameters.
ORASQL_FAILEXEC	&H2&	Raise error and do not create SQL statement object.

Listing 4.26 is an example of creating the OraSQLStmt object.

Listing 4.26

```
1  Dim OraSession As OraSession
2  Dim OraDatabase As OraDatabase
3  Dim OraSqlStmt As OraSqlStmt
4  Set OraSession = _
   CreateObject("OracleInProcServer.XOraSession")
5  Set OraDatabase = OraSession.OpenDatabase( _
   "v8i", "scott/tiger", 0&)
6  Set OraSqlStmt = OraDatabase.CreateSQL( _
   "update emp set job = 'CLERK' where empno = 7839", 0&)
```

Analysis

- Lines 1–3 are Dim statements for the objects being used to connect to the database and to create the OraSqlStmt object.

- Line 4 creates the OraSession object.

- Line 5 creates an OraDatabase object and establishes the connection to the database.

- Line 6 calls the CreateSQL method of the OraDatabase object.

The CreateSQL method executes the statement and returns and OraSQLStmt object. If the SQL statement passed is a Select query, the underlying recordset objects are automatically created, and the methods for manipulating and navigating the data are available. You can also use the OraSQLStmt and CreateSQL method to call PL/SQL stored procedures as demonstrated in Listing 4.27. Listing 4.26 is the Visual Basic code that calls the PL/SQL procedure using the OraSQLStmt object and Refresh method. The Refresh method forces the SQL statement to be re-executed. The procedure EmployeeName.GetEmpName was already created from Listing 4.24.

Listing 4.27

```
1  Dim OraSession As OraSession
2  Dim OraDatabase As OraDatabase
3  Dim OraSqlStmt As OraSqlStmt
4  Set OraSession = _
   CreateObject("OracleInProcServer.XOraSession")
```

```
 5  Set OraDatabase = OraSession.OpenDatabase(
    "v8i", "scott/tiger", 0&)
 6  OraDatabase.Parameters.Add _
    "EMPNO", 7369, 1
 7  OraDatabase.Parameters("EMPNO").ServerType = _
    2 ORATYPE_NUMBER
 8  OraDatabase.Parameters.Add _
    "ENAME", 0, 2
 9  OraDatabase.Parameters("ENAME").ServerType = _
    1   'ORATYPE_VARCHAR2
10  Set OraSqlStmt = OraDatabase.CreateSQL( _
    "Begin EmployeeName.GetEmpName (:EMPNO, :ENAME); end;", 0&)
11 MsgBox OraSqlStmt.SQL
12 MsgBox OraDatabase.Parameters("ENAME").Value
13 OraDatabase.Parameters("EMPNO").Value = 7499
14 OraSqlStmt.Refresh
15 MsgBox OraDatabase.Parameters("ENAME").Value
16 MsgBox OraSqlStmt.SQL
17 OraDatabase.Parameters.Remove ("EMPNO")
18 OraDatabase.Parameters.Remove ("ENAME")
```

Analysis

- Lines 1–3 are Dim statements for the objects being used to connect to the database and to create the OraSqlStmt object.

- Line 4 creates the OraSession object.

- Line 5 creates an OraDatabase object and establishes the connection to the database.

- Line 6 adds a Bind parameter to the Parameter collection for the Empno field.

- Line 7 sets the Empno parameter data type to Number.

- Line 8 adds a Bind parameter to the Parameter collection for the Ename field.

- Line 9 sets the Ename parameter data type to Varchar2.

- Line 10 calls the CreateSQL method of the OraDatabase object.

- Line 11 displays the SQL property of the OraSqlStmt object.

- Line 12 displays the value of the Ename parameter returned from the SQL call to EmployeeName.GetEmpName.

- Line 13 sets the value of the Empno parameter to 7499.

- Line 14 calls the Refresh method of the OraSqlStmt object that executes the SQL call EmployeeName.GetEmpName.

- Line 15 displays the value of the Ename parameter returned from the SQL call to EmployeeName.GetEmpName.

- Line 16 displays the SQL property of the OraSqlStmt object.

- Line 17 removes the Empno parameter from the OraParameters collection.

- Line 18 removes the Ename parameter from the OraParameters collection.

Building a Custom Application Using Dynaset Operations

Now that you have seen the OraDynaset object and the various method calls that allow you to interact with a dynaset object, it's time to build a custom application that uses the various methods described throughout this chapter. You will be using Visual Basic 6. Start by building the GUI (Graphical User Interface) form for the user to interact with.

Designing the GUI Interface for the Dynaset Operations Application

The following steps will guide you in creating the graphical user interface for the Dynaset Operations application.

1. Start Microsoft Visual Basic 6.

2. Choose File ➤ New Project.

3. From the Project window, choose Standard EXE for the target type. Click the OK button.

NOTE Make sure the Project Explorer and toolbox are present. If necessary, use the View menu to make them visible.

Now that you have set up a project with a default form, as seen in Figure 4.1, the next step is to draw the user interface for the Logon screen.

FIGURE 4.1

The Visual Basic Designer with a default form

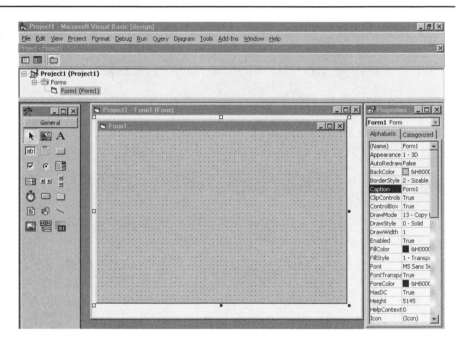

The user interface consists of a form with eight text boxes and four command buttons. The text boxes are used to display the data for the user. The command buttons are used to navigate the user through the dynaset data. To create the command buttons, follow these steps:

1. Click the command button located on the toolbox to give that control the current focus.

TIP You can use the Tool Tips feature to locate the correct control. Position your mouse over a control for a moment or two; the name of the control will appear.

2. Use your mouse pointer to draw a button on the form by holding down the left mouse button and pulling the dotted lines into a rectangle.

3. Repeat the process in step 2 until you have four command buttons on the form.

4. Click each command button, dragging and positioning each on the bottom center of the form.

5. Click the first command button, Command1, to give it the current focus. Locate the Properties dialog box on the right-hand side of the Visual Basic Designer.

6. In the Visual Basic Designer, locate the (Name) property and change the button's name to **FirstBtn**. Change the value by positioning the cursor in the text box to the right of the (Name) property. Use the mouse pointer to highlight the old value. Overwrite the default value and type the new one.

7. Locate the Caption property and change the button's caption to **First Record**.

8. Click the second command button, Command2, to give it the current focus.

9. Locate the (Name) property and change the button's name to **PreviousBtn**.

10. Locate the Caption property and change the button's caption to **Previous Record**.

11. Click the third command button, Command3, to give it the current focus.

12. Locate the (Name) property and change the button's name to **NextBtn**.

13. Locate the Caption property and change the button's caption to **Next Record**.

14. Click the fourth command button, Command4, to give it the current focus.

15. Locate the (Name) property and change the button's name to **LastBtn**.

16. Locate the Caption property and change the button's caption to **Last Record**.

Your form should look like Figure 4.2.

FIGURE 4.2
The user interface with four
navigation buttons

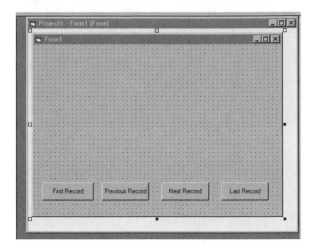

Now that you have the buttons drawn and labeled, as shown in Figure 4.2, you are ready to draw the eight text boxes. These controls will be used to present the data to the user.

1. Choose the text box located on the toolbox to give the control the current focus.

2. Use your mouse pointer to draw a text box on the form by holding down the left mouse button and pulling the dotted lines into a rectangle.

3. Repeat the process in step 2 seven times until you have eight text boxes on the form. Align the text boxes vertically, as shown in Figure 4.3.

FIGURE 4.3
The user interface with
eight text boxes aligned
vertically

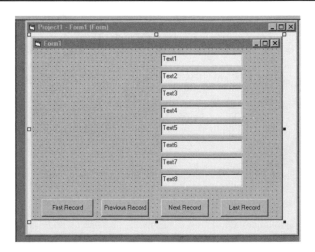

4. Click the Text1 text box to give this object the current focus.

5. In the Visual Basic Properties Designer, locate the (Name) property and change the text box name to **empno_fld**.

6. Click the Text2 text box to give this object the current focus.

7. Locate the (Name) property and change the text box name to **ename_fld**.

8. Click the Text3 text box to give this object the current focus.

9. Locate the (Name) property and change the name to **job_fld**.

10. Click the Text4 text box to give this object the current focus.

11. Locate the (Name) property and change the name to **mgr_fld**.

12. Click the Text5 text box to give this object the current focus.

13. Locate the (Name) property and change the name to **hiredate_fld**.

14. Click the Text6 text box to give this object the current focus.

15. Locate the (Name) property and change the name to **sal_fld**.

16. Click the Text7 text box to give this object the current focus.

17. Locate the (Name) property and change the name to **comm_fld**.

18. Click the Text8 text box to give this object the current focus.

19. Locate the (Name) property and change the name to **deptno_fld**.

Label each text field to give the user a description of the data presented there. To do so, follow these steps:

1. On the toolbox, click Text Label to give this control the current focus. Use your mouse pointer to draw a label on the form by holding down the left mouse button and pulling the dotted lines into a rectangle. Position the label to the left of the first text box.

2. Repeat the process in step 1 until there are eight labels on the form. Align each label next to the appropriate text box.

3. Click the Label1 object to give it the current focus. Locate the (Name) property in the Visual Basic Properties Designer and change the label's name to **empno_lab**.

4. Locate the Caption property in the Visual Basic Properties Designer and change the label's caption to **Employee Number**.

5. Click Label2 to give this object the current focus.

6. Locate the (Name) property and change the label's name to **ename_lab**.

7. Locate the Caption property and change the label's caption to **Employee Name**.

8. Click Label3 to give this object the current focus.

9. Locate the (Name) property and change the label's name to **job_lab**.

10. Locate the Caption property and change the caption to **Job**.

11. Click the Label4 object to give it the current focus.

12. Locate the (Name) property and change the label's name to **mgr_lab**.

13. Locate the Caption property and change the label's caption to **Manager**.

14. Click Label5 to give this object the current focus.

15. Locate the (Name) property and change the name to **hiredate_lab**.

16. Locate the Caption property and change the caption to **Initial Hire Date**.

17. Click the Label6 object to give it the current focus.

18. Locate the (Name) property and change the label's name to **sal_lab**.

19. Locate the Caption property and change the label's caption to **Current Salary**.

20. Click the Label7 object to give it the current focus.

21. Locate the Name property and change the label's name to **comm_lab**.

22. Locate the Caption property and change the label's caption to **Commission Amount**.

23. Click the Label8 object to give it the current focus.

24. Locate the Name property and change the label's name to **deptno_lab**.

25. Locate the Caption property and change the label's caption to **Department Number**.

The completed design for the user interface is shown in Figure 4.4. The next step is to add the program code to make the connection to the database. We'll do that in the next section. The application will provide context-sensitive help and a good error handler to make sure that the user makes the connection successfully.

FIGURE 4.4
The completed user
interface

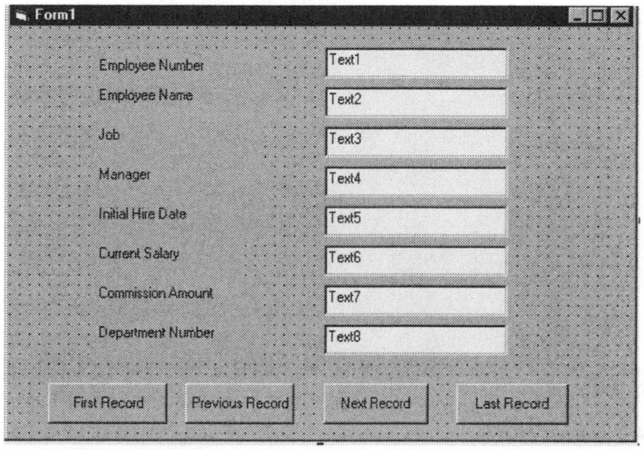

Adding the Program Code

Now that the design of the interface is ready, you can start adding custom code into the event handlers for the controls so that something will actually happen when the user interacts with the text boxes and buttons.

In this application, you are going to use early binding. Therefore, you need to include the reference to the OO4O Type Library so that the types are resolved at compile time (early binding) rather than at runtime (late binding). Early binding will improve performance of the application.

1. In the Visual Basic Designer, choose Project ➤ References.

2. Locate the Oracle InProc Server Type Library in the Available References dialog box. Enable the type library by checking the box on the left. Click the OK button.

3. Click the Form object to give it the current focus.

4. Right-click to display the pop-up menu for the form.

5. From the pop-up menu, choose View Code. The Project Code window appears, as seen in Figure 4.5.

6. Pull down the Objects pick list and select (General).

7. Pull down the Procedures pick list and select (Declarations).

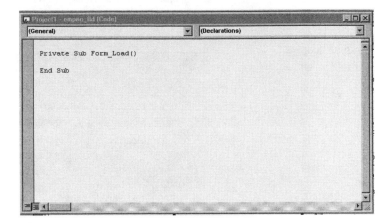

8. Position the in the Project Code window and type the following:

```
Dim OraSession as OraSession
Dim OraDatabase as OraDatabase
Dim OraDynaset as OraDynaset
Dim Connect as String
Dim Database as String
```

9. Pull down the Objects pick list and select Form.

10. Pull down the Procedures pick list and select Load.

11. Position the cursor in the Form_Load procedure and type the code shown in Listing 4.28.

Listing 4.28

```
Set OraSession = _
  CreateObject("OracleInProcServer.XOraSession")
Connect = "scott" + "/" + "tiger"
Database = "v8i"
On Error GoTo HandletheError

 Set OraDatabase = OraSession.OpenDatabase( _
   Database,Connect,&H0&)
```

```
Set OraDynaset = OraDatabase.CreateDynaset( _
"select * from emp",0&)
OraDynaset.MoveFirst

empno_fld.text = OraDynaset.Fields("empno").value
if OraDynaset.Fields("ename").value <> "" then
 ename_fld.text = OraDynaset.Fields("ename").value
else
 ename_fld.text = ""
end if
if OraDynaset.Fields("job").value <> "" then
 job_fld.text = OraDynaset.Fields("job").value
else
  job_fld.text = ""
end if
if OraDynaset.Fields("mgr").value <> "" then
 mgr_fld.text = OraDynaset.Fields("mgr").value
else
 mgr_fld.text = ""
end if
if OraDynaset.Fields("hiredate").value <> "" then
 hiredate_fld.text = OraDynaset.Fields("hiredate").value
else
 hiredate_fld.text = ""
end if
if OraDynaset.Fields("sal").value <> "" then
 sal_fld.text = OraDynaset.Fields("sal").value
else
 sal_fld.text = ""
end if
if OraDynaset.Fields("comm").value <> "" then
 comm_fld.text = OraDynaset.Fields("comm").value
else
 comm_fld.text = ""
end if
deptno_fld.text = OraDynaset.Fields("deptno").value

exit sub
HandletheError:
```

```
If OraSession.LastServerErr = 0 Then
    If Err = 0 Then
     MsgBox("Connected as " & Connect)
    Else
     MsgBox("VB-" & Err & " " & Error)
    End If
Else
    MsgBox(OraSession.LastServerErrText)
End if
```

The next step is to write the code for each of the navigation buttons. To do so, follow these steps.

1. Pull down the Objects pick list and choose FirstBtn.

2. Pull down the Procedures pick list and choose Click.

3. Position the cursor in the FirstBtn_click procedure and type the code shown in Listing 4.29.

4. Pull down the Objects pick list and choose PreviousBtn.

5. Pull down the Procedures pick list and choose Click.

6. Position the cursor in the PreviousBtn_click procedure and type the code in Listing 4.30.

7. Pull down the Objects pick list and choose NextBtn.

8. Pull down the Procedures pick list and choose Click.

9. Position the cursor in the NextBtn_click procedure and type the code in Listing 4.31.

10. Pull down the Objects pick list and choose LastBtn.

11. Pull down the Procedures pick list and choose Click.

12. Position the cursor in the LastBtn_click procedure and type the code in Listing 4.32.

Listing 4.29

```
if OraDynaset.EOF <> True then
    OraDynaset.MoveFirst
empno_fld.text = OraDynaset.Fields("empno").value
```

```
   if OraDynaset.Fields("ename").value <> "" then
    ename_fld.text = OraDynaset.Fields("ename").value
   else
    ename_fld.text = ""
   end if
   if OraDynaset.Fields("job").value <> "" then
    job_fld.text = OraDynaset.Fields("job").value
   else
    job_fld.text = ""
   end if
   if OraDynaset.Fields("mgr").value <> "" then
    mgr_fld.text = OraDynaset.Fields("mgr").value
   else
    mgr_fld.text = ""
   end if
   if OraDynaset.Fields("hiredate").value <> "" then
    hiredate_fld.text = OraDynaset.Fields("hiredate").value
   else
    hiredate_fld.text = ""
   end if
   if OraDynaset.Fields("sal").value <> "" then
    sal_fld.text = OraDynaset.Fields("sal").value
   else
    sal_fld.text = ""
   end if
   if OraDynaset.Fields("comm").value <> "" then
    comm_fld.text = OraDynaset.Fields("comm").value
   else
    comm_fld.text = ""
   end if
   deptno_fld.text = OraDynaset.Fields("deptno").value
End if
```

NOTE   The code that refreshes the text boxes with the current row of data can be placed in a user-defined procedure and then called once you have moved the record pointer.

Listing 4.30

```
if OraDynaset.BOF <> True then
  OraDynaset.MovePrevious
  empno_fld.text = OraDynaset.Fields("empno").value
  if OraDynaset.Fields("ename").value <> "" then
   ename_fld.text = OraDynaset.Fields("ename").value
  else
   ename_fld.text = ""
  end if
  if OraDynaset.Fields("job").value <> "" then
   job_fld.text = OraDynaset.Fields("job").value
  else
   job_fld.text = ""
  end if
  if OraDynaset.Fields("mgr").value <> "" then
   mgr_fld.text = OraDynaset.Fields("mgr").value
  else
   mgr_fld.text =""
  end if
  if OraDynaset.Fields("hiredate").value <> "" then
   hiredate_fld.text = OraDynaset.Fields("hiredate").value
  else
   hiredate_fld.text = ""
  end if
  if OraDynaset.Fields("sal").value <> "" then
   sal_fld.text = OraDynaset.Fields("sal").value
  else
   sal_fld.text = ""
  end if
  if OraDynaset.Fields("comm").value <> "" then
   comm_fld.text = OraDynaset.Fields("comm").value
  else
   comm_fld.text = ""
  end if
  deptno_fld.text = OraDynaset.Fields("deptno").value
end if
```

Listing 4.31

```
if OraDynaset.EOF <> True then
  OraDynaset.MoveNext
  empno_fld.text = OraDynaset.Fields("empno").value
  if OraDynaset.Fields("ename").value <> "" then
   ename_fld.text = OraDynaset.Fields("ename").value
  else
   ename_fld.text = ""
  end if
  if OraDynaset.Fields("job").value <> "" then
   job_fld.text = OraDynaset.Fields("job").value
  else
    job_fld.text = ""
  end if
  if OraDynaset.Fields("mgr").value <> "" then
   mgr_fld.text = OraDynaset.Fields("mgr").value
  else
   mgr_fld.text = ""
  end if
  if OraDynaset.Fields("hiredate").value <> "" then
   hiredate_fld.text = OraDynaset.Fields("hiredate").value
  else
   hiredate_fld.text= ""
  end if
  if OraDynaset.Fields("sal").value <> "" then
   sal_fld.text = OraDynaset.Fields("sal").value
  else
   sal_fld.text = ""
  end if
  if OraDynaset.Fields("comm").value <> "" then
   comm_fld.text = OraDynaset.Fields("comm").value
  else
   comm_fld.text = ""
  end if
  deptno_fld.text = OraDynaset.Fields("deptno").value
end if
```

Listing 4.32

```
OraDynaset.MoveLast
empno_fld.text = OraDynaset.Fields("empno").value
if OraDynaset.Fields("ename").value <> "" then
 ename_fld.text = OraDynaset.Fields("ename").value
else
 ename_fld.text = ""
end if
if OraDynaset.Fields("job").value <> "" then
 job_fld.text = OraDynaset.Fields("job").value
else
   job_fld.text = ""
end if
if OraDynaset.Fields("mgr").value <> "" then
 mgr_fld.text = OraDynaset.Fields("mgr").value
else
 mgr_fld.text = ""
end if
if OraDynaset.Fields("hiredate").value <> "" then
 hiredate_fld.text = OraDynaset.Fields("hiredate").value
else
 hiredate_fld.text= ""
end if
if OraDynaset.Fields("sal").value <> "" then
 sal_fld.text = OraDynaset.Fields("sal").value
else
 sal_fld.text = ""
end if
if OraDynaset.Fields("comm").value <> "" then
 comm_fld.text = OraDynaset.Fields("comm").value
else
 comm_fld.text = ""
end if
deptno_fld.text = OraDynaset.Fields("deptno").value
```

At this stage, all the text boxes and buttons have been coded and are ready for user interaction. The error handler will provide information to help the user troubleshoot any problems. Figure 4.6 shows what is displayed when the application runs.

FIGURE 4.6

The Dynaset Operations application with employee data

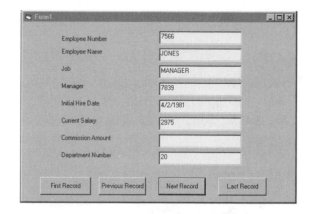

Save your work so you can use what you have created in the next section. In the "Building a Master-Detail Relationship" section, you'll add some functionality to your existing application: a master-detail relationship between the Dept and Emp tables. To save your work, follow these steps:

1. Choose File ➤ Save Project.

2. You will be prompted for a name for both the project and form files.

3. Type **DynasetSample** for both the project and form filename.

4. Click the Save button.

Building a Master-Detail Relationship

Next, let's build a custom application that uses the previous application and builds upon it by implementing a master-detail relationship between two dynasets. A *master-detail relationship* occurs when two tables are joined by a common key. A column in the master recordset is used to determine the set of data that will be displayed in the detail recordset.

In the next example we will build a custom application where the Dept table serves as the master recordset, and the Emp table is the detail recordset. As each new department row is displayed, the Emp table is queried for all employees who work in that department. To build this custom application, we will use Visual

Basic 6. Let's start by building the GUI (graphical user interface) for the user to interact with.

Designing the GUI Interface for the Master-Detail Dynaset Operations Application

The following steps will guide you in creating the graphical user interface for the new Dynaset Operations application that will include a master-detail relationship.

1. Start Microsoft Visual Basic 6.

2. Choose File ➢ Open Project.

3. Browse to the project saved in the last exercise (DynasetSample) and click the Open button.

Currently, the user interface consists of a form with eight text boxes and four command buttons that are used to navigate through the employee data. We are going to add the capability to browse the department data and for the interface to have a relationship with the employee data. The department data will be the master recordset that determines which employees will be a part of the second dynaset, which displays those employees who belong to the current department record.

1. Choose Edit ➢ Select All.

2. Use your mouse pointer to drag the entire selection and position it on the button half of the form. Refer to Figure 4.7 to see how this should look.

FIGURE 4.7
The master-detail form with employee data

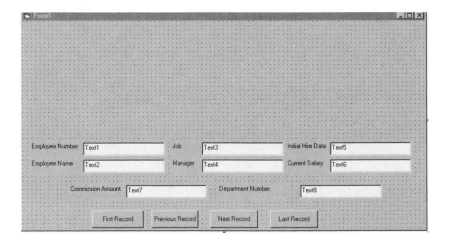

3. On the toolbox, click the Line tool to give it the current focus.

4. Use your mouse pointer to draw a solid line on the form by holding down the left mouse button and pulling the dotted lines into a horizontal line. This will separate the form into two halves, one for the department data and one for the employee data. Figure 4.8 demonstrates how the form should look.

FIGURE 4.8
The Dynaset Operations application with a solid line separating the mployee data and the department data

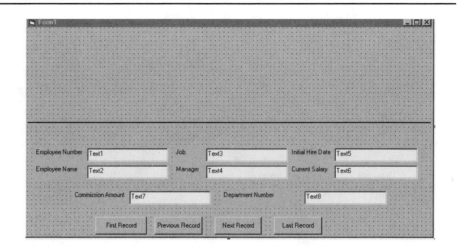

5. On the toolbox, click the command button to give this control the current focus.

TIP

You can use the Tool Tips feature to locate the correct control. Position your mouse over a control for a moment or two, and the name of the control will appear.

6. Use your mouse pointer to draw a button on the form by holding down the left mouse button and pulling the dotted lines into a rectangle.

7. Repeat the process in step 2 until you have four command buttons on the form.

8. Click each command button, dragging and positioning each on the bottom center of the top half of the form.

9. Click the first command button, Command1, to give it the current focus. Locate the Properties dialog box on the right-hand side of the Visual Basic Designer.

10. In the Properties dialog box, locate the (Name) property and change the button's name to **M_FirstBtn**. Change the value by positioning the cursor in the text box to the right of the (Name) property. Use the mouse pointer to highlight the old value. Overwrite the default value by typing in the new name.

11. In the Properties dialog box, locate the Caption property and change the button's caption to **First Record**.

12. Click the second command button, Command2, to give it the current focus.

13. In the Properties dialog box, locate the (Name) property and change the button's name to **M_PreviousBtn**.

14. In the Properties dialog box, locate the Caption property and change the button's caption to **Previous Record**.

15. Click the third command button, Command3, to give it the current focus.

16. In the Properties dialog box, locate the (Name) property and change the button's name to **M_NextBtn**.

17. In the Properties dialog box, locate the Caption property and change the button's caption to **Next Record**.

18. Click the fourth command button, Command4, to give it the current focus.

19. Locate the (Name) property and change the button's name to **M_LastBtn**.

20. Locate the Caption property and change the button's caption to **Last Record**.

FIGURE 4.9
The user interface with four navigation buttons for the department data

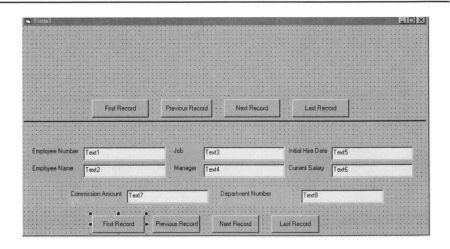

Now that you have the buttons drawn and labeled, as shown in Figure 4.9, you are ready to draw the three text boxes. These controls will be used to present the department data to the user.

1. Choose the text box located on the toolbox to give this control the current focus.

2. Use your mouse pointer to draw a text box on the form by holding down the left mouse button and pulling a rectangle out of the dotted lines.

3. Repeat the process in step 2 two more times until you have three text boxes on the form, aligned vertically, as shown in Figure 4.10.

FIGURE 4.10
The user interface with three text boxes aligned vertically

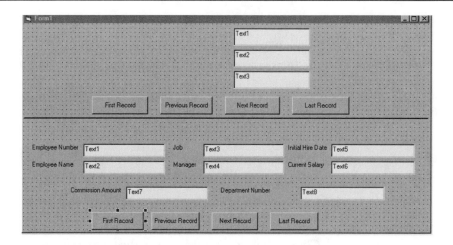

4. Click each text box in turn, dragging and positioning the controls in a vertical row on the form's right side.

5. Click the Text1 text box to give this object the current focus.

6. In the Visual Basic Designer Properties dialog box, locate the (Name) property and change the text box name to **m_deptno_fld**.

7. Click the Text2 text box to give this object the current focus.

8. In the Properties dialog box, locate the (Name) property and change the text box name to **dname_fld**.

9. Click the Text3 text box to give this object the current focus.

10. In the Properties dialog box, locate the (Name) property and change the text box name to **loc_fld**.

In order to give the user a description of the data presented in each text field, label each text box appropriately. To do so, follow these steps:

1. On the toolbox, click Text Label to give this control the current focus.

2. Use your mouse pointer to draw a label on the form by holding down the left mouse button and drawing a rectangle. Position the label to the left of the first text box.

3. Repeat the process in step 2 until there are three labels on the form. Align each label next to the appropriate text box.

4. Click the Label1 object to give it the current focus.

5. In the Properties dialog box of the Visual Basic Properties Designer, locate the (Name) property and change the label's name to **m_dept_lab**.

6. In the Properties dialog box, locate the Caption property and change the label's caption to **Department Number**.

7. Click Label2 to give this object the current focus.

8. In the Properties dialog box, locate the (Name) property and change the label's name to **dname_lab**.

9. In the Properties dialog box, locate the Caption property and change the label's caption to **Department Name**.

10. Click Label3 to give this object the current focus.

11. Locate the (Name) property and change the label's name to **loc_lab**.

12. Locate the Caption property and change the label's caption to **Location**.

The completed design for the user interface is shown in Figure 4.11. The next step is to add the program code to present the department data to the user. We'll do that in the next section. When we're done, this application will provide context-sensitive help and a good error handler to make sure that the user connects successfully.

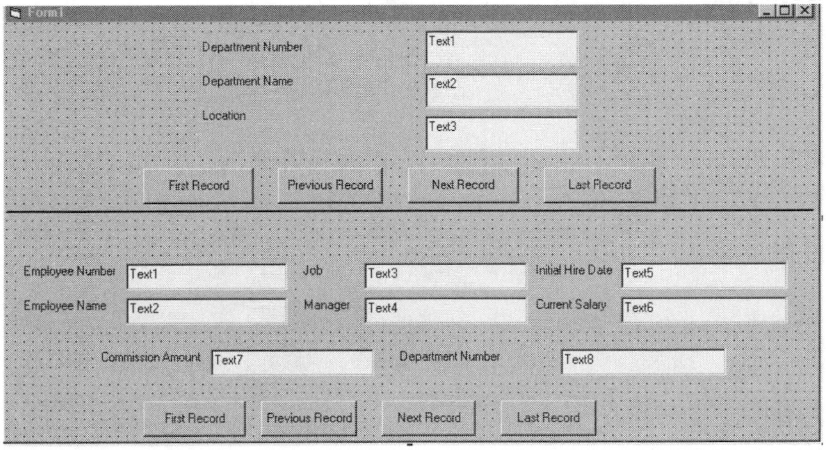

FIGURE 4.11
The completed user interface

Adding the Program Code

Now that the design of the interface is ready, you can start adding custom code into event handlers for the controls so that something will actually happen when the user interacts with the buttons. You will add custom code that will create a link between the master dynaset for the department data and the detail dynaset that holds the employee data.

1. Click the Form object to give it the current focus.

2. Click the right mouse button to display the pop-up menu for the form.

3. From the pop-up menu, choose View Code. The Project Code window appears, as shown in Figure 4.12.

4. Pull down the Objects pick list and select (General).

5. Pull down the Procedures pick list and select (Declarations).

FIGURE 4.12

The Project Code window

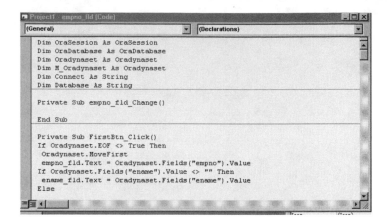

6. Position the cursor in the Project Code window and add the following code:

```
Dim M_OraDynaset as OraDynaset
```

7. Pull down the Objects pick list and select Form.

8. Pull down the Procedures pick list and select Load.

9. Position the cursor in the Form_Load procedure and add the code shown in Listing 4.33 after the code that is already there.

10. Position the cursor in the Form_Load procedure and change the following line of code:

```
Set OraDynaset = OraDatabase.CreateDynaset( _
"select * from emp",0&)
```

to this:

```
Set OraDynaset = OraDatabase.CreateDynaset( _
"select * from emp where deptno= :deptno",0&)
```

Listing 4.33

```
OraDatabase.Parameters.Add _
 "deptno", "10", ORAPARM_INPUT
OraDatabase.Parameters("deptno").ServerType = _
 ORATYPE_NUMBER
```

```
Set M_OraDynaset = OraDatabase.CreateDynaset( _
"select deptno, dname, loc from dept ",0&)
M_OraDynaset.MoveFirst
M_deptno_fld.text = M_OraDynaset.Fields("deptno").value
If M_OraDynaset.Fields("dname").value <> "" then
  dname_fld.text = M_OraDynaset.Fields("dname").value
else
  dname_fld.text = ""
end if
if M_OraDynaset.Fields("loc").value <> "" then
  loc_fld.text = M_OraDynaset.Fields("loc").value
else
  loc_fld.text = ""
end if

OraDatabase.Parameters("deptno").Value = M_deptno_fld.text
```

The next step is to write the code for each of the navigation buttons that you created on the form for the master recordset. To do so, follow these steps:

1. Pull down the Objects pick list and choose M_FirstBtn.

2. Pull down the Procedures pick list and choose Click.

3. Position the cursor in the M_FirstBtn_click procedure and type the code shown in Listing 4.34.

4. Pull down the Objects pick list and choose M_PreviousBtn.

5. Pull down the Procedures pick list and choose Click.

6. Position the cursor in the M_PreviousBtn_click procedure and type the code shown in Listing 4.35.

7. Pull down the Objects pick list and choose M_NextBtn.

8. Pull down the Procedures pick list and choose Click.

9. Position the cursor in the M_NextBtn_click procedure and type the code shown in Listing 4.36.

10. Pull down the Objects pick list and choose M_LastBtn.

11. Pull down the Procedures pick list and choose Click.

12. Position the cursor in the M_LastBtn_click procedure and type the code in Listing 4.37.

Listing 4.34

```
if M_OraDynaset.EOF <> True then
  M_OraDynaset.MoveFirst
  M_deptno_fld.text = M_OraDynaset.Fields("deptno").value
  If M_OraDynaset.Fields("dname").value <> "" then
    dname_fld.text = M_OraDynaset.Fields("dname").value
  else
    dname_fld.text = ""
  end if
  if M_OraDynaset.Fields("loc").value <> "" then
    loc_fld.text = M_OraDynaset.Fields("loc").value
  else
    loc_fld.text = ""
  end if
  call refreshdetail
End if
```

Listing 4.35

```
if M_OraDynaset.BOF <> True then
 M_OraDynaset.MovePrevious
 M_deptno_fld.text = M_OraDynaset.Fields("deptno").value
  If M_OraDynaset.Fields("dname").value <> "" then
    dname_fld.text = M_OraDynaset.Fields("dname").value
  else
    dname_fld.text = ""
  end if
  if M_OraDynaset.Fields("loc").value <> "" then
    loc_fld.text = M_OraDynaset.Fields("loc").value
  else
    loc_fld.text = ""
  end if

 call refreshdetail
end if
```

Listing 4.36

```
M_OraDynaset.MoveNext
M_deptno_fld.text = M_OraDynaset.Fields("deptno").value
If M_OraDynaset.Fields("dname").value <> "" then
  dname_fld.text = M_OraDynaset.Fields("dname").value
else
  dname_fld.text = ""
end if
if M_OraDynaset.Fields("loc").value <> "" then
  loc_fld.text = M_OraDynaset.Fields("loc").value
else
  loc_fld.text = ""
end if
call refreshdetail
```

Listing 4.37

```
M_OraDynaset.MoveLast
M_deptno_fld.text = M_OraDynaset.Fields("deptno").value
If M_OraDynaset.Fields("dname").value <> "" then
  dname_fld.text = M_OraDynaset.Fields("dname").value
else
  dname_fld.text = ""
end if
if M_OraDynaset.Fields("loc").value <> "" then
  loc_fld.text = M_OraDynaset.Fields("loc").value
else
  loc_fld.text = ""
end if
call refreshdetail
```

The last step is to write the code for the procedure to refresh the detail recordset
for the employees.

1. Position the cursor at the end of all the subroutines in the Project Code window. To add the new procedure, type the code shown in Listing 4.38.

Listing 4.38

```
Private sub refreshdetail()
OraDatabase.Parameters("deptno").Value = M_deptno_fld.text
OraDynaset.Refresh
OraDynaset.movefirst
If OraDynaset.Fields("ename").Value <> "" Then
  ename_fld.Text = OraDynaset.Fields("ename").Value
Else
  ename_fld.Text = ""
End If
If OraDynaset.Fields("job").Value <> "" Then
  job_fld.Text = OraDynaset.Fields("job").Value
Else
  job_fld.Text = ""
End If
If OraDynaset.Fields("mgr").Value <> "" Then
  mgr_fld.Text = OraDynaset.Fields("mgr").Value
Else
  mgr_fld.Text = ""
End If
If OraDynaset.Fields("hiredate").Value <>"" Then
  hiredate_fld.Text = OraDynaset.Fields("hiredate").Value
Else
  hiredate_fld.Text = ""
End If
If OraDynaset.Fields("sal").Value <> "" Then
  sal_fld.Text = OraDynaset.Fields("sal").Value
Else
  sal_fld.Text = ""
End If
If OraDynaset.Fields("comm").Value <> "" Then
  comm_fld.Text = OraDynaset.Fields("comm").Value
Else
  comm_fld.Text = ""
End If
deptno_fld.Text = OraDynaset.Fields("deptno").Value
End Sub
```

At this stage, all text boxes and buttons have been coded and are ready to present data to a user. The error handler you provided will display meaningful information to help the user troubleshoot any problems. Take a look at Figure 4.13 for an example of what the application displays when it runs.

FIGURE 4.13
The Dynaset Operations
application with
employee data

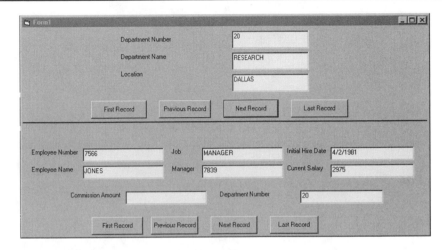

The application presents the master recordset Dept in the top half of the form. You can click the Next Record button to navigate through the master recordset and display the details of all the employees who work in the department that is currently displayed.

Summary

This chapter covered objects, properties, and methods for writing code that displays and manipulates data. You should now know the basics for creating and navigating dynasets, as well as executing SQL and PL/SQL using other approaches, such as calling the ExecuteSQL method of the OraDatabase object. In the next chapter, you will take a look at the Oracle Data Control and the advantages it provides by managing the underlying database objects without you having to write a lot of code.

chapter 5

Using the Oracle Data Control

- Using data aware controls

- Using the Oracle Data Control

- Accessing LOBs with the Oracle Data Control

Data controls are usually ActiveX components that allow your application to simplify the exchange of data between data aware controls and the database. *ActiveX controls* were formerly referred to as OLE controls and are standard interfaces used to provide some functionality or specific kind of service, such as timing services or reporting functionality. They are in-process components that run inside your application's process space. They have high re-use and can be either *visual* or *non-visual controls*. Visual controls usually help with data presentation. Non-visual controls, such as a timer, expose properties and methods called by your application to provide some service.

By placing a data control and some other data aware control, such as a list box, on a form, querying the database is as easy as filling in the connection information and the record source with a valid SQL statement. Data aware controls work with the Oracle Data Control to access, manipulate, and present data to end users. Data aware controls are a special kind of ActiveX control that communicate with the Oracle Data Control to perform queries, inserts, updates, and deletions on the data caused by user interaction or programmed events.

In this chapter, you will take a look at the Oracle Data Control that is bundled with Oracle Objects for OLE and see how to use it to perform the bulk of the work for accessing your data. Let's start with a discussion on data aware controls and the specifics on using them with the Oracle Data Control.

Data Aware Controls

Data aware controls are visual controls that can display data from the database. They are used to create user interfaces for editing and viewing data. A data aware control is bound to a data control; it is considered a bound control once the binding process is complete. Visual Basic offers many data aware controls in Visual Basic 6. Data aware controls are also available through third-party vendors, such as Sheridan and FarPoint.

The following data aware controls have been tested with the Oracle Data Control:

- Visual Basic standard controls version 4, 5, and 6

    - Edit Control

    - Static Text Control

    - Picture Box and Image Control

- Microsoft OLE Container Control

- Microsoft Data Bound List Box Control

- Microsoft Data Bound Combo Box Control

- Microsoft Data Bound Grid Control

- Sheridan Data Widgets 3

  - Sheridan Data Bound Combo Control

  - Sheridan Data Bound Grid Control

  - Sheridan Data Bound Drop Down Control

  - Sheridan Enhanced Data Control

- FarPoint Data Bound Grid Control 2.5.020

NOTE   The information in Table 5.1 is owned by Oracle Corporation and is documented in the Oracle Objects for OLE 8.1.5 release notes.

Known Issues with Data Aware Controls

Table 5.1 outlines some of the known issues with the Oracle Data Control for data aware controls from Microsoft, Sheridan, and FarPoint. These are also documented in the Oracle Objects for OLE 8.1.5 release notes.

T A B L E 5 . 1 : Using Data Aware Controls from Third-Party Vendors

Vendor	Control	Known Issues
Microsoft	Picture Box or Image Control	A Long Raw column accessed through the Oracle Data Control is read only. To insert or update Long Raw data, you must use the AppendChunk method.
Microsoft	List Box Control	When using the List Box Control, you must use the Move methods, MoveNext and MovePrevious, to force an update. The UpdateRecord method will not work.

TABLE 5.1:   Using Data Aware Controls from Third-Party Vendors *(continued)*

Vendor	Control	Known Issues
Microsoft	Combo Box Control	This control does not respond to the UpdateRecord method. Use the MoveNext or MovePrevious methods to force the update.

Microsoft	Grid Control	When the row pointer of the Oracle Data Control's recordset is moved to either EOF or BOF, the Microsoft Grid Control does not re-paint properly. Place logic in your code to move the row pointer to the first or last row in the recordset. For example,
		`If ORADC1.Recordset.BOF =True then`
		`ORADC1.Recordset.MoveLast`
		`ORADC1.Recordset.MoveFirst`
		`Elseif ORADC1.Recordset.EOF = True then`
		`ORADC1.Recordset.MoveFirst`
		`ORADC1.Recordset.MoveLast`
		`Else`
		` 'do nothing`
		`Endif`

Microsoft	Grid Control	The Scroll method will not work.
Microsoft	Grid Control	The Refresh method of the grid will not work. When refreshing data, use ORADC1 .Recordset.Refresh.
Microsoft	Grid Control	When deleting a row from the recordset, use a button and custom code, such as ORADC1 .Recordset. Delete. Using the Delete key causes incorrect behavior.
Microsoft	Grid Control	Microsoft Grid Control bookmarks and Oracle Objects for OLE bookmarks are not compatible. Do not share bookmarks between Oracle objects and the Microsoft Grid Control.
Sheridan	List Box Control	Updates will not work using this control. Use the Microsoft Combo Box Control until this is resolved.

TABLE 5.1: Using Data Aware Controls from Third-Party Vendors *(continued)*

Vendor	Control	Known Issues

Sheridan	Grid Control	When the row pointer of the Oracle Data Control's recordset is moved to either EOF or BOF, the Sheridan Grid Control does not re-paint properly. Place logic in your code to move the row pointer to the first or last row in the recordset. For example,
		`If ORADC1`
		`.Recordset.BOF =True then`
		`ORADC1.Recordset.MoveLast`
		`ORADC1.Recordset.MoveFirst`
		`Elseif ORADC1.Recordset.EOF = True then`
		`ORADC1.Recordset.MoveFirst`
		`ORADC1.Recordset.MoveLast`
		`Else`
		` 'do nothing`
		`Endif`

Sheridan	Grid Control	If you try and insert new rows and all the data has not fetched, an OIP-4119 error occurs. Call the MoveLast method to force all the data to be fetched before inserting new rows. For example, `ORADC1.Recordset.MoveLast`
Sheridan	Grid Control	When refreshing the data, use ORADC1 .Recordset.Refresh. The Refresh method of the Sheridan Grid Control will not work.
Sheridan	Enhanced Data Control	Find functionality does not work properly.
FarPoint	Grid Control	When working with Long Raw data, access violations will occur if the data size minus 118 bytes is a multiple of 32 kilobytes. Contact FarPoint for information about obtaining a fix.
FarPoint	Grid Control	The Reposition event of this control does not work properly after deleting the last row in the recordset. You should call the Refresh method of the Oracle Data Control after deleting rows. For example, `ORADC1.Refresh`

The Oracle Data Control

The Oracle Data Control is an ActiveX component. It acts as the referee between the database and the visual controls to direct and manage information flow. The Oracle Data Control manages various tasks such as navigating, displaying, and updating data. The Oracle Data Control is compatible with the Microsoft Data Control. They both use the same protocol to communicate with other data bound controls. The protocol used for communication between a data control and data aware controls is an open standard. The specification is written and maintained by Microsoft Corporation.

The Oracle Data Control allows you to perform most data access operations without writing a single line of code. In Chapter 4, dynaset operations were discussed, and you examined the various methods available to help manage data. The Oracle Data Control also has various methods, and in addition, the control also responds to events. An *event* is a reaction to a particular action that has taken place. For example, an event occurs after a user clicks a Query button on a form. When a command button is clicked (action), an event is fired (reaction), and code is executed based on that action. Another example is when a user navigates to the next record (action), and an event code (reaction) is executed to validate data.

Behind the scenes, the Oracle Data Control creates and maintains a dynaset. Dynaset operations were discussed in Chapter 4. Now let's take a look at how much easier it is to use the data control than to manipulate an OraDynaset object.

In order to execute a simple query using dynaset operations, you need to build a Visual Basic application that contains, at the minimum, the following lines of code:

```
Dim OraSession as OraSession
Dim OraDatabase as OraDatabase
Dim OraDynaset as OraDynaset
Dim sql_condition as String

Set OraSession = _
CreateObject("OracleInProcServer.Xsession")

Set OraDatabase = OraSession.OpenDatabase( _
  "v8i","scott/tiger",0&)

Set OraDynaset = OraDatabase.CreateDynaset( _
  "Select * from emp",0&)
```

NOTE   The examples in this chapter use the Scott schema, which is owned by Oracle Corporation and is bundled with the Oracle8i client software and the OO4O product.

To present the data, you also have to provide the user interface with navigation buttons or some other means for the user to navigate through the dynaset and view the data, as well as command buttons or menu choices to allow the user to insert and update the dynaset information. All the events for the user interface controls and menu choices have to be programmed by you. Chapter 4 presented the lines of code that you need to write to provide basic functionality. Now, let's see how you can do this by simply dragging and dropping components onto the default form and filling in three properties.

1. Start Visual Basic and create a new project of type Standard Exe.

2. Choose Project ➢ Components and scroll down the list until you find the Oracle Data Control.

3. Choose the component by toggling on the check box, as seen in Figure 5.1. Click OK.

4. Repeat the same process for Microsoft Data Bound Grid Control (data aware control).

NOTE   Microsoft provides several versions of the Grid Control with Visual Basic 6. Make sure that you select the Microsoft Data Bound Grid Control 5.0 (SP3).

FIGURE 5.1

Selecting the Oracle Data Control from the Components dialog box

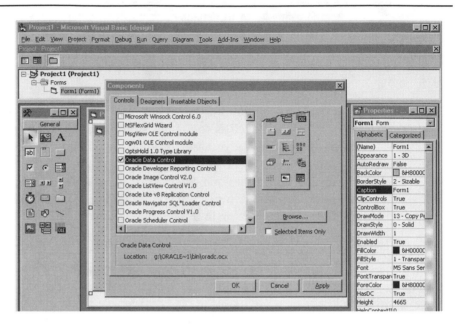

The Oracle Data Control and the Microsoft Grid Control now appear on the toolbox and are available for use by your application. Next, we'll place the data control and the Microsoft Grid Control onto Form1.

1. Choose the Microsoft Grid Control from the toolbox and place it on Form1.

2. Choose the ORADC (Oracle Data Control) component from the toolbox and place it on the form below the Microsoft Grid Control, as shown in Figure 5.2. The Oracle Data Control has a default object name of ORADC1. The actual filename is Oradc.ocx.

FIGURE 5.2

Placing the Microsoft Grid Control and the Oracle Data Control

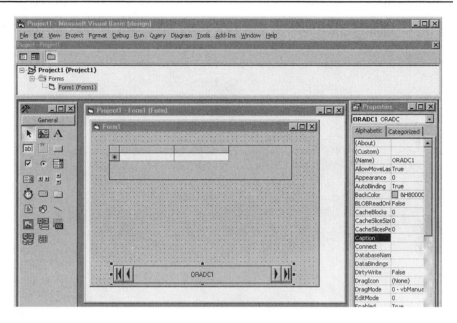

To make a connection to the database, you must fill in the following properties for the data control:

Connect   This is the username and password to be supplied when trying to establish the connection. This property is read/write at design and runtime.

DatabaseName   This is the Net8 service name that has been defined in the TNSNAMES.ORA file using the Net8 Easy Configuration utility.

You can specify the values for these properties at design time by filling in the values in the Properties dialog box of the Visual Basic Designer. Follow these steps to fill in the values at design time:

1. Choose the ORADC1 Control on Form1.

2. In the Properties dialog box, locate the Connect property.

3. Position your cursor within the text box and type in a valid username and password separated by a "/" (forward slash). An example of this is scott/ tiger.

4. In the Properties dialog box, locate the DatabaseName property.

5. Position your cursor in the DatabaseName text box and type in a valid Net8 service name that the control will use to connect to the database. I recommend that you use the one created in Chapter 1 when you installed the Net8 client and OO4O product, v8i. See Figure 5.3 to check your work so far.

FIGURE 5.3

Supplying the Connect and DatabaseName properties at design time

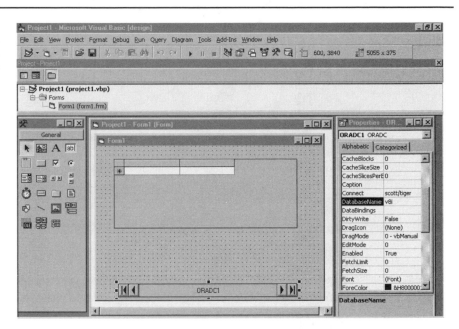

Now that you have supplied the information to the data control for making a connection to the database, you must supply the SQL statement that will execute on the server side and return data back to the Oracle Data Control. The Record-Source property of the Oracle Data Control holds the query to be executed. Follow these steps to set this property at design time:

1. Choose the ORADC1 Control on Form1.

2. In the Properties dialog box, locate the RecordSource property.

3. Position your cursor in the RecordSource text box and type in a valid SQL statement, such as Select From Emp.

The final step is to bind the data control to the data aware control (Microsoft Data Bound Grid Control).

1. Choose the DBGrid1 Control on Form1.

2. In the Properties dialog box, locate the DataSource property.

3. Choose the ORADC1 (Oracle Data Control) component from the DataSource pick list.

That's it. Now, run your application and see the results of your query being executed and presented on the form without you writing a single line of code.

Next, let's examine the properties, methods, and events of the Oracle Data Control.

Oracle Data Control Properties

In this section, we will discuss the properties of the Oracle Data Control. Figure 5.4 shows the Properties dialog box for the Oracle Data Control in the Visual Basic Designer.

FIGURE 5.4
The Properties dialog box
for the Oracle Data Control
(ORADC1)

The following is a list of properties found in the Properties dialog box, along with their description. Each of these properties can be set at design time, runtime, or both. These properties are listed in alphabetical order, with information on when they are available, their value, their default value, and an example of their syntax.

AllowMoveLast

The *AllowMoveLast property* determines whether or not the user is given the capability to move to the last row using the data control's Last Row button.

Availability: Read and write at design and runtime

Value: True, False

Default: True

Syntax: `ORADC1.AllowMoveLast = False`

AutoBinding

The *AutoBinding property* determines whether the automatic binding of database parameters will occur.

Availability: Read and write at design and runtime

Value: True, False

Default: True

Syntax: `ORADC1.AutoBinding = False`

BackColor

The *BackColor property* determines the background color of an object. Visual Basic uses the Microsoft Windows operating environment's Red-Green-Blue (RGB) color scheme.

Availability: Read and write at design and runtime.

Value: See the Microsoft documentation.

Default: Set to the system default color specified by the constant

vbWindowBackground.

Syntax: `ORADC1.BackColor = &H8000`

BLOBReadOnly

The BLOBReadOnly property determines if BLOB data will be read only. This is provided for backward compatibility with previous versions. In previous versions of OO4O, Long Raw data was read only when accessing that data type through the Oracle Data Control.

Availability: Read and write at design and runtime

Value: True, False

Default: True

Syntax: `ORADC1.BLOBReadOnly = False`

CacheBlocks

The *CacheBlocks property* gets or sets the maximum number of cache blocks used for the underlying recordset.

Availability: Read and write at design and runtime

Value: An integer

Default: 0

Syntax: `ORADC1.Database.CacheBlocks = 5`

CacheSliceSize

The *CacheSliceSize property* gets or sets cache slice size used for the underlying recordset.

Availability: Read and write at design and runtime

Value: An integer

Default: 0

Syntax: `ORADC1.Database.CacheSliceSize = 5`

CacheSlicesPerBlock

The *CacheSlicesPerBlock property* gets or sets the cache slice size used per block for the underlying recordset.

Availability: Read and write at design and runtime

Value: An integer

Default: 0

Syntax: `ORADC1.Database.CacheSlicesPerBlock = 5`

Caption

The *Caption property* determines the text description displayed in the Data Control panel.

Availability: Read and write at design and runtime

Value: A string

Default: ORADC1

Syntax: `ORADC1.Caption = "MyOracleDataControl"`

Connect

The *Connect property* determines the username and password used when connecting the data control to an Oracle database. The username and password must be separated by a / (forward slash).

Availability: Read and write at design time and runtime

Value: A string

Default: None

Syntax: `ORADC1.connect = "scott/tiger"`

Database

The *Database property* gets the OraDatabase object associated with the underlying recordset.

Availability: Not available at design time and read only at runtime

Value: OraDatabase object

Default: None

Syntax: `set OraDatabase = ORADC1.Database`

DatabaseName

The *DatabaseName property* determines the Net8 service name used to connect to the database.

> Availability: Read and write at design time and runtime
>
> Value: A string
>
> Default: None
>
> Syntax: `ORADC1.DatabaseName = "v8i"`

DirtyWrite

The *DirtyWrite property* determines whether or not the data control will check for read inconsistencies.

> Availability: Read and write at design and runtime
>
> Value: True, False
>
> Default: False
>
> Syntax: `ORADC1.DirtyWrite = True`

DragIcon

The *DragIcon property* determines the icon to be displayed as the pointer during a drag-and-drop operation.

NOTE   At runtime, the DragIcon property can be set to any object's DragIcon or Icon property, or you can assign it an icon returned by the LoadPicture function.

> Availability: Write at design and runtime
>
> Value: The icon filename and extension format
>
> Default: None
>
> Syntax: `ORADC1.DragIcon = LoadPicture("MyIcon.ico")`

DragMode

The *DragMode property* sets or returns the value that determines whether or not manual or automatic dragging mode is used during a drag-and-drop operation. It can take the following values:

VbManual   Requires using the Drag method to initiate a drag-and-drop operation on the source control.

VbAutomatic   Clicking the source control automatically initiates a drag-and-drop operation. OLE container controls are automatically dragged only when they don't have focus.

Availability: Read and write at design and runtime

Value: 0 or 1

Default: 0 or VbManual

Syntax: `ORADC1.DragMode = 1`

EditMode

The *EditMode property* returns the editing state for the current row selected. It can return the following values:

ORADATA_EDITNONE   No editing is in progress.

ORADATA_EDITMODE   Editing is in progress.

ORADATA_EDITADD   A new record is being added.

Availability: Not available at design time and read-only at runtime

Value: 0, 1, or 2

Default: 0 or ORADATA_EDITNONE

Syntax: `RowState = ORADC1.EditMode`

Enabled

The *Enabled property* determines whether or not the data control is capable of responding to user-generated events.

Availability: Read and write at design and runtime

Value: True, False

Default: True

Syntax: `ORADC1.Enabled = True`

FetchLimit

The *FetchLimit property* sets and gets the fetch array size.

Availability: Read and write at design and runtime

Value: An integer

Default: 0

Syntax: `ORADC1.Database.FetchLimit = 10`

FetchSize

The *FetchSize property* sets and gets the fetch array buffer size.

Availability: Read and write at design and runtime

Value: An integer

Default: 0

Syntax: `ORADC1.Database.FetchSize = 10`

Font

The *Font property* identifies a specific object whose Font property you want to change.

Availability: Read and write at design and runtime

Value: Various

Default: None

Syntax: `ORADC1.Font.Bold = True`

ForeColor

The *ForeColor property* determines the foreground color of an object. Visual Basic uses the Microsoft Windows operating environment's Red-Green-Blue (RGB) color scheme.

Availability: Read and write at design and runtime.

Value: See the Microsoft documentation.

Default: Set to the system default color specified by the constant vbWindowForeground.

Syntax: `ORADC1.BackColor = &H8000`

Height

The *Height property* sets and returns the height of an object that is the Oracle Data Control.

Availability: Read and write at design and runtime

Value: Points

Default: The initial position at design time

Syntax: `ORADC1.Height = 5`

Index

The *Index property* specifies a number that uniquely identifies a control that is part of an object array.

Availability: Available at design time only if the control is part of an array

Value: An integer

Default: No value or not part of an array

Syntax: `pos = ORADC1(i).index`

Left

The *Left property* determines the left edge of the objects and its container.

Availability: Read and write at design and runtime

Value: Points

Default: The initial position at design time

Syntax: `ORADC1.Left = 10`

Name

The *Name property* determines the name used by code to identify an object.

> Availability: Only available at design time
>
> Value: A string
>
> Default: ORADC1
>
> Syntax: Cannot be set programmatically

NoRefetch

The *NoRefetch property* determines whether the default column values set by the server is re-fetched to the local cache or not. If this option is set for the Ora-Database object, the underlying dynaset and recordset will also inherit this trait.

> Availability: Read and write at design and runtime
>
> Value: True, False
>
> Default: False
>
> Syntax: `ORADC1.NoRefetch = True`

Options

The *Options property* determines the options that specify the specific database behavior of the data control and the underlying recordset. This property can take the following values:

ORADB_DEFAULT   Accept the default behavior.

ORADB_ORAMODE   Let Oracle set default field (column) values.

ORADB_NOWAIT   Do not wait on row locks when executing a `Select For Update` statement.

ORADB_NO_REFETCH   Let Oracle set the default field (column) values as in ORADB_ORAMODE, but data is not refetched after the Insert or Update operation.

> Availability: Read and write at design and runtime
>
> Value: A bit flag
>
> Default: ORADB_DEFAULT
>
> Syntax: `ORADC1.options = ORADB_ORAMODE`

OracleMode

The *OracleMode property* determines whether or not changes made to fields are immediately reflected in the local cache. Setting this property has no effect until the Refresh method is called on the Oracle Data Control.

Availability: Read and write at design and runtime

Value: True, False

Default: True

Syntax: `ORADC1.OraMode = False`

ReadOnly

The *ReadOnly property* determines whether the underlying recordset is updateable or not. Setting this property has no effect until the Refresh method is called on the Oracle Data Control.

Availability: Read and write at design and runtime

Value: True, False

Default: True

Syntax: `ORADC1.OraMode = False`

Recordset

The *Recordset property* accepts and returns an OraDynaset object that has been defined by the Connect, DatabaseName, and RecordSource properties. Once this dynaset is returned, all the properties and methods of the OraDynaset object that were discussed in the Chapter 4 are available for use.

Availability: Not available at design time and read only at runtime

Value: The OraDynaset object

Default: None

Syntax: `set OraDynaset = ORADC1.recordset`

or

`Set ORADC1.recordset = OraDynaset`

RecordSource

The *RecordSource property* determines the SQL statement that is sent over to the database.

> Availability: Read and write at design time and runtime
>
> Value: A string
>
> Default: None
>
> Syntax: `ORADC1.RecordSource = "select * from emp"`

Session

The *Session property* returns the Session object associated with the Oracle Data Control.

> Availability: Read only at runtime
>
> Value: The OraSession object
>
> Default: None
>
> Syntax: `MyOraSession = ORADC1.Session`

TrailingBlanks

The *TrailingBlanks property* determines whether or not trailing blanks are stripped from character fields.

> Available: Read and write at design and runtime
>
> Value: True, False
>
> Default: False
>
> Syntax: `ORADC1.TrailingBlanks = True`

Top

The *Top property* determines the distance between the internal top edge of an object and the top edge of its container.

> Availability: Read and write at design and runtime
>
> Value: An integer
>
> Default: The initial position at design time
>
> Syntax: `ORADC1.Top = 10`

Visible

The *Visible property* determines whether an object is visible or hidden on the form.

> Availability: Read and write at design and runtime
>
> Value: True, False
>
> Default: True
>
> Syntax: `ORADC1.visible = False`

Width

The *Width property* determines the width of an object.

> Available: Read and write at design and runtime
>
> Value: Points
>
> Default: The initial position at design time
>
> Syntax: `ORADC1.Width = 10`

Data Control Methods

The following list describes the various methods of the Oracle Data Control and their use in your application. These methods affect the physical appearance of the Oracle Data Control, as well as behavior when working with data aware controls.

Drag

The *Drag method* begins, ends, and cancels a Drag operation. Using the Drag method to control a drag-and-drop operation is required only when the Drag-Mode property of the object is set to zero or manual. The Drag method has the following constants:

VbCancel   Cancels a Drag operation.

VbBeginDrag   Begins dragging.

VbEndDrag   Ends the drag-and-drop operation.

Parameters: A number or one of the previously named constants

Syntax: `ORADC1.drag vbcancel`

Move

The *Move method* moves the Oracle Data Control to a position on the form specified by the Left, Top, Width, and Height parameters.

Left   A value indicating the horizontal coordinate (x-axis) for the left edge of object. Required.

Top   A value indicating the vertical coordinate (y-axis) for the top edge of object. Optional.

Width   A value indicating the new width of object. Optional.

Height   A value indicating the new height of object. Optional.

Parameters: Left, Top, Width, Height

Syntax: `ORADC1.Move 10 20 50 10`

Refresh

The *Refresh method* creates the underlying OraDatabase and OraDynaset objects referenced within the Connect, Database, and RecordSource properties.

Parameters: None

Syntax: `ORADC1.Refresh`

UpdateControls

The *UpdateControls method* gets the current record from the data control's record-set and displays the data in the bound control.

Parameters: None

Syntax: `ORADC1.UpdateControls`

NOTE   The UpdateControls method of the Oracle Data Control is provided for backward compatibility. You should call the method on the Oracle Data Control's Recordset property using the following syntax: `ORADC1.Recordset.UpdateControls`.

UpdateRecord

The *UpdateRecord method* saves the current data values of the bound controls.

Parameters: None

Syntax: `ORADC1.UpdateRecord`

NOTE   The UpdateRecord method of the Oracle Data Cotrol is provided for backward compatibility. You should call the method on the Oracle Data Control's Recordset property using the following syntax: `ORADC1.Recordset.UpdateRecord`.

Zorder

The *Zorder method* places a specified MDIForm, form, or control at the front or back of the z-order in its graphical level. It takes the following parameter:

Position   An integer indicating the position of an object relative to other instances of the same object. If the position is 0 or omitted, the object is positioned at the front of the z-order. If the position is 1, the object is positioned at the back of the z-order.

Parameters: Position

Syntax: `ORADC1.ZOrder 0`

Data Control Events

The following list describes the various events of the Oracle Data Control and their use in your application.

DragDrop

The *DragDrop event* is fired when a drag-and-drop operation is completed as a result of either dragging a control over a form or control and releasing the mouse button, or using the Drag method with its action argument = 2 (Drop).

DragOver

The *DragOver event* is fired when a drag-and-drop operation is in progress. You can use this event to monitor when the mouse pointer enters, leaves, or is directly over a valid target. The mouse pointer position determines which target object receives this event.

Error

The *Error event* is fired whenever an interactive operation causes an error. You can perform some operations directly with the data control, such as using the data control buttons or when the data control refreshes automatically when the form loads. In these cases, the Error event is fired instead of causing a normal run-time error.

MouseDown

The *MouseDown event* is fired whenever a mouse button is pressed (MouseDown) and the mouse pointer is over the data control or has been captured by the data control. The mouse is captured if a mouse button has been previously pressed over the data control until all corresponding MouseUp events have been received.

MouseMove

The *MouseMove event* is fired continuously whenever the mouse pointer moves across the data control. Unless another object has not captured the mouse, the data control recognizes a MouseMove event whenever the mouse position is within its borders.

MouseUp

The *MouseUp event* is fired whenever a mouse button is released (MouseUp) and the mouse pointer is over the Oracle Data Control, or has been captured by the Oracle Data Control. The mouse is captured when a mouse button is pressed over the data control and remains captured until all corresponding MouseUp events are received.

Reposition

The *Reposition event* is fired whenever the database record pointer is successfully repositioned to a new location. This is a good event to use to refresh detail record-sets when your application has a master-detail relationship. In this chapter, you will use the Reposition event to help build a master-detail relationship between the Dept and Emp tables.

NOTE   The Validate event is always fired before the Reposition event.

Validate

The *Validate event* is fired whenever an attempt is made to move to a new record position, to delete a record, to add a record, to move to a bookmark, or to roll back the dynaset changes in the current transaction. Use this event to build in business logic for validating certain values.

NOTE   The Validate event is always called before any operations proceed and any action is taken to move a row pointer or to change the data.

Creating an Application Using the Oracle Data Control

Now that you have examined the properties, methods, and events of the Oracle Data Control, let's put this into practice by writing a small application. The next section guides you through creating a basic application that takes advantage of the Oracle Data Control. As you read through and perform the steps, the properties, methods, and events will be discussed.

Getting Started with the Oracle Data Control

To demonstrate how to use the Oracle Data Control, let's build a small application that binds a data control to the Microsoft Data Bound Grid Control. The following steps will get you started.

1. Start Visual Basic and create a new project of type Standard EXE. Choose Project ➢ Components and scroll down the list until you find the Oracle Data Control.

2. Choose the component by toggling on the check box, as shown in Figure 5.5.

3. Click OK.

4. Repeat the same process for Microsoft Data Bound Grid Control.

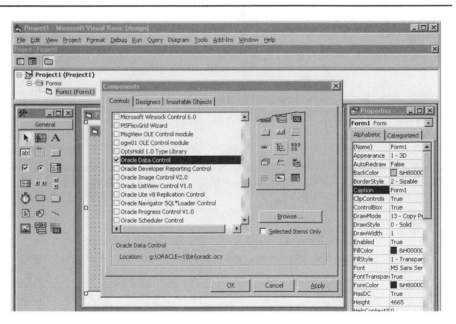

FIGURE 5.5
Selecting the Oracle Data Control from the Components dialog box

The Oracle Data Control and the Microsoft Grid Control now appear on the toolbox and are available for use by your application. Next, place the Oracle Data Control and the Microsoft Grid Control onto Form1.

1. Choose the Microsoft Data Bound Grid Control and place it on Form1.

2. Choose the ORADC (Oracle Data Control) component from the toolbox and place it on the form below the Microsoft Grid Control, as shown in Figure 5.6.

FIGURE 5.6
Placement of the Microsoft Grid Control and the Oracle Data Control

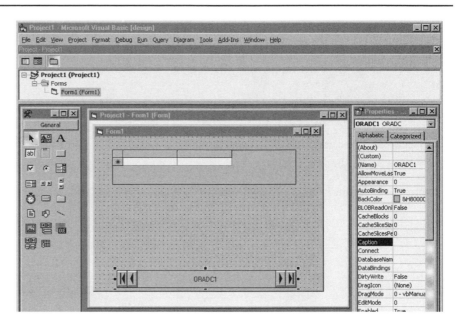

To make a connection to the database, fill in the following properties for the data control:

Connect   This is the username and password to be supplied when trying to establish the connection. This property is read or write at design and runtime.

DatabaseName   This is the Net8 service name that has been defined in the TNSAMES.ORA file using the Net8 Easy Configuration utility. I recommend using "v8i", the service name you defined in Chapter 1 when installing the Net8 client and the OO4O product.

You can either specify the values for these properties at design time by filling in the values on the Properties dialog box in the Visual Basic Designer, or at runtime by programmatically writing the code to supply them. Follow these steps to fill in the values at design time:

1. Choose the ORADC1 Control on Form1.

2. In the Properties dialog box, locate the Connect property.

3. Position your cursor in the Connect text box and type in a valid username and password separated by a "/" (forward slash).

4. In the Properties dialog box, locate the DatabaseName property.

5. Position your cursor in the text box and type in a valid Net8 service name that the control will use to connect to the database. See Figure 5.7 to check your work so far.

FIGURE 5.7

Supplying the Connect and DatabaseName properties at design time

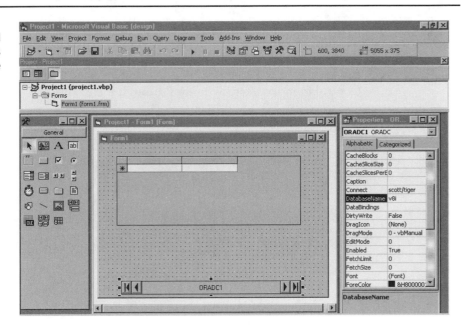

These properties can also be supplied at runtime, which is demonstrated in the "Using Controls in an Application" section later in this chapter.

Now that you have supplied the data control with the information to make a connection to the database, you must supply the SQL statement that will execute on the server side and return data back to the data control. The RecordSource property of the data control holds the query to be executed. Follow these steps to set this property at design time:

1. Choose the ORADC1 Control (Oracle Data Control) on Form1.

2. In the Properties dialog box, locate the RecordSource property.

3. Position your cursor in the RecordSource text box and type in a valid SQL statement, such as Select From Emp.

The final step is to bind the data control to the Microsoft Data Bound Grid Control.

1. Choose the DBGrid1 Control on Form1.

2. In the Properties dialog box, locate the DataSource property.

3. Choose the ORADC1 Control (Oracle Data Control) from the pick list.

The DataSource property is not available at runtime; hence, the property must be set at design time. Run the form and navigate through the recordset by using the directional arrows and the scroll bars associated with the Microsoft Grid Control, as shown in Figure 5.8. You can also use the scroll buttons on the Oracle Data Control to move the row pointer through the recordset.

FIGURE 5.8

The Microsoft Data Bound Grid Control populated with data

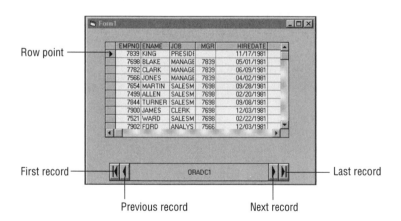

In the next section, you will look at the concepts for programmatic access to the Oracle Data Control. Save your work so you can use it in the next section. To save your project, follow these steps:

1. Choose File ➤ Save Project.

2. You will be prompted for a name for both the project and form files. Type **ORADCSample** for both the project and form filename. Click the Save button after entering the filename for the project and the form.

Using Controls in an Application

In the previous sections, you placed your controls on the default form and supplied values to the Connect, Database, and Recordsource properties. The Connect, Session, Database, and Recordset properties give you explicit control over the connection, navigation, and transaction control of the data. The following example will help demonstrate these concepts.

Programming with the Oracle Data Control

To demonstrate how to program with the Oracle Data Control, let's build a small application that binds a data control to the Microsoft Data Bound Grid Control. The following steps will get you started:

1. Start Visual Basic 6.

2. Choose File ➢ Open Project and browse to the project you created in the previous section, ORADCSample. Click the Open button.

The first concept you will look at is navigational control using the Move methods of the data control's Recordset property. The first step is to set the Connect and Database properties.

1. Double-click the Form object to get the Project Code window to appear. Choose the Activate event from the Form object's Events pick list. This is where you will programmatically set the Connect and DatabaseName properties for the Oracle Data Control. Type the following code to set each property:

```
ORADC1.connect = "scott/tiger"
ORADC1.databasename = "v8i"
```

2. Close the Project Code window.

Next, you will draw four command buttons. The command buttons will be used to navigate through the recordset of the Oracle Data Control. To draw the user command buttons for the application, follow these steps:

1. Click the command button located on the toolbox to give this control the current focus.

> **NOTE** You can use the Tool Tips feature to locate the correct control. Position your mouse over a control, and the name of the control appears.

2. Use your mouse pointer to draw a button on the form. To draw the button, hold down the left mouse button and pull the dotted lines into a rectangle.

3. Repeat the process in step 2 until you have four command buttons on the form.

4. Click each command button, dragging and positioning each on the bottom center of the Microsoft Grid Control.

5. Click the first command button, Command1, to give it the current focus.

6. Locate the Properties dialog box on the right side of the Visual Basic Designer. In the Properties dialog box, locate the (Name) property and change the button's name to **First Btn**. Change the value by positioning the cursor in the (Name) property text box. Use your mouse pointer to highlight the old value. Overwrite the default value by typing in the new name.

7. In the Visual Basic Designer, locate the Caption property and change the button's caption to **First Record**.

8. Click the second command button, Command2, to give it the current focus.

9. Locate the (Name) property and change the button's name to **Next Btn**.

10. Locate the Caption property and change the button's caption to **Next Record**.

11. Click the third command button, Command3, to give it the current focus.

12. Locate the (Name) property and change the button's name to **PrevBtn**.

13. Locate the Caption property and change the button's caption **Prev Record**.

14. Click the fourth command button, Command4, to give it the current focus.

15. Locate the (Name) property and change the button's name to **Last Btn**. Change the value by positioning the cursor in the (Name) property text box. Use your mouse pointer to highlight the old value. Overwrite the default value by typing in the new name.

16. Locate the Caption property and change the button's caption to **Last Record**.

Figure 5.9 shows your progress so far.

FIGURE 5.9

The form with four command buttons below the Microsoft Data Grid Bound Control

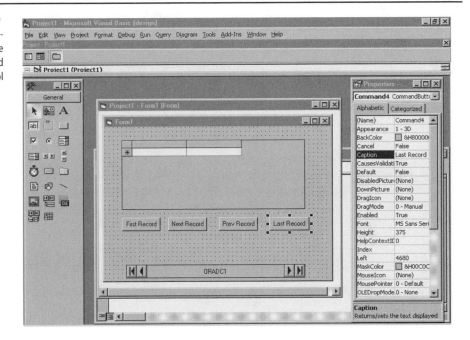

Next, you will provide event code for each button on the form. To do this, use the Move methods of the Oracle Data Control recordset.

1. Click the Form object to give it the current focus.

2. Right-click to display the pop-up menu for the form.

3. Choose View Code. The Project Code window appears.

4. Pull down the Objects pick list and select FirstBtn.

5. Pull down the Procedures pick list and select Click.

6. Position your cursor in the Project Code window and type the following code:

```
ORADC1.Recordset.Movefirst
```

Refer to Figure 5.10 to see the Project Code window.

FIGURE 5.10
The Project Code window
for the Click event of the
First Record button

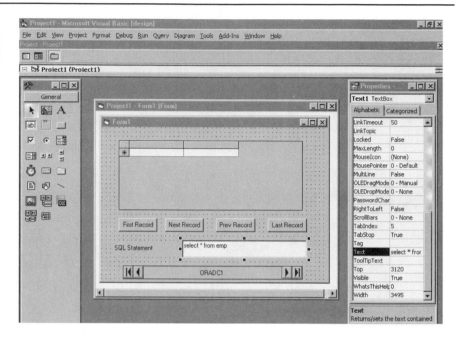

Let's do the same thing for the remaining three command buttons.

1. Pull down the Objects pick list and select NextBtn.

2. Pull down the Procedures pick list and select Click.

3. Position your cursor in the Project Code window and type the following code:

```
if ORADC1.Recordset.EOF = False then
 ORADC1.Recordset.Movenext
Else
   Msgbox "You are positioned at the last record "
End if
```

4. Pull down the Objects pick list and select PrevBtn.

5. Pull down the Procedures pick list and select Click.

6. Position your cursor in the Project Code window and type the following code:

```
if ORADC1.Recordset.BOF = False then
 ORADC1.Recordset.Moveprevious
Else if
    Msgbox "You are positioned at the first record "
End if
```

7. Pull down the Objects pick list and select LastBtn.

8. Pull down the Procedures pick list and select Click.

9. Position your cursor in the Project Code window and type the following code:

```
ORADC1.Recordset.Movelast
```

Now that you have the navigation code in place, you need to provide a place to enter the SQL statement for the data control's record source. To do so, follow these steps:

1. Close the Project Code window.

2. Choose the text box on the toolbox to give this control the current focus.

3. Use your mouse pointer to draw a text box on the form by holding down the left mouse button and pulling the dotted lines into a rectangle. Place this text box below the four navigation buttons.

4. Click TextBox1 to give it the current focus.

5. In the Properties dialog box of the Visual Basic Designer, locate the (Name) property and change the name to **SQL_fld**.

6. In the Properties dialog box of the Visual Basic Designer, locate the Text property and change the default text to **Select * From Emp**. Refer to Figure 5.11 to check your work.

FIGURE 5.11

Form1 with the SQL State-
ment text box

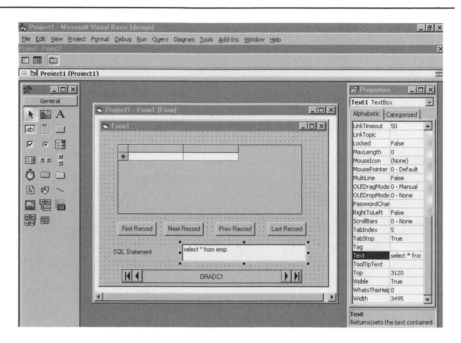

Next, place the text label next to the SQL_fld text box so that the user knows what information to provide when running the application.

1. On the toolbox, click Label to give this control the current focus.

2. Use your mouse pointer to draw a label on the form by holding down the left mouse button and pulling the dotted lines into a rectangle. Position the label to the left of the SQL_fld text box.

3. Click the Label1 object to give it the current focus.

4. In the Properties dialog box of the Visual Basic Designer, locate the (Name) property and change the label's name to **SQL_lab**.

5. In the Properties dialog box of the Visual Basic Designer, locate the Caption property and change the label's caption to **SQL Statement**.

Now, we need one more command button to allow users to refresh the Oracle Data Control's recordset if they choose to change the query in the SQL_fld text box. To create one, follow these steps:

1. On the toolbox, click the command button to give this control the current focus.

2. Use your mouse pointer to draw a button on the form by holding down the left mouse button and pulling the dotted lines into a rectangle. Position the button to the right of the SQL_fld text box.

3. Click the Command4 command button to give it the current focus.

4. In the Properties dialog box of the Visual Basic Designer, locate the (Name) property and change the button's name to **RefreshBtn**.

5. In the Properties dialog box of the Visual Basic Designer, locate the Caption property and change the button's caption to **Refresh**.

6. Pull down the Objects pick list and select RefreshBtn.

7. Pull down the Procedures pick list and select Click.

8. Position your cursor in the Project Code window and type the following code:

```
ORADC1.Recordsource = SQL_fld.text
ORADC1.Refresh
```

9. Pull down the Objects pick list and select Form.

10. Pull down the Procedures pick list and select Activate.

11. Position your cursor in the Project Code window after the line of code that sets the DatabaseName property and type the following code:

```
ORADC1.Recordsource = SQL_fld.text
ORADC1.Refresh
```

This code allows your application to query data for the default value of the RecordSource property when the form activates for the first time. Refer to Figure 5.12 to see the code that you have written so far for the Form object.

FIGURE 5.12
The Project Code window showing the event for the Form object

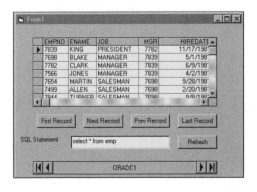

Run your application and test it by using the navigation buttons to move through the recordset. To get a feel for the application's functionality, change the SQL statement and refresh the controls. Figure 5.13 presents data from one record source, and Figure 5.14 shows data from another record source.

FIGURE 5.13

An application displaying data from the Emp table

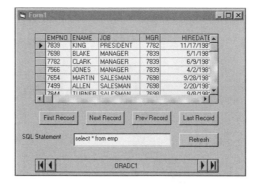

FIGURE 5.14

An application displaying data from the Dept table

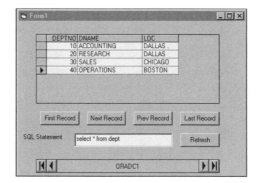

Creating a Master-Detail Relationship

To demonstrate more advanced use of the Oracle Data Control, let's build a small application that uses two tables, the Dept and Emp tables. You will create a master-detail relationship between the two tables using the Text Box Control and the Oracle Data Control.

1. Start Visual Basic and create a new project of type Standard EXE.

2. Choose Project ➢ Components and scroll down the list until you find the Oracle Data Control.

3. Choose the component by toggling on the check box, as seen in Figure 5.15.

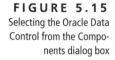

FIGURE 5.15

Selecting the Oracle Data Control from the Components dialog box

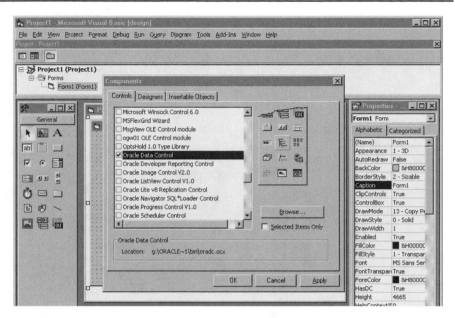

The Oracle Data Control and the Text Box Control now appear on the toolbox and are available for use by your application. Next, place the data control and the three Text Box Controls onto Form1.

1. Choose the text box located on the toolbox to give this control the current focus.

2. Use your mouse pointer to draw a text box on the form by holding down the left mouse button and pulling the dotted lines into a rectangle.

3. Repeat the process in step 2 twice more until you have three text boxes on the form.

4. Click each text box in turn, dragging and positioning the controls in a vertical row on the form's right side.

5. Click the Text1 text box to give it the current focus.

6. In the Visual Basic Designer Properties dialog box, locate the (Name) property and change the text box name to **deptno_fld**.

7. Click the Text2 text box to give this object the current focus.

8. In the Visual Basic Designer Properties dialog box, locate the (Name) property and change the text box name to **deptname_fld**.

9. Click the Text3 text box to give this object the current focus.

10. In the Visual Basic Designer Properties dialog box, locate the (Name) property and change the text box name to **loc_fld**. See Figure 5.16 to check your work so far.

FIGURE 5.16
The user interface with Text Box Controls

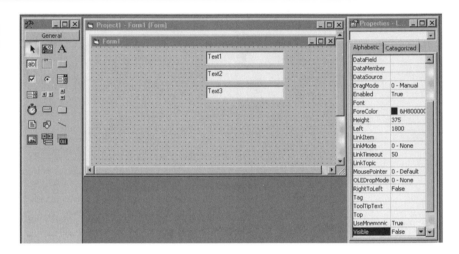

In order to give the user a description of the data presented in each Text Box Control, label each one appropriately.

1. On the toolbox, click Label to give this control the current focus.

2. Use your mouse pointer to draw a label on the form by holding down the left mouse button and pulling the dotted lines into a rectangle. Position the label to the left of the first text box.

3. Repeat the process in step 2 until there are three labels on the form.

4. Click the Label1 object to give it the current focus.

5. In the Visual Basic Properties Designer Properties dialog box, locate the (Name) property and change the label's name to **Deptno_lab**.

6. In the Visual Basic Properties Designer Properties dialog box, locate the Caption property and change the label's caption to **Department Number**.

7. Click Label2 to give it the current focus.

8. In the Visual Basic Properties Designer Properties dialog box, locate the (Name) property and change the label's name to **deptname_lab**.

9. In the Visual Basic Properties Designer Properties dialog box, locate the Caption property and change the label's caption to **Department Name**.

10. Click Label3 to give it the current focus.

11. In the Visual Basic Properties Designer Properties dialog box, locate the (Name) property and change the label's name to **loc_lab**.

12. In the Visual Basic Properties Designer Properties dialog box, locate the Caption property and change the label's caption to **Location**.

13. Choose the ORADC component from the toolbox and place it on the form below the text boxes, as shown in Figure 5.17.

FIGURE 5.17
Placing the Text Box
Controls

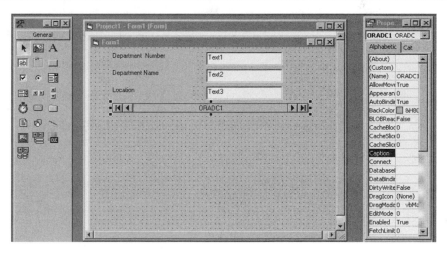

In order for the data control to make a connection to the database, you must fill in the following properties with the appropriate values.

Connect   This is the username and password to be supplied when trying to establish the connection. This property is read/write at design and runtime.

DatabaseName   This is the Net8 service name that has been defined in the TNSNAMES.ORA file using the Net8 Easy Configuration utility. I recommend using "v8i", the service name you defined in Chapter 1 when installing the Net8 client and the OO4O product.

You can either specify the values for these properties at design time by filling in the values in the Properties dialog box of the Visual Basic Designer, or at runtime by programmatically writing the code to supply them. Follow these steps to fill in the properties in at design time:

1. Choose the ORADC1 Control on Form1.

2. In the Properties dialog box, locate the Connect property.

3. Position your cursor in the Connect text box and type in a valid username and password separated by a "/" (forward slash).

4. In the Properties dialog box, locate the DatabaseName property.

5. Position your cursor in the DatabaseName text box and type in a valid Net8 service name that the control will use to connect to the database. See Figure 5.18 to check your work so far.

FIGURE 5.18

Supplying the Connect and DatabaseName properties at design time

Now that you have supplied the Oracle Data Control with the information to make a connection to the database, you must supply the SQL statement that will execute on the server side and return data back to the Oracle Data Control. The RecordSource property of the Oracle Data Control holds the query to be executed. Follow these steps to set this property at design time:

1. Choose the ORADC1 (Oracle Data Control) Control on Form1.

2. In the Properties dialog box, locate the (Name) property.

3. Position your cursor in the text box and type in the name **master**.

4. In the Properties dialog box, locate the RecordSource property.

5. Position your cursor in the text box and type in the Select From Dept SQL statement.

Next, bind the data control to each Text Box Control.

1. Click the Deptno_fld text box to give it the current focus.

2. In the Visual Basic Properties Designer Properties dialog box, locate the DataSource property and change the value to **master** by positioning the text cursor in the text box and typing the new value.

3. In the Visual Basic Properties Designer Properties dialog box, locate the Datafield property and change the value to **DEPTNO**, the actual column name in the Dept table. To change the value, position the cursor in the text box on the right side of the property and type the new value.

4. Click the Deptname_fld text box to give it the current focus.

5. In the Visual Basic Properties Designer Properties dialog box, locate the DataSource property and change the value to **master** by positioning the cursor in the text box and typing the new value.

6. In the Visual Basic Properties Designer Properties dialog box, locate the Datafield property and change the value to **DNAME**, the actual column name in the Dept table. To change the value, position the cursor in the text edit box on the right side of the property and type the new value.

7. Click the Loc_fld text box to give it the current focus.

8. In the Visual Basic Properties Designer Properties dialog box, locate the DataSource property and change the value to **master** by positioning the text cursor in the text box and typing the new value.

9. In the Visual Basic Properties Designer Properties dialog box, locate the Datafield property and change the value LOC to the actual column name in the Dept table. To change the value, position the text cursor in the text box on the right side of the property and type the new value.

The DataSource property is not available at runtime, so the property must be set at design time. Run the form and navigate through the master recordset by using the directional arrows and the scroll bars associated with the Oracle Data Control, as shown in Figure 5.19.

FIGURE 5.19
The Oracle Data Control
and the Text Box Controls
populated with the
master data

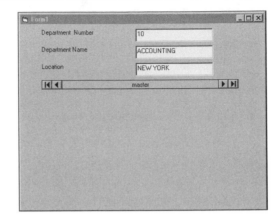

Next, you will finish the user interface by placing the controls for the detail records onto the form.

1. Choose Project ➢ Components and scroll down the list until you find the Microsoft Data Bound Grid Control.

2. Choose the Microsoft Data Bound Grid Control 5.0 (SP3) component by selecting the check box, as seen in Figure 5.20. Click OK.

FIGURE 5.20
Selecting the Microsoft Grid
Control from the Compo-
nents dialog box

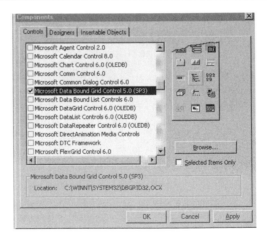

The Oracle Data Control and the Microsoft Grid Control now appear on the toolbox and are available for use by your application. Next, place the data control and the Microsoft Grid Control onto Form1.

1. Choose the Microsoft Data Bound Grid Control and place it on Form1.

2. Choose the ORADC (Oracle Data Control) component from the toolbox and place it on the form below the Microsoft Grid Control, as shown in Figure 5.21.

3. In the Properties dialog box, locate the (Name) property.

4. Position your cursor in the text box and type in the name **detail**.

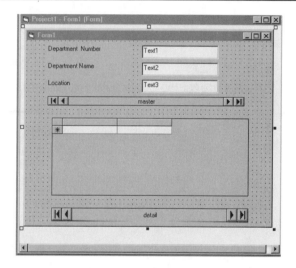

FIGURE 5.21
Placing the Microsoft Grid Control for the detail recordset

The final step is to bind the data control to the Microsoft Data Bound Grid Control.

1. Choose the DBGrid1 Control on Form1.

2. In the Properties dialog box, locate the DataSource property.

3. Choose Detail from the Properties dialog box.

Adding the Program Code

Now that the design of the interface is ready, you can start adding custom code into the event handlers for the controls so that something happens when the user interacts with the navigation buttons on the Oracle Data Control.

In this application, you are going to use early binding. You need to include the reference to the OO4O Type Library so that the types are resolved at compile time (early binding) rather than at runtime (late binding). Early binding will improve the performance of the application.

1. In the Visual Basic Designer, choose Project ➤ References.

2. Locate the Oracle InProc Server Type Library 3 in the Available References section. Enable the type library by checking the box on the left. Click the OK button.

3. Click the Form object to give it the current focus.

4. Click the right mouse button to display the pop-up menu for the form.

5. From the pop-up menu, choose View Code. The Project Code window appears, as seen in Figure 5.22.

6. Pull down the Objects list and select (General).

7. Pull down the Procedures list and select (Declarations).

FIGURE 5.22

The Project Code window

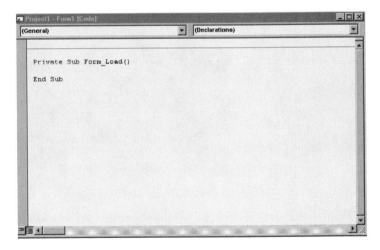

8. Position your text cursor in the Project Code window and type the following code:

```
Dim OraDatabase as OraDatabase
Dim ConnectData as String
Dim DatabaseName as String
Dim MasterQuery as String
Dim DetailQuery as String
```

9. Pull down the Objects list and select Form.

10. Pull down the Procedures list and select Load.

11. Position the text cursor in the Form_Load procedure and type the following lines of code:

```
MasterQuery = "select * from dept"
DetailQuery = "select * from emp where deptno = :deptno"

Detail.Connect = ConnectData
Detail.DatabaseName = DatabaseName
Detail.refresh

Set OraDatabase = detail.Database
OraDatabase.Parameters.Add "deptno",0,1

Detail.RecordSource = DetailQuery
Detail.Refresh

Master.Connect = ConnectData
Master.DatabaseName = DatabaseName
Master.RecordSource = MasterQuery
Master.refresh
```

The last piece of custom code you need to add is for the Reposition event for the master recordset. When the user chooses a new department number, you need to re-query the database for the detail records and update the underlying recordset for the detail data so that your master and detail recordsets are synchronized. To add the Reposition event, follow these steps:

1. Click the Form object to give it the current focus.

2. Right-click to display the pop-up menu for the form.

3. From the pop-up menu, choose View Code. The Project Code window appears, as seen in Figure 5.23.

4. Pull down the Objects list and select Master.

5. Pull down the Procedures list and select Reposition.

FIGURE 5.23

The Project Code window

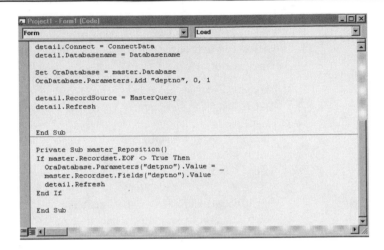

```
detail.Connect = ConnectData
detail.Databasename = Databasename

Set OraDatabase = master.Database
OraDatabase.Parameters.Add "deptno", 0, 1

detail.RecordSource = MasterQuery
detail.Refresh


End Sub

Private Sub master_Reposition()
If master.Recordset.EOF <> True Then
   OraDatabase.Parameters("deptno").Value = _
   master.Recordset.Fields("deptno").Value
   detail.Refresh
End If

End Sub
```

6. Position your text cursor in the Project Code window and type the following:

```
If Master.Recordset.EOF <> True then
   OraDatabase.Parameters("detpno").Value = _
   Master.Recordset.Fields("deptno").value
   Detail.refresh
End if
```

To save your project, follow these steps:

1. Choose File ➤ Save Project.

2. You will be prompted for a name for both the project and form files. Type **ORADCMastDet** for both the project and form filename.

Run the application and use the data control navigation buttons to move through the master and detail recordsets. As you move through the master recordset, the Reposition event is fired and new data is queried for the detail or employee records. Figure 5.24 displays the output generated by this application.

FIGURE 5.24

The department and employee master and detail data

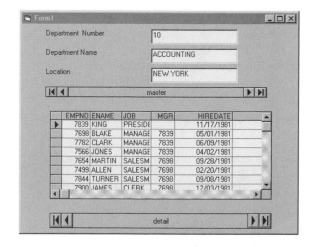

LOB Access with the Oracle Data Control

In previous versions of Oracle Objects for OLE, the Oracle Data Control permitted read-only access for Long Raw data. In version 8i, this limitation has been removed for BLOB data. The Oracle Data Control allows read and write access to BLOB columns. If you need both read and write access, migrate your Long Raw columns to BLOBs. Even in this version, the Oracle Data Control only allows read access to Long Raw and BFILE columns. For backward compatibility, the Oracle Data Control has a new property called *BLOBReadOnly*. When this property is set to True, Write operations are not permitted. If your application starts a Write operation, it is ignored, and no error is generated. OO4O takes advantage of Oracle8i features, and accessing BLOB data is faster than accessing the same data in a Long Raw column. For information on advanced techniques using OO4O and LOB data (Large Objects), see Chapter 9.

NOTE   The Oracle Data Control does not support read or write access for CLOB data.

One easy way to use the Oracle Data Control with BLOBs is to bind the Microsoft OLE Control to the Oracle Data Control so that the state of any OLE object is saved in a BLOB column. Let's create a simple example to show how this is done. The Microsoft OLE Control allows you to edit and update the object. The new state of the object is written to the database when the row position is changed. The demonstration example has two buttons, one that allows you to insert a new image and one that updates the image for the current record. The DDL (Data Definition Language) to create the table follows. Use SQL*Plus to create the table in the Scott schema.

```
CREATE TABLE images (id number, image BLOB)
```

Once the Images table is created, follow these steps to see how this technique works:

1. Start Visual Basic 6 and create a new project of type Standard EXE.

2. Choose Project ➤ Components and scroll down the list until you find the Oracle Data Control.

3. Choose the component by toggling on the check box, as seen in Figure 5.25. Click OK.

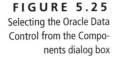

FIGURE 5.25

Selecting the Oracle Data Control from the Components dialog box

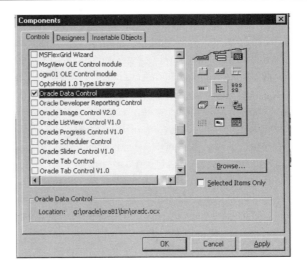

4. Choose the Microsoft OLE Control from the toolbox and place it on Form1.

5. Choose the ORADC (Oracle Data Control) component from the toolbox and place it on the form below the Microsoft OLE Control, as shown in Figure 5.26. The Oracle Data Control has a default object name of ORADC1. The filename is Oradc.ocx.

FIGURE 5.26
Placing the Microsoft OLE Control

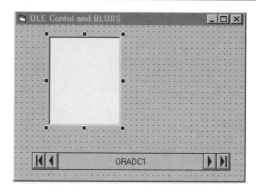

In order for the data control to make a connection to the database, fill in the following properties with appropriate values:

Connect   This is the username and password to be supplied when establishing the connection. This property is read/write at design and runtime.

DatabaseName   This is the Net8 service name that has been defined in the TNSNAMES.ORA file using the Net8 Easy Configuration utility.

You can specify the values for these properties at design time by filling in the values in the Properties dialog box of the Visual Basic Designer. To do so, follow these steps:

1. Choose the ORADC control on Form1.

2. In the Properties dialog box locate the Connect property.

3. Position your cursor in the Connect text box and type in a valid username and password separated by a "/" (forward slash). An example is scott/tiger.

4. In the Properties dialog box, locate the DatabaseName property.

5. Position your cursor in the DatabaseName text box and type in a valid Net8 service name that the control will use to connect to the database. We recommend using "**v8i**", the service name you created in Chapter 1 when installing the Net8 client and OO4O product.

Now that you have supplied the information for the data control to make a connection to the database, supply the SQL statement that will execute on the server side and return data to the Oracle Data Control. The RecordSource property of the

Oracle Data Control holds the query to be executed. Follow these steps to set this property at design time:

1. Choose the ORADC1 control on Form1.

2. In the Properties dialog box, locate the RecordSource property.

3. Position your cursor in the RecordSource text box and type in a valid SQL statement, such as **Select Image From Images**.

The final step is to bind the data control to the data aware control (Microsoft OLE Control). To do so, follow these steps.

1. Choose the OLE1 Control on Form1.

2. In the Properties dialog box, locate the DataSource property.

3. Choose the ORADC1 control (Oracle Data Control) from the DataSource pick list.

4. In the Properties dialog box, locate the Data Field property.

5. Choose the image from the Data Field pick list.

Next, draw the two command buttons that will allow you to choose a new OLE object to either insert or update the current record in the Oracle Data Control recordset.

1. Click the command button located on the toolbox to give this control the current focus.

TIP   You can use the Tool Tips feature to locate the correct control. Position your mouse over a control, and the name of the control appears.

---

2. Use your mouse pointer to draw a button on the form. To draw the button, hold down the left mouse button and pull the dotted lines into a rectangle.

3. Repeat the process in step 2 until you have two command buttons on the form.

4. Click each command button, dragging and positioning each on the right side of the Microsoft OLE Control.

5. Click the first command button, Command1, to give it the current focus.

6. In the Properties dialog box of the Visual Basic Designer, locate the (Name) property and change the button's name to **InsertBtn**. Change the value by positioning the cursor in the (Name) text box. Use the mouse pointer to highlight the old value. Overwrite the default value by typing the new name.

7. In the Properties dialog box of the Visual Basic Properties Designer, locate the Caption property and change the button's caption to **Insert Image**.

8. Click the second command button, Command2, to give it the current focus.

9. Locate the (Name) property and change the button's name to **UpdateBtn**.

10. Locate the Caption property and change the button's caption to **Update Image**. See Figure 5.27 to check your work so far.

FIGURE 5.27
Placing the Insert Image and Update Image buttons on the form

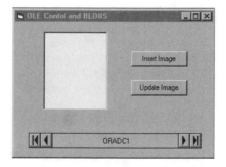

Next, provide the event code for each button on the form. To do so, you will use the methods of the Oracle Data Control Recordset and Database properties.

1. Click the Form object to give it the current focus.

2. Right-click to display the pop-up menu for the form.

3. Choose View Code. The Project Code window appears.

4. Pull down the Objects pick list and select Form.

5. Pull down the Procedures pick list and select Declarations.

6. Position your cursor in the Project Code window and type the following code:

```
Dim Rowcount as Integer
```

7. Pull down the Objects pick list and select Form.

8. Pull down the Procedures pick list and select Activate

9. Position your cursor in the Project Code window and type the following code:

```
ORADC1.recordset.movefirst
Rowcount = 0
```

10. Pull down the Objects pick list and select InsertBtn.

11. Pull down the Procedures pick list and select Click.

12. Position your cursor in the Project Code window and type the following code:

```
rowcount = ORADC1.Recordset.recordcount + 1
SQLString = "insert into images values " & -
"(" & rowcount & ",empty_blob())"
ORADC1.Database.ExecuteSQL SQLString
ORADC1.Recordset.Refresh
ORADC1.Recordset.moveto (rowcount)
OLE1.InsertObjDlg
ORADC1.Recordset.UpdateRecord
```

Refer to Figure 5.28 for a look at the Project Code window.

FIGURE 5.28

The Project Code window for the Click event of the Insert Image button

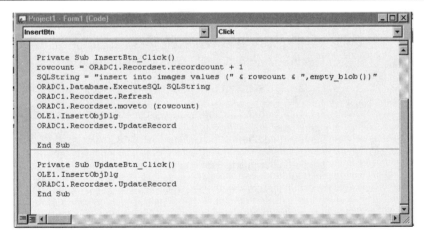

Now, provide the code for the Update Image button.

1. Pull down the Objects pick list and select UpdateBtn.

2. Pull down the Procedures pick list and select Click.

3. Position your cursor in the Project Code window and type the following code:

```
OLE1.InsertObjDlg
ORADC1.Recordset.UpdateRecord
```

Run your application and test it by using the Insert and Update buttons to add an image to the table. When you click the Insert Image button, you will be presented with the Insert Object dialog box, shown in Figure 5.29.

FIGURE 5.29
The Insert Object dialog box

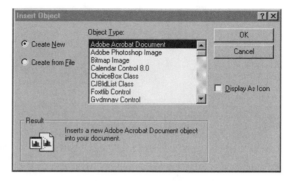

Choose the type of object you wish to insert, such as a bitmap image. Then, choose the option to create the image from file and click the Browse button to find the bitmap image you wish to insert. The Browse dialog box will appear and allow you to select the file. Figure 5.30 shows the Browse dialog box.

FIGURE 5.30
The Browse dialog box

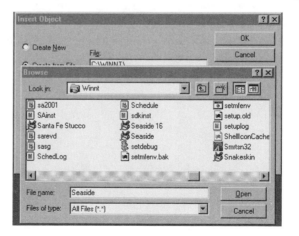

Once you choose the file to insert, click the OK button on the Browse and the Insert Object dialog boxes. The image will appear on the form in the Microsoft OLE control, as shown in Figure 5.31.

FIGURE 5.31
The seaside image displaced in the Microsoft OLE control

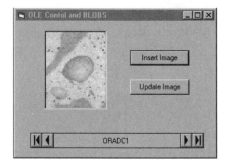

You can experiment with this application and insert several images into the Images table. Then you can scroll through the pictures using the navigation buttons of the Oracle Data Control on the form.

Summary

The Oracle Data Control enables you to build applications that query an Oracle database and present information very rapidly without writing a lot of code. The Oracle Data Control is flexible and exposes the Session, Database, and Recordset properties and methods for advanced programmatic access. It is compatible with the Microsoft Data Control and works with a variety of data bound controls that are available from various vendors.

chapter 6

Error Handling

- Handling errors with the Visual Basic Err object

- Using error-handling techniques

- Troubleshooting common errors

- Enabling SQL Net Tracing

- Additional troubleshooting tips

In this chapter, you will take look at how to handle errors in your application, learn about the various Visual Basic approaches to trapping errors, and learn how to handle errors specific to OO4O. Errors in Visual Basic (VB) and Oracle Objects for OLE (OO4O) can occur during various stages of execution and are grouped into the following categories:

- Visual Basic errors
- OLE Automation errors
- Find Method Parser errors
- Find Method Run-time errors
- Oracle Object Instance errors
- Oracle LOB errors
- Oracle Advanced Queuing errors
- Oracle Collection errors
- Oracle Number errors
- Oracle errors
- Oracle Data Control errors

The Visual Basic Err Object

The *Visual Basic Err object* provides you with the interface that enables your application to trap and make decisions about errors as they are encountered. The Err object contains three properties:

Description   This is the text description of the error.

Number   This is the HRESULT returned by the scripting API.

Source   This is a string that identifies the object that raised the error.

Listing 6.1 demonstrates how the Err object can be implemented in your application. Figure 6.1 demonstrates how your application may present a particular error to a user. The type of error handling shown in Listing 6.1 is referred to as *centralized error handling* because the error handling code is embedded directly into the body of the subroutine. In the top of the subroutine, the On Error clause will cause the execution to branch to the HandletheError line label, which will process and check for specific errors.

Listing 6.1

```
 1  Dim OraSession As OraSession
 2  Dim OraDatabase As OraDatabase
 3  On Error GoTo HandletheError
 4  Set OraSession = _
    CreateObject("OracleInProcServer.XOraSession")
 5  Set OraDatabase = _
    OraSession.OpenDatabase( _
    "v8i", "scott/tiger", 0&)
 6  exit sub
 7  HandletheError:
 8  If OraSession.LastServerErr = 0 Then
 9    If Err = 0 Then
10     MsgBox ("Connected as scott/tiger")
11    Elseif Err = 440 then
12     MsgBox ("OLE Automation Error " + ERROR$)
13    Else
14     MsgBox ("VB-" & Err & " " & Error)
15    End If
16 Else
17     MsgBox (OraSession.LastServerErrText)
18 End If
```

Analysis

- Line 1–2 are the Dim statements for the objects being used to connect to the database.

- Line 3 is an On Error command that directs processing to another section of code whenever an error occurs.

- Line 4 creates the OraSession object.

- Line 5 creates an OraDatabase object and establishes the connection to the database.

- Line 6 is the Exit Sub call.

- Linc 7 is the label for the error-handling routine.

- Line 8 is the If statement to see whether any Oracle error has occurred.

- Line 9 is the inner If statement to see if any Visual Basic error has occurred.

- Line 10 displays a message that the application has successfully connected to the database.

- Line 11 is the Else If statement that checks to see if an OLE Automation error has occurred.

- Line 12 displays a message for the OLE Automation error.

- Line 13 is the Else clause for the inner If statement.

- Line 14 displays a message for the specific Visual Basic error.

- Line 15 is the End If clause for the inner If statement.

- Line 16 is the Else clause for the outer If statement.

- Line 17 displays the Oracle error message that has occurred.

- Line 18 is the End If clause for the outer If statement.

FIGURE 6.1
The Error dialog box

When a run-time error has occurred, the properties of the Err object are set. These properties provide information that identifies the error that has occurred. The Err object's properties are reset after a call in your error-handing routine to any of the following:

Exit Sub   Exits the currently executing subroutine.

Exit Function   Exits the currently executing function.

Resume   Returns control to the statement that caused the error.

Resume Next   Returns control to the statement following the one that caused the error.

The properties of the Err object can also be reset by explicitly making a call to the Clear method. The Err object is automatically created for you and has global scope. Your application does not have to create this object. Visual Basic provides three ways to branch off to various places in your code when an error occurs:

On Error GoTo (Line)   Causes execution to jump to the error-handling code. Line is a label that has the error-handling code.

On Error Resume Next   Causes execution to jump to the next statement after the line that caused the error.

On Error GoTo 0   A special On Error statement that disables the error handler.

Once you have branched into your error handler, there are three different approaches to resume execution: Resume, Resume Next, and Resume (line). Figure 6.2 gives you an idea of the flow of execution when using the Resume and Resume Next statements.

FIGURE 6.2
The logic flow for the Resume and the Resume Next statements

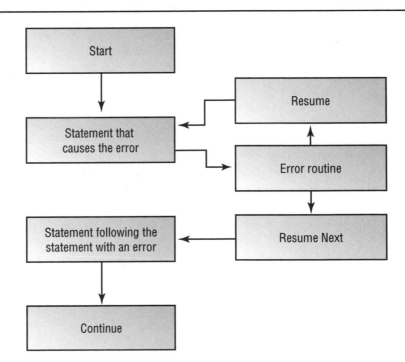

Resume   Gives control to the statement that caused the error.

Resume Next   Returns control to the statement following the one that caused the error.

Resume (Line)   Causes execution to jump to the error-handling code. Line is a label that contains the error-handling code.

The Error-Handling Hierarchy

An *active error handler* is one that is executed or activated (enabled) by some On Error statement. When an error occurs in a procedure that does not have an error handler, Visual Basic searches the current procedure call stack for an enabled error-handling routine. (Remember that an *enabled error handler* is one that has been called by some On Error statement.) The call stack consists of a set of subroutines or procedure calls that lead to the current one that is executing (see Figure 6.3).

FIGURE 6.3
The Visual Basic call stack

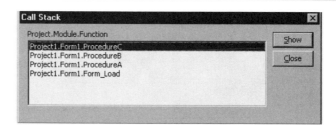

If an error occurs in Procedure C and it does not have an enabled error handler, Visual Basic searches back in the call stack to find one. If one is found, that error handler becomes active, or executing. If one is not found, Visual Basic presents the default Error message dialog box and halts execution, as shown in Figure 6.4.

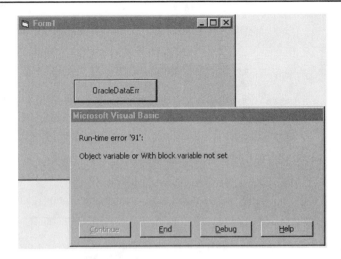

Approaches to Handling Errors

There are three steps involved with error handling:

1. Enable an error handler by telling your application where to jump when the error occurs.

2. Write the error-handling code that responds to the errors you expect in your application.

3. Exit the error handler.

Now let's take a look at four approaches for handling errors in your Visual Basic application and write the code demonstrating each technique. The code you write will use the following methods to branch and resume execution:

- No error handling

- Inline error handling

- Centralized error handling

- Raising an error in your application

No Error Handling

The easiest error-handling approach is to not write any code to handle errors and to let the errors propagate back to the Visual Basic runtime, but this is not practical or useful because you may want to take specific action when errors occur. If you encounter errors, it is desirable to handle them and make decisions about continued execution. If you do not handle the errors with code, you are not allowed these decisions, and the execution of your application halts. An example of not handling errors is shown in Listing 6.2.

NOTE   Examples in this chapter use the Scott schema owned by Oracle Corporation. The schema is bundled with the Oracle8i client software and the OO4O product.

Listing 6.2

```
1  Dim OraSession As OraSession
2  Dim OraDatabase As OraDatabase
3  Dim OraDynaset As OraDynaset
4  Set OraSession = _
     CreateObject("OracleInProcServer.XOraSession")
5  Set OraDatabase = _
     OraSession.OpenDatabase( _
     "v8i", "scott/tiger", 0&)
```

Analysis

- Lines 1–3 are Dim statements for the objects used to connect to the database and to create the dynaset.

- Line 4 creates the OraSession object.

- Line 5 creates an OraDatabase object and establishes the connection to the database.

Inline Error Handling

Inline error handling is when you check for an error after each line instead of using the On Error statement to determine where you will jump to next. Inline error handling is used a lot in the C language because errors are not raised. Instead, they are recorded for you to check later, or each time you return from a call. Listing 6.3 uses this approach in Visual Basic.

Listing 6.3

```
 1  Global OraSession As OraSession
 2  Function CheckLastServerError as long
 3    CheckLastServerError = OraSession.LastServerErr
 4  End Function

 5  Private Sub Form_Load()
 6   Dim OraDatabase As OraDatabase
 7   Dim OraDynaset As OraDynaset
 8   Set OraSession = _
     CreateObject("OracleInProcServer.XOraSession")
 9   Set OraDatabase = _
     OraSession.OpenDatabase( _
     "v8i", "scott/tiger", 0&)
10   TheError = CheckLastServerError
11   If TheError <> 0 then
12     Msgbox "An Error has occurred"
13   end if
14  End sub
```

Analysis

- Line 1 is the statement that declares the OraSession object as global. This line is located in the General Declarations section.

- Line 2 is the Function declaration for the CheckLastServerError function.

- Line 3 returns the value of the OraSession.LastServerErr property.

- Line 4 ends the CheckLastServerError function.

- Line 5 starts the Form_load subroutine.

- Line 6 declares the OraDatabase object.

- Line 7 declares the OraDynaset object.

- Line 8 creates the OraSession object.

- Line 9 creates an OraDatabase object and establishes the connection to the database.

- Line 10 calls the CheckLastServerError function.

- Line 11 is the If statement to check the return value from the CheckLast-ServerError function.

- Line 12 displays a message if an error occurred.

- Line 13 is the End If clause for the If statement.

Centralized Error Handling

Centralized error handling is when you add the error-handling code directly into the body of the subroutine procedure, where the error may occur. This is the easiest method, but may result in having redundant pieces of code in your application. Listing 6.4 demonstrates the centralized error-handling approach.

Listing 6.4

```
1  Dim OraSession As OraSession
2  Dim OraDatabase As OraDatabase
3  Dim OraDynaset As OraDynaset
4  On Error GoTo HandletheError
5  Set OraSession = _
     CreateObject("OracleInProcServer.XOraSession")
6  Set OraDatabase = _
     OraSession.OpenDatabase( _
     "v8i", "scott/tiger", 0&)
7  HandletheError:
8  If OraSession.LastServerErr = 0 Then
9    If Err = 0 Then
10     MsgBox ("Connected as scott/tiger")
11   Elseif Err = 440 then
12     MsgBox ("OLE Automation Error " + ERROR$)
13   Else
14     MsgBox ("VB-" & Err & " " & Error)
15   End If
16 Else
17     MsgBox (OraSession.LastServerErrText)
18 End If
```

Analysis

- Lines 1–3 are Dim statements for the objects used to connect to the database and to create the dynaset object.

- Line 4 is an On Error command that directs processing to another section of code whenever an error occurs.

- Line 5 creates the OraSession object.

- Line 6 creates an OraDatabase object and establishes the connection to the database.

- Line 7 is the label for the error-handling routine.

- Line 8 is the If statement to see whether any Oracle error has occurred.

- Line 9 is the inner If statement to see if any Visual Basic error has occurred.

- Line 10 displays a message if no errors have occurred. This line is actually checking the HRESULT returned.

- Line 11 is the Else If clause for the inner If statement.

- Line 12 displays a message for the OLE Automation error.

- Line 13 is the Else clause for the inner If statement.

- Line 14 displays the Visual Basic error message that has occurred.

- Line 15 is the End If clause for the inner If statement.

- Line 16 is the Else clause for the outer If statement.

- Line 17 displays the Oracle error message.

- Line 18 is the End If clause for the outer If statement.

Raising Errors in Your Application

You can use the Raise method to simulate errors in your application for testing purposes, or if you want to treat a specific error condition the same as other sorts of errors, such as Visual Basic errors. You could also handle all Oracle errors as OLE Automation errors, as demonstrated in Listing 6.5.

Listing 6.5

```
1  Dim OraDatabase As OraDatabase
2  Dim OraDynaset As OraDynaset
3  Set OraSession = _
   CreateObject("OracleInProcServer.XOraSession")
4  Set OraDatabase = _
   OraSession.OpenDatabase( _
   "v8i", "scott/tiger", 0&)
5  On Error GoTo HandleTheError
6  If OraSession.LastServerErr <> 0 Then
7    Err.Raise number=440
8  End if
9  HandleTheError:
10  if Err = 440 then
11    MsgBox ("OLE Automation Error " + ERROR$)
12 Else
13    MsgBox ("VB-" & Err & " " & Error)
14 End If
```

Analysis

- Line 1 is the Dim statement for the objects being used to connect to the database.

- Line 2 is the Dim statement for the objects being used to create the dynaset.

- Line 3 creates the OraSession object.

- Line 4 creates an OraDatabase object and establishes the connection to the database.

- Line 5 is an On Error command that directs processing to another section of code whenever an error occurs.

- Line 6 is the If statement to check the LastServerErr property.

- Line 7 raises an Error 440 if the LastServerErr is not zero.

- Line 8 is the End If clause for the If statement.

- Line 9 is the label for the error-handling routine.

- Line 10 is the If statement to see whether any OLE error has occurred.

- Line 11 displays the OLE error message.

- Line 12 is the Else clause for the If statement.

- Line 13 displays the VB error message.

- Line 14 is the End If clause for the If statement.

Common Errors

The following sections describe the various categories and each error that you may encounter. The tables provide you with three important pieces of information:

- The error number or value

- The error description

- Error troubleshooting tips

OLE Automation Errors

OLE Automation errors result from calling an OO4O object method that does not successfully complete. When this type of error occurs, check the LastServerError property to determine whether an Oracle error has been flagged by the database. Refer to the "Oracle Errors" section later in this chapter for more detailed information on retrieving information on the most recent Oracle error that may have occurred. An OLE Automation error looks like the following:

```
OLE Automation Error (ERR=440, ERROR$=OLE Automation Error)
```

You must scan the ERROR$ string in order to find the specific OLE error number. The error appears in the form of OIP-NNNN, where *N* is one of the following error numbers listed in the tables throughout this chapter. Table 6.1 lists some of the common OLE Automation errors.

TABLE 6.1: Troubleshooting OLE Automation Errors

Error Number	Description of Error	Troubleshooting Hints
4096	Invalid connection.	Make sure the OraDatabase object is valid.
4098	An attempt was made to access a value in an empty dynaset.	Check both EOF and BOF properties, as these both return a True value if the dynaset is empty.
4099	An invalid field name was specified.	Check the OraFields Collection object to verify whether the field exists.
4101	A BeginTrans was specified while a transaction is already in progress.	Either call the CommitTrans or the Rollback method before starting another transaction stream.
4104	A CommitTrans was specified without first executing BeginTrans.	There is no valid transaction to commit. You must first start the transaction by calling BeginTrans.
4105	A rollback was specified without first executing BeginTrans.	There is no valid transaction to roll back. You must first start the transaction by calling BeginTrans.
4106	System attempted to destroy a non-existent dynaset.	The Dynaset object has already been destroyed. This will occur when the object goes out of scope or the reference count reaches zero.
4108	An attempt was made to reference an invalid row.	Check to make sure that EOF and BOF are not True when navigating through a dynaset. Use these properties to determine when you have reached the end of the data.
4109	An error occurred while trying to create a temporary file for data caching.	Check to make sure that the operating system limit on the number of temporary files has not been exceeded. Periodically purge the Temp directory to prevent this error.
4110	An attempt was made to create a named session that already exists using CreateSession or CreateNamedSession.	Check the OraSessions Collection object to see whether the session already exists. Create the new session with a different name if one already exists.
4111	The system attempted to destroy a non-existent session.	The Session object has already been destroyed. This will occur when the object goes out of scope or the reference count reaches zero.

TABLE 6.1: Troubleshooting OLE Automation Errors *(continued)*

Error Number	Description of Error	Troubleshooting Hints
4112	An attempt was made to reference a named object of a collection that does not exist.	Check the spelling of the named object in the collection.
4113	Duplicate connection name.	Change the connection name so that it is unique.
4114	The system attempted to destroy a non-existent connection.	The Connection object has already been destroyed. This will occur when the object goes out of scope or the reference count reaches zero.
4115	An invalid field index was specified.	Check the Fields Collection object to make sure you are referencing a valid field index.
4116	The system attempted to move to a row in an invalid dynaset.	The dynaset object has already been destroyed. This will occur when the object goes out of scope or the reference count reaches zero.
4117	An attempt was made to change the data of a read-only dynaset.	Check the updateable property for the dynaset before attempting to change any data.
4118	An attempt was made to change a field's value without first executing the Edit method.	Call the Edit method before attempting to update the dynaset.
4119	An attempt was made to edit data in the local cache, but the data on the Oracle server has been changed.	After trapping this error, call the Refresh method to sync the local cache with the Oracle server.
4120	Out of memory for data binding buffers.	Check to make sure you are cleaning up objects, such as removing parameters from the collection when they are no longer needed.
4121	An invalid bookmark was specified.	If you have called the Refresh method, all bookmarks are invalid and the row pointer is set to the first row in the dynaset.
4122	Bind variable not enabled.	The OraParameter Add method has not been called for a bind variable that is being used in an SQL statement.

TABLE 6.1: Troubleshooting OLE Automation Errors *(continued)*

Error Number	Description of Error	Troubleshooting Hints
4123	An attempt was made to create a named parameter using Add, but that name already exists.	Navigate the OraParameters collection and remove it from the collection or simply re-use the parameter.
4124	An invalid offset or length parameter was passed to GetChunk, or an internal error has occurred using AppendChunk.	If you are using AppendChunk, report the error to your local technical support group. When using GetChunk, check the offset or length parameter, and make sure it is valid for the file you are working with. You may be trying to read past the end of a binary file.
4125	An attempt was made to use GetChunk or Append Chunk on a field that was not of the type Long or Long Raw.	These methods are specific to fetching Long or Long Raw data. Check your column type by issuing a Describe on the table in SQL*Plus, or by accessing the Type property of the OraField object.
4126	An invalid argument value was entered.	Check to make sure a valid argument was entered for the method being called.
4127	A `Select For Update` statement was specified without first executing the BeginTrans method.	The `Select For Update` SQL statement requires a transaction to be in progress. Call the BeginTrans method before issuing a `Select For Update` statement.
4128	A `Select For Update` statement was specified but the query is non-updateable.	Refer to the rules of updatability in your SQL reference guide.
4129	A commit or rollback was executed while a Select For Update command is in progress.	Before the transaction can be committed or rolled back, all objects that reference the dynaset must be set to "Nothing".
4130	An invalid cache parameter was specified.	The maximum value for cache blocks is 127.
4131	An attempt was made to reference a field that requires a ROWID (Long or Long Raw), but the ROWID was not available.	Check to make sure that the dynaset is updateable.
4132	Out of memory.	Make sure you are recovering allocated memory when objects are no longer being used by setting them to "Nothing" (such as, `OraDynaset = Nothing`).

TABLE 6.1: Troubleshooting OLE Automation Errors *(continued)*

Error Number	Description of Error	Troubleshooting Hints
4135	The element size specified in AddTable exceeds the maximum allowed size for that variable type.	The following ranges are valid: Varchar and string can be 1–1999. Char and Charz can be 1–255.
4136	The dimension specified in AddTable is invalid.	The array parameters used as bind variables in an SQL statement must have the same size. Change the dimensions to be of equal size.
4138	Dimensions of the array parameters used in Insert, Update, or Delete statements are not equal.	The array parameters used as bind variables in an SQL statement must have the same size. Change the dimensions to be of equal size.
4139	Error processing arrays.	For additional details, refer to the 0040Err.log file generated by the InProc Server.
4147	The database pool for this session already exists.	Only one pool can be created per session.
4148	Unable to obtain a free Database object from the pool.	Increase the wait time until a Database object can be obtained from the pool.

Trapping an OLE Automation Error

Listing 6.6 demonstrates an OLE Automation error, OIP-4112 or Named Object Does Not Exist. You can use a very simple error handler to trap and determine the specific error encountered. The error is generated because the Sal column referenced in the SQL statement has not been added to the OraParameter collections by calling the Add method. Since the Add method for enabling the bind variable is never called, an OLE Automation error occurs. Figure 6.5 shows the output from the error handler.

Listing 6.6

```
1   Dim OraSession As OraSession
2   Dim OraDatabase As OraDatabase
3   Dim OraDynaset As OraDynaset
4   On Error GoTo HandletheError
5   Set OraSession = _
    CreateObject("OracleInProcServer.XOraSession")
```

```
6   Set OraDatabase = _
    OraSession.OpenDatabase( _
    "v8i", "scott/tiger", 0&)
7   OraDatabase.Parameters( _
    "sal").serverType = ORATYPE_NUMBER
8   Set OraDynaset = _
    OraDatabase.CreateDynaset( _
    "select * from emp where :sal > 50", 0&)
9   MsgBox "Employee " & _
    OraDynaset.Fields("empno").value _
    & ", #" _
    & OraDynaset.Fields("ename").value
10  HandletheError:
11  If Err = 440 Then
12   If OraDatabase.LastServerErr = 0 then
13    MsgBox ("OLE Automation Error " & ERROR$)
14   Else
15    MsgBox (OraDatabase.LastServerErrText)
16   End if
17  End If
```

Analysis

- Lines 1–3 are Dim statements for the objects being used to connect to the database and to create the dynaset.

- Line 4 is an On Error command, which directs processing to another section of code whenever an error occurs.

- Line 5 creates the OraSession object.

- Line 6 creates an OraDatabase object and establishes the connection to the database.

- Line 7 sets the server type for the Sal parameter to Number.

- Line 8 creates an OraDynaset object based on the employee in the Emp table whose salary is greater than 50.

- Line 9 displays a message box with the employee number and name of the first person matching the find criteria.

- Line 10 is the label for the error-handling routine.

- Line 11 is the If statement to see whether any OLE Automation error has occurred.

- Line 12 is the If statement to see whether any Oracle error has occurred.

- Line 13 displays the actual error message for an OLE Automation error and displays the contents of ERROR$.

- Line 14 is the Else clause for the inner If statement.

- Line 15 displays the actual error message for an Oracle error that has occurred.

- Line 16 is the End If clause for the inner If statement.

- Line 17 is the End If clause for the outer If statement.

FIGURE 6.5

The dialog box showing an OLE Automation error

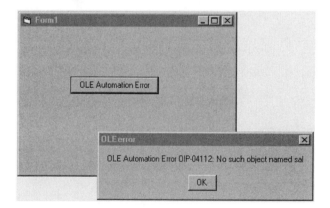

Find Method Parser Errors

When calling the Find method, *Parser errors* occur when the OO4O parser cannot correctly parse out the Where portion or Find clause of the method call. The errors described in Table 6.2 will help you determine what part of the expression has caused the error.

T A B L E 6 . 2 : Troubleshooting Find Method Parser Errors

Error Number	Description of Error	Troubleshooting Hints
4496	Stack overflow	Report this error to your local support center.
4497	Syntax error	Check the syntax of the Find clause and verify that it is valid SQL.
4498	Misplaced parenthesis	Check the location of parenthesis in the Find clause.
4499	Misplaced quotation marks	Check the location of the quotation marks in the Find clause.
4500	Missing closing parenthesis	Check for unbalanced parenthesis in the Find clause.
4501	Open parentheses expected	Check for unbalanced or non-existent parenthesis in the Find clause.
4502	Unknown parser error condition	Report this error to your local technical support group.
4503	Syntax not supported	Check the syntax of the Find clause and make sure it is valid according to the SQL reference guide.
4504	Invalid column name	The Find clause referenced an invalid column name. Check the table definition and make sure the column exists and is spelled correctly.
4505	Maximum token size exceeded in token.	The Find clause is too long.
4506	Unsupported data type	Check to make sure you are referencing a supported data type.
4507	Unexpected token found	Check the syntax of the Find clause.

Trapping an OLE Automation Error Specific to the Find Method

Listing 6.7 demonstrates the Parser error OIP-4504, Column Does Not Exist. This error is specific to calling the Find method. The error is generated because the Ename column is misspelled in the Find clause. Figure 6.6 shows the output from the error handler.

Listing 6.7

```
1  Dim OraSession As OraSession
2  Dim OraDatabase As OraDatabase
3  Dim OraDynaset As OraDynaset
4  On Error GoTo HandletheError
5  Set OraSession = _
   CreateObject("OracleInProcServer.XOraSession")
6  Set OraDatabase = _
   OraSession.OpenDatabase( _
   "v8i", "scott/tiger", 0&)
7  Set OraDynaset = _
   OraDatabase.CreateDynaset( _
   "select * from emp", 0&)
8  OraDynaset.MoveFirst
9  FindClause = "enamr LIKE 'BLAK%'"
10  OraDynaset.FindFirst FindClause
11  If OraDynaset.NoMatch Then
12    MsgBox "Couldn't find rows"
13  else
14    MsgBox OraDynaset.Fields("ename").Value
15  End if
16  HandletheError:
17  If Err = 440 Then
18    If OraDatabase.LastServerErr = 0 then
19      MsgBox ("OLE Automation Error " & ERROR$)
20    Else
21      MsgBox (OraDatabase.LastServerErrText)
22    End if
23  End If
```

Analysis

- Lines 1–3 are Dim statements for the objects being used to connect to the database and to create the dynaset.

- Line 4 is an On Error command that directs processing to another section of code whenever an error occurs.

- Line 5 creates the OraSession object.

- Line 6 creates an OraDatabase object and establishes the connection to the database.

- Line 7 creates an OraDynaset object based on all the employees in the Emp table.

- Line 8 moves the row pointer to the first record in the dynaset.

- Line 9 initializes the Find clause.

- Line 10 calls the FindFirst method to locate the first row in the dynaset that matches the criteria in the Find clause.

- Line 11 is the If statement that checks for no matches found.

- Line 12 displays a message if no rows are found in the search.

- Line 13 is the Else clause for the If statement in line 11.

- Line 14 displays a message for the employee that is found to match the criteria in the Find clause.

- Line 15 is an End If clause for the If statement.

- Line 16 is the label for the error-handling routine.

- Line 17 is the If statement to see whether any OLE Automation error has occurred.

- Line 18 is the If statement to see whether any Oracle error has occurred.

- Line 19 displays the actual error message for an OLE Automation error. It displays the contents of ERROR$.

- Line 20 is the Else clause for the inner If statement.

- Line 21 displays the actual error message for an Oracle error that has occurred.

- Line 22 is the End If clause for the inner If statement.

- Line 23 is the End If clause for the outer If statement.

FIGURE 6.6

The dialog box showing a
Find Parser error

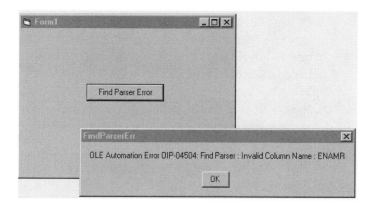

Find Method Run-Time Errors

Parser run-time errors often result when bad code is genereated by the OO4O parser. These errors occur when the system is unable to evaluate an expression in the Where portion or Find clause of the call. Table 6.3 describes these types of errors. These errors rarely occur. There is no troubleshooting tip provided for these types of errors. They should be reported directly to your local technical support center.

TABLE 6.3: Parser Run-Time Errors

Error Number	Description of Error
4516	Internal error: invalid instruction
4517	Stack overflow or underflow
4518	Invalid type conversion
4519	Invalid data type
4520	SQL function missing argument
4521	Invalid comparison
4522	`Select From Dual` statement failed
4523	Invalid data type in `Select From Dual` statement

Oracle Object Instance Errors

Oracle Object Instance errors occur when creating or manipulating object types in an Oracle8i database. These errors can occur when creating an instance of an object, binding object types as parameters, or fetching the object from the database. Table 6.4 describes Object Instance errors.

TABLE 6.4: Troubleshooting Object Instance Errors

Error Number	Description of Error	Troubleshooting Hints
4796	Creating the OraObject object instance in the client-side object cache has failed.	Check to make sure the object exists in the database.
4797	Binding the Oracle object instance to the SQL statement has failed.	Make sure the object reference is valid.
4798	Getting the attribute name of the Oracle object instance has failed.	Make sure the attribute name is valid. Describe the object in SQL*Plus to verify.
4803	Operation on Null Oracle object instance has failed.	Use the IsNull property to make sure the object was created.
4804	Pin operation on Null Ref value has failed.	Use the IsRefNull property to make sure the Ref was created.

Listing 6.8 demonstrates a call to the CreateObject method. This code will fail because the object name is misspelled and does not exist in the database. The actual schema definitions proceed the code example. Use SQL*Plus to create the schema objects needed to run the code. Figure 6.7 shows the output from the error handler.

Listing 6.8

```
CREATE TYPE address AS OBJECT (
street varchar2(200),city varchar2(200),state char(2),
zip varchar2(20));

CREATE TYPE person AS OBJECT (
name varchar2(20), age number, addr address);
```

```
CREATE TABLE person_tab OF person;
CREATE TABLE customers(
account number, aperson ref person);
```

```
1   Dim OraSession as OraSession
2   Dim OraDatabase as OraDatabase
3   Dim OraDynaset as OraDynaset
4   Dim ObjectNew as OraObject
5   On Error GoTo HandletheError
6   Set OraSession = _
    CreateObject("OracleInProcServer.XOraSession")
7   Set OraDatabase = OraSession.OpenDatabase( _
    "v8i", "scott/tiger", 0&)
8   set ObjectNew = OraDatabase.CreateOraObject("ADDRES")
9   HandletheError:
10   If Err = 440 Then
11    If OraDatabase.LastServerErr = 0 then
12     MsgBox ("OLE Automation Error " & ERROR$)
13    Else
14     MsgBox (OraDatabase.LastServerErrText)
15    End if
16   End If
```

Analysis

- Lines 1–4 are Dim statements for the objects being used to connect to the database and to create the OraObject type.

- Line 5 is an On Error command that directs processing to another section of code whenever an error occurs.

- Line 6 creates the OraSession object.

- Line 7 creates an OraDatabase object and establishes the connection to the database.

- Line 8 creates an OraObject of the Address object type.

- Line 9 is the label for the error-handling routine.

- Line 10 is the If statement to see whether any OLE Automation error has occurred.

- Line 11 is the If statement to see whether any Oracle error has occurred.

- Line 12 displays the actual error message for an OLE Automation error. It displays the contents of ERROR$.

- Line 13 is the Else clause for the inner If statement.

- Line 14 displays the actual error message for an Oracle error that has occurred.

- Line 15 is the End If clause for the inner If statement.

- Line 16 is the End If clause for the outer If statement.

FIGURE 6.7
The dialog box showing an Oracle Object Instance error

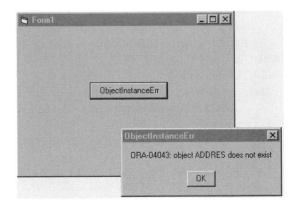

Oracle LOB Errors

Oracle LOB errors occur when you are creating and manipulating OraBLOB, Ora-CLOB, and OraBFILE data. Table 6.5 describes these errors and provides tips for resolving them.

Listing 6.9 demonstrates a call to the Write method of the OraCLOB object. The numbered code will fail because the OraCLOB object is null. The schema definitions proceed the numbered Visual Basic code example. Use SQL*Plus to create the ITEMTABLE and use the DML statements provided to insert data into the table. Figure 6.8 shows the output from the error handler.

TABLE 6.5: Troubleshooting LOB Errors

Error Number	Description of Error	Troubleshooting Hints
4896	Invalid polling amount and chunksize specified for OraBLOB, OraCLOB, and OraNCLOB Read and Write operation.	This value is expressed in bytes for OraBLOB, OraBFILE, or characters for OraCLOB.
4897	Invalid seek value is specified for the LOB Read and Write operation.	This value is expressed in bytes for OraBLOB, OraBFILE, or characters for OraCLOB. The default value is 1. Setting this value to 0 (zero) will raise an error. When the PollingAmount property is not 0 (zero), polling is enabled, the Offset property can only be set before the first Read or Write operation, or after the current polling operation has completed.
4900	Input buffer type is not string for CLOB Write operation.	Change the buffer to the required type. The data type must be String.
4901	Input buffer type is not bytes for BLOB Write operation.	Change the type of the buffer to the required type. The data type must be Byte.
4903	Write, Trim, Append, or Copy operation is not allowed outside the dynaset edit.	Before modifying the content of a LOB column in a row, a row lock must be obtained. If the LOB column is a field of an OraDynaset, the lock is obtained by invoking the Edit method.
4905	Write, Trim, Append, or Copy operation is not allowed for clone LOB object.	No operation that modifies the LOB content of OraBLOB or OraCLOB object can be performed on a clone.
4906	Specified file could not be opened in LOB operation.	Make sure that the file exists and that the name is spelled correctly.
4907	File Read or Write operation failed in LOB operation.	Make sure the disk is not full.
4908	Operation on Null LOB has failed.	Use the IsNull property on OraBLOB, OraCLOB, and OraBFILE object to make sure the object was created.

Listing 6.9

```
CREATE TABLE itemtable (
item_id          number,
```

```
item_name        varchar2(20),
item_desc        clob);

INSERT INTO itemtable values (10,'Engine',EMPTY_CLOB());
INSERT INTO itemtable values (20,'Tires', EMPTY_CLOB());

1   Dim OraSession As OraSession
2   Dim OraDatabase As OraDatabase
3   Dim OraDynaset as OraDynaset
4   Dim ClobData as OraClob
5   On Error GoTo HandletheError
6   Set OraSession = _
    CreateObject("OracleInProcServer.XOraSession")
7   Set OraDatabase = OraSession.OpenDatabase( _
    "v8i","scott/tiger",0&)
8   Set OraDynaset = OraDatabase.CreateDynaset( _
    "select * from itemtable",0&)
9   Set ClobData = OraDynaset.Fields("item_desc").Value
10  OraDynaset.Edit
11  clobdata.CopyFromFile "xxxx.dat"
12  Oradynaset.Update
13  HandletheError:
14  If Err = 440 Then
15   MsgBox ("OLE Automation Error " & ERROR$)
16  Else
17   MsgBox ("VB Error = " & Err & " " & Error)
18  End if
```

Analysis

- Lines 1–3 are Dim statements for the objects being used to connect to the database and to create the dynaset.

- Line 4 is the Dim statement for the object being used to store the CLOB data.

- Line 5 is an On Error command that directs processing to another section of code whenever an error occurs.

- Line 6 creates the OraSession object.

- Line 7 creates an OraDatabase object and establishes the connection to the database.

- Line 8 creates an OraDynaset object based on the item table.

- Line 9 sets the OraCLOB object to the value of the Item_desc object type in the OraDynaset.

- Line 10 calls the OraDynaset edit method.

- Line 11 calls the CopyFrom File method of the CLOBData object.

- Line 12 calls the OraDynaset Update method to flush the changes to the database.

- Line 13 is the label for the error-handling routine.

- Line 14 is the If statement to see whether any OLE Automation error has occurred.

- Line 15 displays the actual error message for an OLE Automation error. It displays the contents of ERROR$.

- Line 16 is the Else clause for the inner If statement.

- Line 17 displays the actual Visual Basic error.

- Line 18 is the End If clause for the If statement.

FIGURE 6.8
The dialog box showing an
Oracle LOB error

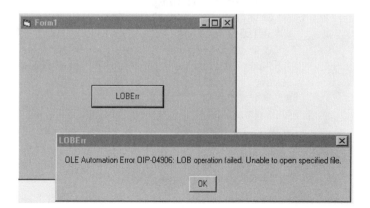

Oracle Advanced Queuing Errors

Advanced Queuing errors result from creating, manipulating, and using the Advanced Queuing interface in Oracle8i. Table 6.6 describes Advanced Queuing errors.

TABLE 6.6: Troubleshooting Advanced Queuing Errors

Error Number	Description of Error	Troubleshooting Hints
4996	Error creating OraAQ Object	Invalid queue name. The queue does not exist in the database.
4997	Error creating AQMsg object	Make sure the OraAQ object is valid.
4998	Error creating Payload object	Make sure the OraAQ object is valid.
4999	Maximum number of subscribers exceeded	The number of subscribers allowed has been exceeded. Increase the maximum size.

Listing 6.10 demonstrates a call to the CreateAQ method. This code will fail because the AppQueue does not exist in the database. Figure 6.9 shows the output from the error handler.

Listing 6.10

```
1  Dim OraSession As OraSession
2  Dim OraDatabase As OraDatabase
3  Dim MyQueue as OraAQ
4  Dim Msg as OraAQMsg
5  On Error GoTo HandletheError
6  Set OraSession = _
   CreateObject("OracleInProcServer.XOraSession")
7  Set OraDatabase = OraSession.OpenDatabase( _
   "v8i","scott/tiger",0&)
8  Set MyQueue = OraDatabase.CreateAQ("AppQueue")
9  Set OraAQMsg = _
   MyQueue.AQMsg(ORATYPE_OBJECT, "MyType","SCOTT")
10  HandletheError:
11 If Err = 440 Then
12  MsgBox ("OLE Automation Error " & ERROR$)
13 Else
14  MsgBox (OraDatabase.LastServerErrText)
15 End If
```

⊃ Analysis

- Lines 1–2 are Dim statements for the objects being used to connect to the database.

- Lines 3–4 are Dim statements for the Advanced Queuing objects.

- Line 5 is an On Error command that directs processing to another section of code whenever an error occurs.

- Line 6 creates the OraSession object.

- Line 7 creates an OraDatabase object and establishes the connection to the database.

- Line 8 calls the CreateAQ method to create an AQ object.

- Line 9 calls the AQMSg method of the OraAQ object.

- Line 10 is the label for the error-handling routine.

- Line 11 is the If statement to see whether any OLE Automation error has occurred.

- Line 12 displays the actual error message for an OLE Automation error. It displays the contents of ERROR$.

- Line 13 is the Else clause for the If statement.

- Line 14 displays the actual error message for an Oracle error that has occurred.

- Line 15 is the End If clause for the If statement.

FIGURE 6.9
The Oracle Advanced Queuing Error dialog box

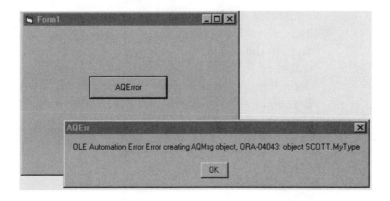

Oracle Collection Errors

Oracle collections are used to house an ordered group of elements. Each element is of the same type and has a unique subscript or index that can be used to access element values. The two types of Oracle collections are VArray and Nested Table. Collection errors are described in Table 6.7.

TABLE 6.7: Troubleshooting Collection Errors

Error Number	Description of Error	Troubleshooting Hints
5196	Operation on Null Oracle collection has failed.	Use the IsNull property to ensure that the collection has been created.
5197	Element does not exist for given index.	Use the Exist method to ensure that the element exists for the given index.
5198	Invalid collection index is specified.	The element at the index specified in the method call does not exist or has been deleted by a call to OraCollection.delete.
5199	Delete operation is not supported for VArray collection type.	The Delete operation is only valid for a Nested Table (ORA_TABLE). You cannot delete an element from a collection type of VArray (ORA_VARRAY). Make sure the type is ORA_TABLE before calling the Delete method.
5200	Variant SafeArray cannot be created from the collection having non-scalar element types.	The collection contains complex data types, such as BLOBs, CLOBs, and REFs. Make sure your collection contains only simple types, such as Varchar, Char, and Number.

Listing 6.11 shows you how to create an OraCollection object. This code will fail because you have specified an invalid index when trying to display the first element in the collection. The index for an OraCollection object starts at 1. First you will need to create the user-defined types and the Departments table. The schema definition proceeds the Visual Basic example in the unnumbered lines of code. Create the schema objects using SQL*Plus. Figure 6.10 shows the output from the error handler.

Listing 6.11

```
CREATE TYPE enamelist  AS varray(20) OF varchar2(30);
CREATE TABLE departments(
 dept_id number(2),
 name varchar2(15),
 enames enamelist);

1  Dim OraSession As OraSession
2  Dim OraDatabase As OraDatabase
3  Dim OraDynaset as OraDynaset
4  Dim TheList as OraCollection
5  On Error GoTo HandletheError
6  Set OraSession = _
   CreateObject("OracleInProcServer.XOraSession")
7  Set OraDatabase = OraSession.OpenDatabase( _
   "v8i","scott/tiger",0&)
8  Set OraDynaset = OraDatabase.CreateDynaset( _
   "select * from departments",0&)
9  set TheList = OraDynaset.Fields("enames").Value
10  msgbox TheList(0)
11  HandletheError:
12  If Err = 440 Then
13  If OraDatabase.LastServerErr = 0 then
14   MsgBox ("OLE Automation Error " & ERROR$)
15  Else
16   MsgBox (OraDatabase.LastServerErrText)
17  End if
18  End If
```

Analysis

- Lines 1–2 are Dim statements for the objects being used to connect to the database.

- Line 3 is the Dim statement for the OraDynaset object.

- Line 4 is the Dim statement for the OraCollections object.

- Line 5 is an On Error command that directs processing to another section of code whenever an error occurs.

- Line 6 creates the OraSession object.

- Line 7 creates an OraDatabase object and establishes the connection to the database.

- Line 8 creates an OraDynaset object based on the Department table.

- Line 9 sets the OraCollection Object to the Enameslist object contained in the database.

- Line 10 displays a message box with the employee name.

- Line 11 is the label for the error-handling routine.

- Line 12 is the If statement to see whether any OLE Automation error has occurred.

- Line 13 is the If statement to see whether any Oracle error has occurred.

- Line 14 displays the actual error message for an OLE Automation error. It displays the contents of ERROR$.

- Line 15 is the Else clause for the inner If statement.

- Line 16 displays the actual error message for an Oracle error that has occurred.

- Linc 17 is the End If clause for the inner If statement.

- Line 18 is the End If clause for the outer If statement.

FIGURE 6.10
The Oracle Collection Error
dialog box

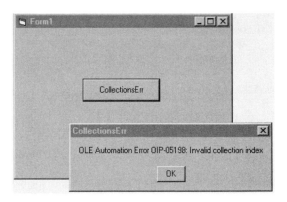

Oracle Numbers Errors

The *Oracle Number object* provides an interface specifically designed for working with Oracle Number columns. This object provides a variety of arithmetical operations and methods to manipulate number types.

TABLE 6.8: Troubleshooting Number Errors

Error Number	Description of Error	Troubleshooting Hints
5296	Operation on Null OraNumber object has failed.	Check to make sure the value of the variant can successfully be converted to a Number. Variant types containing alphanumeric data will result in this error.

Listing 6.12 demonstrates a call to the CreateOraNumber method of the OraSession object. This code will fail because the variant value contains alphanumeric data.

Listing 6.12

```
1  Dim OraSession As OraSession
2  Dim OraDatabase As OraDatabase
3  Dim OraNumber as OraNumber
4  Dim initial_value as Variant
5  On Error GoTo HandletheError
6  Set OraSession = _
   CreateObject("OracleInProcServer.XOraSession")
7  Set OraDatabase = OraSession.OpenDatabase( _
   "v8i","scott/tiger",0&)
8  initial_value = "a12"
9  set OraNumber = _
   OraSession.CreateOraNumber(initial_value)
10 HandletheError:
11 If Err = 440 Then
12  If OraSession.LastServerErr = 0 then
13    MsgBox ("OLE Automation Error " & ERROR$)
14  Else
15    MsgBox (OraSession.LastServerErrText)
16  End if
17 End If
```

⊃ **Analysis**

- Lines 1–2 are Dim statements for the objects being used to connect.

- Line 3 is a Dim statement for the OraNumber object.

- Line 4 is a Dim statement for a variant type that holds the initial value for the OraNumber object.

- Line 5 is an On Error command that directs processing to another section of code whenever an error occurs.

- Line 6 creates the OraSession object.

- Line 7 creates an OraDatabase object and establishes the connection to the database.

- Line 8 initializes the variant initial_value with "a12".

- Line 9 creates the OraNumber object by calling the CreateOraNumber method.

- Line 10 is the label for the error-handling routine.

- Line 11 is the If statement to see whether any OLE Automation error has occurred.

- Line 12 is the If statement to see whether any Oracle error has occurred.

- Line 13 displays the actual error message for an OLE Automation error. It displays the contents of ERROR$.

- Line 14 is the Else statement for the inner If statement.

- Line 15 displays the actual error message for an Oracle error that has occurred.

- Line 16 is the End If clause for the inner If statement.

- Line 17 is the End If clause for the outer If statement.

Oracle Errors

Oracle errors are reported back from the Oracle database to your OO4O application by checking either LastServerErr or LastServerErrText properties on the OraSession or OraDatabase object. The LastServerErr property of the OraSession object reports all Oracle errors that involve connections. These same properties for

OraDatabase report errors on Oracle data. These properties are set as a report of an error that occurred with CreateDynaset, CreateSQL, or ExecuteSQL.

All Oracle messages are formatted with the *ORA-* prefix, a number corresponding to a specific type of error, and a text description of which error has occurred. For example:

```
ORA-01034: Oracle not available
```

In addition to single errors being reported, you may also encounter message stacks where several errors are reported that are related to each other. For example:

```
ORA-06502: PL/SQL: numeric or value error
ORA-06512: at SCOTT.VALUE_ERR, line 1
ORA-06512: at line 1
```

This message stack helps you trace where the error is occurring in the PL/SQL package SCOTT.VALUE_ERR.

Oracle errors involving connections are Oracle network-related issues. These types of errors are caused by passing invalid or incorrect connection parameters to the OpenDatabase method call. Table 6.9 lists some of the common errors that you may encounter. For a more detailed description of the errors, please refer to the *Oracle8i Error Messages Manual Release 8.1.5.*

TABLE 6.9: Troubleshooting Connection Errors

Error Number	Description of Error	Troubleshooting Hints
3121	No interface driver connected; function not performed.	The Oracle Networking components are not installed or the %Oracle-Home%/bin directory does not appear the OS path. Passing the wrong syntax for the Net8 service name can also cause this.
1005	Null password given; logon denied.	Verify that the connect string information is correct when calling the OpenDatabase method. The parameter must contain a valid user account and password separated by a "/" (forward slash).
1014	Oracle shutdown in progress.	The application tried to log on to the database when a shutdown operation was in progress. The logon process is disabled when the instance is shut down.

T A B L E   6 . 9 :   Troubleshooting Connection Errors *(continued)*

Error Number	Description of Error	Troubleshooting Hints
1017	Invalid username or password; logon denied.	Verify that the connect string information is correct when calling the OpenDatabase method. The parameter must contain a valid user account and password separated by a "/" (forward slash).
1034	Oracle not available.	Verify that the database is up and running. Contact your DBA if necessary.
3113	An unexpected end of file was processed on the communication channel.	Check for the existence of a trace file on the server side. This should contain recorded errors that will help determine which errors have occurred.
12154	TNS: could not resolve service name.	Check the value of the database name parameter. This must be a valid Net8 service name defined in **TNSNAMES.ORA**. There may be a problem with the definition of that alias; look for mismatched parenthesis.
12203	TNS: unable to connect to destination. Unable to find the specified protocol adapter, or the listener is not running.	Verify that the listener is running on the server by using the lsnrctl status and verify that the protocol adapter is installed.

An Oracle Connection Error

Listing 6.13 demonstrates a call to the OpenDatabase method for an OraSession object. This code will fail because the database information passed is invalid. The ORA-12154 error will be raised. Figure 6.11 displays the output from the error handler.

Listing 6.13

```
1  Dim OraSession As OraSession
2  Dim OraDatabase As OraDatabase
3  On Error GoTo HandletheError
```

```
4  Set OraSession = _
   CreateObject("OracleInProcServer.XOraSession")
5  Set OraDatabase = OraSession.OpenDatabase( _
   "????","scott/tiger",0&)
6  HandletheError:
7  If Err = 440 Then
8    If OraSession.LastServerErr = 0 then
9      MsgBox ("OLE Automation Error " & ERROR$)
10   Else
11     MsgBox (OraSession.LastServerErrText)
12   End if
13   End If
```

Analysis

- Lines 1–2 are Dim statements for the objects being used to connect to the database.

- Line 3 is an On Error command that directs processing to another section of code whenever an error occurs.

- Line 4 creates the OraSession object.

- Line 5 creates an OraDatabase object and establishes the connection to the database.

- Line 6 is the label for the error-handling routine.

- Line 7 is the If statement to see if any OLE Automation errors have occurred.

- Line 8 is the If statement to see whether any Oracle errors have occurred.

- Line 9 displays the actual error message for an OLE Automation error. It displays the contents of ERROR$.

- Line 10 is the Else clause for the inner If statement.

- Line 11 displays the actual error message for an Oracle error that has occurred.

- Line 12 is the End If clause for the inner If statement.

- Line 13 is the End If clause for the outer If statement.

FIGURE 6.11
The dialog box showing an
Oracle connection error

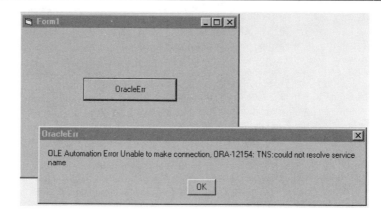

Oracle errors that involve data are reported by the Oracle server when SQL statements are processed. Some of the most common errors are listed in Table 6.10. For a more detailed description of the errors, please refer to the *Oracle8i Error Messages Manual Release 8.1.5* and the "Additional Troubleshooting Tips" section at the end of this chapter.

TABLE 6.10: Troubleshooting Data Errors

Error Number	Description of Error	Troubleshooting Hints
936	Missing expression.	A required part of a clause or expression has been omitted. Check the statement syntax and correct by supplying the missing part.
942	Table or view does not exist.	Verify that the table exists and that the spelling is correct.
955	Name is already in use by an existing object.	Check to make sure that the object name, such as a Table, View, or Index, does not already exist.
957	Duplicate column name.	Check the syntax of the Create or Insert statement and make sure that there are no duplicate column names. Correct the syntax so that all column names are unique.

TABLE 6.10: Troubleshooting Data Errors *(continued)*

Error Number	Description of Error	Troubleshooting Hints
960	Ambiguous column naming in the Select list.	A column name in the Order By list matches more than one column in the Select list. Correct the syntax of the statement so that there are no duplicate column names in the Select list.
972	Identifier is too long.	The name of a schema object in the SQL statement exceeds 30 characters. Correct the statement so that the object name is less than 30 characters.

An Oracle Data Error

Listing 6.14 demonstrates a call to the CreateDynaset method for an OraDatabase object. This code will fail because the table does not exist in the database. The ORA-942 error is raised. Figure 6.12 displays the output from the error handler.

Listing 6.14

```
1  Dim OraSession As OraSession
2  Dim OraDatabase As OraDatabase
3  Dim OraDynaset As OraDynaset
4  On Error GoTo HandletheError
5  Set OraSession = _
   CreateObject("OracleInProcServer.XOraSession")
6  Set OraDatabase = OraSession.OpenDatabase( _
   "v8i","scott/tiger",0&)
7  set OraDynaset = OraDatabase.CreateDynaset( _
   "select * from unknowntable",0&)
8  HandletheError:
9  If Err = 440 Then
10  If OraDatabase.LastServerErr = 0 then
11    MsgBox ("OLE Automation Error " & ERROR$)
12  Else
13    MsgBox (OraDatabase.LastServerErrText)
14  End if
15 End If
```

Analysis

- Lines 1–3 are Dim statements for the objects being used to connect to the database and to create the dynaset object.

- Line 4 is an On Error command that directs processing to another section of code whenever an error occurs.

- Line 5 creates the OraSession object.

- Line 6 creates an OraDatabase object and establishes the connection to the database.

- Line 7 creates an OraDynaset object and passes an invalid SQL statement.

- Line 8 is the label for the error-handling routine.

- Line 9 is the If statement to see whether any OLE Automation errors have occurred.

- Line 10 is the If statement to see whether any Oracle errors have occurred.

- Line 11 displays the actual error message for an OLE Automation error. It displays the contents of ERROR$.

- Line 12 is the Else clause for the inner If statement.

- Line 13 displays the error message for an Oracle error that occurred.

- Line 14 is the End If clause for the inner If statement.

- Line 15 is the End If clause for the outer If statement.

FIGURE 6.12
The Oracle Data Error
dialog box

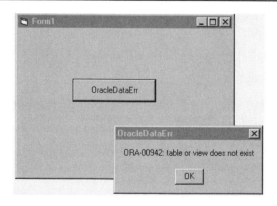

Oracle Data Control Errors

Oracle Data Control errors are specific to the use of the Oracle Data Control. OLE Automation errors that occur during operations will be reported as such. The errors listed in Table 6.7 are reported in the Dataerr parameter of the Error event. The *Error event* is fired whenever an error occurs during operations of the data control, not during execution of your own code. The kinds of operations that cause these errors include:

- A user clicks a data control button.

- The data control automatically opens a database connection and loads a recordset object after the Form Load event.

- A custom data aware control performs a MoveNext, AddNew, or Delete method based on user actions with the control.

Errors that occur before the Form Load procedure is fired are not considered trappable, and they will not cause the Error event to be triggered. Non-trappable errors can result if you set the properties of the data control to connect to an unknown database at design time. Table 6.11 describes the Oracle Data Control errors that may occur.

TABLE 6.11: Troubleshooting Data Control Errors

Error Number	Description of Error	Troubleshooting Hints
28000	Initialization of Oracle InProc Server failed.	Check the Registry for the correct location of Oracle InProc Server.
28001	Internal error. Querying InProc Server interface failed.	Report all internal errors to your local customer support group.
28007	Attempting to access Oracle Data Control prior to initialization.	Try a small delay before attempting to access the Oracle Data Control again.
28009	Bound controls trying to access with invalid field index.	Make sure the field index is valid.
28013	Bound controls trying to access with invalid field name.	Make sure the field name is valid.
28014	Internal error. Failure in allocating memory for the requested bindings from the bound control.	Report all internal errors to your local customer support group.

TABLE 6.11: Troubleshooting Data Control Errors *(continued)*

Error Number	Description of Error	Troubleshooting Hints
28015	Oracle Data Control does not support the requested bookmark type.	An Oracle Data Control bookmark is not compatible with a Visual Basic bookmark. You cannot mix the two.
28016	Oracle Data Control cannot convert field value to requested type.	Check the supported data types.
28017	Setting Session property is not allowed.	This is a read-only property at runtime.
28018	Setting Database property is not allowed.	This is a read-only property at runtime.
28019	Oracle Data Control does not update picture or raw data directly from the bound control.	The Oracle Data Control is not capable of manipulating Long Raw data. Use the AppendChunk method instead or migrate your Long Raw data to BLOBs.
28020	Recordset property cannot be set to a dynaset created with the ORADYN_NOCACHE option.	Using the ORADYN_NOCACHE option results in a forward-only scrolling recordset. The previous rows are unavailable without the presence of a local cache. The data control requires a scrollable recordset.
28021	Recordset property cannot be set to a dynaset created with the ORADYN_NOMOVEFIRST option.	The data control requires the row pointer to be positioned on the first row of the recordset.

An Oracle Data Control Error

Listing 6.15 demonstrates accessing the Oracle Data Control Recordset property. This code will fail because the dynaset we are trying to use as the recordset has been created with the ORADYN_NOCACHE option. The 28020 error is raised. Figure 6.13 displays the output from the error handler.

Listing 6.15

```
1   Dim OraSession As OraSession
2   Dim OraDatabase As OraDatabase
3   Dim OraDynaset As OraDynaset
4   On Error GoTo HandletheError
5   Set OraSession = _
```

```
   CreateObject("OracleInProcServer.XOraSession")
6  Set OraDatabase = OraSession.OpenDatabase( _
   "v8i","scott/tiger",0&)
7  set OraDynaset = OraDatabase.CreateDynaset( _
   "select * from emp",ORADYN_NOCACHE)
8  set ORADC1.recordset = OraDynaset
9  HandletheError:
10 If Err = 440 Then
11  If OraDatabase.LastServerErr = 0 then
12   MsgBox ("OLE Automation Error " & ERROR$)
13 Else
14   MsgBox (OraDatabase.LastServerErrText)
15  End if
16 End If
```

Analysis

- Lines 1–3 are Dim statements for the objects being used to connect to the database and to create the dynase object.

- Line 4 is an On Error command that directs processing to another section of code whenever an error occurs.

- Line 5 creates the OraSession object.

- Line 6 creates an OraDatabase object and establishes the connection to the database. .

- Line 7 creates an OraDynaset object.

- Line 8 sets the ORADC1 Recordset property to the OraDynaset object.

- Line 9 is the label for the error-handling routine.

- Line 10 is the If statement to see whether any OLE Automation errors have occurred.

- Line 11 is the If statement to see whether any Oracle errors have occurred.

- Line 12 displays the actual error message for an OLE Automation error. It displays the contents of ERROR$.

- Line 13 is the Else clause for the inner If statement.

- Line 14 displays the actual error message for an Oracle error that has occurred.

- Line 15 is the End If clause for the inner If statement.

- Line 16 is the If clause for the outer If statement.

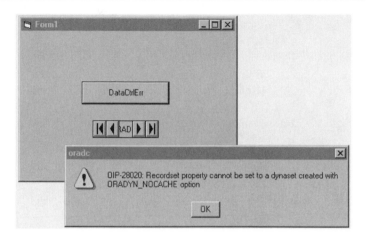

Net8 Tracing

This section will briefly discuss Net8 Tracing and how to turn tracing on and off. The average user may not find the Trace utility useful, but advanced users and developers may find that the information inside a client-side trace file may provide the additional information necessary to help solve problems. The trace files can grow very large and degrade performance of your database applications. Turn tracing on for diagnostic purposes only. The following lists reasons why you may want to turn on this tracing facility:

- To verify the location of the TNSNAMES.ORA file that is opened to resolve the Net8 service name

- To verify the type of connection that is tried, such as TCP/IP or bequeath

- To verify the actual username and password information that is being sent to the server to establish the connection

- To obtain and examine the actual SQL statement that the Oracle Objects for OLE parser is sending to the database

Enabling Client Tracing

In order to enable client-side tracing, you will need to modify the Sqlnet.ora file that is located in the $ORACLEHOME/NETWORK/ADMIN directory. The following parameters must be present and set to the appropriate values:

```
TRACE_LEVEL_CLIENT = 16
TRACE_FILE_CLIENT = cli
TRACE_DIRECTORY_CLIENT = $ORACLEHOME/NETWORK/TRACE
TRACE_CLIENT_UNIQUE = true
```

The TRACE_LEVEL_CLIENT setting is used to determine the detail of the trace. You can set this parameter to the following values:

- Off or 0

- User or 4

- Admin or 10

- Support or 16

The amount of information increases as you move down the list. Support, or 16, provides the most details. The TRACE_DIRECTORY_CLIENT entry can be set to any valid directory path for your environment.

The Net8 Header File

The information in the header file of a Net8 trace file gives you information about the source of the network configuration information in your environment, such as the Sqlnet.ora and TNSNAMES.ORA files. Listing 6.16 is a piece of a Net8 trace file. It shows a packet dump that contains header information. It shows the location of the TNSNAMES.ORA file being used to resolve the service name. You can view a Net8 trace file with the editor of your choice. Browse to the location you specified in the trace_client_directory entry in the Sqlnet.ora file, and open the trace file that has been generated. The file name will be something like Sqlnet??.trc.

Listing 6.16

```
--- TRACE CONFIGURATION INFORMATION FOLLOWS ---
New trace stream is "c:\temp\trace\sqlnet9f.trc"
New trace level is 16
--- TRACE CONFIGURATION INFORMATION ENDS ---
```

```
nigini: entry
nigini: Count in NI global area now: 1
nigini: Count in NI global area now: 1
nrigbi: entry
nrigbni: entry
nrigbni: Unable to get data from navigation file tnsnav.ora
nrigbni: exit
nrigbi: exit
nigini: exit
niqname: Using nnfsn2a() to build connect
descriptor for () database.
nnftboot: entry
nnftboot: exit
nnfoboot: entry
nnfoboot: exit
nnfoboot: entry
nnfoboot: exit
nnfhboot: entry
nnfhboot: exit
nncpmlf_make_local_addrfile:
construction of local names file failed
nncpmsf_make_sys_addrfile:
system names file is
g:\oracle815\network\admin\tnsnames.ora
nncpcin_maybe_init: first request sent to name server will have ID 333
nncpcin_maybe_init: initial retry timeout
for all name servers is 1500 csecs
nncpcin_maybe_init:
max request retries per name server is 1
nngsini_init_streams:
initializing stream subsystem, cache size is 10
nngtini_init_msg:
initializing PDU subsystem, initial pool size is 2
nncpcin_maybe_init:
default name server domain is us.oracle.com
nnfun2a: entry
nlolgobj: entry
nnfgrne: entry
nnftqnm: entry
nnfcagmd: entry
nnfcagmd: Attempting to find metadata for type a.smd
nnfcagmd: Attribute name a.smd
```

```
is a predefined meta type, syntax is 4.
nnfcagmd: exit
nnfotran: Checking local tnsnames.ora file
nnfotran: Checking local tnsnames.ora file
nncpldf_load_addrfile:
initial load of names file
g:\oracle815\network\admin\tnsnames.ora
nncpldf_load_addrfile: success
nnftqnm: Using tnsnames.ora address
(DESCRIPTION = (ADDRESS_LIST
(ADDRESS = (PROTOCOL = TCP)(HOST = mslangor1)
(PORT = 1721)))
(CONNECT_DATA = (SERVICE_NAME = v815
for name V815.us.oracle.com
nnfcraa: entry
nnftans: entry
nnfcran: entry
nnfcran: 64 rrs requested, 1 remaining, 1 total
nnfcran: exit
nnfgrne: exit
```

Packet Information

The Net8 client's main responsibility is to send and receive network packets. With a trace level of Support, or 16, you will be able to see the data packets. This information is not useful to the average person, but it may give additional information about the SQL statements that are being processed by the server. The following is a piece of a Net8 trace file that contains packet information.

The Net8 trace file in Listing 6.17 shows data being sent from the client to the server and from the server to the client. You can see the connection information in this packet dump, such as the connection parameters. Listing 6.18 is a packet dump from a Net8 trace file that shows logon information, such as the username. Listing 6.19 is a packet dump from a Net8 trace file that shows the SQL statement. Listing 6.20 is a packet dump from a Net8 trace file that shows the error messages coming back from the server.

Listing 6.17

```
nspsend: packet dump
nspsend:00 E8 00 00 01 00 00 00  |........|
nspsend:01 36 01 2C 00 00 08 00  |.6.,....|
```

```
nspsend:7F FF A3 0A 00 00 01 00   |........|
nspsend:00 AE 00 3A 00 00 02 00   |...:....|
nspsend:21 21 00 00 00 00 00 00   |!!......|
nspsend:00 00 00 00 00 93 00 00   |........|
nspsend:00 15 00 00 00 00 00 00   |........|
nspsend:00 00 28 44 45 53 43 52   |..(DESCR|
nspsend:49 50 54 49 4F 4E 3D 28   |IPTION=(|
nspsend:41 44 44 52 45 53 53 3D   |ADDRESS=|
nspsend:28 50 52 4F 54 4F 43 4F   |(PROTOCO|
nspsend:4C 3D 54 43 50 29 28 48   |L=TCP)(H|
nspsend:4F 53 54 3D 6D 73 6C 61   |OST=msla|
nspsend:6E 67 6F 72 6C 29 28 50   |ngorl)(P|
nspsend:4F 52 54 3D 31 37 32 31   |ORT=1721|
nspsend:29 29 28 43 4F 4E 4E 45   |))(CONNE|
nspsend:43 54 5F 44 41 54 41 3D   |CT_DATA=|
nspsend:28 53 45 52 56 49 43 45   |(SERVICE|
nspsend:5F 4E 41 4D 45 3D 76 38   |_NAME=v8|
nspsend:31 35 29 28 43 49 44 3D   |15)(CID=|
nspsend:28 50 52 4F 47 52 41 4D   |(PROGRAM|
nspsend:3D 47 3A 5C 6F 72 61 63   |=G:\orac|
nspsend:6C 65 38 31 35 5C 42 49   |le815\BI|
nspsend:4E 5C 53 51 4C 50 4C 55   |N\SQLPLU|
nspsend:53 57 2E 45 58 45 29 28   |SW.EXE)(|
nspsend:48 4F 53 54 3D 4F 52 4C   |HOST=ORL|
nspsend:44 54 2D 50 43 31 35 29   |DT-PC15)|
nspsend:28 55 53 45 52 3D 6A 62   |(USER=jb|
nspsend:65 73 61 77 29 29 29 29   |esaw))))|
nspsend: normal exit
```

Listing 6.18

```
nspsend: packet dump
nspsend:00 CB 00 00 06 00 00 00   |........|
nspsend:00 00 03 76 02 08 E8 10   |...v....|
nspsend:02 05 00 00 00 01 00 00   |........|
nspsend:00 88 E2 12 00 04 00 00   |........|
nspsend:00 58 E0 12 00 44 E4 12   |.X...D..|
nspsend:00 73 63 6F 74 74 0D 00   |.scott..|
nspsend:00 00 0D 41 55 54 48 5F   |...AUTH_|
nspsend:54 45 52 4D 49 4E 41 4C   |TERMINAL|
nspsend:0A 00 00 00 0A 4F 52 4C   |.....ORL|
nspsend:44 54 2D 50 43 31 35 00   |DT-PC15.|
```

```
nspsend:00 00 00 13 00 00 00 13    |........|
nspsend:41 55 54 48 5F 50 52 4F    |AUTH_PRO|
nspsend:47 52 41 4D 5F 4E 4D 00    |GRAM_NM.|
nspsend:41 55 54 0C 00 00 00 0C    |AUT.....|
nspsend:53 51 4C 50 4C 55 53 57    |SQLPLUSW|
nspsend:2E 45 58 45 00 00 00 00    |.EXE....|
nspsend:0C 00 00 00 0C 41 55 54    |.....AUT|
nspsend:48 5F 4D 41 43 48 49 4E    |H_MACHIN|
nspsend:45 14 00 00 00 14 4F 52    |E.....OR|
nspsend:4C 49 4C 41 4E 47 5C 4F    |LILANG\O|
nspsend:52 4C 44 54 2D 50 43 31    |RLDT-PC1|
nspsend:35 00 00 00 00 00 08 00    |5.......|
nspsend:00 00 08 41 55 54 48 5F    |...AUTH_|
nspsend:50 49 44 07 00 00 00 07    |PID.....|
nspsend:31 34 37 3A 31 35 39 00    |147:159.|
nspsend:00 00 00 00 00 00 00 00    |........|
nspsend: normal exit
```

⟳ Listing 6.19

```
nspsend: packet dump
nspsend:00 9F 00 00 06 00 00 00    |........|
nspsend:00 00 11 69 38 D8 97 10    |...i8...|
nspsend:02 01 00 00 00 01 00 00    |........|
nspsend:00 03 5E 39 61 80 00 00    |..^9a...|
nspsend:00 00 00 00 38 B8 10 02    |....8...|
nspsend:13 00 00 00 38 80 10 02    |....8...|
nspsend:0A 00 00 00 00 00 00 00    |........|
nspsend:5C 80 10 02 00 00 00 00    |\.......|
nspsend:01 00 00 00 00 00 00 00    |........|
nspsend:00 00 00 00 00 00 00 00    |........|
nspsend:00 00 00 00 00 00 00 00    |........|
nspsend:00 00 00 00 00 00 00 00    |........|
nspsend:5E 80 10 02 73 65 6C 65    |^...sele|
nspsend:63 74 20 2A 20 66 72 6F    |ct * fro|
nspsend:6D 20 65 6D 70 73 0A 01    |m emps..|
nspsend:00 00 00 00 00 00 00 00    |........|
nspsend:00 00 00 00 00 00 00 00    |........|
nspsend:00 00 00 00 00 00 00 00    |........|
nspsend:00 00 00 01 00 00 00 00    |........|
nspsend:00 00 00 04 00 00 00 00    |........|
nspsend: normal exit
```

Listing 6.20

```
nsprecv:00 8D 00 00 06 00 00 00   |........|
nsprecv:00 00 04 01 00 00 00 00   |........|
nsprecv:AE 03 00 00 00 00 01 00   |........|
nsprecv:0E 00 00 00 00 00 00 00   |........|
nsprecv:00 00 00 00 00 00 00 00   |........|
nsprecv:00 00 00 00 00 00 00 00   |........|
nsprecv:00 00 00 00 00 39 00 00   |.....9..|
nsprecv:01 00 00 00 36 01 00 00   |....6...|
nsprecv:80 F9 1D 00 98 3B 1E 00   |.....;..|
nsprecv:00 00 00 00 00 00 00 00   |........|
nsprecv:00 00 00 00 00 00 00 00   |........|
nsprecv:00 00 00 00 00 00 00 00   |........|
nsprecv:00 00 00 00 28 4F 52 41   |....(ORA|
nsprecv:2D 30 30 39 34 32 3A 20   |-00942: |
nsprecv:74 61 62 6C 65 20 6F 72   |table or|
nsprecv:20 76 69 65 77 20 64 6F   | view do|
nsprecv:65 73 20 6E 6F 74 20 65   |es not e|
nsprecv:78 69 73 74 0A 00 00 00   |xist....|
nsprecv: normal exit
```

Net8 Tracing can provide information to help diagnose problems with your applications. Be careful not to leave Net8 Tracing enabled because it will degrade performance and make your applications seem slow and sluggish.

The next section provides additional tips to troubleshoot errors in your development and run-time environments.

Additional Troubleshooting Tips

This section is a quick reference for compiler, run-time and Oracle error messages and troubleshooting hints.

Compile Error   User-defined type not defined.

Description of error   The data type being used is not defined. This error will occur if you attempt to define a variable as one of the OO4O data types. For example, if you are using the OraSession object (such as Dim OraSession as OraSession) and have not included the type library, you will get this compile error.

Troubleshooting hint   Make sure the type library is included in the project. From the menu bar, choose Project ➤ References and make sure that the "Oracle Objects for OLE 3.0 Type Library" check box is selected.

Compile Error   Argument not optional.

Description of error   A call to a function, procedure or method was attempted and there were missing arguments.

Troubleshooting hint   Double-check the arguments for the procedure, function, or method being called. There may not be enough parameters being passed.

Compile Error   Expected: list separator or).

Description of error   This is a rather general error that may take some digging into to find the real culprit. Generally, it means that there is a missing comma, a missing quote, or a missing closing parenthesis in the argument list when calling a procedure, function, or method.

Troubleshooting hint   Double-check the arguments for the procedure, function, or method being called for an extra or missing parenthesis, comma, or closing quote.

Run-Time error 438   Object doesn't support this property or method.

Description of error   An attempt to execute a method that does not exist was made.

Troubleshooting hint   Double-check the name of the method you are calling to ensure that it is not misspelled or that it does exist as part of the current object instead of as a method for a different object.

Run-Time error 91   Object variable or With Block variable not set.

Description of error   An attempt to access a variable that has been defined but has not yet been assigned an object reference.

Troubleshooting hint   Check the object whose method or attribute is being accessed to verify that it has been assigned an object reference. Assigning an object reference is done using the Visual Basic Set command. For example, the following code will produce this error because although the

OraSession object has been defined, it has not be assigned an object reference prior to accessing its OpenDatabase method:

```
Dim OraSession As OraSession
Dim OraDatabase As OraDatabase
Set OraDatabase = OraSession.OpenDatabase _
        ("v8i", "scott/tiger", 0&)
```

Now take a look at the revised code and notice how the OraSession object is assigned an object reference:

```
Dim OraSession As OraSession
Dim OraDatabase As OraDatabase
Set OraSession = CreateObject _
        ("OracleInProcServer.XOraSession")
Set OraDatabase = OraSession.OpenDatabase _
        ("v8i", "scott/tiger", 0&)
```

ORA-00001 error   A unique constraint has been violated.

Description of error   An SQL statement attempted to insert or update a duplicate primary key.

Troubleshooting hint   Change the primary key value to a value that does not already exist and execute the statement again.

ORA-00054 error   The snapshot is too old.

Description of error   The data contained on the client side does not match the data in the database.

Troubleshooting hint   Refreshing the snapshot frequently would help prevent this error.

ORA-00604 error   Error occurred at recursive SQL level 1

Description of error   This error may be a bit misleading. You will usually encounter this error when working with BFILEs if the DirectoryName alias is greater than 30 characters.

Troubleshooting hint   Double-check the DirectoryName alias and use a smaller name.

ORA-00900 error   The server received an invalid SQL statement.

Description of error   The statement is not recognized as a valid SQL statement. This error can occur if the Procedural option is not installed and an SQL statement is issued that requires this option. You can determine if the Procedural option is installed by starting SQL*Plus. If the PL/SQL banner is not displayed, the option is not installed.

Troubleshooting hint   Correct the syntax or install the appropriate option.

ORA-00901 error   The server received an invalid Create statement.

Description of error   The Create command was not followed by a valid Create option.

Troubleshooting hint   Correct the syntax of the statement.

ORA- 00902 error   The server received an invalid data type.

Description of error   The data type entered in the Create or Alter Table statement is not valid, or the data type of the OO4O parameter does not correlate with data type on the server.

Troubleshooting hint   Correct the syntax of the statement or double-check the data type of the parameters in the database.

ORA-00903 error   The server received an SQL statement that contains an invalid table name.

Description of error   A table or cluster name is invalid or does not exist. This message is also issued if an invalid cluster name or no cluster name is specified in an Alter Cluster or Drop Cluster statement.

Troubleshooting hint   Check your spelling. A valid table name or cluster name must begin with a letter and may contain only alphanumeric characters and the special characters "$" (dollar sign), "_" (underscore), and "#" (pound sign). The name must be less than or equal to 30 characters and cannot be a reserved word.

ORA-00904 error   The server received an SQL statement containing an invalid column name.

Description of error   The column name entered is either missing or invalid.

Troubleshooting hint   Enter a valid column name. A valid column name must begin with a letter, be less than or equal to 30 characters, and consist of only alphanumeric characters and the special characters "$" (dollar sign), "_" (underscore), and "#" (pound sign). If it contains other characters, they must be enclosed in double quotation marks. It may not be a reserved word.

ORA-00905 error   The server received an SQL statement missing a required keyword.

Description of error   A required keyword is missing.

Troubleshooting hint   Correct the syntax of the SQL statement.

ORA-00906 error   The server received an SQL statement missing a left parenthesis.

Description of error   A required left parenthesis has been omitted. Certain commands, such as Create Table, Create Cluster, and Insert, require a list of items enclosed in parentheses. Parentheses also are required around subqueries in Where clauses and in `Update Table Set Column = (SELECT)` statements.

Troubleshooting hint   Correct the syntax by inserting a left parenthesis where required and retry the statement.

ORA-00907 error   The server received an SQL statement missing a right parenthesis.

Description of error   A left parenthesis has been entered without a closing right parenthesis or extra information was contained in the parentheses. All parentheses must be entered in pairs.

Troubleshooting hint   Correct the syntax and retry the statement.

ORA-00908 error   The server received an SQL statement missing the NULL keyword.

Description of error   In a Create Table or Alter Table statement, NOT was entered to specify that no Null values are allowed in that column, but the keyword NULL was omitted. In the IS [NOT] NULL logical operator, the keyword NULL was not found. For example, the following statement generates the Ora-00908 error message:

SELECT * FROM EMP WHERE DEPTNO IS NOT;

The keyword NULL must follow the keywords IS NOT.

Troubleshooting hint   Correct the syntax of the SQL statement.

ORA-00913 error   The server received an SQL statement with too many values.

Description of error   An SQL statement requires two sets of values that are equal in number. This error occurs when the second set of values contains more items than the first set. For example, the subquery in a Where or Having clause may return too many columns, or a Values or Select clause may return more columns than are listed in the Insert statement.

Troubleshooting hint   Check the number of items in each set and change the SQL statement to make them equal.

ORA-00917 error   The server received an SQL statement that is missing a comma.

Description of error   A required comma has been omitted from a list of columns or values in an Insert statement or a list of the form ((C,D),(E,F), ...).

Troubleshooting hint   Correct the syntax of the SQL statement and supply the missing comma.

ORA-00918 error   The server received an SQL statement where the column is ambiguously defined.

Description of error   A column name used in a join exists in more than one table and is thus referenced ambiguously. In a join, any column name that occurs in more than one of the tables must be prefixed by its table name when it is referenced. The column should be referenced as TABLE.COLUMN or TABLE_ALIAS.COLUMN. For example, if tables Emp and Dept are being joined and both contain the column DeptNo, all references to DeptNo should be prefixed with the table name, as in EMP.DEPTNO or E.DEPTNO.

Troubleshooting hint   Prefix references to column names that exist in multiple tables with either the table name or a table alias and a period (.), as in the previous examples.

ORA-00921 error   The server received an SQL statement and encountered an unexpected end of SQL command.

Description of error   The SQL command was not complete. Part of a valid command was entered, but at least one major component was omitted.

Troubleshooting hint   Correct the syntax of the SQL statement.

ORA-00932 error   The server encountered an SQL statement containing inconsistent data types.

Description of error   An attempt was made to perform an operation on incompatible data types. For example, adding a character field to a date field (dates may only be added to numeric fields) or concatenating a character field with a long field.

An attempt was made to perform an operation on a database object (such as a table or view) that is not intended for normal use. For example, system tables cannot be modified by a user. On rare occasions this error occurs because a misspelled object name matched a restricted object's name.

An attempt was made to use an undocumented view.

Troubleshooting hint   If the cause is different data types, use consistent data types. For example, convert the character field to a numeric field with the TO_NUMBER function before adding it to the Date field. Functions may not be used with long fields. If caused by an object that was not intended for normal use, do not access the restricted object.

ORA-00933 error   The server encountered an SQL command that was not ended properly.

Description of error   The SQL statement ends with an incorrect clause. For example, an Order By clause may have been included in a Create View or Insert statement. Order By cannot be used to create an ordered view or to insert in a certain order.

Troubleshooting hint   Correct the syntax by removing the incorrect clauses.

ORA-00934 error   A group function was found and is not allowed in the SQL statement.

Description of error   One of the group functions, such as AVG, COUNT, MAX, MIN, SUM, STDDEV, or VARIANCE, was used in a Where or Group Byclause.

Troubleshooting hint   Remove the group function from the Where or Group By clause. The desired result may be achieved by including the function in a subquery or Having clause.

ORA-00936 error   The server encountered an SQL statement that is missing an expression.

Description of error   A required part of a clause or expression has been omitted. For example, a Select statement may have been entered without a list of columns or expressions or with an incomplete expression. This message is also issued in cases where a reserved word is misused, as in Select Table.

Troubleshooting hint   Check the SQL statement syntax and specify the missing part.

ORA-00942 error   The server received an SQL statement that contains a reference to a table or view that does not exist.

Description of error   The table or view entered does not exist, a synonym that is not allowed here was used, or a view was referenced where a table is required. Existing user tables and views can be listed by querying the data dictionary. Certain privileges may be required to access the table. If an application returned this message, the table that the application tried to access does not exist in the database, or the application does not have access to it.

Troubleshooting hint   Check that the spelling of the table or view name is correct, that a view is not specified where a table is required, and that an existing table or view name exists.

ORA-00955 error   The server received an SQL statement that tried to create an object name that is already used by an existing object

Description of error   An attempt was made to create a database object, such as a Table, View, Cluster, Index, or Synonym, that already exists. A schema's database objects must have unique names.

Troubleshooting hint   Use a unique name for the database object. If you are having difficulty figuring out if the object you are attempting to create already exists, you could simply do a describe on the object. For example, if you wanted to create an object called MYOBJECT and wanted to see if it already existed, you could execute the following through SQL*Plus:

```
DESC MYOBJECT
```

If the object exists, a description of the object is returned. If the object does not exist, an "ORA-04043: object MYOBJECT does not exist" error is returned.

ORA-00957 error   The server received an SQL statement that has a duplicate column name referenced.

Description of error   A column name was specified twice in a Create or Insert statement. Column names must be referenced only once in a Table, View, or Cluster statement.

Troubleshooting hint   Remove one of the duplicate names.

ORA-00960 error   Ambiguous column naming in the Select list.

Description of error   A column name in the Order By list matches more than one of the Select list columns.

Troubleshooting hint   Remove duplicate column name in the Select list.

ORA-01000 error   The maximum number of open cursors has been exceeded.

Description of error   An application attempted to open too many cursors. The initialization parameter OPEN_CURSORS determines the maximum number of cursors per user.

Troubleshooting hint   Increase the OPEN_CURSORS parameter in the Oracle initialization file. The default of 50 may be too low.

ORA-01002 error   Fetch call out of sequence.

Description of error   In an application program, a Fetch call was issued out of sequence. A successful parse and execute must be issued before a Fetch call. This can occur if an attempt was made to fetch after all records have been fetched. This may also be caused by fetching from a Select For Update cursor after issuing a commit.

Troubleshooting hint   Parse and execute an SQL statement before fetching the data.

ORA-01004 error   Default username feature not supported. Logon denied.

Description of error   An attempt was made to use OS authentication on a system that does not support this feature. (OPS$)

Troubleshooting hint   Make sure REMOTE_AUTHENT is set to True in the Oracle initialization file.

ORA-01005 error   A Null password was given. Logon was denied.

Description of error   An invalid password was given when logging on.

Troubleshooting hint   Correct and provide a valid password.

ORA-01008 error   Not all variables are bound.

Description of error   An SQL statement containing substitution variables was executed without all variables bound. All substitution variables must have a substituted value before the SQL statement is executed.

Troubleshooting hint   With OO4O, use the Add Parameter method for each bind variable in the SQL statement.

ORA-01014 error   Oracle shutdown in progress.

Description of error   A user tried to log on to Oracle while an instance shutdown was in progress. Oracle logons are disabled while Oracle is being shut down.

Troubleshooting hint   Wait until Oracle is brought back before attempting to log on.

ORA-01017 error   Invalid username or password; logon denied

Description of error   An invalid username or password was entered in an attempt to log on to Oracle. The username and password must be the same as when the user was created.

Troubleshooting hint   Enter a valid username and password combination in the correct format.

ORA-01019 error   Unable to allocate memory in the user side.

Description of error   The user side memory allocator returned an error.

Troubleshooting hint   Increase the size of the process heap.

ORA-01031 error   Insufficient privileges.

Description of error   This error is general, yet specific. It simply states that you don't have the privileges for the last SQL command that you executed. Whether the last SQL you attempted was some DDL or DML, you require privileges to execute it.

Troubleshooting hint   Check the SQL command that you are attempting to execute and verify with your DBA whether or not the proper permissions can be granted to you.

ORA-01034 error   Oracle not available.

Description of error   The Oracle database was not started.

Troubleshooting hint   Check with your DBA to ensure that the database is up and running.

ORA-01422 error   Exact fetch returns more than requested number of rows.

Description of error   Although one generally does not care how many rows a particular query returns, there are times when returning more than one row of data will result in an error. For example, unless coded correctly, subqueries can only return one row at a time. The same holds true when working with arrays (batch processing) in OO4O. You need to ensure that the SQL being used only returns a single row.

Troubleshooting hint   Ensure that the SQL returns only a single row. To do so, check the SQL in SQL*Plus to verify the number of rows or execute a Select Count command to obtain a count of the number of rows that are processed.

ORA-01460 error   Unimplemented or unreasonable conversion requested.

Description of error   This error can be returned for a number of different reasons. The one most common in this book is when the Directory Alias contains more than 30 characters.

Troubleshooting hint   Ensure the number of characters used for the DirectoryAlias does not exceed 30.

ORA-01555 error   The snapshot is too old.

Description of error   This error is raised when the snapshot is too old.

Troubleshooting hint   Double-check the locks.

ORA-03121 error   The Interface driver is not connected.

Description of error   The application is trying to initiate a connection with the database and the network layer cannot be found.

Troubleshooting hint   Check that the correct Net8 client version is installed and configured. Also make sure the `Oraclehome/bin` directory appears in the OS path.

ORA-1405 error   Fetched column value is null.

Description of error   This error arises when attempting to execute methods of an object that is null. It is more commonly seen when working with LOBs and attempting to execute methods when the column is null.

Troubleshooting hint   Most objects have an IsNull property or a Size property that can be used to make sure that the object referenced does not contain a Null value.

ORA-01843 error   Not a valid month.

Description of error   A date specified an invalid month. Valid months are January–December for the format code MONTH, and Jan–Dec for the format code MON. Check the NLS_DATE_FORMAT and make sure that you are specifying a date in the correct format.

Troubleshooting hint   Enter a valid month value in the correct format.

ORA-02292 error   Integrity constraint.

Description of error   This error arises when attempt to insert, update or delete a field value in one table that is the constraint to a field in another table. Take an employee database as an example: Normally you would not assign an employee to a department that does not exist. To prevent such a thing from happening, a Foreign Key constraint can be created so that any attempt to insert or update an employee with an invalid department will violate the constraint. The error would occur if you attempt to delete a department that currently has employees assigned to it.

Troubleshooting hint   Here is a prime example of the importance of knowing the data and understanding data integrity. Unfortunately there is no hard and fast rule for resolving this error other than to ensure that these constraints are not violated. If you have no idea which constraints correspond to which tables and fields, you can reference some of the system tables to find this information. You can also review one of the Oracle administrator guides.

ORA-06550 error   Displays the line number and column number where the error occurred.

Description of error   This error arises during the execution of a stored procedure or function and will display the line number and column number where the error occurred.

Troubleshooting hint   Alone, this error is usually not very meaningful. The PL/SQL error message that accompanies this error is more accurate. Although the accompanying PL/SQL error will vary depending upon the actual error, it is very reliable in pointing to the exact location of the error when used in conjunction with the line number and column number given with the ORA-06550 error.

ORA-12154 error   Unable to resolve TNS service name.

Description of error   The network layer was unable to find the Net8 service name used to connect to the database.

Troubleshooting hint   Use the Net8 Easy Configuration utility to verify that the Net8 service name exists and is valid.

ORA-22285 error   Non-existent directory or file for file Open operation.

Description of error   The Directory Alias used to reference a BFILE object does not reference a valid directory.

Troubleshooting hint   Double-check the Directory Alias used to make sure that it references a valid directory.

ORA-22288 error   Operation *<method>* failed.

Description of error   Notifies you of a failed operation and replaces *<method>* with the actual method that was executed when the failure occurred. When used with OO4O, it more commonly occurs when referencing a BFILE object that does not exist even though the Directory Alias represents a valid directory.

Troubleshooting hint   Validate the filename for the BFILE and make sure that it can be found in the location reference through the Directory Alias.

ORA-22289 error   Cannot perform file Read operation on an unopened file.

Description of error   One of the prerequisites when reading from a BFILE is that the BFILE is opened for access. Attempting to access the contents of a BFILE without opening it first will result in this error.

Troubleshooting hint   Before attempting to access data in a BFILE object, make sure you use the Open method to open the object.

ORA-24327 error   Need explicit attach before authenticating a user.

Description of error   Occurs when attempting to connect to the database with a specific user without first establishing a physical connection to the database. This error is more likely to occur when using Connection Pooling or Connection Multiplexing.

Troubleshooting hint   Make sure that a physical connection has been established prior to attempting to log on as a specific user.

ORA-24801 error   Illegal parameter value in OCI LOB function.

Description of error   Other than the obvious, which is that there was an illegal parameter used, this error occurs on methods of LOBs when the size happens to be zero even though the object is valid.

Troubleshooting hint   You may have to add code not only to check if the object is valid but also to check the Size property of the LOB to ensure that it's greater than zero.

Summary

Error recovery is important when your application encounters problems. You should always make error handling and recovery a priority when designing your application. Knowing what errors to expect and what possible actions to take is key to setting up an efficient database and supporting it painlessly. You can use the Visual Basic Err object to implement a good error-handling routine for each part of your application for all known, trappable errors. You can also use the troubleshooting hints described throughout this chapter to help you recover from design as well as run-time errors.

chapter 7

Multi-User Concurrency and Transactional Control

- Understanding read consistency and locking

- The effects of the For Update clause and NoWait option

- Transactions and record locking in OO4O

- Data contention

- Using the BeginTrans and RollbackTrans methods

- Potential data conflicts

This chapter will cover the issues related to how Oracle applications handle multiple users who are simultaneously accessing data in the Oracle8i database. The goal of this chapter is to familiarize you with the Oracle8i mechanisms for transactions and read consistency, as well as to cover some of the fundamentals for Oracle client-server application design. In this chapter, you will experience some of the mechanisms for transactions in SQL*Plus, and you will see how to implement transaction control and record locking using OO4O.

The examples used in this chapter make use of the Scott schema and default tables. For more information pertaining to this schema and its tables, you can refer to the introduction for a description or to Chapter 2 for steps on how to create them.

An Overview of Read Consistency and Locking

With Visual Basic, it is very simple and quick to develop a database application using bound controls that allow for editing and viewing of data in the database. This method will work fine for a database application where only one instance of your application will be run, or where each instance of the application will be running against a different schema (or set of tables) in the database.

When an Update operation occurs, there are generally two types of locks that a database can place on a table. The first is a *table lock*. With a table lock, you are essentially locking the entire table during the update. Even if there are one thousand rows in the table and you wish to update only a single row, the database will lock the entire table, preventing all other rows from being updated by other users. The second type of locking is *row-level locking*. This type of locking places a lock only on the particular row being updated. This allows the unlocked rows to be updated by concurrent users. Because Oracle implements row-level locking, even if the same table or tables are used by more than one user, if they are accessing different rows, no conflicts will arise. This means that if two different users make edits to the same database table but to different rows, they do not interfere with one another.

In databases that do not implement row-level locking, as soon as one user attempts to modify one row, the entire table is locked. This means that if two different users access the same database table, as soon as the first user makes an edit, the entire table is locked. In such a case, the second user is not able to access the table until the first user has either committed or rolled back the data. Because Oracle allows row-level locking, this frustrating issue is avoided.

For applications where multiple users will be running the application against the same row data, you need to consider how the users' viewing and editing of the data will interact with each other and devise a method of dealing with any conflicts that may arise in your application.

The best place to start is with a detailed look at how the Oracle RDBMS deals with read consistency and locking and then turn your attention to developmental issues with building client-server applications using this model.

When discussing applications using an RDBMS that can be accessed by multiple users, it is important to understand the concepts involved. What follows is a brief discussion of the terms that will be used to discuss this topic.

Transaction   A transaction refers to a logical set of operations that are performed in a given context. If you begin a transaction and then start modifying the data in the database, you can roll back or undo the changes back to the start of the transaction. To make the changes permanent, a Commit operation is done to finish the current transaction.

Read consistency   Read consistency is the ability of the database to return a set of data that is consistent up to a given point in time, like the beginning of the transaction. When you are updating information but have not yet committed the data, it is possible that the information you edited has changed while you were editing. If a different user comes along and reads the data that you already modified (but have not yet committed), you have what is called a dirty read. It is considered dirty because you have not committed the data, and the data can potentially change either by additional editing or by someone issuing a Rollback command.

Rollback segments   A rollback segment can be thought of as a place in memory in the Oracle8i database where selected data is stored while it is being inserted, updated, or deleted, until it is accepted or rejected by either a Commit or Rollback command. The Oracle8i database insures read consistency by using rollback segments. The database will not allow a dirty read to occur because a transactionally consistent read is always returned. If this cannot be done, perhaps because the data in the rollback segment is overwritten, an error is returned to the user. The following steps show how a transactionally consistent read is always returned:

- When a row is modified, its original contents are moved to the currently active rollback segment. A transaction number is associated with this segment so that it can be located as needed for read consistency for other users or for rolling back any changes to the transaction.

- When a transaction is committed, the rollback segment's resources are freed (the data is unlocked), and the data can be overwritten. The data will not necessarily be lost immediately.

Before the transaction is committed, when other users query the data, they will get the values for the row from the data in the rollback segment.

If the transaction is committed and these rows are no longer locked in the rollback segment, the rows may be overwritten by data from another transaction. When this happens and the user attempts to read the data, the user will receive an ORA-01555 error "Snapshot too old." If this is happening on a regular basis, the DBA may need to increase the size of the rollback segments to decrease the likelihood that the data will be overwritten before the users are finished with a given query.

As long as the transaction remains uncommitted, the rollback segment contains the original copy, which will be provided if someone else (User A for example) tries to read that data block, thus insuring a consistent read. If User B rolls back the data, it is again copied back to the block buffer, and everything is as it was originally. If User B commits the data, the transaction lock on the data in the rollback segment is released, but the original data is still available until it is overwritten by a subsequent transaction. This means that with a large rollback segment, the data may be available for quite some time. If the data in the rollback segment is overwritten by a subsequent transaction, when User A tries to read it, the RDBMS will be unable to provide the unmodified form of the data and will return the ORA-01555 error "Snapshot too old." This insures that User A must refresh the cursor or query to see the newly committed data.

As you can see, at no point is a read of dirty (uncommitted) data allowed. A point-in-time consistent view of the data is also enforced because the user must refresh the cursor if the data is modified and committed long enough before the fetch time that the original data is no longer available.

The Commit and Rollback commands   To start a transaction in the database, a user initiates some change to the data in the database through an Update, Insert, or Delete command, or through a stored procedure or function. To end a transaction, a user must either accept the change(s) or discard the change(s). Different applications have different ways of accepting or discarding the change(s). For example, SQL*Plus uses the *Commit* command to accept and the *Rollback* command to discard any change(s) that may have taken place during the transaction. OO4O also has its own way of accepting or rejecting changes. Table 7.1 lists some of the ways in which OO4O can commit or roll back transactions. These will be covered in depth later in this chapter. As stated in the "An Overview of Read Consistency and Locking" section, the Commit or Rollback command is what essentially ends a transaction. This is true regardless of the application you are using.

TABLE 7.1:   Accepting and Rejecting Changes in OO4O

Accept Changes	Reject Changes
AutoCommit property	Rollback method
CommitTrans method	ExecuteSQL ("Rollback")
ExecuteSQL ("Commit")	

Dirty reads   A dirty read is the ability to read data from a table that has been changed by another user before that user issues a Commit command. A more technical definition is that a dirty read is the ability to view modified data that is currently part of a transaction. Let's say two users (User A and User B) are viewing employee data from the same Employee table, and User A executes an Update command to increase all the salaries by 10% but does not issue a Commit command. The next time User B issues a Select command to view the data, the original data from the Employee table is reviewed. Why? Because User A has not accepted the changes by issuing a Commit command. If User B executed a Select command and was able to see the uncommitted changes, this would be considered a dirty read.

What's wrong with dirty reads? Well, take for example the scenario that was just described. User A wants to increase the salaries by 10%, but instead of hitting the 0 key, she hits the 9 key, and the salaries are increased by 19%. Sure, you wouldn't complain about a 19% increase, but it's pretty likely that someone would. The main point is that if User B produces a report based on a query of this table, the report would contain the new salaries, which are incorrect.

Although there are databases that allow for dirty reads, the Oracle database does not. You could say that Oracle's philosophy is not to allow other users to view modified data unless the changes have been officially accepted by issuing a Commit command. This allows users to massage and manipulate data without affecting what others may see when the data is queried. That is, until they issue a Commit command to accept the changes.

Read Consistency

To illustrate how the concepts of transactions, read consistency, rollback segments, dirty reads, and committing or rejecting changes all come together, let's take a look at an example. To start, open two SQL*Plus sessions and connection both sessions to the user Scott.

You may want to position the screens so they are next to each other, as shown in Figure 7.1. In the text, the screen on the left will be referenced as User 1, and the screen on the right will be referenced as User 2.

FIGURE 7.1
Opening two SQL*Plus sessions

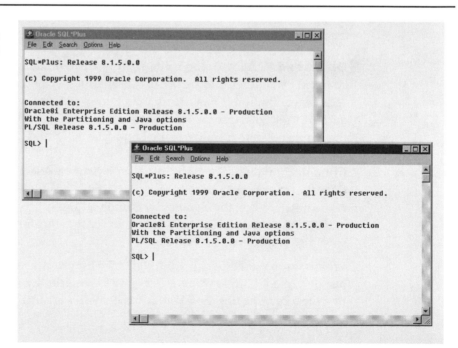

Let's say that User 1 enters the following SQL command at the SQL prompt to view the data in the Emp table.

```
SELECT * FROM EMP;
```

If you are using the demo data provided in the Demobld7.sql file, the results should look something like what you see in Figure 7.2.

FIGURE 7.2

User 1—The results of the Select From Emp command

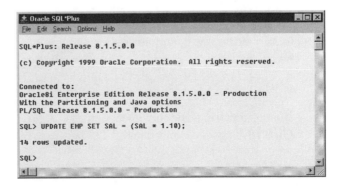

```
SQL> SELECT * FROM EMP;

    EMPNO ENAME      JOB            MGR HIREDATE     SAL      COMM    DEPTNO
    ----- ---------- --------- ------- --------- -------- --------- --------
     7839 KING       PRESIDENT          17-NOV-81    5000                 10
     7698 BLAKE      MANAGER       7839 01-MAY-81    2850                 30
     7782 CLARK      MANAGER       7839 09-JUN-81    2450                 10
     7566 JONES      MANAGER       7839 02-APR-81    2975                 20
     7654 MARTIN     SALESMAN      7698 28-SEP-81    1250     1400        30
     7499 ALLEN      SALESMAN      7698 20-FEB-81    1600      300        30
     7844 TURNER     SALESMAN      7698 08-SEP-81    1500        0        30
     7900 JAMES      CLERK         7698 03-DEC-81     950                 30
     7521 WARD       SALESMAN      7698 22-FEB-81    1250      500        30
     7902 FORD       ANALYST       7566 03-DEC-81    3000                 20
     7369 SMITH      CLERK         7902 17-DEC-80     800                 20
     7788 SCOTT      ANALYST       7566 09-DEC-82    3000                 20
     7876 ADAMS      CLERK         7788 12-JAN-83    1100                 20
     7934 MILLER     CLERK         7782 23-JAN-82    1300                 10

14 rows selected.

SQL>
```

Now, User 2, who is already connected, will begin a transaction against the same Emp table that User 1 just executed a Select command against. For this scenario, let's say that everyone in the company was granted a 10% increase in salary, and now the Emp table must be updated to reflect this increase. To do this, execute the following SQL command in User 2's SQL*Plus session:

```
UPDATE EMP SET SAL = (SAL * 1.10);
```

After executing this command, you should see a reply on the screen confirming that 14 rows have been updated, as shown in Figure 7.3.

FIGURE 7.3

User 2—The Reply screen for the Update command

```
SQL*Plus: Release 8.1.5.0.0

(c) Copyright 1999 Oracle Corporation.  All rights reserved.


Connected to:
Oracle8i Enterprise Edition Release 8.1.5.0.0 - Production
With the Partitioning and Java options
PL/SQL Release 8.1.5.0.0 - Production

SQL> UPDATE EMP SET SAL = (SAL * 1.10);

14 rows updated.

SQL>
```

Remember: User 2 initiated a transaction that updated the salaries for all the employees in the Emp table but has yet to accept or reject this change. User 2 has yet to issue a Commit or Rollback command. Although you may think that the new salaries overwrote the old salaries, what has actually happened behind the scenes is that the old salaries have been written to the rollback segment in the database.

Now, go back to User 1's SQL*Plus session and execute the same Select statement that you entered before. You can either type the SQL again as follows:

```
SELECT * FROM EMP;
```

or, type a / at the SQL prompt and hit Enter. The / is a command in SQL*Plus to tell the system to execute the last SQL statement.

What you should see now, as Figure 7.4 illustrates, is the same output that you saw when you first executed the SQL statement as in Figure 7.2.

FIGURE 7.4

User 1—The results of the Select command

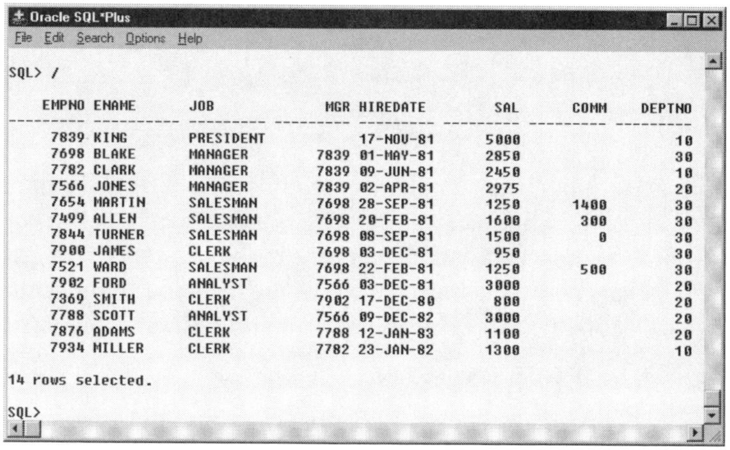

```
SQL> /

    EMPNO ENAME      JOB          MGR HIREDATE       SAL      COMM    DEPTNO
    ----- ---------- --------- ------ --------- -------- --------- ---------
     7839 KING       PRESIDENT        17-NOV-81     5000                  10
     7698 BLAKE      MANAGER     7839 01-MAY-81     2850                  30
     7782 CLARK      MANAGER     7839 09-JUN-81     2450                  10
     7566 JONES      MANAGER     7839 02-APR-81     2975                  20
     7654 MARTIN     SALESMAN    7698 28-SEP-81     1250      1400        30
     7499 ALLEN      SALESMAN    7698 20-FEB-81     1600       300        30
     7844 TURNER     SALESMAN    7698 08-SEP-81     1500         0        30
     7900 JAMES      CLERK       7698 03-DEC-81      950                  30
     7521 WARD       SALESMAN    7698 22-FEB-81     1250       500        30
     7902 FORD       ANALYST     7566 03-DEC-81     3000                  20
     7369 SMITH      CLERK       7902 17-DEC-80      800                  20
     7788 SCOTT      ANALYST     7566 09-DEC-82     3000                  20
     7876 ADAMS      CLERK       7788 12-JAN-83     1100                  20
     7934 MILLER     CLERK       7782 23-JAN-82     1300                  10

14 rows selected.

SQL>
```

The reason User 1 is not able to see the updated record is because User 2 has not committed the change, and User 1 is not able to see modified data in another user's transaction. If the updated record were visible by User 1, it would be considered a dirty read, and as you know by now, a dirty read is not allowed in an Oracle database. In order to maintain read consistency, when User 1 issued a Select command, the original data was actually retrieved from the rollback segment.

Once again, execute the Select command, but this time, execute it from User 2's SQL*Plus session. Don't use the "/" because this will only execute the Update command again and not the Select command. Enter the following Select command at the SQL prompt:

```
SELECT * FROM EMP;
```

Executing the Select command from User 2's session produces a different result than executing it from User 1's session. Figure 7.5 shows the results.

FIGURE 7.5

User 2—The results of the Select command

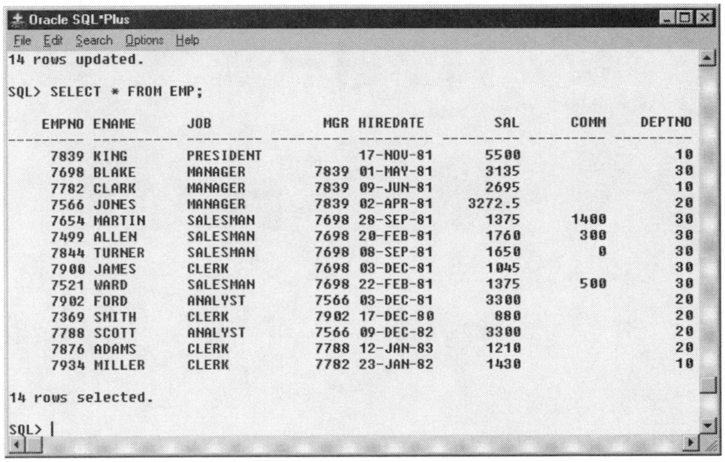

```
★ Oracle SQL*Plus                                          _□X
File  Edit  Search  Options  Help
14 rows updated.

SQL> SELECT * FROM EMP;

    EMPNO ENAME      JOB          MGR HIREDATE      SAL      COMM    DEPTNO
    ----- ---------- --------- ------ --------- -------- --------- --------
     7839 KING       PRESIDENT        17-NOV-81     5500                10
     7698 BLAKE      MANAGER     7839 01-MAY-81     3135                30
     7782 CLARK      MANAGER     7839 09-JUN-81     2695                10
     7566 JONES      MANAGER     7839 02-APR-81   3272.5                20
     7654 MARTIN     SALESMAN    7698 28-SEP-81     1375      1400      30
     7499 ALLEN      SALESMAN    7698 20-FEB-81     1760       300      30
     7844 TURNER     SALESMAN    7698 08-SEP-81     1650         0      30
     7900 JAMES      CLERK       7698 03-DEC-81     1045                30
     7521 WARD       SALESMAN    7698 22-FEB-81     1375       500      30
     7902 FORD       ANALYST     7566 03-DEC-81     3300                20
     7369 SMITH      CLERK       7902 17-DEC-80      880                20
     7788 SCOTT      ANALYST     7566 09-DEC-82     3300                20
     7876 ADAMS      CLERK       7788 12-JAN-83     1210                20
     7934 MILLER     CLERK       7782 23-JAN-82     1430                10

14 rows selected.

SQL> |
```

Notice that User 2 is able to see all the updated salaries. This is because User 2 initiated the transaction. So, only User 2 can see the modified data until the data is officially committed.

At this point, if User 2 decides not to commit the data and instead decides to undo or roll back the changes, this could be done using the Rollback command when executing SQL in SQL*Plus. Once the Rollback command is issued, the transaction is ended, the changes are lost, and the original data is copied back from the database rollback segment. The space in the rollback segment is freed and is available for more transactions. If, during the rollback, both User 1 and User 2 execute the Select From Emp command, they would both see the same results. The results would be the data before the Update command was executed. The results would match Figure 7.2.

Instead of rolling back the data, let's say that User 2 decides to accept the update by issuing a Commit command. In this example, to accept the changes, type the Commit command at the SQL prompt:

```
COMMIT;
```

Now, when User 1 executes the Select command, the output should be similar to Figure 7.6. To execute the Select command in User 1's SQL*Plus session, you can either type the following SQL command or type a / at the SQL prompt.

```
SELECT * FROM EMP;
```

If you take a close look at the output in Figure 7.6, you will notice that it now matches the results that User 2 was seeing after the Update command was issued.

FIGURE 7.6

User 1—The updated Emp table data

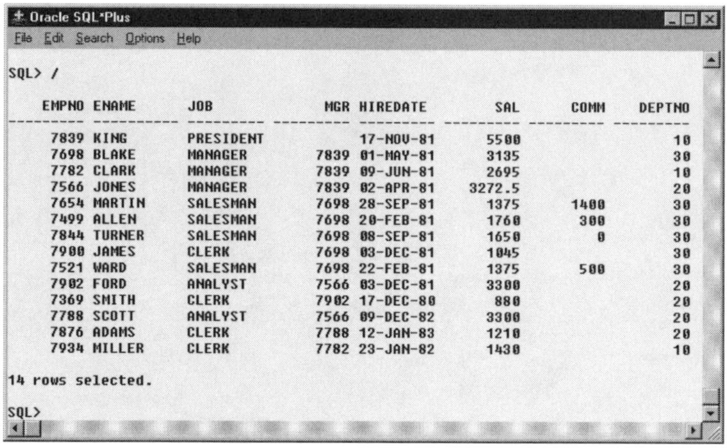

Once User 2 issues the Commit command, the transaction ends. At this point, there are no outstanding transactions, so any subsequent Select commands will produce the same results for each user.

An Overview of Locking

When a given row is being edited (it has been modified but not yet committed), it is considered to be *write locked*. Another user can select (read) it, as you saw in the previous example, but they can't change (edit) it. They *can* edit other rows that have not been locked by other users. If an attempt to lock a row is made on a row that is already locked, one of two possible outcomes will occur:

- The second statement attempting to lock the row will wait until the first user has unlocked the row. This is the default behavior.

- If the SQL statement attempting to lock the row in question was issued with a NoWait clause, it will not wait for the lock to free but instead will return an ORA-00054 error indicating that the row could not be locked for edit.

To illustrate how the locks operate, take a look at the following example. Let's say that User 1 works in the Personnel department, and User 2 works in the Accounting department, and both are logged into the same Scott/Tiger schema through two separate SQL*Plus sessions. User 1 was instructed to make an edit to the Emp table to alter the employee Smith. Apparently Smith has been working so hard that he was recently promoted to salesman. Now, the Emp table must be modified to reflect this change. User 1 from Personnel will have to update the Emp table to change the Job field from clerk to salesman. User 2 from Accounting will have to increase Smith's salary to $1,500 due to his promotion. The promotion and change in title can be accomplished by executing the following SQL command in User 1's SQL*Plus session:

```
UPDATE EMP SET JOB = 'SALESMAN' WHERE EMPNO = 7369;
```

Once executed, you should see the message "1 row updated" appear on the screen. At this time, a Commit or Rollback command has not taken place. As in the previous example, executing the Update command initiated a transaction and wrote the original data to the rollback segment.

One item that was not discussed in the previous section was *row locking*. Once a user has selected a record to update, the row becomes locked by that user. Because a Commit or Rollback command completes a transaction, these commands will also release locks placed on any given row.

To continue with the example, User 2 must now give Smith his increase in salary. This increase can be accomplished by executing the following SQL command in User 2's SQL*Plus session. Remember: User 1 has yet to commit or roll back the update.

```
UPDATE EMP SET SAL = 1500 WHERE EMPNO = 7369;
```

When User 2 enters the Update command and presses the Enter key, the screen locks. Normally, once the Enter key is pressed, the SQL command is executed and an SQL prompt appears on the screen, but not this time. User 1 currently has the row locked while updating Smith's job title, so no other user is able to execute an SQL command that requires a lock of the same row. A given row of data is unable to have more than one lock. So, even though User 2 is attempting to update a different field, the field being updated is part of a row that is already locked.

The only way that the lock can be released is if User 1 commits or rolls back the change. For this example, User 1 commits the change using the following Commit command:

```
COMMIT;
```

You will notice that as soon as User 1 enters the Commit command and presses Enter, the lock on the row is released. Because the lock on the row is released, User 2's Update command can now be processed by the database. A quick glance at User 2's SQL*Plus session reveals an SQL prompt. This means that the database has finished processing and is ready for the next SQL command.

Now, User 2 executes the Select command at the SQL prompt to view the change. You will see not only the changes made by User 2's update but also the update from User 1's session.

```
SELECT * FROM EMP WHERE EMPNO = 7369;
```

The results should look like Figure 7.7.

FIGURE 7.7
The updated Emp table data

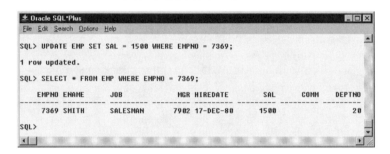

The two things to remember are

- Record locking occurs in the database *implicitly* when an edit occurs or *explicitly* when a user specifies the For Update clause.

- Only one user at a time can acquire a lock on any given row.

For more information on the For Update clause, read the next section.

The For Update Clause

There are two ways that locks can be placed on different rows in a database table:

- Implicitly, by attempting to edit a record

- Explicitly, by specifying the For Update clause

The previous section illustrated an implicit lock. The example in this section illustrates working with an explicit lock. Before jumping into the example, let's take a moment to discuss why you would want to explicitly lock the row(s) of a table. Then, we'll continue to discuss how to explicitly lock rows.

You know from the previous section that once you initiate an edit of a given row, the database places a lock on the row. This prevents other users from updating rows that are currently part of a transaction. In this way, row locking is very important in maintaining read consistency. What if you don't want to initiate a transaction to lock the rows, yet you want to prevent other users from updating the data? Let's say that you are working at Company X and it's the time of year when both bonuses and raises are calculated. The bonuses will be calculated based on a percentage of the employees' new salaries. For this company, the salaries are handled by the Accounting department, and the bonuses are handled by the Personnel department.

As with any company, each employee gets a different percentage increase in salary, and each gets a different bonus percentage. For example, imagine that employee Clark (from the Emp table) has a salary of $5,000 (your actual value may differ) and, due to his outstanding performance, he gets a 15% raise and a 10% bonus. Therefore, Clark's new salary should be ($5,000 × 1.15), or $5,750, and his bonus should be ($5,750 × 1.10), or $6,325. But if the Personnel department calculated the bonus before the Accounting department got to calculate his raise, Clark's bonus would be ($5,000 × 1.10), or $5,500 instead of $6,325. That's a significant difference.

Although the Emp table we have been using only contains a few rows of data, what if the table actually contained many thousands of rows of data? You know that Clark got a 15% raise and a 10% bonus, but what about all the other employees? Picture all this activity happening for each employee in the Emp table. Scott may have gotten a 12% raise and an 8% bonus. James might have excelled in his job and received a 20% raise and a 15% bonus.

With each employee potentially getting a different percentage raise and bonus, it's not likely that you can issue a single Update command to update all the records because the update would be unique for almost all the rows. Yet you do want to make sure that raises are applied prior to calculating the bonuses.

In an extreme case like this, you may have to update each record one at a time. You don't want to get halfway through only to find out that the bonuses have been calculated already. Earlier, you saw how an implicit lock was placed on a row as soon as a transaction was started. In this case, because we may find ourselves having to update one row at a time, there is a very good chance that we may get halfway through the update only to find that the bonuses have been calculated on the rows that were *not* locked.

A way to prevent this frustrating error would be to place a lock on the whole table. This can be done using the For Update clause. The For Update clause is used only in conjunction with a Select statement and allows you to lock all the rows that are part of the Select statement. In the scenario just described, you can prevent the Personnel department from updating any of the employees' records by placing a lock on all the rows. Once the lock is released by issuing either a Commit or Rollback command, Personnel can make their updates.

To see how this works, open two SQL*Plus sessions and position them as you did earlier, similar to Figure 7.1. Set it up with one screen to the left and one to the right. Connect both sessions to the Scott/Tiger account. This time, the screen on the left will be Accounting, which is the department in charge of calculating the raise. The screen on the right will be Personnel, the department in charge of calculating the bonuses. The first thing Accounting will want to do is lock the rows to prevent Personnel from updating them before it's time. Executing the following SQL command in Accounting's SQL*Plus session will lock the rows:

```
SELECT * FROM EMP FOR UPDATE;
```

Once you execute the Select command, your screen should look similar to Figure 7.8.

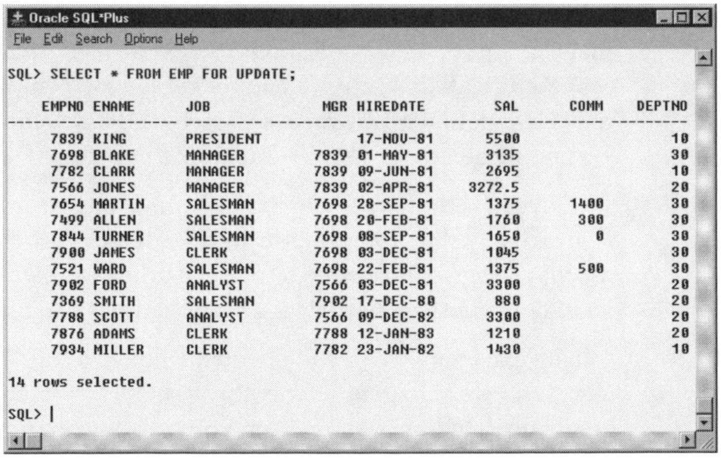

FIGURE 7.8
The results of the Select command

Notice that the result is exactly the same as if a Select command were executed without the For Update clause. The message just above the SQL prompt says that

14 rows have been selected. There is no mention of any row locking. That's because the locking is controlled by the database.

Once the rows are locked, Accounting can go through and edit each row of the Emp table without worrying that Personnel will update a row before Accounting finishes giving raises. Keep in mind that the lock only prevents others from updating—Personnel will still be able to query the data. Take a moment to execute a simple Select command from the Emp table. Do this by executing the following command in Personnel's SQL*Plus session:

```
SELECT * FROM EMP;
```

The results should match the results in Accounting's SQL*Plus session.

The NoWait Option

You now know that the database has a lock on all the rows in the Emp table and will continue to keep the records locked until Accounting commits or rolls back the transaction. You should also remember from the previous section that if any other session attempts to edit a row that is currently locked, that session will wait until the lock is free. The same holds true with the For Update clause. Because the For Update clause locks all the rows returned in the Select command, any other session that attempts to edit a locked row will wait indefinitely until the lock is released.

So, how is Personnel going to know when the locks are freed? If they attempt to execute `Select From Emp For Update` to lock the rows and make calculations for the employee bonuses, the SQL*Plus session will wait indefinitely and will essentially lock SQL*Plus so that no other SQL commands can be executed until the SQL prompt returns. Of course, a new SQL*Plus session can be opened, but it becomes rather cumbersome to have to open a new window every time a session goes into an indefinite wait. After all, there may be other Update, Insert or Select commands that can be processed in other tables instead of waiting.

The NoWait option, which is used in conjunction with the For Update clause, avoids having your session wait indefinitely. If you have been following along and stepped through the "The For Update Clause" section, you should have already executed the Select command with the For Update clause. If not, in Accounting's SQL*Plus session, execute the following SQL command:

```
SELECT * FROM EMP FOR UPDATE;
```

Once this is done, the next step is to use Personnel's SQL*Plus session to execute the following SQL command using the NoWait option:

```
SELECT * FROM EMP FOR UPDATE NOWAIT;
```

The result you see should be similar to Figure 7.9.

FIGURE 7.9
The results of the Select command

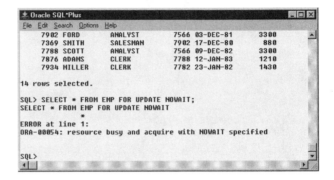

There are two things to notice with the NoWait option. First, notice the ORA-00054 error, which states that the resource is busy and that the NoWait option was specified. The database was unable to lock the resources (the rows of data) and is letting you know. At first, this may be misleading. Because an Oracle error was returned, you might think that an error has occurred when, in fact, the database was informing you that some resources are currently busy. The second and most important thing to notice is that the session did not wait indefinitely, and you were returned to an SQL prompt. You were allowed to continue to use the SQL*Plus session for additional work.

Avoiding Data Conflicts

Here are some of the possible data-contention problems that can occur with multiple users and an explanation of how to avoid them.

The Lost Update Condition

A *lost update condition* occurs when more than one transaction reads the same data and intends to update it. The first Update transaction may change data that the subsequent transaction is unaware of, so the changes will be based on the original data instead of the updated data. If all of the transactions use the For Update clause, only the first transaction will succeed because all the others will be locked out. If the For Update clause is not used, the possibility exists that the old data may be updated instead of updating from the most recent data.

The best way around a lost update is to either use the For Update clause, if you are planning to update a row, or to compare the original row values to the existing ones at the time the update is made (put them into the Where clause of the SQL statement). If the original values have changed, the update will fail, allowing you to re-query the row and refresh the data that the user has updated.

The Incorrect Summary Condition

An *incorrect summary condition* occurs when a first transaction has modified but not committed multiple record items. A second transaction reading this data would not get a consistent view of the data for the items that have been altered. This can be avoided because a transaction-consistent point-in-time Read view is always granted from the database. If this cannot be accomplished, the ORA-01555 error is raised to alert the user to re-query the data.

Because you know that a dirty read can't occur, you need only worry about lock contention when dealing with multi-user concurrency against a given database schema. The simplest approach is to keep the time that any given record will be locked to a minimum; this minimizes the potential for lock contention. You also need to write your application to account for the fact that lock contention might occur, particularly if you choose to not have the users wait for a lock to free itself. This second plan might be a viable alternative if you are certain that the time any given row will be locked will be very short. If you choose this approach, there is very little extra work that you need to do in your application because you are actually leveraging the underlying database behavior. You only need to write your application code so that you are able to ensure that a given row will not be locked for more than a moment.

One final thing to remember is that SQL DDL (Dictionary Data Language) commands (things that will create or destroy existing SQL objects, such as tables and indexes) will force an immediate commit for any outstanding SQL DML commands.

Transactions and Record Locking in OO4O

Now that you have experienced transactions in SQL*Plus, let's explore the mechanisms to control transactions and record locking that are available to you in Visual Basic using Oracle Objects for OLE (OO4O).

Take a moment to think of the potential hazards and conflicts that row locking can cause. Can you image how frustrating it can be for users who, on a daily basis, find themselves constantly waiting for rows to be unlocked by other users so that they can make their updates? Users refer to waiting for locks to release as "hanging." As programmers, you don't become very popular by creating applications that "hang." It is very important to take advantage of OO4O's exposed methods for initiating transactions and record locking so that you can limit record locking and avoid creating an application that frustrates the user.

OO4O offers a number of different ways for initiating transactions and for record locking. The following sections present the advantages and disadvantages of each method.

Record Locking Control

As discussed earlier in this chapter, the For Update clause in an SQL Select command will lock the rows returned as if they were currently being edited. This is a good way to force the locking of a range of rows, or even a single row, but care should be taken in the design of your application when using this method.

If you lock too great a range of rows or for too long a period of time, you run the very real risk that another user will attempt to update rows that are locked. Even if you are minimizing the time and row count for a locking operation, you still need to consider how you will handle a case where the user is prevented from acquiring a lock on a given set of data when another user has the rows locked for updating. You may decide to simply force the second user to wait for the lock to be released. You may opt to have an error returned that prompts the user to wait a moment and then try again. Or you may implement a more complicated algorithm.

Whatever you decide, when you are designing the application, consider how the availability of row locking will affect your users because when users are vying for the same set of data, they may not tolerate having a program hang for long periods of time. (And the definition of long is relative.) Your database design should probably not include any one table or set of data that is constantly under contention by a large number of users because this tends to drive down performance regardless of how you choose to handle it.

Solving hang-time issues requires giving just as careful consideration to the database side of the design (from a usability perspective) as you give to the user interface and client programming. Database performance can vary widely for any given set of data depending upon how the data is structured.

The Edit Method

One of the more common ways in which transactions are initiated and rows are subsequently locked using OO4O is through the Edit method of the OraDynaset object. (For more information on the OraDynaset object, refer to the Oracle Object online documentation.)

When the Edit method is called, OO4O initiates a transaction and locks the current row. Remember that in SQL*Plus, there are two ways that a row can be locked. One way is to issue an Update command. The row becomes locked as soon as the Update is executed. The other way is to execute a Select command with the For Update clause. This places a lock on all the rows returned by the Select command.

With OO4O, as soon as the Edit method of the OraDynaset object is executed, the current row in the dynaset is locked. As we have not issued any type of update yet, this leaves only one other way that OO4O can lock the row. If you guessed that OO4O issues a Select statement using the For Update clause, you are correct.

Minimizing Locked-Row Time

Because calling the Edit method of the OraDynaset object will automatically append a For Update clause onto the SQL statement used to build the dynaset, you need to consider the size of the recordset that will be affected. If you used a Select-style query to build the dynaset, it is almost a sure bet that you will have users frequently colliding when attempting to update. Also, remember that the Lock Wait mode of the Options flag that was used when the OpenDatabase method was called determines whether your program will wait while attempting to lock the rows, or whether it will return an ORA-00054 error if the rows are already locked by another user.

> One possible solution is to use multiple dynasets for scrolling and updating. This allows you to restrict a selection of rows, or perhaps a single row, to be locked at any given time. This approach requires that you keep the view that the user sees is synchronized with the actual database data. There are a number of alternatives for that, as well as other means to control the size of the selection for locking. It is seldom advisable to use a Select-style query to build your dynaset unless the table you will be editing is very small, or unless you do not intend to edit the dynaset used for the selection.

The following example gives you a closer look at the OO4O Edit method. To create this example, do the following:

1. Open Visual Basic.

2. Create a new executable by selecting Standard EXE from the New Project dialog box.

3. Add the Oracle Objects Type Library.

4. Drag and drop a button onto the form.

5. Double-click the button and add the OO4O code contained in Listing 7.1.

Listing 7.1 creates an OraDynaset object based on a Select command of the Dept table. Then it initiates a transaction by executing the Edit command. The Edit command issues a Select using the For Update clause to lock the current row in the dynaset.

Listing 7.1

```
1 Dim OraSession As OraSession
2 Dim OraDatabase As OraDatabase
3 Dim OraDynaset As OraDynaset
4 Set OraSession = CreateObject _
    ("OracleInProcServer.XOraSession")
5 Set OraDatabase = OraSession.OpenDatabase _
    ("v8i", "scott/tiger", 0&)
6 Set OraDynaset = OraDatabase.CreateDynaset _
    ("SELECT * FROM DEPT", 0&)
7 OraDynaset.Edit
8 MsgBox "You have just locked the following record:" & _
        Chr(13) & _
        "Deptno: " & OraDynaset.Fields("Deptno").Value &
        Chr(13) & _
        "Dname : " & OraDynaset.Fields("Dname").Value & _
        Chr(13) & _
        "Loc   : " & OraDynaset.Fields("Loc").Value
```

```
9 OraDynaset.Update
10 MsgBox "All locks should now be released."
```

Analysis

- Lines 1–3 are Dim statements for the objects being used to connect to the database and to create the dynaset.

- Line 4 creates the OraSession object.

- Line 5 creates an OraDatabase object and establishes the connection to the database.

- Line 6 creates the OraDynaset object based on the results returned from the SQL statement `Select From Dept`.

- Line 7 executes the Edit method for the OraDyanset object and issues a lock of the current row.

- Lines 8 displays the contents of the current row and suspends the process to illustrate an important point in the instructions. As you follow along with this example, you will see why this is done.

- Line 9 issues an Update command on the OraDynaset.

- Line 10 displays a message box to notify you that the lock on the row is released.

Before executing this example, open an SQL*Plus session, if one is not already open, and connect to the Scott/Tiger account. Once you have the SQL*Plus session connected, execute the Visual Basic code by pressing the F5 key. When the form appears, press the button. As soon as the button is pressed, OO4O will connect to the database, create the OraDynaset object, and execute the Edit method to issue a lock on the current row of the dynaset. Once the record is locked, a message box will appear (see Figure 7.10), displaying the current row in the dynaset, which also correlates to the row in the database that contains the lock.

FIGURE 7.10

A Locked Row message box

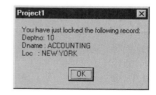

Once the message box appears, do *not* hit OK. Instead, go to the SQL*Plus session and execute the same Select command used in Listing 7.1:

```
SELECT * FROM DEPT;
```

The result should be similar to Figure 7.11.

FIGURE 7.11

The results of the Select From Dept command

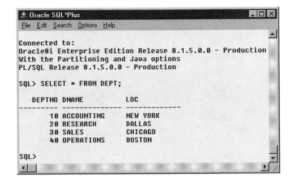

You should be able to match the row displayed in the message box from the Visual Basic example with one of the rows in the SQL*Plus session. In the example illustrated here, it is Department 10.

Once you have matched one of the rows in the message box, execute a Select command in the SQL*Plus session using the For Update clause to attempt to lock the same row. Because the current row is Department 10, SQL*Plus executed the following SQL command:

```
SELECT * FROM DEPT WHERE DEPTNO = 10 FOR UPDATE;
```

As you know from earlier discussions, because OO4O already established a lock on the row, the SQL*Plus session will wait until the lock is released. After executing the SQL command, your screen probably looks like Figure 7.12, which is an SQL*Plus session that is hanging.

FIGURE 7.12
SQL*Plus is waiting.

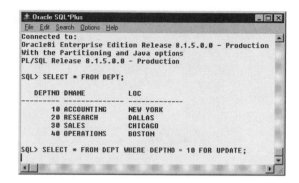

The next step is to go back to the message box display from the Visual Basic example (Figure 7.10) and click the OK button. As soon the button is clicked, the OO4O application executes the Update command, and the database lock is released. The next message box to appear, shown in Figure 7.13, states that the lock is now released.

FIGURE 7.13
The Locks Released mes-
sage box

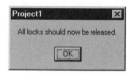

If you turn your attention back to the SQL*Plus session, you will notice that the Select command finally returned a result, and this SQL*Plus session now has a lock on the row. What you see should be similar to Figure 7.14. Before you forget, you should execute a Rollback command in your SQL*Plus session to free the lock from the row so that it can be used in the remaining examples.

FIGURE 7.14

SQL*Plus locks the row.

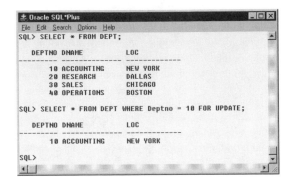

If you are interested in seeing the SQL statements used by OO4O to issue the lock, you can initiate the Net8 Tracing before running the Visual Basic example. Afterward, you can review the trace file that is produced, and you will see an SQL statement that is very similar to the following:

```
SELECT DEPTNO, DNAME, LOC FROM DEPT
    WHERE ROWID = :1 FOR UPDATE
```

Don't try to interpret the SQL statement. Just note that the Select statement contains the For Update clause. For more information on configuring Net8 Tracing, refer to any Oracle Net8 documentation.

The ExecuteSQL Method and AutoCommit Property

ExecuteSQL is a method of the OraDatabase object and a simple way to execute any non-Select SQL statement. The ExecuteSQL method is not a three-stop process like the Edit method is. The three steps for the Edit method are

1. Execute the Edit method.

2. Modify the data.

3. Execute the Update method.

Using the ExecuteSQL method, you simply pass in any Insert, Update, or Delete command. (By the way, the ExecuteSQL command is very useful in executing stored procedures. This is illustrated in Chapter 9.) If you are wondering how the data gets committed, don't. By default, the AutoCommit property of the OraDatabase object is set to True, which means that every SQL command executed with the ExecuteSQL method is automatically followed by a Commit command. This command ends the transaction and releases any locks held by the current session.

The advantage to using the ExecuteSQL method is the minimal amount of time that record(s) may be locked. Listing 7.2 illustrates the use of the ExecuteSQL method.

Listing 7.2

```
1 Dim OraSession As OraSession
2 Dim OraDatabase As OraDatabase
3 Set OraSession = CreateObject _
    ("OracleInProcServer.XOraSession")
4 Set OraDatabase = OraSession.OpenDatabase _
    ("v8i", "scott/tiger", 0&)
5 OraDatabase.ExecuteSQL _
    ("UPDATE DEPT SET DNAME = 'SUPPORT'" & _
        "WHERE DEPTNO = 40")
6 MsgBox "Update complete."
```

Analysis

- Lines 1–2 are Dim statements for the objects being used to connect.

- Line 3 creates the OraSession object.

- Line 4 creates an OraDatabase object and establishes the connection to the database.

- Line 5 calls the ExecuteSQL method.

- Line 6 displays a message box to notify you that the update is complete.

Line 5 executes the update and automatically issues a Commit command. By the time the next line of code is executed and the message box is displayed, the transaction is complete, and the record is updated. If you had an SQL*Plus session open and executed a Select From Dept SQL command, you would see the updated record shown in Figure 7.15.

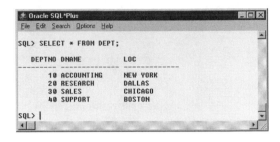

If the AutoCommit property is set to False, you will have to issue either a Commit or a Rollback command to end the transaction. Listing 7.3 illustrates setting the AutoCommit property to False and executing a Commit command to accept the update.

Listing 7.3

```
1  Dim OraSession As OraSession
2  Dim OraDatabase As OraDatabase
3  Set OraSession = CreateObject _
     ("OracleInProcServer.XOraSession")
4  Set OraDatabase = OraSession.OpenDatabase _
     ("v8i", "scott/tiger", 0&)
5  OraDatabase.AutoCommit = False
6  OraDatabase.ExecuteSQL _
     ("UPDATE DEPT SET LOC = 'ORLANDO'" & _
        " WHERE DEPTNO = 40")
7  MsgBox "Update complete."
8  OraDatabase.ExecuteSQL ("COMMIT")
9  MsgBox "Commit complete."
```

Analysis

- Lines 1–2 are Dim statements for the objects being used to connect.

- Line 3 creates the OraSession object.

- Line 4 creates an OraDatabase object and establishes the connection to the database.

- Line 5 sets the AutoCommit property to False.

- Line 6 calls the ExecuteSQL method to update the Dept table.

- Line 7 displays a message box to notify you that the update is complete.

- Line 8 executes the Commit command to end the transaction and to commit the data to the database.

- Line 9 displays a message box to notify you that the Commit operation is complete.

As you can see in line 5, the AutoCommit property is set to False, and you are now required to explicitly end any transaction with either a Commit or a Rollback command. Line 6 executes the update and sets the Loc field in the Dept table to a new value. Line 7 displays a message box (Figure 7.16) once the update is complete.

FIGURE 7.16
The Update Complete
message box

In the previous example, by the time this message box appeared, you were able to view the updated row in SQL*Plus. This time, you won't see any changes because the AutoCommit feature is turned off. In fact, if you execute a `Select From Dept` command in your SQL*Plus session, your results would be the same as in Figure 7.15. Once the OK button is clicked in the message box (as seen in Figure 7.16), the ExecuteSQL method processes the Commit command to end the transaction. Line 9 of Listing 7.3 will then display a second message box informing you that the commit was complete (see Figure 7.17).

FIGURE 7.17
The Commit Complete
message box

Now, if you execute a `Select From Dept` command in your SQL*Plus session, you will see the changes immediately. It should look like Figure 7.18.

FIGURE 7.18
The results of the Select
From Dept command after
the Commit command
is complete

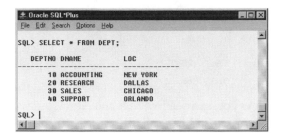

Controlling Transactions

The *OraSession object* exposes the transactional control interfaces. In the newer releases of OO4O, this method is also exposed on the OraDatabase and OraConnection objects. This is a logical place for these to be because the transactions are typically tied to a given session on the RDBMS.

Meta-transaction control or transactional control across multiple sessions or databases is typically done with a Transaction Process Monitor (TPM) product, such as Encina, Tuxedo, or Microsoft Transaction Server (MTS).

NOTE   You are allowed to maintain only one transaction per session.

The BeginTrans Method

The *BeginTrans method* of the OraSession object (or OraConnection/OraDatabase) will explicitly begin a transaction for the session. As with any transaction, this transaction must end with either a Commit or Rollback command. When you use the BeginTrans method to begin a transaction or to end the transaction, you must use one of the following:

The CommitTrans method   To end the transaction and commit any changes to the database.

The ResetTrans method   To end the transaction, but instead of accepting any changes to the data, changes are ignored.

The Rollback method   To end the transaction and ignore any changes. Although the use of this method is valid, it's primarily used for dynasets that were created based on the OraDynaset object of the Oracle Data Control.

With the BeginTrans method, you are only allowed to maintain one transaction per session. This means that you cannot issue a second BeginTrans method to start a second transaction without ending the first transaction. Attempting to issue a second transaction before ending the current transaction will result in an "OIP-04101: Transaction already in progress" error message.

Using the BeginTrans is quite simple. Listing 7.4 shows how to implement this method.

Listing 7.4

```
1   Dim OraSession As OraSession
2   Dim OraDatabase As OraDatabase
3   Dim OraDynaset As OraDynaset
4   Set OraSession = CreateObject _
        ("OracleInProcServer.XOraSession")
5   Set OraDatabase = OraSession.OpenDatabase _
        ("v8i", "scott/tiger", 0&)
6   Set OraDynaset = OraDatabase.CreateDynaset _
        ("SELECT * FROM EMP WHERE EMPNO = 7900", 0&)
7   OraSession.BeginTrans
8   OraDynaset.Edit
9       OraDynaset.Fields("SAL").Value = 2000
10  OraDynaset.Update
11  MsgBox "Check the data."
12  OraSession.CommitTrans
13  MsgBox "Commit complete."
```

Analysis

- Lines 1–3 are Dim statements for the objects being used to connect to the database and to execute the example.

- Line 4 creates the OraSession object.

- Line 5 creates an OraDatabase object and establishes the connection to the database.

- Line 6 creates an OraDynaset object that is essentially a single record from the Emp table.

- Line 7 initiates the transaction using the BeginTrans method.

- Line 8 invokes the Edit method of the OraDynaset object for the current row in the dynaset.

- Line 9 updates the salary field (Sal) to 2000.

- Line 10 executes the Update method of the OraDynaset object.

- Line 11 displays a message box instructing you to check the data. As you follow along, you will see why.

- Line 12 ends the transaction with the CommitTrans method.

- Line 13 displays a message box informing you that the Commit operation is now complete.

Line 7 initiates the BeginTrans method followed by the Edit method of the dynaset. As always, the Edit command initiates the Select For Update command on the current row. But this time, when the Update command (line 10) is executed, the data is not committed. As a result, the change is not viewable by other users (as it was before), and the row is still locked. Once the CommitTrans method is executed, the change is accepted, and the lock is released.

To get a better understanding of how the BeginTrans method affects transactions, you should open an SQL*Plus session and log into the same Scott/Tiger account as you did for the OO4O example. Before running the example, execute the following SQL in SQL*Plus to see the salary data (Sal field) before the update:

```
SELECT * FROM EMP WHERE EMPNO = 7900;
```

Once you have Visual Basic set up, your SQL*Plus session open, and you have viewed the data, execute the example in Listing 7.4. Once the "Check the data" message box appears, execute the previous line of SQL again to view the data. You will notice that the value has not changed. The value of the Sal field is the same as the first time that you executed the SQL.

You'll remember from "The ExecuteSQL Method and the AutoCommit Property" section that as soon as the Update command is executed, the transaction is finished, the locks were released, and the data was visible by any user who queried the table. But this time, it's not visible.

Because a transaction was explicitly started with the BeginTrans method, the transaction will have to be explicitly ended with either the Rollback method or the CommitTrans method. Once you click the OK button on the "Check the data" message box, the CommitTrans method is executed, and you'll see another message box informing you that the Commit operation is complete. Once you see this message box, if you execute the Select From Emp Where Empno = 7900 command again in SQL*Plus, you will see the change. This is because the Commit-Trans method ends the transactions and commits the changes to the database.

TIP

If you have enlisted the OraDatabase object for this session with MTS and it is part of a global MTS transaction in progress, the CommitTrans method has no effect because the MTS transaction will override any local calls.

The RollbackTrans Method

The *RollbackTrans method* of the OraSession object (or OraConnection/OraDatabase) will explicitly end a transaction for the session. As discussed earlier, multiple calls to the BeginTrans method without a subsequent Commit or Rollback command will generate an OIP-4101 "A BeginTrans was specified while a transaction is already in progress" error.

NOTE

OO4O does not currently support setting or using transaction savepoints. *Savepoints* can be thought of as a way to roll back portions of a transaction.

When explicitly creating transactions with the BeginTrans method, you are directly issuing the SQL statements to the database and not using the built-in SQL engine provided by OO4O. There are a few important differences to note in the way other tools, such as SQL*Plus, behave with transactions and the way that OO4O will behave when using the BeginTrans method of transaction control.

NOTE

If you issue explicit transactions via the ExecuteSQL method, as mentioned earlier, OO4O will behave just as SQL*Plus does.

For instance, imagine a scenario where an Update command has failed due to invalid data or due to a constraint violation. Although no data in the row has changed, a lock still exists on the row when executed through OO4O. But, in SQL*PLUS, a failed SQL statement will not issue any locks. The OO4O code in

Listing 7.5 demonstrates a simple scenario in SQL*Plus to see why the behavior differs.

Listing 7.5 illustrates executing an Update command that fails in SQL*Plus. With a failed update, the record does not get locked. If you don't already have two SQL*Plus sessions open, do so now. You may want to position one on the left and the other on the right. The SQL*Plus session on the left will be referred to as User 1 and the second session as User 2.

User 1 attempts to update the Dept table to change the department number from 10 to 15. This update will fail because of a database constraint that prevents department numbers from changing if there are matching values in another table. Because there are rows of data for employees in the Emp table that reference Department 10, the database is smart enough (based on the constraint) not to allow a user to change this number because it could potentially damage the integrity of the data. To change the department from 10 to 15, execute the following SQL in User 1's SQL*Plus session:

```
UPDATE DEPT SET DEPTNO = 15 WHERE DEPTNO = 10;
```

The result of the Update command should be similar to the following bit of code and is due to the fact that rows of data for employees in the Emp table still have references to Department 10.

```
ERROR at line 1:
ORA-02292: integrity constraint (SCOTT.EMP_FOREIGN_KEY)
violated - child record found
```

To verify that there are no locks on the row that are causing the update to fail, in User 2's SQL*Plus session, enter the following SQL:

```
SELECT * FROM DEPT WHERE DEPTNO = 10 FOR UPDATE;
```

You should get one row returned and a lock placed on that row. Remember, if a lock existed, User 2's session would not have returned any results. Instead, it would have waited indefinitely until User 1 issued a Commit or Rollback command.

Now that you have verified that the failed SQL statement did not lock the row in SQL*Plus, let's take a look at how and why OO4O differs. Before doing so, you should release the lock issued by User 2's SQL statement by either closing the session or issuing a Commit or Rollback command.

Listing 7.5 illustrates executing an Update command that fails in OO4O. As you step through this example, you'll verify the failed SQL, verify the lock, and see how you may want to avoid locking rows that you may not be updating. Remember that keeping a row locked unnecessarily is counterproductive, especially when other users may be waiting to update that particular row.

For the example in Listing 7.5, the scenario will be the same as before when you tested with SQL*Plus: User 1 attempts to update the Dept table to change the department number from 10 to 15. You should account for this type of possibility in the error-handling routines that you program for your application. Most likely, you will want to roll back any changes if they were incomplete, but perhaps your application is built in such a way that you want to commit the changes that were completed successfully. The example in Listing 7.5 illustrates how, in OO4O, a failed update (one that results in a constraint violation) still places a lock on the row.

Listing 7.5

```
1    Dim OraSession As OraSession
2    Dim OraDatabase As OraDatabase
3    Dim OraDynaset As OraDynaset
4    Set OraSession = CreateObject _
     ("OracleInProcServer.XOraSession")
5    Set OraDatabase = OraSession.OpenDatabase _
     ("v8i", "scott/tiger", 0&)
6    Set OraDynaset = OraDatabase.CreateDynaset _
     ("SELECT * FROM DEPT WHERE DEPTNO = 10", 0&)
7    OraSession.BeginTrans
8    On Error GoTo GetErrorMessage
9    OraDynaset.Edit
10       OraDynaset.Fields("DEPTNO").Value = 15
11   OraDynaset.Update
12   MsgBox "Continue processing after the error"
13   'There could be additional code here.
14   OraSession.CommitTrans
15   MsgBox "Commit complete."
16   Exit Sub
17   GetErrorMessage:
18     If (OraDatabase.LastServerErr = 2292) Then
19         MsgBox OraDatabase.LastServerErrText
20         'You may opt to end the transaction with a
     'OraSession.Rollback command to free the lock.
           'Then start a new transaction using the
           'OraSession.BeginTrans
21       OraSession.Rollback
22       OraSession.BeginTrans
23     End If
24     Resume Next
```

Analysis

- Lines 1–3 are Dim statements for the objects being used to connect to the database and to execute the example.

- Line 4 creates the OraSession object.

- Line 5 creates an OraDatabase object and establishes the connection to the database.

- Line 6 creates an OraDynaset object based on Department 10.

- Line 7 initiates the transaction using the BeginTrans method.

- Line 8 is an On Error command that directs processing to another section of code whenever an error occurs.

- Line 9 invokes the Edit method of the OraDynaset object for the current row in the dynaset.

- Line 10 attempts to update the department number to 15.

- Line 11 executes the Update method of the OraDynaset object.

- Line 12 displays a message box illustrating that processing is continuing even after encountering the error.

- Line 13 is a comment informing you that additional code can be included here.

- Line 14 ends the transaction with the CommitTrans method.

- Line 15 displays a message box informing you that the Commit operation is now complete.

- Line 16 exits the subroutine. Without this line, processing would continue on to the error routine.

- Line 17 is the label for the error-handling routine.

- Line 18 is the If statement to specifically trap the Oracle error that pertains to the violation constraint.

- Line 19 displays a message box with the error text.

- Line 20 is a comment to inform you that you have unlimited possibilities on what you can do.

- Line 21 releases the lock and ends the transaction.

- Line 22 creates a new transaction.

- Line 23 ends the If statement.

- Line 24 instructs the program to resume processing on the next line after the line that caused the error.

Listing 7.5 starts off like most others and builds the OraDyanset object in line 6 using the record from the Dept table where the department number is 10. This is the specific record you are trying to modify. Once the dynaset is created, line 7 initiates the transaction by executing the BeginTrans method. Line 8 is very important because it will redirect processing whenever an error occurs in this module. (For more information on Error Handling, see Chapter 6.) If line 8 were not included in this particular sample run, you would see a default Error message box with a message similar to what you see in Figure 7.19.

FIGURE 7.19
The default Error
message box

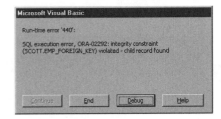

At the least, the default message box allows you to step back into the code by pressing the Debug button. When the application is run as a stand-alone executable, the dialog box displayed simply contains an OK button, as shown in Figure 7.20.

FIGURE 7.20
The standard Error
message box

In either instance, without using the On Error command in line 7, you get the default error handling, which is to display a message box with the error and then quit processing. The On Error command allows you to control the error handling. In Listing 7.5, you forward control to the GetErrorMessage label. For more information on error handling, refer to Chapter 6.

By the time you get to line 9 of Listing 7.5, you know that a transaction has already been initiated, and any locks applied will be held until they are released. If you think back to the SQL*Plus example, no records were locked when the Update command failed; but OO4O acts differently, and line 9 is the key. As discussed earlier in this chapter, once the Edit method of the OraDynaset object is executed, OO4O sends a Select For Update command to the database and locks the row. You can verify this through the Net8 Tracing. Even before any attempt is made to update any data, the record is already locked. Next, line 10 assigns the new value to the Deptno field, and line 11 executes the Update command, which fails due to the constraint violation. At this time, processing continues at the GetErrorMessage label (line 17). Line 18 uses the LastServerErr method to look specifically for error number 2292 "ORA-02292 – integrity constraint violated." Looking for specific errors can be very beneficial because it allows you to apply specific responses to specific errors. Here, we decided to display the error text (line 19) to illustrate that the error encountered is what was expected. The error text returned is shown in Figure 7.21.

FIGURE 7.21

The custom Error message box

Once the message box is displayed, take a moment to open an SQL*Plus session, if you don't already have one open, and execute the following SQL:

```
SELECT * FROM DEPT WHERE DEPTNO = 10 FOR UPDATE;
```

Notice that the SQL*Plus session will end up waiting indefinitely because of the lock applied by OO4O when the Edit method was executed. Even though the update failed, the important thing to note is that the record is still locked, which is different behavior than what you saw in SQL*Plus.

The comment in line 20 lets you know that here is where you determine how to handle the error. Incorporating error handling allows a large number of possibilities in your code. Here are just a few things you can do. For example, you can implement any of the following:

- Issue a Rollback command to free the lock. Don't forget that this will also roll back any other updates that occurred in this transaction.

- Issue a CommitTrans method to free the lock and commit any changes. This too will affect any other updates that occurred in this transaction.

- After the Rollback or Commit command, exit the subroutine.

- After the Rollback or Commit command, continue processing.

- Don't issue any Commit or Rollback command and exit the routine.

- Don't issue any Commit or Rollback command but continue processing.

As you can see, many possibilities are available when implementing error handling. This is why it's very important to have a thorough understanding of not only the data, but also the code and what you are trying to do. Blindly issuing Commit or Rollback commands in the error-handling routine can have adverse effects if data is unexpectedly changed or lost.

In Listing 7.5, I opted to implement the fourth bulleted item:

- After the Rollback or Commit command, continue processing.

We know that no other updates were attempted, so it's safe to issue a Rollback command to free the lock. We do this in line 21. Because the update failed, there is no reason to keep the record locked and prevent other users from making changes. Also, as there is the possibility of making additional updates, a new transaction was initiated in line 22 by calling the BeginTrans method.

Line 23 ends the If condition, and line 24 resumes processing back to line 12. The message box displayed by line 12 illustrates how you are able to resume processing on the line following the line of code that introduced the error. By the time the message box is displayed, the lock is released, and a new transaction has been introduced.

Line 13 simply indicates that, if need be, you can add additional code to continue processing and make any further updates. Line 14 acts as though there is additional code and ends the transaction by issuing a CommitTrans method. If any additional processing or updates occur, any locks will be released, and the data will be updated.

Line 15 displays a message box that notifies you that the Commit operation is complete, the locks are released, and any updates made are now visible to other users.

Line 16 exits the subroutine. Without it, the code would continue processing through the error routine. In this case, it would not have any effect because you are looking for a specific error. If the If condition in line 18 did not exist, the code would continue to process and eventually would display the message box in line 19.

The last error message would appear, as shown in Figure 7.21. This can be misleading because you have already committed the changes successfully, yet you keep getting integrity constraint violations. For more information on Error Handling, refer to Chapter 6.

If you have not already guessed it, one of the bigger decisions that you have to make is not only how to handle transactions and locking in general, but also how to handle them whenever errors occur. As you just saw, there are a number of possibilities, and what may work best for you may not be best for someone else. The key is that you must know your user community. You should have an idea of how many end-users will not only be accessing the application, but also how many will have access at the same time. This bit of information will have a significant bearing on your thinking about transaction and record locking.

Data Conflicts

One of the items discussed in Chapter 2 is the OraDynaset object. Chapter 2 talked about how OO4O caches the data on the client side and the advantages of doing so. One of the issues that can arise when caching data is the potential for the data on the server side to be changed by another user. If this happens, the data in the client-side cache would not be a true representation of the data contained in the database.

Executing queries or running reports is usually not an issue because their purpose is to reflect data at the point in time when they were executed. In an environment that executes queries or running, you would not have to consider changing the underlining data unless your application specifications require it. The difficulty arises when you execute the Edit method of the OraDynaset object on a row in the dynaset where the corresponding row in the database has changed.

Listing 7.6 illustrates how this situation may come about and offers suggestions about how to work with this type of conflict.

Listing 7.6

```
1  Dim OraSession As OraSession
2  Dim OraDatabase As OraDatabase
3  Dim OraDynaset As OraDynaset
4  Set OraSession = CreateObject _
      ("OracleInProcServer.XOraSession")
5  Set OraDatabase = OraSession.OpenDatabase _
      ("v8i", "scott/tiger", 0&)
```

```
6   Set OraDynaset = OraDatabase.CreateDynaset _
        ("select * FROM EMP WHERE EMPNO = 7900", 0&)
7   MsgBox "Now modify the row through SQL*Plus"
8   On Error GoTo GetErrorMessage
9   OraDynaset.Edit
10      OraDynaset.Fields("JOB").Value = "MANAGER"
11  OraDynaset.Update
12  MsgBox "Update complete."
13  Exit Sub
14  GetErrorMessage:
15    If (OraDatabase.LastServerErr = 0) Then
16        If (MsgBox(Error$ & Chr(13) & _
                 "Would you like to try again?", _
                 vbYesNo) = vbYes) Then
17            OraDynaset.Refresh
18            Resume
19        Else
20            Exit Sub
21        End If
22    End If
```

Analysis

- Lines 1–3 are Dim statements for the objects being used to connect to the database and to execute the example.

- Line 4 creates the OraSession object.

- Line 5 creates an OraDatabase object and establishes the connection to the database.

- Line 6 creates an OraDynaset object based on the row of data for the employee in the Emp table whose employee number is 7900.

- Line 7 displays the message box instructing you to modify the same row in the SQL*Plus session.

- Line 8 is an On Error command that directs processing to another section of code whenever an error occurs.

- Line 9 invokes the Edit method of the OraDynaset object for the current row in the dynaset.

- Line 10 attempts to update the Job field for the record.

- Line 11 executes the Update method of the OraDynaset object.

- Line 12 displays a message box illustrating that processing is continuing even after the error is encountered.

- Line 13 exits the subroutine. Without this line, processing would continue on to the error routine.

- Line 14 is the label for the error-handling routine.

- Line 15 is the If statement to see whether any Oracle error has occurred.

- Line 16 displays the actual error message in a message box, along with the text asking you whether you wish to try again.

- Line 17 issues the Refresh command for the dynaset.

- Line 18 resumes processing on the same line that caused the error.

- Line 19 Else statement for the inner If statement.

- Line 20 exits this subroutine if you do not wish to attempt the update.

- Line 21 ends the inner If statement.

- Line 22 ends the outer If statement.

Once Listing 7.6 is set up, and before you actually execute the code, you should open an SQL*Plus session, which will be used to modify the data. Once the OO4O code is executed, a message box will display instructing you to modify the data in SQL*Plus. When it does, execute the following code:

```
UPDATE EMP SET SAL = 1500 WHERE EMPNO = 7900;
```

Once the row is updated, don't forget to commit the change. Not doing so will cause the application to wait for the lock to be released, and that is not what we are trying to illustrate. So, once the row is updated, issue the commit as follows:

```
COMMIT;
```

Once the row is updated through SQL*Plus, in the Visual Basic message box, click the OK button to continue processing. At this time, the client-side cache still has the original data, and the row in the database contains updated data. As the application continues, line 8 will redirect processing to the GetErrorMessage label whenever an error occurs.

The key to this example is line 9, which attempts to edit the current row in the dynaset. This is the same row that has been updated and committed in SQL*Plus. The Edit command is executed and, as you have seen before, a Select For Update command is executed. If this command is successful, what happens next is important. Once the Select For Update command is executed, OO4O compares the data returned from the database with the data that it currently has in the cache. If the data does not match (in this case, it doesn't), an OIP error occurs. Because of the error, processing in the example continues on line 14, which is the error-handling routine.

What happens in the error routine will more than likely vary. It's the turning point in the application. This routine controls whether processing continues or simply stops. Perhaps you don't want to make the decision here. Why not allow the person executing the application to decide what to do next. To create this option, you have to provide the proper prompts for the end user to respond to, as well as the appropriate code to implement the user's request. More information on this type of error handling can be found in Chapter 6.

When entering the error routine, one of the first things you can assume in your code is that an error occurred. The first thing this routine should do is to check to see whether the error was being returned from the database or from the application. In this example, the LastServerErr method (line 15) returns 0 because the Select For Update command executed successfully. This must mean that the error happened on the client side, either in Visual Basic or in OO4O. The Error$ returns the error message. Notice that the message box can be a very handy tool. First, it displays the error message and asks the user if they would like to try again. Second, notice that this time, the message box does not provide just an OK button but rather a message box with a Yes and a No button (see Figure 7.22). In the message box, the first line is the text from the Error$ variable, and the second line is the prompt that you added to find out what the user wants to do. Then, of course, you have the two buttons underneath the text.

FIGURE 7.22
The custom Error
message box

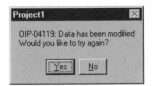

If you click No, processing continues on line 19, moves to line 20, and exits the subroutine. If you select the Yes button, processing continues on line 17, which executes the Refresh method of the OraDynaset object. This will recreate the dynaset based on the original SQL statement used in the CreateDynaset method (line 6), synchronizing the client-side data with the data in the database. Once this is done, the Resume command is executed (line 18), instructing the program to continue processing on the same line of code that originally caused the error. This happens to be line 9. The Edit method is executed, and the row is locked. This time, when the data is returned from the database, it is compared to the data on the client, and they should match.

Processing continues with line 10, which updates the record and then updates the changes with the Update command in line 11. Line 12 displays a message box notifying you that the Update operation is complete. Line 13 exits the subroutine.

Connecting with the NoWait Option

As previous sections illustrated, you have the capability of appending the NoWait options to Select SQL statements. But the *ORADB_NOWAIT* option has not been covered. This option can be used as one of the options available when executing the OpenDatabase method of the OraSession or OraServer object. (For a complete list of available options, refer to the OO4O online documentation.)

The ORADB_NOWAIT option for the connection objects essentially appends a NoWait option to the end of Select SQL statements, such as the ones used to create OraDynaset objects. Listing 7.7 illustrates connecting with the NoWait option.

Listing 7.7

```
1   Dim OraSession As OraSession
2   Dim OraDatabase As OraDatabase
3   Dim OraDynaset As OraDynaset
4   Set OraSession = CreateObject _
      ("OracleInProcServer.XOraSession")
5   Set OraDatabase = OraSession.OpenDatabase _
      ("v8i", "scott/tiger", &H2&)
6   Set OraDynaset = OraDatabase.CreateDynaset _
      ("select * FROM EMP WHERE EMPNO = 7900", 0&)
7   MsgBox "Now lock the row through SQL*Plus"
8   On Error GoTo GetErrorMessage
9   OraDynaset.Edit
10      OraDynaset.Fields("SAL").Value = SAL + 1
11  OraDynaset.Update
12  MsgBox "Update complete."
13  Exit Sub
14  GetErrorMessage:
15    If (OraDatabase.LastServerErr <> 0) Then
16        If (MsgBox(OraDatabase.LastServerErrText & _
              Chr(13) & "Would you like to try again?", _
              vbYesNo) = vbYes) Then
```

```
17          Resume
18      Else
19          Exit Sub
20      End If
21  End If
```

Analysis

- Lines 1–3 are Dim statements for the objects being used to connect to the database.

- Line 4 creates the OraSession object.

- Line 5 creates an OraDatabase object and establishes the connection to the database using the NoWait option.

- Line 6 creates an OraDynaset object based on the row of data for the employee in the Emp table whose employee number is 7900.

- Line 7 displays the message box instructing you to lock either the same row or simply execute a `Select From Emp For Update` statement to lock all the rows.

- Line 8 is an On Error command that directs processing to another section of code whenever an error occurs.

- Line 9 invokes the Edit method of the OraDynaset object for the current row in the dynaset.

- Line 10 attempts to update the salary field (Sal) for the record.

- Line 11 executes the Update method of the OraDynaset object.

- Line 12 displays a message box illustrating that the update was completed.

- Line 13 exits the subroutine. Without this line, processing would continue on to the error routine.

- Line 14 is the label for the error-handling routine.

- Line 15 is the If statement to see whether any Oracle error has occurred.

- Line 16 displays the error message in a message box, along with the text asking if you wish to try again.

- Line 17 issues the Resume command to continue processing on the same line that caused the error.

- Line 18 is the Else statement for the inner If statement.

- Line 19 exits this subroutine if you do not wish to attempt the update again.

- Line 20 ends the inner If statement.

- Line 21 ends the outer If statement.

The key to Listing 7.7 is line 5, which executes the OpenDatabase method. Notice that the last parameter being passed is different from what you have seen in previous examples in this chapter.

When this example is executed, line 7 displays a message box that instructs you to lock the row in the database. You should do so in your SQL*Plus session. If one is currently not open, open one so that you can follow along with the example. Because the dynaset is created based on the row of data for the employee whose employee number (Empno field of the Emp table) equals 7900, you can execute one of the following SQL statements to lock the row. The first SQL statement is as follows:

```
SELECT * FROM EMP WHERE EMPNO = 7900 FOR UPDATE;
```

This SQL statement locks only the one record. The second SQL statement locks the entire table:

```
SELECT * FROM EMP FOR UPDATE;
```

After the lock is applied, go back to the message box and click the OK button to continue processing. Once processing gets to line 9 and the Edit method is executed, it should result in a "ORA-00054: resource busy" error message and force processing to continue at line 14, which is the error-handling routine.

Line 15 checks to see that the error returned is from the database. In this scenario, it is. Processing continues at line 16 and displays a message box with the error message—your own prompt asking the user if they would like to try again. Instead of just an OK button, the message box provides both a Yes and a No button. Figure 7.23 illustrates the message box.

FIGURE 7.23
The custom Error message
box—No Wait

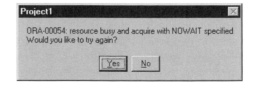

Using Message Boxes Effectively

A message box provides control for the user. The user can choose to continue to update the record or to quit. Keep in mind that you don't have to prompt the user every time. Here is your chance to be creative! For instance, you don't even have to let the user know that a lock occurred. The code can continue to loop through and attempt the updates without prompting the user. Another option is to prompt the user after every three or five attempts. This would actually be more efficient than the design in Listing 7.7, which prompts the user every time.

The important thing is that you must know the users and the data that they will be accessing. For example, what if your application is run in an environment where not only do frequent updates occur, but the users also tend to lock rows for long periods of time? This would not be a good time to set the application to loop continuously while attempting to update a record without notifying the user of the lock. This causes the application to simulate waiting indefinitely (or as we discussed before, a "hang"), which is not appreciated by the users.

On the other hand, if your environment frequently incurs locking conflicts, but these conflicts are very brief, it may be even more frustrating to the user to always be prompted to try again. In such a case, it may be best to loop a few times before prompting. This way, the only time the user is prompted is if there appears to be a serious locking issue.

If you choose the No button, the subroutine will exit. Clicking the Yes button resumes processing on the row that initially caused the error. In Listing 7.7, this is line 9. If the lock still exists, the processing continues the error-handling routine, and the user is prompted to try again. This process continues until either the lock is released or the user decides not to make any more attempts and clicks the No button.

Once a lock is acquired, the record is updated (line 10) and committed (line 11). A message box is then displayed, notifying you that the update is complete.

DDL Automatically Commits

One extremely important topic to discuss is the fact that issuing any Data Dictionary Language (DDL) with the ExecuteSQL method automatically issues a Commit command. That fact that commits are issued when executing these types of SQL statements has nothing to do with OO4O. It is strictly functionality that is built into the database. The Oracle database issues an implicit commit before and after any DDL statement.

DDL pertains to SQL statements that create or alter objects in the database, or SQL statements that grant or revoke privileges and roles. For more information, you may want to refer to the *Oracle8i SQL Reference Manual* and search the index under DDL to locate the specific section. In fact, you should find a table that lists all possible DDL statements.

If you are still unsure as to why this is an issue, take a look at Listing 7.8. It simulates a user (Scott) who, as a joke, decides to give himself a 50% raise. Scott is thinking that because the AutoCommit property of the OraDatabase is set to False and he is prompted for confirmation before committing, he is safe from actually applying his changes. The analysis explains how the codes takes you through safely the first time, but on the second and third time around, an ExecuteSQL method is included to execute a DDL statement showing the potential pitfall.

Listing 7.8

```
1  Dim OraSession As OraSession
2  Dim OraDatabase As OraDatabase
3  Set OraSession = CreateObject _
     ("OracleInProcServer.XOraSession")
4  Set OraDatabase = OraSession.OpenDatabase _
     ("v8i", "scott/tiger", 0&)
5  OraDatabase.AutoCommit = False
6  OraDatabase.ExecuteSQL _
     ("UPDATE EMP SET SAL = SAL * 1.50" & _
       "WHERE EMPNO = 7788")
7  'OraDatabase.ExecuteSQL _
     ("CREATE TABLE TEMP(FIELD1 NUMBER)")
8  If (MsgBox("Are you sure you want to commit?", _
               vbYesNo) = vbNo) Then
9        Exit Sub
10   End If
11  OraDatabase.ExecuteSQL ("COMMIT")
12  MsgBox "Update complete."
```

Analysis

- Lines 1–2 are Dim statements for the objects being used to connect to the database.

- Line 3 creates the OraSession object.

- Line 4 creates an OraDatabase object and establishes the connection to the database.

- Line 5 sets the AutoCommit property to False.

- Line 6 calls the ExecuteSQL method to give Scott a 50% raise.

- Line 7 is currently commented and is the DDL statement that you will uncomment and execute the second and third time through this example.

- Line 8 displays a message box prompting the user to commit the transaction.

- Line 9 exits the subroutine if the user clicks the No button on the message box displayed in line 8.

- Line 10 ends the If statement.

- Line 11 executes a commit.

- Line 12 displays a message box notifying you that the update is complete.

In order to illustrate the example in Listing 7.8 correctly, make sure that line 7 remains a comment for the first execution. To verify when the data is actually updated and rolled back, open an SQL*Plus session, if one is not already open, and connect to the Scott account.

Before executing the sample, take a look a Scott's current salary by executing the following SQL command in the SQL*Plus session:

```
SELECT * FROM EMP WHERE EMPNO = 7788;
```

Notice that once the example is executed, line 5 explicitly turns off the Auto-Commit property, forcing an explicit commit after updating Scott's salary. Processing continues on line 6, which increases Scott's salary by 50%. The first time the example is executed, line 7 should be commented out and, therefore, is not a factor. Line 8 is actually the next line executed and displays the message box shown in Figure 7.24.

FIGURE 7.24

The "Are you sure you want to commit?" message box

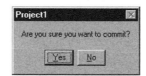

Before clicking the Yes or No button on the message box, go back to the SQL*Plus session and execute another Select From Emp Where Empno = 7788

SQL statement in SQL*Plus to ensure that the data has not changed. Once verified, click the No button on the message box so that Scott won't get in trouble for giving himself such a large raise.

Before executing the code the second time, remove the comment from line 7.

```
OraDatabase.ExecuteSQL _
    ("CREATE TABLE TEMP (FIELD1 NUMBER)")
```

Now run the code again. As before, the AutoCommit property is set to False, and the ExecuteSQL method once again issues an Update command to increase Scott's salary. This time, when line 7 is processed and the DDL statement is processed to create the Temp table, the database issues an implicit commit. If you are following what is happening, you know that even before line 8 is processed and the message box is displayed, the data has already been committed. To verify, once the message box (as seen in Figure 7.24) is displayed, execute the Select From Emp Where Empno = 7788 SQL statement in SQL*Plus.

If you run Listing 7.8 a third time, something a bit different happens, but the outcome will be the same. When you rerun the example and line 7 is processed, you end up with the following error because the table was already created from the previous execution:

```
ORA-00955: name already used by an existing object
```

This time, the example produces an error. If you execute the Select From Emp Where Empno = 7788 SQL statement in SQL*Plus, you will notice that once again the update was indeed committed. Boy, is Scott in a heap of trouble.

Remember, implicit commits are issued *before* and *after* each DDL statement. So, even though the Create statement failed before completion, the implicit commit that occurs before the DDL was executed actually updated the data.

Summary

This chapter discussed how transactions are initiated and ended, as well as row locking and its potential conflicts. The OO4O examples illustrated the different ways that transactions are implemented and how to handle record-locking issues with Visual Basic's error-handling routines. (For more information on Error Handling, refer to Chapter 6.)

If you come away with one thing from this chapter, it should be that before writing your OO4O application, you must know your user community, as well as the data. The number of users running your application and the frequency of updates will affect how you write your code. OO4O provides you with the tools to customize your application for your environment's needs.

chapter 8

Working with Objects and Collections

- Creating object types in the database

- Using collections types in the database

- Working with object types and collection types in OO4O

Oracle Objects for OLE (OO4O) provides a user-friendly way to execute Data Manipulation Language (DML) on tables that contain object and collection types. This chapter provides an overview of how both types are defined in Oracle and illustrates how to interface with these object and collection types in Visual Basic using OO4O.

OO4O created two new objects and added a new method to the OraDatabase object to interface with objects and collections. The two new objects are

- OraObject
- OraCollection

In conjunction with the new objects, a new method was also added to the Ora-Database object:

- CreateOraObject

When executed, the *CreateOraObject method* returns a new OraObject object or a new OraCollection object.

For those who have worked with object types, and especially with collection types, through another means, (such as SQL*Plus or another programmatic interface like the Oracle Call Interface (OCI), you will appreciate the simplistic way that OO4O manipulates both objects and collections. In case you have not had a chance to work with objects and collections before, I have included code in the chapter demonstrating how to execute DML using SQL*Plus. This will help illustrate how much easier OO4O makes working with objects and collections. By the time you complete this chapter, you should have an appreciation of the new objects and the new method.

NOTE   The objects created and examples used in this chapter are from the Scott schema, which is owned by Oracle Corporation and is bundled with the Oracle8i client software and the OO4O product. For more information on this schema, refer to the Introduction.

Object Types in the Database

When creating tables in Oracle, the Oracle database provides what is known as primitive data types. *Primitive data types* are data types that most of us are familiar with. Some of the more commonly used data types are Varchar2, Number, and Date. For a more complete list of the available data types, you can look at any Oracle8i documentation and search the index for data types.

An *object type* is essentially a user-defined type. A *user-defined type* is essentially a type that is not already defined by the database. This object type is usually comprised of primitive data types but at times will include other object types.

For example, if you want to build a table that contains a list of your employees and their spouses, you could first create a new type called Spouse to store the spouse's names and the number of years of marriage. Then, you could create an Employee table based on an employee's number, name, and the Spouse type that was just described. You must create the Spouse type prior to creating the Employee table.

NOTE To create object types, the system privilege Create Any Type is required.

It's very important to remember to define the object type before referencing it. Not doing so will result in an "ORA-00902: invalid datatype" error message. This makes sense because you cannot use a specific type if it has not yet been defined.

NOTE If the type being created already exists and is not referenced by a table or another object, the type can simply be recreated using the Create Or Replace command. But if the type is referenced by some other object, you will not be able to recreate the type without first removing the dependencies. For more information on deleting types with references, you can review the Drop Type command in *The Oracle8i Server SQL Reference Manual*.

To actually create the Spouse type, enter the following SQL code in SQL*Plus:

```
CREATE OR REPLACE TYPE SPOUSE AS OBJECT
   (SpouseName VARCHAR2(20),
   YearsMarried Number(2));
   /
```

Now that the Spouse type is created, create the Employee table. Notice that the last field of the Employee table (SpouseInfo) is of the type Spouse. Before creating the Employee table, you may want to execute the Drop Table Employee command because the Create command will fail if the table already exists. To actually create the table, the following SQL code can be executed in SQL*Plus:

```
CREATE TABLE EMPLOYEE
    (EmployeeNumber NUMBER,
    FullName VARCHAR2(40),
    SpouseInfo SPOUSE);
```

After the table is successfully created, you can insert the following two rows of data in SQL*Plus.

```
INSERT INTO Employee
    VALUES (7900, 'James', Spouse('Lisa', 2));


INSERT INTO Employee
    VALUES (7788, 'Scott', Spouse(NULL, NULL));
```

Figure 8.1 illustrates what your SQL*Plus screen will look like after creating the object and creating the table, and inserting the data.

FIGURE 8.1
Creating an object type in
SQL*Plus

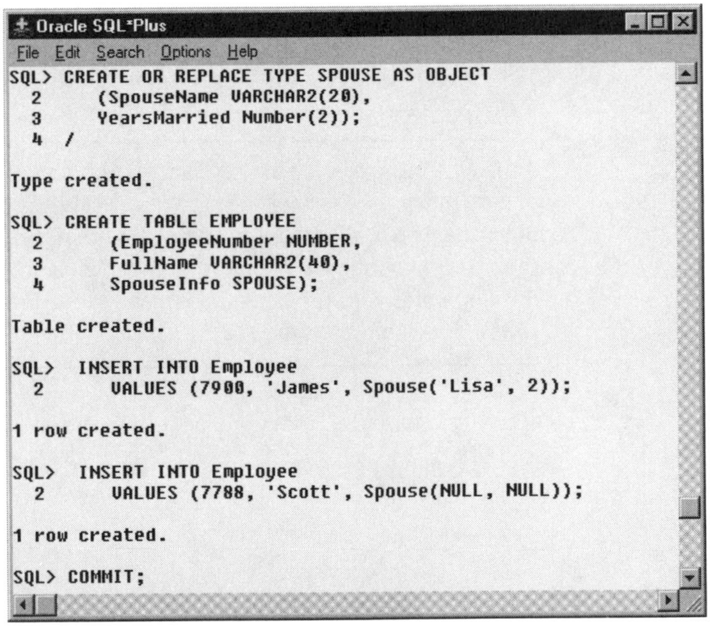

```
Oracle SQL*Plus
File  Edit  Search  Options  Help
SQL> CREATE OR REPLACE TYPE SPOUSE AS OBJECT
  2      (SpouseName VARCHAR2(20),
  3      YearsMarried Number(2));
  4  /

Type created.

SQL> CREATE TABLE EMPLOYEE
  2      (EmployeeNumber NUMBER,
  3      FullName VARCHAR2(40),
  4      SpouseInfo SPOUSE);

Table created.

SQL>  INSERT INTO Employee
  2      VALUES (7900, 'James', Spouse('Lisa', 2));

1 row created.

SQL>  INSERT INTO Employee
  2      VALUES (7788, 'Scott', Spouse(NULL, NULL));

1 row created.

SQL> COMMIT;
```

Notice that the Insert statement may look a bit different than what you are using. When inserting data into an object, be sure to include the object name as a way to cast the data to fit into the object type.

Using DML with Object Types

The introduction of objects has also introduced a different syntax when working with DML (Select, Insert, Update, and Delete). Although executing DML on object types in Oracle Objects for OLE (OO4O) is covered in depth in this chapter, working with objects in other applications, like SQL*Plus, is not. When it comes to executing DML in applications like SQL*Plus, there is too much information to cover in one book, let alone one chapter. When reviewing this section on objects, keep in mind that the book's focus is on interfacing with these objects in Oracle Objects for OLE (OO4O). Therefore, not all code executed in SQL*Plus will contain an explanation. If you are interested in doing more research on using DML with objects, you may want to start with the *Oracle8i Server Application Developer's Guide*.

Once the data has been entered, you can enter the following SQL code in SQL*Plus to see the data:

```
SELECT * FROM Employee;
```

Figure 8.2 illustrates what your SQL*Plus screen will look like after selecting the data.

FIGURE 8.2
Viewing the table data

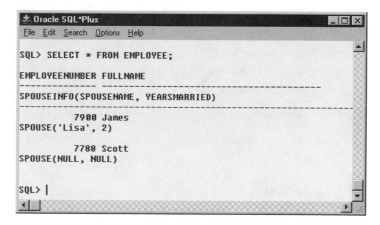

The user-defined type is not new to the Oracle8i database, but it is new to OO4O. If you are not familiar or have not worked with these types, I strongly suggest that you review the *Oracle8i Server Application Developer's Guide*.

Collection Types in the Database

A *collection* can be thought of as a group of elements of the same type for each given record. This type can be either a single primitive type, or it can be an object type. Take for example, defining a collection using the primitive type Number, which consists of an entire group of elements all defined as a Number. If the Spouse object, which was defined in the previous section, were used, you would have an entire group of elements all defined as the Spouse object. When a collection is part of a table definition, that means that each record inserted in the table has its own group.

Whether the group of elements in the collection is a primitive type or an object type, they are categorized into two different groups:

- VArray
- Nested Table

Although the VArray and Nested Table collection types can be defined using the same primitive types or object types, each collection has its own unique characteristics and constraints.

An Overview of the VArray and Nested Table Collections

This section provides an overview of VArray and Nested Table collections in Oracle. If after reading this section you wish to learn more about VArrays and Nested Tables, review any or all of the following Oracle8i documentation:

- *Oracle8i Application Developer's Guide-Fundamentals*
- *Oracle8i SQL Reference*
- *Oracle8i User's Guide and Reference*

A *VArray* can be thought of as a varying array and is very similar to an array in C. Referencing an element in a VArray is done using standard subscripting syntax.

A *Nested Table* can be thought of as a database table. Referencing an element in a Nested Table is also done using standard subscripting syntax, but only after the data has been retrieved.

Creating VArrays and Nested Tables

Creating VArrays and Nested Tables in Oracle will be illustrated in the examples throughout this chapter. This is done not only to build the tables required for the examples in this chapter, but also to provide some exposure to creating and interfacing with collection types using SQL*Plus. Keep in mind that this book is about how OO4O interfaces with the collections in the database and not how to execute DDL and DML on tables using the collection types. So, for more in-depth information on how to create collections in the Oracle database, please refer to the suggested reading listed at the beginning of this section.

Although VArrays and Nested Tables are both collections, they do differ in a number of ways. For example:

- VArrays have a maximum size, but Nested Tables do not.

This is because when you define a VArray, one of the values you must provide is the size, and the size provided is the maximum number of elements that the VArray can hold. As far as Nested Tables are concerned, there is no maximum size. Remember, Nested Tables are similar to database tables. The limitation of Nested Tables is the same as for other database tables.

- VArrays are always dense, but Nested Tables can be sparse.

When we say that VArrays are dense, it means that there are no empty elements between existing elements. For example, if there are five elements in a VArray, you can be sure that elements 1 through 5 will contain data. This also means that if you have five elements, you cannot simply delete the third element. You can only delete the last element of the array.

When we say that Nested Tables are sparse, it means that, as with any database table, you can delete individual rows located throughout the table. You don't have the restriction of being able to delete only the last element.

- VArrays store data inline, while Nested Tables store data in a separate storage table.

Having data stored inline for VArrays makes for quicker retrieval but also makes adding new data a bit involved. Fortunately OO4O simplifies this, as you will see later in the chapter. As for Nested Tables, in order for the collection to find the referencing data, every row in the collection must be mapped to a row in the storage table.

- The data stored in VArrays retain their ordering and subscripting, but Nested Tables do not.

This means that if you have five elements in a VArray, you know that elements with the subscripts 1 through 5 will always return the same data in the same order. With Nested Tables, you have no idea what order the data will be returned in. Unless, of course, you were to add some Order By clause to the SQL code used to return the elements. If you take a moment to think about it, it makes sense. Remember the two earlier comments about Nested Tables? First, data is stored in a separate storage table. And as with any other database table, when you do a Select command without an Order By clause, there is no way to predict the order in which the data will be retrieved. The second comment that data is accessed using subscripting after the data has been retrieved. The subscripting occurs afterward because what was element 1 in a previous Select command may now be element 5 in a current Select command.

With all the differences between VArrays and Nested Tables, there are some similarities between the two collections. First, neither supports the LOB data type. This means that the LOB (BLOB, CLOB, or BFILE) data type cannot be used in a collection. Second, neither collection supports the nesting of collection types. This means that you cannot have a collection type as one of the elements in the VArray or Nested Table.

NOTE   Neither VArrays nor Nested Tables support the LOB data type or the implementation of nested collections.

Working with Collections in SQL*Plus

As you know, VArrays and Nested Tables can be of an existing primitive type or can be of an object type. This section not only helps to draw a parallel between working with VArrays and working with Nested Tables but also helps provide you with examples of working with these types in SQL*Plus.

This section starts off by creating a table using the VArray of a primitive type (we will call this a VArray of a simple type), then illustrates how to insert, select, update, append, and delete data from the collection. The next section creates another table using a VArray of an object type. It then illustrates how to insert, select, update, append, and delete data from this collection of an object type.

To illustrate the similarities between working with VArrays and Nested Tables, we will create two tables using the Nested Table collection. The first is a Nested Table of a simple type and the second is a Nested Table of an object type. Both illustrate how to insert, select, update, append, and delete data from these types.

This section contains a number of examples of working with VArray and Nested Tables in SQL*Plus. To keep the book focused on Oracle Objects for OLE and to keep the page size manageable, this section provides code to manipulate the VArrays and Nested Tables when working in SQL*Plus without going into detail about what each line of code does. The main reason for this section is to expose you to interfacing with collection types outside of OO4O so that you can compare and contrast these methods of working with tables in Visual Basic to using OO4O. The examples implementing DML on collection objects illustrate how user friendly OO4O is when it comes to working with these objects.

Each code example illustrates only one way to implement the DML. The implementation used are designed so that you can draw a parallel between manipulating collections in SQL*Plus and manipulating collections in OO4O. In fact, the tables created in this section will be the same ones used later in the chapter when working with OO4O.

A VArray of a Simple Type

A VArray of a *simple type* can be thought of as a VArray defined using one of the existing data types, similar to Varchar2, Number, or Date. For this example, let's say that you wanted to create a department table, which will hold the department number, department name, and the first names of the employees in the department in a VArray. Let's say that the maximum number of employees for any given department is 20, and that the maximum number of characters for any given employee name is 30 characters. The first step is to create the VArray collection of type Varchar2(30). To create such a type, enter the following SQL code in SQL*Plus:

```
CREATE TYPE EmpVarray AS VARRAY(20) OF VARCHAR2(30);
/
```

Once the VArray collection is created, the next step is to create the department table. For this example, let's name the department table DeptVarry so that we know this is our department table with the VArray implementation. To do so, enter the following SQL code in SQL*Plus:

```
CREATE TABLE DeptVarray
    (Deptno NUMBER(2),
    DeptName VARCHAR2(20),
    EmpNames EmpVarray);
```

To get a pictorial view of what each record could possibly look like with some data, take a look at Figure 8.3. Notice that each record contains an array that can potentially hold 20 employees.

FIGURE 8.3
Creating the DeptVarray
table in SQL*Plus

DeptNested

DeptNo	DeptName	EmpNames	
10	MSLang	Jim	1
		Jenny	2
		Mark	...
			...
			19
			20

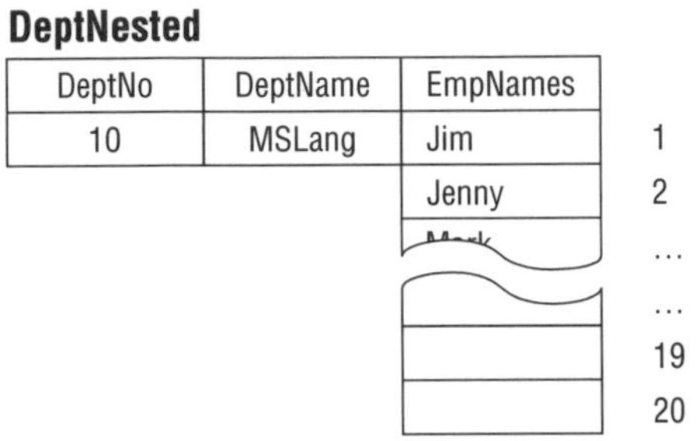

The following sections demonstrate the SQL commands required to execute the DML on the DeptVarray table in SQL*Plus.

Insert

To insert data into a table with a simple type, you need to cast the data for the object type by using the appropriate reference. In this case, it would be EmpVarray. The following code inserts two records into the DeptVarray table:

```
INSERT INTO DeptVarray VALUES
    (10, 'MSLang', EmpVarray('Jim', 'Jenny', 'Mark'));
INSERT INTO DeptVarray VALUES
    (20, 'Accounting', EmpVarray('Lisa', 'Scott', 'John'));
```

To verify that the data was inserted, execute the following SQL command, and you should see the two new records:

```
SELECT * FROM DeptVarray;
```

Update

Updating elements in a VArray requires implementing either an anonymous PL/SQL block or a stored procedure. Since updating VArray elements cannot be done through standard SQL, the entire VArray must be copied into a stand-alone VArray object. This must be done so that you are able to iterate through the elements of the VArray to search for the element(s) to be updated.

The following anonymous PL/SQL block changes the name of one of the elements in the VArray. Notice that once the VArray is copied to the stand-alone VArray element, you still must traverse through each element to find the one that you are planning to update.

```
DECLARE
    EditEmp EmpVarray;
    vIndex Number := 1;
  BEGIN
    SELECT V.EmpNames INTO EditEmp
        FROM DeptVarray V WHERE Deptno = 10;
    LOOP
        IF (vIndex = EditEmp.Count) THEN
            EXIT;
        ELSEIF (EditEmp(vIndex) = 'Jenny') THEN
            EditEmp(vIndex) := 'Jen';
        END IF;
        vIndex := vIndex + 1;
    END LOOP;
    UPDATE DeptVarray V SET V.EmpNames = EditEmp
        WHERE Deptno = 10;
  END;
/
```

To verify that the data was updated, execute the following SQL command, and you should see that the employee name for Department 10 has been changed:

```
SELECT * FROM DeptVarray WHERE Deptno = 10;
```

Update (Append)

In order to add a new element to a VArray of an existing record, you must implementing either an anonymous PL/SQL block or a stored procedure. The entire VArray must be copied into a stand-alone VArray object. This must be done to gain access to the *Extend method*. Executing this method will extend the VArray to one additional element and allocate the space to hold the new value. The following anonymous PL/SQL block adds a new employee name to the VArray collection of the DeptVarray table:

```
DECLARE
    NewEmp EmpVarray;
  BEGIN
    SELECT V.EmpNames INTO NewEmp
```

```
          FROM DeptVarray V WHERE Deptno = 10;
     NewEmp.extend;
     NewEmp(NewEmp.LAST) := 'John';
     UPDATE DeptVarray V SET V.EmpNames = NewEmp
          WHERE Deptno = 10;
   END;
   /
```

To verify that the data was appended, execute the following SQL command, and you should see that Department 10 has an additional employee:

```
SELECT * FROM DeptVarray WHERE Deptno = 10;
```

Delete (Trim)

Deleting elements in a VArray requires implementing either an anonymous PL/SQL block or a stored procedure. The VArray collection must be copied to a stand-alone VArray object. This must be done to obtain access to the Trim method. The *Trim method* actually deletes the element. With the Trim method, you can only Trim elements from the end of the collection.

The following anonymous PL/SQL block deletes one element (the last element) from the VArray:

```
DECLARE
    DeleteEmp EmpVarray;
  BEGIN
    SELECT V.EmpNames INTO DeleteEmp
        FROM DeptVarray V WHERE Deptno = 10;
    DeleteEmp.TRIM(1);
    UPDATE DeptVarray V SET V.EmpNames = DeleteEmp
        WHERE Deptno = 10;
  END;
  /
```

To verify that the data has been deleted, execute the following SQL command, and you should see that Department 10 has one less employee:

```
SELECT * FROM DeptVarray WHERE Deptno = 10;
```

A VArray Collection of an Object Type

A VArray collection of an *object type* can be thought of as a VArray defined using a user-defined object. For this example, let's create a similar department table as in the previous section, which will hold the department number and the department name; but this time, the VArray will not only contain the first name of the employee but also the employee number. In order for a collection to be able to hold more than a single data type, the collection must be based on a new user-defined type. In other words, it has to be based on an object type.

The first step is to create the object. To create such an object, enter the following SQL code in SQL*Plus:

```
CREATE TYPE EmpObj AS OBJECT (Empno NUMBER(5),
     Employee VARCHAR2(30));
/
```

Once the user-defined object (EmpObj) is created, the next step is to create the VArray collection using the EmpObj object. This can be done using the following SQL code in SQL*Plus:

```
CREATE TYPE EmpVarrayObj AS VARRAY(20) OF EmpObj;
/
```

After creating the EmpVarrayObj collection, the table can be created using the following SQL code:

```
CREATE TABLE DeptVarrayObj
     (Deptno NUMBER(2),
     DeptName VARCHAR2(20),
     EmpNames EmpVarrayObj);
```

To get a pictorial view of what each record looks like with data, take a look at Figure 8.4. Notice that each record contains an array, which can potentially hold 20 employees.

FIGURE 8.4
Creating the DeptVarrayObj table in SQL*Plus

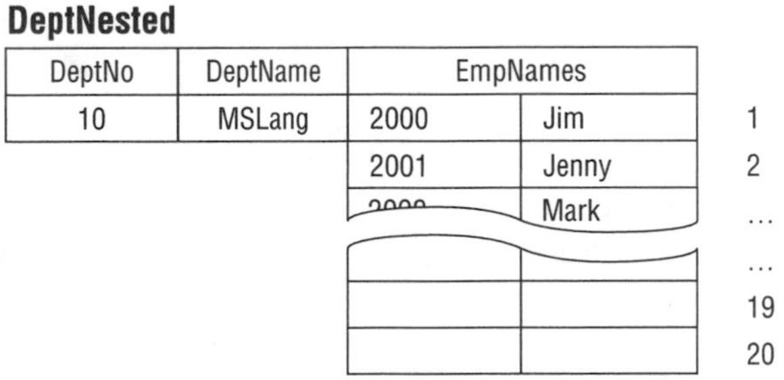

DeptNested

DeptNo	DeptName	EmpNames		
10	MSLang	2000	Jim	1
		2001	Jenny	2
		2002	Mark	...
				...
				19
				20

An important thing to remember is that a collection of objects can be thought of as essentially two separate objects: the first being a collection and the second being an object. In the instance of the DeptVarrayObj table, the EmpNames field, which is defined as EmpVarrayObj, is defined as a VArray of an object. When reviewing these examples, you should notice that they are almost identical to the simple-type examples in the previous sections. The main difference is the extra step(s) required to incorporate the use of an object. The following sections demonstrate the SQL commands required to execute the different DML on the DeptVarrayObj table in SQL*Plus.

Insert

To insert data into a table with a VArray of an object type, you need to cast the data for the collection type and for the object type. The following code inserts two records into the DeptVarrayObj table:

```
INSERT INTO DeptVarrayObj VALUES
    (10, 'MSLang',
        EmpVarrayObj(EmpObj(2000, 'Jim'),
                     EmpObj(2001, 'Jenny'),
                     EmpObj(2003, 'Mark')));
INSERT INTO DeptVarrayObj VALUES
    (20, 'Accounting',
        EmpVarrayObj(EmpObj(3001, 'Lisa'),
                     EmpObj(3002, 'Scott'),
                     EmpObj(3003, 'John')));
```

To verify that the data was inserted, execute the following SQL command, and you should see the two new records:

```
SELECT * FROM DeptVarrayObj;
```

Update

Updating elements in a VArray requires implementing either an anonymous PL/ SQL block or a stored procedure. With VArrays of a simple type, the entire VArray must be copied into a stand-alone VArray object. The same holds true with VArrays of object types, but now there is an additional step required to access the data. Once you have your stand-alone VArray collection, each element of the collection has to be copied to the stand-alone object. This cannot be just any object; the object has to be the one defined and used when creating the VArray. Since the object itself can hold only one element of the collection at a time, you will need to copy the data to the object one at a time as you iterate through the collection.

The following anonymous PL/SQL block changes the name of one of the elements in the VArray. Notice that once the VArray is copied to the stand-alone VArray element, the element of the VArray is copied to the stand-alone object type used when creating the collection. Now, when you reference the data, you do so through the EmpObj object.

```
DECLARE
      EditEmp EmpVarrayObj;
      EditObj EmpObj;
      vIndex Number := 1;
   BEGIN
      SELECT V.EmpNames INTO EditEmp
          FROM DeptVarrayObj V WHERE Deptno = 10;
      LOOP
          EditObj := EditEmp(vIndex);
          IF (vIndex = EditEmp.Count) THEN
              EXIT;
          ELSEIF (EditObj.Employee = 'Jenny') THEN
              EditObj.Employee := 'Jen';
              EditEmp(vIndex) := EditObj;
          END IF;
          vIndex := vIndex + 1;
      END LOOP;
      UPDATE DeptVarrayObj V SET V.EmpNames = EditEmp
          WHERE Deptno = 10;
   END;
   /
```

To verify that the data was updated, execute the following SQL command, and you should see that the employee name for Department 10 has changed:

```
SELECT * FROM DeptVarrayObj WHERE Deptno = 10;
```

Update (Append)

In order to add a new element to a VArray of an existing record, you must implement either an anonymous PL/SQL block or a stored procedure. The entire VArray must be copied into a stand-alone VArray object. This isdone to gain access to the Extend method. Executing this method extends the VArray to one additional element and allocates the space to hold the new value. Since the collection is of an object type, all new data must first be inserted into the object type.

Then the collection is set to the object, which holds the data. The following anonymous PL/SQL block adds a new employee name to the VArray collection of the DeptVarrayObj table:

```
DECLARE
      EditEmp EmpVarrayObj;
   BEGIN
      SELECT V.EmpNames INTO EditEmp
         FROM DeptVarrayObj V WHERE Deptno = 10;
      EditEmp.extend;
      EditEmp(EditEmp.LAST) := EmpObj(2004, 'John');
      UPDATE DeptVarrayObj V SET V.EmpNames = EditEmp
         WHERE Deptno = 10;
   END;
/
```

To verify that the data was appended, execute the following SQL command, and you should see that Department 10 now has an additional employee:

```
SELECT * FROM DeptVarrayObj WHERE Deptno = 10;
```

Delete (Trim)

Deleting elements in a VArray requires implementing either an anonymous PL/SQL block or a stored procedure. The VArray collection must be copied to a stand-alone VArray object. This is done to obtain access to the Trim method. The Trim method deletes the element. There are two items to note when using the Trim method. First, you can only Trim elements from the end of the collection. Second, even with VArrays of object types, the object type used in the collection (EmpObj) is not required as it was with other DML.

The following anonymous PL/SQL block deletes one element (the last element) from the VArray:

```
DECLARE
      EditEmp EmpVarrayObj;
   BEGIN
      SELECT V.EmpNames INTO EditEmp
         FROM DeptVarrayObj V WHERE Deptno = 10;
      EditEmp.TRIM(1);
      UPDATE DeptVarrayObj V SET V.EmpNames = EditEmp
         WHERE Deptno = 10;
   END;
/
```

To verify that the data has been deleted, execute the following SQL command, and you should see that Department 10 has one less employee:

```
SELECT * FROM DeptVarrayObj WHERE Deptno = 10;
```

A Nested Table of a Simple Type

As with a VArray of a simple type, a Nested Table of a *simple type* can be thought of as a Nested Table defined using one of the existing data types, similar to Varchar2, Number, or Date. For this example, let's say that you want to create the same table as you did before. But this time, instead of using a VArray collection, a Nested Table collection will be used. This table will be a department table that will hold the department number, department name, and the first names of the employees in the department in a Nested Table collection. As before, the maximum number of characters for any given employee name is 30 characters. But this time, we don't have the constraint of having 20 people as the maximum number of employees for any given department. Using the Nested Table collection in our table allows for the size of the collection to group dynamically.

The first step is to create a new Nested Table type of the type Varchar2(30). Let's call this type EmpNested. To create such a type, enter the following SQL code in SQL*Plus:

```
CREATE TYPE EmpNested AS TABLE OF VARCHAR2(30);
/
```

Once you have defined the new type, EmpNested, create the department table. For this example, name the department table DeptNested so that we know that this is our department table with the Nested Table collection implementation. To create this table, enter the following SQL in SQL*Plus:

```
CREATE TABLE DeptNested
    (Deptno NUMBER(2),
    DeptName VARCHAR2(20),
    EmpNames EmpNested)
    Nested table EmpNames store as NestedTableSimple;
```

To get a pictorial view of what each record looks like with some data, take a look at Figure 8.5. There are two items to note. First, notice that the data is not actually kept in the DeptNested table, but rather as a reference to the data that is stored in the NestedTableSimple table. Second, notice that the tables show *n* elements in the collection. This is because the Nested Table collection does not have an upper limit to the number of records it can store.

FIGURE 8.5
Creating the DeptNested-
Table table in SQL*Plus

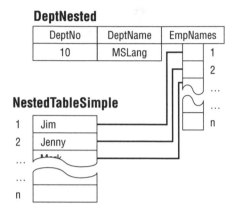

FIGURE 8.5
Creating the DeptNested-
Table table in SQL*Plus

The following sections demonstrate the SQL code required to execute different DML on this table in SQL*Plus.

Insert

To insert data into a table with a simple type, you need to cast the data for the object type using the appropriate reference. In this case, it is EmpNested. The following code inserts two records into the DeptNested table:

```
INSERT INTO DeptNested VALUES
    (10, 'MSLang', EmpNested('Jim', 'Jenny', 'Mark'));
INSERT INTO DeptNested VALUES
    (20, 'Accounting', EmpNested ('Lisa', 'Scott', 'John'));
```

To verify that the data was inserted, execute the following SQL code, and you should see the two new records:

```
SELECT * FROM DeptNested;
```

Update

Just as VArray of simple types required the use of PL/SQL for updating data in a collection type, so does the Nested Table of simple types. Both require implementing either an anonymous PL/SQL block or a stored procedure. Since updating Nested Table elements cannot be done with standard SQL, the entire Nested Table collection must be copied into a stand-alone Nested Table collection object. This allows you to iterate through the elements of the Nested Table collection to search for the element(s) that need to be updated.

The following anonymous PL/SQL block changes the name of one of the elements in the Nested Table collection. Once the Nested Table collection is copied to the stand-alone Nested Tables element, you still must traverse through each element to find the one you want to update.

```
DECLARE
    EditEmp EmpNested;
    vIndex Number := 1;
  BEGIN
    SELECT N.EmpNames INTO EditEmp
        FROM DeptNested N WHERE Deptno = 10;
    LOOP
        IF (vIndex = EditEmp.Count) THEN
            EXIT;
        ELSEIF (EditEmp(vIndex) = 'Jenny') THEN
            EditEmp(vIndex) := 'Jen';
        END IF;
        vIndex := vIndex + 1;
    END LOOP;
    UPDATE DeptNested N SET N.EmpNames = EditEmp
        WHERE Deptno = 10;
  END;
/
```

If you compare this SQL code to the SQL code used to update the DeptVarray table (the department table using the simple VArray type), you notice that only two things have changed. First, this example defines a variable EditEmp as EmpNested, while the example that updated the VArray collection defined it as EmpVArray. Second, the Select and Update commands for this example reference the DeptNested table, while the example that updated the VArray collection referenced the DeptVarray table. Other than that, the PL/SQL code is the same.

To verify that the data was updated, execute the following SQL code, and you should see that the employee name for Department 10 has changed:

```
SELECT * FROM DeptNested WHERE Deptno = 10;
```

Update (Append)

To add a new element to a Nested Table of an existing record, implement either an anonymous PL/SQL block or a stored procedure. As with the previous examples, the collection type must be copied to a stand-alone collection object, which, in turn, enables you to execute the Extend method. This method extends the Nested

Table to include one additional element and allocates the space to hold the new value. The following anonymous PL/SQL block adds a new employee name to the Nested Table collection of the DeptNested table:

```
DECLARE
    NewEmp EmpNested;
  BEGIN
    SELECT N.EmpNames INTO NewEmp
        FROM DeptNested N WHERE Deptno = 10;
    NewEmp.extend;
    NewEmp(NewEmp.LAST) := 'John';
    UPDATE DeptNested N SET N.EmpNames = NewEmp
        WHERE Deptno = 10;
  END;
  /
```

If you compare this SQL code to the SQL code used to append the DeptVarray table (the department table using the simple VArray type), you notice that only two things have changed. First, this Nested Table collection example defines the variable NewEmp as EmpNested, while the example that appends to the VArray collection defined it as EmpVArray. Second, the Select and Update command for this example reference the DeptNested table, while the previous VArray collection example referenced the DeptVarray table. Other than that, the PL/SQL is the same.

To verify that the data was appended, execute the following SQL code, and you should see that Department 10 now has an additional employee:

```
SELECT * FROM DeptNested WHERE Deptno = 10;
```

Delete (Trim)

To delete elements in a collection, implement either an anonymous PL/SQL block or a stored procedure. To do so, The Nested Table collection must be copied to a stand-alone Nested Table object. This is done to obtain access to the Trim method. The Trim method deletes the element. One item to note with the Trim method is that you can only trim one or more elements from the end of the collection.

The following anonymous PL/SQL block deletes one element (the last element) from the Nested Table collection in the DeptNested table:

```
DECLARE
    DeleteEmp EmpNested;
```

```
BEGIN
    SELECT N.EmpNames INTO DeleteEmp
        FROM DeptNested N WHERE Deptno = 10;
    DeleteEmp.TRIM(1);
    DeleteEmp.Delete(1);
    UPDATE DeptNested N SET N.EmpNames = DeleteEmp
        WHERE Deptno = 10;
END;
/
```

Only two things have changed between the SQL code here and the SQL code used to delete the DeptVarray table (the department table using simple VArray type). First, this example defines NewEmp as EmpNested, while the previous VArray example defined it as EmpVArray. Second, the Select and Update command for this example reference the DeptNested table, while the previous VArray example referenced the DeptVarray table. Other than that, the PL/SQL is the same.

To verify that the data was deleted, execute the following SQL code, and you should see that the employee added to Department 10 has been deleted:

```
SELECT * FROM DeptNested WHERE Deptno = 10;
```

The Nested Table of an Object Type

Just as a VArray collection can be created as an object type, a Nested Table can also be defined using a user-defined object. For this example, create a similar department table (as in the "A VArray Collection of an Object Type" section), which will be defined to hold the department number, department name, and a collection type that will contain the employee numbers and first names. Instead of using the VArray collection type, this example will use a Nested Table collection type. For a collection to hold more than a single data type, the collection must be based on a new user-defined type. In other words, it has to be based on an object type.

Normally, the first step is to create the object, but since this object (EmpObj) was created in the previous section, there is no need to create it again.

NOTE   The EmpObj object was created earlier in this chapter.

In case you did not create the EmpObj in the previous section, you can enter the following SQL code in SQL*Plus to create the object:

```
CREATE TYPE EmpObj AS OBJECT (Empno NUMBER(5),
        Employee VARCHAR2(30));
/
```

The next step is to create the Nested Table collection using the EmpObj object. This can be done using the following SQL code in SQL*Plus:

```
CREATE TYPE EmpNestedObj AS TABLE OF EmpObj;
/
```

After creating the EmpNestedObj collection, the table can be created using the following SQL code:

```
CREATE TABLE DeptNestedObj
        (Deptno NUMBER(2),
        DeptName VARCHAR2(20),
        EmpNames EmpNestedObj)
        Nested table EmpNames store as NestedTableObj;
```

To get a pictorial view of what each record looks like, take a look at Figure 8.6. There are two items to note. First, notice that the data is not actually kept in the DeptNestedObj table, but rather as a reference to the data that is stored in the NestedTableObj table. Second, notice that the tables show *n* elements in the collection. This is because the Nested Table collection does not have an upper limit to the number of records it can store.

FIGURE 8.6
Creating the DeptNested-Obj table in SQL*Plus

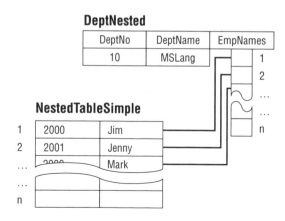

As with VArrays of objects, an important thing to remember when working with Nested Tables of objects is that a collection of objects can be thought of as essentially two separate objects: the first being a collection and the second being an object. In the instance of the DeptNestedObj table, the EmpNames field (which is defined as EmpNestedObj) is defined as a Nested Table of an object. When reviewing the code examples, you should notice that they are almost identical to the examples in the previous section. The main difference is the extra step(s) required to incorporate the use of an object.

The following sections demonstrate the SQL code required to execute DML on the DeptNestedObj table in SQL*Plus.

Insert

To insert data into a table with a Nested Table of an object type, you need to cast the data not only for the collection type but also for the object type. The following inserts two records into the DeptNestedObj table:

```
INSERT INTO DeptNestedObj VALUES
    (10, 'MSLang',
        EmpNestedObj(EmpObj(2000, 'Jim'),
                     EmpObj(2001, 'Jenny'),
                     EmpObj(2003, 'Mark')));
INSERT INTO DeptNestedObj VALUES
    (20, 'Accounting',
        EmpNestedObj(EmpObj(3001, 'Lisa'),
                     EmpObj(3002, 'Scott'),
                     EmpObj(3003, 'John')));
```

To verify that the data was inserted, execute the following SQL code, and you should see the two new records:

```
SELECT * FROM DeptNestedObj;
```

Update

Updating Nested Table collections defined using objects is very similar to updating VArray collections of object types. Both require implementing either an anonymous PL/SQL block or a stored procedure. Both also require an additional step as compared to collections of simple types. The first step in this example is to copy the Nested Table collection to a stand-alone collection type. In this case, it's EmpNestObj. Once you have your stand-alone Nested Table collection, each element of the collection is copied to its stand-alone object type. In this case, it's EmpObj. With collections of objects, access to the data must be done through the object and not through the collection. Since the object itself can hold only one element of the collection at a time, you will need to copy the data to the object one at a time as you iterate through the collection.

The following anonymous PL/SQL block changes the name of one of the elements in the Nested Table collection. Notice that once the Nested Table is copied to the stand-alone Nested Table element, that element of the collection is copied to the stand-alone object type used when creating the collection. Now, as you reference the data, you will be doing so through the EmpObj object type.

```
DECLARE
    EditEmp EmpNestedObj;
    EditObj EmpObj;
    vIndex Number := 1;
BEGIN
    SELECT V.EmpNames INTO EditEmp
        FROM DeptNestedObj V WHERE Deptno = 10;
    LOOP
        EditObj := EditEmp(vIndex);
        IF (vIndex = EditEmp.Count) THEN
            EXIT;
        ELSEIF (EditObj.Employee = 'Jenny') THEN
            EditObj.Employee := 'Jen';
            EditEmp(vIndex) := EditObj;
        END IF;
        vIndex := vIndex + 1;
    END LOOP;
    UPDATE DeptNestedObj V SET V.EmpNames = EditEmp
        WHERE Deptno = 10;
END;
/
```

If you compare this SQL code to the SQL code used to update the DeptVarray-Obj table (the department table using VArrays of object type), you notice that only two things have changed. First, this example defines EditEmp as EmpNestedObj, while the DeptVarrayObj table example defined it as EmpVArrayObj. Second, the Select and Update commands for this example reference the DeptNestedObj table, while the DeptVarrayObj example referenced the DeptVarrayObj table. Other than that, the PL/SQL code is the same.

To verify that the data was updated, execute the following SQL code, and you should see that the employee name for Department 10 has changed:

```
SELECT * FROM DeptNestedObj WHERE Deptno = 10;
```

Update (Append)

To add a new element to a Nested Table collection of an existing record, implement either an anonymous PL/SQL block or a stored procedure. The Nested Table must be copied into a stand-alone Nested Table object. This must be done to gain access to the Extend method. This method will extend the collection to include one additional element and will allocate the space to hold the new value. Since the collection is of an object type, all new data must first be inserted into the object type, and then the collection is set to the object, which holds the data. The following anonymous PL/SQL block adds a new employee name to the Nested Table collection of the DeptNestedObj table:

```
DECLARE
    EditEmp EmpNestedObj;
  BEGIN
    SELECT V.EmpNames INTO EditEmp
        FROM DeptNestedObj V WHERE Deptno = 10;
    EditEmp.extend;
    EditEmp(EditEmp.LAST) := EmpObj(2004, 'John');
    UPDATE DeptNestedObj V SET V.EmpNames = EditEmp
        WHERE Deptno = 10;
  END;
/
```

If you compare this SQL code to the SQL code used to append the DeptVarray-Obj table (the department table using a VArray of an object type), you notice that only two things have changed. First, this example defines NewEmp as EmpNested-Obj, while the DeptVArrayObj example defined it as EmpVArrayObj. Second, the Select and Update commands for this example referenced the DeptNestedObj table, while the DeptVArray example referenced the DeptVarrayObj table. Other than that, the PL/SQL code is the same.

To verify that the data was appended, execute the following SQL code, and you should see that Department 10 now has an additional employee:

```
SELECT * FROM DeptNestedObj WHERE Deptno = 10;
```

Delete (Trim)

Deleting elements in a Nested Table collection requires implementing either an anonymous PL/SQL block or a stored procedure. The Nested Table collection must be copied to a stand-alone Nested Table object. This is done to obtain access to the Trim method. The Trim method deletes the element. There are two items to note when using the Trim method: First, you can only Trim elements from the end of the collection. Second, even with Nested Tables of object types, the object type used in the collection (EmpObj) is not required as it was with other DML.

The following anonymous PL/SQL block deletes one element (the last element) from the Nested Table:

```
DECLARE
     EditEmp EmpNestedObj;
  BEGIN
     SELECT V.EmpNames INTO EditEmp
         FROM DeptNestedObj V WHERE Deptno = 10;
     EditEmp.TRIM(1);
     EditEmp.DELETE(1);
     UPDATE DeptNestedObj V SET V.EmpNames = EditEmp
         WHERE Deptno = 10;
  END;
/
```

If you compare this SQL code to the SQL code used to delete the DeptVarrayObj table (the department table that used the simple VArray of an object type), you notice that only two things have changed. First, this example defines NewEmp as EmpNestedObj, while the DeptVarrayObj example defined it as EmpVArrayObj. Second, the Select and Update commands for this example reference the Dept-NestedObj table, while the DeptVarrayObj example referenced the DeptVarray-Obj table. Other than that, the PL/SQL code is the same.

To verify that the data was deleted, execute the following SQL code, and you see that the employee added to Department 10 with the Append example is now deleted:

```
SELECT * FROM DeptNestedObj WHERE Deptno = 10;
```

Object Types and OO4O

So far, this chapter has discussed objects and collections, as well as how to interact with each in SQL*Plus. This section discusses working with objects in OO4O.

One of the new types that OO4O has introduced is the OraObject type. This object type exposes the same attributes and methods available when working with objects types in SQL*Plus using PL/SQL. The following section goes into more detail about these methods.

OraObject Properties and Methods

The *OraObject object* can be used in OO4O to define any user-defined object types in the database. Table 8.1 lists the available properties and methods for an Ora-Object type.

T A B L E   8 . 1 :   OraObject Methods and Properties

Properties	Methods
Count	Clone
IsNull	
TypeName	

The Count Property

The *Count property* returns the number of attributes in an object. The *attributes* of an object can be thought of as the elements or fields used to create an object. For example, if you are working with an object and are unsure of the number of attributes that it contains but want to view its contents, the following code allows you to scroll through each attribute and display its value in a message box:

```
For Index = 1 To OraObject.Count
    MsgBox OraObject(Index)
OraDynaset.Update
```

The IsNull Property

The *IsNull property* returns a Boolean value depending on whether or not the object is currently null. This is an important property because attempting to access elements in a Null object will result in an error.

The IsNull property can be very useful in error checking.

```
If (OraObject.IsNull = True) Then
    MsgBox "Object is currently NULL", _
        vbInformation, "Null Object"
    Exit Sub
End If
```

The TypeName Property

The *TypeName property* returns the name of the object in the Oracle database that is used to create the OraObject type in OO4O. The name returned is a string value.

To display the name of the object used to create an OraObject object type, use the following code:

```
MsgBox OraObject.TypeName, vbInformation, "Object Name"
```

The Clone Method

The *Clone method* provides a way to copy one OraObject type to a stand-alone OraObject type.

This is an easy way to make a quick copy of an object. Keep in mind that any edits made to the new object will not be reflected in the database. Here is an example of its syntax:

```
Set myClone = OraObject.Clone
```

Collection Types and OO4O

So far, this chapter has discussed objects and collections, as well as how to interact with each in SQL*Plus. This section discusses working with collections in OO4O.

One of the new types OO4O has introduced is the *OraCollection type*. This object type exposes the same attributes and methods available when working with collection types in SQL*Plus using PL/SQL.

Remember that collections can be both a collection of a simple type or a collection of objects. As you saw when working with collections of objects in SQL*Plus, you have to create not only the collection type but also the object type. The same holds true when working in Visual Basic using OO4O. For the collection type, use an OraCollection object. For the object type, use the OraObject object. The OraObject object, together with the OraCollection object, provides a simple way to manipulate collections of object types.

As you continue through this chapter, you will find that from the database perspective, there is considerable difference between the VArray and Nested Table collection types. Even the SQL code for collection types varies a bit. But as you begin to work more with OO4O, you see how user friendly OO4O makes working with the two different collection types by providing a single interface.

OraCollection Properties and Methods

The *OraCollection object* was introduced into OO4O as a means to interface and manipulate the VArray and Nested Table collection types. It does not matter if the collection type you wish to define is a VArray or a Nested Table; as an OraCollection type, either one can be defined in OO4O. Table 8.2 lists the available properties and methods for an OraCollection type.

TABLE 8.2: OraCollection Methods and Properties

Properties	Methods
ElementType	Append
IsLocator	Clone
IsNull	Delete
MaxSize	Exist
SafeArray	Trim
Size	
TableSize	
Type	

The ElementType Property

The *ElementType property* returns the type of the element used in the collection. For example, if the collection is defined as a collection of a simple type like Number, the ElementType property value will be ORATYPE_NUMBER. If the collection is of an object type, the ElementType property will be ORATYPE_OBJECT.

The IsNull Property

The *IsNull property* returns a Boolean value depending on whether or not the collection is currently null. This is an important property because attempting to access elements in a Null collection will result in an error. The same holds true for attempting to execute the methods of the OraCollection object when the collection is null.

The IsNull property is very useful in error checking. Here is an example of its syntax:

```
If (OraCollection.IsNull = True) Then
    MsgBox "Collection is currently NULL", _
        vbInformation, "Null Collection"
    Exit Sub
End If
```

The MaxSize Property

For VArrays, the *MaxSize property* contains the maximum size of the VArray collection. For Nested Tables, the MaxSize property contains the current size of the Nested Table collection.

The MaxSize for the VArray is the size used when the VArray collection was defined. When adding new elements to a VArray, the MaxSize property is a good way to find out how many elements are available.

The MaxSize property contains the current size of the Nested Table and not the maximum size of the collection because Nested Tables do not have an upper limit, as VArrays do. So, returning the current size for a Nested Table makes more sense. You can use the MaxSize property in conjunction with the Size property to see if the VArray has any available elements. The following code does just that. If the MaxSize property is equal to the Size property, all the elements in the VArray have data and attempting to append a new element will result in an error.

```
If (OraVArray.maxSize = OraVArray.Size) Then
    MsgBox "You cannot add any new elements", _
        vbInformation, "VArray Full"
    Exit Sub
End If
```

The SafeArray Property

The *SafeArray property* contains a SafeArray for a given collection type that is of a single element. This means that you cannot create a SafeArray of a collection that is of an Oracle object type. Table 8.3 shows a mapping of the Visual Basic data types to the SafeArray types. Keep in mind that the SafeArray is zero based.

T A B L E 8 . 3 : SafeArray Types

Collection Element Type	SafeArray of
Date	String
Number	String
Char, Varchar2	String
Real	Real
Integer	Integer

The Size Property

The *Size property* contains the current size of the collection.

WARNING   The Size property counts deleted elements.

This sounds simple enough, but there can be some potential confusion when records are deleted. This is predominately true when working with the Delete method and Nested Tables. If you check the size of a Nested Table collection before and after executing the Delete command, the Size property contains the same number until a Refresh is executed on the dynaset. This is different when using the Trim method. If you check the size of any collection before and after executing the Trim method, you see the new size of the collection without having to execute a Refresh.

The TableSize Property

The *TableSize property* contains the current size of Nested Table collection and will exclude records that have been deleted. I recommend using this property to track the size of Nested Table collections, especially when deleting elements. This elevates the potential problem of getting an incorrect record count when deleting items, as you could when using the Size property and deleting elements in the Nested Table collection. This property is not valid for the VArray type.

The Type Property

The *Type property* contains the type code of the collection.

The value contained in the Type property will be one of the following:

- ORATYPE_VARRAY
- ORATYPE_TABLE

The Type property is a straightforward approach for finding out if the collection you currently have is either a VArray or a Nested Table. Here is an example of its syntax:

```
If (OraCollecton.Type = ORATYPE_VARRAY) Then
    MsgBox "The collection type is a VArray", _
        vbInformation, "VArray Type"
    Elseif (OraCollecton.Type = ORATYPE_TABLE) Then
        MsgBox "The collection type is a Nested Table", _
            vbInformation, "Table Type"
End If
```

The Append Method

The *Append method* extends a collection by one element and adds the new value to the end of the collection.

In the case of appending a new string value to the end of a collection that is of type Varchar2, it looks like the following:

```
OraDynaset.Edit
    OraCollection.Append "Append a New String Value"
OraDynaset.Update
```

In the case of appending a new element to the end of a collection that is of an object type, it looks like the following:

```
OraDynaset.Edit
    OraCollection.Append OraObject
OraDynaset.Update
```

The Append method appends only one value. To append more than one value to a collection type, you have to execute the Append method for each new element.

The Clone Method

The *Clone method* provides a way to copy one collection to a stand-alone collection object. This is an easy way to make a quick copy of a collection. Keep in mind that any edits made to the new collection will not be reflected in the database. Here is an example of the syntax used with this method:

```
Set myClone = OraCollection.Clone
```

The Delete Method

The *Delete method* applies only to Nested Tables and allows you to delete elements in a Nested Table collection by simply passing in the subscript of the element you wish to delete. Remember, Nested Tables are sparse and allow you to delete any element in them. For example, if you have 10 elements in a Nested Table collection type and you want to delete the third element, you can do so using the following command:

```
OraDynaset.Edit
    OraNestedTable.Delete 3
OraDynaset.Update
```

Remember that after deleting an element, you must refresh the dynaset object if you wish to obtain the correct record count.

Attempting to execute the Delete method on a VArray collection type will result in a "Delete operation not supported for this collection type" error message.

The Exist Method

The *Exist method* tests whether an element exists at a particular index.

For example, if you want to navigate through a collection to see which elements contain data, do something like the following:

```
For Index = 1 To OraCollection.Size
    If (OraCollection.Exist Index = TRUE) Then
        MsgBox "Data exists for element " & Index & _
          vbInformation, "Does Data Exist"
  Else
        MsgBox "No data exists for element " & Index & _
          vbInformation, "Does Data Exist"
    End If
Next Index
```

The Trim Method

The *Trim method* trims *n* number of elements from the end of a collection.

It may be unclear at first why OO4O has both a Trim method and a Delete method. The Delete method can delete any given element only in a Nested Table collection. The Trim method allows you to trim any number of elements from any collection. The only constraint is that the elements are trimmed from the end of the collection.

Be very careful when working with the Trim method. You may have the tendency to treat Trim as Delete. Just remember, the number you are entering is the number of elements from the end of the collection you wish to trim. Take a look at the following code:

```
OraDynaset.Edit
    OraCollection.Trim 5
OraDynaset.Update
```

This code will trim the last five elements in a collection. It does not delete the fifth element of the collection.

WARNING At the time of this writing, the Trim method subtracts 1 from the number being passed in. This means that if you pass a 1 to Trim the last record, 0 records are trimmed. In the previous example, if you pass in 5, only 4 elements are trimmed. A future release should contain a fix.

CreateOraObject Method

The *CreateOraObject method* (which is a method contained in the OraDatabase object) creates stand-alone objects types in Visual Basic. It's the combination of this method with the two new objects (OraObject & OraCollection) that make inserts and updates of collections possible using OO4O.

The general syntax for creating a new object with the CreateOraObject command is as follows:

```
Set OraObject = _
    OraDatabase.CreateOraObject("DATABASE_OBJECT")
Set OraCollection = _
    OraDatabase.CreateOraObject("DATABASE_COLLECTION")
```

One important thing to note when using the CreateOraObject method is that the object name being passed in must be uppercase. Not using uppercase will result in an "Object not found" error.

WARNING The name of the object being used in the CreateOraObject *must* be uppercase.

The following sections provide more detail on the OraCollection and OraObject objects, and on the CreateOraObject method. These features provide a user-friendly way to manipulate collections in the database.

WARNING At the time of this writing, there is an issue when executing the CreateOraObject method against an 8.0.5 database. In order to use this method, make sure that you are using an 8.1.5 database.

Working with VArrays in Visual Basic

The following sections provide an introduction to working with VArrays in Visual Basic. We begin with a discussion about working with VArrays of simple types and go on to discuss about working with VArrays of object types.

The VArray of a Simple Type

The following examples illustrate working with VArrays of simple types. For this book, simple types are considered to be types that already exist in the database. The table used for these examples is the same one used for the examples working with VArrays of simple types in SQL*Plus. The name of the table is DeptVarray, and the VArray collection used is named EMPVARRAY.

Insert

Listing 8.1 inserts the same three values used for inserting into VArrays in SQL*Plus.

If you have been following along since the beginning of the chapter, delete the records entered earlier. To do so, execute the following SQL command in SQL*Plus:

```
DELETE DeptVarray;
```

Don't forget to execute the Commit command to save the change.

Listing 8.1

```
1  Dim OraSession As OraSession
2  Dim OraDatabase As OraDatabase
3  Dim OraDynaset As OraDynaset
4  Dim DeptCollection As OraCollection
5  Set OraSession = _
       CreateObject("OracleInProcServer.XOraSession")
6  Set OraDatabase = OraSession.OpenDatabase _
       ("v8i", "scott/tiger", 0&)
7  Set OraDynaset = OraDatabase.CreateDynaset _
     ("SELECT * FROM DeptVarray", 0&)
8  Set DeptCollection = _
     OraDatabase.CreateOraObject("EMPVARRAY")
9  DeptCollection(1) = "Jim"
10 DeptCollection(2) = "Jenny"
```

```
11 DeptCollection(3) = "Mark"
12 OraDynaset.AddNew
13    OraDynaset.Fields("DEPTNO").Value = 10
14    OraDynaset.Fields("DEPTNAME").Value = "MSLang"
15    OraDynaset.Fields("EmpNames").Value = DeptCollection
16 OraDynaset.Update
17 MsgBox "Insert Complete"
```

⟂ **Analysis**

- Lines 1–3 are Dim statements for the objects being used to connect to the database and to create the dynaset.

- Line 4 is the Dim statement for the OraCollection object.

- Line 5 creates the OraSession object.

- Line 6 creates an OraDatabase object and establishes the connection to the database.

- Line 7 creates the OraDynaset object based on the DeptVarray table.

- Line 8 creates a stand-alone OraCollection object based on the EMP-VARRAY definition in the database, which is a VArray of a simple type.

- Lines 9–11 assign a value to elements 1 through 3 of the stand-alone collection type.

- Line 12 invokes the AddNew method of the OraDynaset.

- Line 13 inserts 10 into the Deptno field.

- Line 14 inserts "MSLang" into the DeptName field.

- Line 15 inserts the data from the stand-alone OraCollection object into the EmpNames field.

- Line 16 updates the OraDynaset object to commit the Insert operation.

- Line 17 displays a message box after the record is inserted.

The key lines of code to review are lines 8 through 11 and line 15. Line 8 creates the stand-alone VArray collection, lines 9 through 11 populate the collection, and line 15 adds the data to the EmpNames field in the dynaset.

Select

Listing 8.2 selectsfrom a table with a VArray collection to illustrate stepping through the entire collection. It also makes good use of the Size property of the OraCollection object in order to regulate how many elements are contained in the collection.

⟩ Listing 8.2

```
1  Dim OraSession As OraSession
2  Dim OraDatabase As OraDatabase
3  Dim OraDynaset As OraDynaset
4  Dim DeptCollection As OraCollection
5  Set OraSession = _
       CreateObject("OracleInProcServer.XOraSession")
6  Set OraDatabase = OraSession.OpenDatabase _
        ("v8i", "scott/tiger", 0&)
7  Set OraDynaset = OraDatabase.CreateDynaset _
      ("SELECT * FROM DeptVarray", 0&)
8  Set DeptCollection = OraDynaset.Fields("EmpNames").Value
9  For Index = 1 To DeptCollection.Size
10     MsgBox DeptCollection(Index)
11 Next Index
12 MsgBox "Select Complete"
```

Analysis

- Lines 1–3 are Dim statements for the objects being used to connect to the database and to create the dynaset.

- Line 4 is the Dim statement for the OraCollection object.

- Line 5 creates the OraSession object.

- Line 6 creates an OraDatabase object and establishes the connection to the database.

- Line 7 creates the OraDynaset object based on the DeptVarray table.

- Line 8 sets the DeptCollection variable to the content of the current collection type in the database.

- Line 9 starts the For loop to iterate through the elements in the OraCollection object.

- Line 10 displays a message box with the value of the current element in the collection.

- Line 11 increments the counter for the loop.

- Line 12 displays a message box after all the records in the collection have been displayed.

You may want to take a moment to see just how the elements of the VArray collection are being referenced (line 10). Remember, you can use standard subscripting, and, indeed, that's just what we did. The subscript variable is being incremented by the For loop.

Update

This Update example illustrates updating one of the elements in the VArray collection. Due to limitations when selecting and updating collection types, you are required to traverse through each element to find the one you are looking for. This does not mean that your Where clause cannot contain a search criteria based on an element in the collection, but rather, it means that once the record is retrieved and you have the collection that contains the value, you will still have to traverse through the elements of the collection element by element to find the one being searched for.

Listing 8.3 updates the Jenny element and changes it to "Jen".

Listing 8.3

```
1  Dim OraSession As OraSession
2  Dim OraDatabase As OraDatabase
3  Dim OraDynaset As OraDynaset
4  Dim DeptCollection As OraCollection
5  Set OraSession = _
       CreateObject("OracleInProcServer.XOraSession")
6  Set OraDatabase = OraSession.OpenDatabase _
       ("v8i", "scott/tiger", 0&)
7  Set OraDynaset = OraDatabase.CreateDynaset _
     ("SELECT * FROM DeptVarray", 0&)
8  Set DeptCollection = OraDynaset.Fields("EmpNames").Value
```

```
9  For Index = 1 To DeptCollection.Size
10     If DeptCollection(Index) = "Jenny" Then
11          OraDynaset.Edit
12              DeptCollection(Index) = "Jen"
13          OraDynaset.Update
14          MsgBox "Update complete"
15          Exit Sub
16     End If
17 Next Index
18 MsgBox "Data was not updated"
```

Analysis

- Lines 1–3 are Dim statements for the objects being used to connect to the database and to create the dynaset.

- Line 4 is the Dim statement for the OraCollection object.

- Line 5 creates the OraSession object.

- Line 6 creates an OraDatabase object and establishes the connection to the database.

- Line 7 creates the OraDynaset object based on the DeptVarray table.

- Line 8 sets the DeptCollection to the content of the current collection type in the database.

- Line 9 starts the For loop to iterate through the elements in the OraCollection object.

- Line 10 checks to see if the current element of the collection object is equal to value for which you are searching.

- Line 11 edits the OraDynaset object.

- Line 12 sets the current element of the collection to the new value.

- Line 13 updates the OraDynaset object to commit the update.

- Line 14 displays a message box after the data has been committed.

- Line 15 exits the subroutine. No need to continue unless you are expecting more data to update.

- Line 16 ends the If condition.

- Line 17 increments the counter for the loop.

- Line 18 displays a message box if no matching data was found.

The important lines to focus on are lines 9 through 17. Line 9 starts the For loop to traverse through the collection by starting at 1 and using the Size property of the collection object to calculate how many elements exist and will have to be searched. Line 10 is the If condition used to search each element of the collection for "Jenny". Lines 11 through 13 actually edit the record and change the value from "Jenny" to "Jen". Notice that these lines are contained in the If condition, which means that the record will not be edited unless a match is found.

Update (Append)

Listing 8.4 illustrates appending a new element to an existing collection.

Listing 8.4

```
1  Dim OraSession As OraSession
2  Dim OraDatabase As OraDatabase
3  Dim OraDynaset As OraDynaset
4  Dim DeptCollection As OraCollection
5  Set OraSession = _
       CreateObject("OracleInProcServer.XOraSession")
6  Set OraDatabase = OraSession.OpenDatabase _
       ("v8i", "scott/tiger", 0&)
7  Set OraDynaset = OraDatabase.CreateDynaset _
     ("SELECT * FROM DeptVarray", 0&)
8  Set DeptCollection = OraDynaset.Fields("EmpNames").Value
9  OraDynaset.Edit
10     DeptCollection.Append "John"
11 OraDynaset.Update
12 MsgBox "Append complete"
```

Analysis

- Lines 1–3 are Dim statements for the objects being used to connect to the database and for creating the dynaset.

- Line 4 is the Dim statement for the OraCollection object.

- Line 5 creates the OraSession object.

- Line 6 creates an OraDatabase object and establishes the connection to the database.

- Line 7 creates the OraDynaset object based on the DeptVarray table.

- Line 8 sets the DeptCollection to the content of the current collection type in the database.

- Line 9 edits the OraDynaset object.

- Line 10 executes the Append mode of the collection object.

- Line 11 updates the OraDynaset object to commit the Append operation.

- Line 12 displays a message box after the data is committed.

How easy is appending a new value to a VArray of simple types? It's essentially a single line (line 10). The other lines of code are standard for connecting to the database and defining the dynaset. OO4O makes appending a new element to collections of simple types a fairly simple process by providing the Append method.

Delete (Trim)

Listing 8.5 illustrates the use of the Trim method to remove records from a VArray collection type. Keep in mind that the Trim method removes elements from the end of the collection.

Listing 8.5

```
1  Dim OraSession As OraSession
2  Dim OraDatabase As OraDatabase
3  Dim OraDynaset As OraDynaset
4  Dim DeptCollection As OraCollection
5  Set OraSession = _
       CreateObject("OracleInProcServer.XOraSession")
6  Set OraDatabase = OraSession.OpenDatabase _
       ("v8i", "scott/tiger", 0&)
7  Set OraDynaset = OraDatabase.CreateDynaset _
     ("SELECT * FROM DeptVarray", 0&)
8  Set DeptCollection = OraDynaset.Fields("EmpNames").Value
9  MsgBox "Size Of Collection Before: " & _
       DeptCollection.Size
10  OraDynaset.Edit
```

```
11    DeptCollection.Trim 2
12 OraDynaset.Update
12 MsgBox "Size Of Collection After: " & _
      DeptCollection.Size
```

Analysis

- Lines 1–3 are Dim statements for the objects being used to connect to the database and to create the dynaset.

- Line 4 is the Dim statement for the OraCollection object.

- Line 5 creates the OraSession object.

- Line 6 creates an OraDatabase object and establishes the connection to the database.

- Line 7 creates the OraDynaset object based on the DeptVarray table.

- Line 8 sets the DeptCollection to the content of the current collection type in the database.

- Line 9 displays a message box that shows the size of the collection before executing the Trim method.

- Line 10 edits the OraDynaset object.

- Line 11 executes the Trim method.

- Line 12 updates the OraDynaset object to commit the Delete/Trim operation.

- Line 13 displays a message box that shows the size of the collection after executing the Trim method.

NOTE   As of this writing, the Trim method subtracts 1 from the number being passed in. So, although 2 is being passed to the Trim method, only one record is deleted. This should be fixed in a later release of OO4O.

In Listing 8.5, notice that a message box is displayed both before and after executing the Trim method. This is a simple way to illustrate that, unlike the Delete method, the Trim method will update the Size property with the current size without having to execute a Refresh operation.

VArray of an Object Type

The following examples illustrate working with VArrays of object types. The table used for these examples is the same one used for the VArray of object types when working in SQL*Plus. The name of the table is DeptVarrayObj, and the VArray collection used is named EmpVarrayObj. The name of the object used in the collection is EmpObj.

Insert

Listing 8.6 inserts the same three values used for inserting into VArrays of object types in SQL*Plus.

If you have been following along since the beginning of the chapter, delete the records entered earlier. To do so, execute the following SQL command in SQL*Plus:

```
DELETE DeptVarrayObj;
```

Don't forget to execute the Commit command to save the change.

Listing 8.6

```
1   Dim OraSession As OraSession
2   Dim OraDatabase As OraDatabase
3   Dim OraDynaset As OraDynaset
4   Dim DeptCollection As OraCollection
5   Dim EmpObj As OraObject
6   Set OraSession = _
        CreateObject("OracleInProcServer.XOraSession")
7   Set OraDatabase = OraSession.OpenDatabase _
        ("v8i", "scott/tiger", 0&)
8   Set OraDynaset = OraDatabase.CreateDynaset _
        ("SELECT * FROM DeptVarrayObj", 0&)
9   Set EmpObj = OraDatabase.CreateOraObject("EMPOBJ")
10  Set DeptCollection = _
        OraDatabase.CreateOraObject("EMPVARRAYOBJ")
11  'Data for 1st element of the collection
12  EmpObj.EMPNO = 2000
13  EmpObj.EMPLOYEE = "Jim"
14  DeptCollection(1) = EmpObj
15  'Data for 2nd element of the collection
16  EmpObj.EMPNO = 2001
```

```
17 EmpObj.EMPLOYEE = "Jenny"
18 DeptCollection(2) = EmpObj
19 'Data for 3rd element of the collection
20 EmpObj.EMPNO = 2003
21 EmpObj.EMPLOYEE = "Mark"
22 DeptCollection(3) = EmpObj
23
24 OraDynaset.AddNew
25    OraDynaset.Fields("Deptno").Value = 10
26    OraDynaset.Fields("DeptName").Value = "MSLang"
27    OraDynaset.Fields("EmpNames").Value = DeptCollection
28 OraDynaset.Update
29 MsgBox "Insert complete"
```

Analysis

- Lines 1–3 are Dim statements for the objects being used to connect to the database and to create the dynaset.

- Line 4 is the Dim statement for the OraCollection object.

- Line 5 is the Dim statement for the OraObject object.

- Line 6 creates the OraSession object.

- Line 7 creates an OraDatabase object and establishes the connection to the database.

- Line 8 creates the OraDynaset object based on the DeptVarray table.

- Line 9 creates a stand-alone OraObject object based on the EmpObj definition in the database.

- Line 10 creates a stand-alone OraCollection object based on the EmpVarray-Obj definition in the database, which is a VArray of an object type.

- Line 11 is a comment signifying the data for the first element of the collection.

- Lines 12–13 insert data into the two fields of the object.

- Line 14 places the data from the EmpObj object into the first element of the collection.

- Line 15 is a comment signifying the data for the second element of the collection.

- Lines 16–17 insert data into the EmpObj object.

- Line 18 places the data from the EmpObj object into the second element of the collection.

- Line 19 is a comment signifying the data for the third element of the collection.

- Lines 20–21 insert data into the EmpObj object.

- Line 22 places the data from the EmpObj object into the third element of the collection.

- Line 23 is a blank line to make the code easier to read.

- Line 24 invokes the AddNew method of the OraDynaset object.

- Line 25 inserts 10 into the Deptno field.

- Line 26 inserts "MSLang" into the DeptName field.

- Line 27 inserts the data from the stand-alone OraCollection object into the EmpNames field.

- Line 28 updates the OraDynaset object to commit the insert.

- Line 29 displays a message box after the record is inserted.

The key lines of codes are lines 9 through 22 and line 27. Line 9 creates the stand-alone object, and line 10 creates the stand-alone VArray collection. Lines 12 and 13 insert the data into the object. Then, the object data is set to the first element in the collection on line 14. Then, lines 16 and 17 place new data in the object. Since this is data for the second element of the collection, line 18 uses the number 2 subscripting to place the data in the second element of the collection. This same process is followed for the third element. Once the stand-alone collection is populated (DeptCollection), it can be set to the EmpNames field in the dynaset as it is in line 27.

Select

Listing 8.7 illustrates stepping through the entire collection using the Size property of the OraCollection object to regulate how many elements are contained in the collection.

⟳ Listing 8.7

```
1  Dim OraSession As OraSession
2  Dim OraDatabase As OraDatabase
3  Dim OraDynaset As OraDynaset
4  Dim DeptCollection As OraCollection
5  Dim EmpObj As OraObject
6  Set OraSession = _
       CreateObject("OracleInProcServer.XOraSession")
7  Set OraDatabase = OraSession.OpenDatabase _
       ("v8i", "scott/tiger", 0&)
8  Set OraDynaset = OraDatabase.CreateDynaset _
       ("SELECT * FROM DeptVarrayObj", 0&)
9  Set DeptCollection = _
       OraDynaset.Fields("EmpNames").Value
10  For Index = 1 To DeptCollection.Size
11     Set EmpObj = DeptCollection(Index)
12     MsgBox "Employee #: " & EmpObj.EMPNO & _
          Chr(13) & "Employee Name: " & EmpObj.EMPLOYEE
13 Next Index
14 MsgBox "Select Complete"
```

Analysis

- Lines 1–3 are Dim statements for the objects being used to connect to the database and for creating the dynaset.

- Line 4 is the Dim statement for the OraCollection object.

- Line 5 is the Dim statement for the OraObject object.

- Line 6 creates the OraSession object.

- Line 7 creates an OraDatabase object and establishes the connection to the database.

- Line 8 creates the OraDynaset object based on the DeptVarrayObj table.

- Line 9 sets the OO4O collection object to the collection in the dynaset.

- Line 10 starts the For loop to iterate through the collection.

- Line 11 sets the OO4O object to the current element of the collection.

- Lines 12 displays a message box to show the contents of the EmpObj object.

- Line 13 increments the For loop and continues iterating through the collection object.

- Line 14 displays a message box after the record is selected.

You may want to take a moment to see how the elements of the VArray collection of objects are being referenced. Since objects are contained in the collection, accessing the data will take an extra step. This extra step requires copying the collection data to an object first. With the VArrays of simple types example, you accessed the data and display it in a message box using a single line of code, `Msg-Box DeptCollection(1)`. But since this collection type contains objects, using the same command will result in an Automation error. Instead of directly referencing the data, the data must first be copied to an OraObject type, as in line 11. Then, referencing isdone through the OraObject type, as in line 12.

Update

Listing 8.8 updates one of the elements in the VArray of an object collection. As discussed in the VArray of simple types, due to limitations when selecting and updating collection types, you are required to traverse through each element to find the one you are looking for. With VArrays of simple types, you are able to traverse through the collection and search for a matching record. But with VArrays of object types, an extra step is required, which is to extract each record of the collection into its respected object type. This is defined as an OraObject in OO4O. Instead of comparing values against the collection type, you are now comparing values against the object type.

Listing 8.8 updates the Jenny element and changes it to "Jen".

Listing 8.8

```
1  Dim OraSession As OraSession
2  Dim OraDatabase As OraDatabase
3  Dim OraDynaset As OraDynaset
4  Dim DeptCollection As OraCollection
5  Dim EmpObj As OraObject
6  Set OraSession = _
       CreateObject("OracleInProcServer.XOraSession")
```

```
7  Set OraDatabase = OraSession.OpenDatabase _
       ("v8i", "scott/tiger", 0&)
8  Set OraDynaset = OraDatabase.CreateDynaset _
       ("SELECT * FROM DeptVarrayObj", 0&)
9  Set DeptCollection = _
       OraDynaset.Fields("EmpNames").Value
10  For Index = 1 To DeptCollection.Size
11     Set EmpObj = DeptCollection(Index)
12     If EmpObj.EMPLOYEE = "Jenny" Then
13         OraDynaset.Edit
14             EmpObj.EMPLOYEE = "Jen"
15         OraDynaset.Update
16         MsgBox "Update complete"
17         Exit Sub
18     End If
19 Next Index
20 MsgBox "Data was not updated"
```

⤳ Analysis

- Lines 1–3 are Dim statements for the objects being used to connect to the database and to create the dynaset.

- Line 4 is the Dim statement for the OraCollection object.

- Line 5 is the Dim statement for the OraObject object.

- Line 6 creates the OraSession object.

- Line 7 creates an OraDatabase object and establishes the connection to the database.

- Line 8 creates the OraDynaset object based on the DeptVarrayObj table.

- Line 9 sets the DeptCollection to the collection in the DeptVarrayObj table.

- Line 10 starts the For loop to iterate through the elements in the OraCollection object.

- Line 11 sets the OO4O object to the current element of the collection.

- Line 12 checks to see if the object contains the data for which you are searching.

- Line 13 edits the OraDynaset object if a match is found.

- Line 14 sets the value of the Employee field in the object to its new value.

- Line 15 updates the OraDynaset object to commit the change.

- Line 16 displays a message box after the data is committed.

- Line 17 exits the subroutine. No need to continue unless you are expecting to update more data.

- Line 18 ends the If condition.

- Line 19 increments the counter for the loop.

- Line 20 displays a message box if no matching data is found.

The important lines to focus on are lines 10 through 19. Line 10 starts the For loop to traverse through the collection by starting at 1 and using the Size property of the collection object to calculate how many elements exist. Line 11 sets the OraObject variable (EmpObj) to the current reference of the collection based on the subscript of the collection (DeptCollection). Notice that in line 12, instead of executing the If condition against the collection object, it uses the object variable. Lines 13 through 15 actually edit the record and change the value from "Jenny" to "Jen". Notice that these lines are contained in the If condition, which means that the record will not be edited unless a match is found.

Update (Append)

Listing 8.9 appends a new element to an existing collection of an object type.

Listing 8.9

```
1   Dim OraSession As OraSession
2   Dim OraDatabase As OraDatabase
3   Dim OraDynaset As OraDynaset
4   Dim DeptCollection As OraCollection
5   Dim EmpObj As OraObject
6   Set OraSession = _
        CreateObject("OracleInProcServer.XOraSession")
7   Set OraDatabase = OraSession.OpenDatabase _
        ("v8i", "scott/tiger", 0&)
8   Set OraDynaset = OraDatabase.CreateDynaset _
        ("SELECT * FROM DeptVarrayObj", 0&)
9   Set DeptCollection = _
        OraDynaset.Fields("EmpNames").Value
10  Set EmpObj = OraDatabase.CreateOraObject("EMPOBJ")
```

```
11 EmpObj.EMPNO = 2004
12 EmpObj.EMPLOYEE = "John"
13 OraDynaset.Edit
14    DeptCollection.Append EmpObj
15 OraDynaset.Update
16 MsgBox "Append Complete"
```

Analysis

- Lines 1–3 are Dim statements for the objects being used to connect to the database and to create the dynaset.

- Line 4 is the Dim statement for the OraCollection object.

- Line 5 is the Dim statement for the OraObject object.

- Line 6 creates the OraSession object.

- Line 7 creates an OraDatabase object and establishes the connection to the database.

- Line 8 creates the OraDynaset object based on the DeptVarrayObj table.

- Line 9 sets the DeptCollection to the collection in the DeptVarrayObj table.

- Line 10 creates a stand-alone EmpObj object, which is based on the EmpObj object defined in the database.

- Line 11 sets the Empno field of the object to 2004.

- Line 12 sets the Employee field of the object to "John".

- Line 13 edits the OraDynaset object if a match is found.

- Line 14 executes the Append method of the collection using the data in the EmpObj object.

- Line 15 updates the OraDynaset object to commit the change.

- Line 16 displays a message box after the data is appended.

With VArray collections of simple types, you are able to append a new element to the collection by passing in the new value to the Append method. But with VArray of object types, it's the new object that you are passing to the Append method. Notice that line 10 creates a new OraObject object that is used to store the data for the new value. Lines 11 and 12 populate the EmpObj object (of OraObject type) with the data to be appended. Notice that in line 14, the EmpObj object is passed to the Append method.

Delete (Trim)

Listing 8.10 uses the Trim method to remove records from a collection type. The Trim method removes elements from the end of the collection.

Listing 8.10

```
1  Dim OraSession As OraSession
2  Dim OraDatabase As OraDatabase
3  Dim OraDynaset As OraDynaset
4  Dim DeptCollection As OraCollection
5  Dim EmpObj As OraObject
6  Set OraSession = _
       CreateObject("OracleInProcServer.XOraSession")
7  Set OraDatabase = OraSession.OpenDatabase _
       ("v8i", "scott/tiger", 0&)
8  Set OraDynaset = OraDatabase.CreateDynaset _
       ("SELECT * FROM DeptVarrayObj", 0&)
9  Set DeptCollection = _
       OraDynaset.Fields("EmpNames").Value
10 MsgBox "Size Of Collection Before: " & _
       DeptCollection.Size
11 OraDynaset.Edit
12     DeptCollection.Trim 2
13 OraDynaset.Update
14 MsgBox "Size Of Collection After: " & _
       DeptCollection.Size
```

Analysis

- Lines 1–3 are Dim statements for the objects being used to connect to the database and to create the dynaset.

- Line 4 is the Dim statement for the OraCollection object.

- Line 5 is the Dim statement for the OraObject object.

- Line 6 creates the OraSession object.

- Line 7 creates an OraDatabase object and establishes the connection to the database.

- Line 8 creates the OraDynaset object based on the DeptVarray table.

- Line 9 sets the DeptCollection variable to the content of the current collection type in the database.

- Line 10 displays a message box that shows the size of the collection before executing the Trim method.

- Line 11 edits the OraDynaset object.

- Line 12 executes the Trim method.

- Line 13 updates the OraDynaset object to commit the Delete/Trim operation.

- Line 14 displays a message box that shows the size of the collection after executing the Trim method.

NOTE   As of this writing, the Trim method subtracts 1 from the number being passed in. So, although 2 is being passed to the Trim method, only one record is deleted. This should be fixed in a later release of OO4O.

Even though this example uses a VArray of objects, it is almost identical to the Trim example for the VArray of simple types (Listing 8.5). Although this example uses a VArray of object type, there was no extra step required to create the OraObject. Whether the collection is of a simple type or of an object type, there is no need to create an extra object because the Trim method is part of the OraCollection object. The OraCollection object will Trim any type of collection.

Working with Nested Tables in Visual Basic

This section provides an introduction to working with Nested Tables in Visual Basic. First, we discuss working with Nested Tables of simple types. Then we discuss working with Nested Tables of object types.

Nested Tables of a Simple Type

The following examples work with Nested Tables of simple types. For this book, simple types are types that already exist in the database. The table used for these examples is the same as the one used in the examples working with Nested Tables of simple types in SQL.*Plus. The name of the table is DeptNested. The Nested Table collection used is named EmpNested.

Insert

Listing 8.11 inserts the same three values as those used for inserting into the Nested Table in SQL*Plus (from the "Nested Tables of a Simple Type" section earlier in this chapter).

If you have been following along since the beginning of the chapter, delete the records entered earlier. To do so, execute the following SQL command in SQL*Plus:

```
DELETE DeptNested;
```

Don't forget to execute the Commit command to save the change.

Listing 8.11

```
1  Dim OraSession As OraSession
2  Dim OraDatabase As OraDatabase
3  Dim OraDynaset As OraDynaset
4  Dim DeptCollection As OraCollection
5  Set OraSession = _
       CreateObject("OracleInProcServer.XOraSession")
6  Set OraDatabase = OraSession.OpenDatabase _
       ("v8i", "scott/tiger", 0&)
7  Set OraDynaset = OraDatabase.CreateDynaset _
     ("SELECT * FROM DeptNested", 0&)
8  Set DeptCollection = _
     OraDatabase.CreateOraObject("EMPNESTED")
9  DeptCollection(1) = "Jim"
10  DeptCollection(2) = "Jenny"
11 DeptCollection(3) = "Mark"
12 OraDynaset.AddNew
13    OraDynaset.Fields("DEPTNO").Value = 10
14    OraDynaset.Fields("DEPTNAME").Value = "MSLang"
15    OraDynaset.Fields("EmpNames").Value = DeptCollection
16 OraDynaset.Update
17 MsgBox "Insert Complete"
```

Analysis

- Lines 1–3 are Dim statements for the objects being used to connect to the database and to create the dynaset.

- Line 4 is the Dim statement for the OraCollection object.

- Line 5 creates the OraSession object.

- Line 6 creates an OraDatabase object and establishes the connection to the database.

- Line 7 creates the OraDynaset object based on the DeptNested table.

- Line 8 creates a stand-alone OraCollection object based on the EmpNested definition in the database, which is a Nested Table of a simple type.

- Lines 9–11 assign a value to elements 1 through 3 of the stand-alone collection type.

- Line 12 calls the AddNew method of the OraDynaset object.

- Line 13 inserts 10 into the Deptno field.

- Line 14 inserts "MSLang" into the DeptName field.

- Line 15 inserts the data from the stand-alone OraCollection object into the EmpNames field.

- Line 16 updates the OraDynaset object to commit the Insert operation.

- Line 17 displays a message box after the record is inserted.

The key lines of code are lines 8 through 11 and line 15. Line 8 creates the stand-alone Nested Table. Lines 9 through 11 populate the collection. Line 15 adds the data to the EmpNames field in the dynaset.

If you compare this Nested Table of simple types example to the VArray of simple types example (Listing 8.1), you notice that there are only two lines of code that differ (lines 7 and 8). In this listing, line 7 references the DeptNested table instead of the DeptVarray table, and line 8 references the EmpNested collection instead of the EmpVarray collection. This example illustrates how OO4O makes the collection type transparent to you on the back end and provides a simple front end to interface with when working with collections.

Select

Listing 8.12 steps through the entire collection using the Size property of the Ora-Collection object to regulate how many elements are contained in the collection.

Listing 8.12

```
1  Dim OraSession As OraSession
2  Dim OraDatabase As OraDatabase
3  Dim OraDynaset As OraDynaset
4  Dim DeptCollection As OraCollection
5  Set OraSession = _
       CreateObject("OracleInProcServer.XOraSession")
6  Set OraDatabase = OraSession.OpenDatabase _
       ("v8i", "scott/tiger", 0&)
7  Set OraDynaset = OraDatabase.CreateDynaset _
     ("SELECT * FROM DeptNested", 0&)
8  Set DeptCollection = OraDynaset.Fields("EmpNames").Value
9  For Index = 1 To DeptCollection.Size
10      MsgBox DeptCollection(Index)
11 Next Index
12 MsgBox "Select Complete"
```

Analysis

- Lines 1–3 are Dim statements for the objects being used to connect to the database and to create the dynaset.

- Line 4 is the Dim statement for the OraCollection object.

- Line 5 creates the OraSession object.

- Line 6 creates an OraDatabase object and establishes the connection to the database.

- Line 7 creates the OraDynaset object based on the DeptNested table.

- Line 8 sets the DeptCollection to the content of the current collection type in the database.

- Line 9 starts the For loop to iterate through the elements in the OraCollection object.

- Line 10 displays a message box with the value of the current element in the collection.

- Line 11 increments the counter for the loop.

- Line 12 displays a message box after all the records in the collection have been displayed.

Take a moment to see how the elements of the Nested Table collection are referenced (line 10). Remember, you can use standard subscripting, and, indeed, that's what is done. The subscript variable is incremented by the For loop.

If you compare this Nested Table of simple types example to the VArray of simple types example (Listing 8.2), you notice that only one line of code differs. This is line 7, which references the DeptNested table instead of the DeptVarray table. This example illustrates how, when working with either VArrays or Nested Tables, OO4O allows you to use a generic interface (OraCollection object) to view and manipulate data.

Update

This example of the Update method illustrates updating one of the elements in the Nested Table collection. Due to limitations when selecting and updating collection types, you are required to traverse through each element to find the one you are looking for. As with VArray collections, this does not mean that your Where clause cannot contain a search criteria based on an element in the collection, but rather, it means that you will still have to traverse through the collection once retrieved.

Listing 8.13 updates the Jenny element and changes it to "Jen".

Listing 8.13

```
1  Dim OraSession As OraSession
2  Dim OraDatabase As OraDatabase
3  Dim OraDynaset As OraDynaset
4  Dim DeptCollection As OraCollection
5  Set OraSession = _
       CreateObject("OracleInProcServer.XOraSession")
6  Set OraDatabase = OraSession.OpenDatabase _
       ("v8i", "scott/tiger", 0&)
```

```
 7  Set OraDynaset = OraDatabase.CreateDynaset _
       ("SELECT * FROM DeptNested", 0&)
 8  Set DeptCollection = OraDynaset.Fields("EmpNames").Value
 9  For Index = 1 To DeptCollection.Size
10     If DeptCollection(Index) = "Jenny" Then
11          OraDynaset.Edit
12              DeptCollection(Index) = "Jen"
13          OraDynaset.Update
14          MsgBox "Update complete"
15          Exit Sub
16     End If
17 Next Index
18 MsgBox "Data was not updated"
```

Analysis

- Lines 1–3 are Dim statements for the objects being used to connect to the database and to create the dynaset.

- Line 4 is the Dim statement for the OraCollection object.

- Line 5 creates the OraSession object.

- Line 6 creates an OraDatabase object and establishes the connection to the database.

- Line 7 creates the OraDynaset object based on the DeptNested table.

- Line 8 sets the DeptCollection to the content of the current collection type in the database.

- Line 9 starts the For loop to iterate through the elements in the OraCollection object.

- Line 10 checks to see if the current element of the collection object is equal to the value for which you are searching.

- Line 11 edits the OraDynaset object.

- Line 12 sets the current element of the collection to the new value.

- Line 13 updates the OraDynaset object to commit the Update operation.

- Line 14 displays a message box after the data is committed.

- Line 15 exits the subroutine. No need to continue unless you are expecting more data to update.

- Line 16 ends the If condition.

- Line 17 increments the counter for the loop.

- Line 18 displays a message box if no matching data is found.

The important lines to focus on are lines 9 through 17. Line 9 starts the For loop to traverse through the collection by starting at 1 and using the Size property of the collection object to calculate how many elements exist and will have to be searched. Line 10 is the If condition used to search each element of the collection for "Jenny". Lines 11 through 13 edit the record and change the value from "Jenny" to "Jen". Notice that these lines are contained in the If condition, which means that the record will not be edited unless a match is found.

As with the previous example, if you compare this Nested Table of simple types example to the VArray of simple types example (Listing 8.3), you notice that only one line of code differs. As before, this is line 7, which references the DeptNested table instead of the DeptVarray table. This example illustrates how, when working with either VArrays or Nested Tables, OO4O allows you to use a generic interface (OraCollection object) to view and manipulate data.

Update (Append)

The Update method example in Listing 8.14 appends a new element to an existing collection.

Listing 8.14

```
1  Dim OraSession As OraSession
2  Dim OraDatabase As OraDatabase
3  Dim OraDynaset As OraDynaset
4  Dim DeptCollection As OraCollection
5  Set OraSession = _
       CreateObject("OracleInProcServer.XOraSession")
6  Set OraDatabase = OraSession.OpenDatabase _
       ("v8i", "scott/tiger", 0&)
7  Set OraDynaset = OraDatabase.CreateDynaset _
     ("SELECT * FROM DeptNested", 0&)
8  Set DeptCollection = OraDynaset.Fields("EmpNames").Value
```

```
9  OraDynaset.Edit
10    DeptCollection.Append "John"
11 OraDynaset.Update
12 MsgBox "Append complete"
```

Analysis

- Lines 1–3 are Dim statements for the objects being used to connect to the database and to create the dynaset.

- Line 4 is the Dim statement for the OraCollection object.

- Line 5 creates the OraSession object.

- Line 6 creates an OraDatabase object and establishes the connection to the database.

- Line 7 creates the OraDynaset object based on the DeptNested table.

- Line 8 sets the DeptCollection to the content of the current collection type in the database.

- Line 9 edits the OraDynaset object.

- Line 10 executes the Append mode of the collection object.

- Line 11 updates the OraDynaset object to commit the appended data.

- Line 12 displays a message box after the data is committed.

How easy is appending a new value to a Nested Table of simple types? It's essentially the same as appending a new value to a VArray of a single type, and this happens to be a single line of code (line 10). The other lines of code are standard for connecting to the database and defining the dynaset. OO4O makes appending a new element to collections of simple types a fairly simple process by providing the Append method. If you compare this example to the Append example for the VArray of simple types (Listing 8.4), you find that line 7 is the only line that is different, and this is because the examples are referencing two different tables.

Delete

The example uses the Delete method to remove a given record from a Nested Table collection type. This method is only valid against a Nested Table collection type and not against a VArray collection type.

Listing 8.15 uses the Delete method to remove a record from the collection. Although this number can reference any valid subscript in the collection, it can only delete one record at a time. So, if you wish to delete more than one element from the collection, the Delete method must be executed once for each element.

Listing 8.15

```
1  Dim OraSession As OraSession
2  Dim OraDatabase As OraDatabase
3  Dim OraDynaset As OraDynaset
4  Dim DeptCollection As OraCollection
5  Set OraSession = _
       CreateObject("OracleInProcServer.XOraSession")
6  Set OraDatabase = OraSession.OpenDatabase _
       ("v8i", "scott/tiger", 0&)
7  Set OraDynaset = OraDatabase.CreateDynaset _
      ("SELECT * FROM DeptNested", 0&)
8  Set DeptCollection = OraDynaset.Fields("EmpNames").Value
9  MsgBox "Value in Size property: " & _
          DeptCollection.Size & Chr(13) & _
          "Value in TableSize property: " & _
          DeptCollection.TableSize, , "Before"
10  OraDynaset.Edit
11    DeptCollection.Delete 2
12 OraDynaset.Update
13 MsgBox "Value in Size property: " & _
          DeptCollection.Size & Chr(13) & _
          "Value in TableSize property: " & _
          DeptCollection.TableSize, , "After"
```

Analysis

- Lines 1–3 are Dim statements for the objects being used to connect to the database and to create the dynaset.

- Line 4 is the Dim statement for the OraCollection object.

- Line 5 creates the OraSession object.

- Line 6 creates an OraDatabase object and establishes the connection to the database.

- Line 7 creates the OraDynaset object based on the DeptNested table.

- Line 8 sets the DeptCollection to the content of the current collection type in the database.

- Line 9 displays a message box displaying both the Size property and the TableSize property of the collection before executing the Delete method.

- Line 10 edits the OraDynaset object.

- Line 11 executes the Delete method.

- Line 12 updates the OraDynaset object to commit the Delete operation.

- Line 13 displays a message box that shows both the Size property and the TableSize property of the collection after executing the Delete method.

This is an excellent example, which illustrates not only the use of the Delete method but also the difference in the values held in the Size property and the TableSize property of the OraCollection object after executing the Delete method without executing a Refresh operation.

Delete (Trim)

Listing 8.16 uses the Trim method to remove records from a Nested Table collection type. Keep in mind that the Trim method removes elements from the end of the collection.

Listing 8.16

```
1  Dim OraSession As OraSession
2  Dim OraDatabase As OraDatabase
3  Dim OraDynaset As OraDynaset
4  Dim DeptCollection As OraCollection
5  Set OraSession = _
       CreateObject("OracleInProcServer.XOraSession")
6  Set OraDatabase = OraSession.OpenDatabase _
       ("v8i", "scott/tiger", 0&)
7  Set OraDynaset = OraDatabase.CreateDynaset _
     ("SELECT * FROM DeptNested", 0&)
8  Set DeptCollection = OraDynaset.Fields("EmpNames").Value
9  MsgBox "Size Of Collection Before: " & _
         DeptCollection.Size
```

```
10  OraDynaset.Edit
11    DeptCollection.Trim 2
12 OraDynaset.Update
13 MsgBox "Size Of Collection After: " & _
     DeptCollection.Size
```

Analysis

- Lines 1–3 are Dim statements for the objects being used to connect to the database and to create the dynaset.

- Line 4 is the Dim statement for the OraCollection object.

- Line 5 creates the OraSession object.

- Line 6 creates an OraDatabase object and establishes the connection to the database.

- Line 7 creates the OraDynaset object based on the DeptNested table.

- Line 8 sets the DeptCollection to the content of the current collection type in the database.

- Line 9 displays a message box that shows the size of the collection before executing the Trim method.

- Line 10 edits the OraDynaset object.

- Line 11 executes the Trim method.

- Line 12 updates the OraDynaset object to commit the Trim operation.

- Line 13 displays a message box that shows the size of the collection after executing the Trim method.

NOTE   As of this writing, the Trim method subtracts 1 from the number being passed in. So, although 2 is being passed to the Trim method, only one record is deleted. This should be fixed in a later release of OO4O.

In the example in Listing 8.16, notice that a message box is displayed both before and after executing the Trim method. This is a simple way to illustrate that unlike the Delete method, the Trim method will update the Size property with the new size without having to execute a Refresh operation.

Other than the different tables being referenced when creating the dynaset, this example is essentially the same as the one used when illustrating the use of the Trim method for the VArray of simple types (Listing 8.5).

A Nested Table of an Object Type

The following examples illustrate working with Nested Table of object types. The table used for these examples is the same as the one used for the Nested Table of object types example when working in SQL*Plus. The name of the table is Dept-NestedObj, and the Nested Table collection used is named EmpNestedObj. The name of the object used in the collection is EmpObj.

Insert

Listing 8.17 inserts the same three values used for inserting into VArrays of object types in SQL*Plus.

If you have been following along since the beginning of the chapter, delete the records entered earlier. To do so, execute the following SQL command in SQL*Plus:

```
DELETE DeptNestedObj;
```

Don't forget to execute the Commit command to save the change.

Listing 8.17

```
1   Dim OraSession As OraSession
2   Dim OraDatabase As OraDatabase
3   Dim OraDynaset As OraDynaset
4   Dim DeptCollection As OraCollection
5   Dim EmpObj As OraObject
6   Set OraSession = _
        CreateObject("OracleInProcServer.XOraSession")
7   Set OraDatabase = OraSession.OpenDatabase _
        ("v8i", "scott/tiger", 0&)
8   Set OraDynaset = OraDatabase.CreateDynaset _
        ("SELECT * FROM DeptNestedObj", 0&)
9   Set EmpObj = OraDatabase.CreateOraObject("EMPOBJ")
10  Set DeptCollection = _
        OraDatabase.CreateOraObject("EMPNESTEDOBJ")
11 'Data for 1st element of the collection
```

```
12 EmpObj.EMPNO = 2000
13 EmpObj.EMPLOYEE = "Jim"
14 DeptCollection(1) = EmpObj
15 'Data for 2nd element of the collection
16 EmpObj.EMPNO = 2001
17 EmpObj.EMPLOYEE = "Jenny"
18 DeptCollection(2) = EmpObj
19 'Data for 3rd element of the collection
20 EmpObj.EMPNO = 2003
21 EmpObj.EMPLOYEE = "Mark"
22 DeptCollection(3) = EmpObj
23
24 OraDynaset.AddNew
25    OraDynaset.Fields("Deptno").Value = 10
26    OraDynaset.Fields("DeptName").Value = "MSLang"
27    OraDynaset.Fields("EmpNames").Value = DeptCollection
28 OraDynaset.Update
29 MsgBox "Insert complete"
```

Analysis

- Lines 1–3 are Dim statements for the objects being used to connect to the database and to create the dynaset.

- Line 4 is the Dim statement for the OraCollection object.

- Line 5 is the Dim statement for the OraObject object.

- Line 6 creates the OraSession object.

- Line 7 creates an OraDatabase object and establishes the connection to the database.

- Line 8 creates the OraDynaset object based on the DeptNestedObj table.

- Line 9 creates a stand-alone OraObject object based on the EmpObj object definition in the database.

- Line 10 creates a stand-alone OraCollection object based on the EmpNested-Obj definition in the database. EmpNestedObj is a Nested Table of an object.

- Line 11 is a comment signifying the data for the first element of the collection.

- Lines 12–13 insert data into the two fields of the object.

- Line 14 places the data from the EmpObj object into the first element of the collection.

- Line 15 is a comment signifying the data for the second element of the collection.

- Lines 16–17 insert data into the EmpObj object.

- Line 18 places the data from the EmpObj object into the second element of the collection.

- Line 19 is a comment signifying the data for the third element of the collection.

- Lines 20–21 insert data into the EmpObj object.

- Line 22 places the data from the EmpObj object into the third element of the collection.

- Line 23 is a blank line to make the code easier to read.

- Line 24 invokes the AddNew method of the OraDynaset object.

- Line 25 inserts 10 into the Deptno field.

- Line 26 inserts "MSLang" into the DeptName field.

- Line 27 inserts the data from the stand-alone OraCollection object into the EmpNames field.

- Line 28 updates the OraDynaset object to commit the Insert operation.

- Line 29 displays a message box after the record is inserted.

The key lines of the code are lines 9 through 22 and line 27. Line 9 creates the stand-alone object, and line 10 creates the stand-alone Nested Table collection. When inserting the data, notice that lines 12 and 13 insert the data into the object. Then the object data is set to the first element in the collection on line 14. Lines 16 and 17 place new data in the object. Since this is data for the second element of the collection, line 18 uses the number 2 subscripting to place the data in the second element of the collection. This same process is followed for the third element. Once the stand-alone collection is populated (DeptCollection), it can be set to the EmpNames field in the dynaset, as is done in line 27.

Comparing this example to the VArray of object types example (Listing 8.6) reveals that only two lines of code differ. These are lines 8 and 10. Line 8 uses the DeptNestedObj table instead of the DeptVarrayObj, and line 10 creates the Emp-NestedOjb object instead of the EmpVarrayObj object.

Select

Listing 8.18 steps through the entire collection using of the Size property of the Ora-Collection object to regulate how many elements are contained in the collection.

Listing 8.18

```
1  Dim OraSession As OraSession
2  Dim OraDatabase As OraDatabase
3  Dim OraDynaset As OraDynaset
4  Dim DeptCollection As OraCollection
5  Dim EmpObj As OraObject
6  Set OraSession = _
       CreateObject("OracleInProcServer.XOraSession")
7  Set OraDatabase = OraSession.OpenDatabase _
       ("v8i", "scott/tiger", 0&)
8  Set OraDynaset = OraDatabase.CreateDynaset _
       ("SELECT * FROM DeptNestedObj", 0&)
9  Set DeptCollection = _
       OraDynaset.Fields("EmpNames").Value
10  For Index = 1 To DeptCollection.Size
11     Set EmpObj = DeptCollection(Index)
12     MsgBox "Employee #: " & EmpObj.EMPNO & _
          Chr(13) & "Employee Name: " & EmpObj.EMPLOYEE
13 Next Index
14 MsgBox "Select Complete"
```

Analysis

- Lines 1–3 are Dim statements for the objects being used to connect to the database and to create the dynaset.

- Line 4 is the Dim statement for the OraCollection object.

- Line 5 is the Dim statement for the OraObject object.

- Line 6 creates the OraSession object.

- Line 7 creates an OraDatabase object and establishes the connection to the database.

- Line 8 creates the OraDynaset object based on the DeptVarrayObj table.

- Line 9 sets the OO4O collection object to the collection in the dynaset.

- Line 10 starts the For loop to iterate through the collection.

- Line 11 sets the OO4O object to the current element of the collection.

- Lines 12 displays a message box to show the contents of the EmpObj object.

- Line 13 increments the For loop and continues iterating through the collection object.

- Line 14 displays a message box after the record is selected.

Take a moment to see how the elements of the Nested Table collection of objects in this example are referenced. Since objects are contained in the collection, accessing the data takes an extra step. This extra step is copying one element of the collection data to an object. With the Nested Table of simple types example, you were able to access the data and display it in a message box using a single line of code, `MsgBox DeptCollection(1)`. But since this collection type contains objects, using the same command results in an Automation error. Instead of directly referencing the data, the data must first be copied to an OraObject type, as in line 11. Then referencing is done through the OraObject type, as in line 12.

If you compare this Select example with the VArray of object's Select example (Listing 8.7), you find that only one line of code is different. This is line 7, which creates a dynaset based on the DeptNestedObj table instead of on the DeptVarray-Obj table.

Update

This Update method example illustrates updating one of the elements in the Nested Table of object type collection. Due to limitations when selecting and updating collection types, you are required to traverse through each element to find the one you are looking for. With Nested Table of simple types, you are able to traverse through the collection and search for a matching record. But with Nested Table of object types, an extra step is required, which extracts each record of the collection into its respective object type. This is defined as an OraObject in OO4O. Instead of comparing values against the collection type, you are now comparing values against the object type.

Listing 8.19 updates the Jenny element and changes it to "Jen".

Listing 8.19

```
1  Dim OraSession As OraSession
2  Dim OraDatabase As OraDatabase
3  Dim OraDynaset As OraDynaset
4  Dim DeptCollection As OraCollection
5  Dim EmpObj As OraObject
6  Set OraSession = _
      CreateObject("OracleInProcServer.XOraSession")
7  Set OraDatabase = OraSession.OpenDatabase _
      ("v8i", "scott/tiger", 0&)
8  Set OraDynaset = OraDatabase.CreateDynaset _
      ("SELECT * FROM DeptNestedObj", 0&)
9  Set DeptCollection = _
      OraDynaset.Fields("EmpNames").Value
10  For Index = 1 To DeptCollection.Size
11     Set EmpObj = DeptCollection(Index)
12     If EmpObj.EMPLOYEE = "Jenny" Then
13         OraDynaset.Edit
14             EmpObj.EMPLOYEE = "Jen"
15         OraDynaset.Update
16         MsgBox "Update complete"
17         Exit Sub
18     End If
19 Next Index
20 MsgBox "Data was not updated"
```

Analysis

- Lines 1–3 are Dim statements for the objects being used to connect to the database and to create the dynaset.

- Line 4 is the Dim statement for the OraCollection object.

- Line 5 is the Dim statement for the OraObject object.

- Line 6 creates the OraSession object.

- Line 7 creates an OraDatabase object and establishes the connection to the database.

- Line 8 creates the OraDynaset object based on the DeptNestedObj table.

- Line 9 sets the DeptCollection to the collection in the DeptNestedObj table.

- Line 10 starts the For loop to iterate through the elements in the OraCollection object.

- Line 11 sets the OO4O object to the current element of the collection.

- Line 12 checks to see if the object contains the data for which you are searching.

- Line 13 edits the OraDynaset object if a match is found.

- Line 14 sets the value of the Employee field in the object to its new value.

- Line 15 updates the OraDynaset object to commit the change.

- Line 16 displays a message box after the data is committed.

- Line 17 exits the subroutine. No need to continue unless you are expecting to update more data.

- Line 18 ends the If condition.

- Line 19 increments the counter for the loop.

- Line 20 displays a message box if no matching data is found.

The important lines to focus on are lines 10 through 19. Line 10 starts the For loop to traverse through the collection by starting at 1 and using the Size property of the collection object to calculate how many elements exist. Line 11 sets the OraObject variable (EmpObj) to the current reference of the collection based on the subscript of the collection (DeptCollection). In line 12, instead of executing the If condition against the collection object, the object variable is used. Lines 13 through 15 actually edit the record and change the value from "Jenny" to "Jen". These lines are contained in the If condition, which means that the record will not be edited unless a match is found.

Update (Append)

Listing 8.20 appends a new element to an existing collection of an object type.

Listing 8.20

```
1  Dim OraSession As OraSession
2  Dim OraDatabase As OraDatabase
3  Dim OraDynaset As OraDynaset
```

```
4  Dim DeptCollection As OraCollection
5  Dim EmpObj As OraObject
6  Set OraSession = _
       CreateObject("OracleInProcServer.XOraSession")
7  Set OraDatabase = OraSession.OpenDatabase _
       ("v8i", "scott/tiger", 0&)
8  Set OraDynaset = OraDatabase.CreateDynaset _
       ("SELECT * FROM DeptNestedObj", 0&)
9  Set DeptCollection = _
       OraDynaset.Fields("EmpNames").Value
10  Set EmpObj = OraDatabase.CreateOraObject("EMPOBJ")
11 EmpObj.EMPNO = 2004
12 EmpObj.EMPLOYEE = "John"
13 OraDynaset.Edit
14     DeptCollection.Append EmpObj
15 OraDynaset.Update
16 MsgBox "Append Complete"
```

Analysis

- Lines 1–3 are Dim statements for the objects being used to connect to the database and to create the dynaset.

- Line 4 is the Dim statement for the OraCollection object.

- Line 5 is the Dim statement for the OraObject object.

- Line 6 creates the OraSession object.

- Line 7 creates an OraDatabase object and establishes the connection to the database.

- Line 8 creates the OraDynaset object based on the DeptNestedObj table.

- Line 9 sets the DeptCollection object to the collection in the DeptNestedObj table.

- Line 10 creates a stand-alone EmpObj object, which is based on the EmpObj object defined in the database.

- Line 11 sets the Empno field of the object to 2004.

- Line 12 sets the Employee field of the object to "John".

- Line 13 edits the OraDynaset object if a match is found.

- Line 14 executes the Append method of the collection using the data in the EmpObj object.

- Line 15 updates the OraDynaset object to commit the change.

- Line 16 displays a message box after the data has been appended.

With Nested Table collections of simple types, you are able to append a new element to the collection by passing in the new value to the Append method. With Nested Table of object types, the new object is passed to the Append method. Line 10 creates a new OraObject object, which stores the data for the new value. Lines 11 and 12 populate the EmpObj with the data to be appended. In line 14, the EmpObj is passed to the Append method.

Comparing this example to the Append method example for the VArray of object (Listing 8.9), you find that the only line of code that differs is the one that creates the dynaset.

Delete

This Delete method example uses the Delete method to remove a given record from a Nested Table collection type. The Delete method is only valid against a Nested Table collection type and not with a VArray collection type.

Listing 8.21 uses the Delete method to remove a record from the collection. Although this number can reference any valid subscript in the collection, it can only delete one record at a time. If you wish to delete more than one element from the collection, the Delete method must be executed for each one.

Listing 8.21

```
1  Dim OraSession As OraSession
2  Dim OraDatabase As OraDatabase
3  Dim OraDynaset As OraDynaset
4  Dim DeptCollection As OraCollection
5  Set OraSession = _
       CreateObject("OracleInProcServer.XOraSession")
6  Set OraDatabase = OraSession.OpenDatabase _
       ("v8i", "scott/tiger", 0&)
7  Set OraDynaset = OraDatabase.CreateDynaset _
     ("SELECT * FROM DeptNestedObj", 0&)
8  Set DeptCollection = OraDynaset.Fields("EmpNames").Value
```

```
9  MsgBox "Value in Size property: " & _
          DeptCollection.Size & Chr(13) & _
          "Value in TableSize property: " & _
          DeptCollection.TableSize, , "Before"
10  OraDynaset.Edit
11    DeptCollection.Delete 2
12 OraDynaset.Update
13 MsgBox "Value in Size property: " & _
          DeptCollection.Size & Chr(13) & _
          "Value in TableSize property: " & _
          DeptCollection.TableSize, , "After"
```

Analysis

- Lines 1–3 are Dim statements for the objects being used to connect to the database and to create the dynaset.

- Line 4 is the Dim statement for the OraCollection object.

- Line 5 creates the OraSession object.

- Line 6 creates an OraDatabase object and establishes the connection to the database.

- Line 7 creates the OraDynaset object based on the DeptNested table.

- Line 8 sets the DeptCollection object to the content of the current collection type in the database.

- Line 9 displays a message box that shows both the Size property and the TableSize property of the collection before executing the Delete method.

- Line 10 edits the OraDynaset object.

- Line 11 executes the Delete method.

- Line 12 updates the OraDynaset object to commit the Delete operation.

- Line 13 displays a message box that shows both the Size property and the TableSize property of the collection after executing the Delete method.

This example illustrates using of the Delete method and the difference in the values held in the Size property versus the TableSize property of the OraCollection object after executing the Delete method without executing a Refresh operation.

Although the table in this example is a Nested Table of an object type, except for the table name used, it's identical to the Delete example for the Nested Table of a simple type (Listing 8.15). This is because the Delete method is part of the Ora-Collection object, and there is no requirement to access any of the underlying objects. After all, the objects are going to be deleted.

Delete (Trim)

Listing 8.22 uses the Trim method to remove records from a collection type. The Trim method removes elements from the end of the collection.

⟳ Listing 8.22

```
1  Dim OraSession As OraSession
2  Dim OraDatabase As OraDatabase
3  Dim OraDynaset As OraDynaset
4  Dim DeptCollection As OraCollection
5  Dim EmpObj As OraObject
6  Set OraSession = _
       CreateObject("OracleInProcServer.XOraSession")
7  Set OraDatabase = OraSession.OpenDatabase _
       ("v8i", "scott/tiger", 0&)
8  Set OraDynaset = OraDatabase.CreateDynaset _
       ("SELECT * FROM DeptNestedObj", 0&)
9  Set DeptCollection = _
       OraDynaset.Fields("EmpNames").Value
10  MsgBox "Size Of Collection Before: " & _
        DeptCollection.Size
11 OraDynaset.Edit
12      DeptCollection.Trim 2
13 OraDynaset.Update
14 MsgBox "Size Of Collection After: " & _
        DeptCollection.Size
```

⟳ Analysis

- Lines 1–3 are Dim statements for the objects being used to connect to the database and to create the dynaset.

- Line 4 is the Dim statement for the OraCollection object.

- Line 5 is the Dim statement for the OraObject object.

- Line 6 creates the OraSession object.

- Line 7 creates an OraDatabase object and establishes the connection to the database.

- Line 8 creates the OraDynaset object, which is based on the DeptNestedObj table.

- Line 9 sets the DeptCollection object to the content of the current collection type in the database.

- Line 10 displays a message box that shows the size of the collection before executing the Trim method.

- Line 11 edits the OraDynaset object.

- Line 12 executes the Trim method.

- Line 13 updates the OraDynaset object to commit the Trim operation.

- Line 14 displays a message box that shows the size of the collection after executing the Trim method.

NOTE   As of this writing, the Trim method subtracts 1 from the number being passed in. Although 2 is being passed to the Trim method, only one record is deleted. This should be fixed in a later release of OO4O.

Although this example uses a Nested Table of an object type, it is almost identical to the Trim example for the Nested Table of simple types. Even though this example uses a Nested Table of an object type, there was no extra step required to create the OraObject object. This is because regardless of whether the collection is of a simple type or of an object type, there is no need to create an extra object because the Trim method is part of the OraCollection object. The OraCollection object will trim any type of collection whether it's a simple type or an object type.

Summary

After completing this chapter, you may start think that there is not much difference between the VArray and Nested Table examples, or much difference between a collection of a simple type and a collection of an object type. If so, you have learned two important things:

- There is not much difference between interfacing with VArrays and Nested Tables.

- Working with collections of an object type may require using the Create-OraObject method to create stand-alone objects, which must be used to interface with the data, as opposed to being able to directly reference the data through the collection.

Even if the topic of collections is still a bit hazy, the examples in this chapter are available when you want to review how to work with collections.

chapter 9

Advanced Programmatic Interfaces

- Using stored procedures and functions

- Using arrays and stored procedures

- Working with object types and member functions

- Passing objects to stored procedures

- Using sequences

- Using the OraParameters collection and OraParamArray objects

- Using the Returning clause

- Working with dates

In previous chapters, we concentrated on working with OO4O doing simple Data Manipulation Language (DML), but that's only a very small portion of OO4O's capabilities. OO4O provides a number of features that many users don't know are even possible. For example, not only can you execute stored procedures and functions in the database using OO4O, but you can also return one or more result sets from a stored procedure or function. Another important feature is batch processing. These and other topics will be addressed in this chapter.

As you work through this chapter, you will notice that there is some overlap between the sections. For example, the OraParameters collection is covered when we discuss how to make a program more dynamic, as well as when discussing interfacing with stored procedures and functions. The same is true for the section on the OraParamArray object, which describes the objects functionality in creating arrays and then discusses using arrays in stored procedures and functions.

Overall, this chapter shows a number of neat features that you may not have known existed. For those who know about these features but are not sure how they work, this chapter will get you on your way.

NOTE   The objects created and the examples in this chapter use the Scott schema and some of its default tables. For more information pertaining to this schema and default tables, refer to the Introduction.

Stored Procedures and Functions

OO4O provides the functionality to interface with stored procedures and functions in the database. So what's the big deal? A lot. For example, if an application requires an enormous amount of calculations to be computed and subsequent queries to be processed before returning a result, would you rather have the client or the server handle all the processing? Why not pass the initial information to the database once, have the database handle all the heavy processing, and then when it's finished, let it return the result. This is especially sensible if producing the result requires querying a table, and you are using the result as the criteria for subsequent queries. Think of the network traffic that could potentially be saved!

Stored procedures and functions also provide a central location for storing business logic and rules. Having the stored procedures and functions in the database means that the database administrator, rather than the programmer, can control the business rules.

Business Rules

Business rules are the constraints or restrictions placed on the data when executing DML. For example, if bonuses are provided by your company twice a year and you want to ensure that no one's bonus exceeds 10 percent of their salary, you can apply this constraint as one of your business rules and prevent anyone from receiving more than the allotted percentage.

Changing business rules, which are located in the database, is simpler and more convenient than changing an application. What happens if each time bonuses are given the percentage changes? You would have to edit and rebuild your application each time. When the business rules are located in the database, the rules can be changed freely without having to touch the client application. Of course, if a new procedure or function is created, or if the number of parameters or the parameter type change, the client application has to be modified, as well.

Keeping the logic and business rules in the database and using stored procedures or functions to handle the logic alleviates many of the headaches associated with working in an environment where the requirements are always changing. Any inserts, updates, and deletions can be processed through the stored procedures and functions and will only be carried out if none of the data violated any of the business rules. Also, if any of the business rules change, the stored procedures and functions can be modified easily without having to touch the OO4O application.

Calling a Simple Stored Procedure

Calling a stored procedure from OO4O is not much different from calling it using SQL*Plus. In fact, if the stored procedure does not contain any parameters, the SQL used to execute a stored procedure in OO4O is identical to the SQL used in SQL*Plus.

Let's create a table to use for a simple example. Open an SQL*Plus session and enter the following SQL code to create a table that will be updated by the stored procedure:

```
CREATE TABLE HOLD_MESSAGE
   (MESSAGE_FIELD VARCHAR2(50));
```

The reason that the table needs to be created first is because any reference to a database object in a procedure or function without the object actually existing results in a compilation error.

Once the table is created, continue by entering the following SQL in SQL*Plus to create the stored procedure:

```
CREATE OR REPLACE PROCEDURE
  INSERT_MESSAGE(MESSAGE_IN IN VARCHAR2)
  IS
   BEGIN
     INSERT INTO HOLD_MESSAGE VALUES (MESSAGE_IN);
     COMMIT;
   END;
 /
```

This stored procedure accepts a string value as an input parameter and then uses the input parameter to insert the string value into the HOLD_MESSAGE table. The stored procedure will first be executed from SQL*Plus and then again from OO4O. The only difference between the SQL used in SQL*Plus from the SQL used in OO4O is the string that is passed to the stored procedure. Afterward, the table will be queried to confirm that both inserts were successful.

Once the stored procedure is compiled successfully, execute it using the following syntax in SQL*Plus:

```
BEGIN INSERT_MESSAGE('From SQL*Plus'); END;
 /
```

Listing 9.1 illustrates how the same stored procedure is executed in OO4O. Don't forget to add the OO4O Type Library before running the example.

Listing 9.1

```
1  Dim OraSession As OraSession
2  Dim OraDatabase As OraDatabase
3  Dim OraDynaset As OraDynaset
4  Set OraSession = CreateObject _
        ("OracleInProcServer.XOraSession")
5  Set OraDatabase = OraSession.OpenDatabase _
        ("v8i", "scott/tiger", 0&)
6  OraDatabase.ExecuteSQL _
        ("BEGIN INSERT_MESSAGE('From OO4O'); END;")
7  MsgBox "Validate the data from SQL*Plus"
```

> **Analysis**

- Lines 1–3 are Dim statements for the objects being used in the sample.

- Line 4 creates the OraSession object.

- Line 5 creates an OraDatabase object and establishes the connection to the database.

- Line 6 executes the SQL statement to call the Insert_Message stored procedure.

- Line 7 displays a message box when the procedure is completed.

Notice that the ExecuteSQL command is sending almost the identical SQL statement. The only difference is that the text being passed is changed to identify the application from which the stored procedure is called.

After executing the stored procedure twice, once from SQL*Plus and once from OO4O, type the following SQL statement in SQL*Plus to verify that two records were entered:

```
SELECT * FROM HOLD_MESSAGE;
```

The output should look something like the following:

```
MESSAGE_FIELD
--------------------------------------------------
From SQL*Plus
From OO4O
```

Notice that the same SQL statement is used to execute a stored procedure from two different applications. One important item to note is that when executing stored procedures or functions using the ExecuteSQL statement in OO4O, an implicit commit is sent to the database.

Calling a Simple Stored Function

The difference between a stored procedure and a function is that not only do functions return a value, but they also can be part of an expression. Have you ever executed the following SQL statement in SQL*Plus?

```
SELECT USER FROM DUAL;
```

USER is actually a function provided by the database. Executing the User function returns the name of the user who is logged in. If you are logged into the Scott account and type the previous SQL, you will see the following:

```
USER
------------------------------
SCOTT
```

Functions do not always have to be used in expressions; they can be executed in anonymous PL/SQL blocks, just as the stored procedures can. The following code demonstrates executing the User function in an anonymous PL/SQL block. Before executing, an SQL*Plus environment variable needs to be set to display the value from the DBMS_OUTPUT.PUT_LINE command. At the SQL*Plus prompt, type the following command:

```
SET SERVEROUTPUT ON
```

This will allow the return value to be displayed. Entering the following SQL statement in SQL*Plus demonstrates calling the User function in an anonymous PL/SQL blockL:

```
DECLARE
    X VARCHAR2(40);
    Begin X := USER;
    DBMS_OUTPUT.PUT_LINE (X);
    END;
  /
```

The "/" will execute the code and should return the username that you are logged in as.

One of the differences you may notice is the inclusion of the Declare statement. The Declare statement creates the bind variable *X*, which is used to store the return value from the User functions.

Sysdate is another function in the database. Executing the following Sysdate function in SQL*Plus returns the current date.

```
SELECT SYSDATE FROM DUAL;
```

If today is the 1st of August in the year 2000 and this SQL statement is executed, the following date information is displayed:

```
SYSDATE
---------
01-AUG-00
```

Although the default date format is set to display the data in the day-month-two-digit-year (DD-MON-YY) format, the format of the date on your machine may differ because it is controlled by the NLS_DATE_FORMAT parameter.

The *User function* (which returns the user who is currently logged in) and the *Sysdate function* (which returns the current date in the database) are standard functions provided by Oracle.

Let's create our own function to get a further understanding of how stored functions work. Enter the following code in an SQL*Plus session:

```
CREATE OR REPLACE FUNCTION FunctionSample
   Return VARCHAR2
   IS
   BEGIN
      RETURN 'OO4O is easy';
   END;
   /
```

This function returns the string "OO4O is easy". Just as the User and Sysdate functions were used to return a value, the newly created function FunctionSample can also return a value. This means that you should be able to execute the function just as you executed the User and Sysdate functions. Enter the following SQL statement in the SQL*Plus session:

```
SELECT FUNCTIONSAMPLE FROM DUAL;
```

Executing the FunctionSample function returns the following:

```
FUNCTIONSAMPLE
----------------------------------------------------
OO4O is easy
```

Listing 9.2 illustrates how the same stored function can be called in OO4O. Don't forget to add the OO4O Type Library before running the example.

Listing 9.2

```
1   Dim OraSession As OraSession
2   Dim OraDatabase As OraDatabase
3   Dim OraDynaset As OraDynaset
4   Set OraSession = CreateObject _
        ("OracleInProcServer.XOraSession")
5   Set OraDatabase = OraSession.OpenDatabase _
        ("v8i", "scott/tiger", 0&)
```

```
6   Set OraDynaset = OraDatabase.CreateDynaset _
        ("select FUNCTIONSAMPLE from DUAL", 0&)
7   MsgBox OraDynaset.Fields("FUNCTIONSAMPLE").Value, _
        vbOKOnly, "Function Sample"
```

Analysis

- Lines 1–3 are Dim statements for the objects being used in this example.

- Line 4 creates the OraSession object.

- Line 5 creates an OraDatabase object and establishes the connection to the database.

- Line 6 executes the SQL statement to call the FunctionSample stored function.

- Line 7 displays the return values from the function.

The code from Listing 9.2 displays the message box shown in Figure 9.1.

FIGURE 9.1
The "0040 is easy"
message box

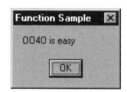

As demonstrated, functions can be called from an SQL Select statement, as well as from an anonymous PL/SQL block. Listing 9.2 demonstrates how a single row of data can be returned. Functions can also be used to inherently process multiple rows of data. Create the following function (DoubleSalary) in an SQL*Plus session. The function uses the Emp table in the Scott schema.

```
CREATE OR REPLACE FUNCTION
  DoubleSalary(p_Empno Emp.empno%TYPE)
  RETURN Emp.Sal%TYPE
  IS
     v_Sal Emp.Sal%TYPE;
  BEGIN
    SELECT SAL INTO v_Sal
    FROM EMP WHERE EMPNO = p_Empno;
    RETURN (v_Sal * 2);
END;
/
```

This function takes the salary for a particular employee and doubles it. Like the previous functions, this function can be executed to return a single result. The first SQL statement demonstrates the function being executed in an expression in SQL*Plus:

```
SELECT DoubleSalary(7788) "New Salary" FROM DUAL;
```

This SQL statement returns the new salary for a particular employee. The same function can be used to return the new salary for all employees with a single SQL statement.

```
SELECT ENAME "Employee", SAL "Old Salary",
  DoubleSalary(EMPNO) "New Salary"
  FROM EMP ORDER BY SAL;
```

The output for this example looks like the following:

```
Employee   Old Salary New Salary
---------- ---------- ----------
SMITH             800       1600
JAMES             950       1900
ADAMS            1100       2200
MARTIN           1250       2500
WARD             1250       2500
MILLER           1300       2600
TURNER           1500       3000
ALLEN            1600       3200
CLARK            2450       4900
BLAKE            2850       5700
JONES            2975       5950
FORD             3000       6000
SCOTT            3000       6000
KING             5000      10000
```

By now, you have realized that although there are similarities between procedures and functions, there are definitely differences, too. There is a wealth of information available specifically on stored functions and procedures. If you wish to read more, review Oracle's *PL/SQL User's Guide and Reference*.

The OraParameters Collection

When calling a stored procedure, there is nothing wrong with passing a hard-coded value, but it does not make a very dynamic application. Every time you want to change the value being passed to the procedure, the application needs to be recompiled. Another issue when working with hard-coded values is what to do if the hard-coded value is modified by the stored procedure. How would you manage to return the new value? The same holds true when using a stored function: How would a function return the value from the database? The answer to this is fairly simple: Use bind variables. If you remember from the previous section, when a function is executed in SQL*Plus, a bind variable is created in the anonymous PL/SQL block to hold the return value.

Bind variables provide a way to pass data from the Visual Basic application to the database and also allow the database to pass data back to the Visual Basic application. The bind variable takes the place of a hard-coded value. It's essentially a placeholder. The actual value of the bind variable can be set during application runtime, which negates the need to rebuild the application each time the value changes.

With OO4O, when it comes to bind parameters, think of it as registering a parameter. You need to provide the name and the data type that the bind variable will map to in Oracle. On the client side, OO4O maps the Oracle data type back into a Visual Basic data type for the bind parameter. Keep in mind that attempting to bind a Visual Basic variable directly into OO4O when passing SQL statements to the database will result in an "ORA-01008: not all variables bound" error because of the way Visual Basic and OO4O differ internally in allocating the memory for their variables.

Bind variables are not only used with stored procedures and functions, but they can also be used in SQL statements to execute Select, Insert, and even Update statements.

OraParameters collection provides a way to bind a variable used to pass a value to a stored procedure or function, or even in an SQL statement. Using the OraParameters object in SQL statements allows the OO4O application to be quite dynamic.

There are five potential parameters used when creating a bind parameter:

```
OraDatabase.OraParameters.Add  "<Parameter Name>" _
  <Initial Value>, <OraParameter Type>, <Server Type> _
  <Database Object Name>
```

The first parameter, *<Parameter Name>*, is the name of the bind parameter being created. This can be any string value. It's usually best to create a parameter with a meaningful name. For example, if the parameter being created is used for passing an employee's salary to a stored procedure, the parameter name could be EmployeeSal, EmpSal, or even Salary.

The second parameter, *<Initial Value>*, is the initial value and determines the type of the parameter in Visual Basic. If a numeric value is used for this parameter, VB treats the parameter being created as a Variant/Number type. If a string value is used or if no value is entered, VB treats the parameter as a Variant/String type.

The third parameter, *<OraParameter Type>*, defines the type of the bind variable. This does not pertain to the data type but to how the variable will actually be used. There are three types:

ORAPARM_INPUT   Means that the data being passed in will not be modified. Attempting to modify the contents of a parameter of this type will result in an Oracle error.

ORAPARM_OUTPUT   Means that the variable defined will be used to return a value from the database. Any value assigned to this variable on the client side will be disregarded by the database.

ORAPARM_BOTH   Means that the parameter can be used to not only pass a value to the database but also to return a value.

The fourth parameter, *<Server Type>*, is the Oracle data type that the parameter maps to. The available types range from the simple data types (Varchar2, Number, Char) to the new data types (CLOB, BLOB, BFILE, VArrays, and even Nested Tables). For a complete list of available types, refer to the OO4O online help.

The fifth parameter, *<Database Object Name>*, is the actual name of an object in the database and is required if the fourth parameter, <Server Type>, is one of the following:

- ORATYPE_OBJECT
- ORATYPE_REF
- ORATYPE_TABLE
- ORATYPE_VARRAY

These types are defined in the `Oraconst.txt` file. This file must be included in the VB project when using any of the OO4O constant variables. The `Oraconst.txt` file contains all the definitions of the constant variables used by OO4O. Using these predefined variables without including the file in the Visual Basic application will result in an error.

WARNING Not including the `Oraconst.txt` file in the VB project when using OO4O constants will result in an error when using OO4O's predefined variables.

Adding a Simple Parameter

For clarity reasons, when creating bind parameters, it's best to give them meaningful names. Let's say that you need to create a parameter to return an employee's last name from a stored procedure or function. Just knowing that you need to return an employee's last name from the database is enough information to create an OraParameter object. For the first parameter, a meaningful name could be LastName. Although a default value entered is disregarded by the database, you are still required to enter a value. The third parameter would be ORAPARM_OUTPUT because you know that the parameter will be used to return a value. The fourth parameter is simply an ORATYPE_VARCHAR2 because last names are usually text. No value is required for the last parameter (<Server Type>) because the fourth parameter (Varchar2) is not any of the new types.

Creating the parameter can be done in one of two ways. The first and most common method is to create a bind variable in a single statement:

```
OraDatabase.Parameters.Add  "LastName", , _
        ORAPARM_OUTPUT, ORATYPE_VARCHAR2
```

The second method actually executes faster because fewer objects are referenced. Here is the same example using the second method:

```
Dim OraParameters As OraParameters
        :
        :
Set OraParameters = OraDatabase.Parameters
OraParameters.Add "LastName", 0, ORAPARM_OUTPUT, _
    ORATYPE_VARCHAR2
```

Many examples in this chapter will define parameters. As you go along, the advantages of using these bind parameters will become increasingly evident.

The OraParameters Collection and Stored Procedures

In Listing 9.1, the Insert_Message stored procedure example was executed using a hard-coded value. The string value was passed into the stored procedure and then inserted into a table.

When you use a hard-coded value, each time you want a different string value, the OO4O application has to be modified and rebuilt. Well, what about situatuons where using a hard-coded value is not very desirable?

This is where the OraParameters collection comes into play. Defining a parameter essentially creates a placeholder. Instead of a hard-coded value, the bind variable that is created is passed. By changing the value of the parameter, you change the value passed to the stored procedure.

Take a look at Listing 9.1 and see how it differs with the incorporation of a parameter used in Listing 9.3. Listing 9.3 executes the same stored procedure twice, passing in a new value each time. Don't forget to add the OO4O Type Library before running the example.

Listing 9.3

```
1  Dim OraSession As OraSession
2  Dim OraDatabase As OraDatabase
3  Dim OraDynaset As OraDynaset
4  Set OraSession = CreateObject _
        ("OracleInProcServer.XOraSession")
5  Set OraDatabase = OraSession.OpenDatabase _
        ("v8i", "scott/tiger", 0&)
6  OraDatabase.Parameters.Add "InsertData", _
            "1st Insert - Default Value", _
            ORAPARM_INPUT, ORATYPE_VARCHAR2
7  For InsertSample = 1 To 2
8      OraDatabase.ExecuteSQL _
        ("BEGIN INSERT_MESSAGE(:InsertData); END;")
9      OraDatabase.Parameters _
        ("InsertData").Value = "2nd Insert - New Value"
10  Next InsertSample
11  OraDatabase.Parameters.Remove "InsertData"
12  MsgBox "Execution Complete"
```

⟳ Analysis

- Lines 1–3 are Dim statements for the objects being used in this example.
- Line 4 creates the OraSession object.
- Line 5 creates an OraDatabase object and establishes the connection to the database.
- Line 6 creates the parameter being used as the placeholder.
- Line 7 starts the loop.
- Line 8 executes the stored procedure.
- Line 9 sets the parameter to a new value.
- Line 10 increments the loop.
- Line 11 deletes the InsertData parameter.
- Line 12 displays a message box when finished.

Notice that the stored procedure is executed twice; both times, a new value is passed.

Entering the following SQL statement in SQL*Plus will not only display the data entered in Listing 9.1 but also the new data created by Listing 9.3:

```
SELECT * FROM HOLD_MESSAGE;
```

Although parameters are being implemented, technically, hard-coded values are still used: In order to change the value, the code needs to be recompiled. To finalize the example and make it dynamic, the parameter can be bound to a text box on a form. This is the next and final step.

Start with a new project in Visual Basic. Before adding any components, the OO4O Type Library must be added to the project. To do this, click the References menu item, which can be found on the menu bar in the Project drop-down list (see Figure 9.2).

FIGURE 9.2

Finding the References dialog box

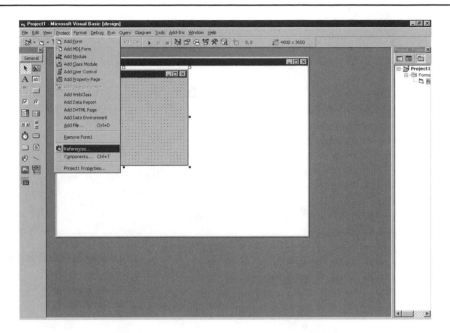

Once the References dialog box appears, scroll down until you see the Oracle Objects Type Library. Once it's found, select the Oracle Objects For OLE 3.0 Type Library check box and click the OK button to return to the form (see Figure 9.3).

FIGURE 9.3

The References dialog box

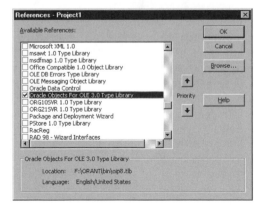

Next, select and place a text box and a command button on the form. Your form should look like Figure 9.4.

FIGURE 9.4

The VB form

Click the button while you're still in Design mode to activate the Properties dialog box. Edit the (Name) property and Caption property so that the button reads "Execute," as shown in Figure 9.5.

FIGURE 9.5

The Button's properties

(Name) property ———

Caption property ———

Click the Textbox field on the form and scroll through the Properties dialog box until you see the Text property. Visual Basic uses the default value Text1. Place the cursor in the Text property and delete this value, leaving this field empty. The highlighted Text property in Figure 9.6 is the one that you will make blank.

FIGURE 9.6
The Text property

Text property

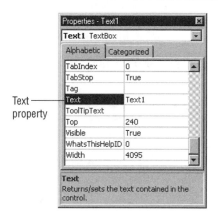

Double-click the Button Control on the form, and Visual Basic will create an Execute_Click() method. Place the OO4O code in Listing 9.4 in the Execute_Click method.

Listing 9.4

```
1   Private Sub Execute_Click()
2   Dim OraSession As OraSession
3   Dim OraDatabase As OraDatabase
4   Dim OraDynaset As OraDynaset
5
6   Set OraSession = CreateObject _
        ("OracleInProcServer.XOraSession")
7   Set OraDatabase = OraSession.OpenDatabase _
        ("v8i", "scott/tiger", 0&)
8   OraDatabase.Parameters.Add "InsertData", _
    "Default_Value", _
        ORAPARM_INPUT, ORATYPE_VARCHAR2
9   OraDatabase.Parameters("InsertData").Value = Text1.Text
10  OraDatabase.ExecuteSQL _
        ("BEGIN INSERT_MESSAGE(:InsertData); END;")
```

```
11 MsgBox "Finished executing the Stored Procedure"
12 OraDatabase.Parameters.Remove "InsertData"
13 End Sub
```

Analysis

- Line 1 is the procedure name created by Visual Basic when the button on the form is double-clicked.

- Lines 2–4 are Dim statements for the objects being used to connect to the database.

- Line 5 is a blank space to make the code easier to read.

- Line 6 creates the OraSession object.

- Line 7 creates an OraDatabase object and establishes the connection to the database.

- Line 8 creates the InsertData parameter.

- Lines 9 sets (binds) the contents of the text box on the form to the parameter.

- Line 10 executes the stored procedure.

- Line 11 displays a message box when the stored procedure is complete.

- Line 12 deletes the parameter when the OO4O code is finished.

- Line 13 is the End Sub statement for this procedure.

Once you've entered the code into the Execute_Click method, execute the program. Place a text value in the field and click the Execute button. When the message box is displayed, the stored procedure is completed, new text can be entered, and the Execute button can be clicked again. Each time the button is clicked, the new string value in the text box is passed to the parameter and then to the stored procedure without having to modify the code or rebuild the project.

To verify that the data entered actually exists, log into the database as the same user as in the OO4O application and use SQL*Plus to execute the following SQL statement:

```
SELECT * FROM HOLD_MESSAGE;
```

You should see all the values passed in through the text field. This SQL statement displays all the data entered in the table in Listing 9.4, as well as the data entered in the previous listings in this chapter.

Returning a Value from a Stored Procedure or Function

Both stored procedures and functions provide a way to return a value or values. Stored procedures can return a value through one or more of the parameters in their parameter list. Stored functions can return values in one of two ways. The first is the same as procedures, which is to return one or more values through one of the parameters in the parameter list. The second is to return a single value as a return value. Returning a value from a function using its return value was demonstrated in the "Calling a Simple Stored Function" section. This section revisits returning a value from a function and demonstrates how to return a value from a procedure.

We'll create both a procedure and a function. Each will accept a numeric value and then pass back the square of that value. If you pass in a 4, the return value will be 16. The function will return the result as its return value, and the procedure will return the result in the same parameter used to pass in the value.

To begin, start an SQL*Plus session and enter the following SQL commands to create the stored function:

```
CREATE OR REPLACE FUNCTION SQUARE_FUNCTION
     (VALUE_IN IN NUMBER)
RETURN NUMBER
IS
BEGIN
RETURN (VALUE_IN * VALUE_IN);
END;
/
```

Now enter the following SQL commands to create the stored procedure:

```
CREATE OR REPLACE PROCEDURE SQUARE_PROCEDURE
     (VALUE_IN IN OUT NUMBER)
IS
BEGIN
VALUE_IN := VALUE_IN * VALUE_IN;
END;
/
```

Figure 9.7 illustrates what your SQL*Plus session will look like after entering these SQL commands to create the stored function and procedure.

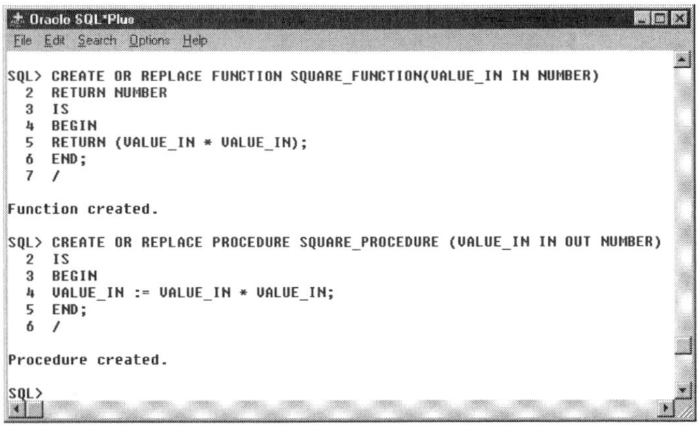

FIGURE 9.7
Creating a stored function
and procedure

```
Oracle SQL*Plus
File  Edit  Search  Options  Help

SQL> CREATE OR REPLACE FUNCTION SQUARE_FUNCTION(VALUE_IN IN NUMBER)
  2    RETURN NUMBER
  3    IS
  4    BEGIN
  5    RETURN (VALUE_IN * VALUE_IN);
  6    END;
  7  /

Function created.

SQL> CREATE OR REPLACE PROCEDURE SQUARE_PROCEDURE (VALUE_IN IN OUT NUMBER)
  2    IS
  3    BEGIN
  4    VALUE_IN := VALUE_IN * VALUE_IN;
  5    END;
  6  /

Procedure created.

SQL>
```

Now that the function and procedure are created, we'll create an OO4O application to execute each one. For the function, two parameters will be created. One parameter is for passing the numeric value to the function, and the other parameter is for the numeric value being returned. For the procedure, only one parameter will be created. This single parameter will represent the numeric value being passed in, as well as the value being passed out. How does one variable represent two values? It doesn't. When the value is passed to the procedure, the new value overwrites the old, and the parameter is passed back with the new value.

The OO4O example in Listing 9.5 demonstrates executing the stored function and procedure shown in Figure 9.7 using different methods. The function is executed using two different calling conventions, and the procedure is executed once. In either case, the correct value is returned.

Listing 9.5 illustrates how OO4O implements both the function and the procedure. Don't forget to add the OO4O Type Library before running this example.

Listing 9.5

```
1  Dim OraSession As OraSession
2  Dim OraDatabase As OraDatabase
3
4  Set OraSession = CreateObject _
        ("OracleInProcServer.XOraSession")
5  Set OraDatabase = OraSession.OpenDatabase _
        ("v8i", "scott/tiger", 0&)
```

```
6   OraDatabase.Parameters.Add "ProcNumber", 12, _
         ORAPARM_BOTH, ORATYPE_NUMBER
7   OraDatabase.Parameters.Add "FuncInNumber", 12, _
         ORAPARM_INPUT, ORATYPE_NUMBER
8   OraDatabase.Parameters.Add "FuncRetNumber", 0, _
         ORAPARM_OUTPUT, ORATYPE_NUMBER
9   OraDatabase.ExecuteSQL _
         ("Begin :FuncRetNumber := " & _
         "SQUARE_FUNCTION(:FuncInNumber); END;")
10  MsgBox "The Square of " & _
         OraDatabase.Parameters("FuncInNumber").Value & _
         " = " & OraDatabase.Parameters("FuncRetNumber").Value
11  'Demonstrates executing the same function
12  'using a different method
13  OraDatabase.ExecuteSQL _
         ("Begin Select SQUARE_FUNCTION(:FuncInNumber) " & _
         "INTO :FuncRetNumber From DUAL; END;")
14  MsgBox "The Square of " & _
         OraDatabase.Parameters("FuncInNumber").Value & " = " & _
         OraDatabase.Parameters("FuncRetNumber").Value
15
16  X = OraDatabase.Parameters("ProcNumber").Value
17  OraDatabase.ExecuteSQL _
         ("Begin SQUARE_PROCEDURE(:ProcNumber); END;")
18  MsgBox "The Square of " & X & " = " & _
         OraDatabase.Parameters("ProcNumber").Value
19
20  OraDatabase.Parameters.Remove "ProcNumber"
21  OraDatabase.Parameters.Remove "FuncInNumber"
22  OraDatabase.Parameters.Remove "FuncRetNumber"
```

Analysis

- Lines 1–2 are Dim statements for the objects being used in this example.

- Line 3 is a blank space to make the code easier to read.

- Line 4 creates the OraSession object.

- Line 5 creates an OraDatabase object and establishes the connection to the database.

- Line 6 creates the ProcNumber parameter to be used for the procedure.

- Line 7 creates the FuncInNumber parameter to pass in the value to the function.

- Line 8 creates the FuncRetNumber parameter to be used for return value from the function.

- Line 9 executes the function using an anonymous PL/SQL block to pass the FuncRetNumber and FuncInNumber parameters.

- Line 10 creates a message box that shows the number passed in, as well as its squared value.

- Lines 11–12 are both comments that the same function will be executed a second time using a different method.

- Line 13 executes the same function but uses a Select statement to retrieve the value.

- Line 14 creates a message box that shows the number passed in, as well as its squared value.

- Line 15 is a blank space to make the code easier to read.

- Line 16 creates a variable to hold the original value of the ProcNumber parameter.

- Line 17 executes the procedure passing the ProcNumber parameter.

- Line 18 creates a message box that shows the number passed in, as well as its squared value.

- Line 19 is a blank space prior to removing the parameters.

- Lines 20–22 delete the parameters created earlier in the code.

Notice how the parameter passed to the procedure was overwritten with the new value, and how, in order to retain the original value, the original value has to be copied into the X variable.

If retaining the original value is crucial, the procedure can easily be modified to accept two parameters instead of one. The first parameter passes in the value, and the second parameter is used as an Out parameter to return the value. As with the function, two parameters are required. For more information on the different parameter types (In, Out, In Out), see the Oracle's *PL/SQL User's Guide and Reference*.

Although this example uses hard-coded values, it can easily be modified to accept its value from a field on a form. The real decision between whether or not to use a procedure or a function will be contingent upon the requirements of your implementation.

Returning Result Sets

A popular feature of OO4O is the ability to return a result set from a stored procedure or function. Be careful not to confuse a result set with a dynaset.

Once a stored procedure or function is called and the PL/SQL cursor is opened, there needs to be a way to return the cursor from the stored procedure or function. What's returned is not the actual PL/SQL cursor but rather a reference to that cursor. In order to return a Reference cursor from the database, the stored procedure or function must be created in a package. For more information on creating packages, see Oracle's *PL/SQL User's Guide and Reference*.

As you have seen previously, OraDynaset objects can be created very easily with a simple call to the CreateDynaset method. From OO4O's perspective, result sets are just as easy to create using the CreatePLSQLDynaset method.

The Server-Side Setup

Before creating a PL/SQL dynaset in OO4O, a package and procedure must be created in the database. We suggest using SQL*Plus to do this. Whenever user-defined data types are used in a procedure or a function, the stored procedure, function, and data type variable must be created in a package.

Listing 9.6 creates the package. Before creating the package, you must make sure that the Customer table exists. If not, you can find the table definition along with some data in the `Demobld7.sql` file, which can be found in the OO4O directory. Once it is verified that the table exists, Listing 9.6 can be entered in SQL*Plus to create the package.

Listing 9.6

```
1 CREATE OR REPLACE PACKAGE RefCurPackage AS
2     CURSOR DB_Cursor is select * from CUSTOMER;
3     TYPE RefCursorType is REF CURSOR return
4         DB_Cursor%rowtype;
5 PROCEDURE RefCurProcedure
6     (ProcedureCursor in out RefCursorType);
7 END RefCurPackage;
8 /
```

Analysis

- Line 1 creates a Package Spec with the name RefCurPackage. This package will accommodate the definition of the Reference cursor, as well as the prototype for the actual stored procedure.

- Line 2 defines a cursor called DB_Cursor, which is based on the Customer table.

- Lines 3–4 create a new Ref Cursor type based on the cursor created in step 1. This Reference Cursor type that will be passed back to the OO4O application.

- Lines 5–6 are the prototypes of the stored procedure used to return the cursor. The actual definition is implemented in the package body.

- Line 7 ends the package specification (RefCurPackage).

- Line 8 executes the package creation.

Lines 2 and 3 are the essentail steps to return the result set by its reference. Notice that in line 3, the type actually being returned for the cursor created in line 2 is of RowType. *RowType* is a PL/SQL operator that will actually create a type based on the table definition. Line 2 shows that DB_Cursor is a cursor for the Customer table. In line 3, a Ref Cursor type is created based on DB_Cursor%rowtype. So, the Ref Cursor type actually resolves to reference a row that is defined to match the definition of a row for the Customer table. These are the essential steps required to return the result set by its reference.

NOTE   For more information on the RowType command, see Oracle's *PL/SQL User's Guide and Reference*.

Once the package specification is created, the package body follows. The package specification contains the prototype of the stored procedure, and the package body contains the actual definition. Listing 9.7 shows the SQL used in SQL*Plus to create the package body.

Listing 9.7

```
1 CREATE OR REPLACE PACKAGE BODY RefCurPackage AS
2    PROCEDURE RefCurProcedure
3      (ProcedureCursor in out RefCursorType) IS
4    BEGIN
5      OPEN ProcedureCursor for SELECT * FROM CUSTOMER;
6    END RefCurProcedure;
7  END RefCurPackage;
8  /
```

Analysis

- Line 1 creates a package body with the name RefCurPackage. The name of the package specification must match the name of the package body.

- Lines 2–3 start defining the RefCurProcedure procedure.

- Line 4 begins the procedure.

- Line 5 opens the cursor.

- Line 6 ends the procedure (RefCurProcedure).

- Line 7 ends the package body (RefCurPackage).

- Line 8 executes the package creation.

NOTE The project that contains this example also includes an additional example that demonstrates how to subset the data returned by passing in a parameter for a Where clause.

Once the package specification and package body are created, the next step is to set up OO4O to call the procedure and return the Reference cursor.

The Client-Side Setup

OraDynaset objects are created using the CreateDynaset method of the OraDatabase object. Result sets are created by making a call to the CreatePLSQL-Dynaset method. Both CreateDynaset and CreatePLSQLDynaset are methods in the OraDatabase object.

NOTE The CreateDynaset and CreatePLSQLDynaset method both produce an OraDynaset object.

The following code shows that the CreatePLSQLDynaset method takes three parameters:

```
CreatePLSQLDynaset (StoredProcedure, _
                CursorName, _
                Options)
```

The first parameter for the CreatePLSQLDynaset is a bit different than for the CreateDynaset method. Here, you don't pass a Select statement but rather a call to a stored procedure or function. The call must be placed in an anonymous PL/SQL block.

The second parameter is the name of the cursor being passed back by the stored procedure. Because you know that the CreatePLSQLDynaset method returns a Ref cursor, this parameter must match the name of one of the parameters in the stored procedure or function used to return the Ref cursor. For example, in the following OO4O code, notice that the second parameter, RefCursor, matches the RefCursor parameter passed in to the procedure.

```
Set OraDynaset = OraDatabase.CreatePLSQLDynaset _
    ("Begin Package.Procedure (:RefCursor); end;", _
    "RefCursor", ORADYN_DEFAULT)
```

If a match cannot be found, an error will result. At times, you may be executing a procedure or function that accepts more than one parameter. This will not cause a problem as long as the second parameter of the CreatePLSQLDynaset matches one of the parameters being passed to the stored procedure or function. Take a look at the following:

```
Set OraDynaset = OraDatabase.CreatePlsqlDynaset _
    ("Begin Package.Procedure " & _
    "(:Param1, :Param2, :Param3); end;", _
    "Param2", ORADYN_DEFAULT)
```

Notice that the second parameter of the CreatePLSQLDynaset method is Param2. The first test is to verify that Param2 matches one of the bind parameters in the parameter list of the stored procedure. Sure enough, it does; it matches the second bind variable (:Param2). Next, OO4O is expecting that the bind parameter (:Param2) will be the Ref cursor returned from the stored procedure. If any of the two criteria fail, an Oracle error will be returned.

The third parameter is the available options and functionality for the resulting OraDynaset object. Table 9.1 lists the other available options. For more information on each option, refer to the OO4O online help.

TABLE 9.1:   Options for the CreatePLSQLDynaset Method

String Value	Hexadecimal Value
ORADYN_DEFAULT	0&
ORADYN_NO_BLANKSTRIP	2&
ORADYN_NOCACHE	8&
ORADYN_NO_MOVEFIRST	40&

Listing 9.8, with its brief description, demonstrates a bit more of what is going on. Don't forget to add the OO4O Type Library before running the example.

Listing 9.8

```
1   Dim OraSession As OraSession
2   Dim OraDatabase As OraDatabase
3   Dim OraDynaset As OraDynaset
```

```
4  Set OraSession = CreateObject _
       ("OracleInProcServer.XOraSession")
5  Set OraDatabase = OraSession.OpenDatabase _
       ("v8i", "scott/tiger", 0&)
6 Set OraDynaset = OraDatabase.CreatePlsqlDynaset _
       ("Begin RefCurPackage.RefCurProcedure " & _
       "(:RefCursor); end;", "RefCursor", ORADYN_DEFAULT)
7 MsgBox "There are " & OraDynaset.RecordCount & _
       " records in the Customer table."
```

Analysis

- Lines 1–3 are the Dim statements for the objects being used in this example.

- Line 4 creates the OraSession object.

- Line 5 creates an OraDatabase object and establishes the connection to the database.

- Line 6 executes the CreatePLSQLDynaset method to call a stored procedure that returns the PL/SQL Dynaset.

- Line 7 creates a message box that shows the number of records in the OraDynaset.

This example executes the CreatePLSQLDynaset method and returns an Ora-Dynaset type. It also demonstrates the actual call to the CreatePLSQLDynaset method (line 6). Remember that the first parameter is the call to the stored procedure (see the "Server-Side Setup" section of "Returning Result Sets" for details). Here, the call to the stored procedure is placed in an anonymous PL/SQL block. The bound parameter being passed is RefCursor.

By now, you may be asking how you can pass a bind variable without it being defined. If you remember from the previous sections, all bound variables were defined as part of the OraParameters collection. Well, they actually get implicitly defined for you. Take a close look at the statement in line 6 of Listing 9.8. Notice the second parameter, RefCursor. OO4O expects this parameter to be the name of the Reference cursor returned and expects to find a matching parameter in the parameter list that is passed to the stored procedure. This means that if the stored procedure contains a number of parameters, OO4O will search the parameter list for one that matches the second parameter.

WARNING	If the second parameter cannot find a match with one of the parameters in the parameter list, an error will result.

Arrays

Normally, every Insert, Update, or Delete command that is executed results in an expense in the form of network traffic. If you insert *n* number of rows of data into a table, as the number of inserts (*n*) increases, so does the number of network round-trips to the database. Wouldn't it be great to be able to execute one SQL statement to insert *n* number of rows and only make one network round-trip? This is what arrays provide for you: a way to do DML on a number of records with just one SQL statement.

This section uses the following table definition in its examples. You can enter the following SQL in SQL*Plus to create the table:

```
CREATE TABLE ArraySample
    (RowNumber NUMBER, RowText VARCHAR2(50));
```

OraParamArray

As always, any parameter used in an SQL statement in OO4O has to be defined, and arrays are no exception. Instead of using the Add method to create a variable of a simple type, like with the OraParameters collection, the AddTable method must be called. Actually setting up the arrays is a two-step process. First, a Parameter table is required. Second, an array needs to be defined, based on the table created in the first step. The AddTable method creates a Parameter table and takes up to six parameters:

```
OraDatabase.OraParameters.AddTable "<Table Name>", _
        <OraParameter Type>, <Server Type>, _
        <Array Size>, <String Size>, <Database Object Name>
```

- The first parameter, *<Table Name>*, is the name of the table being created.

- The second parameter, *<OraParameter Type>*, defines how the array is to be used. This defines whether the array will be used for input, for output, or for both. The following are the three available values that can be passed:

  ORAPARM_INPUT   Means that the array being passed in will not be modified. In fact, attempting to modify the contents of a parameter of this type will result in an Oracle error.

  ORAPARM_OUTPUT   Means that the array being defined will be used to return a value from the database. Any value assigned to this variable on the client side will be disregarded by the database.

  ORAPARM_BOTH   Means that the array can be used not only to pass values to the database but also to return a value.

- The third parameter, *<Server Type>*, is the Oracle data type to which the array maps. The available types range from the simple data types (Varchar2, Number, Char) to the new data types (CLOB, BLOB, BFILE, VArrays and even Nested Tables). For a complete list of available types, refer to the OO4O online help.

- The fourth parameter, *<Array Size>*, is the maximum number of elements in the array. Defining a table smaller than the number of elements accessed by the array will result in an "Invalid argument value" error message. Defining a table larger than the number of elements accessed by the array can potentially cause problems. For example, if you pass in an array size of five and then only define four elements in the array, the database will attempt to process all five elements. The database will attempt to insert a 0 as a numeric type and a blank for character data for the empty element.

WARNING   Make sure the <Array Size> variable is defined to be the exact size you need. Creating an <Array Size> variable smaller or larger than what you actually need will result in either an error or erroneous results.

- The fifth parameter, *<String Size>*, is only valid if the server type is character data and represents the maximum number of characters for each element. Exceeding this limit will result in an "Invalid argument value" error.

- The sixth parameter, *<Database Object Name>*, is the actual name of an object in the database and is required if the fourth parameter, <Server Type>, is one of the following:

  - ORATYPE_OBJECT

  - ORATYPE_REF

  - ORATYPE_TABLE

  - ORATYPE_VARRAY

For example, to define a parameter called SampleTableType as an input parameter of type Varchar2, and the table will hold a maximum of 10 elements with each element no larger than 25 characters, the AddTable method looks like the following:

```
OraDatabase.Parameters.AddTable "SampleAddTable", _
    ORAPARM_INPUT, ORATYPE_VARCHAR2, 3, 25
```

The next step in defining the array after executing the AddTable method is to create the OraParamArray object from the table created in the first step. For example, using the SampleAddTable parameter that was just created, the OraParamArray is created as the following:

```
Set SampleArray = OraDatabase.Parameters("SampleAddTable")
```

Now that the array is created, each element of the array needs to be populated. This can be done using the Visual Basic's format for populating arrays.

```
SampleArray(0) = "Array Element 1"
SampleArray(1) = "Array Element 2"
SampleArray(2) = "Array Element 3"
```

NOTE   Arrays in OO4O are zero based.

Defining the arrays using a one-based array element will result in an error. The following example is incorrect and will result in an "Invalid argument value" error.

```
SampleArray(1) = "Array Element 1"
SampleArray(2) = "Array Element 2"
SampleArray(3) = "Array Element 3"
```

Once the arrays have been established, they can be used in an Insert, Update, or Delete SQL statements.

Listing 9.9 uses the ArraySample table created earlier in the "Arrays" section. Two OraParamArray objects are defined and used in an Insert, Update, and Delete SQL statement. This example is set up to display a message box after the DML statement so that you can execute a Select statement in SQL*Plus to verify that each was successful. The first part of the example inserts three rows of data and displays a message box when the insert is complete.

Execute a `Select From ArraySample` statement to verify that the data was inserted. Once verified, click the OK button on the message box so the example continues. The next part of the Listing 9.9 executes an Update operation using arrays. Once the update is complete, another message box appears. At this time, you can execute another `Select From ArraySample` statement to verify that the data was updated. Once verified, click the OK button on the message box so that the example can finish executing a Delete operation using an array. Once the delete is complete, the final message box appears. At this time, you can execute one final `Select From ArraySample` statement to verify that the data was deleted. Once verified, click the OK button on the message box so that the example can complete.

If you follow along and execute the `Select From ArraySample` SQL statement after each pause, your output should look similar to Figure 9.8. Don't forget to add the OO4O Type Library before running the example in Listing 9.9.

FIGURE 9.8
The array output

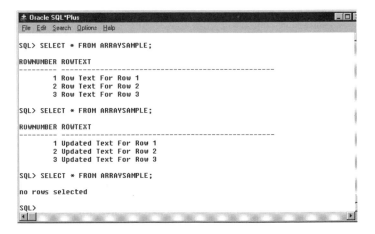

Listing 9.9

```
1  Dim OraSession As OraSession
2  Dim OraDatabase As OraDatabase
3  Dim RowNumberArray As OraParamArray
4  Dim RowTextArray As OraParamArray
5
6  Set OraSession = CreateObject _
       ("OracleInProcServer.XOraSession")
7  Set OraDatabase = OraSession.OpenDatabase _
       ("v8i", "scott/tiger", 0&)
8
9  OraDatabase.Parameters.AddTable "RowNumberTable", _
       ORAPARM_INPUT, ORATYPE_NUMBER, 3
10  OraDatabase.Parameters.AddTable "RowTextTable", _
       ORAPARM_INPUT, ORATYPE_VARCHAR2, 3, 25
11
12 Set RowNumberArray = OraDatabase.Parameters("RowNumberTable")
13 Set RowTextArray = OraDatabase.Parameters("RowTextTable")
14
15 'Populates Array Elements For the Insert
16 RowNumberArray(0) = 1
17 RowTextArray(0) = "Row Text For Row 1"
18 RowNumberArray(1) = 2
19 RowTextArray(1) = "Row Text For Row 2"
20 RowNumberArray(2) = 3
21 RowTextArray(2) = "Row Text For Row 3"
22 'Initiates Array Insert
23 OraDatabase.ExecuteSQL ("INSERT INTO ArraySample " & _
       "VALUES (:RowNumberTable, :RowTextTable)")
24 MsgBox "Verify the INSERT from SQL*Plus", vbOKOnly, _
       "Insert Complete - Check Data"
25
26 'Populates Array Elements For the Update
27 RowTextArray(0) = "Updated Text For Row 1"
28 RowTextArray(1) = "Updated Text For Row 2"
29 RowTextArray(2) = "Updated Text For Row 3"
30 'Initiates Array Update
31 OraDatabase.ExecuteSQL ("UPDATE ArraySample " & _
       "SET RowText = :RowTextTable " & _
       "WHERE RowNumber = :RowNumberTable")
```

```
32 MsgBox "Verify the UPDATE from SQL*Plus", vbOKOnly, _
      "Update Complete - Check Data"
33
34 'Initiates Array Delete
35 OraDatabase.ExecuteSQL _
      ("DELETE ArraySample WHERE RowNumber = :RowNumberTable")
36 MsgBox "Verify the DELETE from SQL*Plus", vbOKOnly, _
      "Delete Complete - Check Data"
37 OraDatabase.Parameters.Remove "RowNumberTable"
38 OraDatabase.Parameters.Remove "RowTextTable"
```

Analysis

- Lines 1–4 are Dim statements for the objects being used in this example.

- Line 5 is a blank space to make the code easier to read.

- Line 6 creates the OraSession object.

- Line 7 creates an OraDatabase object and establishes the connection to the database.

- Line 8 is a blank space to make the code easier to read.

- Line 9 creates the table type RowNumberTable.

- Line 10 creates the table type RowTextTable.

- Line 11 is a blank space to make the code easier to read.

- Line 12 creates the first array, RowNumberArray, as an OraParamArray object.

- Line 13 creates the second array, RowTextArray, as an OraParamArray object.

- Line 14 is a blank space to make the code easier to read.

- Line 15 is a comment signifying populating the OraParamArray object.

- Lines 16–17 assign values to the first element of the array.

- Lines 18–19 assign values to the second element of the array.

- Lines 20–21 assign values to the third element of the array.

- Line 22 is a comment signifying the array insert.

- Line 23 executes the array insert.

- Line 24 displays a message box when the array insert is finished.

- Line 25 is a blank space to make the code easier to read.

- Line 26 is a comment signifying the array update.

- Lines 27–29 assign a new value to the elements of the RowTextArray parameter.

- Line 30 is a comment signifying the array update.

- Line 31 executes the array update.

- Line 32 displays a message box when the array update using arrays is finished.

- Line 33 is a blank space to make the code easier to read.

- Line 34 is a comment signifying the array delete.

- Line 35 executes the array delete.

- Line 36 displays a message box when the Delete operation is finished.

- Lines 37–38 delete the parameters.

This example modifies only the array containing the text and not the array containing numeric values. This allows for the Update and Delete operations to occur on the correct rows.

Once again, be careful to match the array size with the number of elements in the array. In Listing 9.9, consider what would happen if there were only two elements defined for the Insert operation, as shown here:

```
RowNumberArray(0) = 1
RowTextArray(0) = "Row Text For Row 1"
RowNumberArray(1) = 2
RowTextArray(1) = "Row Text For Row 2"
```

In this case, OO4O still attempts to insert three rows of data because that's the size defined when the Array parameter is created. A zero is inserted for the numeric value, and the string value is empty.

Play around with this example. Try inserting more array elements than are defined. Afterward, try inserting fewer and see what happens. Try removing the

Where clause from the Update statement. You will notice that no error is returned, but the results may not be what you are expecting.

When executing Update and Delete operations using arrays, make sure that the values for the Where clauses in the arrays actually exist. If a value for a particular array element does not exist, the Update or Delete methods will result in an "OIP-04139: Error occurred while processing Arrays." error message. You can verify the values in the Where clause by placing the following line of code before the Execute-SQL command for either the Update or Delete method:

```
RowNumberArray(2) = 21
```

Because the ArraySample table in the database does not contain any RowNumber fields with a value 21, the Update or Delete method will result in the OIP-04139 error. It may be best to provide some error trapping so that if this does happen, your application won't fail, but rather the user will be presented with a message telling them to verify all array elements. Modify this example using incorrect element values in the array to see what happens. For example, even though an error is produced, do the other elements get processed? Are the changes committed? Check it out to find out more about how arrays work.

Arrays with Stored Procedures and Functions

By now, you know how arrays work and how they can potentially save time by decreasing the network traffic to the database. You also know how using stored procedures and functions allows the server to handle some of the workload for the client. Both features are very efficient, and this section will discuss using them together. Using arrays with stored procedures and functions can potentially make for an extremely efficient application.

When the types of parameters were discussed in the "OraParamArray" section, one of the types was an ORATYPE_TABLE. This type creates the PL/SQL table. Although it's called a PL/SQL table, it's actually an array of a single data type.

NOTE   PL/SQL tables are actually arrays of a single data type.

This quirky definition tends to cause some confusion because many users are inclined to think that a table means a collection of rows, and each row can consist of more than one data type. In fact, a PL/SQL table is a collection of rows, but each row consists of only a single data type. As seen in the previous section, to return an actual row of data (a row that consists of more than one data type), a Ref cursor is required. Whe working with arrays, you are still able to work with multiple rows, but each array consists of a single data type.

The previous section illustrated working directly with arrays. This section takes it a step further and illustrates working with arrays and stored procedures. The example in Listing 9.10 uses a table definition that can be created in SQL*Plus using the following SQL command:

```
CREATE TABLE ArraySample2
  (RowNumber NUMBER, RowText VARCHAR2(50));
```

As with any OO4O application that accesses a stored procedure or function, there must be some initial setup on the server.

Server-Side Setup

Before writing any OO4O code, there should be a stored procedure in place on the database to handle the arrays. Because there are no existing predefined array types on the database, they must be created. Using the ArraySample2 table as the demo table, you can see that there are two columns. The first is of type Number, and the second is of type Varchar2. In order to create an array to interface with this table, a PL/SQL table must be created for each field used in the operations.

Because Listing 9.10 uses both fields in the table, we'll create a PL/SQL table of type Number and of type Varchar2. As with any user-defined types, the types must be defined in a package specification. Listing 9.10 illustrates the SQL commands to create the required package in the database in SQL*Plus.

Listing 9.10

```
1 CREATE OR REPLACE PACKAGE ArraySamplePackage AS
2    TYPE RowNumArrayType IS TABLE OF
3        ArraySample2.RowNumber%TYPE
4        INDEX BY BINARY_INTEGER;
5    TYPE RowTextArrayType IS TABLE OF
6        ArraySample2.RowText%TYPE
```

```
7        INDEX BY BINARY_INTEGER;
8     PROCEDURE ArraySampleProc1
9        (NumOfElements IN NUMBER,
10        RowNumArray IN RowNumArrayType,
11        RowTextArray IN RowTextArrayType);
12    PROCEDURE ArraySampleProc2
13        (NumOfElements IN NUMBER,
14        RowNumArray IN RowNumArrayType,
15        RowTextArray OUT RowTextArrayType);
16  END;
17  /
```

Analysis

- Line 1 creates a package specification with the name ArraySamplePackage. This package will accommodate the definition of the PL/SQL tables for each column being used, as well as the prototype for the actual stored procedures.

- Lines 2–4 define the first PL/SQL table type to be of the same type as the RowNumber field in the ArraySample2 table.

- Lines 5–7 define the second PL/SQL table type to be of the same type as the RowText field in the ArraySample2 table.

- Lines 8–11 are the prototype for the first procedure. This procedure will do the array Insert operation.

- Lines 12–15 are the prototype for the second procedure. This procedure will do the array Select operation.

- Line 16 ends the specifications.

- Line 17 compiles the specifications.

Each procedure is defined with three parameters. Although the reason for passing in the NumOfElements parameter is not obvious, it will be clear once the procedures are defined.

- The first parameter will pass in the number of elements in the array.

- The second parameter for each procedure is the array to hold the Row-Number field.

- The third parameter for each is the array for the RowText field.

The second procedure defines the RowTextArray parameter as an Out parameter. This is because the second procedure uses the values from the RowNumber arrays in the Where clause of the Select statement used to populate the RowText array. This can be seen in the Where clause in line 22 of Listing 9.11.

Listing 9.11 is the actual definition of the procedures.

Listing 9.11

```
1 CREATE OR REPLACE PACKAGE BODY ArraySamplePackage AS
2  PROCEDURE ArraySampleProc1
3       (NumOfElements IN NUMBER,
4        RowNumArray IN RowNumArrayType,
5        RowTextArray IN RowTextArrayType) IS
6  BEGIN
7    FOR ArrayElement IN 1..NumOfElements LOOP
8       INSERT INTO ArraySample2 VALUES
9          (RowNumArray(ArrayElement),
10             RowTextArray(ArrayElement));
11     END LOOP;
12   END ArraySampleProc1;
13  PROCEDURE ArraySampleProc2
14       (NumOfElements IN NUMBER,
15        RowNumArray IN RowNumArrayType,
16        RowTextArray OUT RowTextArrayType) IS
17   BEGIN
18     FOR ArrayElement IN 1..NumOfElements LOOP
19       SELECT RowText
20       INTO RowTextArray(ArrayElement)
21       FROM ArraySample2
22       WHERE RowNumber = RowNumArray(ArrayElement);
23     END LOOP;
24   END ArraySampleProc2;
25  END ArraySamplePackage;
26 /
```

Analysis

- Line 1 creates a package body with the name ArraySamplePackage. The name of the package body must match the name of the package specification.

- Lines 2–5 begin the definition of the ArraySampleProc1 procedure.

- Line 6 begins the body of the procedure.

- Line 7 starts the loop.

- Lines 8–10 execute the Insert command.

- Line 11 ends the loop.

- Line 12 ends the ArraySampleProc1 procedure.

- Lines 13–16 begin the definition of the ArraySampleProc2 procedure.

- Line 17 begins the body of the second procedure.

- Line 18 starts the loop.

- Lines 19–22 execute the Select command to populate the array.

- Line 23 ends the loop.

- Line 24 ends the ArraySampleProc2.

- Line 25 ends the package body.

- Line 26 executes the package creation.

The loop used in each procedure is provided to allow the Insert and Select statements to iterate through each element in the array.

Using arrays with Select statements takes a bit more planning than for other types of SQL. You need to make sure that when doing a Select operation using an array, each element in the array must return only a single value. If any one Select statement returns more than one row, an ORA-01422 error will be returned.

WARNING Returning more than one row for any given Select statement will result in the "ORA-01422: Exact fetch returns more than requested number of rows." error message.

Client-Side Setup

Once the table isdefined and the package and procedures are created, it's time to generate the client-side code in Visual Basic. The following OO4O example in Listing 9.12 will insert two rows into the ArraySample2 table using an array and the

ArraySampleProc1 procedure. The following three parameters are passed. The parameter type is shown in parentheses.

- (In)The first parameter is the number of elements in the array.

- (In) The second parameter is an array of values for the RowNumber field.

- (In) The third parameter is an array of values for the RowText field.

After the first procedure completes (ArraySampleProc1), the example selects data from the ArraySample2 table using an array and the ArraySampleProc2 procedure. The following three parameters are used:

- (In) The first parameter is the number of elements in the array.

- (In) The second parameter is an array of values for the RowNumber field.

- (Out) The third parameter is an array of values for the RowText field.

The only difference in the parameters between the two procedures is the third parameter for ArraySampleProc2. This parameter is an Out parameter type and the third parameter for the ArraySampleProc1 is an In parameter type. The Out parameter in the second procedure allows values to be passed from the procedure in the database to the client application. The data being returned in Listing 9.12 is the data queried from the ArraySample2 table. Even though more than one row is inserted and selected, the example will make just two round- trips to the database, one for each call.

Don't forget to add the OO4O Type Library before running the code in Listing 9.12.

Listing 9.12

```
1   Dim OraSession As OraSession
2   Dim OraDatabase As OraDatabase
3   Dim RowNumberArray As OraParamArray
4   Dim RowTextArrayIN As OraParamArray
5   Dim RowTextArrayOUT As OraParamArray
6   Dim arraySize As Integer
7   arraySize = 2
8
9   Set OraSession = CreateObject _
        ("OracleInProcServer.XOraSession")
10  Set OraDatabase = OraSession.OpenDatabase _
```

```
                ("v8i", "scott/tiger", 0&)
11  OraDatabase.Parameters.Add "NumOfElements", _
          arraySize, ORAPARM_INPUT
12  OraDatabase.Parameters.AddTable "RowNumber", _
          ORAPARM_INPUT, ORATYPE_NUMBER, arraySize
13  OraDatabase.Parameters.AddTable "RowTextIN", _
          ORAPARM_INPUT, ORATYPE_VARCHAR2, arraySize, 50
14  OraDatabase.Parameters.AddTable "RowTextOUT", _
          ORAPARM_OUTPUT, ORATYPE_VARCHAR2, arraySize, 50
15  Set RowNumArray = OraDatabase.Parameters _
          ("RowNumber")
16  Set RowTextArrayIN = OraDatabase.Parameters _
          ("RowTextIN")
17  Set RowTextArrayOUT = OraDatabase.Parameters _
          ("RowTextOUT")
18
19  RowNumArray(0) = 1
20  RowNumArray(1) = 2
21  RowTextArrayIN(0) = "Row 1 Text"
22  RowTextArrayIN(1) = "Row 2 Text"
23
24  OraDatabase.ExecuteSQL _
      ("Begin ArraySamplePackage.ArraySampleProc1 " & _
      "(:NumOfElements, :RowNumber, :RowTextIN); End;")
25  MsgBox "Insert Complete. Validate Data then hit " & _
          "enter to continue with the second procedure."
26  OraDatabase.ExecuteSQL _
      ("Begin ArraySamplePackage.ArraySampleProc2 " & _
      "(:NumOfElements, :RowNumber, :RowTextOUT); End;")
27
28  MsgBox "The first element of the array: " & _
          RowTextArrayOUT(0)
29  MsgBox "The second element of the array: " & _
          RowTextArrayOUT(1)
30  OraDatabase.ExecuteSQL ("DELETE ArraySample2")
```

⤵ Analysis

- Lines 1–5 are Dim statements for the OO4O objects being used in this example.

- Line 6 is the Dim statement for the ArraySize variable that will hold the number of elements in the array.

- Line 7 sets the number of elements in the array to 2.

- Line 8 is a blank space to make the code easier to read.

- Line 9 creates an OraSession object.

- Line 10 creates an OraDatabase object and establishes the connection to the database.

- Line 11 creates the NumOfElements parameter to be used to pass the number of elements in the array to the stored procedures.

- Line 12 creates the RowNumber array parameter using the AddTable method.

- Line 13 creates the RowTextIN array parameter using the AddTable method.

- Line 14 creates the RowTextOUT array parameter using the AddTable method.

- Lines 15–17 set the parameter created in lines 12–14 to their parameter array objects.

- Line 18 is a blank space before inserting data into the arrays.

- Line 19 sets the value of the first element in the RowNumArray array.

- Line 20 sets the value of the second element in the RowNumArray array.

- Line 21 sets the value of the first element in the RowTextArrayIN array.

- Line 22 sets the value of the second element in the RowTextArrayIN array.

- Line 23 is a blank space before executing the stored procedures.

- Line 24 is the ExecuteSQL method used to execute the first procedure that will insert the data from the RowNumArray and the RowTextArrayIN arrays.

- Line 25 displays a message box to stop processing so you can verify that the data was actually inserted into the ArraySample2 table.

- Line 26 is the ExecuteSQL method used to execute the second procedure that will select the data based on the data from the RowNumArray array and return the results in the RowTextArrayOUT array.

- Line 27 is a blank space before displaying the data.

- Lines 28–29 display the data in the two elements of the RowTextArrayOUT array.

- Line 30 cleans up by deleting the data just inserted in case the example is run more than once.

Objects Types and Member Functions

As stated in Chapter 8, "Working with Objects and Collections," an object type is essentially a user-defined type. But it is still an object, and like any object, it can have both attributes and methods. The methods can be either a procedure or a function. The previous chapter created objects with only attributes. This section creates a new object that has attributes and is a member of a function. If you are not familiar or have not worked with these object types, review the *Oracle8i Server Application Developer's Guide*.

Let's create an object with a built-in function. Let's say that you need to create a table to store employee and spouse information. This employee information includes the employee number, the employee name, and spouse information. For this example, the information for the spouse is placed in an object that contains the spouse's name and the number years of marriage. Because not all employees are married, a member function will be created for the object so that there is a quick and easy way to determine which employees are married and which are not.

The following SQL code creates an object called SpouseObj. It contains a SpouseName field for the name of the spouse and a YearsMarried field for the number of years that the employee has been married. A member function named Is_Married will return a string value of "Is Married" if the employee is married and "Is Not Married" if the employee is not.

Creating an object with a built-in function is a two-step process, which is very similar to creating packaged stored procedures. First, you create the prototype or the specification, and then you create the body.

Entering the following SQL code at the SQL*Plus prompt creates the specification for the object and the function prototype:

```
CREATE OR REPLACE TYPE SpouseObj AS OBJECT(
    SpouseName VARCHAR2(20),
    YearsMarried Number(2),
    Member FUNCTION Is_Married Return VARCHAR2,
    pragma RESTRICT_REFERENCES
    (Is_Married, WNDS, RNPS, WNPS));
    /
```

Once the specification is created for the object, create the body of the Is_Married() function for the SpouseObj object. The following SQL code defines how the function is implemented. Enter the following SQL commands to create the SpouseObj object and its Is_Married function:

```
CREATE OR REPLACE TYPE BODY SpouseObj IS
    MEMBER FUNCTION Is_Married RETURN VARCHAR2 IS
      BEGIN
        IF YearsMarried > 0 THEN
            RETURN ('Is Married');
        END IF;
      RETURN ('Is Not Married');
      END;
    END;
    /
```

Figure 9.9 illustrates what your SQL*Plus screen looks like after creating the object.

FIGURE 9.9

The object type in SQL*Plus

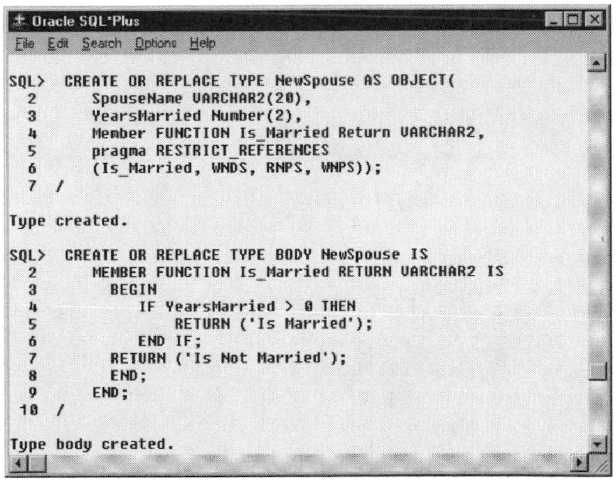

Once the type and the body of the function are defined, a table can be created using the SpouseObj object type. Before creating the Employee table, execute the `Drop Table Employee` SQL command because the Create command will fail if the table already exists. The following code creates a table using the SpouseObj object type:

```
CREATE TABLE Employee
    (EmpNumber NUMBER,
    FirstName VARCHAR2(40),
    Spouse SpouseObj);
```

After the table is successfully created, insert the following two rows of data:

```
INSERT INTO Employee
    VALUES (2000, 'Jim', SpouseObj('Lisa', 2));

INSERT INTO Employee
    VALUES (2001, 'Ken', SpouseObj(NULL, NULL));
```

Don't forget to commit your changes as follows:

```
COMMIT;
```

Built-In Methods in Functions

The introduction of objects has not only introduced a different syntax when working with DML (selects, inserts, updates, and deletes), but has also introduced the fact that you can create objects with built-in methods designed to be either procedures or functions. Much of this information is outside the scope of this book. Although executing built-in functions in OO4O is covered later in this chapter, creating objects with built-in methods is not. When reviewing this section, keep in mind that the book's focus is on interfacing with these objects in Oracle Objects for OLE (OO4O). If you are interested in doing more research, start with the *Oracle8i Server Application Developer's Guide*.

After inserting the data, the new function can be tested by entering the following SQL statement:

```
SELECT E.FirstName "Employee",
    E.Spouse.Is_Married() "Marriage Status"
    FROM Employee E;
```

Figure 9.10 illustrates what your SQL*Plus screen looks like after creating the table, inserting the record, and executing the Select statement in SQL*Plus.

FIGURE 9.10
Executing the member
function execution

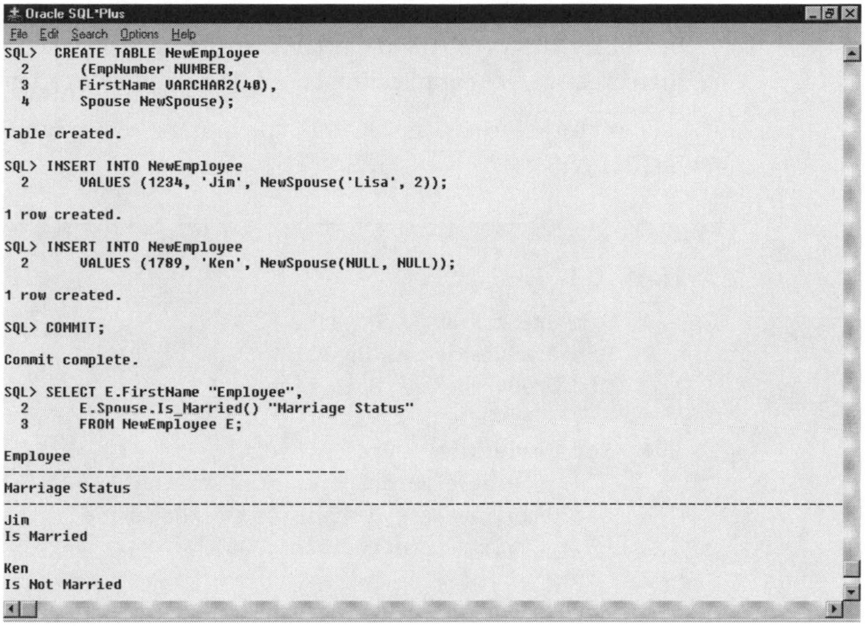

```
 Oracle SQL*Plus                                                    _ 8 X
File  Edit  Search  Options  Help
SQL>   CREATE TABLE NewEmployee
    2       (EmpNumber NUMBER,
    3        FirstName VARCHAR2(40),
    4        Spouse NewSpouse);

Table created.

SQL> INSERT INTO NewEmployee
    2      VALUES (1234, 'Jim', NewSpouse('Lisa', 2));

1 row created.

SQL> INSERT INTO NewEmployee
    2      VALUES (1789, 'Ken', NewSpouse(NULL, NULL));

1 row created.

SQL> COMMIT;

Commit complete.

SQL> SELECT E.FirstName "Employee",
    2       E.Spouse.Is_Married() "Marriage Status"
    3       FROM NewEmployee E;

Employee
-------------------------------------------------
Marriage Status
-------------------------------------------------
Jim
Is Married

Ken
Is Not Married
```

Listing 9.10 returns the value in the FirstName field from the Employee table and the result from the function. Notice the E.Spouse.Is_Married() portion of the SQL statement. This reference calls the function. The Is_Married function is executed for each row that is processed. The function assesses the value held in the YearsMarried field of the Spouse_Object type and returns a value.

OO4O and Objects Types with Member Functions

So far, you have seen how to access the object's method in SQL*Plus. Now, try it in OO4O. Because inserting into the object type is the same with or without any member functions, Listing 9.13 focuses on accessing the function that is created. Actually, you'll do that twice. The first time, the function is accessed using an Ora-Dynaset object. The example then loops through each record displaying the results in a message box. The second time you insert into the object type, the function is accessed using a parameter in an ExecuteSQL call to find the results for a particular employee. Notice that both methods return the same value.

OO4O usually provides more than one way to accomplish a given task. This flexibility allows OO4O to work toward your application's requirements, rather than creating your application based on a product's capabilities or lack thereof.

Don't forget to add the OO4O Type Library before running the example code in Listing 9.13.

Listing 9.13

```
1  Dim OraSession As Object
2  Dim OraDatabase As Object
3  Dim OraDynaset As OraDynaset
4
5  Set OraSession = CreateObject _
        ("OracleInProcServer.XOraSession")
6  Set OraDatabase = OraSession.OpenDatabase _
        ("v8i", "scott/tiger", 0&)
7
8  Set OraDynaset = OraDatabase.CreateDynaset _
        ("SELECT E.FirstName, E.Spouse.Is_Married() " & _
        "FROM Employee E", 0&)
9  For rowIndex = 1 To OraDynaset.RecordCount
10     MsgBox OraDynaset.Fields("FirstName").Value & _
        " - " & OraDynaset.Fields("E.Spouse.Is_Married()").Value
11     OraDynaset.MoveNext
12 Next rowIndex
13
14 OraDatabase.Parameters.Add "Status", , _
        ORAPARM_OUTPUT, ORATYPE_VARCHAR2
15 OraDatabase.ExecuteSQL _
        ("BEGIN SELECT E.Spouse.Is_Married() " &
        "INTO :Status FROM Employee E " & _
        "WHERE E.FirstName='Jim'; END;")
16 MsgBox "Jim - " & OraDatabase.Parameters("Status").Value
```

Analysis

- Lines 1–3 are Dim statements for the objects being used in this example.

- Line 4 is a blank space to make the code easier to read.

- Line 5 creates the OraSession object.

- Line 6 creates an OraDatabase object and establishes the connection to the database.

- Line 7 is a blank line before creating the OraDynaset object.

- Line 8 executes the CreateDynaset method of the OraDatabase object.

- Line 9 starts to loop through the OraDynaset.

- Line 10 displays a message box with the employee name and their marriage status.

- Line 11 moves to the next record in the OraDynaset object.

- Line 12 increments the counter for the loop.

- Line 13 is a blank line before the next select.

- Line 14 creates the parameter to hold the return value.

- Line 15 executes the ExecuteSQL method to return the value of a single employee.

- Line 16 displays the results.

Using Objects and Stored Procedures

A common request among programmers is for a way to pass recordsets to and from a stored procedure. Doing so allows a single parameter to return more than one column of data. Image having to return or pass in a row of data that contained 10 columns. Without the ability to return a recordset, you have to create a stored procedure with 10 different parameters, one for each column in the row. Although this feature is not yet implemented, including objects in the Oracle database and the OraObject object in OO4O allows using an object type to return or pass in a row of data.

This section covers two examples. This first is Listing 9.14, which illustrates inserting a row of data into the Dept table using an object type. Listing 9.15 illustrates returning a row of data from the Emp table through a single object.

There is a lot of information to learn when it comes to working with objects. Although this section provides you with the SQL code to create the object types and stored procedures, the focus will be on the OO4O code. For more information on objects, object types, and stored procedures, you refer to the Oracle manuals. As you will soon find out, a number of different manuals discuss objects and object types. If you want one that gives an overview of objects, object types, and stored procedures, take a look at Oracle's *PL/SQL User's Guide and Reference* .

Passing Objects to a Stored Procedure

Before passing an object to a stored procedure, the object type that is being passed in must exist in the database. If the object type does not exist, when compiled, the stored procedure will return errors for each line that references the absent object type variable. In Listing 9.14, an object named DeptObj is created. Its attributes are defined using the same data types that are in the Dept table. To create the DeptObj object, execute the following SQL code in your SQL*Plus session:

```
CREATE TYPE DeptObj AS OBJECT
   (DeptNo NUMBER(2),
    DeptName VARCHAR2(14),
    Location VARCHAR2(13));
/
```

Once the object type is created, take a moment to review the fields that make up the Dept table. You can accomplish this by executing the Describe command in SQL*Plus:

```
DESC DEPT
```

The Desc Dept command returns the definition of the Dept fields by displaying the fields and their data types. The output looks like the following:

```
Name                        Null?     Type
------------------------- -------- -----------
DEPTNO                      NOT NULL NUMBER(2)
DNAME                                VARCHAR2(14)
LOC                                  VARCHAR2(13)
```

Notice that the DeptObj object is created with the same data types as the fields in the Dept table, yet the fields themselves can have different names.

Once the object type is created, you can create the stored procedure that accepts the object type just defined and uses it in the Insert SQL statement. The following is the SQL code required. Execute the following code in SQL*Plus to compile and build the stored procedure:

```
CREATE OR REPLACE PROCEDURE ObjectSample
      (DeptObj DeptObj)
AS
BEGIN
   INSERT INTO DEPT VALUES
       (DeptObj.DeptNo,
        DeptObj.DeptName,
        DeptObj.Location);
COMMIT;
END;
/
```

Notice that the stored procedure accepts a single parameter, yet the Insert command actually inserts three different values. The three different values are attributes of the object.

Once the object type is created and the stored procedure is compiled, you are ready to execute the stored procedure in OO4O, as shown in Listing 9.14.

Listing 9.14

```
1  Dim OraSession As OraSession
2  Dim OraDatabase As OraDatabase
3  Dim OraDynaset As OraDynaset
4  Dim DeptObj As OraObject
5
6  Set OraSession = _
     CreateObject("OracleInProcServer.XOraSession")
7  Set OraDatabase = OraSession.OpenDatabase _
     ("v8i", "scott/tiger", 0&)
8
9  OraDatabase.Parameters.Add "DeptObjParm", Null, _
        ORAPARM_INPUT, ORATYPE_OBJECT, "DEPTOBJ"
10  Set DeptObj = OraDatabase.CreateOraObject("DEPTOBJ")
11 DeptObj.DeptNo = 51
12 DeptObj.DeptName = "MSLang"
```

```
13 DeptObj.Location = "Orlando"
14
15 OraDatabase.Parameters("DeptObjParm").Value = DeptObj
16 OraDatabase.ExecuteSQL _
      ("BEGIN ObjectSample(:DeptObjParm); END;")
17 OraDatabase.Parameters.Remove "DeptObj"
18 MsgBox "Done"
```

Analysis

- Lines 1–3 are Dim statements for the objects being used in this example.

- Line 4 is the Dim statement for the OraObject object.

- Line 5 is a blank space to make the code easier to read.

- Line 6 creates the OraSession object.

- Line 7 creates an OraDatabase object and establishes the connection to the database.

- Line 8 is a blank line before creating the OraDynaset object.

- Line 9 creates the DeptObjParm parameter being used as the placeholder.

- Line 10 creates the DeptObj object.

- Lines 11–13 set the attributes of the DeptObj object.

- Line 14 is a blank line before creating the OraDynaset object.

- Line 15 sets the value of the DeptObjParm parameter to the DeptObj object.

- Line 16 executes the ObjectSample procedure, which passes in the DeptObjParm parameter.

- Line 17 removes the parameter.

- Line 18 displays a message box when finished.

There are a couple of items to note in this example. Line 9 creates the parameter used to pass to the stored procedure. The first value passed to the Add method is the name of the parameter being created. In this case, it's DeptObjParm. The fourth value passed in is ORATYPE_OBJECT. Essentially, line 9 defines DeptObjParm as an object type. Because the fourth value passed in is of an ORATYPE_OBJECT type, you must pass in the name of the object as the fifth value. In Listing 9.14, it's DEPTOBJ. It's very important to remember that this value is case sensitive. Entering a value that does not match a value in the database will result in an error during execution.

Line 10 creates the stand-alone object that will contain the data to pass to the stored procedure. The DeptObj being created in Visual Basic is of the DEPTOBJ object type, which is contained in the database. Don't forget that the value passed to the CreateOraObject method is case sensitive and must match exactly or else an error will be returned.

Once the DeptObj is populated with data, as in lines 11–13, you can set the value of the DeptObjParm parameter to the DeptObj object. When the stored procedure is executed, as in line 16, the DeptObjParm passes the data to the DeptObj object.

To verify that the data was entered successfully, enter the following SQL statement at the SQL*Plus prompt:

```
SELECT * FROM DEPT;
```

To run the example in Listing 9.14 more than once, you have to either delete the record just entered or change the Deptno value to be a different value because the Deptno field of the Dept table is a unique index constraint. This means that the Deptno field cannot contain duplicate values.

Returning Objects from a Stored Procedure

Listing 9.15 returns an object from a stored procedure. Before beginning the example, the object type being passed must be defined. If the object type is not defined, the stored procedure will not compile because the database will not know how the references to the types are defined.

The object type for Listing 9.15 is defined almost the same as in the Emp table in the Scott schema. To create this object type, enter the following SQL code in SQL*Plus:

```
CREATE TYPE EmployeeObj AS OBJECT
(EmpNo NUMBER(4),
Ename VARCHAR2(14),
Job VARCHAR2(9),
Salary NUMBER(7,2),
Comm NUMBER(7,2),
DeptNo NUMBER(2));
/
```

Once the EmployeeObj object type is created, review the fields that make up the Emp table by executing the Describe command in SQL*Plus:

```
DESC EMP
```

The Desc Emp command returns the definition of the Emp fields by displaying the fields and their data types. The output looks like the following:

```
Name                          Null?    Type
----------------------------- -------- -------------
EMPNO                         NOT NULL NUMBER(4)
ENAME                                  VARCHAR2(10)
JOB                                    VARCHAR2(9)
MGR                                    NUMBER(4)
HIREDATE                               DATE
SAL                                    NUMBER(7,2)
COMM                                   NUMBER(7,2)
DEPTNO                        NOT NULL NUMBER(2)
```

If you compare these fields to the ones described in the Emp table, you notice that there is a match for all the attributes in the EmployeeObj object type except for HIREDATE and MGR. This just goes to show that the object type created does not have to be identical to the row you wish to return. You are able to pick and choose only the fields relevant to what you are trying to accomplish.

Once the object type is created, create the stored procedure that will return a variable of the EmployeeObj object type. The following is the SQL code that is required. Execute this code in SQL*Plus to compile and build the stored procedure:

```
CREATE OR REPLACE PROCEDURE GetObjectSample
      (EmpNum NUMBER, Employee IN OUT EmployeeObj)
AS
BEGIN
   SELECT EMPNO, ENAME, JOB, SAL, COMM, DEPTNO
   INTO
   Employee.EmpNo,
   Employee.Ename,
   Employee.Job,
   Employee.Salary,
   Employee.Comm,
   Employee.Deptno
  FROM EMP WHERE Empno = EmpNum;
END;
/
```

Once the object type is created and the stored procedure is successfully compiled, execute the stored procedure using OO4O, as shown in Listing 9.15.

Listing 9.15

```
1  Dim OraSession As OraSession
2  Dim OraDatabase As OraDatabase
3  Dim OraDynaset As OraDynaset
4 Dim EmpObj As OraObject
5
6  Set OraSession = _
     CreateObject("OracleInProcServer.XOraSession")
7  Set OraDatabase = OraSession.OpenDatabase _
     ("v8i", "scott/tiger", 0&)
8
9  OraDatabase.Parameters.Add "EmpNoValue", 7788, _
     ORAPARM_INPUT, ORATYPE_NUMBER
10  OraDatabase.Parameters.Add "EmpObjParm", Empty, _
     ORAPARM_OUTPUT, ORATYPE_OBJECT, "EMPLOYEEOBJ"
11 OraDatabase.ExecuteSQL _
     ("BEGIN GetObjectSample(:EmpNoValue, :EmpObjParm); END;")
12 Set EmpObj = OraDatabase.Parameters("EmpObjParm").Value
13 MsgBox "Empno: " & EmpObj.Empno & Chr(13) & _
          "Ename: " & EmpObj.Ename & Chr(13) & _
          "Job: " & EmpObj.Job & Chr(13) & _
          "Salary: " & EmpObj.Salary & Chr(13) & _
          "Comm: " & EmpObj.Comm & Chr(13) & _
          "Deptno: " & EmpObj.Deptno
14 OraDatabase.Parameters.Remove "EmpObjParm"
15 OraDatabase.Parameters.Remove "EmpNoValue"
```

Analysis

- Lines 1–3 are Dim statements for the objects used in this example.

- Line 4 is the Dim statement for the OraObject object.

- Line 5 is a blank space to make the code easier to read.

- Line 6 creates the OraSession object.

- Line 7 creates an OraDatabase object and establishes the connection to the database.

- Line 8 is a blank line before creating the OraDynaset object.

- Line 9 creates the EmpNoValue parameter being used as the placeholder for the employee number that is queried.

- Line 10 creates the EmpObjParm parameter being used as the placeholder.

- Line 11 executes the GetObjectSample procedure passing in two parameters. One is the employee number, and the second is the object that will contain the data that is returned.

- Line 12 sets the EmpObj object to the EmpObjParm parameter so that the values can be retrieved.

- Line 13 displays a message box with all the attributes and data of the object that is returned.

- Lines 14–15 remove the parameters.

This example creates two parameters. One parameter is for the employee number (line 9) passed to the stored procedure that is used in the Where clause to select the employee that will be returned. The employee data selected will return to the OO4O application via the second parameter (line 10) EmpObjParm.

Line 11 executes the ExecuteSQL method to call the stored procedure. Once executed, it returns to the OO4O application, and the EmpObjParm parameter should contain the data you opted for. Before accessing the data, you will need to create an OraObject of the same type as in line 12, which creates an EmpObjParm parameter. (For more information on objects and the CreateOraObject method, see Chapter 8.) Once the OraObject is created, set it to the OO4O parameter. In this case, it's EmpObjParm. Now, referencing can be done as with any other object, which is *<objectname>.<attribute>*. As you can see in line 13, this is done to display the value of all the attributes in the EmpObj object.

Using Sequences and the Returning Clause

Working with sequences is not really a complex topic but tends to generate the same questions often enough that it is well worth the time to create a simple example to demonstrate how it works. It also allows us to demonstrate another new feature released in this version of OO4O, called the Returning clause. Actually, there is no official name per say. It's been called the Returning clause or sometimes the Returning…Into clause. This new feature makes working with sequences easier than before. The two most common questions when working with sequences are

- How do I insert a record that uses a sequence?

- How do I return the sequence number that is generated?

The answer to the first question is easy and is demonstrated in Listing 9.16. The way in which sequence numbers are inserted has not changed from the previous version of OO4O to this version, but implementing the answer to the second question has.

Prior to this release, the user had to get creative and implement different procedures to obtain the sequence number used to insert a new record. For example, prior to this release, users would sometimes connect to the database, generate a new sequence number, return the value, and then use it to insert a new record into a table. This was obviously not the most efficient method because it required two network trips to the database to insert a record. The first trip was to obtain the sequence number, and the second trip actually inserted the sequence number. Another way is to pass the data to be inserted to a stored procedure or function and have it obtain the next sequence number, place it in a variable, use it as part of the insert, and then return the number used to the application. This does limit the process to a single network round-trip, but it still requires multiple steps.

The *Returning clause*, which can be used in conjunction with Insert and Update operations, allows you to return information from the database without having to execute an additional statement. Of course, what is being returned is limited to the row that is currently being inserted or updated.

Listing 9.16 executes an Insert operation using a sequence generator to generate a number, and then uses the Returning clause to return the number that is used.

Before executing this example, you need to create a sequence and a table. The following code contains the SQL commands to generate a very simple sequence in SQL*Plus:

```
CREATE SEQUENCE SequenceSample
INCREMENT BY 1
  START WITH 1;
```

NOTE   To create sequences, the system privilege Create Any Sequence is required.

Once the sequence is generated, use the following SQL to create the table:

```
CREATE TABLE SequenceTest (EmployeeNumber NUMBER,
  EmployeeName VARCHAR2(50));
```

Once the sequence and table are created, you can experiment with the following OO4O example. Don't forget to add the OO4O Type Library before running the code in Listing 9.16.

Listing 9.16

```
1  Dim OraSession As OraSession
2  Dim OraDatabase As OraDatabase
3
4  Set OraSession = CreateObject _
        ("OracleInProcServer.XOraSession")
5  Set OraDatabase = OraSession.OpenDatabase _
        ("v8i", "scott/tiger", 0&)
6
7  OraDatabase.Parameters.Add "SequenceNumber", , _
        ORAPARM_OUTPUT, ORATYPE_NUMBER
8  OraDatabase.ExecuteSQL _
        ("INSERT INTO SequenceTest values " & _
        "(SequenceSample.NextVal, 'John Doe') " & _
        "RETURNING EmployeeNumber INTO :SequenceNumber")
9  MsgBox "The sequence number used for" & _
        " the Insert was " & _
        OraDatabase.Parameters("SequenceNumber").Value
```

Analysis

- Lines 1–2 are Dim statements for the objects being used in this example.

- Line 3 is a blank space to make the code easier to read.

- Line 4 creates the OraSession object.

- Line 5 creates an OraDatabase object and establishes the connection to the database.

- Line 6 is a blank space prior to creating the SequenceNumber parameter.

- Line 7 creates the parameter that will house the return value from the Insert statement.

- Line 8 executes the Insert statement that contains the Returning clause.

- Line 9 displays a message box that simply shows the sequence number returned from the Insert statement.

As you can see, there really is not much to the code. This latest release of OO4O has simplified this functionality. To make this example more dynamic, you can create a bind parameter in place of the hard-coded value "John Doe" and use Visual Basic's Textbox Control to populate the parameter. This way, each Insert operation can contain not only a unique number but also a different name.

To check the data inserted, execute the following SQL in SQL*Pus:

```
SELECT * FROM SequenceTest;
```

Using Dates

Like sequences, working with dates is not that complicated, but it tends to generate a number of questions that primarily deal with obtaining the hours and minutes of a given Date field. The next OO4O example in Listing 9.17 does a number of things. First, it inserts different dates using a different date format for each. Next, the dates are displayed using the default MM/DD/YY format. In the last step, the same dates are displayed, but this time, the date format is MONTH-DD-YYYYHH:MI:SSAM.

Before testing the example, create a table with a Date field. Enter the following SQL in SQL*Plus to create a table with a single field:

```
CREATE TABLE Date_Table (DateField DATE);
```

The DateField field will be of a Date data type.

NOTE

Without specifying a specific date format, the date will be displayed in a VB-specific format that tends to map to the format found in the Registry under `HKEY_CURRENT_USER\Control Panel\International\sShortDate`.

Don't forget to add the OO4O Type Library before running Listing 9.17.

Listing 9.17

```
1  Dim OraSession As Object
2  Dim OraDatabase As Object
3  Dim Oradynaset As Object
4  Dim HireDateArray As OraParamArray
5
6  Set OraSession = CreateObject _
       ("OracleInProcServer.XOraSession")
7  Set OraDatabase = OraSession.OpenDatabase _
       ("v8i", "scott/tiger", 0&)
8
9  OraDatabase.Parameters.AddTable "DummyDate", _
       ORAPARM_BOTH, ORATYPE_DATE, 5
10  Set HireDateArray = OraDatabase.Parameters("DummyDate")
11 HireDateArray(0) = "14-FEB-1999 12:10:32"
12 HireDateArray(1) = "12:34:56 Mar-17-1999 "
13 HireDateArray(2) = "99-Dec-27"
14 HireDateArray(3) = "1-1997-August 5:30 PM"
15 HireDateArray(4) = "1-Jan-00 12:00:01 AM"
16 OraDatabase.ExecuteSQL _
       ("INSERT INTO Date_Table VALUES (:DummyDate)")
17
18 MsgBox "Using the default date format."
19 Set Oradynaset = OraDatabase.CreateDynaset _
       ("SELECT * FROM Date_Table", 0&)
20 For rowIndex = 1 To Oradynaset.RecordCount
21     MsgBox Oradynaset.Fields("DateField").Value, _
             vbOKOnly, "Dates"
22     Oradynaset.MoveNext
23 Next rowIndex
24
```

```
25 MsgBox "Using the following data format: " & _
        "MONTH-DD-YYYYHH:MI:SSAM"
26 Set Oradynaset = OraDatabase.CreateDynaset _
        ("SELECT TO_CHAR(DateField, " & _
        "'Month-DD-YYYY HH:MI:SS AM') FROM Date_Table", 0&)
27 For rowIndex = 1 To Oradynaset.RecordCount
28      MsgBox Oradynaset.Fields _
        ("TO_CHAR(DATEFIELD,'MONTH-DD-YYYYHH:MI:SSAM')") _
        .Value, vbOKOnly, "Dates"
29      Oradynaset.MoveNext
30 Next rowIndex
31 OraDatabase.Parameters.Remove "HireDate"
32 OraDatabase.ExecuteSQL ("DELETE DATE_TABLE")
```

Analysis

- Lines 1–4 are Dim statements for the objects being used in this example.

- Line 5 is a blank space to make the code easier to read.

- Line 6 creates the OraSession object.

- Line 7 creates an OraDatabase object and establishes the connection to the database.

- Line 8 is a blank space to make the code easier to read.

- Line 9 creates the table type DummyDate.

- Line 10 creates the OraParamArray HireDateArray.

- Lines 11–15 populate the array with a number of different dates and formats.

- Lines 16 uses the array to insert the dates into the Date_Table table, which is created earlier in this section.

- Line 17 is a blank space to make the code easier to read.

- Line 18 displays a message box signifying the section that displays the dates using the default date format.

- Line 19 creates an OraDynaset object based on the Date_Table table.

- Line 20 starts the loop that will iterate through each date.

- Line 21 displays the Date field.

- Line 22 moves to the next row in the OraDynaset object.

- Line 23 increments the loop.

- Line 24 is a blank space to make the code easier to read.

- Line 25 displays a message box signifying the section that displays the dates using the MONTH-DD-YYYYHH:MI:SS AM date format.

- Line 26 creates an OraDynaset object based on the Date_Table table.

- Line 27 starts the loop that will iterate through each date.

- Line 28 displays the Date field.

- Line 29 moves to the next row in the OraDynaset object.

- Line 30 increments the loop.

- Line 31 deletes the HireDate parameter.

- Line 32 cleans up by deleting the dates just inserted in case this example is run more than once.

Summary

We hope that this chapter gave you a good understanding of the versatility of OO4O by discussing a variety of programmatic interfaces. We discussed a number of topics, including stored procedures and functions, creating parameters and arrays, and integrating these with each other. Another popular feature, returning result sets from the database, was also discussed. On the lighter side, we addressed some common-interest topics, such as working with sequences and working with dates. This chapter introduced you to how to integrate OO4O's powerful features to increase the flexibility and functionality of your applications.

chapter 10

Working with Large Objects (LOBs)

- Initializing LOBs

- Implementing OraLOB's properties and methods

- Performing piecewise Read and Write operations with LOBs

- Working with Directory Aliases

This chapter discusses how Oracle Objects for OLE (OO4O) interfaces with LOBs in the database. During this discussion, the properties and methods of the OraLOB objects (OraBLOB, OraCLOB, and OraBFILE) will be covered. The OraLOB object types are new to OO4O with this release of Oracle8i. LOBs pertain to the CLOB, BLOB, and BFILE data types found in an Oracle8i database and are discussed in depth in the next section. *OraLOBs* are objects introduced in the 8i release of OO4O that interface with LOBs in the database. Although LOBs existed in earlier releases of the Oracle database, the OraLOB objects did not exist for OO4O. This is why the earlier versions of OO4O were unable to interface with database LOBs. The OraLOB objects are definitely one of the best characteristics of OO4O because of how easy they make it to manipulate LOBs in the database.

Before discussing the new OraLOB objects, we will discuss LOBs in the database. The remainder of the chapter will review and discuss the equivalent OraLOB objects in OO4O.

NOTE   The examples used in this chapter make use of the Scott schema, which is owned by Oracle and is bundled with OO4O. For more information pertaining to this schema and its tables, refer to the Introduction for a description of the schema, or to Chapter 2 for steps on how to create the tables.

LOBs in the Database

Large Objects (LOBs) were introduced in the first official release (version 8.0.3) of the Oracle8 database but were not available with OO4O until the current release of Oracle8i. (The first production release of OO4O to contain the new OraLOB objects is 8.1.5.3.3.) Since the first release of Oracle8, Oracle has provided a DBMS_LOB package to use to manipulate Large Object data types. The four types of LOBs are

CLOB   Character Large Objects

NCLOB   National Character Large Objects

BLOB   Binary Large Objects

BFILE   Binary Files, which are a particular kind of Large Object

LOB objects are different from simple data types (simple data types include Number, Integer, Varchar2, and Char) in the size of the data that they can store, as well as the way in which the database actually stores the data.

The initial version of the Oracle8 database (version 8.0.3) would not allow LOB data to be inserted without explicitly initializing the LOB field using one of the functions provided by Oracle. LOBs have to be initialized because they are not kept inline like simple data types are. Therefore, the database requires the LOB to be initialized and set to an Empty value before inserting data.

This version of the Oracle8i database (version 8.1.5) has enhanced working with LOBs. You now have the option of storing LOBs either inline (like other data types) or out-of-line, as they were originally designed. The storage method is decided when creating the database table. For more information on doing this, look for the Create Table command in the *Oracle8i SQL Reference*.

The LOB field does not always have to be initialized. For example, if the value of the data is less than 4,000 bytes, the database will store the data inline. In this case, the LOB field does not have to be initialized.

What happens when LOBs are initialized? Essentially, the initializing process allocates space and returns what is called a *LOB locator*. The LOB locator refers to the actual location of the LOB in the database. Let's look at how a table with simple data types works and then see how a table defined with a LOB data type (stored out-of line) works.

If a table (SimpleTable) is defined with two fields, one a Number(5) and the other a Varchar2(100), the database stores the data in each row (inline). This looks like Figure 10.1.

FIGURE 10.1
Simple data type data storage

SimpleTable

Number (5)	Varchar2 (100)
101	Test data 1
102	Test data 2
103	Test data 3

With LOBs, characteristics of data storage are a bit different. For starters, the LOBs can be stored either inline or out-of-line. This is controlled by the database and is usually determined by the size of the LOB data. Figure 10.2 illustrates a table (MyLOBTable) that is defined with a Number(5), a CLOB, and a Varchar2(100).

FIGURE 10.2

CLOB data type data
storage

MyLOBTable

Number (5)	CLOB	Varchar2 (100)
101		Test data 1
102		Test data 2
103		Test data 3

The CLOB column in Figure 10.2 is not really a column defined to hold data as the Number or Varchar2 fields are. Instead, this CLOB stores a reference (LOB locator) to where the actual data is stored. Figure 10.3 illustrates how this looks.

FIGURE 10.3

CLOB data storage

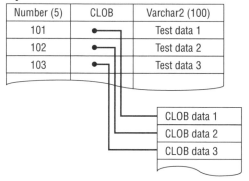

MyLOBTable

Notice how each CLOB column does not contain any actual data but rather a pointer to where the data is stored in the database. Oracle provides low-level control of LOB storage by allowing the LOBs to be stored in other table spaces or even other physical drives in the Oracle database. Allowing this type of control helps with performance and with fine-tuning the database.

Another advantage of LOBs over Long and Long Raw data types is that you can have more than one LOB in a table. This option was not available with Long and Long Raw data types. Keep in mind that the LOB data types were created to eventually replace the Long and Long Raw data types.

The Move from Long and Long Raw Data Types to LOBs

LOBs (CLOB, NCLOB, BLOB) are Oracle8's version of the Long and Long Raw data types from the Oracle7 database. Actually, the Long and Long Raw data types still exist in both Oracle8 and Oracle8i, but only for backward compatibility. Oracle makes the statement in a number of documents that the Long and Long Raw data types may not exist in a future release of Oracle.

One of the biggest disadvantages of the Long and Long Raw data types is the fact that any given table can only contain one Long or Long Raw field. This means that if a company creates a database of their employees that contains each individual's resume and an image of each employee, this will require at least two tables. You need one to store the resume (Long field) and the other to store the image in a Long Raw field. With the LOB data types, a single table can be created to store the resume in a CLOB field *and* the employee's image in a BLOB field.

The LOB's design allows a table to contain more than one LOB data type. The one component that makes this happen is the LOB locator. Figure 10.4 illustrates how a table with more than one LOB type looks.

FIGURE 10.4
A table with CLOB and BLOB fields

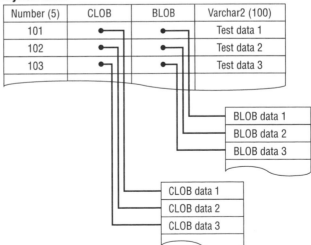

> **NOTE**   Interfacing with a LOB is done through the locator. In fact, executing a Select statement on any LOB field returns the LOB locator and not the data; the locator is used to access the data.

Initializing a LOB

When a table contains a CLOB or a BLOB field, these fields must be initialized before inserting data. Initializing simply allocates the LOB locator. There are two ways to initialize a LOB field. The first is to explicitly initialize the LOB using either the EMPTY_BLOB() or the EMPTY_CLOB() functions.

> **NOTE**   Although EMPTY_CLOB() and EMPTY_BLOB() are called functions, they do not return any values.

The EMPTY_CLOB() and EMPTY_BLOB() functions exist in both the Oracle8 and Oracle8i databases. The *EMPTY_CLOB() function* initializes the LOB locator for CLOB fields. The *EMPTY_BLOB() function* initializes the LOB locator for the BLOB fields. The following code is an example of explicitly initializing both a CLOB and a BLOB field.

Before executing the code, open SQL*Plus and connect to the Oracle8i database. Once you are successsfully connected, enter the following:

```
CREATE TABLE MYTABLE (FIELD_INDEX NUMBER(5),
    BLOB_FIELD BLOB, CLOB_FIELD CLOB);
```

Once the table is created, you can execute an Insert statement to pass in the EMPTY_BLOB() and EMPTY_CLOB() functions as values. From the SQL prompt, an insert into this table looks like this:

```
INSERT INTO MYTABLE VALUES (1, EMPTY_BLOB(),EMPTY_CLOB());
```

Once the Insert statement is executed using the EMPTY_CLOB() and the EMPTY_BLOB() functions, the LOB fields (BLOB_FIELD and CLOB_FIELD) in the table are initialized. This means that the LOB locator has been established and the LOBs are ready to be populated with data. To populate the LOB fields using SQL*Plus, execute an SQL statement on one or both of the LOBs using the Update command in conjunction with the DBMS_LOB package. The later sections in this chapter cover how to update the LOB fields with data in OO4O. For more information on updating LOBs in SQL*Plus and on the DBMS_LOB package, can review the *Oracle8i Application Developer's Guide—Large Objects (LOBs)* manual.

The second way to initialize a LOB field is to do it implicitly. To implicitly initialize the LOB fields, insert data into the fields (using SQL) without using the EMPTY_CLOB() or the EMPTY_BLOB() functions. Using the example table that we used previously, a second Insert statement is executed, using the following SQL statement, to implicitly initialize both a CLOB and a BLOB field. If you don't already have an SQL*Plus session open, open one now. If you still have an SQL*Plus session available, at the SQL prompt, enter the following:

```
INSERT INTO MYTABLE VALUES (1, HEXTORAW('FFFF'),
  'Hello World');
```

Let's take a moment to review the last two Insert statements to clarify two major points:

- To explicitly initialize a LOB, you must first execute an Insert statement using the EMPTY_CLOB() and the EMPTY_BLOB() functions and then execute an Update command to populate the field. Basically, it's a two-step process.

- To implicitly initialize a LOB, you only have to execute an Insert statement and include the data, without having to follow with an Update command. Basically, it's a one-step process.

If you can implicitly initialize a LOB and insert data all in a single command, why would anyone want to use any other method? Why are there two separate methods? Good questions. First, you can only implicitly initialize a LOB field if the size of the field is less than 4K. If the size of the data is greater than 4K, you must first explicitly initialize the LOB field and then perform an Update command to populate the field with data. Also, implicitly initializing a LOB causes the database to store the data inline; explicitly initializing a LOB causes the database to store the data out-of-line.

Character Large Objects (CLOBs) and National Character Large Objects (NCLOBs)

Both the CLOB and NCLOB data types contain character data. The difference between the two types is that the *CLOB data type* contains single-byte characters, and the *NCLOB data type* contains multi-byte characters.

The multi-byte characters contained in NCLOB objects are a fixed width. This means that varying-width character sets are not supported in any version of Oracle.

The CLOB and NCLOB data types can store up to 4GB of data and are primarily used for storing character data. This is a significant increase from the Long data type, which is only capable of storing up to 2GB of data.

Although Long data types are present in Oracle8i, they are provided mainly for backward compatibility. The new CLOB and NCLOB data types should be used instead.

Remember that Oracle8i provides the Long data type primarily for backward compatibility, and it will no longer exist in some future (not yet known) release of the Oracle8i database. The fact that tables can be created with more than one CLOB or NCLOB field, and that CLOBs and NCLOBs can store up to 4GB of data, makes the Long data type obsolete.

Binary Large Objects (BLOB)

The *BLOB data type* contains binary data not character data like the CLOB and NCLOB data type. This means that BLOB data is impervious to any character set conversions like the CLOB and NCLOB data may experience. The BLOB data type provides more storage capacity (4GB) than the Long Raw data type (2GB).

Although the Long Raw data type is present in Oracle8i, it is provided mainly for backward compatibility. The new BLOB data type should be used instead.

Like the Long data type, the Long Raw data type is provided by Oracle8i for backward compatibility and will no longer exist in some future (not yet known) release of the Oracle8i database. The fact that tables can be created with more than one BLOB field and that BLOBs can store up to 4GB of data makes the Long Raw data type obsolete.

Binary Files (BFILE)

The *BFILE data type* is new to the Oracle8 and Oracle8i databases and is a reference to a file external to the database. Although the file is external to the database, the file is still located on the same physical machine as the database. The file in reference cannot be located on a remote machine. Because the file is external to the database, restrictions to the size are controlled not by the database but by the operating system where the external file is stored.

Just as the CLOB and BLOB data types use a LOB locator to point to their respective data, the BFILE uses a LOB locator to point to its data. In contrast, the LOB locator for the CLOB and BLOB data types reference data that is stored out-of-line. The BFILE data type uses a LOB locator to reference a file stored on the operating system. Figure 10.5 illustrates a table that contains both a CLOB and a BFILE data type. Notice how the LOB locator for the CLOB references data in the database but out-of-line with the rest of the table data. The LOB locator for the BFILE references files (`MyFile1.BMP` and `MyFile2.BMP`) that are external to the database.

FIGURE 10.5
A table with a BFILE field

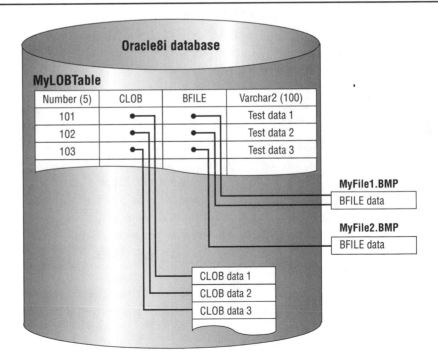

Because the BFILE can reference a given file on the operating system, the file can contain any type of data, but the data contained in the file will be treated like a BLOB. This means that the data contained in the file will not undergo any character set conversions like CLOB and NCLOB data will.

Additional user privileges are required when working with BFILEs that are not necessary for the other data types. In the following section, you'll learn how to properly initialize the BFILE object, what user privileges are required, and about some common stumbling blocks when working with the BFILE data type.

Initializing a BFILE

Just as the CLOB and BLOB data types use the EMPTY_CLOB() and EMPTY_BLOB() functions to initialize the LOB locators for their respective data, the BFILE data type uses the BFILENAME function.

Unlike the EMPTY_CLOB() and EMPTY_BLOB() functions, which don't take any parameters, the BFILENAME function takes two parameters. The first parameter is a Directory Alias and the second parameter is the name of the external file located on the operating system.

The first parameter of the BFILENAME function is the Directory Alias and is the reference to a directory located externally to the database but still on the same operating system as the database. Generally, you'll want to exercise a little caution when creating these aliases. You don't want to start creating Directory Aliases for every single file you want to reference. That could result in a huge number of Directory Aliases, and it would be a nightmare to maintain them all.

At the same time, you don't want to create Directory Aliases that make reference to numerous drives and directories on the operating system. Not only would that create a maintenance nightmare for tracking each alias, but it would also increase the potential for someone to accidentally delete one of the referenced directories on the operating system. A better idea is to organize a central location where all BFILE references can be found.

For example, you can create a BFILE directory on the D drive and use this as a location to store BFILEs, or you can take it a step further and create a subdirectory under the BFILE directory for each user. The structure would theoretically look like one of the directory structures in Figure 10.6.

FIGURE 10.6
Two options for setting up a file directory

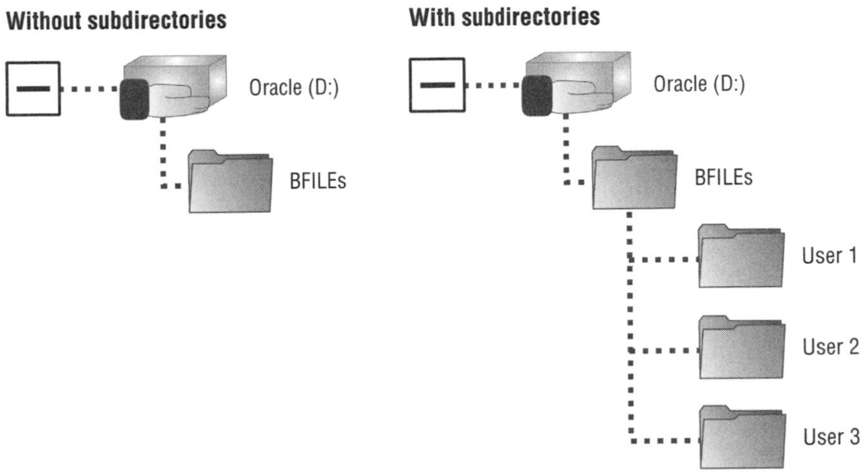

One of the benefits of having external files congregated in a specific area is that it makes locating these files more intuitive. Another advantage is that you'll have simpler backups. Because these external files are located under some single root directory, you can select to backup the root directory and any or all subsequent directories or files.

NOTE   To create a Directory Alias you must have the Create Any Directory system privilege.

Before creating any Directory Aliases in the database, you must have Create Any Directory privileges. To see how this works, let's say you are working in a database as the user Scott. Your DBA would use the following SQL at the SQL prompt in SQL*Plus to grant Scott the ability to create aliases:

```
GRANT CREATE ANY DIRECTORY TO SCOTT;
```

Once user Scott obtains the grant, different aliases can be created. Using the shorter scenario in Figure 10.6 (without subdirectories), the following SQL statement can be entered at the SQL prompt in SQL*Plus to create a Directory Alias called BFILE_DIR:

```
CREATE OR REPLACE DIRECTORY BFILE_DIR AS 'D:\BFILES';
```

In the case where subdirectories are present, the following SQL can be used:

```
CREATE OR REPLACE DIRECTORY BFILE_DIR AS 'D:\BFILES\USER1';
```

The Directory Aliases are global for the system. This means that if an alias called BFILE_DIR is created in one schema, another user can create the same Directory Alias in their own schema with the same name. The new location being referenced will override the old one. Every time a user creates a new alias, the database updates the system-owned All_Directories table with the alias name and the directory it references. So, if two users create an alias with the same name, the last entry made is the one found in the table. To prevent this, you can query the All_Directories table to see if any records exist. If the query returns any records, you know that the alias already exists.

To see how this global alias works in SQL*Plus, let's see whether the BFILE_DIR alias that was just created actually exists. To do so, enter the following at the SQL prompt:

```
SELECT * FROM ALL_DIRECTORIES
WHERE DIRECTORY_NAME = 'BFILE_DIR';
```

There is an example in this chapter that demonstrates how to implement a validation in VB using OO4O. If you want to skip ahead, see Listing 10.1.

A global Directory Alias allows other developers or users to access them as long as they have Read privileges on the Directory Alias. Creating a Directory Alias in your own schema automatically grants you Read privileges. For example, if you are working in Scott's schema and want to use the new Directory Alias name that was created by another user, such as BFILE_DIRECTORY, the DBA would have to provide Read privileges using the following SQL statement in SQL*Plus:

```
GRANT READ ON DIRECTORY_BFILE_DIRECTORY TO SCOTT;
```

NOTE   To use a Directory Alias created by another user, you must have Read privileges on the Directory Alias.

Once the Directory Alias is defined, the only other piece of information required for the BFILENAME function is the second parameter, which is the name of the external file.

The following example creates a new table named LOB_TABLE that will contain four fields. The first field is defined as a Number data type for easy reference to each record, and the remaining three fields are defined for each of the LOB data types (BLOB, CLOB, and BFILE). For the following example, when initializing the BFILE field, you will pass in `MyFile1.BMP` as the external filename for the second parameter of the BFILENAME function when initializing the BFILE field. In SQL*Plus, enter the following SQL code at the SQL prompt to create the required table:

```
CREATE TABLE LOB_TABLE
(INDEX_FIELD NUMBER,
BLOB_FIELD BLOB,
CLOB_FIELD CLOB,
BFILE_FIELD BFILE);
```

Once the table is created, the next step is to insert a record. The BLOB and CLOB field will be initialized using the EMPTY_BLOB() and the EMPTY_CLOB() functions. The BFILE file will be initialized using the BFILENAME function. The two parameters required for initializing the BFILE are the Directory Alias and a filename. Use the BFILE_DIR alias defined earlier as the Directory Alias and the external filename `MyFile1.BMP` for the parameters for the BFILENAME function. The SQL to insert a record should look like this:

```
INSERT INTO LOB_TABLE VALUES
    (1, EMPTY_BLOB(), EMPTY_CLOB(),
    BFILENAME('BFILE_DIR', 'MyFile1.BMP'));
```

Once again, the first parameter of the BFILENAME function is a valid Directory Alias. In this example, BFILE_DIR is used. The second parameter is the actual filename being referenced.

Take a moment to review the second parameter (`MyFile1.BMP`) for the BFILE-NAME function. Don't worry whether or not the file `MyFile1.BMP` exists. It's actually OK to insert a BFILE object with reference to a file that currently does not exist but may exist at a later time. The file can be copied to the location referenced by the BFILE_DIR alias at your convenience, but any attempt to access a BFILE object in SQL*Plus, OO4O, or any other method, before the file actually exists will result in an error.

It is usually wise to make sure that the file exists before attempting to access the data. When working with BFILEs in SQL*Plus, the database contains a DBMS_LOB package that provides a FILEEXISTS function to verify that the BFILE field references an existing file. For information on this function and the DBMS_LOB package, you refer to the *Oracle8i Application Developer's Guide—Large Objects*

(LOBs). Just as the database provides its own function for verifying BFILE references, so does OO4O. Although the process for verifying a file's existence is not the same, the purpose is the same: to validate the BFILE's existence. Further information on how OO4O implements this is covered later in the chapter.

As stated earlier in this section, the file referenced by the BFILE field is actually a physical file on the operating system. Because the operating system controls this file, the file size will be limited not by the database but by the operating system. In fact, the actual files can be added, deleted, and modified without having to interface with the database at all. As long as you have permission on the operating system and the directory where the file is located, the database does not have to be online in order to modify the file.

Using LOBs in OO4O

LOBs were introduced in the first version of the Oracle8 database. At that time, the only way to insert and update them was either to use the DBMS_LOB package provided by the Oracle8 database or to use Oracle's native API call, Oracle Call Interface (OCI).

The DBMS_LOB package is fairly simple and straightforward. The downside with using the DBMS_LOB package is that the code has to be executed in a stored procedure on the database. This means that there is no simple way to return LOBs to the client. But, with OCI, you can not only bypass using the DBMS_LOB package and its restrictions, but you can also retrieve the LOBs from the database and use them on the client for further manipulation.

The downside with using OCI is that it uses a complex language and usually requires a lot of code to do basic manipulation of LOBs. For more on the DBMS_LOB package, review the *Oracle8i Application Developer's Guide—Large Objects (LOBs)*. For more information on OCI, review the *Oracle Call Interface—Programmer's Guide* (Volumes 1 and 2) for more information.

Some clever developer at Oracle was probably thinking how great it would be if there were an interface for working with LOBs that was as fully functional as OCI yet as simple as the DBMS_LOB package. This is where Oracle Object for OLE (O4OO) comes into the picture. OO4O provides a very simple approach for working with LOBs and provides full functionality. Keep in mind that OO4O is not new to Oracle8i. In fact, OO4O existed when Oracle7 was the last version of the database. It's just that OO4O did not have the capability to work with LOBs until the version released with Oracle8i.

In order for OO4O to interface with the database LOBs, OO4O has to introduce a few new objects of its own. The OraLOB objects provide this link between the LOB objects and OO4O functionality. The OraLOB object provides a mapping in a one-to-one relationship with the LOB objects in the database. Table 10.1 lists OO4O's new data types and how they map to their corresponding data type in the database.

Initializing LOBs Using OO4O

When working with LOBs using OO4O's OraLOB objects, first, you must initialize the LOB whether the data will kept inline or out-of-line in the the database. Ora-LOBs cannot be manipulated prior to initializing them. Two of the easier ways to initialize the LOB fields is either to use the EMTPY_CLOB() and EMPTY_BLOB() functions for CLOB and BLOB fields (and the BFILENAME function for the BFILE fields), or to use the Empty value when adding a new record to a dynaset. (Refer to Chapter 4 for more information on dynasets.)

Access to the EMPTY_BLOB(), EMPTY_CLOB(), and BFILENAME functions can be used to initialize an OraLOB, but only if you are executing SQL statements using OO4O's ExecuteSQL command. Using the LOB_TABLE created in the "Initializing a BFILE" section, the following bit of code inserts and initializes LOBs in OO4O. Keep in mind that this is just a single line of OO4O code extracted from a Visual Basic application to demonstrate using the ExecuteSQL command. The complete example will be discussed later in this chapter.

```
OraDatabase.ExecuteSQL ("INSERT INTO LOB_TABLE VALUES " & _
        "(2, EMPTY_BLOB(), EMPTY_CLOB(), " & _
        "BFILENAME('BFILE_DIR', 'MyFile1.BMP'))")
```

If you are manipulating data using a dynaset, the LOB fields can be initialized using the Visual Basic variable Empty. Keep in mind that the following is just a bit of OO4O code extracted from a Visual Basic application to demonstrate using the Empty value when adding a new record to a dynaset. The complete example will be discussed later in this chapter.

```
OraDynaset.AddNew
        OraDynaset!BLOB_FIELD = EMPTY
        OraDynaset!CLOB_FIELD = EMPTY
        'Remember to match case with the DirectoryName
```

```
        OraBFILE.DirectoryName = "BFILE_DIR"
        OraBFILE.FileName = "MyFile1.BMP"
OraDynaset.Update
```

An Empty value is not the same as a Null value; these cannot be used interchangeably. An *Empty value* will initialize the LOB for you and represents an object with no contents. A *Null value* does not initialize the LOB because a Null value represents an object that has no value, similar to zero. Using a Null value instead of an Empty value will cause subsequent calls to an object's methods to fail. For more information on the Empty value, you can review Visual Basic's online help.

Just as the database provides the DBMS_LOB package to interface with the LOB objects, OO4O's OraLOB objects provide their own set of properties and methods. These will be covered in the section "An Overview of OraLOB Properties and Methods" ater in this chapter.

With the NCLOBs in the database, although the data will be stored as a double byte, with OO4O, you will only be able to insert and manipulate single byte data. Complete functionality should be available in a later release.

An Overview of OraLOB Properties and Methods

The OraBLOB, OraCLOB, and OraBFILE objects that OO4O provides for interfacing with the LOBs in the database are designed so that there is a one-to-one mapping of OO4O LOB data types with the database LOB data types with one exception. The OraCLOB object in OO4O maps to both the database CLOB and NCLOB object. Table 10.1 illustrates this mapping.

TABLE 10.1: Comparable OO4O Objects and Database LOB Objects

OO4O LOB Objects	Database LOB Objects
OraBLOB	BLOB
OraCLOB	CLOB/NCLOB
OraBFILE	BFILE

The CLOB and NCLOB objects are, for the most part, the same. The only difference is that the NCLOB data type supports wide characters. For more information on the CLOB and NCLOB data types, refer to the "Character Large Objects (CLOBs) and National Character Large Objects (NCLOBs)" section earlier in this chapter.

TIP   Although OraCLOBs can be used to interface with NCLOBs in the database, complete functionality does not exist. Expect this functionality to be available in a later release of OO4O.

Along with the new objects provided by OO4O come new properties and methods for each. Tables 10.2 and 10.3 provide an overview of the properties and methods available for each object. You'll find discussions of each method and how they're used in the following sections.

TABLE 10.2: OraLOB Properties

Properties	OraBLOB/OraCLOB	OraBFILE
DirectoryName	No	Yes
Exists	No	Yes
FileName	No	Yes
IsNull	Yes	Yes
IsOpen	No	Yes
OffSet	Yes	Yes
PollingAmount	Yes	Yes
Size	Yes	Yes
Status	Yes	Yes

TABLE 10.3: OraLOB Methods

Methods	OraBLOB/OraCLOB	OraBFILE
Append	Yes	No
Clone	Yes	Yes

TABLE 10.3: OraLOB Methods *(continued)*

Methods	OraBLOB/OraCLOB	OraBFILE
Close	No	Yes
CloseAll	No	Yes
Compare	Yes	Yes
CopyFromFile	Yes	No
CopyFromBFile	Yes	No
CopyToFile	Yes	Yes
DisableBuffering	Yes	No
EnableBuffering	Yes	No
Erase	Yes	No
FlushBuffer	Yes	No
MatchPos	Yes	Yes
Open	No	Yes
Read	Yes	Yes
Trim	Yes	No
Write	Yes	No

A quick glance at Tables 10.2 and 10.3 reveals that the OraBLOB and OraCLOB have the same five properties and fifteen methods. This is because the OraBLOB and OraCLOB objects are closely related. The main difference is that the CLOB data type is exposed to character set conversion. Other than that, interfacing with either data type is the same. Therefore, the properties and methods in the OraBLOB and OraCLOB objects are the same. As discussed in the "Binary Files (BFILE)" section earlier in this chapter, the BFILE data type is very different from the BLOB and CLOB types. Therefore, it is necessary to have different properties and methods in the OraBFILE object.

One major advantage of the new objects in OO4O is that each object has enough properties and methods to make it easy to manipulate the various LOBs in the database.

You'll become familiar with each OraLOB object as you review the sections describing their properties and methods. Also, you will notice that the additional methods found in the OraCLOB and OraBLOB objects, but not in the OraBFILE object, are the ones that manipulate the data. The extra methods in the OraLOB objects allow the user to physically modify the data by appending, copying, trimming, or overwriting data. Although the OraBFILE object provides access to its data, the access is limited to copying. The only manipulation available to the OraBFILE object is changing the external file reference.

Although the number of properties and methods varies between the OraBFILE object and the other OraLOB objects, there is plenty of overlap. The properties and methods that are contained in each object provide the same functionality. In order to avoid redundant text, we'll just point out the exceptions.

OraBLOB, OraCLOB, and OraBFILE Properties and Methods

Tables 10.2 and 10.3 provided a quick reference to the available properties and methods for the OraLOB objects. The following sections will discuss each property and method for the OraBLOB, OraCLOB, and OraBFILE data types. As each property is discussed, you will realize how easy OO4O makes interfacing with database LOBs.

OraLOB Properties

The properties described here are all the properties available to the OraLOB objects. Each property listing itemizes the object(s) (OraCLOB, OraBLOB, or OraBFILE) that support it, as well as whether the property is read only or if it is read and write capable. The descriptions tell what each property does, along with one or two lines of code demonstrating the syntax. If there are any potential snags, they will be discussed, as well.

The DirectoryName Property

The *DirectoryName property* is the alias defined in the database for the location of the BFILE(s). The alias will point to a physical location where the BFILE(s) is found on the operating system. The DirectoryName property is valid for OraBFILE objects only and is read and write at runtime.

```
OraBFILE.DirectoryName = "BFILE_DIR"
```

In this code, BFILE_DIR resolves to a directory on the operating system of the machine where the database is located. If a valid Directory Alias has not been defined, or if you are unsure of how to set it, review the "Initializing a BFILE" section earlier in this chapter.

If you wish to create a Directory Alias in OO4O instead of using SQL*Plus, the ExecuteSQL method of the OraDatabase object can be used:

```
OraDatabase.ExecuteSQL _
        ("CREATE DIRECTORY BFILE_DIR AS 'D:\BFILES'")
```

When setting the DirectoryName property, OO4O does not validate and will allow the user to enter any string value for the DirectoryName. This can be useful because it allows the user to enter a value now and define the corresponding alias in the database at a later time.

Due to this lack of validation, there are four potential stumbling blocks. First, although OO4O will accept a large alias as a DirectoryName, the database will only allow an alias of 30 characters or fewer. So, if an alias of more than 30 characters is entered for the DirectoryName property in OO4O, there will be no way to retrieve the data from the database. In fact, if you try to view the Exists property of an OraBFILE object where the DirectoryName is greater than the allotted 30 characters, two Oracle errors will be returned. The first is "ORA-00604: error occurred at recursive SQL level 1," and the second error message is "ORA-01460: unimplemented or unreasonable conversion requested." If this happens, the record has to be modified to use a valid DirectoryName property before retrieving data from the BFILE is feasible.

The second stumbling block is what happens if a valid alias exists, but it gets mistyped when setting the DirectoryName property. Let's say that the alias BFILE_DIR is defined in the database, and, when setting the DirectoryName property, it is accidentally misspelled as "BFILE_DRI". The user may be unaware of the problem until they notice that the Exists property (the Exists property is described later this is section) returns False, or until the BFILE is accessed using the Open method. (The Open property is described later in this section.) When accessing a BFILE with an invalid DirectoryName property, the Open method returns the Oracle error "Ora-22285: non-existent directory or file for FILEOPEN operation."

The third stumbling block is when the DirectoryName property is set with a string value that has mixed case. When a Directory Alias is created in SQL*Plus and the alias name is not placed in quotes, the database executes an Upper function call on the alias to force the name to be stored in the database in all capital letters. Let's take a moment to see just how and when the Directory Alias will and will not be converted by the Upper command when creating a Directory Alias in SQL*Plus and in OO4O. First, let's take a look at when an Upper command will be executed on the SQL in SQL*Plus and in OO4O. We will then discuss how to reserve the case of the Directory Alias in SQL*Plus and in OO4O.

Uppercase

If you enter the following Create Directory command at the SQL prompt in SQL*PLUS:

```
CREATE OR REPLACE DIRECTORY Bfile_Dir AS 'C:\BFILES';
```

the database will execute the Upper command and store the string value in the database in uppercase as "BFILE_DIR".

You can accomplish the same thing if you execute the following ExecuteSQL command in OO4O:

```
OraDatabase.ExecuteSQL ("CREATE OR REPLACE DIRECTORY " & _
        "Bfile_Dir AS 'D:\BFILES'")
```

In both instances, the Directory Alias is stored in the database as "BFILE_DIR".

Reserving Case

If you place the alias in double quotation marks (" "), the database will retain its case. For example, if the following Create Directory command is executed at the SQL prompt in SQL*Plus:

```
CREATE OR REPLACE DIRECTORY "Bfile_Dir" AS 'C:\BFILES';
```

the database will store the string value as "Bfile_Dir".

You can accomplish the same results if you execute the following ExecuteSQL command in OO4O:

```
OraDatabase.ExecuteSQL _
    ("CREATE OR REPLACE DIRECTORY ""Bfile_Dir"" AS 'D:\BFILES'")
```

In both instances, the Directory Alias is stored in the database as "Bfile_Dir".

Validating the DirectoryName Property in OO4O

The fourth stumbling block is that the same alias name is defined ("BFILE_DIR" and "Bfile_Dir"), but each one can reference a different location on the server.

Because most developers are not aware of using double quotation marks, case retention is usually not an issue.

If you want to incorporate validation of a DirectoryName (Directory Alias) in OO4O, Listing 10.1 will definitely come in handy. Keep in mind that although static values are used in this example, the code can be modified to handle dynamic values.

Listing 10.1

```
1  'Create a temporary Dynaset to hold any returned rows.
2  Dim valDirName As OraDynaset
3  mySQL = "SELECT * FROM ALL_DIRECTORIES " & _
        "WHERE DIRECTORY_NAME = 'BFILE_DIR'"
4  Set valDirName = OraDatabase.CreateDynaset(mySQL, 0&)
5  If (valDirName.RecordCount = 0) Then
6      MsgBox "BFILE_DIR is an invalid directory name in " & _
        "the Database", vbCritical, "Invalid Directory"
7      Exit Sub
8  End If
9  'Continue Processing
```

Analysis

- Line 1 is a comment describing this section of code.

- Line 2 is the Dim statement for the OraDyanset object being used to create the dynaset. This object will contain any results returned from the database.

- Line 3 is the SQL used to query the All_Directories table for a particular Directory Alias. Keep in mind that, for demonstration purposes, this example uses a hard-coded value, BFILE_DIR, for demonstration purposes. In your actual code, you will want to make the string dynamic by using a variable.

- Line 4 executes the SQL to create the OraDynaset object.

- Line 5 uses the If statement to see whether any records were returned by inspecting the RecordCount property. If the value returned is 0 (zero), you know that the Directory Alias is not valid.

- Line 6 is the message box displayed if the Directory Alias does not exist.

- Line 7 exits the current subroutine. Here you can opt to exit the subroutine if the Directory Alias is invalid, or you can prompt the user for a new Directory Alias. Use the method that best fits your purpose.

- Line 8 ends the If condition.

- Line 9 is a comment that this routine is finished and you can continue.

Listing 10.1 creates an OraDynaset object based on a Select statement from the All_Directories table where the directory name equals BFILE_DIR. If the record count of the dynaset is zero, you know that the Directory Alias is not valid. Once it has been established that the directory name is invalid, you can provide a message box warning the user that the directory name does not exist.

Another option is to provide an error message and force the user to enter an alias that already exists. Or, if you want to be adventurous, you can provide either a combo box or list box with a list of values. Listing 10.2 demonstrates how to populate a combo box with a list of current aliases.

Listing 10.2

```
1  Set OraDynaset = OraDatabase.CreateDynaset _
      ("select * from All_Directories " & _
      "order by directory_name", 0&)
2  While Not OraDynaset.EOF
3      Combo1.AddItem _
          OraDynaset.Fields("Directory_name").Value
4      OraDynaset.MoveNext
5  Wend
```

Analysis

- Line 1 creates an OraDynaset object, ordered by directory_name, to house all the data in the All_Directories table.

- Line 2 starts the While loop to step through each record in the dynaset. Each record of the dynaset must be added to the combo box one at a time.

- Line 3 executes the AddItem method of the combo box. The AddItem method allows you to add a new value to the combo box. For more information on populating combo boxes, refer to the Visual Basics online help. The dynaset value used to add a new element to the combo box is the Directory_name field. Combo1 is the name used in this example for the combo box object on a form. The name you use may differ.

- Line 4 navigates to the next record in the dynaset so that it can be added to the combo box.

- Line 5 ends the While loop.

Listing 10.2 does a Select statement, sorts all the available directory names in alphabetical order, and places them in a combo box. This allows the user to select a valid Directory Alias.

It is valid to use a Directory Alias that does not exist because validation of the Directory Alias does not occur until the BFILE object in the database is being accessed. It's up to the developer to decide whether or not to allow users to enter a Directory Alias that does not exist or whether to require that only existing Directory Aliases are used.

The FileName Property

The *FileName property* is the actual name of the file residing on the server in the directory referenced by the DirectoryName alias. A neat feature is that the file does not have to exist. It can be placed there at a later time. The FileName property is valid for OraBFILE objects only and is read and write at runtime.

```
OraDynaset.Edit
OraBFILE.FileName = "MyPicture.GIF"
OraDynaset.Update
```

The Exists Property

The *Exists property* provides a simple way to validate a file's existence on the server and is valid for OraBFILE objects only. The Exists property is read only at runtime.

Executing any OraBFILE method when the Exists property is False and the DirectoryName property contains a valid alias will return an "ORA-22288: operation <method> failed" error, along with the message that the specified file does not exist. In this error message, *<method>* will name the actual method being executed. The following code can be used to prevent such errors:

```
If (OraBFILE.Exists = False) Then
    MsgBox "File does not exist", _
            vbInformation, "Missing File"
    Exit Sub
End If
```

Be aware that the Exists property expects the value stored in the DirectoryName property or the OraBFILE to be valid. If it's not, the Exists property will return an error.

NOTE   To prevent the problems associated with an invalid Directory Alias, review the DirectoryName property for OraBFILE objects, discussed earlier in this chapter.

The IsNull Property

The *IsNull property* is an excellent way to validate whether an object has been initialized. If IsNull equals True, the object has not yet been initialized and must be prior to use. The IsNull property is valid for all OraLOB objects (OraCLOB, OraBLOB, and OraBFILE) and is read only at runtime.

OraBFILEs are not initialized in the same manner as OraCLOBs and OraBLOBs. OraCLOBS and OraBLOBs are initialized with the Empty value first before actually inserting data. The BFILEs aren't: Data can be inserted without first setting it to an Empty value. The key point is that, in either case, before updating the OraLOB object, you must be working with an object that already contains data or has at least been initialized.

The IsNull property is an excellent way to prevent errors in an application because executing certain methods on an OraLOB that is not initialized will result in an Oracle error. Because the IsNull property is valid for all OraLOB objects, it can be used to validate that the OraCLOB, OraBLOB, and OraBFILE objects have been initialized.

The following code demonstrates how to avoid errors when working with Null objects.

```
If (OraCLOB.IsNull = True) Then
    MsgBox "Object has not been initialized", _
        vbInformation, "Null Object"
    Exit Sub
End If
```

While executing the CopyFromFile method on objects whose IsNull property is True results in an ORA-01403 error, executing the CopyToFile method will not. One item to note for the CopyToFile method is that no error is returned at all, and the application will appear to function successfully when only an empty file is generated.

How would you know if an error prevented the data from being written, or if there is or should be any data? You have to do a bit more than just check the value of the IsNull property. You may also want to check the size of the OraLOB object. If the size is zero, you can either make a default entry into the file to signify that the CopyToFile method worked but there was no data, or you can simply bypass creating a file. The following code checks not only the IsNull property but also the Size property to ensure that they are greater than zero. If both of these properties are not greater than zero, the CopyToFile method is not executed.

```
If (OraLOB.IsNull = FALSE) AND (OraLOB.Size > 0) Then
        OraLOB.CopyToFile "C:\CopyFileSample.txt"
End If
```

TIP   Executing specific methods on objects where IsNull is False may result in an "ORA-01403: no data found" error. Checking the IsNull property can prevent many errors.

The IsOpen Property

All OraBFILE objects require the object to be opened for access prior to executing any OraBFILE methods. The *IsOpen property* provides a simple way of validating whether an OraBFILE object is currently open and available for access. The IsOpen property is valid for OraBFILE objects only and is read only at runtime.

For example, executing the CopyToFile method of an OraBFILE object when the IsOpen property is False results in the Oracle error "ORA-22289: cannot perform FILEREAD operation on an unopened file." The following code validates whether or not an OraBFILE object is open:

```
If (OraBFILE.IsOpen = FALSE) Then
        OraBFILE.Open
End If
```

If the OraBFILE object is not already opened, a simple call to the Open method will open the object and prevent errors, such as the ORA-22289 error.

The PollingAmount Property

The *PollingAmount property* is required and must be set to the total amount of data to be read or written when piecewise operations are executed. (An example of piecewise operations will be included later in the chapter.) The PollingAmount property is valid for all OraLOB objects (OraCLOB, OraBLOB, and OraBFILE) and is read and write at runtime.

If reading or writing the entire object in a piecewise operation, the total amount can easily be set by setting the PollingAmount property equal to the Size property of the object, like this:

```
OraCLOB.PollingAmount = OraCLOB.Size
```

The default value for the PollingAmount property is 0 (zero). Not setting the PollingAmount property to the amount you want can result in an incomplete Read or Write operation. Although results were inconsistent, some preliminary tests show that when the PollingAmount is not set and piecewise Read or Write operations are executed, the last piece of the operation is omitted. So, if you are executing piecewise Read or Write operations and it appears that not all the pieces exist, double-check that the PollingAmount property is set.

The Offset Property

The *Offset property* signifies the position (in bytes) in an OraLOB object where the piecewise Read and Write operations should start. The Offset property is valid for all OraLOB objects (OraCLOB, OraBLOB, and OraBFILE) and is read and write at runtime.

The Offset property is one-based with a default value of 1. If an OraCLOB object is 100 bytes in length and you only wish to operate on the last 25 bytes, the Offset property would be set to 76 using the following command:

```
OraLOB.OffSet = 76
```

An example is included at the end of the chapter to demonstrate the different ways that the Offset property can affect a Read or Write operation.

Once an operation has started, the Offset property can be set to a new value, but the new value will be disregarded until the current operation completes. The new value takes effect at the onset of the next operation.

The Size Property

The *Size property* is not only an excellent way to set the PollingAmount property of an object but is also an excellent way to prevent errors. The Size property is valid for all OraLOB objects (OraCLOB, OraBLOB, and OraBFILE) and is read only at runtime.

This property is simple and straightforward but very useful because it returns the size of the OraLOB object.

For example, executing the Compare method of an OraLOB object whose Size property is zero results in the Oracle error "ORA-01405: fetched column value is NULL." To prevent an error like this, the following code can be executed to validate that an object's Size property is not zero:

```
If (OraLOB.Size = 0) Then
    MsgBox "Object has no data", _
        vbInformation, "No Data"
    Exit Sub
End If
```

The Status Property

This *Status property* is used to provide the status of piecewise Read and Write operations. The Status property is valid for all OraLOB objects (OraCLOB, OraBLOB, and OraBFILE) and is read only at runtime.

When doing piecewise operations, OO4O needs to know when the last piece was read or written. First, OO4O uses the PollingAmount property as its guideline on how many bytes there are. Second, OO4O continually adds each piece processed until the total bytes processed equals the PollingAmount property. After each piece is processed, the Status property is automatically updated with one of the following three statuses:

- ORALOB_NEED_DATA

- ORALOB_NODATA

- ORALOB_SUCCESS

A common use for the Status property is to check its value programmatically after each Read or Write operation. If the Status property is ORALOB_NEED_DATA, the LOB operation is incomplete and must continue. Normally, the LOB operation continues until an ORALOB_SUCCESS is returned. Once this happens, the piece-wise operation is complete. The following code checks the Status property. The piecewise example at the end of the chapter will provide a more complete sample.

```
If (OraLOB.Status = ORALOB_NEED_DATA) Then
     'Continue processing LOB operation
     ElseIf (OraLob.Status = ORALOB_SUCCESS) Then
     'LOB Operation completed
End If
```

TIP   Initiating another LOB operation before a current piecewise Read or Write operation with a status of ORALOB_SUCCESS completes will result in the Oracle error "ORA-03130: the buffer for the next piece to be fetched is required."

Most piecewise operations are executed in some sort of loop (For, Do, While), and the loop terminates when the Status property equals ORALOB_SUCCESS. It is very important to check the Status property after each piece is processed during a piecewise operation. If a piecewise Read operation is executed in a loop and the Status property is not checked, the Read operation will not terminate. Instead, it will read until it reaches the end of the data and then continue reading from the beginning of the OraLOB object once again.

OraLOB Methods

The following sections list all of the methods available to the OraLOB objects. Each method lists the object(s) (OraCLOB, OraBLOB, or OraBFILE) that support it and a brief description of what each does. If there are any potential snags with a method, they will be discussed, as well.

The Append Method

The *Append method* appends the contents of one OraLOB object to another and is valid only for the OraCLOB and OraBLOB objects.

When executing the Append method, the two objects must be of the same type. For example, when executing the Append method of an OraCLOB object, the object being passed in must also be of an OraCLOB type.

The following code shows how simple it is to append one OraLOB object to another.

```
OraDynaset.Edit
    OraCLOB1.Append OraCLOB2
OraDynaset.Update
```

The Clone Method

The *Clone method* instantiates a stand-alone copy of an OraLOB object. The Clone method is available for all OraLOB objects (OraCLOB, OraBLOB, and OraBFILE).

A cloned object is a stand-alone OraLOB object. A *stand-alone object* is one that is not bound to an object in the database (usually through a dynaset). Even if the data of a cloned object could be modified, any changes to these objects would not be reflected in the database.

When OraBFILE objects are cloned, instead of copying the data, OO4O actually copies the reference (or BFILE locator) into the new object automatically.

Cloned OraLOB objects cannot execute all the methods available to non-cloned objects. The methods still exist, but executing particular methods will result in an Oracle error.

Because cloned objects are not bound objects (they are not bound to any objects in the database; cloned objects are strictly stand-alone), it may be best to think of cloned objects as read-only objects. Executing an OraLOB.Append or OraLOB .CopyFromFile method of a cloned object will result in an error. Some of the methods available to a clone are

- Clone (Yes, a clone of a cloned object may exist.)

- Compare

- CopyToFile

- MatchPos

- Read

Some of the methods that result in an error if executed on a clone are

- CopyFromFile

- Write

- Append

- Copy

Be careful when cloning objects. If a bound OraLOB (OraLOB1) is assigned to be a clone of another object (OraLOB2), OraLOB1 will no longer be bound. This may seem confusing at first, but take a moment to look at this example, and it might make a little more sense.

```
Set OraCLOB1 = OraDynaset.Fields("CLOBField1").Value
    :
    :
'OraCLOB1 is no longer bound to an object in the database
Set OraCLOB1 = OraTempCLOB.Clone
```

Notice that the second Set command reassigns the OraCLOB1 object. If modification to the OraCLOB1 object were possible, any changes would no longer be reflected in the database. This reassignment of a bound object is an easy mistake to make. You may find yourself accidentally doing this when you're looking for a quick and easy way to copy the contents of a temporary LOB into the database.

The Close Method

The *Close method* closes an OraBFILE object that has previously been opened using the Open method. The Close method is available only for OraBFILE objects.

To successfully execute particular operations, most OraBFILE objects require the object to be open. The following code illustrates how to close a BFILE object:

```
OraBFILE.Close
```

The CloseAll Method

The *CloseAll method* is a simple way to close all OraBFILE objects that were opened using the Open method. The CloseAll method is available only for OraBFILE objects.

The CloseAll method will only close opened OraBFILE objects associated with a particular OraDatabase object.

For example, let's say that two connections to the database are established (OraDatabase1 and OraDatabase2). In the OraDatabase1 session, three OraBFILE objects are created (OraBFILE1, OraBFILE2, OraBFILE3). In the OraDatabase2 session, another three OraBFILE objects are created (OraBFILE4, OraBFILE5, OraBFILE6).

Executing the CloseAll method on any single object will close all objects in that session. So, executing the OraBFILE2.CloseAll command will close OraBFILE1, OraBFILE2, and OraBFILE3 only. Executing the OraBFILE5.CloseAll command will close OraBFILE4, OraBFILE5, and OraBFILE6 only.

The following code illustrates how to use the CloseAll method to close all open OraBFILE objects associated with a particular OraDatabase object:

```
OraBFILE.CloseAll
```

The Compare Method

The *Compare method* allows you to compare all or part of an OraLOB object with all or part of another OraLOB object. The Compare method is available to all OraLOB objects (OraCLOB, OraBLOB, and OraBFILE).

The Compare method returns a True value if the comparison finds the same object and False if it does not.

The Compare method takes up to four parameters; the first parameter is mandatory, and the subsequent parameters are optional.

```
CompareResult = OraLOB1.Compare(OraLOB2, _
                    AmountToCompare, _
                    OffSetOfOraLOB1, _
                    OffSetOfOraLOB2)
```

- The first parameter is another LOB object and must be of the same type as the calling object.

- The second parameter (optional) is the total amount to compare to each object. The default value is the size of the LOB being compared. In the code shown here, this would be OraLOB2.

- The third parameter (optional) is the OffSet parameter of the base LOB. The default value is 1.

- The fourth parameter (optional) is the OffSet parameter of the LOB being compared. The default value is 1.

The OffSet parameters allow the Compare method to start at different bytes in an object.

Although all OraLOB objects have a Compare method, they can only be used to compare objects of the same type. This means that doing a compare of an Ora-CLOB object with an OraBLOB object will result in an error.

Let's take a look at a few scenarios. If OraCLOB1 equals "123ABCDEF" and OraCLOB2 equals "ABCDEFG", the following code returns False because the objects are clearly not the same:

```
'Scenario 1
CompareResult = OraLOB1.Compare (OraLOB2)
MsgBox "Are the objects the same --> " & CompareResult
```

```
'Scenario 2
CompareResult = OraLOB1.Compare (OraLOB2,,4)
MsgBox "Are the objects the same --> " & CompareResult
```

In the next example, although setting the Offset to 4 for OraCLOB1 starts the comparison for both objects at the letter A, OraLOB2 contains an extra letter (G), so this Compare method will also return False:

```
'Scenario 3
CompareResult = OraLOB1.Compare (OraLOB2,,4,6)
MsgBox "Are the objects the same --> " & CompareResult
```

By entering a 6 for the last parameter, essentially we are telling OO4O to compare only 6 bytes of data. This Compare method will return a True value.

The Copy Method

The *Copy method* allows the user to copy all or part of one OraLOB object with all or part of another OraLOB object. This method is available to only the OraCLOB and OraBLOB objects.

The Copy method takes up to four parameters; the first parameter is mandatory, and the subsequent parameters are optional.

```
OraLOB1.Copy OraLOB2, _
             AmountOfLobToCopy, _
             OffSetOfOraLOB1, _
             OffSetOfOraLOB2
```

- The first parameter is the OraLOB object that is being copied.

- The second parameter (optional) is the total amount to copy. The default value is the entire size.

- The third parameter (optional) is the OffSet parameter of the OraLOB object executing the Copy method. This allows the contents of one LOB to be copied into a specific portion of another LOB. The default value is 1.

- The fourth parameter (optional) is the OffSet parameter of the LOB being copied. The default value is 1.

The Copy method is that it will overwrite an object but will not resize an object if its size is smaller. An example can help make this concept clearer.

If the contents of OraCLOB1 are "1234567890", and the contents of OraCLOB2 are "ABCDEFGHIJKLMNOP", executing the following code sets OraLOB1 equal to "ABCDEFGHIJKLMNOP":

```
OraCLOB1.COPY OraCLOB2
```

OO4O resizes the OraCLOB1 object to fit the new data, which is what would be expected.

If we switch this around so that instead of the OraCLOB1 calling the Copy method, OraCLOB2 executes it, the following code sets OraLOB2 equal to "1234567890KLMNOP":

```
OraDynaset.Edit
OraCLOB2.COPY OraCLOB1
OraDynaset.Update
```

Although the size of the data being copied is smaller, OO4O will not resize the OraCLOB2 object. You may not have expected this result, but it is the correct behavior.

Although both the OraCLOB and OraBLOB objects have a Compare method, they can only be used to compare objects of the same type. This means that doing a compare of an OraCLOB object with an OraBLOB object will result in an error.

The CopyFromBfile Method

The *CopyFromBfile method* allows all or a part of the contents of an OraBFILE object to be copied into either an OraBLOB or an OraCLOB object. The CopyFromBfile method is available only to OraCLOB and OraBLOB objects.

If you remember, BFILEs are external to the database, therefore, updating the contents of a BFILE is not feasible. The CopyFromBfile method allows a fast, simple way to copy data stored externally (in BFILEs) and place it in the database. From there, the data can actually be manipulated. This method has four parameters; one is mandatory, and three are optional.

```
OraLOB.CopyFromBfile OraBFILE, _
        AmountToCopy, _
        OraLobOffset, _
        OraBFileOffset
```

- The first parameter is an OraBFILE object.

- The second parameter (optional) is the amount to copy. The default is the entire contents.

- The third parameter (optional) is the Offset parameter of the OraCLOB or OraBLOB object. The default is 1.

- The fourth parameter (optional) is the Offset parameter of the BFILE object. The default is 1.

The CopyFromBfile functions in the same manner as the Copy method when it comes to resizing.

The following code illustrates the CopyFromBfile method in its simplest form. It simply uses the default values to copy the content of the BFILE into the LOB object.

```
OraDynaset.Edit
    OraLOB.CopyFromBfile OraBFILE
OraDynaset.Update
```

The CopyFromFile Method

The *CopyFromFile method* copies all or a part of a file to either an OraCLOB or an OraBLOB object. This method is available only to OraCLOB and OraBLOB objects.

This method is definitely a programmer's dream because it makes writing data to the database from a file simple. This functionality is definitely one of OO4O's strong points. This method takes four parameters, and like the other methods, only the first is mandatory.

```
OraLOB.CopyFromFile "<directory>:\<filename>", _
        AmountToCopy, _
        Offset, _
        ChunkSize
```

- The first parameter is the location of an existing file on the local machine.

- The second parameter (optional) is the amount to copy. The default is the entire file.

- The third parameter (optional) is the Offset parameter with the file. The default is 1.

- The fourth parameter (optional) is primarily used with piecewise operations and is the size of each piece to copy. The default is to copy the entire content in one piece.

Here is how a CopyFromFile method may look:

```
OraDynaset.Edit
    OraLOB.CopyFromFile "D:\OO4O\Examples\TestData.txt"
OraDynaset.Update
```

In its simplest form, all that is required when executing the method is the directory and filename to copy from. The directory must be valid, and the file must exist. If not, an error is returned. All the hard stuff is executed by OO4O.

The CopyFromFile method functions in the same manner as the Copy method when it comes to resizing.

The CopyToFile Method

The *CopyToFile method* copies all or part of an OraLOB to a file. This method is available for all OraLOB objects (OraCLOB, OraBLOB, and OraBFILE).

This method is even simpler than the CopyFromFile method because it does not require an actual file to exist. This method takes four parameters, and like the other methods, only the first is mandatory.

```
OraLOB.CopyToFile "<directory>:\<filename>", _
        AmountToCopy, _
        Offset, _
        ChunkSize
```

- The first parameter is the location and filename of where the data will be written.

- The second parameter (optional) is the amount to copy. The default is the entire contents of the object.

- The third parameter (optional) is the Offset parameter of the object. The default is 1.

- The fourth parameter (optional) is primarily used with piecewise operations and is the size of each piece to copy. The default is to copy the entire contents in one piece.

In its simplest form, all that is required when executing this method is to provide a valid directory. If an invalid directory is used, an error is produced. If the file does not exist, OO4O will create it. If the file does exist, the contents will be overwritten. Here is an example of using the CopyToFile method:

```
OraLOB.CopyToFile "C:\SimpleSample.txt"
```

The DisableBuffering Method

The *DisableBuffering method* turns off buffering that has been invoked by the EnableBuffering method. The DisableBuffering method is available only for the OraCLOB and OraBLOB objects.

Refer to "The EnableBuffering Method" section that follows for more information. Here is an example of using the DisableBuffering method:

```
OraLOB.DisableBuffering
```

The EnableBuffering Method

The *EnableBuffering method* limits the number of network round-trips by buffering the data being read or written. The EnableBuffering method is available only for the OraCLOB and OraBLOB objects.

OO4O holds the data in the buffer until the FlushBuffer method (covered later in this section) is executed. If you think this sounds too good to be true, you are pretty close. There are many restrictions placed on this function, along with many qualifications that must be met for this to be really beneficial. If you are interested in pursuing this method, or if you want more information, refer to the OO4O online help.

Here is an example of using the EnableBuffering method:

```
OraLOB.EnableBuffering
```

The Erase Method

The *Erase method* removes all or part of an OraCLOB or OraBLOB object. The Erase method is available only for the OraCLOB and OraBLOB objects.

There are two parameters for this method; the first is mandatory, and the second is optional.

```
OraLOB.Erase Amount, Offset
```

- The first parameter is the amount of the object to erase.

- The second parameter (optional) is the Offset parameter. The default is 1.

One thing to remember is that the Erase method does not truncate the data. The Trim method truncates the data. The size of the object before and after an Erase operation will be the same.

For example, look at what happens to the contents of OraCLOB1 (1234567890) when the following Erase method is executed:

```
'BEFORE - Contents "1234567890" (Size = 10)
OraDynaset.Edit
    OraCLOB.Erase 3, 5
OraDynaset.Update
'AFTER - Contents are now "1234   890" (Size still 10)
```

The FlushBuffer Method

The *FlushBuffer method* is called to flush out the data held in the buffer when buffering is enabled. The FlushBuffer method is available only for the OraCLOB and OraBLOB objects.

Refer to the EnableBuffering method earlier in this section for more information. Here is an example of using the FlushBuffer method:

```
OraLOB.FlushBuffer
```

The MatchPos Method

The *MatchPos method* returns the Offset parameter (or position) of the occurrence of a particular value in a LOB. The MatchPos method is available for all OraLOB objects (OraCLOB, OraBLOB, and OraBFILE).

There are three parameters, and all are required.

```
MatchingOffset = OraLOB.MatchPos ("<value>", _
    Offset, _
    WhichOccurrence)
```

- The first parameter is the specific value to search for. For OraCLOBs, the value would be a string value, and for OraCLOBs the value would be a byte array.

- The second parameter is the Offset parameter. Use 1 to start at the beginning of the object.

- The third parameter controls which occurrence to find. Use 1 to find the first occurrence, or 2 to find the second. If no match is found, 0 (zero) is returned.

If an OraCLOB object contains the string value 12345678901234567890, here is how the code will look:

```
'Returns 1
MatchingOffset = OraLOB1.MatchPos ("123", 1, 1)
```

If the Offset parameter is changed to be 2, the search starts at the second byte; in this case, it's the number 2. From here, the first occurrence is found starting at the 11th byte.

```
'Returns 11
MatchingOffset = OraLOB1.MatchPos ("123", 2, 1)
```

What happens if the Offset parameter is changed back to 1, so that the search starts at the beginning, and a 3 is entered for the last parameter? The 3 instructs OO4O to search for the third occurrence.

```
'Returns 21
MatchingOffset = OraLOB1.MatchPos ("123", 1, 3)
```

The Open Method

The *Open method* opens an OraBFILE object for access. This method is available for only OraBFILE objects.

A prerequisite to executing almost any OraBFILE method is that the OraBFILE object is open. Not using the Open method will result in an error stating that the object is currently not open for access. To open an OraBFILE object, use the following code:

```
OraBFILE.Open
```

The only confusing part with the Open method is that it returns the same Oracle error "ORA-22285: non-existent directory or file for FILEOPEN operation" for different problems. This can be a bit troublesome if you don't know what to look for. For example, each of the following items will return the same ORA-22285 error:

- Invalid filename reference (FileName property)

- Invalid alias (DirectoryName property)

- Invalid alias reference (Defined in the database)

> **NOTE**   See the issues on how to avoid the ORA-22285 error in the Open method in "The DirectoryName Property" section earlier in this chapter.

The Read Method

The *Read method* is used to read the contents of an OraLOB object into a buffer. The Read method is available for all OraLOBs objects (OraCLOB, OraBLOB, and OraBFILE).

There are two parameters for this method. The first parameter is mandatory, and the second is optional. The return value will be the amount of data read.

```
AmountRead = OraLOB.Read (Buffer, ChunkSize)
```

- The first parameter is the buffer variable.

- The second parameter (optional) is primarily used for piecewise operations and is the size of each piece to read. If left blank, the data will be read as one piece and placed into the buffer.

Reading the contents of a LOB object is usually done to either display the value or to write the value to a file. Writing the contents to a file can be done in one of two ways.

First, you can use Visual Basic's new file system object for working with files. The following chunk is a section of code that reads an OraCLOB object as one piece and then writes to a file using Visual Basic's new file system object:

```
Dim Buffer As Variant
    :
    :
Set FileObject = CreateObject _
    ("Scripting.FileSystemObject")
Set txtFile = FileObject.CreateTextFile _
    ("C:\ReadTest2.txt", True)
AmountRead = OraCLOB.Read(Buffer)
txtFile.write (Buffer)
txtFile.Close
```

For more information on Visual Basic's new file system object and the methods available, you may wish to review Visual Basic's online help. One of the issues with the new file system object is its inability to support the creation of binary files. For this, you must use the old file system commands, like Open.

The second way to write the content to a file is to use the older file system commands. The only issue with this file system command is its inability to write Variant data types, which simply means that you have to copy the data from a variant variable to a string variable.

NOTE   If you're using the Read method to insert data into a file, the buffer must be declared as a variant variable and copied into a string variable. Then, the string variable must be written to the file.

The following code is an example of reading an OraCLOB object as one piece and writing it to a file:

```
'The following Dim statements should already be done.
'Dim Buffer As Variant
'Dim BufferToString As String
        :
        :
FileNumber = FreeFile
Open "C:\ReadTest.txt" For Binary As #FileNumber
        :
AmountRead = OraCLOB.Read (Buffer)
BufferToString = Buffer
Put #FileNumber, , BufferToString
Close FileNumber
```

For a complete example on read and writing to a file as piecewise operations, see the "Piecewise Write Operations with OraLOBs" and "Piecewise Read Operations with OraLOB" sections later in this chapter.

The Trim Method

The *Trim method* truncates the contents of an OraCLOB or OraBLOB object. This method is available only for OraCLOB and OraBLOB objects. Executing this method will actually resize the object.

```
OraLOB.Trim newSize
```

Be careful: you may want to pass in the amount of data you wish trim, when, in fact, the value being passed in should be the actual new size of the object.

For example, if OraCLOB1 has a size of 50, executing the following Trim method does not truncate the last 10 characters to give a size of 40. What actually happens is that OO4O truncates the data down to a size of 10 characters.

```
OraDynaset.Edit
    OraCLOB1.Trim 10
OraDynaset.Update
```

The Write Method

The *Write method* writes the contents of a buffer to an OraLOB object. The Write method is available for only the OraCLOB and OraBLOB objects.

There are three parameters for this method. The first parameter is mandatory; the second and third are optional. The return value will be the amount of data written into the buffer.

```
AmountWritten = OraLOB.Write (Buffer, _
        ChunkSize, _
        WhichPiece)
```

- The first parameter is the buffer variable where the OraCLOB or OraBLOB object will write from.

- The second parameter (optional) is primarily used with piecewise operations and is the size of each piece to write. If a value is not passed, OO4O will write the contents of the buffer to the OraCLOB or OraBLOB object in one piece.

- The third parameter (optional) is primarily used for piecewise Write operations. For piecewise operations, this parameter notifies the database which piece is currently being processed. This parameter can be one of the following values:

    - ORALOB_ONE_PIECE is the default value and is used if the Write operation is done in one piece. If no value is passed, OO4O uses the default value and executes the Write operation as one piece.

    - ORALOB_FIRST_PIECE establishes the beginning of a piecewise operation and is the first piece written to the OraLOB object.

- ORALOB_NEXT_PIECE establishes the next piece to be written to the OraLOB object. After writing the first piece, all subsequent calls (except the last) will require this value.

- ORALOB_LAST_PIECE establishes the final piece to be written to the OraLOB object. This is required to notify the OraLOB object that the Write operation is complete.

The following code demonstrates two possible ways to execute a single-piece Write operation. Both will produce the same results.

```
'Sample 1
LobBuffer = "Hello World"
OraDynaset.Edit
    AmountWritten = OraLOB1.Write (LobBuffer)
OraDynaset.Update

'Sample 2
LobBuffer = "Hello World"
OraDynaset.Edit
AmountWritten = OraLOB1.Write(LobBuffer, , _
        ORALOB_ONE_PIECE)
OraDynaset.Update
```

If you are not sure of the size of the buffer, it may be best to leave the second parameter blank. This defaults to writing the entire buffer because if a smaller size is passed, an incorrect amount of data may be written.

The following example uses a chunk size of 7, but since the third parameter is set to ORALOB_ONE_PIECE, OO4O will write only seven bytes of data even though the buffer contains more than seven bytes.

```
'The following will write "Hello W"
LobBuffer = "Hello World"
OraDynaset.Edit
AmountWritten = OraLOB1.Write(LobBuffer, 7, _
        ORALOB_ONE_PIECE)
OraDynaset.Update
```

This example will not write the entire "Hello World" string. Instead, only the first seven bytes, "Hello W", will be written.

For more information and examples on piecewise Write operations, check out the "Piecewise Write Operations with OraLOBs" section.

The Write method functions in the same manner as the Copy method when it comes to writing data that is either larger or smaller than its original size.

The data used to write to the OraLOB object can stem from either a field on a form or from a file on your computer. The following code reads data from a file and writes the content to an OraLOB object in one piece, using Visual Basic's new file system object. For more information on this new file system, review Visual Basic's online help.

```
Set FileObject = CreateObject _
        ("Scripting.FileSystemObject")
Set txtFile = FileObject.OpenTextFile _
        ("C:\WriteTest.txt", 1)
Buffer = txtFile.Read _
        (FileObject.GetFile("c:\WriteTest.txt").Size)
OraDynaset.Edit
    OraCLOB.Write (Buffer)
OraDynaset.Update
```

If you decide to stick with Visual Basic's old method of working with files, the following code reads data from a file located on the current machine and writes the contents in a single piece to an OraLOB object.

```
Dim Buffer As String
        :
        :
FileNumber = FreeFile
Open "C:\WriteTest.txt" For Binary As #FileNumber
Get #FileNumber, , Buffer
OraDynaset.Edit
    OraClob.Write (Buffer)
OraDynaset.Update
Close FileNumber
```

Using OraLOB Objects in Your Applications

This section provides examples implementing most of what has been covered in this chapter. The examples guide you through a broad spectrum of OraLOB concepts, starting from creating a Directory Alias for BFILE objects and initializing the database CLOB and BLOB objects, to reading the data back out and writing it to a file.

Figure 10.7 is a screen shot of what the application form looks like with all the buttons.

FIGURE 10.7
The example program with buttons

The form has seven buttons, and each button demonstrates some of the important topics discussed in this chapter.

It is important to run the examples in order because the first example creates the table and Directory Alias that will be used in the following examples. These examples are all part of a single application and can be found on the CD-ROM in the Chapter 10 folder. The application has a single form with a number of Button Controls. Each button will execute one of the examples.

In order for the examples to be precise and to the points made in this chapter, the number of lines of code were kept to a minimum. For example, no error checking is done unless it is specifically showing how to prevent or capture a particular error. A prime example of how to prevent errors was demonstrated by showing how to validate whether a Directory Alias exists (Listing 10.1). For more information on capturing errors, review tChapter 6.

Another reason why the number of lines in the example code is limited is because they use hard-coded values for a number of variables. For example, the Update example uses hard-coded values for the Directory Alias. These values do not have to be hard-coded; they can be passed in from other procedures or from a Field Control located on a form.

Also, in order to create the stand-alone code in these examples, each will establish a new connection. As you get more comfortable with OO4O and Visual Basic, you may find it best to establish a single connection at the start of the application.

Although the use of hard-coded values helps keep the number of lines of code to a minimum, it does not allow for a dynamic example. So, if you wish to run the examples more than once, the data in the table should be removed. This can be accomplished easily by executing the DeleteData procedure. This procedure is included in the Chapter 11 project on the CD-ROM but is not discussed here.

Other key items to note when viewing the examples are

- All the examples use the Scott schema and connect using v8i as the connect string.

- CLOB data is used when demonstrating Update, Insert, Read, and Write operations, so if you decide to step through the code with the debugger, you can follow what is going on and validate the data.

- The examples show how to execute non-select SQL statements and DDL statements using the ExecuteSQL method.

Creating a Directory Alias and Table

The primary focus of Listing 10.3 is to create a Directory Alias, but it also demonstrates one of the many uses of the ExecuteSQL method. The ExecuteSQL method is primarily used for non-select SQL statements. So, this is the perfect method to use for creating a Directory Alias and a table in an OO4O application. For further information on the ExecuteSQL method, refer to the OO4O online help. Don't forget, Create Directory privileges are required to create the Directory Alias, and Create Table privileges are required to create the table.

There are two things to notice in the SQL code used to create the Directory Alias. First, in line 9, the SQL statement CREATE DIRECTORY BFILE_DIR AS 'D:\BFILES_DIRECTORY' is the same SQL code used if you are creating a Directory Alias in SQL*Plus. Second, the code CREATE DIRECTORY BFILE_DIR AS 'D:\BFILES_DIRECTORY' is used instead of the statement CREATE OR REPLACE DIRECTORY BFILE_DIR AS 'D:\BFILES_DIRECTORY'. The only difference between the two SQL statements is that the second statement does a Replace operation if the Directory Alias exists.

The reason to do a Create operation without a Replace operation is so that you can check for an "ORA-00955: name is already used by an existing object" error. If you don't check whether there is an error and blindly execute a Create operation with a Replace operation, you can write over someone else's alias.

For a refresher on the potential stumbling blocks when working with the Directory Alias, you may want to take a moment to refer to the "Binary Files (BFILE)" section earlier in the chapter, which discusses the BFILE object.

Listing 10.3

```
1   Private Sub CreateTableAndAlias_Click()
2   'Declare objects being used.
3   Dim OraSession As OraSession
4   Dim OraDatabase As OraDatabase
5
6   Set OraSession = CreateObject _
        ("OracleInProcServer.XOraSession")
7   Set OraDatabase = OraSession.OpenDatabase _
        ("v8i", "scott/tiger", 0&)
8
9   'Do NOT use the CREATE OR REPLACE command here.
10  OraDatabase.ExecuteSQL _
        ("CREATE DIRECTORY BFILE_DIR " & _
         "AS 'D:\BFILES_DIRECTORY'")
11  OraDatabase.ExecuteSQL _
        ("CREATE TABLE 0040_LOB_TABLE " & _
            "(INDEX_FIELD NUMBER, " & _
            "CLOB_FIELD CLOB, " & _
            "BLOB_FIELD BLOB, " & _
            "BFILE_FIELD BFILE)")
12  MsgBox "This section is complete.", vbOKOnly, _
        " Create Directory Alias and Table"
13  End Sub
```

Analysis

- Line 1 is the procedure name created by Visual Basic.

- Line 2 is a comment marking the start of the Dim statement for the objects used in the example.

- Lines 3–4 are Dim statements for the objects being used in this example.

- Line 5 is a blank space to make the code easier to read.

- Line 6 creates the OraSession object.

- Line 7 creates an OraDatabase object and establishes the connection to the database.

- Line 8 is a blank space to make the code easier to read.

- Line 9 is a comment reminding you not to use the Create or Replace SQL command.

- Line 10 executes the SQL statement to create the Directory Alias.

- Line 11 executes the SQL to create the OO4O_LOB_TABLE table in the database.

- Line 12 displays a message box letting you know that the procedure is complete.

- Line 13 is the End Sub statement for this procedure.

Once this example is executed, there is no need to execute it again, as this procedure will not overwrite the Directory Alias or table. Executing the procedure without dropping the Directory Alias or the table will result in an error saying that the objects already exist.

Initializing OraLOBs

Listing 10.4 demonstrates how to initialize the OraCLOB and OraBLOB objects using Visual Basic's Empty value. Two records are inserted into the table named OO4O_LOB_TABLE. The only difference between the two inserts is the way the fields are referenced. The first reference is done using the "!" notation: `Ora-Dynaset!Clob_Field`. The second is done using the "." notation: `OraDynaset .Fields("Clob_Field").Value`. Both are correct. For additional information on the different notations, refer to the OO4O online help.

Listing 10.4

```
1   Private Sub Insert_Click()
2   'Declare objects being used.
3   Dim OraSession As OraSession
4   Dim OraDatabase As OraDatabase
5   Dim OraDynaset As OraDynaset
6   Dim OraBFILE As OraBFILE
7   Dim directoryAlias As String
```

```
8  Dim bfileName As String
9
10  Set OraSession = CreateObject _
        ("OracleInProcServer.XOraSession")
11 Set OraDatabase = OraSession.OpenDatabase _
        ("v8i", "scott/tiger", 0&)
12 Set OraDynaset = OraDatabase.CreateDynaset _
        ("SELECT * FROM OO4O_LOB_TABLE", 0&)
13
14 ' Adds the first record
15 OraDynaset.AddNew
16     OraDynaset!Index_Field = 1
17     OraDynaset!Clob_Field = Empty
18     OraDynaset!Blob_Field = Empty
19 OraDynaset.Update
20 ' Adds the second record
21 OraDynaset.AddNew
22     OraDynaset.Fields("Index_Field").Value = 2
23     OraDynaset.Fields("Clob_Field").Value = Empty
24     OraDynaset.Fields("Blob_Field").Value = Empty
25 OraDynaset.Update
26 MsgBox "This section is complete.", vbOKOnly, _
        "Insert Complete"
27 End Sub
```

Analysis

- Line 1 is the procedure name created by Visual Basic.

- Line 2 is a comment marking the start of the Dim statement for the objects used in the example.

- Lines 3–8 are Dim statements for the objects being used.

- Line 9 is a blank space to make the code easier to read.

- Line 10 creates the OraSession object.

- Line 11 creates an OraDatabase object and establishes the connection to the database.

- Line 12 creates an OraDynaset object based on the Select statement against the table OO4O_LOB_TABLE.

- Line 13 is a blank space to make the code easier to read.
- Line 14 is a comment line stating that this is the start of the first insert.
- Line 15 initiates the first record insert.
- Line 16 inserts a 1 into the first field of the first record.
- Lines 17–18 initialize the CLOB and BLOB objects with Visual Basic's Empty value.
- Line 19 executes the update of the OraDynaset object.
- Line 20 is a comment line stating that this is the start of the second Insert operation.
- Line 21 initiates the second record insert.
- Line 22 inserts a 2 into the first field of the second record.
- Lines 23–24 initialize the CLOB and BLOB objects with Visual Basic's Empty value.
- Line 25 executes the update for the OraDynaset object.
- Line 26 displays a message box letting you know that this procedure is complete.
- Line 27 is the End Sub statement for this procedure.

You may have noticed that OraBFILE object was not referenced in this example. That's because they do not have to be initialized, as the CLOB and BLOB objects do. Inserting into the BFILE object will be demonstrated in the Update example later in the chapter.

If you plan to execute this procedure more than once, execute the DeleteData procedure included in the project first.

Piecewise Write Operations with OraLOBs

Listing 10.5 demonstrates a piecewise Write operation to an OraCLOB object. Using the OraCLOB object, as opposed to an OraBLOB object, allows you to step through the code and check the data in Visual Basic's Debug windows so that you can get an in-depth view of the data as each piece is written. This should help you understand how the piecewise Write operation works.

Although hard-coded values are used for variables like chunkSize and testData, the data could vary when pulled from fields on a form. For example, Visual Basic's Text Box Controls can be placed on a form to allow a user to enter a desired chunk size and string value for the test data being written to the database.

To obtain a further understanding of how the different chunk sizes and string lengths affect the piecewise Write operation, enter different values for the chunk-Size variable (line 22) and for the testData variable (line 24). See what happens when you increase the chunkSize variable. Try making the chunkSize variable larger then the string length used for the testData variable. You may notice that even when attempting piecewise Write operations, the data may still be written in one piece if the size of the data is actually smaller than the chunk size being used.

Listing 10.5

```
1   Private Sub PiecewiseWrite_Click()
2   'Declare objects being used.
3   Dim OraSession As OraSession
4   Dim OraDatabase As OraDatabase
5   Dim OraDynaset As OraDynaset
6   Dim OraCLOB As OraCLOB
7   Dim OraBLOB As OraBLOB
8   Dim chunkSize As Integer
9   Dim amountOfData As Integer
10   Dim movePointer As Integer
11  Dim testData As String
12  Dim tempTestData As String
13
14  Set OraSession = CreateObject _
        ("OracleInProcServer.XOraSession")
15  Set OraDatabase = OraSession.OpenDatabase _
        ("v8i", "scott/tiger", 0&)
16
17  'Use a WHERE clause to specifically query the first record.
18  Set OraDynaset = OraDatabase.CreateDynaset _
        ("SELECT * FROM OO4O_LOB_TABLE " & _
        "WHERE INDEX_FIELD = 1", 0&)
19  Set OraCLOB = OraDynaset.Fields("Clob_Field").Value
20
21  'Change the chunkSize value to alter the
    'piecewise operation
```

```
22 chunkSize = 5
23 movePointer = chunkSize
24 testData = "This sample demonstrates a simple " & _
               "Piecewise insert (using the Write method) " & _
               "for an OraCLOB."
25
26 'Required for navigation
27 tempTestData = testData
28 amountOfData = Len(tempTestData)
29 OraCLOB.PollingAmount = amountOfData
30 If chunkSize > amountOfData Then
31  WriteStatus = ORALOB_ONE_PIECE
32  movePointer = chunkSize = amountOfData
33 Else
34  WriteStatus = ORALOB_FIRST_PIECE
35 End If
36 'Retrieves the pieces of data in appropriate chunks
37 tempTestData = Mid(testData, 1, chunkSize)
38 ' Lock the row
39 OraDynaset.Edit
40  amount_written = OraCLOB.Write _
        (tempTestData, chunkSize, WriteStatus)
41  ' Status property will = ORALOB_NEED_DATA if
    'more than one piece is required
42  While OraCLOB.Status = ORALOB_NEED_DATA
43      'Re-Establish how much data to be written
44      amountOfData = amountOfData - chunkSize
45      If chunkSize > amountOfData Then
46          WriteStatus = ORALOB_LAST_PIECE
47          chunkSize = amountOfData
48      Else
49          WriteStatus = ORALOB_NEXT_PIECE
50      End If
51      tempTestData = _
            Mid(testData, movePointer + 1, chunkSize)
52      amount_written = OraCLOB.Write _
            (tempTestData, chunkSize, WriteStatus)
53      movePointer = movePointer + chunkSize
54  Wend
55 OraDynaset.Update
56 MsgBox "This section is complete.", vbOKOnly, _
        "Piecewise Write"
57 End Sub
```

Analysis

- Line 1 is the procedure name created by Visual Basic.

- Line 2 is a comment marking the start of the Dim statement for the objects used in the example.

- Lines 3–7 are Dim statements for the objects being used.

- Lines 8–11 are the Dim statements for the variables used throughout the piecewise Write operation. These will be used to track the chunk sizes of each piece of data, as well as how much data to write.

- Line 13 is a blank space to make the code easier to read.

- Line 14 creates the OraSession object.

- Line 15 creates an OraDatabase object and establishes the connection to the database.

- Line 16 is a blank space to make the code easier to read.

- Line 17 is a comment stating that a Where clause is used to ensure that a particular record is selected.

- Line 18 creates an OraDynaset object based on the Select statement against the OO4O_LOB_TABLE table.

- Line 19 binds the OraCLOB object to its associated field in the OraDynaset object.

- Line 20 is a blank space to make the code easier to read.

- Line 21 is a comment suggesting that you change the chunkSize variable when you want to change the size of chunks to use for this piecewise Write operation.

- Line 22 sets the chunkSize variable to 5. This means that this procedure will be writing data to the OraCLOB objects 5 bytes at a time.

- Line 23 sets the movePointer variable to be equal to the chunkSize variable. The movePointer variable will move a pointer along the data and will be used as a placeholder so that when the next piece is written, you know where the last Write operation ended and where the next one should begin.

- Line 24 sets the testData variable to the text string so this example will write to the OraCLOB object.

- Line 25 is a blank space to make the code easier to read.

- Line 26 is a comment to let us know what variables are being initialized and will be used to guide the piecewise operation.

- Line 27 sets the tempTestData variable to the contents of the testData variable, which is actually the string value that will be written.

- Line 28 sets the amountOfData variable to the length of the string data.

- Line 29 sets the PollingAmount property of the OraCLOB object. As stated in "The PollingAmount Property" section, setting this property is very important.

- Line 30 checks to see if the total size of the chunk size used is greater than the size of the data being written. If so, the data will be written in one piece.

- Line 31 sets the WriteStatus variable to ORALOB_ONE_PIECE if the data is less than the chunk size used. This will be used to tell the Write operation that only one piece is required.

- Line 32 sets the movePointer and the chunkSize variable to be equal to the amount of data to be written.

- Line 33 is the Else statement for the If statement in line 30.

- Line 34 sets the WriteStatus variable to ORALOB_FIRST_PIECE if the data is greater than the chunk size used. This will be used to tell the Write operation that this is the first piece and more pieces will follow.

- Line 35 ends the If statement started in line 30.

- Line 36 is a comment to describe the next line.

- Line 37 sets the tempTestData variable to the first chunk of data.

- Line 38 is a comment to signify where row locking is happening.

- Line 39 starts the edit of the OraDyanset object.

- Line 40 executes the Write method for the OraCLOB object. The Write method passes in the data to be written, the chunk size being used, and whether there is only one piece or if this is the first piece of data. The amount of data actually written will be returned in the amount_written variable.

- Line 41 is a comment explaining why the Status property is being checked in line 42.

- Line 42 starts the loop if more pieces are to be written and will continue until the last piece is written.

- Line 43 is a comment stating that the amount of data to be written must be re-established after each piece is written.

- Line 44 sets the amountOfData variable to establish the amount of data to be written.

- Line 45 executes another If statement to determine whether this is the last piece to be written.

- Line 46 sets the WriteStatus variable to "ORALOB_LAST_PIECE" if this is the last piece to be written.

- Line 47 sets the chunkSize variable to the remaining amount of data if this is the last piece.

- Line 48 is the Else statement for the If statement in line 45.

- Line 49 sets the WriteStatus variable to "ORALOB_NEXT_PIECE" if this is the next piece to be written.

- Line 50 is the End If statement for the If statement in line 45.

- Line 51 sets the tempTestData variable to the actual data that will be written in the next operation.

- Line 52 executes the Write method of the next piece for the OraCLOB object. The Write method passes in the next chunk of data to be written, the chunk size being used, and whether this is the next piece or the last piece of data. The amount of data actually written will be returned in the amount_written variable.

- Line 53 sets the movePointer variable so that the next chunk of data can be extracted.

- Line 54 is the Wend statement for the While loop that starts on line 42.

- Line 55 executes the Update command that actually commits the changes to the database.

- Line 56 displays a message box letting you know that this procedure is complete.

- Line 57 is the End Sub statement for this procedure.

Piecewise Read Operations with OraLOB

Listing 10.6 demonstrates a piecewise Read operation from an OraCLOB object. Using the OraCLOB object, you can step through the code and check the data in Visual Basic's Debug windows so that you can get an in-depth view of the data as each piece is read. This should help in understanding more about how the piecewise Read operations work.

Although hard-coded values are used for variables, like chunkSize, and for the filename being used, the data could vary when pulled from a field on a form. For example, Visual Basic Text Box Controls could be placed on a form to allow a user to enter a desired chunk size and a filename to read the data to.

To obtain a further understanding of how the different chunk sizes affect the piecewise operation, enter different values for the chunkSize variable (line 21). See what happens when you increase the chunkSize variable. Try making the chunkSize variable larger than the string length in the OraCLOB object. You may notice that even if you're attempting to do a piecewise Read operation, the data may still be read in one piece if the size of the data is actually smaller than the chunk size being used.

There are two items to note in this example. First, notice that the file C:\ReadTest.txt does not have to exist. If it exists, Visual Basic will overwrite it. If it does not exist, Visual Basic will create it. The second and most important item to note is how each piece is read into a variable that is defined as a Variant data type and then copied into a variable defined as a String data type. This is because the Read method of the OraLOB object requires a variable of type Variant to be passed in. Unfortunately, Visual Basic's Put command has difficulty with these types, so they must be converted. For character data, as with the OraCLOB object, the Variant data type must be converted to a String data type. And for binary data, as with the OraBLOB object, the Variant data type must be converted to a byte array.

Listing 10.6

```
1    Private Sub PiecewiseRead_Click()
2    'Declare objects being used.
3    Dim OraSession As OraSession
4    Dim OraDatabase As OraDatabase
5    Dim OraDynaset As OraDynaset
6    Dim OraCLOB As OraCLOB
```

```
 7  Dim OraBLOB As OraBLOB
 8  Dim chunkSize As Integer
 9  Dim amountOfData As Integer
10   Dim testData As String
11  Dim tempTestData As String
12  Dim variantBuffer As Variant
13  Dim stringBuffer As String
14
15  Set OraSession = CreateObject _
        ("OracleInProcServer.XOraSession")
16  Set OraDatabase = OraSession.OpenDatabase _
        ("v8i", "scott/tiger", 0&)

17  'Use a WHERE clause to specifically query
    'the first record.
18  Set OraDynaset = OraDatabase.CreateDynaset _
        ("SELECT * FROM 0040_LOB_TABLE " & _
         "WHERE INDEX_FIELD = 1", 0&)
19  Set OraCLOB = OraDynaset.Fields("Clob_Field").Value

20  'Change the chunkSize value to alter the
    'piecewise operation
21  chunkSize = 5
22  OraCLOB.PollingAmount = OraCLOB.Size
23
24  'Standard Visual Basic File commands.
25  FileNumber = FreeFile
26  Open "C:\ReadTest.txt" For Binary As #FileNumber
27
28  AmountRead = OraCLOB.Read(variantBuffer, chunkSize)
29  stringBuffer = variantBuffer
30  Put #FileNumber, , stringBuffer
31
32  While OraCLOB.Status = ORALOB_NEED_DATA
33   AmountRead = OraCLOB.Read(variantBuffer, chunkSize)
34   stringBuffer = variantBuffer
35   Put #FileNumber, , stringBuffer
36  Wend
37  Close FileNumber
38  MsgBox "This section is complete.", vbOKOnly, _
            "Piecewise Read"
39  End Sub
```

Analysis

- Line 1 is the procedure name created by Visual Basic.

- Line 2 is a comment marking the start of the Dim statement for the objects used in the example.

- Lines 3–7 are Dim statements for the OO4O objects being used in this example.

- Lines 8–12 are the Dim statements for the variables used throughout the piecewise Read operation. These will be used to track the chunk size of each piece of data, as well as the amount of data to read.

- Line 14 is a blank space to make the code easier to read.

- Line 15 creates the OraSession object.

- Line 16 creates an OraDatabase object and establishes the connection to the database.

- Line 17 is a comment stating that a Where clause is used to ensure that a particular record is selected.

- Line 18 creates an OraDynaset object based on the Select statement against the table OO4O_LOB_TABLE.

- Line 19 binds the OraCLOB object to its associated field in the OraDynaset object.

- Line 20 is a comment suggesting that you change the chunkSize variable when you want to change the size of chunks for this piecewise Read operation.

- Line 21 sets the chunkSize variable to 5. This means that this procedure will be reading data from the OraCLOB objects five bytes at a time.

- Line 22 sets the PollingAmount property of the OraCLOB object. As stated in "The PollingAmount Property" section, setting this property is very important during piecewise Read operations.

- Line 23 is a blank space to make the code easier to read.

- Line 24 is a comment to let you know that the FreeFile command is a Visual Basic command.

- Line 25 sets the FileNumber variable to a file number provided by Visual Basic.

- Line 26 uses the Visual Basic Open command to open a file. As the data is read from the OraCLOB object, it will be written out to this file. If the file does not exist, one will be created.

- Line 27 is a blank space to make the code easier to read.

- Line 28 executes the Read method for the OraCLOB object. The Read method passes in the variable to hold the data that is read and the chunk size that is used. The amount of data actually read is returned in the amount-Read variable.

- Line 29 copies the contents of the buffer defined as a Variant data type and copies it to the buffer defined as a String data type.

- Line 30 executes the Visual Basic Put command to actually write the data just read to a file.

- Line 31 is a blank space to make the code easier to read.

- Line 32 initiates a While loop to continue reading from the OraCLOB object until all the data is read.

- Line 33 executes the OraCLOB.Read method for the next piece being read.

- Line 34 copies the contents of the buffer defined as a Variant data type to the buffer defined as a String data type.

- Line 35 executes the Visual Basic Put command to actually write the next piece of data that was just read to a file.

- Line 36 is the Wend statement for the While loop that starts on line 32.

- Line 37 closes the file once all the data is written.

- Line 38 displays a message box letting you know that this procedure is complete.

- Line 39 is the End Sub statement for this procedure.

Updating OraLOB

Listing 10.7 demonstrates a number of important items. For starters, this is the first example in the chapter to work with the OraBFILE object and demonstrates setting the reference to an external file by updating the DirectoryName and FileName properties. It also shows the suggested way to validate whether a DirectoryName exists. To validate, a Select statement is executed against the All_Directories table using the DirectoryName property. If no match is found, a message box is displayed telling you that an invalid directory name was issued. If a match is found, the DirectoryName property is valid and a message box is displayed with the message that the name is valid. Normally, if the name is valid, a message box is not displayed, but, in this example, the message box helps demonstrate a point. Modify the directoryAlias variable (line 19) to use different values to test the validation in your own system.

Listing 10.7

```
1  Private Sub UpdateSample_Click()
2  'Declare objects being used.
3  Dim OraSession As OraSession
4  Dim OraDatabase As OraDatabase
5  Dim OraDynaset As OraDynaset
6  Dim OraCLOB As OraCLOB
7  Dim OraBFILE As OraBFILE
8  Dim directoryAlias As String
9  Dim bfileName As String
10
11 Set OraSession = CreateObject _
       ("OracleInProcServer.XOraSession")
12 Set OraDatabase = OraSession.OpenDatabase _
       ("v8i", "scott/tiger", 0&)
13 Set OraDynaset = OraDatabase.CreateDynaset _
       ("SELECT * FROM 0040_LOB_TABLE", 0&)
14
15 Set OraCLOB = OraDynaset.Fields("CLOB_FIELD").Value
16 Set OraBFILE = OraDynaset.Fields("BFILE_FIELD").Value
17
18 'Sets the variables used for the BFILE object.
19 directoryAlias = "BFILE_DIR"
20 bfileName = "MYFILE.TXT"
21 Dim testDynaset As OraDynaset
22 mySQL = "select * from all_directories " & _
           "where DIRECTORY_NAME = '" _
           & UCase(directoryAlias) & "'"
23 Set testDynaset = OraDatabase.CreateDynaset(mySQL, 0&)
24 If (testDynaset.RecordCount = 0) Then
```

```
25    MsgBox directoryAlias & " is an invalid " & _
            "directory name in the Database", _
            vbCritical, "Invalid Directory"
26    Exit Sub
27 Else
28    MsgBox directoryAlias & _
            " is valid and references " & _
            testDynaset.Fields("directory_path").Value
29 End If
30
31 OraDynaset.Edit
32    OraDynaset!Index_Field = 4
33    OraCLOB.Write "OO4O CLOB Sample"
34    OraBFILE.DirectoryName = directoryAlias
35    OraBFILE.FileName = bfileName
36 OraDynaset.Update
37 MsgBox "This section is complete.", vbOKOnly, _
        "Update Complete"
38 End Sub
```

⊃ Analysis

- Line 1 is the procedure name created by Visual Basic.

- Line 2 is a comment marking the start of the Dim statement for the objects used in the example.

- Lines 3–7 are Dim statements for the OO4O objects being used in this example.

- Lines 8–9 are the Dim statements for the variables used to insert data into the OraBFILE object.

- Line 10 is a blank space to make the code easier to read.

- Line 11 creates the OraSession object.

- Line 12 creates an OraDatabase object and establishes the connection to the database.

- Line 13 creates an OraDynaset object based on the Select statement against the OO4O_LOB_TABLE table.

- Line 14 is a blank space to make the code easier to read.

- Lines 15–16 set (bind) the OraLOB objects to their associated fields in the OraDynaset object.

- Line 17 is a blank space to make the code easier to read.

- Line 18 is a comment line for setting the variables used in the OraBFILE object.

- Line 19 sets the directoryAlias variable to the Directory Alias BFILE_DIR.

- Line 20 sets the bfileName variable to "MYFILE.TXT" which is the name of a file on the server. Keep in mind that the file does not have to exist at this time.

- Line 21 is the Dim statement to define a temporary OraDynaset object that will be used to validate the Directory Alias.

- Line 22 sets the mySQL variable, which will be used to create the SQL statement that will validate the directory name.

- Line 23 creates an OraDynaset with the name testDynaset. If the directory name already exists, the OraDynaset object will have a RecordCount greater than 0 (zero). If no data is returned, you know that the Directory Alias does not exist, and you may want to prompt the user to provide a valid name.

- Line 24 executes an If statement to check whether any data is returned.

- Line 25 will display a message box if no data is returned in the testDynaset object.

- Line 26 will exit this procedure if the Directory Alias is invalid. Without exiting, an invalid Directory Alias may be entered and cause problems later when accessing the OraBFILE object.

- Line 27 is an Else statement to the If statement for line 26.

- Line 28 displays a message box if the Directory Alias used is valid. This is just for testing purposes, to let you know that validation is taking place. Normally, you would only provide information if the Directory Alias is invalid.

- Line 29 ends the If statement started in line 26.

- Line 30 is a blank space to make the code easier to read.

- Line 31 starts the edit of the OraDyanset object.

- Line 32 sets the Index_Field to 4.

- Line 33 updates the OraCLOB object with text. Keep in mind that the data does not have to be hard coded; it could be from a text field on the form or from a file.

- Line 34 sets the DirectoryName property of the OraBFILE object.

- Line 35 sets the FileName property of the OraBFILE object.

- Line 36 executes the Update command, which commits the changes in the database.

- Line 37 displays a message box letting you know that this procedure is complete.

- Line 38 is the End Sub statement for this procedure.

Using the CopyFromFile and CopyToFile Methods

Listing 10.8 is a basic example highlighting two of OO4O's new features: the CopyFromFile and the CopyToFile methods for the OraLOB object. Although the example uses an OraCLOB object, the execution is identical for all the other OraLOB objects, with the exception of the CopyFromFile method for the OraBFILE object. As noted earlier in the chapter, this method is not part of the OraBFILE object.

There are a couple of items to note in this example: First, lines 16–20 are primarily there to create the data and file used in the example, so don't pay too much attention to them.

Second, the example can easily be modified to copy from a different file on your machine by changing the filename in line 23 to one that currently exists.

Third, by changing the object reference in line 6 from OraCLOB to OraBLOB, you can test the CopyFromFile and CopyToFile methods using a binary file.

Overall, you will find the CopyFromFile and CopyToFile methods very pleasant to work with.

Listing 10.8

```
1   Private Sub CopyToCopyFromSample_Click()
2   'Declare objects being used.
```

```
3  Dim OraSession As OraSession
4  Dim OraDatabase As OraDatabase
5  Dim OraDynaset As OraDynaset
6  Dim OraCLOB As OraCLOB
7  Dim stringBuffer As String
8
9  Set OraSession = CreateObject _
       ("OracleInProcServer.XOraSession")
10  Set OraDatabase = OraSession.OpenDatabase _
       ("v8i", "scott/tiger", 0&)
11 Set OraDynaset = OraDatabase.CreateDynaset _
       ("SELECT * FROM OO4O_LOB_TABLE", 0&)
12 Set OraCLOB = OraDynaset.Fields("Clob_Field").Value
13
14 'Standard Visual Basic File commands.
15 'Creates a file and data to use in the sample.
16 FileNumber = FreeFile
17 Open "C:\CopyFrom.txt" For Binary As #FileNumber
18 stringBuffer = "This is all too easy."
19 Put #FileNumber, , stringBuffer
20 Close FileNumber
21
22 OraDynaset.Edit
23     OraCLOB.CopyFromFile "C:\CopyFrom.txt"
24 OraDynaset.Update
25 OraCLOB.CopyToFile "C:\CopyTo.txt"
26 MsgBox "This section is complete.", vbOKOnly, _
       " CopyToFile/CopyFromFile "
27 End Sub
```

Analysis

- Line 1 is the procedure name created by Visual Basic.

- Line 2 is a comment marking the start of the Dim statement for the objects used in the example.

- Lines 3–7 are Dim statements for the OO4O objects being used in this example.

- Line 8 is a blank space to make the code easier to read.

- Line 9 creates the OraSession object.

- Line 10 creates an OraDatabase object and establishes the connection to the database.

- Line 11 creates an OraDynaset object for the table OO4O_LOB_TABLE.

- Line 12 sets (binds) the OraCLOB objects to their associated fields in the OraDynaset object.

- Line 13 is a blank space to make the code easier to read.

- Line 14 is a comment stating that the File commands are Visual Basic commands and not OO4O commands.

- Line 15 is a comment stating that the data used in this example is currently being created.

- Line 16 sets the FileNumber variable to a file number provided by Visual Basic.

- Line 17 uses the Visual Basic Open command to open a file.

- Line 18 sets the stringBuffer variable to the data.

- Line 19 executes the Visual Basic Put command to write the data (stringBuffer variable) to the `CopyFrom.txt` file.

- Line 20 closes the file after all the data has been written.

- Line 21 is a blank space to make the code easier to read.

- Line 22 edits the OraDynaset object.

- Line 23 executes the CopyFromFile method, which copies the data from the `CopyFrom.txt` file.

- Line 24 commits the change to the database.

- Line 25 executes the CopyToFile method, which copies the data from the OraCLOB object to the `CopyTo.txt` file.

- Line 26 displays a message box letting you know that this procedure is complete.

- Line 27 is the End Sub statement for this procedure.

Summary

In this chapter, we discussed a number of items. First we discussed the new data types introduced in OO4O. These are the OraCLOB, OraBLOB, and OraBFILE objects. We also discussed how simple these objects have made the task of manipulating LOBs in the database. Next, we covered some potential stumbling blocks and ways to avoid them.

This chapter demonstrated the ease with which OO4O interfaces with LOBs in the database. The more experience you gain working with LOBs using other applications, the more you will come to appreciate this new feature.

chapter 11

Connection Pooling
and Connection Multiplexing

- How to monitor connections

- Implementing Connection Pooling

- Using the new OraServer object

- How to perform Multiplexing

Programmers are always trying to find ways to make applications faster, particularly when it comes to working with data. They will do things like invoke batch processing, use the customizing features of dynasets, or use stored procedures and functions to have the database handle certain tasks. But, one item that tends to get overlooked is the overhead involved with making each database connection. Making a database connection is a very expensive and labor-intensive task for the database, even on a small scale. This chapter introduces Connection Pooling and Multiplexing as methods to minimize the overhead costs of making these database connections.

Connection Pooling is when you create a "block" of connections that stay open in order to save search, open, and validation time for each individual connection. This is an especially useful feature if you can't predict when users will be accessing the database, such as with a company catalog that is available on the Internet. Sharing an open resource minimizes the time it takes for an individual to access data.

Multiplexing is when a single physical connection is shared by multiple users. Although many users can share the same physical connection to the database, only one user at a time can be active, so you have to plan carefully and take the time during the design phase to make sure that you will not create a backlog in your application.

Connection Pooling exists in the previous release of Oracle Objects for OLE (OO4O). Connection Multiplexing is a new feature introduced for the first time in this release. Although these concepts are entirely different from each other, both of these features create a more efficient and functional application.

Connection Monitoring

Both the Connection Pooling and Connection Multiplexing models discussed in this chapter relate to database connections in one way or another. Let's begin with a description of how to monitor the database processes and connections for each model. This will help you understand how each model works and how they differ from one another.

Whether you are using OO4O, SQL*Plus, or another vendor's product to connect to an Oracle database, there are a number of system views that get updated in the database. The two views of primary interest are the V_$PROCESS view and the V_$SESSION view. Both views are actually called *dynamic performance* views because their data is constantly altered by the database as users and processes connect and disconnect from the database. Because only the user Sys can view the actual tables, there are public synonyms with very similar names. The public synonym for V_$PROCESS is V$PROCESS. For V_$SESSION, the public synonym is V$SESSION.

NOTE   Because V$PROCESS and V$SESSION are public synonyms, any user should be able to view them. If not, you will have to connect as the Sys user to view the contents of the actual tables.

The V$PROCESS synonym shows a new record every time there is a new physical connection to the database. The new record contains general information about the connection. When a physical connection is lost, the record containing the information about that connection is deleted by the system.

The V$SESSION synonym will also show a new record every time a new session is opened in the database. The new record contains general information about the session. When the session is closed, that record is deleted by the system.

To view the contents of V$SESSION, you can execute a `Select * From V$SESSION` SQL statement, but this tends to return more information then is really necessary. To find the number of records, a `Select Count * From V$SESSION` statement can be executed. This returns the number of sessions logged into the database. Executing either a `Select Count * From V$SESSION` or a `Select Count * From V$PROCESS` statement will be sufficient for viewing the data that you'll need for this chapter.

It's not uncommon to think that the number of records displayed by both V$SESSION and V$PROCESS should be the same. After all, it sounds logical that each session has its own process and vice versa. This is not necessarily true. After reading this chapter and running the examples, you should understand why.

When you run the first example from the "Connection Pooling" section, you may want to open an SQL*Plus session to monitor the contents of both the V$SESSION and V$PROCESS synonyms. This will provide a good indication of when the initial connections are made, when additional connections are made, and when idle connections are closed.

When you run the example from the "OraServer Object" section, you will notice that there are two fields on the form created for this example that monitor the

V$SESSION and V$PROCESS synonyms for you. Each time a connection is made or closed, their associated fields are updated with the latest number of rows.

Connection Pooling

What better way to describe Connection Pooling than that it's simply a pool of connections? Actually, it is a bit more involved than that. First, you need to understand what Connection Pooling is, and why and when to use it. Second, you need to know how to create the pool, and third, you'll want to know how to retrieve a connection from the pool.

What Is Connection Pooling and Why Use It?

With OO4O, each database connection results in the creation of an OraDatabase object. Think of Connection Pooling as a collection of these OraDatabase objects, or database connections. In even the smallest OO4O application that connects to the database, you will notice a delay during the connection phase when the application is executed. This delay increases as the number of users increases.

Normally, even in a large company, a given application connects once to a database, completes one or more transactions, and logs off when finished. Any delays that are encountered are usually just tolerated. The one place where slow connections are not tolerated is on the Internet. A slow Web page can actually cost a company both customers and money. All too often, a slow-processing Web page will deter an existing customer or a potential customer, which results in loss of revenue. Now that OO4O is being used as a vital part of the development of Web pages for the Internet, you can see how important it is to eliminate the overhead in time that is encountered when connecting to a database.

Although all of the overhead encountered when connecting to a database can't be avoided, you can incur this cost at a time when it will not affect the user. For example, if you have an application that, when executed, instantiates numerous database connections and holds them open and available for other applications upon request, the connection to the database seems to be almost instantaneous. The application you'd use in this case would be a Web server. To establish Connection Pooling, you must first create a pool of connections.

How to Create a Pool of Connections

Before jumping in and describing how to create a pool of connections, take a moment to review how applications that are not using Connection Pooling establish a database connection:

```
Dim OraSession As OraSession
Dim OraDatabase As OraDatabase
Set OraSession = CreateObject _
    ("OracleInProcServer.XOraSession")
Set OraDatabase = OraSession.OpenDatabase _
    ("v8i", "scott/tiger", 0&)
```

NOTE   The examples in this chapter use the Scott schema, which is owned by Oracle Corporation and is bundled with the Oracle8i client software and the OO4O product.

First, an OraSession object is instantiated by making a call to the CreateObject command, which invokes the InProc Server. Then, an OraDatabase object is created using the OpenDatabase method of the OraSession object to represent the connection to the database.

Now, take a look at how an application that uses Connection Pooling creates a database pool. You still need to create the OraSession object first, but this time, the CreateDatabasePool method is called instead of the OpenDatabase method. When the CreateDatabasePool method is called, it does not return an OraDatabase object. In fact, the CreateDatabasePool method does not return anything at all. Instead, this method creates the OraDatabase objects and holds them in a pool until a request to retrieve a connection is made. (Retrieving a connection is discussed in the next section.) Take a look at how a pool of connections is created:

```
Dim OraSession As OraSession
Set OraSession = CreateObject _
    ("OracleInProcServer.XOraSession")
OraSession.CreateDatabasePool initPoolSize,
            maxPoolSize,
            idleTimeOut,
            Net8Alias,
            UsernamePassword,
            options
```

The CreateDatabasePool method takes six parameters:

- initPoolSize
- maxPoolSize
- idleTimeOut
- Net8Alias
- UsernamePassword
- Options

The *initPoolSize parameter* is the initial size of the pool or, rather, the number of OraDatabase objects initially created in the pool when the CreateDatabasePool method is executed.

The *maxPoolSize parameter* is the maximum number of OraDatabase objects allowed to be created for a particular application. If the maxPoolSize is set to 50, when a request for the 51st OraDatabase object is made, an error is returned.

The *idleTimeOut parameter* determines how much idle time each OraDatabase object should allow before disconnecting.

The *Net8Alias parameter* is the alias or service name defined for connecting to the database.

The *UsernamePassword parameter* contains the username and password for whom the connection is to be made. The username and password is passed in as a string separated by a "/", as with "Scott/Tiger". This is the only location to specify a username, which means that all the connections in a given pool pertain to one user. If you want to use multiple users, you have to create a separate pool for each user. Each pool needs to be created with its own OraSession object.

NOTE   All OraDatabase objects in a given pool pertain to a single user.

The final parameter is the *Options parameter*. This parameter allows the OraDatabase objects to be created with a specific option. The options available here are the same as for the OpenDatabase method for the OraSession object. For more information on each option and what they do, see the OO4O online documentation.

Figure 11.1 illustrates a Connection Pooling model.

FIGURE 11.1
Connection Pooling

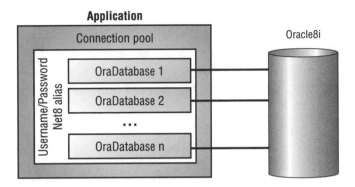

In Figure 11.1, there are a couple of items to note. First, as we just mentioned, although there may be numerous OraDatabase connections, they are all connected to the same schema. Second, each OraDatabase object is independent of any other; therefore, each OraDatabase object has its own connection. Figure 11.1 illustrates the pool of connections that are contained in an application. In order for the application to access the database, an OraDatabase object has to be retrieved from the pool.

Retrieving a Connection from the Pool

Once the pool of connections is created, OO4O provides a convenient method for obtaining an OraDatabase object from the pool. This method is simply called *Get-DatabaseFromPool* and takes a single parameter. The single parameter is the amount of time to wait (in seconds) for the return of an OraDatabase object. Here is an example of its syntax:

```
'The following line of code waits 30 seconds
'for the return of an OraDatabase object
Set OraDatabase = OraSession.GetDatabaseFromPool(30)
```

If no OraDatabase object is returned after the allotted time, or if there are no more available OraDatabase objects, the following error will result:

```
OERROR_GETDB Unable to obtain a free database object from the pool.
```

A Connection Pooling Application

The concept of Connection Pooling has already been implemented on the Internet in Web pages that require immediate connections to a database or that need to avoid the overhead associated with connecting. Since the majority of people reading this book will probably not have a Web server readily available, we will use a simple example to demonstrate Connection Pooling methodology.

Figure 11.2 expands upon Figure 11.1's concepts by illustrating two different front ends accessing their own separate pool of connections. One application uses a Web server and the other uses Connection Pooling as an ActiveX executable. The example for this chapter creates Connection Pooling with an ActiveX executable.

FIGURE 11.2
A Connection Pooling model with two different applications

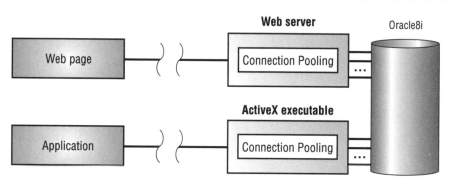

The top portion of Figure 11.2 illustrates implementing Connection Pooling with a Web page. The bottom portion of Figure 11.2 uses a front-end application that connects to an ActiveX executable and illustrates implementing Connection Pooling with the example that we'll get to in a minute.

Creating the Pool

In order to create the example, you need to start the Visual Basic (VB) IDE. As part of VB's start-up, you are prompted for the type of application to create. The dialog box in Figure 11.3 illustrates the available applications.

FIGURE 11.3
The New Project dialog box

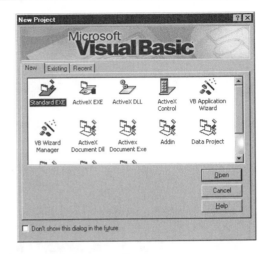

Usually, Standard EXE is the type of project selected. But this time, select ActiveX EXE, as seen in Figure 11.4, and click the Open button.

FIGURE 11.4
Choosing ActiveX EXE for your new project type

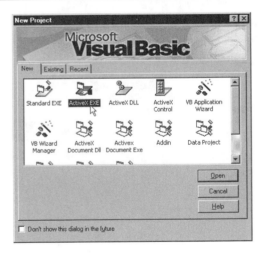

Once the Open button is pressed, VB opens a new project and opens a default Class Module, as seen in Figure 11.5.

FIGURE 11.5
Choosing the default Class
Module

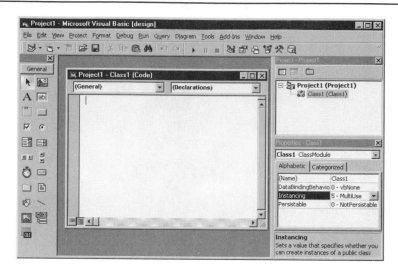

First, you need to add a new module to the project. This module will house the Main routine of the server and will be executed each time the application is started. It will also be used to create the pool of connections. To add a new module, select Project from the Visual Basic menu bar and then select the Add Module menu (see Figure 11.6).

FIGURE 11.6
Using the
Add Module menu

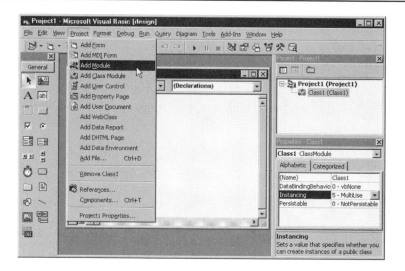

As you add a new module to the project, VB will provide an Add Module dialog box asking whether a new module is to be created or if an existing module should be opened. For this example, create a new module, as shown in Figure 11.7, and click the Open button.

FIGURE 11.7

The Add Module dialog box

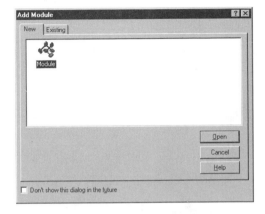

Once the new module is added to the project, your screen should resemble Figure 11.8.

FIGURE 11.8

An empty module

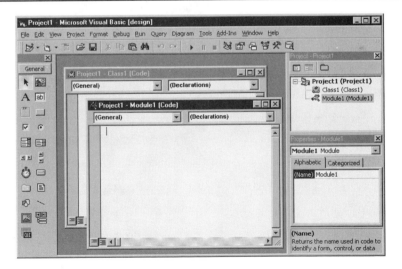

Before you write any code for your new module, the Oracle Objects for OLE Type Library must be included in the project. This is primarily so that you can use early binding. To include the type library, select the References item in the Project drop-down menu on the VB menu bar (see Figure 11.9).

NOTE   See Chapter 3 for more information on early binding.

FIGURE 11.9
Adding the type library reference from the References menu

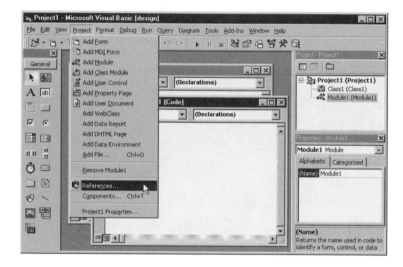

When the References menu item is selected, VB displays a Reference dialog box that lists all the available libraries. The References dialog box is shown in Figure 11.10. Keep in mind that the items displayed in this dialog box may vary from machine to machine.

FIGURE 11.10
The References dialog box:
Yours may differ.

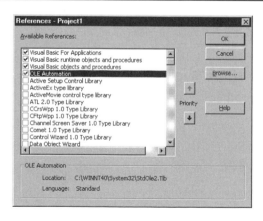

The References dialog box provides an alphabetic listing of the available type libraries. If you scroll down, you will see the Oracle Objects for OLE Type Library, as shown in Figure 11.11.

FIGURE 11.11
The OO4O 3.0 Type Library

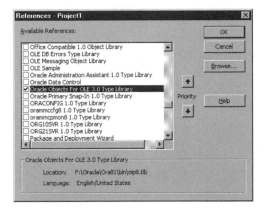

If Oracle Objects for OLE (OO4O) is not installed, the type library will not appear in the References dialog box.

Select the Oracle Objects For OLE 3.0 Type Library check box and click OK. Be sure that a check mark is present before clicking OK. Highlighting the field will not include the type library; a check mark must be present. Once the OK button is pressed, you will return to the VB project.

The next step is to rename the project. To rename the project, select the Project1 (Project1) listing in the Project Explorer window. Normally, the Project Explorer can be found as a smaller window on the right side of the VB workspace. If the Project Explorer window is not visible or if you are not sure of its location, press CTRL+R, and the window will gain focus. In this window, select the Project1 (Project1) item, as shown in Figure 11.12.

TIP

You can make the Project Explorer window gain focus by pressing CTRL+R.

FIGURE 11.12
The Project Explorer
window

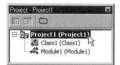

Once the Project is highlighted in the Project Explorer, the Properties dialog box will display the name of the project, as shown in Figure 11.13. The Properties dialog box, similar to the Project Explorer window, is usually found as a smaller window on the right side of the VB workspace. If the Properties dialog box is not visible or if you are unsure of its location, press F4, and the window will gain focus.

TIP   You can make the Properties dialog box gain focus by pressing F4.

FIGURE 11.13
The Project Properties
dialog box

Change the name of the project to **ConnPoolProject** by typing in the new project name and hitting the Return key. This will change the name of the project to ConnPoolProject, as shown in Figure 11.14. The new project name is short for Connection Pool Project.

FIGURE 11.14
The new project name is
ConnPoolProject.

The next step is to rename the Class Module, just as you did with the project name. First, highlight Class1 in the Project Explorer window. In the Properties dialog box, change the name from Class1 to **ConnPoolClass** and hit the Return key.

Once the project and Class Module are renamed, the next step is to add the required declaration. In Module1, place the following line of code under the (General) (Declarations) section.

```
Global OraSession As OraSession
```

This line defines a global OraSession object called OraSession. This variable will house the pool of connections created in this application. It's defined as a global object to allow the class (soon to be created) to reference and pass back the requested OraSession to the calling application.

Now, we are ready to add the OO4O code that will create the pool of connections. Keep in mind that this is a DLL and not an executable. As a result, when this application is first loaded into memory, the Main subroutine is executed. So, we need to create the Main subroutine and place the code in Listing 11.1 into Module1. This code will create the pool of connections.

Listing 11.1

```
1  Sub Main()
2  Dim initSizeOfPool As Integer
3  Dim maxSizeOfPool As Integer
4  Dim idleTimeOut As Integer
5  initSizeOfPool = 2
6  maxSizeOfPool = 4
7  idleTimeOut = 20
8  Set OraSession = CreateObject _
        ("OracleInProcServer.XOraSession")
9  OraSession.CreateDatabasePool initSizeOfPool, _
                                 maxSizeOfPool, _
                                 idleTimeOut, _
                                 "v8i", "scott/tiger", 0
10  MsgBox "A DatabasePool has been established " & _
        "with the following setting:" & vbCrLf & _
        "initSizeOfPool = " & initSizeOfPool & vbCrLf & _
        "maxSizeOfPool = " & maxSizeOfPool & vbCrLf & _
        "idleTimeOut = " & idleTimeOut, , _
        CreateDatabasePool
11 End Sub
```

Analysis

- Line 1 defines the Main subroutine.

- Lines 2–4 define the variables used in defining the pool of connections.

- Line 5 sets the initSizeOfPool variable to 2, which is the initial number of OraDatabase objects created when the pool in initialized.

- Line 6 sets the maxSizeOfPool variable to 4, which is the maximum number of OraDatabase objects to be created.

- Line 7 sets the idleTimeOut variable to 20 seconds, which is the amount of time for a connection to remain idle before the OraDatabase object is disconnected from the database.

- Line 8 executes the CreateObject command to load the Oracle InProc Server and returns the interface for the OraSession object.

- Line 9 executes the CreateDatabasePool method of the OraSession object, which creates the pool of connections.

- Line 10 is a message box that is displayed each time this application is instantiated. The message box is included so you can see when the pool is actually created and serves as a reminder of the initial size and the maximum size of the pool, as well as when the timeouts for idle connections occur.

- Line 11 signifies the end of the Main subroutine.

The message box created in line 10 is not required, but it's especially useful in signifying when this application is loaded. After completing this chapter, feel free to change the values of any of the variables used in lines 5 through 7 to see how the different values can affect the calling application. If you change the values of these variables, the message box also serves as a reminder of the values used when creating the connection pool.

When you're finished defining the global variable, the Main subroutine, and the code to create the connection pool, Module1 should look something like Figure 11.15.

FIGURE 11.15
The completed Module1

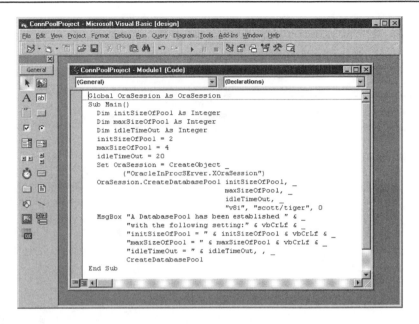

When Module1 is completed, the next step is to complete the code for the Class Module, which was named ConnPoolClass. The only code necessary is the code in Listing 11.2, which is required to return the OraSession object to the calling application. After returning the OraSession object, the calling application can retrieve a connection to the pool. To complete the Class Module, place the code in Listing 11.2 in the ConnPoolClass module.

Listing 11.2

```
1   Property Get GetConnectionFromPool() As OraSession
2     Set GetConnectionFromPool = OraSession
3   End Property
```

Analysis

- Line 1 defines the Get method of the class that will be used to call the application that retrieves the OraSession object.

- Line 2 returns the OraSession object.

- Line 3 ends the Get method definition.

Once the code is entered, the project's properties must be edited so that when the application starts, the Main subroutine, which was created earlier, will be called. To do this, you must access the ConnPoolProject Properties menu item. The ConnPoolProject Properties menu item can be found in the Project drop-down menu, as shown in Figure 11.16.

FIGURE 11.16
The ConnPoolProject–
Properties menu

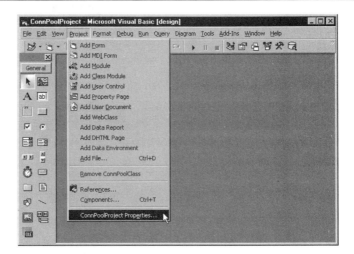

Once this menu item is selected, the dialog box in Figure 11.17 is displayed.

FIGURE 11.17
The Project Properties
dialog box

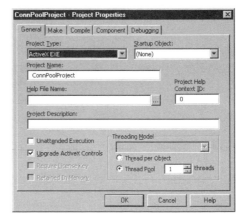

Next, make two entries in this dialog box. First, make sure that the Main subroutine is called. To do this, select the Sub Main option from the Startup Object list box, as shown in Figure 11.18.

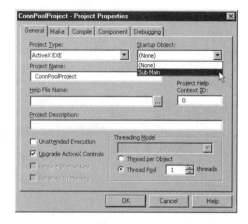

The second entry is the project description. It may not sound important, but the description entered here is used to create the reference name. You will see this name in the References dialog box. The importance of this requirement will be evident when the calling application is created. Enter the following code in the Project Description field and click OK:

```
Connection Pooling Sample (Simulating Web Server)
```

If you have not already done so, save the application. The location is not important, so save it to anywhere you like.

The final step is to actually build the application. To do this, execute the Make ConnPoolServer.exe option under the File drop-down menu on the Visual Basic menu bar, as shown in Figure 11.19.

NOTE   If you used the Visual Basic project ConnPoolProject on the CD-ROM instead of following the steps in this section, you may encounter an error when opening the project (Unable to set the version compatible component...). If so, simply click OK and continue. Rebuilding the project on your machine will remedy this issue.

FIGURE 11.19
The Make
ConnPoolServer.exe option

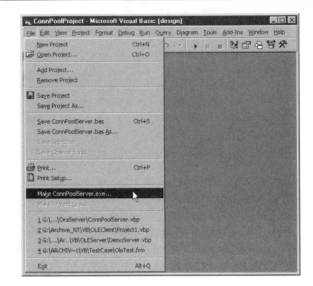

This will provide you with a Make Project dialog box, which will prompt you for the location in which to build the EXE file. The location can be any place on your machine.

Creating the Client Application

When the server portion is completed, the next step is to create the calling application that will retrieve the OraDatabase objects from the pool. To do so, start the VB IDE application. If you have just completed the previous section, VB is already running, and you can simply create a new project by selecting the New Project option from the File drop-down menu on the Visual Basic menu bar. In either case, you are prompted for the type of application to create.

Create this application as a Standard EXE type. Standard EXE is the default type, so you can just click the OK button to continue. This will automatically provide you with a new form, called Form1. Once the form is visible, drag and drop a CommandButton object onto the form. Click the button once to give it the current focus and to activate the Properties dialog box. In the Properties dialog box, change the caption on the button by typing the new name, **Run Test**, into the Caption text box, as shown in Figure 11.20.

FIGURE 11.20

Changing the name of a
button caption

Before entering any code, the reference to the server application created in the "Creating the Pool" section and the Oracle Objects For OLE 3.0 Type Library must be included in this project. To do so, access the Reference dialog box by selecting the References menu item from the Project drop-down menu on the VB menu bar. Figure 11.9 shows the References menu item, and Figure 11.10 illustrates the References dialog box. This time, select the new reference that was created when the first application was compiled. Figure 11.21 illustrates which reference to include.

FIGURE 11.21

Choosing the new refer-
ence for the server
application

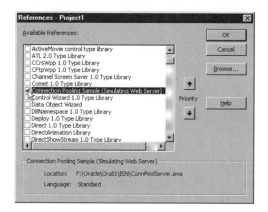

After selecting the reference to the Connection Pooling Sample library, scroll further down the list and select the Oracle Objects For OLE 3.0 Type Library. Once both are selected, click the OK button to return to the form.

Now that the reference to the first application is made, you are able to return the OraSession object created to obtain a connection from the pool. If you double-click the button on the form, a new window (Code Module) will open where you can enter the code used to obtain the OraSession object. When the button on the form is double-clicked, the Code Module will appear and display a Command1_Click()

subroutine by default. Before entering any code in this subroutine, two variables must be declared. These two variables are declared in the (General) (Declarations) section of the Code Module. Make sure that these two variables are defined in the (General)(Declarations) section and not in the Command1_Click event or you will get different results when executing the application.

The first variable created is the ConnPoolClass, which will be of the ConnPoolClass type. This class was created in the first application. Selecting the references in this project through the Reference dialog box allows for early binding. Enter the following line of code to define the first variable, which is actually a class:

```
Dim ConnPoolClass As New ConnPoolClass
```

Figure 11.22 illustrates the ConnPoolClass reference found in the list of available types. Access to ConnPoolClass is available once the reference is included.

FIGURE 11.22
The ConnPoolClass reference

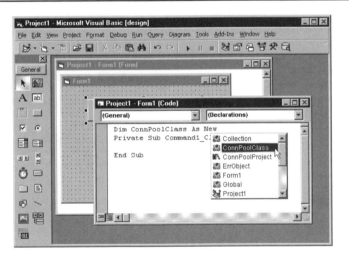

The second object needed is an OraSession object. Because this object will be returned from the server application, a placeholder is required in the client application. Add the following line after the ConnPoolClass definition:

```
Dim OraSession As OraSession
```

Now that the variables are defined, you can enter the code from Listing 11.3 to the Command1_Click event. This code will obtain the connection from the pool and use it in the example application.

Listing 11.3

```
 1 Private Sub Command1_Click()
 2   Set OraSession = ConnPoolClass.GetConnectionFromPool()
 3   On Error GoTo errhandler
 4   Set OraDatabase = OraSession.GetDatabaseFromPool(10)
 5   Set OraDynaset = OraDatabase.CreateDynaset _
        ("select * from emp", 0&)
 6   MsgBox OraDynaset.Fields("ENAME").Value
 7   Exit Sub
 8  errhandler:
 9   MsgBox "VB:" & Err & " " & Error(Err)
10 End Sub
```

Analysis

- Lines 1 and 10 are created automatically when the CommandButton is dou-ble-clicked and the Code Module appears.

- Line 2 calls the GetConnectionFromPool method of the ConnPoolClass object. If you remember, this method was defined in the first application and simply returns the OraSession object created when the application is loaded.

- Line 3 controls error handling by processing any errors that occur, instead of allowing the application to abort. The error handler used in this example captures and displays the error returned when a database object cannot be obtained from the pool.

- Line 4 executes the GetDatabaseFromPool command.

- Line 5 uses the newly obtained database object to create a dynaset object and retrieve data from the Emp table.

- Line 6 displays the employee name.

- Line 7 ends the subroutine.

- Line 8 is the label for the error handler.

- Line 9 displays a message box with the error message.

- Line 10 ends the subroutine.

For demonstration purposes, the message box in line 6 is used to lock the database object. Without the message box halting the processing, the subroutine would just end, and the database object would be released.

Using Message Boxes to Suspend an Application

Using a message box to suspend an application is the primary reason for creating the example in this chapter, instead of creating a Web page and using a Web server. Because you can't suspend the Web page during loading and accessing of the OraDatabase objects, it is very difficult to demonstrate when the pool is loaded or when new OraDatabase objects are created. This is because the Web page accesses the OraDatabase object and releases it so quickly that you are not able to see the pool being created with its OraDatabase objects. It is also difficult to see the additional OraDatabase objects being created without opening an exorbitant number of Web pages. Besides, but then again, the objects are released too quickly for us to view the V$PROCESS and V$SESSION synonyms and see how they are affected.

After entering the code, the next step is to build an EXE. Sure, you can run the application from VB, but to provide a more in-depth understanding, an EXE must be built so that the multiple instances of the application can be spawned. To build the EXE, select the Make Project1.exe... option under the File drop-down menu. To make the application easy to find, save the EXE file on one of your root drives. Locate the `Project1.exe` file on your file system and spawn five instances of the application. Each application will be identical to the next. You should now have five dialog boxes on your screen that look similar to the one in Figure 11.23.

FIGURE 11.23
A client application that is a
Run Test button

Once you have five instances available, spread them out across the screen to give each plenty of room. Click the Run Test button on any one of the five applications. The first screen you will see is the message box from the server application informing you of the values used to create the pool of connections. It should look like Figure 11.24.

FIGURE 11.24
A message box with the values used to create the pool of connections

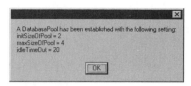

Almost immediately after the dialog box appears, you should also see the message box that displays the employee name of the first record, as shown in Figure 11.25.

FIGURE 11.25
The Employee message box

Although you may be tempted, don't close the message box that displays the employee name. The message box suspends the processing and places a lock on the database object, preventing it from returning to the pool. Instead, click the Run Test button on any three of the four remaining applications. This should result in a total of four visible message boxes, each with an Employee's name. Before clicking the Run Test button on the fifth and final application, think about what is currently happening and what will happen when the last button is clicked.

Remember that the maximum size of the pool created in the server application is four, and as there are currently four applications that have hold on a database object, it's safe to say that there are no more database objects available. Clicking the Run Test on the fifth application will produce a dialog box with an error message, as shown in Figure 11.26.

FIGURE 11.26
A Connection Pool error message

Keep track of which application produced the error, and click OK to clear the error message box. Next, click OK on any one of the other Employee message boxes. This should allow the code to complete and release the OraDatabase back to the pool. Now, go back to the application that earlier produced the error and click the Run Test button again. This time, you should not get an error. Instead, the employee name should appear inside a message box. Why did this happen?

When you clicked OK on one of the Employee message boxes, one of the OraDatabase objects was released back to the pool, allowing it to be accessed by another application.

Connection Pooling Monitoring

Before running the example created in the "A Connection Pooling Example" section, you may want to open an SQL*Plus session and log on as System so that you can see the V$PROCESS and V$SESSION synonyms before the example is executed and again after the pool of connections are created. You will notice that once the pool is created, the number of processes and the number of sessions increase in size, and that size growth matches the value passed in as the parameter for the initial pool size. As the number of required connections exceeds the initial amount, you will also notice that the number of records in V$PROCESS and V$SESSION increase with each access.

If you leave the pool idle long enough (the time in idleTimeOut parameter), you will notice that when the connections are closed, the number of records contained in the V$PROCESS and V$SESSION synonyms decreases.

Multiplexing

Multiplexing is when there is a single physical connection that is shared by multiple users. This is quite different from many connections maintained in an open state. One of the new objects released with this version of OO4O is the *OraServer object*. The purpose of this object is to allow the implementation of Multiplexing in an OO4O application. Figure 11.27 illustrates how this may look.

FIGURE 11.27
A multiplexed object using the OraServer object

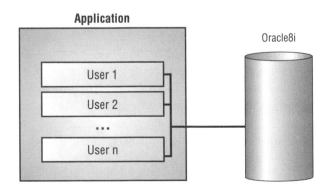

As discussed earlier in the chapter, connecting and disconnecting to a server is a fairly expensive action in terms of processing time. If an application is required to connect with multiple users throughout its execution, there could be a degradation of performance because each user requires a separate database connection. OraServer provides a way for one or more users to share a physical database connection. This does not mean that multiple users can access the database concurrently. Although many users can share the same physical connection to the database, only one user can actually be active at any given time.

OraServer Object

The previous section defined Multiplexing as the ability for many users to share one physical connection. The OraServer object was incorporated into this release to make Multiplexing possible. Each OraServer object represents one physical connection. Because the OraServer object is new, there are a couple of items you should note.

First, when creating an OO4O application, instead of creating the OracleInProcServer.XOraSession object, you must instead create the OracleInProcServer.XOraServer object. In most of the examples in other chapters, you will notice that the OracleInProcServer.XOraSession object is created. This is usually done with the following command:

```
Set OraSession = CreateObject _
        ("OracleInProcServer.XOraSession")
```

When using Multiplexing, you have to create the OracleInProcServer.XOraServer object using the following command:

```
Set OraServer = CreateObject _
        ("OracleInProcServer.XOraServer")
```

There is a subtle difference between the two previous code snippets. In the first one, the CreateObject command references the XOraSession class, while the second CreateObject command references the XOraServer class.

The second item to note is that the physical connection is to a single database. If an application requires Multiplexing to multiple databases, you have to create an OraServer object for each database connection.

Another important item to note is that although many users can use this one physical connection, only one user can be connected at a time. This means that if User1 is using the connection to process a query, User2 can't access the database until User1 is finished. Therefore, you must take the time when designing your application to make sure that you will not create a backlog.

There is a big expense when it comes to connecting and disconnecting to a database. If your application requires connections to multiple schemas, using the OraServer object may make sense.

OraServer Properties

Because the OraServer object simply creates the physical connection to the database, there is really not much information to gather. This is one reason why the OraServer object has only three properties:

- Databases
- Name
- Session

The *Databases property* returns an object that contains a Count property. The Count property tracks the number of different sessions open for a given OraServer object.

The *Name property* is the database or service name used to open the connection to the database.

The *Session property* returns an OraSession object.

For more in-depth information on these properties, you can review the OO4O online documentation.

OraServer Methods

Once the OraServer object is created, there are three methods provided by the OraServer object that allow you to change the password for a given user, open the connection to the database, and open a user session. The methods for doing these are

- ChangePassword
- Open
- OpenDatabase

The *ChangePassword method* allows you to change the password for a given user. The OO4O online documentation provides an example of how to implement changing a user's password.

The *Open method* takes a single parameter. The parameter is the Net8 alias or service name used to open the physical connection to the database. For example, if you use the v8i alias created in the previous chapter to open the physical connection, the code looks like this:

```
OraServer.Open "v8i"
```

The *OpenDatabase method* opens a session for a particular user and uses the database connection created with the Open method. There are two parameters involved. The first parameter is the username/password. The second parameter is the optional modes available for the particular connection. The OO4O online documentation provides a list of the available modes. The following line of code can be used to create a session for the user Scott whose password is Tiger:

```
Set OraDB1 = OraServer.OpenDatabase _
        ("scott/tiger", 0)
```

Attempting to create a session before actually opening a physical connection to the database will result in the "ORA-24327: need explicit attach before authenticating a user" error.

An Application Using Multiplexing

The example created in this section demonstrates how more than one user can share a single database connection using the Multiplexing feature provided by the OraServer object. We will create a form that is divided into three users that will all share the same database connection. One of the users should be the user System, who is required to obtain access to the V$SESSION and V$PROCESS synonyms. If the V$SESSION and V$PROCESS synonyms can be accessed from another user, using that one is fine. These synonyms are used to show the number of processes and the number of sessions established in the database. See the

"Connection Monitoring" section at the beginning of the chapter for more information on how these values are obtained.

The other two users can be whomever you wish. These two users will execute different SQL to validate their connection.

Before working with this example application, there are a couple of items to note:

- In order to limit the number of lines in the application, there is no error checking other than to see if access to the V$SESSION and V$PROCESS synonyms exists. If a syntactically incorrect SQL statement is entered, the application will terminate. To keep it simple, you can enter one of the following SQL commands (which should work for all users, regardless of who you are logged in as): Select Count * From User_Tables or Select User From Dual.

- When you run the application, log in and out a number of times and watch the values in the Number of Processes field and the Number of Sessions fields on the form increment or decrement with each log in.

- To get a good feel for using the OraServer object, use different users in the code and see if you notice how quickly each user can process a query without having to reestablish a database connection for each.

- To keep the application simple, the message box that displays the data is designed to simply list the value of the first field in the dynaset.

Now that the preliminary information is out of the way, it's time to start building the application.

If the VB IDE is not already running, start a new instance. As before, VB prompts for the type of application to create. The dialog box in Figure 11.3 illustrates the available types. Select a Standard EXE application type. Next, the Oracle Objects for OLE Type Library must be included. If you are unsure of how to do this, refer to the "Creating the Pool" section and review Figures 11.9 and 11.10.

The next step is to place the required components on the form. This form requires the following:

- six Command buttons
- four Text Box Controls
- one line

- one frame

- two labels

Figure 11.28 illustrates how these components should be arranged.

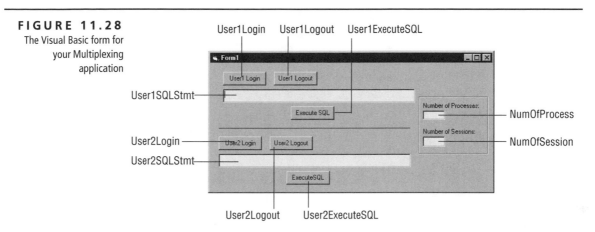

FIGURE 11.28
The Visual Basic form for your Multiplexing application

Figure 11.28 also illustrates how the (Name) property should be set for each item. Each component requiring a specific name has a line drawn to it with the name to use. The names used are very important because the code makes reference to specific objects. Not using the names provided will result in errors when the application is executed, unless you make similar alterations to the code. Some components, like the line, frame, and labels, are primarily for aesthetic reasons and do not require a specific name.

Once the components are placed on the form and the required names are changed, the next step is to add the underlying code. Right-click the form to view the Context menu. One of the options is View Code. Select this item.

The first section of code is placed in the (General) (Declarations) section to allow each OraDatabase object to exist for the life of the application. The following is the code required to run the application:

```
Dim OraServer As OraServer
Dim OraDB As OraDatabase
Dim OraDB1 As OraDatabase
Dim OraDB2 As OraDatabase
```

Listing 11.4 makes an initial connection to the database and is used to update the number of processes and sessions shown on the form. This code is executed once the form is loaded into memory and just before being displayed on the screen.

Listing 11.4

```
1  Private Sub Form_Load()
2    Set OraServer = CreateObject _
        ("ORacleInProcServer.XOraServer")
3    OraServer.Open "v8i"
4    Set OraDB = OraServer.OpenDatabase _
        ("SYSTEM/MANAGER", 0)
5    User1Logout.Enabled = False
6    User1ExecuteSQL.Enabled = False
7    User1SQLStmt.Enabled = False
8    User2Logout.Enabled = False
9    User2ExecuteSQL.Enabled = False
10    User2SQLStmt.Enabled = False
11   UpdateData
12 End Sub
```

Analysis

- Line 1 defines the Form_Load subroutine.

- Line 2 creates the OraServer option.

- Line 3 opens the connection to the database used by the OraServer object by calling the Open method and passing the service name created in the previous chapter.

- Line 4 opens the connection to the actual user. The user System is used to allow access to the V$SESSION and V$PROCESS synonyms.

- Lines 5–10 disable the various components until the user actually logs into the database.

- Line 11 executes the UpdateData subroutine. This subroutine is discussed later in this section.

- Line 12 is the end of the subroutine.

There are a couple of important items to note in this listing. In line 1, the XOra-Server object, rather than the XOraSession object, is created. The XOraServer object allows Multiplexing to occur. The second important item is that, in line 4, the initial connection is established by the user System. This is because access to the V$PROCESS and V$SESSION synonyms are required for this particular example.

The last important item is in line 3. The string "v8i" is the Net8 connection string. This is the alias defined in the TNSNAMES.ORA file.

The next couple of subroutines are used for enabling and disabling User1's components. The first subroutine defined for User1, shown in Listing 11.5, is the User1Login_Click event. The code in Listing 11.5 is processed each time the User1 Login button is pressed.

Listing 11.5

```
1 Private Sub User1Login_Click()
2    Set OraDB1 = OraServer.OpenDatabase("SCOTT/TIGER", 0)
3    User1Login.Enabled = False
4    User1Logout.Enabled = True
5    User1ExecuteSQL.Enabled = True
6    User1SQLStmt.Enabled = True
7    UpdateData
8 End Sub
```

Analysis

- Line 1 defines the User1Login_Click event.

- Line 2 opens the connection for a particular user. For this example, any valid user is appropriate.

- Lines 3–6 enable the components related to User1.

- Line 7 executes the UpdateData subroutine. This subroutine is discussed later in this section.

- Line 8 ends the subroutine.

For this example, the username and password used in line 2 can be any valid username and password. If the database was installed with the default settings, user Scott should already exist. If not, line 2 has to be modified to use a username and password that already exists.

The second subroutine designed for User1 is the User1Logout_Click event, which is shown in Listing 11.6. The code in Listing 11.6 is processed each time the User1 Logout button is pressed.

Listing 11.6

```
1 Private Sub User1Logout_Click()
2   Set OraDB1 = Nothing
3   User1Login.Enabled = True
4   User1Logout.Enabled = False
5   User1ExecuteSQL.Enabled = False
6   User1SQLStmt.Enabled = False
7   UpdateData
8 End Sub
```

Analysis

- Line 1 defines the User1Logout_Click event.

- Line 2 sets the OraDB1 object for User1 to "Nothing", which closes the database connection for User1.

- Line 3 enables the Login button for User1.

- Lines 4–6 disable the components related to User1.

- Line 7 executes the UpdateData subroutine. This subroutine is discussed later in this section.

- Line 8 ends the subroutine.

The final subroutine defined for User1 is the User1ExecuteSQL event, shown in Listing 11.7. The code in Listing 11.7 is processed each time the ExecuteSQL button for User1 is pressed.

Listing 11.7

```
1 Private Sub User1ExecuteSQL_Click()
2   Dim OraDynaset1 As OraDynaset
3   Set OraDynaset1 = OraDB1.CreateDynaset _
      (User1SQLStmt.Text, 0)
4   MsgBox OraDynaset1.Fields(0).Value
5 End Sub
```

Analysis

- Line 1 defines the User1ExecuteSQL_Click event.

- Line 2 creates the OraDynaset object.

- Line 3 creates a dynaset based on the SQL statement entered in the Text Box component for User1.

- Line 4 displays a message box with the value of the first field in the dynaset.

- Line 5 ends the subroutine.

Make sure that the SQL entered in the Text Box component is valid because there is no validation in the code. Incorrect syntax or invalid table names will cause the application to close. The SQL used here should not end with a semicolon.

Once the code is created for User1 (Listing 11.7), enter the code for User2 (Listing 11.8). As with User1, the first subroutine defined for User2 is code to log into the database, which is handled by the User2Login_Click event. The code in Listing 11.8 is processed each time the User2 Login button is pressed.

Listing 11.8

```
1 Private Sub User2Login_Click()
2     Set OraDB2 = OraServer.OpenDatabase _
          ("SYSTEM/MANAGER", 0)
3     User2Login.Enabled = False
4     User2Logout.Enabled = True
5     User2ExecuteSQL.Enabled = True
6     User2SQLStmt.Enabled = True
7     UpdateData
8 End Sub
```

Analysis

- Line 1 defines the User2Login_Click event.

- Line 2 opens the connection for a particular user. This example uses the user System, but any valid user is appropriate.

- Lines 3–6 enable the components related to User2.

- Line 7 executes the UpdateData subroutine. This subroutine is discussed later in this section.

- Line 8 ends the subroutine.

For this example, the username and password used in line 2 can be any valid username and password. This example uses a different username and password for User2 than for User1, which is an excellent way to demonstrate Multiplexing. If System/Manager is not a valid username and password, this line of code must be modified to use a username and password that already exists.

The second subroutine designed for User2 is the User2Logout_Click event, shown in Listing 11.9. The code in Listing 11.9 is processed each time the User2 Logout button is pressed.

Listing 11.9

```
1 Private Sub User2Logout_Click()
2    Set OraDB2 = Nothing
3    User2Login.Enabled = True
4    User2Logout.Enabled = False
5    User2ExecuteSQL.Enabled = False
6    User2SQLStmt.Enabled = False
7    UpdateData
8 End Sub
```

Analysis

- Line 1 defines the User2Logout_Click event.

- Line 2 sets the OraDB2 object for User2 to "Nothing", which closes the database connection for this user.

- Line 3 enables the Login button for User2.

- Lines 4–6 disable the components related to User2.

- Line 7 executes the UpdateData subroutine. This subroutine is discussed later in this section.

- Line 8 ends the subroutine.

The final subroutine defined for User2 is the User2ExecuteSQL event, shown in Listing 11.10. The code in Listing 11.10 is processed each time the ExecuteSQL button for User2 is pressed.

Listing 11.10

```
1 Private Sub User2ExecuteSQL_Click()
2    Dim OraDynaset2 As OraDynaset
3    Set OraDynaset2 = OraDB2.CreateDynaset _
         (User2SQLStmt.Text, 0)
4    MsgBox OraDynaset2.Fields(0).Value
5 End Sub
```

Analysis

- Line 1 defines the User1ExecuteSQL_Click event.

- Line 2 creates the OraDynaset object.

- Line 3 creates a dynaset based on the SQL statement entered in the Text Box component for User2.

- Line 4 displays a message box with the value of the first field in the dynaset.

- Line 5 ends the subroutine.

The last piece of code for this example is the *UpdateData subroutine*, shown in Listing 11.11. This subroutine is the method by which the number of processes and the number of sessions are retrieved from the database and displayed on the form. The connection to the database used in this subroutine was established during the Form_Load event. This is why it's important that the username and password used in the Form_Load event have access to the V$SESSION and V$PROCESS synonyms.

Listing 11.11

```
1  Private Sub UpdateData()
2     Dim OraDynaset As OraDynaset
3     On Error GoTo checkUser
4     Set OraDynaset = OraDB.CreateDynaset _
         ("Select count(*) from V$PROCESS", 0)
```

```
5    NumOfProcess.Text = OraDynaset.Fields(0).Value
6    Set OraDynaset = OraDB.CreateDynaset _
          ("Select count(*) from V$SESSION", 0)
7    NumOfSession.Text = OraDynaset.Fields(0).Value
8    Exit Sub
9 checkUser:
10    If OraDB.LastServerErr = 942 Then
11        MsgBox "You do NOT have access to the " & _
          "V$SESSION & V$PROCESS tables." & vbCrLf & _
          "The Number of Process and Number of Sessions" & _
          "will NOT be updated.", vbExclamation
12    End If
13 End Sub
```

Analysis

- Line 1 defines the UpdateData subroutine.

- Line 2 creates the OraDynaset object.

- Line 3 redirects the process to another section of code in the event of an error.

- Line 4 creates a dynaset based on the number of records found in the V$PROCESS synonym.

- Line 5 displays the number of records found into the NumOfProcess Text Box component.

- Line 6 creates a dynaset based on the number of records found in the V$SES-SION synonym.

- Line 7 displays the number of records found in the NumOfSession Text Box component.

- Line 8 exits the subroutine.

- Line 9 creates the label for the error-handling code.

- Line 10 checks for a specific error code. If the error code is 942, the username and password used in the Form_Load event does not have access to the V$PROCESS and V$SESSION synonyms.

- Line 11 is the message box and text displayed if the 942 error code is returned.

- Line 12 ends the If statement.

- Line 13 ends the subroutine.

Once again, it's important to ensure that the username and password used in the Form_Load event have access to the V$PROCESS and V$SESSION synonyms. Having access to these tables allows this example to demonstrate the increments and decrements of the number of processes and sessions in the database.

At this point, the project can be built and an executable can be created. The executable can be saved anywhere on the machine. Either run the application as a single instance or try running multiple instances. Remember that each application has only one OraServer object. You should notice that the number of processes in the database increases by one for each OraServer object. For each application instance, you will notice that the number of processes also increases by one. As each user logs in and out of the database, you will notice that the processes remain constant and only the number of sessions increases and decreases.

As soon as User1 or User2 is logged in, execute an SQL statement to validate that you are actually connected. Remember that there is no validation of the SQL entered. An incorrect SQL statement or a Select statement on a table that does not exist will cause the application to close. If you are unsure of what tables exist for which users, try one of the following SQL statements that use a system table applicable for any valid user.

NOTE   When entering SQL in the form, you do not have to include the semicolon at the end. Doing so will result in an "ORA-00911:invalid character" error message.

This Select statement returns the number of rows from the USER_TABLES table:

```
SELECT COUNT(*) FROM USER_TABLES
```

The following Select statement returns the table names for all the tables owned by the user:

```
SELECT TABLE_NAME FROM USER_TABLES
```

Once the SQL statement is entered, press the ExecuteSQL button. The application will display the value of the first field in the dynaset. Remember that this code isn't necessarily practical—the primary idea is to help you understand Multiplexing.

Multiplexing Monitoring

There is a very simple way to observe the concept of Multiplexing in action. Notice that the form created in the previous section has two text boxes in a field on the right side of the form (see Figure 11.28). One text box is called Number of Processes, and the other is called Number of Sessions. The Number of Processes field displays the number of processes connected to the database by counting the number of records in the V$PROCESS synonym. The Number of Sessions field displays the number of sessions in the database by doing a count of the number of records in the V$SESSION synonym. For more information on the V$PROCESS or V$SESSION synonyms, review the "Connection Monitoring" section earlier in the chapter or review the *Oracle8i Reference* manual.

As you connect through the Login button and disconnect through the Logout button, the number in the Number of Sessions field increments and decrements with each activity, yet the number in the Number of Processes field does not change. Even if both users are logged in at the same time, the number of processes does not change. This should help confirm that the two users are indeed sharing the same connection.

If you start a second or third instance of the example, or if some other application connects to the database, the number of processes increases when the field is refreshed.

Summary

This chapter covered two topics. One is an existing feature, Connection Pooling, and the other is a new feature, Multiplexing. We also discussed the overhead incurred when connecting and disconnecting to a database and how these features help to minimize this cost. We also discussed the differences and advantages of these different ways of allowing multiple users to access the same data. Although the examples provided are fairly straightforward, they should assist you in fully understanding the functionality of these two concepts.

chapter 12

Advanced Queuing

- Introduction to Advanced Queuing

- Understanding Advanced Queuing

- Creating the Queue Administrator and users

- Creating the message queue

- Using Advanced Queuing in OO4O

- Building an Advanced Queuing application

This chapter covers using the new Oracle8i Advanced Queuing feature in your Visual Basic applications. The Oracle *Advanced Queuing feature* (AQ) was introduced with version 8 of the RDBMS and offers a "publish and subscribe" mechanism for passing messages (publishing information or data) between database applications by using message queues. These queues provide a powerful and flexible architecture for managing the delivery of information between various applications. Until the release of OO4O 8.1, accessing these features was done through database-side programming using PL/SQL, or through a low-level client API, such as the Oracle Call Interface (OCI), using C/C++. Some platforms (not Microsoft Windows) allowed for these APIs to be accessed in other languages, such as PASCAL or COBOL, but access to these features on a Microsoft Windows platform from a high-level language (such as Visual Basic) was not feasible without writing your own custom extensions. With the release of OO4O 8.1, these features are now accessible in any tool that supports Visual Basic for Applications (VBA) or from Visual Basic itself. The message recipients can be widely separated, and this feature allows applications to coordinate activities and data by passing messages to one another.

An Introduction to Advanced Queuing

Advanced Queuing in Oracle uses the Publish and Subscribe model for propagating messages. This means that message-queue-enabled applications can publish messages to one or more queues (or lists of messages) that can then be received by other applications subscribing to that queue. Messages are *published*, or placed in the queue by applications generating content for delivery and are retrieved from the queue by *consumers*, or applications that accept messages and content for processing. Message consumers may also be message publishers, and the reverse is also true: Publishers may also be consumers.

> **NOTE**   The term *agent* is also used to describe a message producer or subscriber. An agent can be either another application or an individual user.

In a distributed environment, the messages may come to or from multiple applications or even from different servers in a distributed environment. Messages can be of any user-defined type or of type Raw, which is the same as the table column type Raw. Messages can be made persistent in the database via user queue tables or can be non-persistent via system queue tables. *Persistent queues* store their messages until they are dequeued by a client application, however long that might take. Because they can be persistent, the messages can be retained after consumption. This retention time is controlled by the Queue Administrator. A rich amount of history information is kept for each message, including enqueue time, dequeue time, and who it was dequeued by.

Messages can be *asynchronous*, that is, they are delivered when requested by the client rather than immediately upon processing by the server. Message queue consumers may specify rules to determine whether a message will be routed to them based on content (Rule-Based Subscription), or they can order messages by priority or by some other identification (see the correlation properties discussed in this chapter).

With the 8.1 release of Oracle Objects for OLE, native support for Advanced Queuing is introduced, as well (with version 8, the applications using Advanced Queuing had to be written entirely in OCI or PL/SQL). Refer to the *Oracle8i Application Developers Guide* for more details of Advanced Queuing, including specifics at the database level.

In this chapter, you will approach Advanced Queuing from the perspective of using the message queues for information distribution among database applications, as shown in the Advanced Queuing model in Figure 12.1.

WARNING   DBA access to the RDBMS will be required initially to enable the Advanced Queuing features and to set up an Advanced Queuing Administrator account. See the "Creating the Queue Administrator and Users" section for more information.

FIGURE 12.1
Advanced Queuing Model

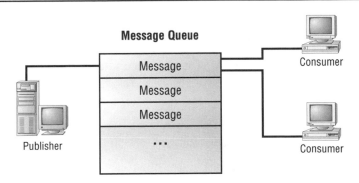

If you are already familiar with the Advanced Queuing feature of the database itself, this chapter will show you how easy it is to access this feature using OO4O and Visual Basic.

NOTE   Using the Advanced Queuing feature will require some database-side interaction to create and manage the queue users and queues themselves. It is assumed that you are familiar with using SQL*Plus to access the database.

Creating the Queue Administrator and Users

Using the Advanced Queuing feature of the Oracle database will require some DBA interaction. The DBA will need to create a user for maintaining the Advanced Queuing (AQ) features, or perhaps more than one if many different AQ applications are needed. This user is known as the Queue Administrator. Additionally, there may need to be AQ user accounts created or certain new roles granted to existing user accounts to allow them to use the AQ features.

NOTE   *Roles* are sets of predefined RDBMS permissions that may be granted to database user accounts. Refer to the *Oracle8i Administrator's Guide* for more details on roles and database permissions.

The AQ Administrator account is normally the user account that will create the queues and perform maintenance on them. The Queue Administrator account will need the special role AQ_ADMINISTRATOR_ROLE granted to it. This role contains the necessary database permissions for performing the queue administration functions. The user accounts are usually the actual message publisher and subscribers themselves. In the example that will be discussed in this chapter, the Queue Administrator account is also the queue user account.

To create a queue administrative account and a queue for use by the applications in SQL*Plus, follow these steps:

1. Connect as System or as another account with DBA access.

   ```
   connect system/manager;
   ```

Exercise caution when connecting to the RDBMS as System or as another DBA account. Incorrect use of such an account may cause the RDBMS to fail to function or may cause permanent data loss or corruption.

2. Create the administrative user account for the queue. The TESTAQ user will be created and used in the example presented here.

   ```
   create user TESTAQ identified by TESTAQ;
   ```

3. Grant the necessary privileges to the user, as shown here:

   ```
   grant connect, resource, aq_administrator_role to TESTAQ;

   grant execute on dbms_aq to TESTAQ;

   grant execute on dbms_aqadm to TESTAQ;
   ```

NOTE   In addition to the normal Connect and Resource privileges, you also grant the role AQ_ADMINISTRATOR_ROLE. Additionally, you need to grant execute privileges on the DBMS_AQ and DBMS_AQADM packages, as these are where the AQ administrative functions are located. The DBMS_AQADM package is needed only for the Queue Administrator. A queue user would need to access only the DBMS_AQ package. Because you will be using the same account for both the AQ Administrator and the AQ user in this example, no user specific accounts will be created.

4. Grant the queue privileges to the TESTAQ user. The RDBMS System, AQ Administrator, or other DBA account must be used. To do this in SQL*Plus, execute the following code:

   ```
   execute
       dbms_aqadm.GRANT_SYSTEM_PRIVILEGE(
       'ENQUEUE_ANY','TESTAQ',FALSE);

   execute
       dbms_aqadm. GRANT_SYSTEM_PRIVILEGE(
       'DEQUEUE_ANY', 'TESTAQ', FALSE);
   ```

The DBMS_AQADM.GRANT_SYSTEM_PRIVILEGE() procedure is executed to grant both ENQUEUE_ANY and DEQUEUE_ANY privileges to the TESTAQ user. This allows the specified user to enqueue or dequeue messages. You can limit this to DEQUEUE_ANY if the user needs only Read Message (or Consumer) access to the queue. Likewise, you can limit this to ENQUEUE_ANY if the user will only be posting or publishing messages to the queue. If you were not using the Queue Administrator account to send and receive messages, you would continue to grant the ENQUEUE_ANY, DEQUEUE_ANY, and Execute privileges to the DBMS_AQ package to additional users as needed. These then become the normal AQ user accounts.

TIP   The DBMS_AQADM.GRANT_TYPE_ACCESS() procedure is no longer needed in 8.1.5 because all internal AQ objects are now accessible to Public, or all users. This was not true for AQ in 8.0.

Access to the DBMS_AQ package allows normal message queue functions (after the ENQUEUE_ANY/DEQUEUE_ANY grant is completed). Access to the DBMS_AQADM package allows administration of the message queue. A typical message queue application would have the Execute privilege on the DBMS_AQ package in addition to the ENQUEUE_ANY and DEQUEUE_ANY grants provided via the DBMS_AQADM.GRANT_SYSTEM_PRIVILEGE() procedure.

Normally, a single user account is assigned the role of Queue Administrator for a given set of message queues. Many other user accounts can be assigned the role of queue users. In the example in the "Advanced Queuing Example" section, the TESTAQ user will administer this queue for the user accounts that are participating in the message queue and sending and receiving the messages.

The accounts are now prepared for you to begin using the Advanced Queuing features.

Creating the Message Queue

To create the message queue to be used by the TESTAQ user that you defined in the previous section "Creating the Queue Administrator and Users," follow these steps:

TIP   If you are not using the TESTAQ user from the previous section, you must connect with an account that has queue administrative permissions, which means that it has access to the DBMS_AQADM package and has been granted the AQ_ADMINISTRATOR_ROLE role.

1. Connect as the TESTAQ user in SQL*Plus. The example in the "Advanced Queuing Example" section demonstrates a user-defined object or type as the message payload. You need to first create the type used by the queue messages before the queue itself can be created. To do so, enter the command shown here:

```
connect testaq/testaq

CREATE type BBS_POST_TYPE as
    object (
            posted DATE,
            subject  VARCHAR2(80),
            body VARCHAR2(4000)
            );
```

This is the object type definition of the messages posted between users in our example program. The message payload can be of any user-defined type. This type was created to serve the purposes of this example. Note that the type contains the basic structure for the message information to be passed. The type is not the data itself, but it is a blueprint for the data in that it defines the structure of the data. Our example application will use a Date property to track the time that the message is posted to the queue. We will also set properties for the message data itself. The Message Subject property confines the subject to 80 characters. The Message Body property confines the message body to 4,000 characters.

2. Next, create the RDBMS data structures for the message queue. These are the message-queue-specific structures that allow the queuing feature to function. First, create the message queue table used for the message persistence. In this example, the messages will be made persistent by using user queue tables. By *persistent*, we mean that a message will be stored in the queue table until it is delivered to the specified user, or users, via a Dequeue operation from the client application. This table is managed by the Advanced Queuing system itself, it isn't simply created via an SQL DDL command, as a normal table is. Instead, the DBMS_AQADM package is used to accomplish this task, as shown in the following SQL*Plus command sequence:

```
EXECUTE
        dbms_aqadm.create_queue_table (
            queue_table => 'TESTAQ.BBS_MSG',
            sort_list => 'PRIORITY,ENQ_TIME',
            queue_payload_type => 'TESTAQ.BBS_POST_TYPE');
```

This command creates the queue table BBS_MSG in the TESTAQ schema, which will contain message records of type BBS_POST_TYPE. Each row will be an item of BBS_POST_TYPE, the user-defined type we just created. This table is managed by the AQ packages and will not directly be manipulated by the user of the account. Enqueue operations will add rows to the table, and Dequeue operations will remove them. If further manipulation, such as dropping and recreating the table, is required, only the AQ Administrator user can do this. If your application uses these features, other options, such as multiple consumers options, sort options, and even the Table Storage clause, may be specified here as a parameter to this command.

NOTE   Multiple consumers are discussed in the "Multiple Consumers" section. Sort options are covered in the "Building an Advanced Queuing Application" section later in this chapter.

3. Using the DBMS_AQADM package in SQL*Plus, create the message queue itself and associate it with the queue table created in the previous step. This will actually create the queue that will be used to pass the messages to and

from the clients. To create the message queue, enter this command via SQL*Plus:

```
EXECUTE
  dbms_aqadm.create_queue (
      queue_name  => 'BBS_MSG_QUEUE',
      queue_table => 'TESTAQ.BBS_MSG');
```

4. In SQL*Plus, start the message queue you just created, using this command:

```
EXECUTE
          dbms_aqadm.start_queue (
              queue_name  => 'BBS_MSG_QUEUE');
```

Your message queue is now created and is ready for use.

When starting the queue, the default is to start it for both Enqueue and Dequeue operations. If you need to start it for only one of these operations, specify both the Dequeue => and Enqueue => parameters. The following SQL*Plus code starts the queue MY_MSG_QUEUE for Dequeue operations only:

```
EXECUTE
          dbms_aqadm.start_queue (
              queue_name  => 'MY_MSG_QUEUE',
              dequeue => 'TRUE',
              enqueue => 'FALSE');
```

For more detailed information on this subject, refer to the *Oracle8i Application Developers Guide – Advanced Queuing* manual.

Advanced Queuing in OO4O

Native support for Advanced Queuing is new with release 8.1 of OO4O. New COM objects and new methods were added on existing objects. In the last section, "Building an Advanced Queuing Application," a working program was provided to demonstrate some of the Advanced Queuing features. In this section, the new AQ objects and methods will be discussed in detail.

OraAQ

The OraAQ object represents a message queue in RDBMS and is created as a part of calling the CreateAQ() method of an OraDatabase object. The *OraAQ object* contains the properties and methods that allow you to control the queue itself from your VB application. All of the properties associated with reading messages from the queue are available on this object. These methods and properties are demonstrated in the "Building an Advanced Queuing Application" section and in the OO4O documentation.

Because Enqueue operations are specific to the message itself (for the most part), most of the message enqueue options are associated with the OraAQMsg object. The following properties are available on the OraAQ object:

Consumer   The message consumer name

Correlate   The message correlation ID

DequeueMode   How the messages are dequeued

DequeueMsgId   The AQ Message ID

Navigation   The queue position control

RelMsgId   The position for enqueuing new messages

Visible   Transaction control

Wait   Dequeue delay

The OraAQ object also contains the following methods:

AQMsg   Creates a message object.

Enqueue   Posts a message.

Dequeue   Retrieves a message.

MonitorStart   Event notification.

MonitorStop   Event notification.

> **WARNING** In OO4O 8.1.5, calling the CreateAQ() method of the OraDatabase object with an invalid queue name will not return an error. Subsequent use of the invalid OraAQ object can result in ORA-25205 "Invalid Queue" errors. Be prepared to trap this in your error handler if the queue name can possibly be in error.

OraAQ Properties

Here are the properties exposed by the OraAQ object and a brief discussion of what they represent. The *OraAQ object* represents the Advanced Queue on the database and is used to control the queue from the client.

Consumer   This property is used during a Dequeue operation to specify the consumer name for the messages to be retrieved. The Consumer property is valid only for a queue created with the Multiple Consumer option. The default action for a multi-consumer queue is to retrieve messages created for all consumers only. Messages that are sent to a specific user will not be dequeued unless the Consumer property is set to the name of the consumer for whom the message was enqueued.

Correlate   This property is used during a Dequeue operation and allows you to assign a correlation identifier that will be used for ordering messages during Dequeue operations. The default correlation is RELATIVE_MSG_ID, which uses the AQ-generated message ID to order or organize the messages retrieved. If you specify another value here, it should be a string that was set on the Correlation property of an OraAQMsg object during a previous Enqueue operation. If you do not specify a correlation identifier, you will see all messages regardless of their correlation identifier. If you specify a correlation identifier, you will only dequeue messages for which the identifiers match. You can think of this as a Where clause condition in an SQL statement: If it isn't specified, you see everything; if it is specified, you only get what you asked for. See the description of the OraAQMsg object Correlation property later in this chapter.

DequeueMode   This property controls how messages are treated during a Dequeue operation. Use this property to specify the way the messages will be locked when retrieved. The default method (ORAAQ_DQ_REMOVE) reads the message and removes (delete) it from the queue. You can also specify ORAAQ _DQ_BROWSE, which will read the message without removing it from the queue. The message is also left unlocked, meaning that someone else can read it, lock it, or remove it. You can also specify ORAAQ_DQ_LOCKED, which allows you to browse the messages (not remove them) while locking them so that another user can't remove them. The lock is removed by a transaction Commit operation.

DequeueMsgId   This property is used during a Dequeue operation and allows you to set the specific message ID of a message to be retrieved. (A Message ID is unique to a single message.) This is really only useful if you have stored the message ID during a previous Enqueue operation. Using the Where clause example from the Correlate property, you can compare this to specifying a specific ROWID (and Oracle unique row identifier) in the Where clause condition.

NOTE   The Enqueue method of the OraAQ object will return the message ID as a byte array. A call to Dequeue() with an invalid message ID will result in an ORA-25263 error, "No message in queue X with message ID Y", being returned in the OraDatabase object.

Navigation   This property is used during a Dequeue operation to control the starting position for the messages to be retrieved from the queue. The default value is ORAAQ_DQ_NEXT_MSG. This will cause the Dequeue operation to return the next available message. The ORAAQ_DQ_FIRST_MSG will jump to the start of the message queue and subsequent Dequeue operations will return the first matching message. The ORAAQ_DQ_NEXT_TRANS value causes the remainder (if any) of the current transaction group to be skipped, and a subsequent Dequeue operation will return the first message in the next transaction group.

NOTE   For the ORAAQ_DQ_NEXT_TRANS option to be valid, the message queue must have been created in a queue table that is enabled for transaction grouping. Setting the Message_grouping parameter in the call to "DBMS_AQADM.CREATE_QUEUE_TABLE" and setting that equal to "TRANSACTIONAL" accomplishes this. (Add a parameter to the command like so: GROUPING=>TRANSACTIONAL. See the "Creating the Message Queue" section earlier in this chapter). For more details, refer to the *Oracle8i Application Developers Guide – Advanced Queuing* manual.

RelMsgId   This property is used during an Enqueue operation to specify a relative message before the next one that will be enqueued. Thus, if you previously enqueued Message A and stored its message ID, you can set the RelMsgId property to the value of the message ID for Message A, and the next call to the Enqueue() method will cause Message B (the next message) to be enqueued ahead of Message A, even though Message A was enqueued first.

Visible   This property is used during an Enqueue operation to set the message queue to transaction visibility (ORAAQ_ENQ_ON_COMMIT), which uses Oracle's transaction mechanism to control when the messages will be published to the subscribers or to immediate visibility (ORAAQ_ENQ_IMMEDIATE). Using transactional visibility allows multiple messages to be enqueued and published all at once when the transaction commits, or to be canceled and never published by issuing a transaction rollback. The alternative value for this parameter (ORAAQ_ENQ_IMMEDIATE) makes each message available immediately upon the call to the Enqueue() method. The default behavior is ORAAQ_ENQ_IMMEDIATE.

Wait   This property is used during a Dequeue operation and specifies the amount of time, in seconds, to wait for a message to become available, if one is not available at the time of the call to Dequeue(). If the time expires and a message is still not available, an ORA-25228 error "Timeout or end-of-fetch during message dequeue" is returned in the OraDatabase object. Two predefined constants exist in the Oraconst.txt file that you can also use:

- ORAAQ_DQ_NOWAIT will fail immediately if a message is not available for dequeuing.

- ORAAQ_DQ_WAIT_FOREVER will cause the Dequeue operation to hold until a message becomes available.

TIP   The default value for the Wait Dequeued property of the OraAQ object is ORAAQ_DQ_NOWAIT, although the documentation supplied with the 8.1.5 version of OO40 indicates that the default value is ORAAQ_DQ_WAIT_FOREVER.

OraAQ Methods

Next, we will discuss the methods exposed by the OraAQ object and give a brief discussion of what features they implement. We will also include code to demonstrate these methods.

The AQMsg Method

The *AQMsg method* creates an OraAQMsg object for the specified input parameters. This method takes two parameters, as follows:

msgtype This can be either of two values:

> **ORATYPE_RAW** The message payload is of type Raw.

> **ORATYPE_OBJECT** The message payload is a user-defined type.

typename A string specifying the user-defined type of the message payload. This parameter is not used for a message payload of type Raw. It has one parameter:

> **schema** A string specifying the User schema where the user-defined type is defined. This parameter is not used for a message payload of type Raw and is not needed if the object type is defined in the schema for the user you are connected as.

Here is an example of using this method:

```
Set MyMsg = OraQ.AQMsg(ORATYPE_OBJECT,  _
                       "BBS_POST_TYPE",  _
                       "TESTAQ")
```

In this example, BBS_POST_TYPE is a user-defined type in the TESTAQ schema (see the "Building an Advanced Queuing Application" section later in this chapter).

WARNING With OO4O version 8.1.5.0.0, an attempt to call AQMsg() with an invalid object type name specified will result in an OLE Automation error with an HRESULT of – 2147417848.

The Enqueue Method

The *Enqueue() method* is used to post messages to the queue associated with this OraAQ object. It works by using the last associated OraAQMsg object (created with the AQMsg() method). The return value from the Enqueue method is the message identifier as a byte array. This unique identifier can be used elsewhere to control Enqueue and Dequeue operations. As an example, if you were to set the RelMsgId property of the OraAQ object to a given message ID and call the Enqueue method, the new message would be enqueued *ahead* of the message specified by the Message ID property (the message that was previously queued). For more information, see the RelMsgId property in the "OraAQ Properties" section earlier in this chapter.

WARNING   With OO4O version 8.1.5, an attempt to call Enqueue() without having any valid OraAQMsg objects created will result in an OLE Automation error with an HRESULT of –2147417848.

The Dequeue Method

The *Dequeue method* is used to dequeue, or retrieve, messages from the RDBMS message queue associated with the OraAQ object. If it succeeds, the associated OraAQMsg object will contain the message payload for the message that is retrieved. The return value from this method will give you the message ID for the message that was read. If you have multiple OraAQMsg objects that were created via the AQMsg() method for this OraAQ object, they will *all* be updated to contain the payload of the message.

NOTE   With OO4O version 8.1.5, an attempt to call Dequeue() without having any valid OraAQMsg objects created will result in an OLE Automation error with an HRESULT of –2147417848.

MonitorStart

If you create your own OLE object that exposes the NotifyMe interface, you can use the *MonitorStart method* to have the OraAQ object asynchronously dequeue messages and pass them to the interface. The interface is of the form

```
void NotifyMe(LPDISPATCH)
```

where the LPDispatch (or IDispatch pointer/VB object reference) is to an OraAQMsg object containing the message payload. Calling this method starts a message monitor thread to call your NotifyMe interface. The object containing the NotifyMe() interface method must be created before this method is called because a reference to it must be passed into the NotifyMe call. Use the MonitorStop() method to stop the callbacks. You must call the MonitorStop() method before destroying the object that contains your NotifyMe Interface.

Here is a Visual Basic example of the MonitorStart method. Assume that you have created your own control called MyNotify, which exposes the NotifyMe interface; that you have included this control in your project; and that the Test queue exists for the user schema that you are connecting as.

```
Dim MyQ as OraAQ
Dim Notifier as MyNotify
Dim DB as OraDatabase
Dim OraS as Object
      .
      . ' connect to the RDBMS and initialize the session
      .
Set MyQ = DB.CreateAQ("TEST")
Set Notifier = new MyNotify

MyQ.MonitorStart(Notifier)
```

You will then get a copy of an OraAQMsg object associated with the message being dequeued that is passed into the NotifyMe interface of the Notifier object. You can then manipulate the OraAQMsg object as needed to process the message.

WARNING   In version 8.1.5.0.0 of Oracle Objects for OLE, the MonitorStart method was broken. The NotifyMe function was always called with a Null input parameter, making this feature unusable. This should be fixed in a patch release to 8.1.5.x and in version 8.1.6.

MonitorStop

The *MonitorStop method* is used to stop the message queue monitoring threads created via the call to the MonitorStart (see the MonitorStart method description) method.

OraAQMsg

The *OraAQMsg object* represents a message to be enqueued or dequeued from an Oracle Advanced Queue. This object is created via a call to the AQMsg() method of the OraAQ object. The OraAQMsg object represents the actual data payload for the message and the properties of the associated message in the RDBMS when it was queued.

The OraAQMsg object contains the following properties:

Correlation   Is used for organization when a message is enqueued.

Delay   Is used as a time delay before the message is enqueued.

ExceptionQueue   Specifies another queue to be used for error messages.

Expiration   Sets an expiration for the message.

Priority   Assigns a priority to the message.

The OraAQMsg object contains only one method:

AQAgent   Creates an OraAQAgent object

OraAQMsg Properties

The *OraAQMsg object* represents a message in a queue. Here are the properties exposed by the OraAQMsg object and a brief description of what they represent:

Correlation   This property is used when a message is enqueued. It specifies a correlation identifier that can be used to control the dequeuing of specific messages. The value of this property can be any string up to 128-bytes long. You might use this to assign a group identifier to a message or messages. The Dequeue operation can then be made specific to only one of the groups at a time by setting the correlate property of the OraAQ object to the group identifier you wish to retrieve messages for. Setting this property is optional. If the code that dequeues the messages does not use the OraAQ correlate property, it will not affect the message processing because it will be ignored. (See the description of the Correlate property of the OraAQ object earlier in this chapter.)

Delay   This property is used when the message is enqueued. It specifies an optional delay time, in seconds, before the message will be enqueued. The default is 0 (ORAAQ_MS_NO_DELAY), but it can be set to any positive integer value. For example, if it is set to 60, after the call to Enqueue() on the OraAQ object, it will be 60 seconds before a subsequent Dequeue() call will return this message.

ExceptionQueue   This property is used when a message is enqueued. It specifies the name of another Oracle Advanced Queue where this message should be posted if an error occurs during dequeuing. This will occur if the maximum number of dequeue attempts as specified in the DBMS_AQADM.CREATE_QUEUE() call is exceeded (see the max_retries parameter in the *Oracle8i Application Developers Guide – Advanced Queuing* manual), or if the message has expired (see the Expiration property of the OraAQMsg object later in this section). This allows for automatic routing of messages in the event that a message-related error occurs, such as a message expiring without being read by a consumer.

NOTE   In version 8.1.5 of the RDBMS, the default value for the max_retries parameter is 5.

Expiration   This property is used when a message is being enqueued. It specifies a time in seconds after which the message will expire and no longer be available for Dequeue operations. If a message expires, it may be sent to an exception queue (see the ExceptionQueue property of the OraAQMsg object). The default value is 0 (ORAAQ_MSG_NO_EXPIRE), in which case the message will never expire and will remain in the queue until it is read. This time is added to the delay time, so if 60 seconds is specified for both the delay and expiration times, the message will expire 120 seconds after the call to enqueue, and 60 seconds after it is available to be dequeued.

Priority   This property is used when a message is enqueued and allows you to force a sort order to the messages. This priority relates to the messages themselves and not to the users dequeuing them. A higher priority message is dequeued before a lower priority message. There is no way to prioritize which user will be the first to receive a message. The values of the Priority property are arbitrary integer values. Smaller numbers indicate a higher priority than larger ones. Negative numbers may be used, as well. If two messages have the same priority, the first one enqueued will be the first one dequeued (First In, First Out). If the Message Queue table was not created to use priority as a sort order item, the messages are sorted by their relative message ID (RelMsgId), which will sort them by their time of entry.

TIP In order to use the Priority property, the Message Queue table should be created with the Priority column specified in the SORT_LIST argument; otherwise, it will be ignored. Refer to the *Oracle8i Application Developers Guide – Advanced Queuing* manual for more details.

OraAQMsg Methods

The OraAQMsg has one method:

AQAgent This method will create and return an instance of an OraAQAgent for this message (see the "OraAQAgent" section later in this chapter). Each message can have a list of up to the value of ORAAQ_MAX_AGENTS associated with it.

NOTE The ORAAQ_MAX_AGENTS constant is defined in the `Oraconst.txt` file located in the OO4O installation Home directory. In version 8.1.5 of OO4O, the value for this is 10.

The AQAgent method accepts a single parameter, which is a string (30 bytes maximum) containing the name of the agent. (See also the "AQAgent Object" section later in this chapter for details on its use.) An example of using this method in Visual Basic follows:

```
Dim MyAgent as OraAQAgent
Dim OraQ as OraAQ
Dim OraM as OraAQMsg
.
. ' connect, create OraQ object & OraM object
.
Set MyAgent = OraM.AQAgent("SCOTT")
.
. ' other message specific operations
.
OraQ.Enqueue
```

In this example, Scott is a user to be associated with this message.

NOTE   Any database user can be specified, but only a user with Dequeue permissions on this particular queue will be able to see the message. For the purpose of the previous example, assume that user Scott has Dequeue permissions on the queue being used.

OraAQAgent

The *AQAgent object* represents an Advanced Queuing agent (a specified consumer of messages in this context). The AQAgent object is valid only for an Advanced Queue that was created with the Multiple Consumer option enabled (for more information, see the *Oracle8i Application Developer's Guide – Advanced Queuing* manual). Attempting to use an OraAQAgent object on a queue that was not created for multi-consumer use will generate an ORA-24039 error, "Queue *x* Not created in Queue table for Multiple Consumers," when the Enqueue() method is called on the OraAQ object. In this error message, *x* is the name of the queue being used.

OraAQAgent Properties

Here is a list of the properties available in OraAQAgent and a brief discussion of the functions that they perform:

Address   This property refers to the address of agents via a specific protocol (for more information, see the discussion on this in the *Oracle8i Application Developer's Guide – Advanced Queuing* manual). This property is currently not implemented for OO4O, so setting it has no effect.

Name   This is the name of a specific consumer. Because the OraAQAgent objects are associated with a specific OraAQMsg object, it will set a consumer name for the specified message. This controls the consumer name that will be used during the Enqueue operation. You use the Consumer property of the OraAQ object to specify the consumer name to be used for Dequeue operations (see the "OraAQ Object" section earlier in this chapter).

Building an Advanced Queuing Application

The example application will use the message queue created earlier in this chapter (see the "Creating the Message Queue" section) to send and receive messages via the RDBMS. The message content will actually be an Oracle ADT (the BBS_POST_TYPE object) that contains the data. In this example, only the TESTAQ user defined in the earlier section will be used. The example application assumes that you have already installed and configured OO4O (version 8.1.5 or later) and that the message queue and users discussed in previous sections have also been created.

The Basic Message Queue Functionality

Let's begin by creating an example application to demonstrate the basic message queue functionality. Start by opening the Visual Basic Designer's development environment and selecting a new project for a standard executable. You will see a default form (see Figure 12.2).

FIGURE 12.2
The VB Designer with a Standard EXE default form

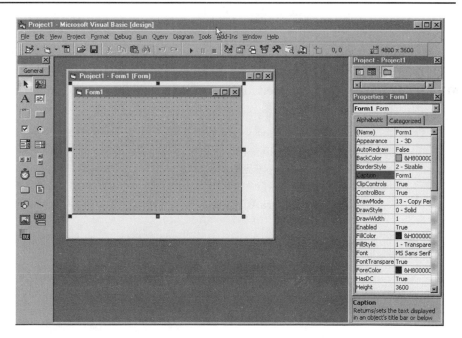

From the Project drop-down menu, select the References menu item. Scroll down the list and choose the Oracle Objects For OLE 3.0 Type Library check box (see Figure 12.3). Selecting this option allows early binding of the OO4O objects. (For more information on bound controls, see Chapter 5.)

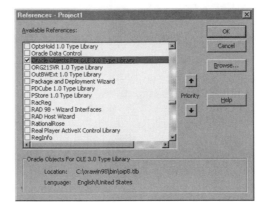

Add two Text Box Controls to the form, one above the other. Make the upper one single-line and the bottom one multiline. Expand the Bottom Control to allow several lines of visible text. Name the upper control ENQsubject and name the lower control ENQtext (where *ENQ* stands for Enqueue). Place a button directly under the lower Text Box Control and change the caption to Enqueue (see Figure 12.4). You can also place labels beside the form text fields if you like. This will be the enqueue portion of the application, where the messages are generated and submitted to the queue for processing.

Use a Line Control to split the form horizontally. Below the line, add three more Text Box Controls, one above the other. The top two should be single line; the bottom one should be multiline. Name the top one DEQdate, name the middle one DEQsubject, and name the bottom one DEQtext (where *DEQ* stands for Dequeue). As before, you can use Label Controls on the side of the text boxes to identify them to the user. Add a button below the bottom multiline Text Box Control. Label the button Dequeue (see Figure 12.5).

FIGURE 12.4
The Enqueue button
caption

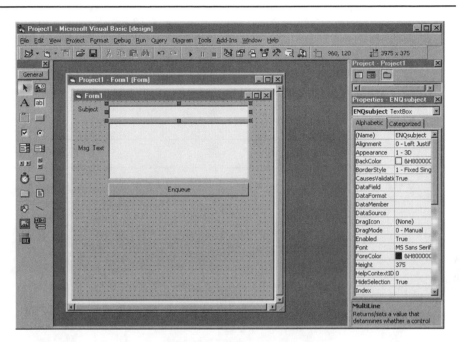

FIGURE 12.5
The Dequeue button
caption

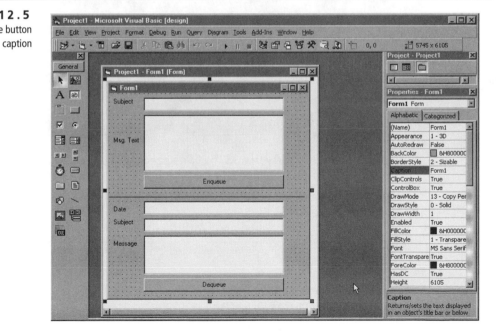

In the Project Navigator window, right-click the project name. From the Context menu, select Add and then select Add File. Scroll to the OO4O installation directory (normally, \Oracle81\OO4O) and select the Oraconst.txt file to include in the project (see Figure 12.6).

NOTE   The Oraconst.txt file contains all of the ORAAQ_XXXX constants used throughout the code.

FIGURE 12.6
The *Oraconst.txt* file

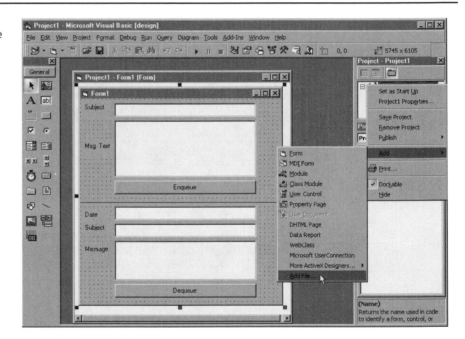

You are now ready to add the code needed to make the application function. Double-click the form to open the code-editing window. Pull down the Objects pick list and choose (General). Add the code in Listing 12.1 to the (Declarations) section of the form.

Listing 12.1

```
10 Dim MsgQ As OraAQ
20 Dim MsgObj As OraAQMsg
```

```
30 Dim MsgAgent As OraAQAgent
40 Dim OraObj As OraObject
50 Dim OraSession As Object
60 Dim OraDB As OraDatabase
```

NOTE   The numbering convention used in this chapter will allow you to build the basic AQ application and add functionality, such as priority messaging and correlation indentifiers. The gaps in the numbering represent the sequence you can use to merge the code together to create a single application.

Pull down the Object pick list and choose Form. Position the cursor in the Form_Load event and add the code in Listing 12.2.

Listing 12.2

```
100 ' Create an Oracle Session Object
110 Set OraSession = CreateObject( _
                           "OracleInProcServer.XOraSession")

120 ' Create an Oracle Database object for this session
130 ' MyAlias should be the actual TNS alias for the
140 ' database you are using
150 Set OraDB = OraSession.OpenDatabase("v8i", _
                      "testaq/testaq", 0&)

160 ' Create an AQ Object for the Queue to be used
170 Set MsgQ = OraDB.CreateAQ("BBS_MSG_QUEUE")


180 ' Create the message. BBS_POST_TYPE is a user
190 ' defined type
200 ' (ADT) in the "TESTAQ" schema
210 Set MsgObj = MsgQ.AQMsg(ORATYPE_OBJECT, _
                      "BBS_POST_TYPE", _
                      "TESTAQ")
```

Pull down the Objects pick list and choose Enqueue. Position the cursor in the Enqueue_Click event and add the code in Listing 12.3.

Listing 12.3

```
300 ' Set an error handler
310 On Error GoTo error_catch

340 If (ENQsubject.Text = "") Then
350  MsgBox ("Cannot Enqueue an Empty Message")
360  Exit Sub
370 End if

380 If (ENQtext.Text = "") Then
390  MsgBox (Cannot Enqueuq an Empty Message")
400  Exit Sub
410 End if

420 ' hourglass the cursor
430 Screen.MousePointer = vHourglass

440 ' begin the transaction
450 OraSession.BeginTrans

500 ' set the visibility of the messages. Since we have
510 ' an active transaction, we can use the
520 ' ORAAQ_ENQ_ON_COMMIT
530 ' mode for the visible property
540 MsgQ.Visible = ORAAQ_ENQ_ON_COMMIT

600 ' Create the ADT object for the message payload
610 Set OraObj = OraDB.CreateOraObject("BBS_POST_TYPE")

700 ' Populate the values for the object
710 ' note that these match the attributes we defined
720 ' for the BBS_POST_TYPE.
730 ' get the system date and format it to match the RDBMS
740 ' you can change the format to suit your needs
750 OraObj("posted").Value = Format(Date, "dd-mmm-yy")

800 ' Get the subject from the text field on the form
810 OraObj("subject").Value = ENQsubject.Text
```

```
900 ' get the message body from the text field
910 ' on the form
920 OraObj("body").Value = ENQtext.Text

1000 ' Set the value of the message to the ADT
1010 ' itself since
1020 ' this is the desired payload (The object)
1030 MsgObj.Value = OraObj

1480 ' Enqueue the message
1490 Msgid = MsgQ.Enqueue

1500 ' commit the transaction
1510 OraSession.CommitTrans

1600 ' clear the fields
1610 ENQsubject.Text = ""
1620 ENQtext.Text = ""

1700 ' un-hourglass the cursor
1710 Screen.MousePointer = vbDefault

1800 Exit Sub

1900 ' this is the error handling block
1910 error_catch:
1920 ' un-hourglass the cursor
1930 Screen.MousePointer = vbDefault
1940 ' Check to see if an Oracle error has occurred
1950 If OraDB.LastServerError <> 0 Then
1960    ' Yes, an Oracle error occurred
1970       MsgBox OraDB.LastServerErrText
1980 Else
1990       ' No, it was a different error
2000       MsgBox Err & " : " & Error(Err)
2010 End If
2020 Exit Sub
```

Even though it isn't required for this example, in line 450 of Listing 12.3, a transaction is started. In line 170 of Listing 12.2, an OraAQ object is created. In line 210 of Listing 12.3, this object is associated with the message queue created in the previous section (see the "Creating the Message Queue" section). In line 540 of Listing 12.3, transactional visibility is enabled for the messages being sent.

Enabling transaction visibility requires that you start and end a transaction (which is done in this example). Line 210 of Listing 12.3 is where the message is created. In line 610 of Listing 12.3, the message payload is created (the BBS_POST_TYPE). Lines 750 through 930 of Listing 12.3 populate the values on the message payload object (the BBS_POST_TYPE object) from the text fields on the form. In line 1030 of Listing 12.3, the message payload is set to the object. Line 1490 of Listing 12.3 performs the message Enqueue operation. In line 1510 of Listing 12.3, the commit that will make the message visible is issued. If the Visible property of the OraAQ object is left at the default value of ORA_ENQ_IMMEDIATE, the commit is not necessary. Lines 1600 through 1710 of Listing 12.3 restore the form to the defaults and restore the normal cursor so that the user will have a visual indication that the procedure is complete.

Lines 1900 through 2020 of Listing 12.3 are used only if an error is generated by OO4O or Visual Basic in the execution of the subroutine. Line 1930 of Listing 12.3 restores the cursor so that an error doesn't leave the busy cursor set. Line 1950 of Listing 12.3 checks the OracleDatabase object to see whether an Oracle error occurred. If so, the error information is displayed in line 1970 of Listing 12.3. If it wasn't an Oracle error, the error number and error text are displayed in line 2000 of Listing 12.3.

Return to the form by double-clicking the form name in the Project Navigator window. Double-click the Dequeue button to open the code-editing window. Add the code associated with the Dequeue button, as shown in Listing 12.4.

Listing 12.4

```
300 ' setup an error routine
310 On Error GoTo error_catch

400 ' hourglass the cursor
410 Screen.MousePointer = vbHourglass
420 ' clear the display of any previous values
430 DEQdate.Text = ""
440 DEQsubject.Text = ""
450 DEQtext.Text = ""
```

```
700 ' call dequeue to retrieve the message and populate
710 ' the OraAQMsg object
720 MsgQ.Dequeue

800 ' populate the OracleObject (ADT) from the value of
810 ' the message (the payload is of type ADT)
820 Set OraObj = MsgObj.Value

900 ' populate the date field from the POSTED
910 ' value of the object
920 DEQdate.Text = OraObj("posted").Value

1000 ' populate the subject field from the SUBJECT
1010 ' value of the object
1020 DEQsubject.Text = OraObj("subject").Value

1100 ' populate the msg. Text from the BODY
1110 ' value of the object
1120 DEQtext.Text = OraObj("body").Value

1200 ' done
1210 ' un-hourglass the cursor
1220 Screen.MousePointer = vbDefault
1230 Exit Sub

1300 ' here begins the error handler
1310 error_catch:
1320 ' un-hourglass the cursor
1330 Screen.MousePointer = vbDefault
1340 ' Check to see if an Oracle error has occurred.
1350 If OraDB.LastServerErr <> 0 Then
1360     ' are we at the end of the queue?
1370     If OraDB.LastServerErr = 25228 Then
1380         ' yes, display an informative message
1390             ' rather than an Oracle error
1400         MsgBox "Nothing to Dequeue"
1410     Else
1420         ' no, some other Oracle error occurred
1430         MsgBox OraDB.LastServerErrText
1440     End If
1450 Else 'Non-Oracle error
1460     MsgBox "VB:" & Err & " " & Error(Err)
```

```
1470 End If
1480 ' end of error handler
1490 Exit Sub
```

Lines 400 through 450 of Listing 12.4 clear the display fields of any previous values and set the cursor to busy so that the user has visual feedback that the subroutine is executing.

Line 720 of Listing 12.4 dequeues the message. In line 820 of Listing 12.4, the OraObject is created that represents the user-defined object that is the message payload (the BBS_POST_TYPE object). Lines 900 through 1120 of Listing 12.4 populate the form text fields with the data in the message payload. Lines 1200 through 1230 of Listing 12.4 are the clean-up and normal exit from the subroutine. Note that the cursor is returned to normal before exiting, giving the user a visual indication that the subroutine is complete.

Lines 1300 through 1490 of Listing 12.4 are only used when an error is generated by OO4O or Visual Basic in the execution of the subroutine. Line 1330 of Listing 12.4 restores the cursor so that an error doesn't leave the busy cursor set. Line 1350 of Listing 12.4 checks the OracleDatabase object to see if an Oracle error occurred. We can expect one normal error to occur: the ORA-25229 error. This error indicates that there are no further messages to retrieve. In line 1400 of Listing 12.4, this error is replaced with a more informative text message for the user. If another Oracle error occurs, it is displayed at line 1430 of Listing 12.4. If it isn't an Oracle error, the error number and error text are displayed at line 1450 of Listing 12.4.

NOTE   This example shows connecting to the database in the scope of the Form Load events. The OraSession and OraDatabase objects are defined in the (Declarations) section of the VB project.

You are now ready to run the application and test the Advanced Queuing features. On the Run menu, select the Start menu item from your project. Enter several messages and enqueue them. Use some way of identifying their order, perhaps with a unique subject line, such as Message #1, Message #2, and so on (see Figure 12.7).

FIGURE 12.7
Creating subject lines to
uniquely identify each
message

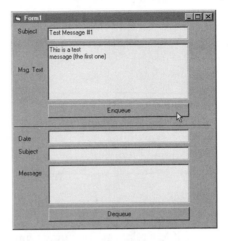

Now, try a Dequeue operation (see Figure 12.8). Do not dequeue all of the messages you sent, only the first one or two.

FIGURE 12.8
The Dequeue operation in
action

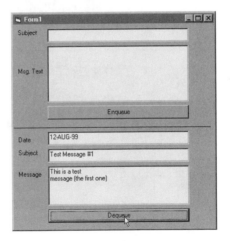

You should be able to retrieve and read the messages from the queue.

Priority and Correlation

Now, let's extend the previous application to include message priority and message correlation identifiers to demonstrate how to group and order messages as they are dequeued.

NOTE

For the Priority setting to be used during a Dequeue operation, the Queue table must be created with the Priority option set on the sort_order parameter of the DBMS_AQADM.CREATE_QUEUE_TABLE procedure. For more information, see the section "Creating the Message Queue," earlier in this chapter.

Start with resizing the form to allow enough space to add two more Text Box Controls and a set of radio buttons. Next, add a single-line Text Box Control and name it ENQcorrelation. You may want to add a Label Control for this form, as well. Add a Frame Control and size it to hold three option buttons. Set the caption for the Frame Control to Priority. Add the three Option Button Controls. Name them OptionLow, OptionNormal, and OptionHigh. Set the captions to Low, Normal, and High respectively (see Figure 12.9). Set the Value property of the Normal option button to True and leave the others at the default of False.

FIGURE 12.9
Adding the Priority frame, which has three buttons

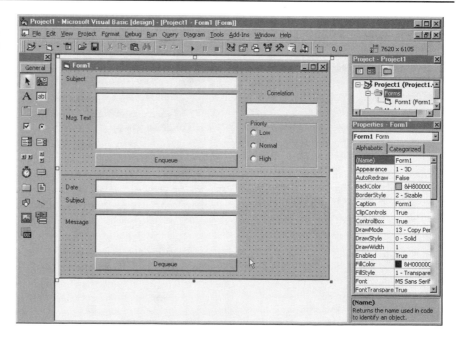

Switch to the code-editing window for the Enqueue button by double-clicking the button in the form editor. Add the code in Listing 12.5 to the Enqueue button. Click subroutine just before the call to MsgQ.Enqueue.

Listing 12.5

```
1100 ' set the priority of the message
1110 If OptionLow.Value Then
1120    MsgObj.Priority = ORAAQ_MSG_PRIORITY_LOW
1130 ElseIf OptionNormal.Value Then
1140    MsgObj.Priority = ORAAQ_MSG_PRIORITY_NORMAL
1150 ElseIf OptionHigh.Value Then
1160    MsgObj.Priority = ORAAQ_MSG_PRIORITY_HIGH
1170 End If

1200 ' set a correlation ID for the message if
1210 ' one was entered
1220 If Len(ENQcorrelation.Text) > 0 Then
1230    MsgObj.Correlation = ENQcorrelation.Text
1240 End If
```

Here, the use of the predefined priority constants is shown in lines 132, 134, and 136. You need not use these because any numeric value will work. The lower the value, the higher the priority. Negative values are perfectly legal, as well. The predefined values from the Oraconst.txt file are

```
ORAAQ_MSG_PRIORITY_LOW      =  10
ORAAQ_MSG_PRIORITY_NORMAL   =   0
ORAAQ_MSG_PRIORITY_HIGH     = -10
```

With a value of –10, the ORAAQ_MSG_PRIORITY_HIGH constant is the lowest value and, consequently, has the highest assigned priority.

Next, add a new single-line Text Box Control to the Dequeue section of the form (add a label for it if desired) and name it DEQcorrelation (see Figure 12.10).

FIGURE 12.10
Adding the Correlation
text box

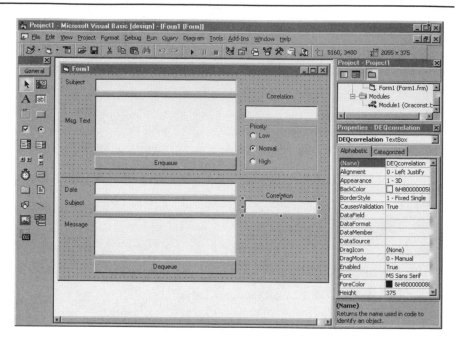

Open the code-editing window for the Dequeue button and add the code from
Listing 12.6 just before the call to MsgQ.Dequeue.

Listing 12.6

```
500 ' check for a correlation ID and set it if used
510 If Len(DEQcorrelation.Text) > 0 Then
520    MsgQ.Correlate = DEQcorrelation.Text
530 End If
```

Run the form and send several messages as follows:

- A message with a correlation ID, normal priority (see Figure 12.11)

FIGURE 12.11

A normal priority message with correlation

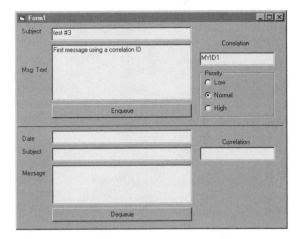

- A message without a correlation ID, high priority (see Figure 12.12)

FIGURE 12.12

A high priority message with no correlation

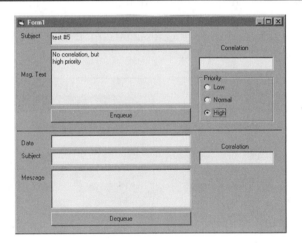

- A message with a correlation ID and a high priority (see Figure 12.13)

FIGURE 12.13
A high priority message
with correlation

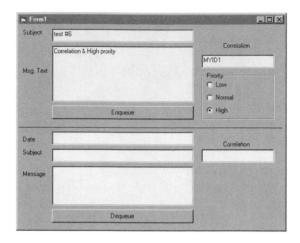

Again, use a unique subject line to identify how the messages are sent. Dequeue the next message without specifying a correlation ID. Because there were some messages left queued from the previous section, without the Priority field enabled, you expect the next message to be the first one dequeued. Instead, you see that the first high-priority message without a correlation ID is the one dequeued (see Figure 12.14).

FIGURE 12.14
A high priority message is
dequeued.

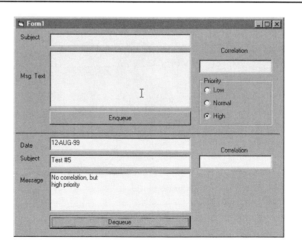

Dequeue the next message using a correlation ID. Use the same one specified on the Enqueue operation. The high-priority message with the correlation ID is the first one dequeued (see Figure 12.15).

FIGURE 12.15
Dequeuing the correlation
ID message

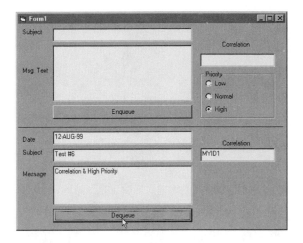

Dequeue the next message leaving the correlation ID value set. The normal-priority message sent using the correlation ID is the next message retrieved (see Figure 12.16).

FIGURE 12.16
Retrieving the next
message

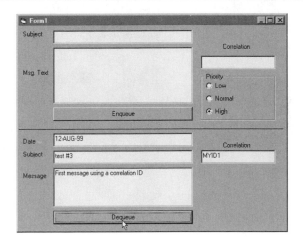

Click the Dequeue button again, leaving the correlation ID entered. You should see the message indicating that you are at the end of the queue. There are no further messages matching the specified correlation ID waiting to be dequeued (see Figure 12.17).

FIGURE 12.17
You're finished dequeuing.

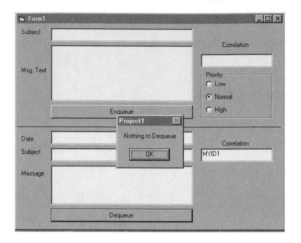

Finally, remove the correlation identifier (clear the Text Box Control) and dequeue the next message or messages. At last, the messages sent previously without a priority specified are seen (see Figure 12.18).

FIGURE 12.18
The previous messages are now seen.

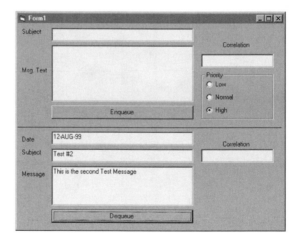

That's how the priority and correlation identifiers can be used to order and group messages in a specified queue.

Multiple Consumers

The message queue created for the previous example (see the section in this chapter titled "Creating the Message Queue") was a single-consumer queue. This means that only one agent reads the messages posted to the queue. If you want multiple agents subscribed to a queue and to be able to control message delivery to a specific agent, you need to alter the way the queue is created.

Altering the Example Queue

Using the example from the "Creating the Message Queue" section, the following steps allow you to alter the BBS_MSG_QUEUE (see the "Creating the Message Queue" section) to be a multi-consumer queue. First, run SQL*Plus and connect to the RDBMS as the TESTAQ user, then execute the following commands:

1. Stop the queue.

   ```
   EXECUTE dbms_aqadm.stop_queue(queue_name => 'BBS_MSG_QUEUE');
   ```

2. Next, drop the queue by entering this command at the SQL prompt:

   ```
   EXECUTE dbms_aqadm.drop_queue(queue_name => 'BBS_MSG_QUEUE');
   ```

3. Now, drop the queue table itself. It must be recreated with the multiple_consumer option set to True because multi-consumer is enabled at the Queue table level.

   ```
   EXECUTE dbms_aqadm.drop_queue_table(queue_table =>
   'TESTAQ.BBS_MSG');
   ```

4. Now, you can recreate the Queue table as a multi-consumer table by entering this command at the SQL prompt:

   ```
   EXECUTE
         dbms_aqadm.create_queue_table (
           queue_table => 'TESTAQ.BBS_MSG',
           Multiple_consumers => TRUE,
           sort_list => 'PRIORITY,ENQ_TIME',
           queue_payload_type => 'TESTAQ.BBS_POST_TYPE');
   ```

Notice that the only thing you have altered is the way the Message Queue table is defined.

5. Now, recreate the message queue and restart it by entering these commands at the SQL prompt:

```
EXECUTE
  dbms_aqadm.create_queue (
     queue_name  => 'BBS_MSG_QUEUE',
     queue_table => 'TESTAQ.BBS_MSG');

EXECUTE
        dbms_aqadm.start_queue (
           queue_name  => 'BBS_MSG_QUEUE');
```

In addition to altering the way the table is defined, if you are going to take advantage of the multi-consumer option, you need to alter your message-handling code slightly. You do not have to alter your code if you want every message to be delivered to every subscriber because this is the default behavior. But if the queue has no subscribers defined, you will get an Oracle error if you attempt an Enqueue operation without specifying at least one consumer. Likewise, if you attempt a Dequeue operation on a multi-consumer queue without first specifying a consumer name, an Oracle error will be returned because a multi-consumer queue must know who is consuming the message.

Use this anonymous PL/SQL block to add a named subscriber to the queue (for the purposes of this example, add at least one named subscriber):

```
declare
subscriber sys.aq$_agent;
begin
subscriber := sys.aq$_agent('FIRST', null, null);
dbms_aqadm.add_subscriber(queue_name => 'BBS_MSG_QUEUE', subscriber =>
subscriber);
end;
```

Refer to the *Oracle8i Application Developers Guide – Advanced Queuing* manual for the specific details of setting up messages queues and subscribers.

Here is a quick summary of the DBMS_AQADM.ADD_SUBSCRIBER() procedure. The parameters for the procedure are as follows:

Queue_name   This is the name of the queue the subscriber will be added to (a Varchar parameter).

Subscriber   This is an Oracle ADT (definition owned by user Sys) that describes the subscriber you are adding. The object is of type aq$_agent with the following members:

- name Varchar2(30)
- address Varchar2(1024)
- protocol Number

Rule   This is an optional Varchar parameter specifying a rule to apply to messages that will then decide if they are to be routed to the subscriber. For example, you might specify that only messages with a priority greater (or less) than a certain number are sent to the subscriber.

Altering the Example Application

Let's modify the example application code to support a multi-consumer queue. We'll start by enlarging the form and re-arranging some of the fields a bit to give you room to add more fields (see Figure 12.19).

FIGURE 12.19
Arranging the fields

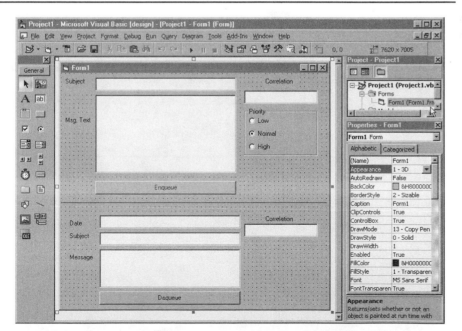

In the Enqueue section at the top of the form, add a new single-line Text Box Control and name it ENQconsumer. You can add a label if you like. Likewise, at the bottom of the form, in the Dequeue section, add a single-line Text Box Control and name it DEQconsumer (see Figure 12.20).

FIGURE 12.20
Adding the Text Box Controls to the form

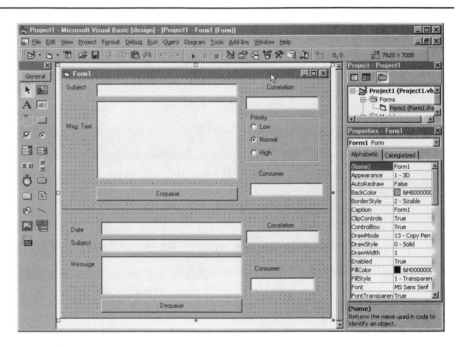

Next, add the following code just before the call to MsgQ.Enqueue (see Listing 12.3):

```
1300   ' set an agent if a consumer is specified
1310   If Len(ENQconsumer.Text) > 0 Then
1320     Set MsgAgent = MsgObj.AQAgent(ENQconsumer.Text)
1330   End If
```

NOTE   Up to 10 OraAQAgent objects can be associated with a single message in this fashion, each having a different subscriber specified.

In the Dequeue button command subroutine, add the following code just before the call to MsgQ.Dequeue (Listing 12.2):

```
600  ' set a consumer name if specified
610  If Len(DEQconsumer.Text) > 0 Then
620     MsgQ.Consumer = DEQconsumer.Text
630  End If
```

You are now ready to test the multi-consumer queue. Run the example application and enter a test message without specifying a consumer name (see Figure 12.21). This will enqueue the message to the default subscribers you associated with the DBMS_AQADM.ADD_SUBSCRIBER() procedure in the previous section, "Altering the Example Queue."

FIGURE 12.21

Running the example application

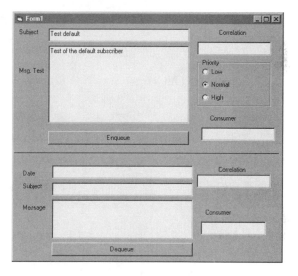

Next, send a message to a specific consumer by populating the ENQconsumer Text Box Control and selecting the Enqueue button (see Figure 12.22).

FIGURE 12.22

Sending a message to the consumer

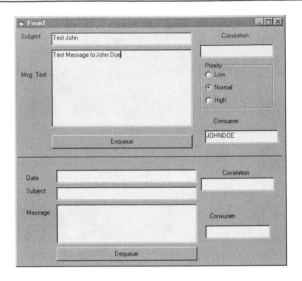

Populate the DEQconsumer Text Box Control with the name of the consumer you used in the previous step and select the Dequeue button (see Figure 12.23). You should be able to dequeue the message sent to that consumer.

FIGURE 12.23

Dequeue the message.

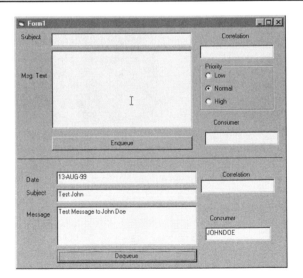

Substitute the name of the default consumer previously defined and select the Dequeue button (see Figure 12.24). You should see the message retrieved that was sent with no consumer name specified.

FIGURE 12.24
The retrieved message

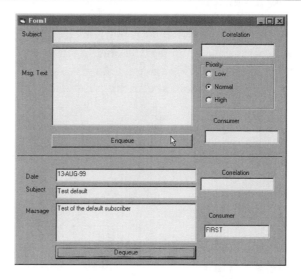

Finally, leave the DEQconsumer Text Box Control blank and select the Dequeue button. You should receive an Oracle error ORA-25231 (see Figure 12.25).

FIGURE 12.25
The Oracle error

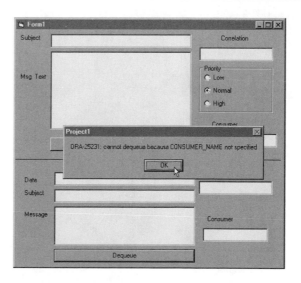

You have successfully created and demonstrated the use of a multi-consumer queue with OO4O.

Summary

In this chapter, you stepped through creating and using the Oracle Advanced Queuing features. The introduction of this feature into OO4O has opened the door to a much broader range of developers—previously only PL/SQL and OCI developers could take advantage of this technology. OO4O makes it extremely easy to access and manipulate the queuing mechanism in the RDBMS, and the completely customizable message payload gives you the ability to design a messaging application to suit your specific requirements.

chapter 13

Deploying Your Application

- Deployment considerations

- Using the Package and Deployment Wizard

- Using InstallShield™ with the Oracle ISV Development Kit

- Using InstallShield™ without the Oracle ISV Development Kit

- Troubleshooting installation problems

Once you have developed your application, the final step is to get it bundled up for delivery to your end users. In this chapter, we will cover the deployment and installation of your application onto the target systems.

Deployment Considerations

Deployment is generally the last, but certainly not the least, of the steps in developing an application. This is the stage where it all comes together and you deliver your application to the end user, which is the reason you wrote it. While you can resort to simply having the user copy files to their systems from your distribution media, this is hardly an optimal approach. A professional installation makes a much more positive first impression. A properly built installation will not only correctly install the product on the target systems but will also provide a method to uninstall the application should it need to be removed. Visual Studio 6 includes a Package and Deployment Wizard that can be used to build an installable package for your application. You can also use products, such as InstallShield™, to create your application distribution files. In this chapter, we will discuss both approaches to distribution.

TIP   It is a good idea to have "clean" machines available that you can do test deployments on to ensure that your installation is working as expected.

If you are distributing an application built using OO4O, you will need to include redistribution of these components in addition to any other third-party controls that you have used. The following is an installation checklist for the redistribution of an OO4O application. You need to make sure that the following components are installed on the target machine:

- Your application code and object dependencies, such as other OCX controls.

- The Oracle InProcess Server (Oip80.dll), Type Library (Oip8.tlb), Oraansi.dll, and Data Control (Oradc.ocx) if used. The InProcess Server and Data Control must be registered on the system, along with any other controls. Registry scripts are provided in the Oraipsrv.reg and OO4Oparm.reg files.

- Oracle client software. The `Oracle_Home\Bin` directory must also be included in the operating system search path.

- The Microsoft OLE redistributable common files should be updated to match the version distributed with Oracle Objects for OLE if any of the components on the target system are older. For a list of redistributable Microsoft components, refer to the Visual Studio installation CD-ROM. Look at the `Redist.txt` file in the `Common\Redist` directory.

- Internet Explorer 4.0 Service Pack 1 must be installed because some components included with this installation are required. There is no other authorized redistribution kit from Microsoft that contains these components.

If the machines on which your application will be deployed already have the Oracle client software installed and configured, it is important to match the version of the Oracle Required Support Files (RSF) to the version used by OO4O. For example, the 8.0.5.x version of OO4O requires that the 8.0.5.x version of the RSF and Net8 be installed on the target machine. The 8.1.x version requires the 8.1.x RSF and Net8 (version 8.1.x). Also make sure that any database connection information required by your program is updated on the target machine. If your application is expecting to use a specific Net8 service name or SQL*Net alias, make sure that the client has the same alias or service name configured.

The only supported way to install the Oracle client software is through the Oracle Installer. Creating your own custom installation scripts for the Oracle products can result in an Oracle installation that will not be recognized by the Oracle Installer as valid. This will preclude ever using the Oracle Installer to add, remove, or update any of the Oracle software on that machine. You can launch the Oracle Installer as part of your installation process or require that it already be installed. Oracle also provides the Oracle8i ISV Development Kit, which allows you to easily integrate the Oracle installation process with your own. This kit is available from Oracle directly (contact your account representative) or from the Oracle Technology Network (OTN) via the Internet at `http://technet.oracle.com/`. Registration for OTN is free.

WARNING The Oracle client software is a licensed product. Your target machines must have the necessary Oracle client licenses if you intend to redistribute Oracle software with your application.

We will look at the following deployment scenarios:

- Oracle client software is already installed. The installation is done via the Package and Deployment Wizard included with Visual Studio 6.

- Oracle client software is not installed. The installation is done with InstallShield™ and the Oracle ISV Development Kit to include installation of the Oracle software.

If the Oracle client is already installed, you can simply use the Package and Deployment Wizard to bundle the required files for the application and create an installation package. If the Oracle client software is not installed, you must use another method to combine installation of your own application with that of the Oracle software or simply require the Oracle Client installation to be performed first. The Oracle ISV Development Kit discussed here is one such option. OO4O includes a Minimal Install (or run-time) option that you can use via the Oracle Installer to ensure that the target machines have the correct versions of the OO4O libraries and Required Support Files installed.

Using the Package and Deployment Wizard

You will now step through building a deployment package of an OO4O application using the Package and Deployment Wizard.

TIP
For this example, you will be deploying one of the programs included with the OO4O installation (`Empgrid.exe`). As a preparation step to deployment, open the file containing the older project file (`Empgrid.mak`) in Visual Basic and choose the Save Project As option from the File menu to save the project as a Visual Basic 6 project file (`Empgrid.vbp`).

Launch the Package and Deployment Wizard from the Visual Studio 6.0 Tools menu item on the system Start menu. You will see the screen in Figure 13.1.

FIGURE 13.1

The Package and
Deployment Wizard

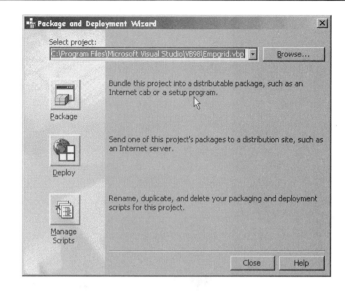

Use the Browse button to select the project file to be deployed. If the executable has not been built or if the project file revision date is newer than the executable build date, you will be prompted to build (or rebuild) the executable. The wizard will then analyze the project file for its dependencies. When the wizard has analyzed the project file, it will prompt you for the type of package you wish to create, as shown in Figure 13.2.

FIGURE 13.2

The Package and
Deployment Wizard –
Package Type screen

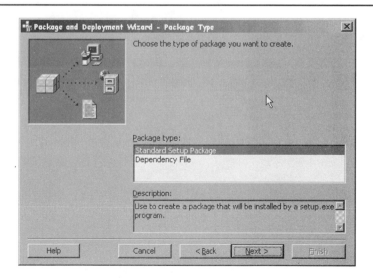

In the Package Type field, choose the Standard Setup Package option to create a deployment package for a normal executable application or program. The Dependency File is used when you are building components that will later be included in other deployment packages, such as OCX Controls or libraries. These dependency files will assist the wizard in quickly identifying all of the resources needed to deploy your custom components. It is advantageous to use these dependency files because the wizard can't automatically detect all dependencies.

After selecting the package type and clicking the Next button, you are prompted to select a folder in which to store the generated deployment package, as shown in Figure 13.3.

FIGURE 13.3
The Package and Deployment Wizard – Package Folder screen

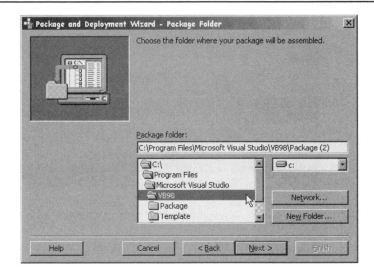

This screen sets the location where the wizard will store the generated Cab files, Setup.exe, and other files used during the installation process. If the folder does not exist, you are prompted to create it. Click the Next button to continue.

Since the project to be deployed uses the Oracle Data Control, you are presented with a dialog that warns you about missing dependency information, as shown in Figure 13.4.

FIGURE 13.4
The Missing Dependency
Information dialog box

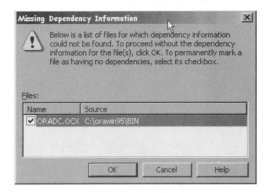

You can select the check box to prevent the wizard from warning you of this again in future deployments of OO4O projects. You will manually add the OO4O components and their dependent files, so select OK to proceed.

NOTE   If you already have or are intending to deploy the run-time version of OO4O using the Oracle Installer, you can overlook the OO4O dependency information and redistribution discussion here. Simply omit the steps referring to the OO4O components (and the files themselves) from the installation process.

You are now presented with a list of the files to be included in the deployment package, as seen in Figure 13.5.

FIGURE 13.5
The Package and
Deployment Wizard –
Included Files screen

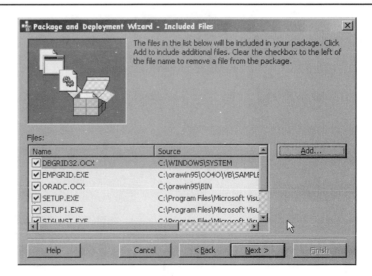

Make sure that the list includes the VB6 Runtime and OLE Automation components and that they are checked. If it does not, click the Add button and select this for inclusion in the project. Click the Add button and browse to the Oracle_Home\ Bin directory. Select the following files (one at a time) to be added to the deployment package:

- Oip8.dll
- Oip8.tlb
- Oraansi.dll
- Oraipsrv.reg
- OO4Oparm.reg

Once you have added all of these files to the package, click the Next button to proceed.

Editing the Registry Scripts

The Oraipsrv.reg and OO4Oparm.reg files require manual editing to correct the drive and path information. If you choose to install the Oip80.dll into the System/System32 directory, you need not include any path information for it. For example,

```
[HKEY_CLASSES_ROOT\CLSID\{3893B4A0-FFD8-101A-ADF2-
04021C007002}\InProcServer32]

@="c:\\orant\\bin\\oip8.dll"

"ThreadingModel"="Both"
```

becomes

```
[HKEY_CLASSES_ROOT\CLSID\{3893B4A0-FFD8-101A-ADF2-
04021C007002}\InProcServer32]

@="oip8.dll"

"ThreadingModel"="Both"
```

For the other entries, you must know the destination paths, such as the Oracle_Home directory location, on the target machine. Due to these restrictions, it is generally preferable to use the ISV kit unless you are in an environment where the configuration of the target machines is the same.

You are now presented with a screen prompting you to configure how the deployment package will deal with the included Registry scripts, as shown in Figure 13.6.

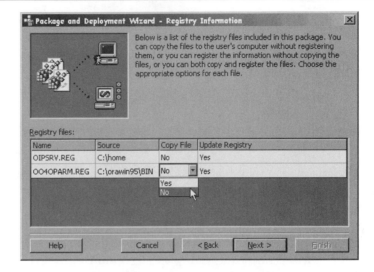

You do not need the files to actually reside on the target machine at runtime, only for them to be applied to the Registry during installation. If you do wish for these files to exist on the machine, select Yes for the Copy File option. In either case, the Update Registry option must be set to Yes for the program to operate correctly after installation.

When the Registry information is complete, select the Next button. The Options screen will appear, as shown in Figure 13.7. In this screen, you can select how the distribution Cab files are created.

FIGURE 13.7
The Package and
Deployment Wizard – Cab
Options screen

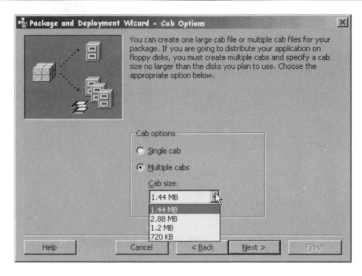

FIGURE 13.7
The Package and
Deployment Wizard – Cab
Options screen

If you will be distributing via a CD-ROM or other media large enough to hold the entire deployment package, you should choose the Single Cab option. Otherwise, choose the Multiple Cabs option and select the size appropriate to the media you will use for distribution. Select Next when you are done.

In the Installation Title text box, enter the file for your installation package, as shown in Figure 13.8. This will be displayed to the user when launching the setup program.

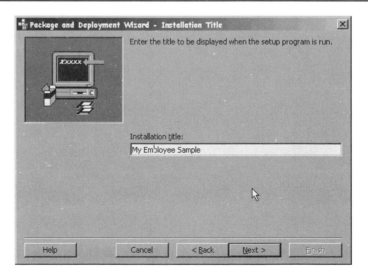

FIGURE 13.8
The Package and
Deployment Wizard –
Installation Title screen

When you are finished, click the Next button. The Start Menu Items screen appears, as shown in Figure 13.9. In the Start Menu Items field, select the Start Menu folder that will be created when your program is installed by editing the properties for the items.

FIGURE 13.9
The Package and
Deployment Wizard – Start
Menu Items screen

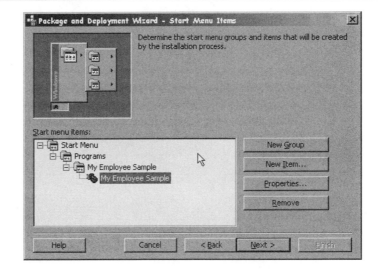

If you were deploying a Readme.txt file or multiple application executables, you can add menu items for them by selecting the New Item button and associating this item with the appropriate file from your package. You can also optionally change the folder that will be used for the default working directory of the program item to be executed.

When you have selected the appropriate Start menu items, click the Next button. The Install Location screen will appear, as shown in Figure 13.10. In this screen, you can alter the installation directories for the executables and any associated controls included in your package. By default, OCX Controls will be deployed into the Windows\System directory indicated by the $(WinSysPath) macro in the Install Location drop-down menu.

Normally, you don't alter the default locations for these components. If you wish to alter their location, a list of predefined macros is available to choose from. See the help included with the Package and Deployment Wizard for a detailed description of each macro.

FIGURE 13.10

The Package and
Deployment Wizard –
Install Locations screen

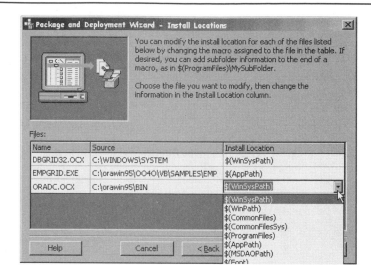

When you have selected the installation locations for the components, select the Next button. The Shared Files screen will appear, as shown in Figure 13.11. In this screen, choose the executables (if any) in your deployment package that are to be shared files. Since the executable in this example is not a shared component, you should leave the check box blank.

FIGURE 13.11

The Package and
Deployment Wizard –
Shared Files screen

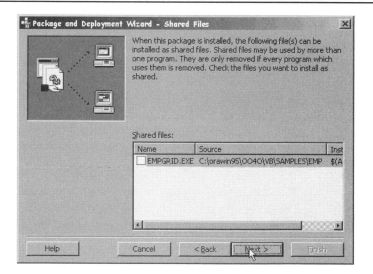

Click the Next button. The Finished! screen will appear, as shown in Figure 13.12. The last step before the package is created is to choose a name for the script used to create this package. Enter the name in the Script Name text box.

FIGURE 13.12
The Package and Deployment Wizard – Finished! screen

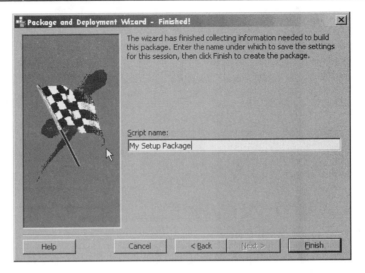

When you have entered the name, click the Finish button to start the deployment process. The packaged files will be copied into the deployment folder specified previously. When the deployment is complete, you will see a Packaging report detailing what was created, as seen in Figure 13.13.

FIGURE 13.13
The Packaging Report dialog box

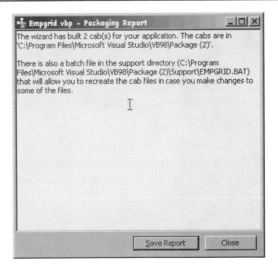

> **TIP**
> If File Not Found or other errors occur during packaging, the wizard may appear to hang while trying to display the report. You can simply close the Working dialog and return to the Deployment wizard to correct any errors.

Your installation is now ready to distribute and deploy. Simply copy the files from the deployment directory onto your distribution media. As you saw, the wizard is a fairly straightforward way to package and distribute your application. It doesn't offer as many options for the installation as InstallShield™ or some other installation programs do, but it will certainly do the job for most standard application installations.

Using InstallShield™ with the Oracle ISV Development Kit

> **NOTE**
> For more information on InstallShield™, try the following Web sites: `http://www.installshield.com` or `http://www.installsite.org`. Or review the documentation that is available with the product.

In this section, you will step through using InstallShield™ and the Oracle8i ISV Development Kit (IDK) to create the distribution package for your application. These instructions assume that you are already familiar with using InstallShield™ for packaging applications. It would require another book this size to discuss InstallShield™ in detail. But, we will discuss the basic use of InstallShield™ so that if you are considering using it, you can get a good idea of what is involved. But, the details of using the product will not be covered. InstallShield Professional™ version 5 will be used for this discussion.

The IDK consists of two main components: the deployment client and the InstallShield™ kit. The InstallShield™ kit has the files needed to integrate launching the Oracle Installer from InstallShield™ to install the necessary Oracle components in Silent mode. This makes the installation appear to be a single process.

Oracle Installer Silent Mode Operation

The Oracle Installer (version 3.x) has always contained a way to do "batch-type" installation (no prompting of the user for input) with a pre-built response file. This is referred to as *Silent mode installation*. If you need to do the exact same installation on many computers, you could go through the interactive mode once and generate the response file. This response file can be used in lieu of user interaction on subsequent installations. The details of this were not generally publicized because it was not supported by Oracle for customer use. The new Universal Installer for 8i products also supports this type of scripting, but the details of this were unavailable at the time of this writing.

The following is an example session using the 3.x Installer via the command line:

```
REM - THIS COMMAND WOULD INSTALL THE 7.3 REQUIRED SUPPORT FILES
ONLY
REM - AND GENERATE THE RESPONSE FILE. THE PRODUCT CODES ARE LISTED
REM - IN THE SPECIFIED PRD FILE

ORAINST /PRD D:\INSTALL\NT.PRD /INSTALL RSF73 /RSPDEST
C:\MYINSTALL\MINE.RSP

REM - THIS COMMAND WOULD USE THE SPECIFIED RESPONSE FILE AGAINST
THE
REM - SPECIFIED PRODUCT (PRD) FILE TO INSTALL THE 7.3 RSF

ORAINST.EXE /SILENT /PRD D:\INSTALL\NT.PRD /INSTALL RSF73 /RSPSRC
C:\MYINSTALL\MINE.RSP
```

To begin using InstallShield™ and the Oracle8i ISV Development Kit (IDK) to create the distribution package for your application, launch the InstallShield™ program. The initial screen is shown in Figure 13.14.

FIGURE 13.14
The InstallShield™ main
screen

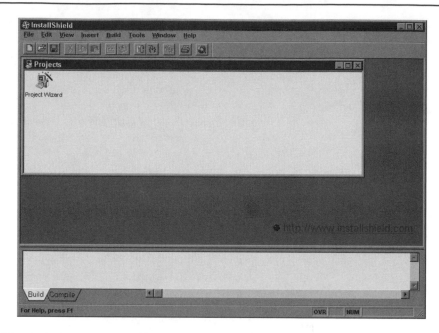

Double-click the Project Wizard to start building your installation. The Welcome screen will appear, as shown in Figure 13.15.

FIGURE 13.15
The Project Wizard –
Welcome screen

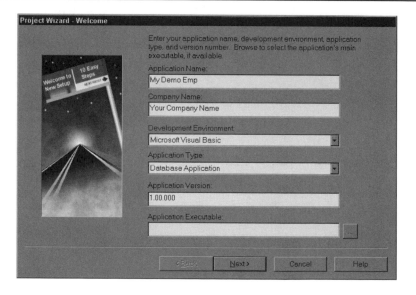

This is where you will specify the general information about your program. Use the Browse (…) button to locate the installation executable file. (We are again using `Empodc.exe` for this demonstration.) Select the Next button when you have filled in the appropriate information. The Choose Dialogs screen will appear, as shown in Figure 13.16.

FIGURE 13.16
The Project Wizard –
Choose Dialogs screen

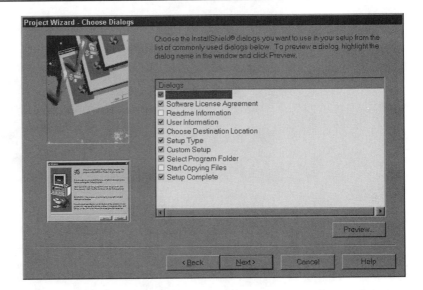

Here you choose the basic style and layout of the installation package. This screen controls the types of information dialogs that the user is required to select during the setup. For example, you may require them to accept a license agreement before completing the installation. For the purpose of this example, simply accept the default check boxes that are selected. When you are finished, click the Next button. The Choose Target Platforms screen will appear, as shown in Figure 13.17.

In the Operating System field, choose the operating systems that you wish InstallShield™ to support with your distribution. This allows you to configure differing versions of the components to be targeted for the various operating systems. Selecting the operating systems will highlight the chosen platforms. This example will use only Windows NT 4 and Windows 95/98 as target platforms.

FIGURE 13.17
The Project Wizard –
Choose Target Platforms
screen

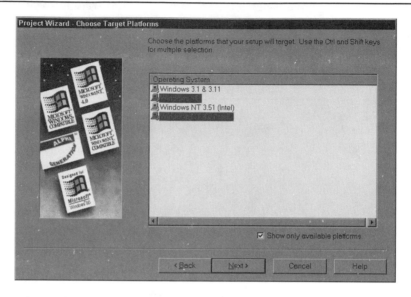

When you have chosen the appropriate operating systems, click the Next button. The Specify Languages screen will appear, as shown in Figure 13.18.

FIGURE 13.18
The Project Wizard – Specify
Languages screen

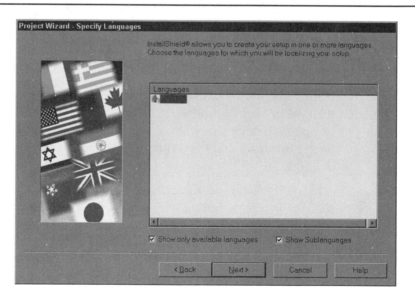

In the Languages field, select the languages that will be supported by your installation package. InstallShield™ (depending upon the version purchased) can generate installation kits for many different languages, allowing you to provide international support. Selecting the languages to be used will highlight them. English is the default language. Currently, the Oracle ISV kit supports only English, so this is all that will be discussed for this example.

When you have selected the appropriate languages, click the Next button. The Specify Setup Types screen will appear, as shown in Figure 13.19.

FIGURE 13.19
The Project Wizard – Specify Setup Types screen

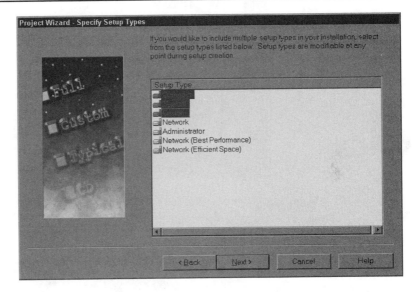

In the Setup Type field, select the types of installations you want to generate support for. The common ones are Typical, Compact, or Custom. But you can choose from several other options here, and you can create your own after the wizard completes. A Compact installation might omit example files or help files. The Custom install lets the user define which components to include. You must choose at least Typical for the purposes of this example, although you may choose more if you like.

When you have chosen the appropriate setup type, click the Next button. The Specify Components screen will appear, as shown in Figure 13.20.

In the Components field, you can define the program groups that will exist in your installation kit. The groups defined here will later be associated with the installation types that were previously defined (see Figure 13.19). The program groups you define will in turn contain file groups (the specific files to be installed). The wizard lists typical groups for you to select from. You can create your own by using the Add button. For the purposes of this example, simply use the defaults.

FIGURE 13.20

The Project Wizard – Specify Components screen

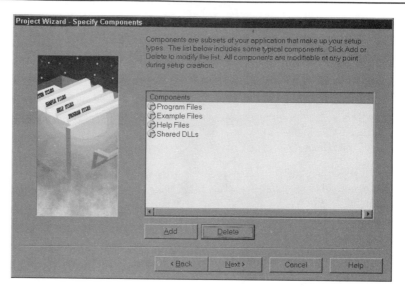

When you have specified the appropriate components, click the Next button. The Specify File Groups screen will appear, as shown in Figure 13.21.

FIGURE 13.21

The Project Wizard – Specify File Groups screen

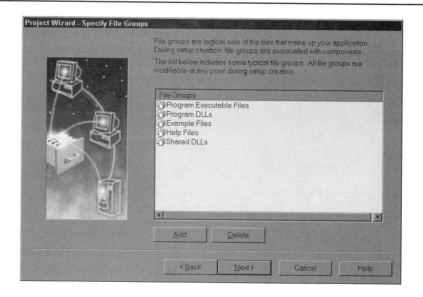

In the File Groups field, select which component groups will exist. There is often a one-to-one mapping for the component groups to the file groups used, but not always. If you have an Examples component group, it might contain several different file groups (perhaps Visual Basic examples and C++ examples). This is simply a logical relationship to assist the developer during deployment. You can add more groups by using the Add button. For the purpose of this example, use the defaults.

When the file groups are specified, click the Next button. The Summary screen will appear, as shown in Figure 13.22.

FIGURE 13.22
The Project Wizard –
Summary screen

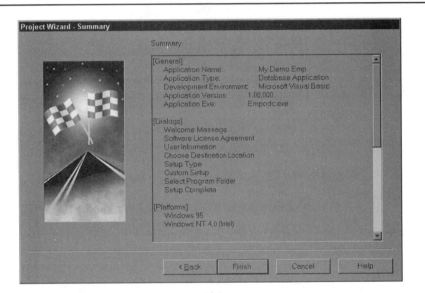

The Summary field lists the options that the wizard will generate for your project. If all is in order, select the Finish button to create the shell project. Figure 13.23 shows the completed project.

FIGURE 13.23
The Project Wizard is
finished.

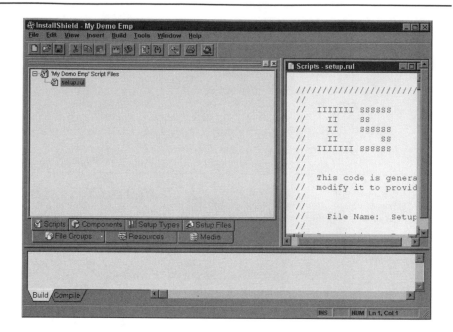

At this point, you have a shell project completed and ready to begin building your deployment package. If you run through the setup as it exists now, you will be presented with all the dialogs and choices that you selected, but no files would actually be installed. There are several more steps yet to complete before you will have a working installation. There are two possibilities at this point: Either you already have a working Oracle installation on the target machine and you only need to distribute your application, or you must redistribute some or all of the Oracle client software with your application. First, we will cover getting your application-specific components to install; then we will use the Oracle ISV Development Kit to include all or part of the Oracle software with your installation.

Starting from the shell project that you created, select the File Groups tab in the project folder. Expand the Program Executable Files group folder and select the Links icon. This is where links to the files for this component are entered. This link tells InstallShield™ where to locate the files for this project. Right-click the Links icon and select Insert Files. . ., as shown in Figure 13.24.

FIGURE 13.24
Selecting the Insert Files. . .
menu item

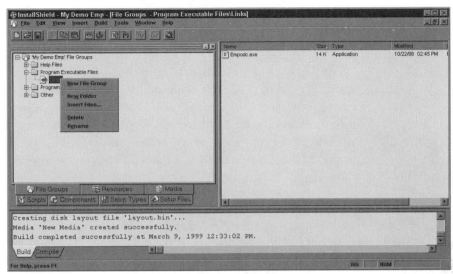

Browse to the location of the application executable (`Empodc.exe` for this example), select it, and confirm that the link was entered into the group. You will see the `Empodc.exe` listed in the Links Properties dialog box. Select the Program Executable Files group folder. In the Properties dialog box, you will see the options for files in this group, such as shared, compressed, or self-registered.

WARNING   Select the Self-Registered option only if *all* of the files in this group can be self-registered. Otherwise, an error will be returned during the installation process.

For this application executable, the only option you will use is Compressed. Set this option to Yes. If any help or documentation files are to be included, they can be added into the Help Files group folder. Since this group folder is not used for this example, it can be deleted (right-click and select Delete). Likewise, all other groups, except the Program Executable Files group, can be deleted.

The next step associates a given program group with a logical group—the installation components. Any one component can contain one or more program groups. The installation component groups are what the user sees as selectable items during a Custom installation. The group File Need property controls the importance of the individual group to the installation. Some files are critical (without them, the installation will not function), while others are optional components that do not affect the installed program's operation.

For this example, associate the program executable with the Program Files group. To do this, select the Components tab, highlight the Program Files component group, and double-click the Included File Groups in the Properties dialog box. You can also navigate here by right-clicking the Program Files component, selecting the Properties item from the context menu, and then selecting the Included File Groups tab. Click the Add button and select the Program Executable Files group.

TIP
Without this step, InstallShield™ will not actually copy any files during the installation since it has no information about which parts of the program belong to the component groups. If your installation silently fails to deploy anything, this is the first place to check for an error.

For your own programs, you would continue to add the other program groups to the various component groups as appropriate for your installation.

You are now ready to include the Oracle components. For the purposes of this example, it is assumed that you already have the Oracle ISV Deployment Kit, which includes both the InstallShield™ kit and the DeploymentClient or DeploymentServer kits, in a staging directory.

Staging the Deployment Client

When you extract the DeploymentClient archive, it will extract a number of files under the Win32 directory tree relative to the staging folder. When you are staging these files on your own media, you should include the Win32 directory tree and all the files in it under the root directory for your installation executable (**Setup.exe**). For example, if your setup is to be launched from a **\Install** subdirectory on a CD-ROM, the **\Win32** directory tree will exist directly under the **\Install** directory (**\Install\Win32**...). The scripts used presume that this directory structure exists when executing.

The DeploymentClient kit includes more components than you may require to customize the installation of the Oracle products to suit your needs, such as JDBC drivers, ODBC drivers, and a Web publishing assistant. You must edit the Orainst.ini file included with the ISV kit. Look for the [SETUP_GROUP] section:

```
[SETUP_GROUP]
clientnt=Client;nt;20,5,18,19,8,3,10,23,24,27,28
server=Server;nt;5,18,19,24,27,28,7,12,25,23
client95=Client;w9x;29,18,19,24,27,28,30
```

These are the setup types that will be presented to the user during the installation script.

NOTE   Only one type of client will be offered, based upon the platform. The Installer will automatically determine the operating system being used (NT or 9x).

The numbers in the list are the associated Oracle components that will be installed. Look for the [COMPONENTS] section:

```
[COMPONENTS]
1=dbassist;Oracle Database Assistant
2=dbmig;Oracle Data Migration Assistant
3=jdbc;Oracle8 JDBC Drivers
4=ntagent;Oracle Intelligent Agent
5=ntinstall;Oracle Installer
6=ntnames80;Oracle Names Server
7=ntnetsrv80;Oracle Net8 Server
8=ntobject80;Oracle Objects for OLE Runtime
9=ntoco80;Oracle8 ConText Cartridge
10=ntodbo3220;Oracle8 ODBC Driver
11=ntperfmon;Oracle8 Performance Utility
12=ntrdbms80;Oracle8 Server
13=ntsnmp80;Oracle SNMP Agent
14=owast20;Oracle Web Publishing Assistant
15=w32a2owiz80;Oracle Migration Assistant for Microsoft Access
16=w32ctx;Oracle8 ConText Cartridge Workbench
17=w32doc80;Oracle Documentation
18=w32net8a80;Oracle Net8 Assistant
19=w32netclt80;Oracle Net8 Client
20=w32oci80;Oracle Call Interface
```

```
21=w32oem10;Oracle Enterprise Manager
22=w32oemsdk10;Oracle Enterprise Manager SDK
23=w32plus80;SQL*Plus
24=w32tcp80;Oracle TCP/IP Protocol Adapter
25=w32util80;Oracle8 Utilities
26=w32vom;Oracle Administrator Toolbar
27=w32nmp80;Oracle Named Pipes Protocol Adapter
28=w32spx80;Oracle SPX Protocol Adapter
29=w95install;Oracle Installer
30=w95odbo3220;Oracle8 ODBC Driver
31=w95object80;Oracle Objects for OLE Runtime
```

The [COMPONENTS] section breaks out the individual components to be installed (note that some are operating-system specific) and corresponds to the numbers in the lists for each of the installation types.

For a minimal installation of OO4O, you will need the following:

- SQL*Net/Net8 (including the appropriate protocol adapters)
- Oracle Objects for OLE Runtime
- Oracle Required Support Files

You should have a [GROUP_LIST] section similar to the following:

```
[SETUP_GROUP]
clientnt=Client;nt;5,19,24,27,28,8
client95=Client;w9x;29,19,24,27,28,31
```

The server item is completely omitted since you are only interested in a working client. The example [GROUP_LIST] section shown previously installs the following items:

- Oracle Installer
- Net8 client
- TCP/IP, Named Pipes and SPX protocol adapters
- Oracle Objects for OLE Runtime

If you so desire, you need include only the protocol adapter(s) specific to your network.

WARNING   You still must stage the entire Deployment Client package on your distribution media. The Oracle Installer will only install the specified components.

Select the Scripts tab from the InstallShield™ project screen. From the menu that appears, select Insert, then select Files Into Script Files. Browse to the ISV kit staging directory and insert both the `Orainst.rul` and `Orainst.h` files into the script files section, as shown in Figure 13.25. You insert them by double-clicking the files you want to insert.

FIGURE 13.25

Inserting the script files

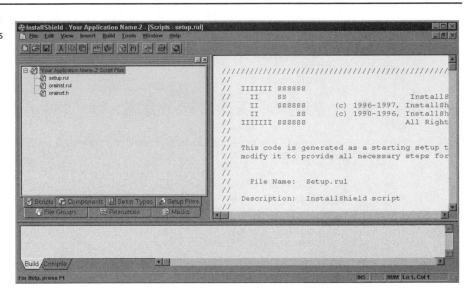

Select the Setup Files tab in InstallShield™. In the Language Independent\ Operating System Independent group (see Figure 13.26), insert the following files from the ISV kit:

- `Orainst.ini`
- `Oralogo.bmp`
- `Startus.bmp`

FIGURE 13.26
Inserting the BMP files

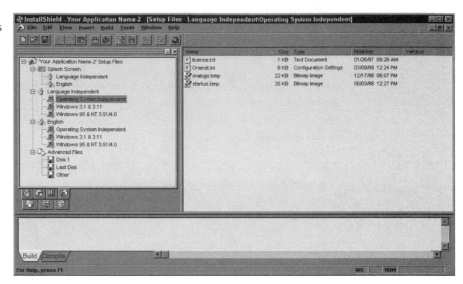

Return to the Scripts tab. Double-click the Setup.rul file. This is your setup script. Look for these lines near the beginning of the file:

```
// Include header file
#include "sdlang.h"
#include "sddialog.h"
```

and change them to the following:

```
// Include header file
#include "sdlang.h"
#include "sddialog.h"
#include "orainst.h"
#include "winsub.h"
```

Now, look for the following lines near the end of the file:

```
// --- include script file section ---
#include "sddialog.rul"
```

and change them to read as follows:

```
// --- include script file section ---
#include "sddialog.rul"
#include "orainst.rul"
#include "winsub.rul"
```

You are now ready to add the code to your script to invoke the Oracle Installer as part of your installation. Typically, the Installer is called with the MoveFile-Data() function, although you can invoke it at any point during the installation script processing. The default MoveFileData() function processes the Component-MoveData() function, which extracts the setup files from the compressed distribution (Cab) files and puts them into the target directory. Listing 13.1 calls the MoveFileData() function to launch the Oracle Installer:

Listing 13.1

```
//////////////////////////////////////////////////////
// Function:  MoveFileData
//  Purpose:  This function handles the data movement for
//            the setup. //
//////////////////////////////////////////////////////
function MoveFileData()
    NUMBER nResult, nDisk;
 begin
  // Initialize control variables.
  // These variables take precedence
  // over other ways of passing information
  // to be used to install Oracle.
  // If these variables have an empty value,
  // as below, the call to
  // install_oracle() will read orainst.ini
  // to get its values, if it is
  // not found in the .ini file, it will ask
  // the user for it (by displaying dialog boxes).
  svORACLE_HOME = "";
  svORACLE_SOURCE = "";
  svCOMPANY_NAME = "";
  svSEED_DATABASE = "";
  svDOC_ON_DISK = "";
  svSETUP_TYPES = "";
  svCOMPONENTS_LIST = "";
  nDisk = 1;
  SetStatusWindow( 0, "" );
  Disable( DIALOGCACHE );
  Enable( STATUS );
```

```
StatusUpdate( ON, 100 );
nResult = ComponentMoveData( MEDIA, nDisk, 0 );

HandleMoveDataError( nResult );

Disable( STATUS );
if (nResult = 0) then
  // Installs Oracle if ComponentMoveData succeeded
  install_oracle();
endif;

return nResult;

end;
```

Listing 13.1 will launch the Oracle installation steps if the ComponentMove-Data() function is successful in extracting your installation package.

Figure 13.27 shows the Select Install Directory dialog box. This screen shows the path where Oracle will be installed.

FIGURE 13.27

The Select Install Directory dialog box

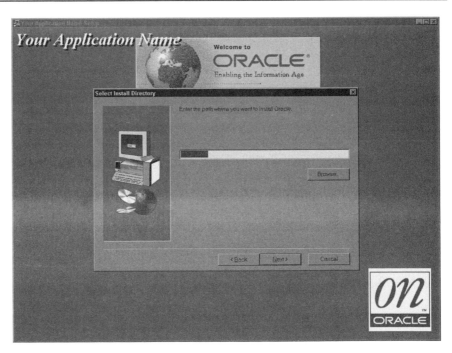

Next, the Oracle Source dialog box appears, as shown in Figure 13.28. This dialog box shows the default source path for the Oracle installation.

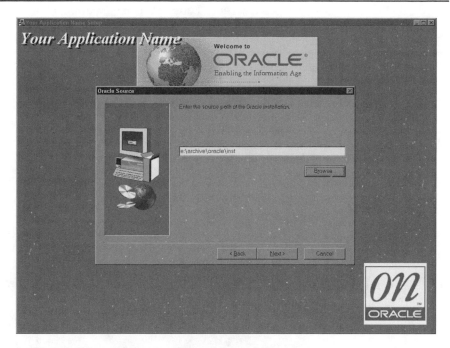

Next, the User Information screen appears, as shown in Figure 13.29. This screen shows the user information entered on installation.

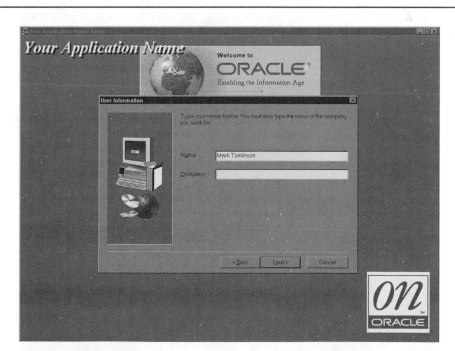

Next, the Select Oracle Type Setup screen appears, as shown in Figure 13.30. This screen shows the Oracle installation type that was specified.

FIGURE 13.30
The Oracle Type Setup screen

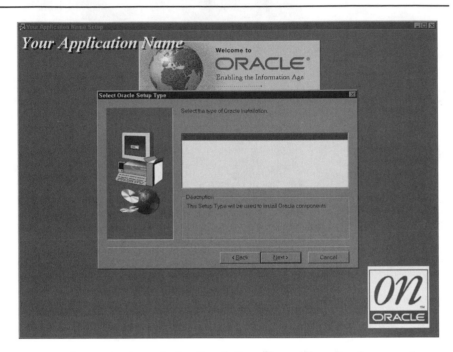

Select the Next button to launch the Oracle Installer with no further user intervention required. The Oracle Installer will install the appropriate client packages and return control back to InstallShield™. You must now compile the source and then build the distribution media, and you will be ready to deploy your program using a setup program created by InstallShield™.

WARNING Remember that one of the conditions for using the ISV Development Kit is that your target machines do *not* have an existing Oracle installation. Deploying into an existing Oracle installation can result in an unusable Oracle client. This will likely change with later versions of the ISV kit.

Using InstallShield™ without the Oracle ISV Development Kit

If you choose, you can redistribute just your application and a version of the OO4O run-time distribution files using only InstallShield™. The redistribution challenges to this type of bundling are

- Ensuring that the target machines have an Oracle client (of the correct version) correctly installed and configured

- Registering the InProcess Server component

- Preventing a conflict with any pre-existing OO4O applications

If you know that all of your target machines are already going to have an Oracle client (including OO4O installed), none of these issues will matter. Assuming that the correct Oracle client is already installed, another option is to register the InProcess Server (using the values in the `Oraipsrv.reg` file) via the InstallShield™ Registry APIs. Substitute the correct path information where required. This will require that you prompt the user to determine the location of the Oracle Home directory. You can always install the InProcess Server into the `Windows\System` directory, which would obviate the need for much of the path information. But in doing so, you run the risk of conflict with another installation of OO4O (either already existing or installed later).

There are future plans to incorporate a run-time only installation of OO4O in the development seat installation. This gives you a single executable to include with your installation that can be launched as a part of your installation and will install only the run-time components of OO4O.

Troubleshooting Installation Problems

Installation problems for applications using Oracle Objects for OLE can be roughly divided into three types:

- Problems with the application installation

- Problems with the Oracle client installation

- Problems with the OO4O redistribution

Identifying the correct problem area will help you to quickly resolve it.

At the beginning of this chapter, there is a note about the advantages of having a "clean" machine on which to test your installation procedures. What exactly does the word *clean* mean? It means that the machine or machines to be used for testing represent the typical fresh installation of your expected client base. For example, if you expect that your clients will have both Windows 98 and Windows NT installed as the operating system, you should have one of each to test on. The installed software should be set up and configured the same as your clients will be. For example, if they already have a certain version of the Oracle client software installed, you should have the same installation prestaged on your test systems.

Problems with the Application Installation

If the Installer is simply not installing the correct components, or is installing them in the wrong places, you need to revisit the installation scripts. Carefully examine these to ensure that you have correctly specified the actions that you desire. It is very easy, particularly with InstallShield™, to make an error in the scripts or to skip a step needed for the installation to be successful. If you are using the Deployment Wizard, make sure that you have correctly identified all of the dependencies for your application.

If the Installer is causing a General Protection Fault (GPF) or other access violations, make sure that you have the latest version of the Installer component, including any service packs or patches. You need to do the same for the operating system, as well. Also, look at the machine hardware configuration and make sure that it is sufficient for the Installer to run correctly. Access violations or GPFs are usually caused by a hardware problem, such as insufficient memory.

Problems with the Oracle Client Installation

If your application cannot connect to the Oracle database, check the following:

- You have the alias correctly configured for the TNSNAMES.ORA entry or that the Net Names Server alias is defined.

- The \Bin directory just below the Oracle Home directory (for example, \OraWin95\Bin) is in the system search path. As you will see, not having this correctly set can also lead to other problems.

If you have SQL*Plus also installed on the client, this is the best tool to test your client installation and connectivity with. If you do not have this installed, the client installation also includes a command line utility called TNSPING, which can be used to test connectivity for a specified TNS alias. The command line syntax for the program is as follows:

```
TNSPING myalias
```

where myalias is the alias to be tested. Here is a sample session:

```
C:>TNSPING testORCL
TNS Ping Utility for 32-bit Windows: Version 8.1.5.0.0 - Production on
25-MAR-00
   17:00:43

(c) Copyright 1997 Oracle Corporation.  All rights reserved.

Attempting to contact
(ADDRESS=(PROTOCOL=TCP)(HOST=127.0.0.1)(PORT=1521))
   OK (340 msec)

C:\>
```

If this fails, you need to troubleshoot the Oracle client installation. Most likely, the TNSNAMES (or Net NAMES server) configuration is wrong. Check what you have entered for the alias configuration using the Net8 Easy Config application and verify that the protocol, machine name, and SID (or Net8 service name) are all correct. If you are using TCP/IP, try to ping the other machine's host name or IP address, as shown here:

```
C:>ping www.oracle.com

Pinging www.us.oracle.com [205.227.44.44] with 32 bytes of data:

Reply from 205.227.44.44: bytes=32 time=210ms TTL=240
Reply from 205.227.44.44: bytes=32 time=210ms TTL=240
Reply from 205.227.44.44: bytes=32 time=200ms TTL=240
Reply from 205.227.44.44: bytes=32 time=200ms TTL=240

Ping statistics for 205.227.44.44:
    Packets: Sent = 4, Received = 4, Lost = 0 (0% loss),
Approximate round trip times in milli-seconds:
    Minimum = 200ms, Maximum =  210ms, Average =  205ms

C:>
```

If you can't successfully ping the machine, your TCP/IP networking is incorrectly installed or configured.

Problems with the OO4O Redistribution

If you are receiving OO4O OLE Automation errors when attempting to run your application, you have a problem with the OO4O redistribution. First, verify that you did redistribute all of the required components, including any needed updates to the OLE common files.

NOTE   The OLE common files dependency is generally picked up for you if you use the Package and Deployment Wizard or InstallShield™.

TIP   The most common problems are failure to set the system search path to include the `Oracle_Home\Bin` directory and failure to have the correct version of the Oracle networking components installed.

Check to make sure that the required Registry entries were made and are pointing to the correct locations for the OO4O binaries.

The following lines are the Registry entries for OO4O version 8.1.5 as they appear in a Registry script file. If you are using a version other than 8.1, check your version's installation Registry scripts for specifics.

NOTE   These defaults in the `Oraipsrv.reg` file assume that the Oracle Home directory is `C:\Oracle\Ora81`.

```
[HKEY_CLASSES_ROOT\OracleInProcServer.XOraSession]
@="Oracle Objects For OLE 3.3"
[HKEY_CLASSES_ROOT\OracleInProcServer.XOraSession\Clsid]
@="{3893B4A0-FFD8-101A-ADF2-04021C007002}"

; Version independent registration for OraServer
[HKEY_CLASSES_ROOT\OracleInProcServer.XOraServer]
@="OraServer"

[HKEY_CLASSES_ROOT\OracleInProcServer.XOraServer\Clsid]
@="{5CEA8296-F9B9-11d1-9E07-00C04FC2BED8}"
```

```
; Class ID registration for OraSession
[HKEY_CLASSES_ROOT\CLSID\{3893B4A0-FFD8-101A-ADF2-04021C007002}]
@="Oracle Objects For OLE 3.3"

[HKEY_CLASSES_ROOT\CLSID\{3893B4A0-FFD8-101A-ADF2-
04021C007002}\InProcServer32]
 @="c:\\oracle\\ora81\\bin\\oip8.dll"
 "ThreadingModel"="Both"

[HKEY_CLASSES_ROOT\CLSID\{3893B4A0-FFD8-101A-ADF2-04021C007002}\ProgID]
@="OracleInProcServer.XOraSession.3"

[HKEY_CLASSES_ROOT\CLSID\{3893B4A0-FFD8-101A-ADF2-
04021C007002}\VersionIndependentProgID]
 @="OracleInProcServer.XOraSession"

; Class ID registration for OraServer
[HKEY_CLASSES_ROOT\CLSID\{5CEA8296-F9B9-11d1-9E07-00C04FC2BED8}]
@="OraServer"

[HKEY_CLASSES_ROOT\CLSID\{5CEA8296-F9B9-11d1-9E07-
00C04FC2BED8}\InProcServer32]
 @="c:\\oracle\\ora81\\bin\\oip8.dll"
 "ThreadingModel"="Both"

[HKEY_CLASSES_ROOT\CLSID\{5CEA8296-F9B9-11d1-9E07-00C04FC2BED8}\ProgID]
@="OracleInProcServer.XOraServer.1"

[HKEY_CLASSES_ROOT\CLSID\{5CEA8296-F9B9-11d1-9E07-
00C04FC2BED8}\VersionIndependentProgID]
 @="OracleInProcServer.XOraServer"

; TypeLib registration for OraServer
[HKEY_CLASSES_ROOT\TypeLib\{F2D4ED20-FFD3-101A-ADF2-04021C007002}]

[HKEY_CLASSES_ROOT\TypeLib\{F2D4ED20-FFD3-101A-ADF2-04021C007002}\3.0]
@="Oracle Objects For OLE 3.0 Type Library"

[HKEY_CLASSES_ROOT\TypeLib\{F2D4ED20-FFD3-101A-ADF2-
04021C007002}\3.0\0]
```

```
[HKEY_CLASSES_ROOT\TypeLib\{F2D4ED20-FFD3-101A-ADF2-
04021C007002}\3.0\0\win32]
  @="c:\\oracle\\ora81\\bin\\oip8.tlb"

[HKEY_CLASSES_ROOT\TypeLib\{F2D4ED20-FFD3-101A-ADF2-
04021C007002}\3.0\409]

[HKEY_CLASSES_ROOT\TypeLib\{F2D4ED20-FFD3-101A-ADF2-
04021C007002}\3.0\409\win32]
  @="c:\\oracle\\ora81\\bin\\oip8.tlb"

[HKEY_CLASSES_ROOT\TypeLib\{F2D4ED20-FFD3-101A-ADF2-
04021C007002}\3.0\HELPDIR]
  @=";US english"

[HKEY_LOCAL_MACHINE\SOFTWARE\ORACLE]
"OO4O"="c:\\oracle\\ora81\\OO4O\\mesg"

;OO4O home
[HKEY_LOCAL_MACHINE\SOFTWARE\ORACLE\OO4O]
"CacheBlocks"="20"
"FetchLimit"="100"
"FetchSize"="4096"
"HelpFile"="C:\\oracle\\ora81\\MSHELP\\oracleo.hlp"
"PerBlock"="16"
"SliceSize"="256"
"OO4O_HOME"="C:\\oracle\\ora81\\oo4o"
"TempFileDirectory"="c:\\temp"
```

Summary

Getting OO4O and the Oracle client installed and configured correctly is as essential to a working application as the application code itself. There are a few challenges that need to be overcome with a run-time installation of OO4O, particularly if you do not use the Oracle ISV kit bundled with your installation. But, the steps needed to install the runtime are fairly straightforward once you understand what all the dependencies are. This chapter covered what you need to know to successfully deploy your application. A professional deployment is the final step in delivering the power and functionality of your application to your end users.

chapter 14

Using the Oracle OLE DB Provider

- An overview of OLE DB

- Connecting to an Oracle database in your application

- Querying the database using the ADO command and recordset objects

- Working with BLOBs, CLOBs, and BFILEs

- Working with the ADO Data Control

- An overview of transactional support

This chapter focuses on how to write Visual Basic applications using the ADO object model and the Oracle OLE DB Provider. *OLE DB* is Microsoft's new data access model for accessing and manipulating data. ADO stands for ActiveX Data Objects, and it enables you to write an application to access data in a database using an OLE DB Provider. The benefits of using ADO are good performance, a simple programming model, and the minimal system resources required to run applications efficiently. In Chapter 2, you reviewed the ADO model and should have a good understanding of this interface. The Oracle OLE DB Provider is being released as a production driver with Oracle version 8.1.6 for Windows NT.

An Overview of OLE DB

OLE DB is a specification written by Microsoft Corporation. It describes an API that allows applications to connect and retrieve data from a persistent store. This persistent store can be an SQL database or a flat file. The specification is some-times referred to as the universal strategy for data access. This standard was writ-ten to replace the ODBC specification that has been in existence for many years and will probably be deprecated if OLE DB follows the same path. OLE DB com-prises two basic components, a consumer and a Provider, as seen in Figure 14.1. The *consumer* is an application, and the *provider* is a driver or middleware that translates the data into viewable form.

FIGURE 14.1
OLE DB components

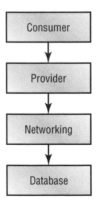

The Oracle OLE DB Provider is actually a set of COM interfaces that imple-ments the OLE DB specification. The Provider has attributes specific to Oracle, like PLSQLRSet, which are discussed later in this chapter. Let's start by looking at the installation and system requirements.

Installation and Oracle System Requirements

To use the Oracle OLE DB Provider, you need to have access to an Oracle Database version 7.3.4 or later and an Oracle 8.1.6 client. Your system also must meet the following requirements:

- Windows 95/98, Windows NT 4, Windows 2000
- Oracle Server release 7.3.4 or later
- Oracle8i client release 8.1.6 or later

Installing the Oracle OLE DB Provider

To start using the Oracle OLE DB Provider with your Visual Basic application, you will need the following component installed:

- Net8 client 8.1.6
- Oracle OLE DB Provider 8.1.6

If this is your first Oracle installation, the Universal Installer will install the selected products and will also guide you through the process of configuring a Net8 service name. After the initial installation, the Universal Installer will not take you through the net configuration and will install only the products that you selected. This section will guide you through the installation of the OLE DB Provider but will assume that you already have a basic Oracle client installed. If this is a new installation, refer to Chapter 1 for guidance on installing the Oracle client pieces.

NOTE   You must have Administrator privileges to complete the installation.

Place the Oracle8i CD-ROM in the CD-ROM drive. There are three ways to begin the installation:

- Use the Autostart function.
- Use the Windows Explorer to launch the Setup.exe file.
- Use the Run command to launch the Setup.exe file.

If the CD-ROM autostarts, you will see the image in Figure 14.2. From here, click the Install/Deinstall Products button. The next screen is the Welcome dialog box.

FIGURE 14.2

The Oracle Universal
Installer main installation
screen

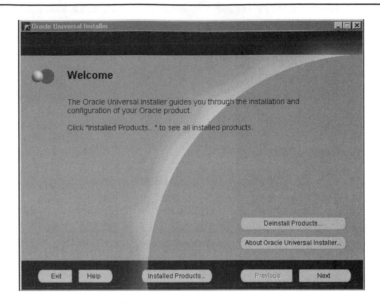

If the CD-ROM does not autostart, you can use Windows Explorer to start the setup application. Use the Windows Explorer to navigate to the CD-ROM drive and click the drive letter to refresh the screen with the directories and files from the CD-ROM. Figure 14.3 illustrates how the directory structure should look.

FIGURE 14.3

The directory listing of the
CD-ROM drive

Once the screen is refreshed, locate the Setup.exe file. Figure 14.4 has the Setup.exe file highlighted. Execute this file by double-clicking it. The Welcome screen will appear.

FIGURE 14.4
The *Setup.exe* file

If you wish to run the installation without using Windows Explorer, you can use the Run command to type in the location and name of the setup application. Figure 14.5 illustrates how this looks if the CD-ROM is located on the F drive. When finished, click the OK button, and the Universal Installer will display the Welcome screen.

FIGURE 14.5
Using the Run command to run the Universal Installer

The main installation screen provides you with a number of different buttons. The Deinstall Products and Installed Products buttons enable you to de-install products or get a list of products that are already installed in the Oracle8i Home. Click the Installed Products button to see a list of currently installed products, as shown in Figure 14.6.

FIGURE 14.6
A list of installed products

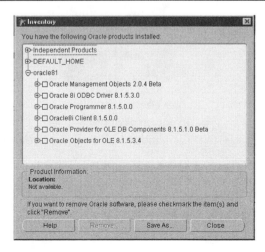

Once you have verified that the Oracle client components are installed, click the Back button to return to the main installation screen. Click the Next button to continue.

Figure 14.7 displays the next screen for the installation. The File Locations screen is the first screen where you will provide input. The Source field is the file system path, or location to the file that lists the products that are available to install. The Destination field describes where the Oracle Home is physically located and also defines the name of the Oracle Home. Since you are installing on a machine with an existing version of the Oracle8i client, make sure that the location and name for your Oracle8i Home are selected.

The Path area is the physical path where the products will be installed. Once you have verified that the location is correct, click the Next button to continue to the next screen.

FIGURE 14.7

The Oracle Universal Installer File Locations screen

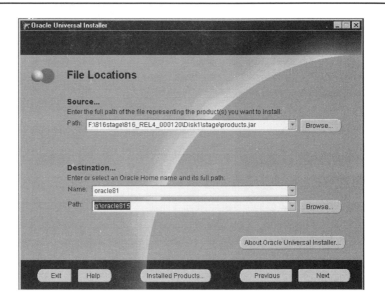

When the Next button is clicked, you are notified that the Universal Installer is loading information about products. Figure 14.8 displays the dialog box that shows that the Universal Installer is preparing for the installation.

FIGURE 14.8
The Loading Product Information dialog box

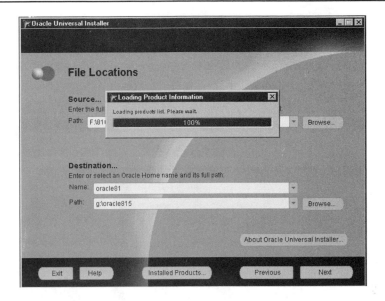

Once the Universal Installer is ready, the screen in Figure 14.9 appears, providing you with three different installation options and a brief explanation of each. You can choose from the following options:

- Oracle8i Enterprise Edition 8.1.6.0.0

- Oracle8i Client 8.1.6.0.0

- Oracle Programmer 8.1.6.0.0

NOTE   At the time of this writing, only the Oracle8i Enterprise Edition CD-ROM was available. In the future, there may be an Oracle8i Client CD-ROM or Programmer CD-ROM. In any case, these installation options may differ.

Choosing the Oracle8i Client option allows you to install the Oracle OLE DB Provider, which is the component you are interested in.

FIGURE 14.9

The Oracle Universal
Installer Available Products
screen

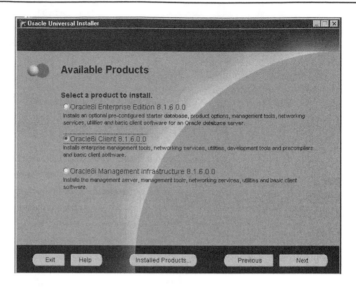

The next screen prompts you for the installation type. Figure 14.10 shows you the available types. The first three options are default pre-determined installations, and the last option is a Custom installation. Select a Custom installation to get the products in this chapter installed quickly and easily. After selecting the Custom installation option, click the Next button.

FIGURE 14.10

The Oracle Universal
Installer Installation Types
screen

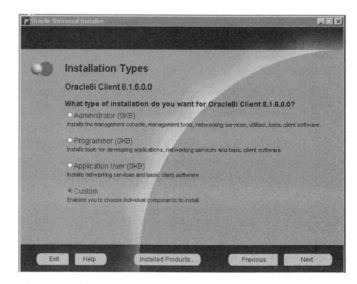

Figure 14.11 illustrates the next screen, which lists the products installed and the products available for installation. Look to the right of each product for a status of

the components. The screen provides an overview of the products to be installed along with other information. Scroll down through the list and locate the OLE DB Provider. Choose the product by selecting the check box to the left of the label. Click the Next button to continue.

FIGURE 14.11

The Oracle Universal Installer Available Product Components screen

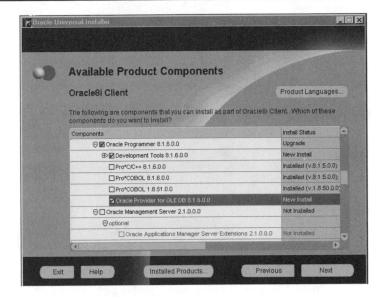

When the Next button is clicked, the Universal Installer will display a message indicating that it is loading product information, as seen in Figure 14.12.

FIGURE 14.12

The Available Product Components screen with the Loading SQL*Plus progress bar

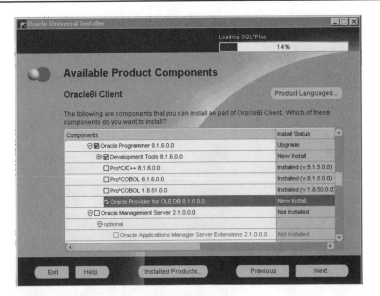

The next screen is the Component Locations screen, where you specify the location of the Runtime Environment (see Figure 14.13). Click Next to continue.

FIGURE 14.13
The Oracle Universal
Installer Component
Locations screen

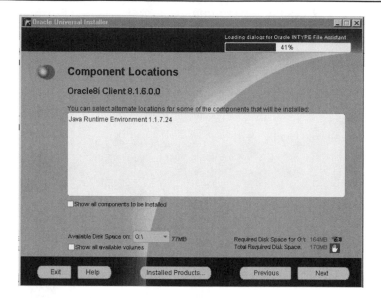

The next screen presents you with an Install button to actually start the installation. The Summary screen displays a list of products to be installed. Once the Install button is clicked, the Universal Installer displays the screen in Figure 14.14. This screen provides a progress bar to update you on the status of the installation. When the initial installation is complete, the End Of Installation screen appears.

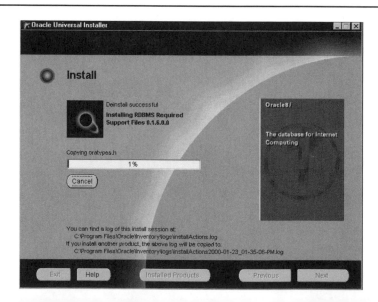

This final screen is the End Of Installation screen. From this screen, you can view the installed products, install additional products, or click the Exit button to exit the Universal Installer. If you click the Exit button, the Exit dialog box will appear to confirm that you want to exit, as seen in Figure 14.15.

FIGURE 14.15
The Exit dialog box

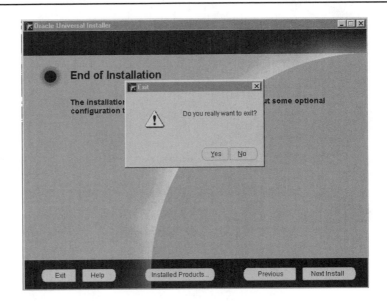

Click the Yes button to exit the Universal Installer.

NOTE   After installing on Windows 95/98, the machine must be rebooted.

If your installation is on Windows 95/98, the machine will need to be rebooted so that the environment variable path can be updated. On Windows NT, this is already taken care of. The reboot only has to be done the first time Oracle products are installed.

Once the installation is complete, view the changes that the Universal Installer has made to the machine. The changes include the addition of an OLE DB directory underneath the Oracle Home directory. Table 14.1 shows the files installed on the system that enable the Provider to work properly.

TABLE 14.1:   Oracle OLE DB Provider Installation Summary

File	Description	Destination
OraOLEDB.dll	The Oracle OLE DB Provider	Oracle_home/bin
OraOLEDBrfc.dll	The Oracle rowset file cache manager	Oracle_home/bin
OraOLEDBrmc.dll	The Oracle rowset memory cache manager	Oracle_home/bin
OraOLEDBrst.dll	The Oracle rowset	Oracle_home/bin
OraOLEDBgmr.dll	The Oracle ODBC SQL parser	Oracle_home/bin
OraOLEDBpus.dll	Property descriptions	Oracle_home/bin
OraOLEDButl.dll	The Oracle OLE DB utility	Oracle_home/bin
OraOLEDB.tlb	The Oracle OLE DB Type Library	Oracle_home/bin
OraOLEDB.h	The Oracle OLE DB header file	Oracle_home/oledb/
OraOLEDB.lib	The Oracle OLE DB import library	Oracle_home/oledb/
Readme.txt	The Oracle OLE DB Provider release notes	Oracle_home/oledb/
Oledb.pdf	The Oracle OLE DB Provider User's Guide in PDF format	Oracle_home/oledb/
.html files	The Oracle OLE DB Provider User's Guide in HTML format, including TOC.html	Oracle_home/oledb/

NOTE   The OraOLEDB.h and OraOLEDB.lib files are for use with MSVC ++ 6 and the Native OLE DB interface.

The second change is the new menu items added to the System menu. These changes can be viewed by clicking the Start button on the desktop and navigating to the Programs menu item. From the Programs item, you will see Oracle-OraHome81 if you accepted the default value. If not, you will still see Oracle, but it will be followed by the name you provided. Under this menu item, there are two more menu items, Application Development and Network Administrator, which represent the products selected during the installation in the previous section.

The Application Development menu item houses SQL*Plus and Oracle OLE DB product shortcuts. Figure 14.16 shows how the menu layout may look.

FIGURE 14.16
Application Development
shortcuts

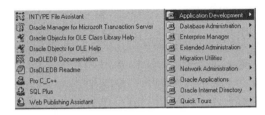

The Network Administrator menu item houses the following three applications:

- Net8 Assistant

- Net8 Configuration Assistant

- Net8 Easy Config

Its layout looks similar to Figure 14.17.

FIGURE 14.17
The Network Administrator

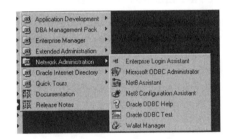

Now that you have successfully installed the Oracle OLE DB Provider, you are ready to use the Provider in your Visual Basic applications. The next section discusses how to use the ADO connection object to make the connection to your Oracle database.

Connecting to an Oracle Database in Your Application

In order to run or execute any SQL statements using the OLE DB Provider, you must first make a connection to the Oracle database. You will use the ADO connection object to make this connection and set Provider specific attributes. Listing 14.1 shows you how to create the connection object and what attributes to set with the Oracle OLE DB Provider. At a minimum you will need to set the Provider, Data Source, User ID, and Password attributes to make a successful connection.

Listing 14.1

```
1  Dim democon As ADODB.Connection
2  Set democon = New ADODB.Connection
3  democon.ConnectionString = "Provider=OraOLEDB.Oracle; " _
   & "Data Source=v8i;" _
   & "User ID=scott;Password=tiger;"
4  democon.Open
```

Analysis

- Line 1 declares the ADO connection object.

- Line 2 creates an instance of the ADO connection object.

- Line 3 sets the ConnectionString property of the ADO connection object, using the following Provider attributes:

  - Provider = OraOLEDB.Oracle

  - Data Source = v8i

  - User ID = scott

  - Password = tiger

- Line 4 calls the Open method to establish the connection to the database.

The Oracle OLE DB Provider has several other Provider-specific attributes that can be set in the connection string property of the ADO connection object. Table 14.2 lists the attributes and their definitions.

TABLE 14.2: Oracle OLEDB Provider Connection String Attributes

Attribute	Definition
FetchSize	This attribute is used to set the size of the array fetch. This determines how much data will be fetched in a network round-trip.
CacheType	This attribute is used to set the type of cache used to store the rowset on the client side. CacheType can be either memory or file.

TABLE 14.2:   Oracle OLEDB Provider Connection String Attributes *(continued)*

Attribute	Definition
ChunkSize	This attribute specifies the size of Long or Long Raw data stored in a Provider-specific cursor.
OSAuthent	The attribute is used to specify if OS authentication is going to be used when connecting to an Oracle database.
PLSQLRSet	This attribute is used to enable parsing of PL/SQL blocks. This attribute must be set to 1 if you want to call a stored procedure that returns a result set.
PwdChgDlg	This attribute is used to enable or disable the Change Password dialog box displayed by the Provider when a logon attempt fails because the user's password has expired.

The default values for these attributes are stored in the Registry at \\HKEY_LOCAL_MACHINE\SOFTWARE\ORACLE\OLEDB.

The default values are listed here:

- FetchSize = 100
- CacheType = Memory
- OSAuthent = 0
- PLSQLRSet = 0
- ChunkSize = 100
- PwdChgDlg = 1

Connecting Using OS Authentication

The Provider gives you a specific attribute or property to set when you want your application to connect to the database using OS authentication. This attribute is called OSAuthent. OSAuthent is set to either 0 (zero) or 1. The default is 0, which means do not use OS authentication. If this attribute is set to 1, you do not need to pass a username and password. The Provider will pass the appropriate OS logon information to the security manager on the server. The server will then authenticate you or return an error to the Provider. A second approach would be to pass a "/" (forward slash) in the User ID attribute before calling the Open method. You can find additional information on using OS authentication in the *Oracle8i Enterprise Edition Getting Started Release 8.1.5.0.0 for Windows NT* manual.

Listing 14.2 demonstrates a simple ADO program that connects to the Oracle database using OS authentication.

Listing 14.2

```
1  Dim democon As ADODB.Connection
2  Set democon = New ADODB.Connection
3  democon.ConnectionString = "Provider=OraOLEDB.Oracle;OSAuthent=1;" _
   & "Data Source=v8i"
4  democon.Open
```

Analysis

- Line 1 declares the ADO connection object.

- Line 2 creates an instance of the ADO connection object.

- Line 3 sets the ConnectionString property of the ADO connection object, using the following Provider attributes:

  - Provider = OraOLEDB.Oracle

  - OSAuthent = 1

  - Data Source = v8i

- Line 4 calls the Open method to establish the connection to the database.

Passing Parameters to the Open Method Call

The ADO connection object has a Provider property that is used to indicate which specific OLE DB Provider you are using in your application. When calling the Open method of the connection object, you can also pass connection-specific attributes, such as User ID, password, and data source, instead of setting these in the connection string property of the ADO connection object. The attributes are enclosed in single quotation marks and are passed directly as string literals when making the Open method call. Listing 14.3 shows you how this may be done.

Listing 14.3

```
1  Dim democon As ADODB.Connection
2  Set democon = New ADODB.Connection
3  democon.Provider = OraOLEDB.Oracle
4  democon.Open "v8i","scott","tiger"
```

Analysis

- Line 1 declares the ADO connection object.

- Line 2 creates an instance of the ADO connection object.

- Line 3 sets the Provider property of the ADO connection object to Ora-OLEDB.Oracle.

- Line 4 calls the Open method to establish the connection to the database. Three parameters are passed to the Open method call directly overriding the ConnectionString property:

  - Data Source as "v8i"

  - User ID as "scott"

  - Password as "tiger"

WARNING   Be careful when passing parameters to the Open method of the connection object as this will override all attributes that may have been set in the ConnectionString property. For a demonstration of this problem, see Listing 14.4.

Listing 14.4 demonstrates how passing connection parameters directly to the Open method can cause errors. In Listing 14.4, the PLSQLRSet attribute is set to 1 to allow the Provider to enable result sets in the application. (PLSQLRSet will be discussed in detail in the section titled, "Returning Result Sets from Stored Procedures.") But we also passed the data source, username, and password directly to the Open method, so the PLSQLRSet attribute is overridden. Instead of getting set to 1, the PLSQLRSet attribute stays at the default of 0 (zero). If you want to return a result set, you must set the PLSQLRSet attribute to 1 so that the Provider knows to handle the details of returning result sets to the Visual Basic program. Because we passed parameters directly to the Open method, an error occurs when the application tries to return a result set from a stored procedure.

Listing 14.4

```
1  Dim democon As ADODB.Connection
2  Set democon = New ADODB.Connection
3  democon.Provider = OraOLEDB.Oracle
4  democon.ConnectionString = PLSQLRSet=1
5  democon.Open "v8i","scott","tiger"
```

Analysis

- Line 1 declares the ADO connection object.

- Line 2 creates an instance of the ADO connection object.

- Line 3 sets the Provider property of the ADO connection object to "Ora-OLEDB.Oracle".

- Line 4 sets the ConnectionString property of the connection object. The Provider attribute PLSQLRSet is set to 1.

- Line 5 calls the Open method to establish the connection to the database. Three parameters are passed to the Open Method call directly overriding the ConnectionString property:

  - Data Source as "v8i"

  - User ID as "scott"

  - Password as "tiger"

Enabling the Password Expiration Feature

The Oracle OLE DB Provider has an attribute to turn on and off the Oracle8i Password Expiration feature. The attribute name is PwdChgDlg, and it enables and disables the OraOLEDB Password Change dialog box generated by the Provider when the user's password has expired. The OraOLEDB Password Change dialog box, shown in Figure 14.18, allows the user to change their password whenever the logon password has expired. When the attribute is set to 1, the feature is enabled. When it is set to 0 (zero), the feature is disabled. The default is enabled, or 1.

FIGURE 14.18
The OraOLEDB Password
Change dialog box

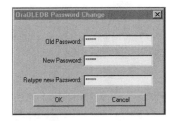

Listing 14.5 demonstrates how to disable the Password Expiration feature. If you chose to disable it, you will need to trap the ORA-28001, "The password has expired" error that is returned by the Oracle server in your application and provide a way to handle such an error. You may want to present your own custom Change Password dialog box or simply trap the error and display something to the user.

Listing 14.5

```
1  Dim democon As ADODB.Connection
2  Set democon = New ADODB.Connection
3  democon.ConnectionString = "Provider=OraOLEDB.Oracle; " _
   & "Data Source=v8i;" _
   & "User ID=scott;Password=tiger;PwdChgDlg=0"
4  democon.Open
```

Analysis

- Line 1 declares the ADO connection object.

- Line 2 creates an instance of the ADO connection object.

- Line 3 sets the ConnectionString property of the ADO connection object, using the following Provider attributes:

  - Provider = OraOLEDB.Oracle

  - Data Source = v8i

- User ID = scott

- Password = tiger

- PwdChgDlg = 0

- Line 4 calls the Open method to establish the connection to the database.

Once you have established a successful connection, you are ready to start executing SQL statements. The next section demonstrates using the ADO command and recordset objects to query the database.

Querying the Database Using the ADO Command and Recordset Object

The command object has properties and methods that allow you to query the database more efficiently by defining parameterized queries or using bind variables. The command object is used to describe your query and its parameters. The ADO recordset object is the container that houses data that is returned from your query. You cannot use the following data types as command parameters in your parameterized queries:

- BLOB

- CLOB

- NLOB

- NChar

- NVarchar2

NOTE   The Oracle OLE DB Provider only supports positional binding. This means that you must pass the parameters in the order they are expected.

Listing 14.6 uses the command and recordset objects to return the results of a parameterized query. The example executes `Select From Emp Where Deptno = ?`. The ? is actually the placeholder for a bind variable that is supplied by the user or application. In the example application, `Deptno` is set to 30 by default when the ADO parameter is created for the parameterized query. You can prompt the user to provide the department number to be used as input into the query.

Listing 14.6

```
1  Dim democon As ADODB.Connection
2  Dim democmd As New ADODB.Command
3  Dim demorset As New ADODB.Recordset
4  Dim demoparam1 As New ADODB.Parameter
5  Set democon = New ADODB.Connection
6  democon.ConnectionString = _
   "Provider=OraOLEDB.Oracle; " _
   & "Data Source=v8i;User ID=scott;Password=tiger;"
7  Set demoparam1 = democmd.CreateParameter _
   ("demoparam1", adSmallInt, adParamInput, , 30)
8  democmd.Parameters.Append demoparam1
9  democon.Open
10  democmd.ActiveConnection = democon
11  Set demorset = New ADODB.Recordset
12  democmd.CommandText = "select * from emp where deptno = ?"
13  Set demorset = democmd.Execute
14  While Not demorset.EOF
15   MsgBox demorset(1)
16   demorset.MoveNext
17  Wend
18  demorset.Close
19  democon.Close
```

Analysis

- Line 1 declares the ADO connection object.

- Line 2 declares the ADO command object.

- Line 3 declares the ADO recordset object.

- Line 4 declares the ADO parameter object.

- Line 5 creates an instance of the ADO connection object.

- Line 6 sets the ConnectionString property of the ADO connection object. It sets the following Provider attributes:

  - Provider = OraOLEDB.Oracle

  - Data Source = v8i

  - User ID = scott

  - Password = tiger

- Line 7 creates a parameter object for the Deptno field.

- Line 8 appends the parameter object to the Parameters collection.

- Line 9 calls the Open method to establish the connection to the database.

- Line 10 sets the ActiveConnection property of the command object to the active connection, democon.

- Line 11 creates an instance of the ADO recordset object.

- Line 12 sets the commandText property of the command object to `"Select From Emp Where Deptno = ?"`.

- Line 13 calls the Execute method of the command object. This call executes the SQL statement and returns the data.

- Line 14 starts a While loop to navigate through the recordset.

- Line 15 displays the contents of the Empno field (first column in the recordset object) to the screen.

- Line 16 calls the MoveNext method of the recordset object. This moves the row pointer to the next row in the recordset.

- Line 17 ends the While loop.

- Line 18 closes the recordset object.

- Line 19 closes the connection object.

NOTE   The QueryTimeout property of the command and recordset objects is not supported by the Oracle OLE DB Provider at this time.

By default, ADO creates a non-updateable recordset. In order to update the data, you must set the Updatability property to a value that allows the rows to be changed. The following list outlines the values available when setting this property of the command object:

- 1 = Allow update on rows.

- 2 = Allow deletions.

- 3 = Allow updates and deletions.

- 4 = Allow inserts.

- 5 = Allow inserts and updates.

- 6 = Allow inserts and deletions.

- 7 = Allow inserts, deletions, and updates

Listing 14.7 shows you how to set the properties of the ADO command object to allow a user to change the data in the recordset.

Listing 14.7

```
1  Dim democon As New ADODB.Connection
2  Dim democmd As New ADODB.Command
3  Dim demorset as New ADODB.Recordset
4  democon.ConnectionString = _
   "Provider=OraOLEDB.Oracle; " _
   & "Data Source=v8i;User ID=scott;Password=tiger;"
5  democon.Open
6  democmd.ActiveConnection = democon
7  democmd.CommandText = "Select * from Dept"
8  democmd.CommandType = adcmdText
9  democmd.Properties("IrowsetChange") = True
10 democmd.Properties("Updatability") = 7
11 Set demorset = democmd.Execute
12 demorset.Close
13 democon.Close
```

Analysis

- Line 1 declares and creates an instance of the ADO connection object.

- Line 2 declares and creates an instance of the ADO command object.

- Line 3 declares and creates an instance of the ADO recordset object.

- Line 4 sets the ConnectionString property of the ADO connection object. It sets the following Provider attributes:

  - Provider = OraOLEDB.Oracle

  - Data Source = v8i

  - User ID = scott

  - Password = tiger

- Line 5 calls the Open method to establish the connection to the database.

- Line 6 sets the ActiveConnection property of the command object to the active connection, democon.

- Line 7 sets the commandText property of the command object to "Select * From Dept".

- Line 8 sets the commandType property of the command object to "adcmdText".

- Line 9 sets the IRowsetChange property of the command object to True.

- Line 10 sets the Updatability property of the command object to 7 to allow inserts, updates, and deletions.

- Line 11 calls the Execute method of the command object. This call executes the SQL statement and returns the data.

- Line 12 closes the recordset object.

- Line 13 closes the connection object.

Querying the Database Using the ADO RecordSet Object

The *ADO recordset object* is the container that houses data that is returned from your query. It has a set of properties and methods that allow you to execute an SQL statement without involving the command object. The recordset object has the following properties and methods that are useful when querying the database:

ActiveConnection property   This property holds a reference to an ADO connection object.

Source property   This property holds the SQL statement to be executed.

Open method   This method creates the recordset object by executing the SQL defined in the RecordSource property.

Listing 14.8 illustrates how to work with ADO recordsets. It executes Select From Emp and navigates through the recordset displaying each Empno field until the end of the data is reached.

Listing 14.8

```
1  Dim democon As ADODB.Connection
2  Dim demorset As New ADODB.Recordset
3  Set democon = New ADODB.Connection
4  democon.ConnectionString = _
   "Provider=OraOLEDB.Oracle; " & _
   "Data Source=v8i;User ID=scott;Password=tiger;"
5  democon.Open
6  Set demorset = New ADODB.Recordset
7  demorset.ActiveConnection = democon
8  demorset.Source = "select * from emp"
9  demorset.open
10  While Not demorset.EOF
11  MsgBox demorset(1)
12   demorset.MoveNext
13 Wend
14 demorset.Close
15 democon.Close
```

Analysis

- Line 1 declares the ADO connection object.

- Line 2 declares the ADO recordset object.

- Line 3 creates an instance of the ADO connection object.

- Line 4 sets the ConnectionString property of the ADO connection object. It sets the following Provider attributes:

  - Provider = OraOLEDB.Oracle

  - Data Source = v8i

  - User ID = scott

  - Password = tiger

- Line 5 calls the Open method to establish the connection to the database.

- Line 6 creates an instance of the ADO recordset object.

- Line 7 sets the ActiveConnection Property of the recordset object to our connection object, democon.

- Line 8 sets the Source property of the recordset object to "Select From Emp".

- Line 9 calls the Open method of the recordset object. This call executes the SQL statement and returns the data.

- Line 10 starts a While loop to navigate the recordset.

- Line 11 displays the contents of the Empno field (first column in the recordset object) to the screen.

- Line 12 calls the MoveNext method of the recordset object. This moves the row pointer to the next row in the recordset.

- Line 13 ends the While loop.

- Line 14 closes the recordset object.

- Line 15 closes the connection object.

Filtering the Data with the Filter Property of the Recordset Object

The ADO library gives you the capability to filter your data by using the Filter property of the recordset object. The Filter property can be used to filter records based on user-defined criteria without having to use the command object and create parameterized queries. This property saves you time and code. Examine Listing 14.9 to get a feel for how this is done. Listing 14.9 uses a command type of adCmdTable and passes the name of the table to the Open method of the connection object.

Listing 14.9

```
1  Dim demorset As ADODB.Recordset
2  Dim connectStr As String
3  Dim demorsetCount As Integer
4  Dim Deptno As Integer
5  Dim Message As String
6  strCnn = "Provider=oraoledb.oracle;" & _
   "Data Source=v8i;User ID=scott;Password=tiger;"
7  Set demorset = New ADODB.Recordset
8  demorset.CursorType = adOpenStatic
9  demorset.Open "emp", strCnn, , , adCmdTable
```

```
10  intdemorsetCount = demorset.RecordCount
11 Deptno = Trim(InputBox( _
   "Enter a Deptno to filter on:"))
12 If Str(Deptno) <> "" Then
13  Set demorset = _
    CustomFilter(demorset, "Deptno", str(Deptno))
14  If demorset.RecordCount = 0 Then
15    MsgBox "No Employees from that Department."
16  Else
17    Message = "Employees in original recordset: " & _
vbCr & demorsetCount & vbCr & _
      "Employees in filtered recordset " & vbCr & _
      demorset.RecordCount
18    MsgBox Message
19  End If
20 demorset.Close
21 End If

22 Public Function CustomFilter(rsetTemp As ADODB.Recordset, _
     strField As String, strFilter As String) _
     As ADODB.Recordset
23  rsetTemp.Filter = strField & " = " & strFilter
24  Set CustomFilter = rsetTemp
25 End Function
```

Analysis

- Line 1 declares the ADO recordset object.

- Line 2 declares a string to hold the connection parameters.

- Line 3 declares an integer to hold the record count for the recordset.

- Line 4 declares an integer to hold the department number that is used as an input parameter.

- Line 5 declares a string to hold a message that will be displayed to the user.

- Line 6 sets the Provider attribute of the ADO connection object, using the following attribute:

  - Provider = OraOLEDB.Oracle

Line 6 also constructs the contents of the ConnectionString property of the ADO connection object. It sets the following Provider attributes:

- Data Source = v8i

- User ID = scott

- Password = tiger

- Line 7 creates a new instance of the ADO recordset object.

- Line 8 sets the cursor type for the recordset object to adOpenStatic.

- Line 9 calls the Open method of the recordset object. This passes the table name, connection attributes, and the command type of adTable.

- Line 10 sets the variable demorsetcount to the total number of records returned in the recordset object.

- Line 11 prompts the user for the department number to filter.

- Line 12 is the outer If statement to check for a Null department number.

- Line 13 calls the CustomFilter function to filter the recordset. You must pass the following parameters:

  - The name of recordset to filter

  - The column name to filter

  - The actual value to filter

- Line 14 is the inner If statement, which checks for an empty recordset and returns a message to the user if no records are found.

- Line 15 displays message if no records are found.

- Line 16 is the Else clause for the inner If statement.

- Line 17 sets a string variable called Message to the record count for the original recordset with all employees and the record count for the filtered recordset based on the actual department number entered by the user.

- Line 18 calls the Visual Basic Msgbox function to display the record counts.

- Line 19 is the End If clause for the inner If statement.

- Line 20 calls the Close method for the recordset object.

- Line 21 is the End If clause for the outer If statement.

- Line 22 starts the user-defined function CustomFilter.

- Line 23 sets the Filter property of the recordset object to the actual department number entered by the user.

- Line 24 sets the temporary recordset object to the newly filtered recordset object.

- Line 25 ends the CustomFilter function.

Calling Stored Procedures

When calling stored procedures using the Oracle OLE DB Provider, you must use either the Oracle Native call syntax or the ODBC SQL calling convention. The Oracle OLE DB Provider does not support the command type of adcmdStoredProc. You must specify the command type as adcmdtext and use one of the following calling methods:

Method 1: Oracle Native syntax   This syntax involves using the BEGIN and END keywords as you would when calling the stored procedure from a native Oracle application. An example of this type of call is shown here:

```
BEGIN myprocedurename(100); END;
```

Method 1: ODBC SQL syntax   This method involves using the call specifier enclosed in left and right curly braces, or an Escape character sequence when calling the stored procedure. An example of this type of call is shown here:

```
{CALL myprocedurename(100) }
```

Listing 14.10 uses the Oracle Native syntax to call a stored procedure using the Execute method of the connection object. The stored procedure simply updates an employee record. The PL/SQL code to create the stored procedure is provided in the unnumbered lines of Listing 14.10. Use SQL*Plus to create the EmpUpdate procedure. The actual Visual Basic code that demonstrates the Oracle Native syntax is numbered and analyzed in Listing 14.10. This code will call the EmpUpdate procedure to update an employee record.

Listing 14.10

```
CREATE OR REPLACE PROCEDURE EmpUpdate(
 inempno IN NUMBER, indeptno IN NUMBER)
AS
BEGIN
 UPDATE emp SET deptno = indeptno WHERE empno = inempno;
END EmpUpdate;
/


1  Dim democon As New ADODB.Connection
2  democon.Provider = "OraOLEDB.Oracle"
3  democon.ConnectionString = _
 "Data Source=v8i;" _
 & "User ID=scott;Password=tiger;"
4  democon.Open
5  democon.Execute("BEGIN EmpUpdate(7934,20); END; ")
6  democon.Close
```

Analysis

- Line 1 declares the ADO connection object.

- Line 2 sets the Provider attribute of the ADO connection object to OraOLEDB.Oracle

- Line 3 sets the ConnectionString property of the ADO connection object. It sets the following Provider attributes:

  - Data Source = v8i

  - User ID = scott

  - Password = tiger

- Line 4 calls the Open method to establish the connection to the database.

- Line 5 calls the Execute method of the connection object and passes the Oracle Native syntax for calling a stored procedure.

- Line 6 calls the Close method of the ADO connection object.

Returning a Result Set from a Call to a Stored Procedure

The Oracle OLE DB Provider gives you the capability to return a result set from a stored procedure in the form of an ADO recordset that you can navigate and present to the end user. The results returned by the call are read-only recordsets and cannot be updated. If you want to use this feature, you must set the Provider attribute PLSQLRSet to 1. This tells the Provider to parse the PL/SQL blocks and determine if the call is returning a result set from a Ref Cursor variable of a stored procedure. The Oracle OLE DB Provider maps the results of a PL/SQL Ref cursor to an ADO recordset object. A Ref Cursor variable is not defined in the OLE DB specification so this specific data type is not bound in your application like other parameters or bind variables. If you try and bind this parameter, you will receive an error. The Provider will bind the Ref cursor for you when you set the PLSQLRSet attribute to 1.

> **NOTE**   In order to use this feature, the stored procedure must be called using the ODBC SQL syntax. You cannot use the adcmdStoredProc command type.

You must also create your PL/SQL procedures using a specific format. Here are some guidelines to use with this feature:

- Set PLSQLRSet = 1.

- A package must be created to declare the Ref cursors.

- A procedure is implemented in the body of the package that uses the Ref cursor and returns it to the calling program.

Listing 14.11 demonstrates how to call a stored procedure that returns a result set to your Visual Basic application. The unnumbered lines provide you with the PL/ SQL code to create the package. Use SQL*Plus to create the package. Listing 14.11 demonstrates the Visual Basic code to return a result set from a call to an Oracle stored procedure. This example passes in a department number and returns all employees who are assigned to that department.

> **NOTE**   With the first release of the Oracle OLE DB Provider, returning multiple result sets is not supported.

Listing 14.11

```
CREATE OR REPLACE PACKAGE EmpByDept
AS
TYPE empcur IS REF CURSOR;
PROCEDURE GetEmpByDept(p_cursor OUT empcur, indeptno IN NUMBER);
END EmpByDept;
/
CREATE OR REPLACE PACKAGE BODY EmpByDept
AS
PROCEDURE GetEmpByDept(p_cursor OUT empcur,
indeptno IN NUMBER) IS
BEGIN
OPEN p_cursor FOR SELECT * FROM emp WHERE deptno = indeptno
ORDER BY empno;
END GetEmpByDept;
END EmpByDept;
/
```

```
1  Dim democon As New ADODB.Connection
2  Dim demorset As New ADODB.Recordset
3  Dim democmd As New ADODB.Command
4  Dim demoparam1 As New ADODB.Parameter
5  democon.Provider = "OraOLEDB.Oracle"
6  democon.ConnectionString = _
   "Data Source=v8i;" _
 & "User ID=scott;Password=tiger;PLSQLRSet=1;"
7  democon.Open
8  democmd.ActiveConnection = democon
9  Set demoparam1 = democmd.CreateParameter _
 ("demoparam1", adSmallInt, adParamInput, , 30)
10  democmd.Parameters.Append demoparam1
11 democmd.CommandText = "{CALL "_
 & "EmpByDept.GetEmpByDept(?)}"
12 Set demorset = democmd.Execute
13 While Not demorset.EOF
14  MsgBox demorset(1)
15  demorset.MoveNext
16 Wend
17 demorset.Close
18 democon.Close
```

⟩ **Analysis**

- Line 1 declares the ADO connection object.
- Line 2 declares the ADO recordset object.
- Line 3 declares the ADO command object.
- Line 4 declares the ADO parameter object for param1.
- Line 5 sets the Provider attribute of the ADO connection object to OraOLEDB.Oracle.
- Line 6 sets the ConnectionString property of the ADO connection object. It sets the following Provider attributes:
    - Data Source = v8i
    - User ID = scott
    - Password = tiger
    - PLSQLRSet = 1
- Line 7 calls the Open method to establish the connection to the database.
- Line 8 sets the ActiveConnection property for the command object to democon.
- Line 9 creates the Demoparam1 object for the Deptno column.
- Line 10 calls the Append method to add the Demoparam1 object to the Parameters collection of the command object.
- Line 11 sets the CommandText property of the command object to the correct ODBC SQL syntax for calling the stored procedure.
- Line 12 calls the Execute method of the command object. This call executes the SQL statement and returns the data to our recordset object.
- Line 13 starts a While loop to navigate the recordset.
- Line 14 displays the contents of the Empno field (the first column in the recordset object) to the screen.
- Line 15 calls the MoveNext method of the recordset object. This moves the row pointer to the next row in the recordset.
- Line 16 ends the While loop.
- Line 17 closes the recordset object.
- Line 18 closes the connection object.

In the next section, we will examine ways to work with Oracle8i advanced data types. These data types include BLOBs, CLOBs, and BFILEs.

NOTE   Oracle8i objects are not supported with the Oracle OLE DB Provider.

Working with BLOBs, CLOBs, and BFILEs

The Oracle OLE DB Provider has support for BLOBs, CLOBs, and BFILEs implemented through the ISequential stream interface of the OLE DB specification. The OLE DB Provider gives you read and write access to BLOBs and CLOBs as long as the Select statement used to create the result set does not contain a Join statement.

NOTE   The Oracle OLE DB Provider only gives read-only capability for BFILEs.

There are a couple of different ways to manipulate LOB data using the ADO object model. The first method involves using the AddNew and Update methods to insert data into a LOB column. The second method involves using the Append-Chunk method of the recordset object to stream data and piece the LOB data together.

Using the Update Method to Insert CLOB Data

Listing 14.12 demonstrates the Visual Basic code necessary to work with CLOB data in your ADO recordset. Use the SQL code provided in the unnumbered lines to create a demo table that contains a CLOB column. Use SQL*Plus or SQL Worksheet to execute the DDL (Data Definition Language) provided to create the table. Listing 14.12 shows you how to call the AddNew and Update methods to save data to a CLOB column in the Oracle database.

Listing 14.12

```
CREATE TABLE clobtable (
clobid number(4),
clobdata clob);
```

```
1   Dim democon As New ADODB.Connection
2   Dim demorset As New ADODB.Recordset
3   democon.Provider = "OraOLEDB.Oracle"
4   democon.Open "v8i", "scott", "tiger"
5   demorset.Open "clobtable", democon, adOpenStatic, _
    adLockOptimistic, adCmdTable
6   demorset.AddNew
7   demorset.Fields("CLOBID").value = 1
8   demorset.Fields("CLOBDATA").value = _
    "This is an example of inserting into a lob field"
9   demorset.Update
10   demorset.Close
11  democon.Close
```

⊃ Analysis

- Line 1 declares the ADO connection object.

- Line 2 creates an instance of the ADO connection object.

- Line 3 sets the Provider property of the ADO connection object to "OraOLEDB.Oracle".

- Line 4 sets the ConnectionString property of the connection object. The Provider attribute PLSQLRSet is set to 1.

- Line 5 calls the Open method to establish the connection to the database. This line passes parameters to the Open method directly, overriding the ConnectionString property.

- Line 6 calls the AddNew method of the recordset object. This adds a new row to the recordset.

- Line 7 sets the ClobID field to 1.

- Line 8 sets the Clob1 field to "This is an example of inserting into a lob field" by assignment.

- Line 9 calls the Update method of the recordset object to write the changes to the database.

- Line 10 closes the recordset object.

- Line 11 closes the database connection.

Using the AppendChunk Method to Insert CLOB Data

Another approach you can use in ADO to insert LOB data into an Oracle table is called *streaming*. This is accomplished by calling the AppendChunk method of the recordset object to append pieces of the data together and then calling the Update method to write these to the Oracle database. Listing 14.13 demonstrates how this technique works.

Listing 14.13

```
1  Dim democon As New ADODB.Connection
2  Dim demorset As New ADODB.Recordset
3  democon.Provider = "OraOLEDB.Oracle"
4  democon.Open "v8i", "scott", "tiger"
5  demorset.Open "clobtable", democon, adOpenStatic, _
 adLockOptimistic, adCmdTable
6  demorset.AddNew
7  demorset.Fields("CLOBID").value = 2
8  demorset.Fields("CLOBDATA").AppendChunk _
 "This is an example of inserting into a lob field "
9  demorset.Fields("CLOBDATA").AppendChunk _
 "using the append chunk method"
10  demorset.Update
11 demorset.Close
12 democon.Close
```

Analysis

- Line 1 declares the ADO connection object.

- Line 2 creates an instance of the ADO connection object.

- Line 3 sets the Provider property of the ADO connection object to "OraOLEDB.Oracle".

- Line 4 sets the ConnectionString property of the connection object. The Provider attribute PLSQLRSet is set to 1.

- Line 5 calls the Open method to establish the connection to the database. This line passes parameters to the Open method directly, overriding the ConnectionString property.

- Line 6 calls the AddNew method of the recordset object. This adds a new row to the recordset.

- Line 7 sets the value of the ClobID field to 1.

- Line 8 sets the value of the Clob1 field to "This is an example of inserting into a lob field" by calling the AppendChunk method.

- Line 9 appends the value "This is an example of inserting into a lob field" to the Clob1 field by calling the AppendChunk method.

- Line 10 calls the Update method of the recordset object to write the changes to the database.

- Line 11 closes the recordset object

- Line 12 closes the database connection.

Using the AppendChunk Method to Insert BLOB Data

The Oracle OLEDB Provider is also capable of providing you with read and write access to BLOB columns. Listing 14.14 demonstrates writing binary data to the database. This example will read the data from an operating system file and use the AppendChunk method to place the contents of the file into a BLOB column in the database.

Use the SQL code provided in the unnumbered lines to create a demo table that contains a BLOB column. Use SQL*Plus or SQL Worksheet to execute the DDL (Data Definition Language) provided to create the table. The numbered lines demonstrate the Visual Basic code to read data from a file and save it in the BLOB table using the AppendChunk method of the ADO recordset object.

Listing 14.14

```
CREATE TABLE blobtable (
blobid number(4),
bloblength number,
blobdata blob);

1  Dim democon As ADODB.Connection
2  Dim demorset As ADODB.Recordset
3  Const ChunkSize = 4096
```

```
4   Dim BlobData() As Byte
5   Dim DataLength As Long
6   Dim FileOffset As Long
7   Set democon = New ADODB.Connection
8   Set demorset = New ADODB.Recordset
9   democon.Provider = "OraOLEDB.Oracle"
10   democon.Open "v8i", "scott", "tiger"
11  demorset.Open "blobtable", democon, _
 adOpenStatic, adLockOptimistic, adCmdTable
12 Open "C:\demo.zip" For Binary Access Read As #1
13 demorset.AddNew
14 demorset.Fields("blobid").Value = 1
15 DataLength = LOF(1)
16 demorset.Fields("bloblength").Value = DataLength
17 FileOffset = 1
18 Do
19   If FileOffset + ChunkSize <= DataLength Then
20       ReDim BlobData(ChunkSize)
21   Else
22       ReDim BlobData(DataLength - FileOffset + 1)
23   End If
24   Get #1, FileOffset, BlobData()
25   demorset.Fields("blobdata").AppendChunk BlobData()
26   FileOffset = FileOffset + ChunkSize
27 Loop While FileOffset < DataLength
28 Close #1
29 demorset.Update
30 demorset.Close
31 democon.Close
```

Analysis

- Line 1 declares the ADO connection object.

- Line 2 declares the ADO recordset object.

- Line 3 sets a constant variable for the ChunkSize.

- Line 4 declares the BlobData variable as Byte.

- Line 5 declares the DataLength variable as Long.

- Line 6 declares the FileOffset variable as Long.

- Line 7 creates a new instance of the connection object.

- Line 8 creates a new instance of the recordset object.

- Line 9 sets the Provider property of the ADO connection object to "OraOLEDB.Oracle".

- Line 10 calls the Open method to establish the connection to the database. This line passes parameters to the Open method directly, overriding the ConnectionString property.

- Line 11 calls the Open method for the recordset object using the command type of adTable.

- Line 12 opens a binary file for reading.

- Line 13 calls the AddNew method of the recordset object. This adds a new row to the recordset.

- Line 14 sets value of the BlobID field to 1.

- Line 15 sets the DataLength variable to the length of the file.

- Line 16 stores the actual length of the file to the BlobLength column of the BLOB table.

- Line 17 initializes the FileOffset variable to 1.

- Line 18 starts a Do loop to read in the file.

- Line 19 is the outer If statement to test for the end of the data.

- Line 20 re-allocates the BlobData variable for the amount of data to be read in.

- Line 21 is the Else clause for the outer If statement.

- Line 22 allocates the exact amount of storage for the last piece of data to be read.

- Line 23 is the End If clause for the outer If statement.

- Line 24 reads the data from the file.

- Line 25 calls the AppendChunk method to append the data read in from the binary file.

- Line 26 computes the FileOffset variable.

- Line 27 is the Do While loop condition that tests to see if the end of the file has been reached.

- Line 28 closes the binary file.

- Line 29 calls the Update method for the recordset object.

- Line 30 closes the recordset object.

- Line 31 closes the connection object.

Using the GetChunk Method to Read BLOB Data

In Listing 14.14, you saw how to use the AppendChunk method to write data into the database. You may also wish to read this data back out and write it to a binary file to use in your application. You can do this with the GetChunk method of the recordset object. Listing 14.15 demonstrates the Visual Basic code that reads the data from the BLOB table and writes its contents to a file. The code reads the BlobData column of the first row of the recordset and writes it back to a file.

Listing 14.15

```
1  Dim democon As ADODB.Connection
2  Dim demorset As ADODB.Recordset
3  Const ChunkSize = 4096
4  Dim BlobData() As Byte
5  Dim DataLength As Long
6  Dim FileOffset As Long
7  Set democon = New ADODB.Connection
8  Set demorset = New ADODB.Recordset
9  democon.Provider = "OraOLEDB.Oracle"
10  democon.Open "v8i", "scott", "tiger"
11 demorset.Open "blobtable", democon, _
  adOpenStatic, adLockOptimistic, adCmdTable
12 demorset.MoveFirst
13 Open "C:\demoout.zip" For Binary Access Write As #1
14 Dim DataTemp As Variant
15 FileOffset = 1
16 DataLength = demorset.Fields("bloblength").Value
17   Do
18     DataTemp = _
  demorset.Fields("blobdata").GetChunk(ChunkSize)
```

```
19      BlobData() = DataTemp
20      Put #1, FileOffset, BlobData()
21      FileOffset = FileOffset + LenB(DataTemp)
22    Loop While LenB(DataTemp) = ChunkSize
23 Close #1
24 demorset.Close
25 democon.Close
```

Analysis

- Line 1 declares the ADO connection object.

- Line 2 declares the ADO recordset object.

- Line 3 declares a constant named ChunkSize and initializes its value to 4096 bytes. This determines how big the chunk size will be for the reads.

- Line 4 declares the BlobData variable as Byte.

- Line 5 declares the DataLength variable as Long.

- Line 6 declares the FileOffset variable as Long.

- Line 7 creates a new instance of the connection object.

- Line 8 creates a new instance of the recordset object.

- Line 9 sets the Provider property of the ADO connection object to "OraOLEDB.Oracle".

- Line 10 calls the Open method to establish the connection to the database. This line passes parameters to the Open method directly, overriding the ConnectionString property.

- Line 11 calls the Open method for the recordset object using the adTable command type.

- Line 12 calls the MoveFirst method for the recordset object. This positions the row pointer to the beginning of the recordset.

- Line 13 opens a binary file for writing.

- Line 14 declares a variable to hold the data read in from the binary file stored in the BlobLength column of the BLOB table.

- Line 15 initializes the FileOffset variable to 1.

- Line 16 initializes the DataLength variable to the file size.

- Line 17 starts a Do loop to read in the file.

- Line 18 calls the GetChunk method to read a piece of data.

- Line 19 sets the BlobData variable to the contents fetched by calling the GetChunk method.

- Line 20 writes the data from the file.

- Line 21 computes the new FileOffset variable.

- Line 22 is the Do While loop condition that tests to see if all the data has been read.

- Line 23 closes the binary file.

- Line 24 closes the recordset object.

- Line 25 closes the connection object.

In the next section, we will examine using the ADO Data Control with the Oracle OLE DB Provider. The ADO Data Control handles a lot of the work that your application normally provides in the code.

Working with the ADO Data Control

The ADO Data Control can be used to bring data back to bound controls with little or no code. The ADO Data Control is very simple to use and performs a lot of the work for your application. To demonstrate its simplicity and usefulness, we are going to create a small ADO application that uses the ADO Data Control and the Oracle OLE DB Provider. This application will query the Emp table in the Scott schema.

Follow the steps outlined here to create the sample application:

1. Start Microsoft Visual Basic 6.

2. Choose File ➤ New.

3. From the Project window, choose Standard EXE for the target type and click the OK button. Make sure that the Project Explorer and toolbox are present. If necessary, use the View menu to make them visible.

NOTE	Make sure that the Project Explorer and toolbar are present when you are opening VB 6 in Standard target type. If necessary, use the View menu to make them visible.

Now that you have set up a project with a default form, as seen in Figure 14.19, the next step is to place the bound control and ADO Data Control on the form.

FIGURE 14.19
The default project with a main form

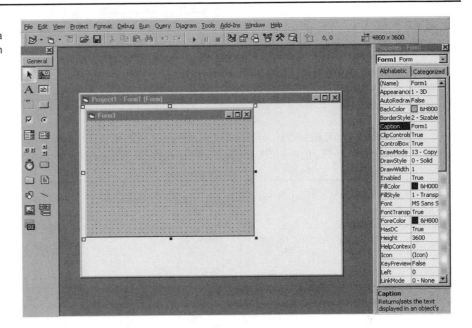

To place the bound control and the ADO Data Control on the form, follow these steps:

1. From the Project menu, choose Project ➢ Components.

2. Choose the ADO Data Control (OLEDB) and the ADO Data Grid (OLEDB) component by toggling the check box next to each item in the Components dialog box. Refer to Figure 14.20 to check your work so far.

FIGURE 14.20

The Components dialog box with the ADO Data Control and ADO Data Grid components selected

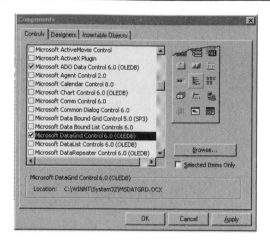

3. Click OK, and the components will be available on the toolbox for selection. Figure 14.21 shows the new components on the toolbox.

FIGURE 14.21

The new toolbox with ADO Data Control and Data Grid icons

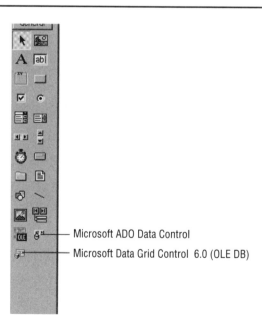

— Microsoft ADO Data Control

— Microsoft Data Grid Control 6.0 (OLE DB)

4. Choose the ADO Data Control from the toolbox and drag it onto the bottom of the form.

You can use Help to locate a component on the toolbox. Move your cursor over a component, and the name will be displayed.

5. Choose the ADO Data Grid component from the toolbox and drag it onto the top of the form, as shown in Figure 14.22.

FIGURE 14.22
Adodc1 and Datagrid1 placed on the form

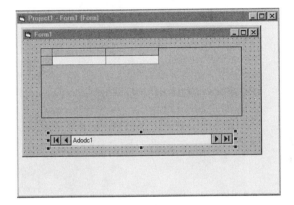

6. Click the Datagrid1 object on the form to give it the current focus. Locate the DataSource property on the Properties dialog box and set this property by pulling down the pick list and choosing Adodc1.

7. Click the ADO Data Control object named Adodc1 on Form1 to give it the current focus. Right-click and choose ADODC properties. The Property Pages dialog box appears, as shown in Figure 14.23.

FIGURE 14.23
ADO Data Control Property Pages dialog box

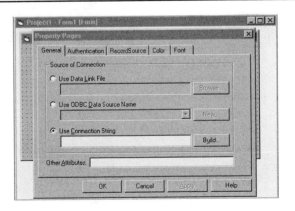

8. Choose the Use Connection String radio button as the source of the connection. Click the Build button to build the ConnectionString property of the ADO Data Control. The next screen is the Data Link Properties dialog box, as shown in Figure 14.24.

FIGURE 14.24
The Data Link Properties dialog box

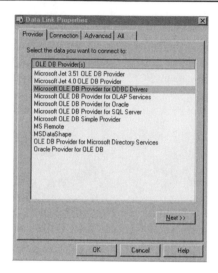

9. Choose the Provider tab. You will see the Oracle OLE DB Provider in the list of available choices. Figure 14.25 shows the available providers. Click the Oracle OLE DB Provider to give it the current focus.

FIGURE 14.25
The list of available providers

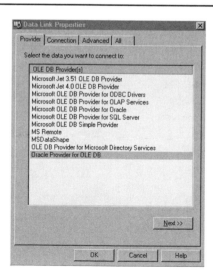

10. Choose the Connection tab, as shown in Figure 14.26. This section allows you to specify the connection information that the OLE DB Provider will use to make the connection.

FIGURE 14.26
The Data Link Properties
Connection tab

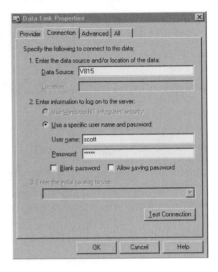

11. Fill in the Server Name, Username, and Password properties. Place your cursor in the text fields and type the appropriate values. Using the Scott schema, the values would be as follows:

- v8i
- scott
- tiger

At this point, you have supplied enough information to test the connection using the ADO Data Control and the Oracle OLE DB Provider. Test the connection by clicking the Test Connection button on the bottom of the screen, as shown in Figure 14.27. If you receive any errors, you may want to go to SQL*Plus and try the connection there with the same parameters. You can also refer to Chapter 6 for additional troubleshooting references.

FIGURE 14.27
The Test Connection button

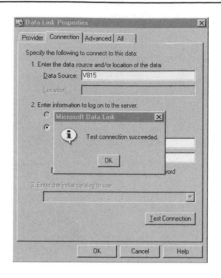

After you have tested the connection, click the OK button to apply the selections you've made so far. This will bring you back to the Property Pages dialog box where you can now see the contents of the Use Connection String text box. This text box contains the value of the ConnectionString property that you built by filling in previous properties (see Figure 14.28).

FIGURE 14.28
The Property Pages dialog box with the Connection-String property built

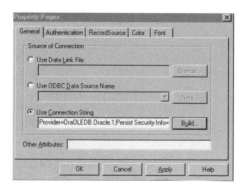

The next step is to specify the RecordSource property by clicking the Record-Source tab. This will allow you to enter an SQL statement to execute when the application runs. The RecordSource tab contains two other pieces of information: the command types and a text box to supply the table or stored procedure name. For the first two command types, adcmdunknown and adcmdtext, you are required to put a Select statement in the Command text box. The last two types, adCmdTable and adcmdStoredProc, require that you supply either the table name or the name of the stored procedure. The Table or Stored Procedure Name text boxes are not activated unless you choose the two command types that require them to be supplied. Follow these steps to complete the application:

1. Choose the RecordSource tab.

2. In the Command Type drop-down list, choose 1-adCmdText.

3. Enter the SQL statement `Select From Emp` in the Command Text (SQL) text box. Figure 14.29 demonstrates how this should look.

FIGURE 14.29
The ADO Data Control RecordSource tab

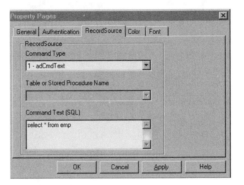

> **NOTE** The Oracle OLE DB Provider currently does not support calling a stored procedure using the command object. Thus, you must use the ODBC call syntax and set the command type to adcmdtext. Refer to the section "Returning a Result Set from a Call to a Stored Procedure" for additional details.

4. Choose Run ➤ Start to run the form and see the list of employee names displayed in the data grid component. Figure 14.30 shows the correct output.

FIGURE 14.30
The ADO Data Control
application results

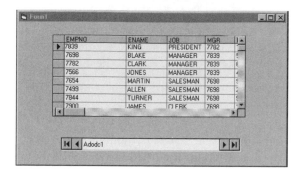

You can navigate through the employee records by clicking the navigation buttons on the ADO Data Control or using the scroll bars on the Microsoft Data Bound Grid Control.

Transactional Support

A *transaction* is basically a change that has been recorded and time stamped. These changes can be made permanent by issuing a commit, or they can be rolled back, and the old values will be restored. The OLE DB Provider supports local and distributed transactions. *Distributed transactions* are monitored by software known as a transaction monitor or transaction coordinator. *Local transactions* are managed by your application.

The key thing to know about transactions is that once you have started a global transaction, you cannot start a local transaction in the same session and vice versa. You can enlist in global transactions or manage local ones in your application but not both. You have to make a choice. The Oracle OLE DB Provider is supported with the Microsoft Transaction Server. You must write the code to enlist your application in global transactions with MTS. Although there is no special programming involved other than setting the object transaction's required property in your application, you must install and configure the Oracle Services for MTS version 8.1.6 . Refer to the Oracle 8.1.6 documentation titled "Using the Oracle Services for MTS" for additional information on installation and configuration.

Nested transactions are not supported by the OLE DB Provider. The transaction stream is either committed or rolled back as a whole.

The Oracle OLE DB Provider commits all local transactions by default. Auto-Commit must be turned off by calling the BeginTrans method of the connection object. Once the transaction has been started, you must use the CommitTrans and RollbackTrans methods of the connection object to either save or undo any changes. Listing 14.16 demonstrates how to use these transactional methods with the Oracle OLE DB Provider. The program allows a user to make changes to a column in the recordset and to choose whether to commit or roll back the updates.

Listing 14.16

```
1  Dim democon As New ADODB.Connection
2  Dim demorset As New ADODB.Recordset
3  democon.Provider = "OraOLEDB.Oracle"
4  democon.Open "v8i", "scott", "tiger"
5  demorset.Open "EMP", democon, adOpenStatic, _
   adLockOptimistic, adCmdTable
6  democon.BeginTrans
7  Do Until demorset.EOF
8   If Trim(demorset!Comm) < 500 Then
9     strComm = demorset!Comm
10    strMessage = "Commission is " & strComm & vbCr & _
        "Increase to 1000?"
11    If MsgBox(strMessage, vbYesNo) = vbYes Then
12      demorset!Comm = 1000
13      demorset.Update
14    End If
15  End If
16  demorset.MoveNext
17 Loop
18 If MsgBox("Save all changes?", vbYesNo) = vbYes Then
19   democon.CommitTrans
20 Else
21   democon.RollbackTrans
22 End If
23 demorset.Close
24 democon.Close
```

⤵ Analysis

- Line 1 declares the ADO connection object.

- Line 2 declares the ADO recordset object.

- Line 3 sets the Provider property of the ADO connection object to "Ora-OLEDB.Oracle".

- Line 4 calls the Open method to establish the connection to the database. This line passes parameters to the Open method directly, overriding the ConnectionString property.

- Line 5 calls the Open method for the recordset object. Passing in the name of the table, connection object, and command type of adTable.

- Line 6 starts a new transaction by calling the BeginTrans method of the connection object. This will turn off AutoCommit and allow transactional control of the updates.

- Line 7 starts the Do loop to navigate through the recordset object.

- Line 8 is the outer If statement, which tests for commissions less than 500.

- Line 9 sets the variable strComm variable to the value of the Commission column of the current row in the recordset.

- Line 10 creates a message to display to the user. This message prompts the user to confirm changes to the Commission column.

- Line 11 is the inner If statement to display the message and check the response from the user.

- Line 12 sets the commission value to 1,000 if the user's response is yes.

- Line 13 calls the Update method of the recordset object.

- Line 14 is the End If clause for inner If statement.

- Line 15 is the End If clause for the outer If statement.

- Line 16 calls the MoveNext method of the recordset object to move the row pointer to the next record.

- Line 17 is the end Loop clause.

- Line 18 is the last If statement that determines whether to commit or roll back the changes based on a decision made by the user.

- Line 19 calls the CommitTrans method and commits the changes if the answer is yes.

- Line 20 is the Else clause for the last If statement.

- Line 21 calls RollbackTrans method to roll back the changes if the answer is no.

- Line 22 is the End If clause.

- Line 23 closes the recordset object

- Line 24 closes the connection object.

Error Handling

Anytime an error occurs that has been thrown by the underlying components, such as the Oracle OLE DB Provider, the ADO error's collection object is populated with detailed information on the error. The error object provides you with an error number, the source, and a description. Listing 14.17 demonstrates how to navigate through the Error collection to extract the most detailed information about the error that has occurred. This example displays error information to the screen by calling the Msgbox function. The parameters passed to the Open method are invalid in order to force an error to occur.

Listing 14.17

```
1  Dim democon As New ADODB.Connection
2  Dim demoErr As Errors
3  Dim i As Integer
4  On Error GoTo AdoError
5  democon.Provider = "OraOLEDB.Oracle"
6  democon.Open "x", "scott", "tiger"
7  Done:
8  If democon.State = adStateOpen Then
9    democon.Close
10  End If
11 Set democon = Nothing
12 Exit Sub
13 AdoError:
```

```
14 Dim errLoop As Error
15 Dim strError As String
16 On Error Resume Next
17 i = 1
18 msgbox "VB Error # " & Str(Err.Number)
     & " Generated by " & Err.Source
     & " Description " & Err.Description
19 Set demoErr = democon.Errors
20 For Each errLoop In demoErr
21  With errLoop
22  msgbox "Error #" & i
       & " ADO Error #" & .Number
       & " Description " & .Description
       & " Source " & .Source
23  i = i + 1
24  End With
25 Next
26 On Error Resume Next
27 GoTo Done
```

Analysis

- Line 1 declares the ADO connection object.

- Line 2 declares the ADO Errors object.

- Line 3 declares integer variable i. This variable is used as a counter to determine the total number of errors reported.

- Line 4 is the OnError event to trap errors.

- Line 5 sets the Provider property of the ADO connection object to Ora-OLEDB.Oracle.

- Line 6 calls the Open method for the recordset object, passing in the name of the table, connection object, and command type of adTable.

- Line 7 is the Done Line label. This label contains code that cleans up system resources.

- Line 8 is the outer If statement that checks for an open connection.

- Line 9 closes the connection if it is already open.

- Line 10 is the End If clause.

- Line 11 sets the connection object to "Nothing".

- Line 12 calls the Exit sub command to exit the current subroutine.

- Line 13 is the line label AdoError. This starts the error-handling code.

- Line 14 declares an error object.

- Line 15 declares a string variable.

- Line 16 sets the error trap to resume if an error occurs when navigating through the Errors collection.

- Line 17 initializes the variable i to 1.

- Line 18 displays the Visual Basic Err object number, source, and description.

- Line 19 sets the variable demoerr to the number of errors in the collection.

- Line 20 starts the For loop to navigate through the Error collections.

- Line 21 is the With statement for the Loop clause.

- Line 22 displays the error number, description, and source from the Error collection object.

- Line 23 increments the variable i by 1.

- Line 24 ends the With statement for the Loop clause.

- Line 25 is the Next command to loop back if more errors exist.

- Line 26 sets the error trap to `Resume Next` if any errors occur.

- Line 27 calls the GoTo method and branches to the Done line label.

This example demonstrates how to extract error information from the ADO Error collection object, as well as the Visual Basic Err object. The ADO error object will contain error information returned by the Oracle OLE DB Provider where the Visual Basic Err object will contain any Visual Basic runtime-related error, such as error 91.

Summary

This chapter presented techniques and concepts that enable you to write Visual Basic applications using ADO and the Oracle OLE DB Provider. It demonstrated the major features available with the first release of the Provider. The chapter covered the basics, such as connecting to the Oracle database, as well as some more advanced techniques like manipulating BLOBs and calling stored procedures that return ADO recordsets. This chapter gives you a first look at the Oracle OLE DB Provider and what its capabilities are in Visual Basic.

This book gives you the knowledge to start writing basic as well as complex applications that manipulate an object-oriented database design. We hope that the material in this book helps you to master the OO4O programming model and to write applications with simple interfaces that use Oracle8i's advanced features.

INDEX

Note to the Reader: Page numbers in **bold** indicate the principal discussion of a topic or the definition of a term. Page numbers in *italic* indicate illustrations.

B

(

D

E

F

M

N

O

S

W

Z

What's on the CD-ROM

This book's companion CD-ROM contains a wealth of information and tools to help you in your Visual Basic and Oracle development efforts. We've included reusable code to help you work through the examples presented throughout the text. We've also included free and shareware Oracle and Visual Basic utilities. Instructions for installing the following tools are included on the CD-ROM's Readme.txt file:

Sample code   We've included every significant example presented in the book in a readily usable format so that you can easily work with the ideas and concepts presented in each chapter. Specific setup instructions are provided in the corresponding Readme.txt files.

Assistant Series   FinSys Consultants Inc. presents the Assistant Series software suite, which includes the Research, Join, Query, SQL, and AOL Assistants. This software is written specifically for Oracle applications to assist developers in tasks, such as finding source database columns, joining tables, and building queries.

EZSQL   This EZSQL product is a powerful, easy-to-use Oracle database development and administrative tool. It allows you to create and modify almost every kind of database object, edit tables, monitor database performance, export data to text files, extract DDL statements, and much more.

Oracle 8 SQL Help   Another great tool from FinSys, this is a Windows help file for all Oracle 8 SQL*Plus and PL/SQL commands. You can use this file as an online cheat sheet for SQL syntax.

SQL Designer 1.4   From Core Lab, this program executes, tests, and debugs SQL and PL/SQL statements.

Time to Win   The MCR Co. created this compilation of functionality for Visual Basic 4, 5, and 6. Time to Win is a multithreaded DDL with 970 functions and subroutines to use in your VB applications.

WinSQL   The Summit Data Group offers this utility that allows you to run SQL commands in any ODBC-compliant database. With this program, you can connect to multiple databases simultaneously. It includes many powerful features, such as enhanced error handling, an SQL Query Wizard, an HTML publisher that allows you to export the results of an SQL query to the Web, and much more.

NOTE   This CD-ROM can be viewed on Windows 95, 98, and NT. You also need to be running Oracle8i to access the tools on this CD-ROM.
